Gazetteer

and

Business Directory

of

Otsego County, N.Y.

for

1872-3

Compiled and Published by

Hamilton Child

Author of Wayne, Ontario, Seneca, Cayuga, Tompkins, Onondaga, Madison,
Cortland, Chemung, Schuyler, Oneida, Steuben, Orleans, Niagara, Genesee,
Chenango, Monroe, Herkimer, Saratoga, Montgomery and Fulton,
Albany and Schenectady, Rensselaer, Washington, Wyoming,
Columbia, Ulster, Schoharie, Sullivan, Broome,
and Other County Directories.

HERITAGE BOOKS
2024

HERITAGE BOOKS

AN IMPRINT OF HERITAGE BOOKS, INC.

Books, CDs, and more—Worldwide

For our listing of thousands of titles see our website
at
www.HeritageBooks.com

A Facsimile Reprint
Published 2024 by
HERITAGE BOOKS, INC.
Publishing Division
5810 Ruatan Street
Berwyn Heights, MD 20740

Syracuse:
Printed at the Journal Office,
23 &24 E. Washington Street
1872

— Publisher's Notice —
Pages 165 and 166 are missing.
In reprints such as this, it is often not possible to remove
blemishes from the original. We feel the contents of this
book warrant its reissue despite these blemishes and
hope you will agree and read it with pleasure.

International Standard Book Number
Paperbound: 978-0-7884-2652-0

GAZETTEER

AND

BUSINESS DIRECTORY

OF

OTSEGO COUNTY, N. Y.

FOR

1872-3.

COMPILED AND PUBLISHED BY

HAMILTON CHILD.

AUTHOR OF WAYNE, ONTARIO, SENECA, CAYUGA, TOMPKINS, ONONDAGA, MADI-
SON, CORTLAND, CHEMUNG, SCHUYLER, ONEIDA, STEUBEN, ORLEANS, NIAG-
ARA, GENESEE, CHENANGO, MONROE, HERKIMER, SARATOGA, MONT-
GOMERY AND FULTON, ALBANY AND SCHENECTADY, RENSSELAER,
WASHINGTON, WYOMING, COLUMBIA, ULSTER, SCHOHARIE,
SULLIVAN, BROOME, AND OTHER COUNTY DIRECTORIES.

Permanent Office, 23 & 24 E. Washington St., Syracuse, N. Y.

"He that has much to do, will do something wrong, and of that wrong must suffer
the consequences; and if it were possible that he should always act rightly, yet when
such numbers are to judge of his conduct, the bad will censure and obstruct him by
malevolence, and the good sometimes by mistake."—SAMUEL JOHNSON.

SYRACUSE:

PRINTED AT THE JOURNAL OFFICE, 23 & 24 E. WASHINGTON STREET.
1872.

INDEX TO PUBLISHER'S NOTICES.

Three Mile Point House is located on the banks of Otsego Lake, three miles from Cooperstown, and is under the able management of Mr. A. W. Thayer, who, as a "host," has had seven years experience, and consequently must "know how to keep a hotel," as his numerous patrons can testify. Otsego Bass and Trout, and Game Dinners, are served here at all hours of the day. Pleasure parties will find Mr. T. a good man to stop with. See card, page 164.

B. F. Murdock & Bro., proprietors of the Cash and Accommodation Store, at Cooperstown, deal in Dry Goods Groceries, Crockery, Looking Glasses, Carpets, Oil Cloths and everything usually kept in a country store. They are honorable, fair-dealing men, keep a good supply of goods, and are bound not to be undersold. Try them once and you will call again. See card on page 174.

The Schenevus Monitor, J. J. & J. L. Multer, editors and proprietors, is published every Saturday, at Schenevus. It was established in 1864 and is a worthy exponent of Democratic politics. Mr. J. L. Multer is also the publisher of the *Schoharie County Democrat*, at Richmondville. Both sheets are neatly printed and are worthy of the patronage bestowed upon them. See card on page 148.

James Bowes, Plumber, Steam and Gas Fitter, at Cory's Stone Store, Cooperstown, keeps an excellent assortment of Plumbers', Gas and Steam Fitters' Materials, Wrought Iron, Lead Pipe, and everything usually found in a first-class establishment of this kind. Those of our readers who wish their houses furnished in the best manner, will do well to call on Mr. Bowes, who gives his personal supervision to all work. His card appears on page 182.

INTRODUCTION.

In presenting to the public the "Gazetteer and Business Directory of Otsego County," the publisher desires to return his sincere thanks to all who have so kindly aided in obtaining the information it contains, and without whose aid it would have been impossible to collect it in the brief space of time in which it is essential that all such works should be completed. Especially are our thanks due to the several Editors of the County papers, for the uniform kindness which has been evinced in calling attention to the author's efforts; and to the following persons, viz., Hon. W. W. Campbell, Cherry Valley; Rev. E. H. Saunders, Burlington; Rev. C. Ayer, Morris; Ashley Hotchkin, Schenevus; E. Blakeley and Elisha S. Saunders, Otego; Hon. Samuel S. Edick, County Judge, Cooperstown; and John B. Hooker, Assistant Assessor Internal Revenue, Fly Creek; for essential aid in furnishing material for the work. Many others have kindly volunteered their assistance, to all of whom we return our sincere thanks.

The following works have been consulted in its preparation: French's, Gordon's and Spafford's Gazetteers of the State of New York; Lossing's "Pictorial Field Book of the Revolution;" Campbell's "Annals of Tryon County;" "History of Cooperstown;" Campbell's "Centennial Address," Cherry Valley; and many others.

That errors have occurred in so great a number of names and dates as are here given is probable; and that names have been omitted which should have been inserted is quite certain. We can only say that we have exercised more than ordinary diligence and care in this difficult and complicated feature of book-making. Of such as feel aggrieved in consequence of errors or omissions we beg pardon, and ask the indulgence of the reader in marking such as have been observed in the subsequent reading of the proofs, and which are found in the ERRATA, following the Introduction.

It was designed to give a brief history of all the church organizations in the County, but owing, in some cases, to the negligence of those who alone were able to give the necessary information, and in others, to the inability of any one to do so, we have been obliged to omit many or indefinitely delay the completion of the work.

We would suggest that our patrons observe and become familiar with the explanations at the commencement of the Directory.

The Map of the County was engraved with great care by Messrs. Weed, Parsons & Co., of Albany, and will, it is believed, prove a valuable acquisition to the work.

The ADVERTISERS represent some of the leading business men and firms of this and other counties; and we most cheerfully commend them all to the patronage of those under whose observation these pages may come.

With thanks to our friends generally, we leave our work to secure the favor which earnest endeavor ever wins from a discriminating public.

HAMILTON CHILD.

ERRATA.

ADDITIONS AND CORRECTIONS.

GAZETTEER.

County.—THE OTEGO RECORD is now published by Alpheus S. Foote.

Edmeston.—*The West Edmeston Seventh Day Baptist Church* was organized Sept. 28, 1823, with 78 members. Rev. Daniel Coon was the first pastor. The first house of worship was erected in 1823 ; the present one, which will seat 250, in 1843, at a cost of $800. The present value of Church property is $1,200. The present number of members is about 100, and the pastor, Rev. J. B. Clarke.

The Second Baptist Church in Edmeston, located at Edmeston Center, was organized, May 1846, with 21 members. The first pastor was Rev. J. H. Wells. The house of worship, which will seat 250, was erected in 1853 at a cost of $1,600. The present value of Church property is $5,000. The present number of members is 115, and the pastor, Rev. G. E. Flint.

Milford.—*Milford Center*, near the center, contains a hotel, store, Baptist church, blacksmith shop and a few dwelling houses.

Oneonta.—*West Oneonta* (p. v.) contains a hotel, three stores, a tailor shop, millinery shop, two wagon shops, a cooper shop, two blacksmith shops, a Free Will Baptist church, a shoe shop, two saw mills, a foundry, a brick manufactory and from one to two hundred inhabitants.

Oneonta Plains, about two miles west of Oneonta, contains a creamery, a Methodist church and eight or ten houses.

The Second Free Will Baptist Church, located at Oneonta, was organized, with 17 members, in February 1856, by Rev. O. T. Moulton, its first and present pastor, assisted by Revs. P. Scramling and D. Greene. The house of worship, which will seat 300. was erected in 1858 at a cost of $3,500. The present value of the Church property is $6,000. The present number of members is 70. This Church has had four pastors. The present one was its first pastor for five years, and is now on his second engagement. A good Sabbath School is connected with the Church.

Otego.—In 1783, Adam Kalden built a log house, about at the present center of the village of Otego.

Otsego.—The physicians of the Thanksgiving Hospital are Dr. W. T. Bassett and Dr. M. A. Bassett.

Springfield.—*The Springfield Baptist Church*, located at Springfield Center, was organized by Elder Bostwick, with nine members, about January 15, 1787. The first pastor was Elder Furman. The first house of worship was erected about 1790. The present house was erected in 1855 at a cost of $3,350 ; it will seat 250. The present value of Church property is $6,250. The present number of members is 65, and the pastor, Rev. S. J. Douglass. This was the first Baptist Church organized west of the Hudson River, and contributed much in planting other Baptist Churches in the surrounding country.

DIRECTORY.

Burlington.—Breese, Lewis, (West Burlington,) postmaster.

Kelsey, Silas L., (Burlington Flats,) saw and grist mills.

Cherry Valley.—Clearwatter, Joseph, (Saltspringville, Montgomery Co.,) general merchant.

Flint, Daniel, (Saltspringville, Montgomery Co.,) farmer 200.

MERRITT, GEO., (Cherry Valley,) loan commissioner, physician and surgeon, Main.

Nestell, George, (Saltspringville, Montgomery Co.,) farmer 92.

Peaslee, Joseph B., (Saltspringville, Montgomery Co.,) farmer 175.

Prime, John H., (Saltspringville, Montgomery Co.,) farmer 73.

Scott, Chas. W., (Cherry Valley,) post master and general agent for Empire State Life Insurance Co., for Otsego Co.

Walrad, Jonas, (Saltspringville, Montgomery Co.,) farmer 50.

Walradt, James, (Saltspringville, Montgomery Co.,) farmer 210.

Weller, Hiram, (Saltspringville, Montgomery Co.,) grist and saw mills.

Middlefield.—Davidson, Robert, (Middlefield Center,) post master.

Francis, Samuel, (Phœnix Mills,) post master and supt. for Scott, Ernst & Co.

GILBERT, FAYETTE L., (Middlefield,) post master, dealer in dry goods and groceries, agent for Singer Sewing Machines and farmer 43.

Morris.—LULL, ADIN, (Morris,) (*Lull & Steele*.)

LULL & STEELE, (Morris,) (*Adin Lull and H. C. Steele,*) general merchants.
STEELE, H. C., (Morris,) (*Lull & Steele.*)

Otsego.—AVERY, DAVID A., (Cooperstown,) county treasurer and director Second National Bank of Cooperstown.

BOWEN, SAMUEL A., (Cooperstown,) district attorney, attorney and counselor at law, Main.

Westford.—Drake, John, (Westford,) physician and coroner.

The Buckeye Mowing and Reaping Machines—When the great U. S. Trial of Mowers and Reapers was held at Syracuse in 1857, this admirable machine, which had just been brought out, surprised everybody by its novelty and many excellencies, and won the highest awards. At that time the valuable patents under which it was built were secured for several States by the enterprising firm which now continues its manufacture, Adriance, Platt & Co. At the second great trial of Mowers and Reapers, made by the N. Y. State Agricultural Society in 1866, the Buckeye again carried off the highest honors, showing that in the years intervening it had not gone backward in the race for superiority. Every new suggestion is thoroughly weighed, *improvements* only are adopted. The verdict of the people is nearly as unanimous as that of the learned and practical committees who made these awards, for its sales far exceed those of any other machine in the sections supplied by Adriance, Platt & Co. In fact they increase so *fast*, that the demand is almost always in excess of the supply. The Self-Raking Attachment on the Buckeye Machine has met with a success corresponding to that of the Mower, and has surpassed all others in the perfection of its operation. One great secret of the success of Adriance, Platt & Co., as manufacturers, has been in the conscientious manner in which they have built their machines, and the great durability of the Buckeye machine has been largely due to the excellence of the material used and the mechanical perfection of the workmanship. See advertisement on Map.

Dr. Kingsley, of Rome, justly celebrated for the many cures he has effected of that most distressing disease, Cancer, publishes a notice on page 1. He is prepared to treat all scrofulous diseases, and others of long standing, and assures his patients that they will not be charged a heavy bill and dismissed without receiving any benefit. Persons who cannot conveniently call upon him in person, can address him by letter, and will receive prompt attention. Dr. K. is a graduate, with an experience of over fourteen years in the practice of medicine. Let the afflicted give him a call.

Henry Bayer, Merchant Tailor and dealer in Gentlemen's Furnishing Goods, Cooperstown, publishes an appropriately illustrated card on page 190. Those who want a good suit of clothes, made up in fashionable style and in a workmanlike manner, we recommend to call on Mr. Bayer, who will give you *fits* every time and charge you a reasonable price.

R. Russell & Co., proprietors of the Central Cash Store, at Cooperstown, N. Y., advertise on page 156. Messrs. R. & Co. are too well known to need any commendation from us. They have been established over ten years, command a large trade, and keep a general assortment of Dry Goods, Groceries, and all other goods usually found in a first-class country store, and which they sell at New York prices. Call on them when you go to Cooperstown.

Hinds & Parshall, Butchers and proprietors of Meat Market, Cooperstown, N. Y., keep a good supply of all kinds of Meats, constantly on hand, which they dispose of at such reasonable rates that no one need go hungry. See card on page 164.

Otsego Iron Works, located at Fly Creek, are largely engaged in the manufacture of Steam Engines, Turbine Water Wheels, Circular Saw Mills, Flour Mills, Threshers and Cleaners, Plows, Scrapers, Castings and Machinery in general. The Works cover an area of two acres, and were started in 1812. Mr. Shepherd, the present proprietor, is the successor of Metcalf & Shepherd, and has been connected with the Works since 1869. He gives his personal attention to the business, employs none but good workmen, uses good materials and turns out first-class work. See advertisement on page 148.

Ackerman & Son, Edmeston, keep a good assortment of Lumber, and everything in their line, constantly on hand, and manufacture Doors, Sash, Blinds, and everything necessary to finish a first-class house. They are enterprising, energetic men, and can be depended upon to fulfill whatever they promise. Being Builders themselves, they know just what is wanted for a house, and how to finish it. Give them your patronage if you would have everything in first-class style. See card on page 156.

The Freeman's Journal, published at Cooperstown, by S. M. Shaw, was established in 1808. It is a live family newspaper and enjoys a liberal patronage. Its extensive circulation makes it an excellent advertising medium, a fact which business men should not fail to make a note of. See card on page 198.

Geo. W. Borden, Schenevus, dealer in Clocks, Watches and Jewelry, is prepared to furnish his customers with Silver and Plated Ware, Musical Instruments, Fishing Tackle, and a variety of other articles too numerous to mention. If you want a good timekeeper, or the old one repaired, give him a call. See card on page 198.

GENERAL CONTENTS.

INDEX TO BUSINESS DIRECTORY.

INDEX TO ADVERTISEMENTS.

The Empire Agricultural Works of Minard Harder, located in the village of Cobleskill, Schoharie Co., N. Y., were established in 1859 by Messrs. R. & M. Harder. Like most great enterprises, its beginnings were small and only a small number of machines were sold the first year; but the business has constantly increased until they now give employment to about twenty-five hands and sell about $50,000 worth annually. Mr. Minard Harder, one of the original proprietors, is now the sole owner of these works and is manufacturing some of the best Threshing Machines in the country, as well as other Implements. At the Great National Implement Trial at Auburn, N. Y., in July 1866, a gold medal was awarded to Messrs. Harder for the best Combined Thresher and Cleaner. The Committee, in speaking of the Endless Chain Horse Powers made by Mr. Harder, say, that "It works more equably, more smoothly and with less waste of power than any machines that we have ever met with. * * * The construction of this machine is such as to produce a sufficient speed for threshing, by a very slow and easy movement, of the horses," while the mechanical execution of this power is deserving of the highest commendation. The best of materials and the best workmanship are combined in all machines coming from Mr. Harder's establishment. The Combined Thresher and Cleaner has several new features, rendering it superior to any other in use. Mr. Harder also manufactures Fanning Mills, Wood Saws, Seed Sowers and Planters. Farmers, it will pay you to make a visit to Cobleskill, and visit the Empire Agricultural Works, and inspect his machines. If you cannot make it convenient to do so, write to Mr. Harder for a Catalogue, which he will cheerfully send you by mail, free. But first of all, read his advertisement, which you will find inside the first cover of this work.

Jay L. Comstock, Surveyor and Conveyancer, Richfield Springs, publishes his card on page 246. Mr. C. is a gentleman of experience in his profession, and all who require his services may rest assured of the efficient performance of his work.

Newell & Pank, Builders and Jobbers, manufacturers of Sash, Doors and Blinds, opposite the Depot, Cooperstown, publish a card on page 18. They have a large establishment, where Planing, Sawing, Moulding and Turning is done, and all material prepared for building in the best manner. They have had 15 years' experience in the erection of all classes of buildings, Stair Building &c. During 1871 over twenty buildings were erected by this firm, besides furnishing materials for many more. Messrs. Newell & Pank are successors to C. A. Newell & Co., Mr. Pank having lately entered the firm and brought to the business the capital of experience and means acquired during seven years in a similar establishment at Rockville, Conn. Newell & Pank have commenced with enlarged capital, and have begun a further addition to their factory, adding new and improved machinery, and systematizing their business to insure promptitude as well as efficiency in all its departments. It will be to the interest of those contemplating building, to consult them before letting their work or purchasing materials.

Dodge's Model Printing Offices are advertised on page 230. Mr. G. A. Dodge is the proprietor of three separate printing offices, all located on the line of the Albany and Susquehanna Railroad, viz., the *Otsego Democrat*, published at Oneonta; *Home and Abroad*, at Unadilla; and the *Saturday Review*, at Bainbridge. These papers are ably conducted, contain forty columns each, and have a combined circulation of 4,000 copies. Business men should not fail to note this. Connected with each office is a well arranged Job Department, where all kinds of Job Printing is neatly executed at reasonable rates.

C. B. Fuller, Richfield Springs, manufacturer of Saddles, Harness and Trunks, prints an appropriately illustrated card on page 246. Anything in the harness dealers' line can be procured of Mr. Fuller at moderate rates. His work is always well executed and consequently gives satisfaction, as his numerous patrons will testify. Mr. F. also does Upholstering in all its branches with neatness and dispatch. Try him.

OTSEGO COUNTY OFFICERS.

Coroners.
P. O. ADDRESS
Bunn, Albert C. ....Morris
Drake, John............ .. ..Westford
Hills, Lyman H....... ....Schuyler's Lake
Packard, Edward M.... .... Unadilla

County Clerk.
Hills, E. Delevan .. .. .Cooperstown

County Judge.
Edick, Samuel S.............Cooperstown

County Treasurer..
Avery, David A..............Cooperstown

District Attorney.
Bowen, Samuel A ....Cooperstown

Justices of Sessions.
P. O. ADDRESS
Best, Henry W..............Cherry Valley
Shaffer, Isaac ....

Loan Commissioners.
Jenks, James W. ....Oneonta
Merritt, Geo................Cherry Valley

School Commissioners.
Clinton, E. R. Jr............. Butternuts
Thompson, Chas. F.......Schuyler's Lake

Sheriff.
Franklin, Daniel............Cooperstown

Surrogate.
Scofield, Byron J............Cooperstown

Courts in Otsego County.—1872–3.
TO BE HELD AT THE COURT HOUSE IN COOPERSTOWN.

	1872.	1873
Third Monday in January	BALCOM, Justice	BOARDMAN, Justice
Third Monday in June	MURRAY, Justice	BALCOM, Justice
Third Monday in September	MURRAY, Justice	BOARDMAN, Justice
Fourth Tuesday in March*	BALCOM, Justice	BOARDMAN, Justice

*Special Term without a Jury.

COUNTY COURTS AND COURTS OF SESSIONS.
SAMUEL S. EDICK, COUNTY JUDGE.

Second Monday in...March
Third Monday in...April
Second Monday in...July
Second Monday in..August
Last Monday in..October
First Monday in...December

United States Officers in Otsego County.
ASSISTANT ASSESSOR.
P. O. ADDRESS
John B. Hooker ....Fly Creek

DEPUTY COLLECTORS.
Elias C. Mather..Garrattsville
Fred. L. Palmer...Cooperstown

DEPUTY MARSHAL.
E. A. Olendorf...Fly Creek

REGISTER OF BANKRUPTCY.
Edwin Countryman...Cooperstown

UNITED STATES JUDGE.
Hon. Samuel Nelson ....Cooperstown

Post Offices and Post Masters in Otsego County.

POST OFFICE.	TOWN.	POST MASTER
Burlington	Burlington	T. A. Rutherford
Burlington Flats	Burlington	Newton A. Marcy
Butternuts	Butternuts	E. N. Cobb
Center Valley	Roseboom	Sawyer F. Pearson
Chaseville	Maryland	Simon B. Wilson
Cherry Valley	Cherry Valley	Chas. W. Scott
Colliersville	Milford	Abram Diefendorf
Cooperstown	Otsego	Thos. S. Blodgett
Decatur	Decatur	Daniel Day
East Springfield	Springfield	Geo. R. Fowler
East Worcester	Worcester	N. Thurber
Edmeston	Edmeston	Truman Bootman
Elk Creek	Maryland	Edmund Kelley
Exeter	Exeter	Wm. P. Jones
Fly Creek	Otsego	Silas W. Alger
Garrattsville	New Lisbon	Edward S. Hoag
Hartwick	Hartwick	Elisha Robinson
Hartwick Seminary	Hartwick	Wm. C. Davison
Laurens	Laurens	Milton Gurney
Maple Grove	Morris	Loring Barker
Maryland	Maryland	Lysander Draper
Middlefield	Middlefield	Fayette L. Gilbert
Middlefield Center	Middlefield	Robert Davison
Milford	Milford	David Wilber
Morris	Morris	H. Sergeant
Mount Vision	Laurens	Chauncey Wright
New Lisbon	New Lisbon	G. I. Peck
Oaksville	Otsego	J. H. Steere
Oneonta	Oneonta	G. W. Reynolds
Otego	Otego	M. Wilcox
Otsdawa	Otego	G. A. Chamberlain
Phœnix Mills	Middlefield	Samuel Francis
Pittsfield	Pittsfield	Chester Card
Pleasant Brook	Roseboom	Othelbert Low
Portlandville	Milford	Eli Van Etten
Richfield	Richfield	Joseph M. Hyde
Richfield Springs	Richfield	Eugene A. Hinds
Roseboom	Roseboom	John W. Sterricker
Schenevus	Maryland	S. H. Gurney
Schuyler's Lake	Exeter	Lucius O. Veber
South Edmeston	Edmeston	Nelson W. Matterson
South Hartwick	Hartwick	Laselle L. Hubbard
South Valley	Roseboom	D. A. Finch
South Worcester	Worcester	Ira B. Olmstead
Spooner's Corners	Plainfield	Francis B. Smith
Springfield	Springfield	Zina E. Lay
Springfield Center	Springfield	John Losee
Toddsville	Hartwick	Sands Shumway
Unadilla	Unadilla	Edward M. Packard
Unadilla Center	Unadilla	Hiram Cole
Unadilla Forks	Plainfield	Albert B. Crumb
Wells' Bridge	Unadilla	Wm. H. White
West Burlington	Burlington	Lewis Breese
West Edmeston	Edmeston	Elias Andrews
West Exeter	Exeter	O. H. Wilcox
Westford	Westford	W. H. Tyler
West Laurens	Laurens	Daniel Mills
West Oneonta	Oneonta	Benjamin Culver
Westville	Middlefield	John Post
Worcester	Worcester	H. H. Smith

PUBLISHER'S NOTICES.

N. F. Ruso & Son, Produce Commission Merchants, Albany, N. Y., are extensive dealers in all kinds of Farm Produce. We commend Messrs. R. & Son to the favorable consideration of all interested parties, feeling assured that all who may deal with them will find them honorable business men. They are located at 28 Madison Avenue, corner of Church Street, opposite Albany & Susquehanna R. R. Passenger Depot. See card on page 14.

"The Buckeye," J. M. Childs & Co., proprietors, office 10 and 12 Fayette Street, Utica. It is hardly worth while to discuss the merits of this celebrated Mowing and Reaping Machine, at this late day. So perfect and complete was the Machine as originally invented, that its principles have never been changed. Improvement in parts, it is true, have been made, as experience showed them to be requisite. When it is understood that notwithstanding the great number of machines thrown upon the market for public favor, more than 130,000 of the "Buckeyes" have been sold, it will be universally conceded that the majority are in favor of this as a labor-saving implement. We will not attempt to detail its merits, but would recommend the reader to call and inspect the machine for himself, or send for a circular to J. M. Childs & Co., Utica. Messrs. C. & Co. also keep on hand a full assortment of Agricultural Implements, such as Threshing Machines, Fanning Mills, Horse Rakes, Cultivators, Plows, Cider Mills, &c., &c. Read their advertisement on colored page 271.

The Republican & Democrat, published at Cooperstown, N. Y., by James I. Hendryx, is advertised on page 268. It is a 36-column paper, Republican in politics, and for over forty years has been a welcome weekly visitor to the homes of a large number of the citizens of Otsego County. Mr. Hendryx is ably assisted by his son, Chas. F. Hendryx, in the editorial management of the paper. A good Job Office is connected with the establishment.

Bassett & Bailey, Cooperstown, Druggists, publish a card on page 246. They keep a good assortment of Drugs and Medicines, and put up Prescriptions in a careful manner. They are both young, energetic men, but thoroughly posted in the Drug trade, and are deserving of a liberal patronage.

George H. Gross, manufacturer of Horse Powers, Threshers and Cleaners, Fanning Mills &c., Fly Creek, Otsego Co., N. Y., advertises on page 156. Mr. Gross is the successor of E. W. Badger, having purchased the works in August 1871. He is a practical mechanic, thoroughly understands his business and is thoroughly prepared to render all work satisfactory. Repairing in all its branches, promptly attended to. We commend Mr. Gross to the favorable attention of all our readers.

Hartwick Theological and Classical Seminary presents rare advantages for the education of the young. It was incorporated in 1816, and endowed with $80,000 by John Christopher Hartwick. It is situated four miles from Cooperstown, near Hartwick Station, on the Cooperstown & Susquehanna Valley Railroad. It is liberally supplied with every means neccessary for the education of its pupils, and under the superintendency of its able Principal, Rev. T. T. Titus, A. M., assisted by a competent corps of teachers, its continued prosperity is assured. For further particulars, we refer the reader to page 198.

Tanner & Son, Cooperstown, Watchmakers and Jewelers, keep fully stocked with all goods pertaining to the Watch and Jewelry trade, which they dispose of at the most reasonable rates; and if you should be so unfortunate as to have your sight impaired, whether by advancing years or otherwise, you will find all varieties of artificial aids by calling on the Messrs. Tanner, where you cannot fail to get suited. See card on page 6.

Central New York Burr Mill Stone Manufactory, Utica, N. Y., Munson Bros., proprietors, is advertised on page 14. This firm manufactures the celebrated Burr Mill Stones, Munson's Patent Portable Mills, and deal in Steam Engines, Boilers, Saw Mills, Corn Crackers, Smut Machines, and all kinds of mill furnishings. This enterprising firm is too well known to require any commendation from us. They employ none but experienced workmen, consequently every article of their manufacture is well executed and bound to give satisfaction. They sell at the lowest cash prices. Give them a call.

The Morris Chronicle, L. P. Carpenter, editor and proprietor, is advertised on page 214. The *Chronicle* is a neatly printed and worthy local paper, its Local and Miscellaneous columns are well sustained, and we cheerfully commend it to the favor of the citizens of Morris and vicinity. All kinds of Job Printing is neatly executed at this office.

Miss M. E. Comstock, of Richfield Spa, keeps a good assortment of Millinery, Straw and Fancy Goods, a fact to which we wish to call the attention of the ladies. Her prices too are always reasonable. Call and see her, at Church Street, three doors from Main Street, if you wish anything in the above line. See card on page 246.

C. C. Shaver, manufacturer of Solid Silver Ware and dealer in Plated Ware of all kinds, No. 9 Broad Street, Utica, N. Y., advertises on colored page 273. Mr. Shaver keeps a splendid assortment of first-class goods, which he sells at prices which cannot fail to satisfy. Cash paid for old Silver. Call and see his splendid Tea Sets, and other elegant goods.

Richfield Springs Mercury is published at Richfield Springs every Saturday by C. Ackerman & Son. It is ably managed, is neatly printed and enjoys an extended circulation. The Job Department has every facility for doing all kinds of Book and Job Work with neatness and dispatch, and no pains are spared to make it a model printing office. See card on page 262.

Rockwell, Fitch & Co., proprietors of the Wholesale, Retail and Custom Woolen Mills, Mount Upton, Chenango Co., advertise on colored page 272. This is an old and well established manufactory, that has gained a wide reputation for manufacturing good all-wool goods. Experience has taught most of us that it is better to buy good cloth, though it cost a little more, than to invest in shoddy that will not pay for making. The establishment was started in 1832 as a custom mill, and as a woolen manufactory in 1849. They use only the best qualities of wool, entirely free from waste or shoddy, and employ only experienced and careful workmen, who strive to maintain the reputation their goods have ever borne. Farmers, Mechanics and business men generally, can make good bargains by calling at the factory.

C. W. Smith & Co., Bankers, Iron Clad Building, Cooperstown, N. Y., publish a card on page 164. They deal in Government Bonds and all first-class Securities, pay interest on Deposits, negotiate Loans, sell Drafts on foreign countries, issue Passage Tickets to and from Europe, make Collections &c., &c. Their facilities for doing a general banking business are such as to warrant the confidence of all desiring the services of a banker.

Peter Bundy, Otego, publishes his card on page 230. Mr. Bundy deals quite extensively in Flagging Stone, all sizes of which he keeps constantly on hand. Building Stone, in any quantity, can also be procured of him at reasonable rates. Builders and others would do well to give him a call. His Quarry is three miles north of Otego village.

We would respectfully call the attention of our readers to the card of Messrs. **J. & H. C. Walter,** published on colored page 271. Messrs. Walter are extensive dealers in Watches Jewelry, Silver Ware, Musical Instruments, Fancy Goods &c., a large assortment of which goods may always be seen at their store at Richfield Springs. If you want a good, reliable timekeeper, either Gold or Silver, at a fair price, Walters' is the place to get it. Their assortment of Jewelry, Solid Silver and Silver Plated Ware is very fine. Call and see them and you will be well repaid.

McIntosh & Haynes, Attorneys and Counselors at Law, Cooperstown, N. Y., publish their card on page 164. They pay particular attention to business in Surrogate and Justices' Courts.

O. J. & J. Walrath, Jobbers and Builders, and dealers in Ready-made Houses, publish a card on page 190. They are enterprising business men, good workmen, and allow no work to go out of their hands imperfectly executed. Parties proposing to build should not fail to call on them. Their office is near the Railroad Crossing, Cooperstown.

Chancey Williams, Cooperstown, proprietor of Saw, Shingle and Cider Mills, publishes a card on page 190. Mr. W. has had a large experience in the different branches which he advertises, and has been in business over six years. Lumber and Shingles, in any quantity, may be had of him at the most reasonable rates. He manufactures Cider to order. Mr. W. has also the entire right of the County in the Saw Guming business. Give him a call when you want anything in his line.

Morris Livery Stable, at Morris, N. Y., John W. Still, proprietor, is advertised on page 214. Mr. S. keeps a good supply of Saddle and Carriage Horses, and his Carriages, Sleighs &c., are of the best manufacture. His charges are always reasonable. Call on him when you want anything in his line.

J. W. Still, M. D., at Morris, is a graduate of Buffalo Medical College and has had a long and successful experience as a physician in the treatment of all forms of disease. We commend Dr. Still to the favor of those of our readers who may be so unfortunate as to require the services of a skillful physician. See card on page 214.

J. Gale & Sons, manufacturers of Horse Rakes, Bent Felloes, Chairs, Broom Handles &c., Barnerville, N. Y., advertise on page 2. This firm carry on a great variety of business, manufacturing Chairs extensively and doing all kinds of Turning. They are good workmen, use good timber and turn out good work. We commend them to the liberal patronage of all our readers, believing that they are worthy men.

M. De V. Martin, Furniture Dealer and Undertaker, Richfield Springs, advertises on page 230. Mr. M. keeps a good assortment of Furniture, to meet the varied wants and tastes of his patrons, and sells at the lowest living prices. Everything in the line of Undertaking is promptly attended to. Give him a call.

LLAGES.	Burlington Flats.	Butternuts.	Cherry Valley.	Clarksville.	Cooperstown.	Edmeston.	East Springfield.	East Worcester.	Fly Creek.	Garrattsville.	Hartwick Seminary.	Hartwick.	Jacksonville.	Laurens.	Maryland.	Milford.	Morris.	Monticello.	New Berlin.	Otego.	Oneonta.	Portlandville.	Richfield Springs.	Roseboom.	Schuyler's Lake.	South New Berlin.	Springfield.
gton Flats....																											
uts......	17.																										
Valley......	18.8	31.2																									
rille.....	15.1	24.5	7.4																								
rtown....	11.5	21.9	9.2	8.6																							
ton.......	3.7	13.6	21.8	17.4	13.8																						
pringfield....	16.6	30.4	3.3	8.4	9.	20.																					
orcester.....	23.2	29.7	10.7	8.3	11.6	25.1	13.7																				
eek........	8.9	20.5	10.8	6.2	2.7	11.3	9.8	14.4																			
tsville.......	5.6	12.1	20.	14.4	11.1	4.3	18.7	21.6	9.1																		
ck Seminary	11.2	18.6	12.7	5.9	3.7	12.5	12.7	12.5	4.2	9.																	
ck......	7.5	16.2	15.3	9.3	6.3	8.7	14.8	16.3	4.3	5.4	3.7																
nville......	10.9	13.1	18.8	11.3	9.1	10.5	18.	16.8	8.5	6.3	5.5	4.6															
s........	12.6	10.9	21.	13.9	11.9	11.4	20.8	18.8	4.3	7.3	8.2	7.3	2.7														
nd........	17.7	19.8	16.	8.9	9.5	18.4	17.8	10.1	11.	14.2	6.6	10.1	8.2	9.2													
l........	13.4	17.9	14.5	7.2	6.3	14.	15.	12.	7.2	10.1	2.9	5.7	4.9	7.	4.4												
ello.......	11.7	5.6	25.8	19.4	16.6	8.7	24.9	25.4	15.1	6.7	18.5	10.8	8.4	6.9	16	13.2											
erlin.......	8.9	25.6	13.1	13.4	10.8	12.6	10.1	21.3	9.	13.4	13.4	10.7	16.4	18.9	20.2	16.2	20.1										
a.........	8.9	9.1	26.4	21.1	17.8	5.3	24.8	28.2	15.6	6.6	15.6	12.	11.6	10.4	30.	16.3	5.7	17.9									
dville.......	19.9	8.	29.3	22.	20.4	17.6	29.4	25.2	20.	14.3	16.7	15.9	11.4	8.6	15.	14.7	9.1	27.3	14.7								
ld Springs...	17.4	11.4	23.9	16.5	15.3	16.	24.3	19.5	15.3	12.	11.6	11.6	7.1	4.8	9.3	9.2	9.6	23.5	15.	5.7							
om.........	15.6	16.	18.	10.6	10.	15.5	18.7	13.7	10.7	11.3	6.7	8.2	5.	5.5	8.8	3.6	12.3	19.6	16.5	11.6	6.						
er's Lake....	10.4	26.5	10.9	11.8	9.7	14.	7.8	19.6	8.3	14.3	12.5	11.7	16.3	16.	19.3	15.5	21.	2.2	19.8	27.6	23.4	19.					
om.........	7.2	22.2	11.6	9.5	6.6	10.6	9.4	17.8	4.4	10.	8.5	7.3	11.9	14.5	15.6	10.5	16.7	4.7	15.6	23.1	19.	14.9	4.5				
New Berlin	15.1	4.	31.2	25.1	22.1	11.3	30.1	31.1	20.3	11.3	19.2	16.2	14.1	12.5	21.7	19.	5.7	24.	6.4	11.6	14.3	17.8	25.8	28.9	21.2		
ield.........	13.9	28.4	5.8	8.4	7.8	17.3	2.8	15.1	7.9	16.3	11.4	12.2	16.4	16.2	17.	14.1	22.8	7.3	22.3	27.9	28.	17.8	5.1	7.1	6.8	27.7	
Valley......	20.5	30.	5.6	5.8	9.2	23.	8.6	5.2	11.7	20.3	11.5	14.8	16.8	19.2	12.2	12.3	25.1	17.1	26.9	26.8	21.1	15.1	15.1	3.3	14.3	30.8	10.3
vus.........	19.6	22.7	14.6	8.2	9.8	20.5	16.5	7.4	12.	16.5	8.4	11.8	10.7	12.	2.8	6.3	18.8	20.7	22.5	17.7	12.	6.7	19.6	11.1	36.3	24.5	16.6
a Forks......	6.6	22.2	21.	19.5	16.1	8.7	18.2	27.7	13.6	12.	16.9	13.8	17.5	19.	23.9	19.5	17.4	8.2	13.2	26.2	24.	22.	10.4	21.	9.9	19.6	15.3
a.........	24.8	8.5	36.5	29.3	27.5	21.7	36.4	32.6	26.7	19.6	28.8	22.4	18.8	15.5	22.5	22.	13.1	33.1	17.6	7.5	18.2	19.1	33.7	33.5	29.2	16.8	
dmeston......	4.3	17.2	22.6	19.4	15.7	4.2	20.2	27.5	13.1	8.2	15.4	10.7	14.4	15.5	21.8	17.5	12.7	11.3	8.1	21.8	20.2	19.8	13.2	21.8	10.9	14.	17.4
le.........	14.6	21.2	11.3	4.	4.5	16.1	12.2	9.1	6.7	12.5	3.5	7.8	8.1	10.3	5.2	3.4	16.5	15.3	19.	18.1	12.6	6.7	14.2	8.	10.8	22.2	11.
rd.........	17.7	25.2	8.7	2.9	6.1	19.5	10.6	5.6	8.7	16.2	7.1	9.8	12.	14.9	7.4	7.4	20.5	16.8	22.8	21.8	16.1	10.1	14.8	5.2	12.5	26.2	11.
ter.........	20.9	26.2	11.9	7.	9.8	22.4	14.2	3.5	12.4	18.7	9.8	13.6	18.1	15.3	6.6	8.8	22.	20.4	25.1	21.6	15.9	10.2	18.7	8.6	16.4	27.7	15.

THE STATES,

THEIR SETTLEMENT, ADMITTANCE TO THE UNION, POPULATION,

SUFFRAGE LAWS, ETC.

ALABAMA was settled near Mobile, in 1702, by the French; was formed into a Territory by act of Congress, approved March 3, 1817, from the eastern portion of the Territory of Mississippi; framed a Constitution August 2, 1819, and was admitted into the Union December 14 of the same year. Area 50,722 square miles, or 32,462,080 acres.— Population in 1860, 964,201, of whom 435,080 were slaves. Population in 1870 was 996,175. It is the chief cotton growing State of the Union. Male citizens who have resided one year in the State and three months in the county, are entitled to vote. An election for a Convention was held December 24, 1860, and a majority of over 50,000 votes cast for secession; the Convention met January 7, 1861, and on the 11th passed the ordinance of secession, by a vote of 61 to 39, which was followed on the 21st by the resignation of its members of Congress.

ARKANSAS was settled at Arkansas Post in 1685, by the French, and was part of the Louisiana purchase ceded by France to the United States, April 30, 1803. It was formed into a Territory by act of Congress, March 2, 1819, from the southern part of the Territory of Missouri; its western boundary was settled May 26, 1824, and its southern, May 19, 1828. Having adopted a Constitution, a memorial was presented in Congress, March 1, 1836, and an act for its admission into the Union passed June 15 of the same year. Area 52,198 square miles, or 33,406,-720 acres. In 1860 its population was 435,450, of whom 111,115 were slaves. Population in 1870 was 473,174. It is an agricultural State, its staples being corn and cotton. Citizenship and residence in the State for six months, qualify voters in the county and district where they reside.— January 16, 1861, its Legislature ordered a State Convention, which assembled, and on May 6, voted to secede, 69 to 1. January 4, 1864, a Convention assembled in Little Rock, which adopted a new Constitution, the principle feature of which consisted in a clause abolishing slavery. The Convention adjourned January 22. This body also inaugurated a Provisional Government. The Constitution was submitted to the people, and 12,177 votes cast for it, to 226 against it. The State was reorganized under the plan contained in the Amnesty Proclamation of President LINCOLN, in pursuance of which an election was held March 14, 1864. The vote required under the Proclamation was 5,405. About 16,000 votes were cast.

B

CALIFORNIA was settled at Diego in 1768, by Spaniards, and was part of the territory ceded to the United States by Mexico, by the treaty concluded at Guadaloupe Hidalgo, February 22, 1848. After several ineffectual attempts to organize it as a Territory or admit it as a State, a law was passed by Congress for the latter purpose, which was approved September 9, 1850. Area 188,981 square miles, or 120,947,784 acres. Population in 1870, 549,808. It is the most productive gold mining region on the continent, and also abounds in many other minerals. Male citizens of the United States, and those of Mexico who may choose to comply with the provisions of the treaty of Queretaro, of May 30, 1848, who have resided in the State six months and in the county or district thirty days, are entitled to vote.

CONNECTICUT was settled at Windsor, in 1633, by English Puritans from Massachusetts, and continued under the jurisdiction of that Province until April 23, 1662, when a separate charter was granted, which continued in force until a Constitution was formed, September 15, 1818. It was one of the original thirteen States, and ratified the United States Constitution, January 9, 1788. Area 4,674 square miles, or 2,991,360 acres. Population in 1870, 537,417. It is one of the most densely populated and principal manufacturing States in the Union. Residence for six months, or military duty for a year, or payment of State tax, or a freehold of the yearly value of seven dollars, gives the right to vote.

DELAWARE was settled at Wilmington, early in 1638, by Swedes and Finns; was granted to William Penn, in 1682, and continued under the government of Pennsylvania until the adoption of a Constitution, September 20, 1776; a new one was formed June 12, 1792. It was one of the original thirteen States, and ratified the United States Constitution, December 7, 1787. Area 2,120 square miles, or 1,356,800 acres.— Population, in 1860, 112,216, of whom 1,798 were slaves. Population in 1870 was 125,015. It is a grain and fruit growing State, with some extensive manufactories. Residence in the State one year, and ten days in the election district, with payment of a State or county tax assessed ten days prior to an election, gives the right to vote, except that citizens between twenty-one and twenty-two years of age need not have paid the tax.

FLORIDA was settled at St. Augustine, in 1565, by Spaniards; was formed from part of the territory ceded by Spain to the United States by treaty of February 22, 1819; an act to authorize the President to establish a temporary government was passed March 3, 1819; articles of surrender of East Florida were framed July 10, and of West Florida, July 17, 1821, and it was then taken possession of by General Jackson as Governor. An act for the establishment of a Territorial Government was passed March 30, 1822, and by act of March 3, 1823, East and West Florida were constituted one Territory. Acts to establish its boundary line between Georgia and Alabama were passed May 4, 1826, and March 2, 1831. After several ineffectual attempts to organize it into two Territories, or into a State and Territory, an act for its admission into the Union was passed March 3, 1845. Area 59,268 square miles, or 37,930,520 acres. Population, in 1860, 140,425, of whom 61,745 were slaves. Population in 1870 was 189,995. It is an agricultural State, tropical in its climate and products. Every male citizen, who has resided in the State two years and in the county six months, and has been enrolled in the militia (unless exempt by law,) is qualified to vote; but no soldier, seaman or marine can vote unless qualified before enlistment. Its Legislature called a Convention, December 1, 1860, which met January 3, 1861, and passed a secession ordinance on the 10th by a vote of 62 to 7.

GEORGIA was settled at Savannah, in 1733, by the English under General Oglethorpe. It was chartered June 9, 1732; formed a Constitution February 5, 1777; a second in 1785 and a third May 30, 1798.— It was one of the original thirteen States, and ratified the United States Constitution January 2, 1788. Area 58,000 square miles, or 37,120,000 acres. Population, in 1860, 1,057,286, of whom 462,198 were slaves. Population in 1870 was 1,174,832. It is a large cotton and rice growing State. Citizens of the State, six months resident of the county where voting, who have paid taxes the year preceding the election, are entitled to vote. November 18, 1860, its Legislature ordered an election for a State Convention, which assembled and passed a secession ordinance January 19, 1861, by a vote of 208 to 89, and on the 23d of the same month its members of Congress resigned.

ILLINOIS was settled at Kaskaskia, in 1683, by the French, and formed part of the northwestern territory ceded by Virginia to the United States. An act for dividing the Indiana Territory and organizing the Territory of Illinois, was passed by Congress, February 3, 1809; and an act to enable it to form a State Constitution, Government, &c., was passed April 18, 1818; a Constitution was framed August 26, and it was admitted into the Union December 23 of the same year. Area 54,405 square miles, or 64,819,200 acres. Population, in 1870, 2,529,410. It is the chief "prairie" State, and the largest grain growing and second largest cattle raising State in the Union. All male inhabitants, who have resided in the State one year and election district sixty days, can vote in the district where actually residing.

INDIANA was settled at Vincennes, in 1690, by the French, and formed part of the northwestern territory ceded by Virginia to the United States. It was organized into a Territory May 7, 1800, from which the Territory of Michigan was set off in 1805, and Illinois in 1809. An act was passed to empower it to form a State Constitution, Government, &c., April 19, 1816, and it was admitted into the Union December 11 of the same year. Area 33,809 square miles, or 21,637,760 acres. Population, in 1870, 1,655,675. It is an agricultural State, chiefly devoted to grain growing and cattle raising. A residence of one year in the State entitles males of 21 years of age to vote in the county of their residence.

IOWA was first settled at Burlington by emigrants from the Northern and Eastern States. It was part of the region purchased from France; was set off from the Territory of Wisconsin and organized as a separate Territory June 12, 1838; an act for its admission as a State was passed and approved March 3, 1845, to which the assent of its inhabitants was to be given to be announced by Proclamation of the President, and on December 28, 1846, another act for its admission was passed. Area 50,914 square miles or 32,584,960 acres. Population, in 1870, 1,181,359. It is an agricultural State, resembling Illinois, and contains important lead mines. Male citizens of the United States, having resided in the State six months and county twenty days, are entitled to vote.

KANSAS was formed out of the original Louisiana purchase, and organized into a Territory by act of Congress, May 30, 1854, and after several ineffectual attempts was finally admitted into the Union in January, 1861. Area 78,418 square miles, or 50,187,520 acres. Population, in 1870, 379,-497. It is an agricultural State, with a soil of rich and deep black loam, except the central portion, which is partly a desert. The western portion is a fine grazing country, well wooded. Residence in the State six months, and in the township or ward thirty days, confers the right of suffrage on male citizens. It also abounds in minerals.

KENTUCKY was settled in 1775, by Virginians; formed into a Territory by act of the Virginia Legislature, December 18, 1789, and admitted into the Union June 1, 1792, by virtue of an act of Congress passed February 4, 1791. Area 37,680 square miles, or 24,115,200 acres.—Population in 1860, 1,155,684, of whom 225,483 were slaves. Population in 1870 was 1,320,407. It is an agricultural State, raising more flax and hemp than any other. Loyalty, a residence of two years in the State and one in the county are the requirements to vote.

LOUISIANA was settled at Iberville, in 1699, by the French, and comprised a part of the territory ceded by France to the United States, by treaty of April 30, 1803, which purchase was erected into two Territories by act of Congress March 26, 1804, one called the Territory of Orleans, the other the District of Louisiana, afterwards changed to that of Missouri.—Congress, March 2, 1806, authorized the inhabitants of Orleans Territory to form a State Constitution and Government when their population should amount to 60,000; a Constitution was adopted January 22, 1812, and the State admitted into the Union April 8 of the same year, under the name of Louisiana. Area 41,255 square miles, or 26,403,200 acres. Population in 1860, 708,002, of whom 331,726 were slaves. Population in 1870 was 734,420. It is the chief sugar producing State of the Union. Two years' residence in the State and one in the parish are the qualifications of voters. December 10, 1860, the Legislature ordered a State Convention to be held, which assembled and passed an ordinance of secession January 26, 1861, by a vote of 113 to 17. The people voted on the question, and on March 28 the following was announced as the result: For, 20,448; against, 17,296; a majority of 3,152. The Convention ratified the 'Confederate' Constitution March 11, 1861, by a vote of 107 to 7, and refused to submit it to the people by 94 to 10. On the 11th day of January, 1864, Maj. Gen. Banks issued a Proclamation for an election of State officers and delegates to a Constitutional Convention, for the purpose of affecting a reconstruction of the State Government under the plan suggested in the Amnesty Proclamation of President Lincoln. The election was held on the 22d day of February, 1864. The officers thus elected were installed March 4. The total vote cast was 10,725. The vote requisite under the Proclamation, was 5,051. The Convention amended the Constitution so as to abolish slavery. The new Constitution was adopted by the people by a vote of 6,836 for, to 1,566 against.

MAINE was settled at York, in 1623, by the English, and was formerly under the jurisdiction of Massachusetts. October 29, 1819, the inhabitants of the District of Maine framed a Constitution; applied for admission December 8, 1819. Congress passed an act March 3, 1820, and it was admitted as a State March 15, of the same year. Area 31,766 square miles, or 20,330,240 acres. Population, in 1870, 628,719. It is largely engaged in the lumber trade and ship building. Citizens of the United

States, except paupers and persons under guardianship, who have resided in the State for three months next preceding the election, are entitled to vote.

MARYLAND was settled at St. Mary, in 1634, by Irish Roman Catholics, having been chartered June 20, 1632. It was one of the original thirteen States; formed a Constitution August 14, 1776, and ratified the Constitution of the United States April 28, 1788. Area 11,124 square miles, or 7,119,260 acres. Population in 1860, 687,049, of whom 87,189 were slaves. Population in 1870 was 790,095. It is mainly an agricultural State, producing grain and tobacco. A residence of one year in the State, and six months in the county, gives the right to vote to every male citizen who takes the oath of allegiance prescribed in the Constitution. January 28, 1864, a bill passed the Legislature submitting to the people the question of a Convention to revise the Constitution of the State. The popular vote on the question was as follows: For Convention, 32,203; against, 18,337. The Convention assembled and adopted a Constitution abolishing slavery, which was submitted to and adopted by the people; and in accordance with its provisions, on the 29th of October, 1864, the Governor issued his Proclamation declaring the slaves in that State free from the 1st day of November.

MASSACHUSETTS was settled at Plymouth, November 3, 1620, by English Puritans, and Charters were granted March 4, 1629, January 13, 1630, August 20, 1726, and October 7, 1731. It was one of the original 13 States; adopted a Constitution March 2, 1780, which was amended November 3, 1820, and ratified the Constitution of the United States February 6, 1788. Area 7,800 square miles, or 4,992,000 acres. Population in 1870, 1,457,351. It is a largely commercial, the chief manufacturing and most densely populated State in the Union. A residence of one year in the State, and payment of State or county tax, gives the right to vote to male citizens of 21 years and upward, except paupers and persons under guardianship.

MICHIGAN was settled at Detroit in 1670, by the French, and was part of the territory ceded to the United States by Virginia. It was set off from the territory of Indiana, and erected into a separate Territory January 11, 1805; an act to attach to it all the territory of the United States west of the Mississippi river, and north of the State of Missouri, was passed June 28, 1834. Wisconsin was organized from it April 30, 1836. In June of the same year an act was passed to provide for the admission of the State of Michigan into the Union, and a Constitution having been adopted, it was admitted January 26, 1837. Area 56,243 square miles, or 35,995,552 acres. Population in 1870, 1,184,653. It is a grain growing and cattle rearing State, with rich and extensive mines of copper and iron in the Northern Peninsula. In the vicinity of Saginaw, salt is extensively manufactured. A residence in the State of six months preceding the election, entitles male citizens to vote.

MINNESOTA was settled about 1846, chiefly by emigrants from the Northern and Western States. It was organized as a Territory by act of Congress approved March 3, 1849, and admitted into the Union February 26, 1857. Area 95,274 square miles, or 60,975,536 acres. Population in 1870, 424,543 whites. It is an agricultural State, chiefly devoted to Northern grains. The right to vote is extended to male persons of 21 years of age, of the following classes, if they have resided in the United States one year, the State four months, and the election district ten days: citizens of the United States, and those of foreign birth who have declared their intention to become citizens ; persons of mixed white and Indian blood who have adopted the customs of civilization, and those of pure Indian blood who have been pronounced capable by any district court of the State.

MISSISSIPPI was settled at Natchez, in 1716, by the French, and was formed out of part of the territory ceded to the United States by South Carolina in 1787, and Georgia in 1802. It was organized as a Territory by act of Congress, April 7, 1789, and enlarged on the north March 27, 1804, and on the south May 14, 1812. After several unsuccessful attempts to enter the Union, Congress finally passed an act March 1, 1817, enabling the people of the western part of the Territory to form a State Constitution and Government, which being complied with August 15, it was admitted December 10 of the same year. Area 47,156 square miles, or 30,179,840 acres. Population in 1860, 791,305, of whom 436,631 were slaves. Population in 1870 was 842,056. It is the second cotton growing State of the Union. Citizens who have resided one year in the State, and four months in the county, and having performed military duty or paid taxes, are entitled to vote. A Convention met January 7, 1861, and on the 9th passed an ordinance of secession by a vote of 84 to 15.

MISSOURI was settled at Genevieve in 1763, by the French, and was part of the territory ceded by France by treaty of April 30, 1803. It was created under the name of the District of Louisiana, by an act approved March 26, 1804, and placed under the direction of the officers of the Indiana Territory, and was organized into a separate Territory June 4, 1812, its name being changed to that of Missouri; and was divided March 2, 1819, the Territory of Arkansas being then created. An act authorizing it to form a State Constitution and Government was passed March 6, 1820, and it was admitted into the Union December 14, 1821. Area 67,380 square miles, or 43,123,200 acres. Population in 1860, 1,182,012, of whom 114,931 were slaves. Population in 1870 was 1,691,-693. An act of gradual emancipation was passed July 1, 1863, by a vote of 51 to 30. On the 6th of January, 1865, a Constitutional Convention assembled in St. Louis, and on the 8th of April adopted a new Constitution, declaring the State free, prohibiting compensation for slaves, and adopting many other radical changes. On the 6th of June the Constitution was adopted by the people by a vote of 43,670 to 41,808, and pursuant to a Proclamation issued on the 1st of July, the Constitution went into effect July 4, 1865. It is an agricultural and mining State. Citizens of the United States who have resided in the State one year, and county three months, are entitled to vote. By an act passed by the Legislature of 1863, voting by ballot was adopted, and the *viva voce* system abolished.

NEBRASKA was settled by emigrants from the Northern and Western States, and was formed out of a part of the territory ceded by France, April 30, 1803. Attempts to organize it were made in 1844 and 1848, but it was not accomplished until May 30, 1854. Area 75,955 square miles, or 44,796,160 acres. Population in 1870 116,888, besides a few roving tribes of Indians. A Convention adopted a State Constitution Feb. 9, 1866, which was submitted to the people on the 22d of June, and adopted by a vote of 3,938 for, to 3,838 against, and State officers were elected. A bill was passed by Congress, July 27th, admitting the State, but the President withheld his signature. In Feb. 1867, Congress passed an act imposing certain conditions to admission, which were promptly accepted, and the territory became a State. It is an agricultural region, its prairies affording boundless pasture lands.

NEVADA was organized as a Territory March 2, 1861. Its name signifies snowy, and is derived from the Spanish word *nieve* (snow.) It comprises 81,539 square miles, or 52,184,960 acres, lying mostly within the Great Basin of the Pacific coast. Congress, at its session in 1864, passed an act which was approved March 21, to enable the people of the Territory to form a Constitution and State Government, in pursuance of which a Government was organized and the Territory admitted as a State by Proclamation of the President, October 31, 1864. At the time of its organization the Territory possessed a population of 6,857 white settlers. Population in 1870 was 42,456. The development of her mineral resources was rapid and almost without parallel, and attracted a constant stream of immigration to the Territory. As the population has not been subject to the fluctuations from which other Territories have suffered, the growth of Nevada has been rapid and steady. At the general convention election of 1863, 10,934 votes were cast. During 1864 great accessions to the population were made. It is probably the richest State in the Union in respect to mineral resources. No region in the world is richer in argentiferous leads. It also contains an immense basin of salt, five miles square. Quartz mills are a very important feature in mining operations. The State is barren for agricultural purposes, and is remarkably healthy.

NEW HAMPSHIRE was settled at Dover, in 1623, by English Puritans, and continued under the jurisdiction of Massachusetts until September 18, 1679, when a separate charter was granted. It was one of the original thirteen States, and ratified the United States Constitution June 21, 1788; its State Constitution was framed January 5, 1776, and amended in 1784 and 1792. Area 9,280 square miles, or 5,939,200 acres. Population in 1860, 326,073; in 1870, 317,710, showing a decrease in ten years of 8,363. It is a grazing and manufacturing State. All male citizens, except paupers, are allowed to vote.

NEW JERSEY was settled at Bergen, in 1624, by the Dutch and Danes; was conquered by the Dutch in 1655, and submitted to the English in 1664, being held thereafter under the same grants as New York, until it was surrendered to the Crown in 1702. It was one of the original thirteen States, adopted a State Constitution July 2, 1776, and ratified the United States Constitution December 18, 1787. Area 8,320 square miles, or 5,324,800 acres. Population in 1870, 903,044. It is a grain and fruit growing region, its orchard and market products being relatively greater than those of any other State. A residence of one year in the State gives the right to vote, except to paupers, &c.

NEW YORK was settled at Manhattan, in 1614, by the Dutch; was ceded to the English by grants to the Duke of York, March 20, April 26, and June 24, 1664; was retaken by the Dutch in 1673, and surrendered again by them to the English, February 9, 1674. It was one of the original thirteen States; ratified the United States Constitution July 26, 1788; framed a Constitution April 20, 1777, which was amended October 27, 1801, and November 10, 1821; a new one was adopted November 3, 1846. Area 47,000 square miles, or 30,080,000 acres. Population in 1870, 4,370,846. It is the most populous, wealthy and commercial of the States. Male citizens of the United States, who have resided in the State one year, in the county four months, and election district thirty days, are entitled to vote.

NORTH CAROLINA was settled at Albemarle, in 1650, by the English, and was chartered March 20, 1663. It was one of the original thirteen States, and ratified the United States Constitution, November 21, 1789 ; its State Constitution was adopted December 18, 1776, and amended in 1835. Area 50,704 square miles, or 32,450,560 acres. Population in 1860, 992,622, of whom 331,059 were slaves. Population in 1870 was 1,016,954. It is an agricultural State, with some mines and extensive pine forests. Males of 21 years of age, having resided one year in any county in the State, may vote for a member of the House of Commons, but must own fifty acres of land to vote for a Senator. A State Convention passed an ordinance of secession May 21, 1861. An election for delegates to a State Convention took place September 21, 1865. The Convention assembled October 2. On the 2d of October it passed an ordinance forever prohibiting slavery. The Legislature ratified the Constitutional amendment December 1. An election was held on the first Thursday of November, for Governor, Members of Congress and the Legislature.

OHIO was settled at Marietta, in 1788, by emigrants from Virginia and New England ; was ceded by Virginia to the United States October 20, 1783; accepted by the latter March 1, 1784, and admitted into the Union April 30, 1802. Area 39,964 square miles, or 25,576,960 acres. Population in 1870, 2,652,302. It is the most populous and wealthy of the agricultural States, devoted principally to wool growing, grain and live stock. A male of 21 years of age, who has resided in the State one year, and has paid or been charged with a State or county tax, is eligible to vote.

OREGON, although it had previously been seen by various navigators, was first taken possession of by Capt. Robert Gray, who entered the mouth of its principal river May 7, 1792, naming it after his vessel, the Columbia, of Boston. Exploring expeditions soon followed, and fur companies sent their trappers and traders into the region. In 1811 a trading post was established at the mouth of the Columbia river by the American Fur Company, who named it Astoria. For some time a Provisional Territorial Government existed, but the boundary remained unsettled until the treaty with Great Britain in 1846, when the 49th parallel was adopted. It was formally organized as a Territory August 14, 1848 ; was divided March 2, 1853, on the 46th parallel, the northern portion being called Washington and the southern Oregon. November 9, 1857, a State Constitution was adopted, under which it was admitted February 14, 1859, about one-third of it on the east being added to Washington Territory, its northern boundary following the Columbia river until its intersection with latitude 46° north. Area 102,606 square miles, or 65,667,840 acres. Population in 1870, 90,878. It is an agricultural State, possessed of a fertile soil, extensive pastures, genial climate, and is well wooded. Gold and other precious metals are found in considerable abundance.

PENNSYLVANIA was settled at Philadelphia, in 1681, by English Quakers, and was chartered February 28 of the same year. It was one of the original thirteen States, ratifying the United States Constitution December 12, 1787 ; adopted a State Constitution September 28, 1776, and amended it September 2, 1790. Area 46,000 square miles, or 29,440,000 acres. Population in 1870, 3,511,543. It is the second State in wealth and population, and the principal coal and iron mining region in the

Union. Residence in the State one year, and ten days in the election district, with payment of a State or county tax assessed ten days prior to an election, gives the right to vote; except that citizens between 21 and 22 years of age need not have paid the tax.

RHODE ISLAND was settled at Providence in 1636, by the English from Massachusetts, under Roger Williams. It was under the jurisdiction of Massachusetts until July 8, 1662, when a separate charter was granted, which continued in force until the formation of a Constitution in September, 1842. It was one of the original thirteen States, ratifying the United States Constitution May 29, 1790. Area 1,306 square miles, or 835,840 acres. Population in 1870, 217,356. It is largely engaged in manufactures. A freehold possession of $13; or, if in reversion, renting for $7, together with a residence of one year in the State and six months in the town; or, if no freehold, then a residence of two years in the State and six months in the town, and payment of $1 tax or military service instead, are the qualifications of voters.

SOUTH CAROLINA was settled at Port Royal, in 1670, by the English, and continued under the charter of Carolina, or North Carolina, until they were separated in 1729. It was one of the original thirteen States, ratifying the United States Constitution May 23, 1798; it framed a State Constitution March 26, 1776, which was amended March 19, 1778, and June 3, 1790. Area 29,385 square miles, or 18,806,400 acres. Population in 1860, 703,708, of whom 402,406 were slaves, an excess of 101,270 over the whites. Population in 1870, 705,789. It is the principal rice-growing State. Males residing in the State two years and district six months, and having a freehold of fifty acres of land, or have paid a State tax, are entitled to vote. December 17, 1860, a Convention assembled in Columbia, adjourned to Charleston, and on the 24th unanimously adopted an ordinance of secession, which was followed the next day by a Declaration of Causes claimed to be sufficient to justify the act. An election for delegates to a State Convention was held September 4, 1865. The Convention assembled September 13, and adjourned on the 28th. It repealed the ordinance of secession, abolished slavery, equalized the representation of the Senate and taxation throughout the State, giving the election of Governor and Presidential electors to the people, ordered voting in the Legislature by *viva voce*, endorsed the Administration unanimously, and directed a commission to submit a code to the Legislature for the protection of the colored population. The Legislature ratified the Constitutional Amendment November 13, 1865.

TENNESSEE was settled at Fort Donelson, in 1756, by emigrants from Virginia and North Carolina; was ceded to the United States by North Carolina, December, 1789, conveyed by the Senators of that State February 25, 1790, and accepted by act of Congress April 2 of the same year; it adopted a Constitution Feb. 6, 1796, and was admitted into the Union the 1st of June following. Area 45,600 square miles, or 29,184,000 acres. Population in 1860, 1,109,601, of whom 275,179 were slaves. Population in 1870 was 1,225,937. It is a mining and agricultural State, and is largely productive of live stock. Citizens of the United States who have resided six months in the county are entitled to vote. A military league was formed between the Governor, Isham G. Harris, and the rebel States, May 7, 1861, ratified the same day by the Senate by a vote of 14 to 6, and a Declaration of Independence submitted to the people, the election to be held June 8, the result of which was declared by the Governor, June 24, to be 104,913 for, and 47,238 against. This movement not being acceptable to the people of East Tennessee, which had declared against separation by a vote of 32,923 to 14,780, they, in a Convention held at Greenville, June 18–21, repudiated it. Andrew Johnson, Provisional Governor of the State, called a State Convention to be held in Nashville the second Monday in January. Delegates were elected, the Convention met, declared slavery forever abolished, prohibited compensation to owners of slaves, and abrogated the secession ordinances. These amendments of the Constitution were submitted to the people 22d of February, 1865, with the following result: For ratification, 22,197; rejection, 63. The United States Constitutional Amendment was ratified April 5, 1865.

TEXAS was first settled at Bexar, in 1694, by Spaniards; formed a part of Mexico until 1836, when she revolted from that Republic and instituted a separate Government, under which she existed until admitted into the Union by a joint resolution approved March 1st, 1845, imposing certain conditions, which were accepted, and a Constitution formed July 4 of the same year, and another joint resolution adopted by Congress, consummating the annexation, was approved December 29, 1845. Area 237,504 square miles, or 152,002,500 acres. Population in 1860, 604,215, of whom 182,566 were slaves. Population in 1870 was 795,500. It is an agricultural region, principally devoted to grain, cotton and tropical fruits. Male citizens of 21 years of age, who have resided in the State one year and district six months are entitled to vote. A Convention assembled at Galveston January 28, 1861, and on February 1 passed an ordinance of secession, by a vote of 166 to 7, to be submitted to the people February 23, and on March 4 they declared the State out of the Union, and Gov. Houston issued a Proclamation to that effect.

VERMONT was settled in 1724, by Englishmen from Connecticut, chiefly under grants from New Hampshire; was formed from a part of the territory of New York, by act of its Legislature March 6, 1769; framed a Constitution December 25, 1777, and was admitted into the Union March 4, 1791, by virtue of an act of Congress passed February 18 of the same year. Area 10,212 square miles, or 6,535,680 acres. Population in 1870, 330,582. It is a grazing region, producing more wool, live stock, maple sugar, butter, cheese and hay, in proportion to its population, than any other State. Any citizen of the United States who has resided in the State one year, and will take the oath of allegiance, is entitled to vote.

VIRGINIA was settled at Jamestown, in 1607, by the English, and was chartered April 10, 1606, May 23, 1609, and March 12, 1612. It was one of the original thirteen States, ratifying the United States Constitution June 25, 1788; it framed a State Constitution July 5, 1776, which was amended January 15, 1830. The State was divided in 1863. Present area 37,352 square miles. Population in 1860, 1,314,532, of whom 481,-410 were slaves. Population in 1870 1,211,442. It is a large corn producing, and the chief tobacco growing State. Every male citizen of the age of 21 years, who has been a resident of the State for one year, and of the county, city or town where he offers to vote for six months next preceding an election, and has paid all taxes assessed to him, after the adoption of the Constitution, under the laws of the Commonwealth, after the re-organization of the county, city or town where he offers to vote, is qualified to vote for members of the General Assembly and all officers elective by the people. A Convention sitting in Richmond on the 17th of April, 1861, passed an ordinance of secession, by a vote of 88 to 55, which was submitted to the people at an election held May 23, the result of which was announced June 25 to be 128,824 for, and 32,134 against.

The State Government was re-organized by a Convention which met at Wheeling, May 11, 1861. Upon the division of the State in 1863, the seat of Government was removed to Alexandria. A State Constitutional Convention, March 10, 1864, adopted a section abolishing slavery.

WEST VIRGINIA.—On the passage of the ordinance of secession by the Virginia Convention, a Convention of the western and other loyal counties of the State was held at Wheeling, which assembled May 11, 1861, and on the 17th unanimously deposed the then State officers and organized a Provisional Government. On the 26th of November, 1861, a Convention representing the western counties assembled in Wheeling and framed a Constitution for West Virginia, which was submitted to the people on the 3d of May, 1862, and adopted by them by a nearly unanimous vote. The division of the State was sanctioned by the Legislature May 13, 1862, and ratified by Congress by an act approved December 31, 1862, conditioned on the adoption of an amendment to the Constitution providing for the gradual abolition of slavery, which was done on the 24th of March, 1863, by a vote of the qualified electors of the proposed State, 28,318 voting in favor of the amendment, and 572 against it.. In pursuance of the act of Congress, the President issued a Proclamation, April 20, 1863, admitting the State sixty days from the date thereof, and on the 20th of June the new State Government was formally inaugurated. Area 24,000 square miles. Population in 1860, 350,599, of whom 12,754 were slaves. Population in 1870 was 441,094. It is a large corn producing State, and abounds in coal and other minerals. The Alexandria Legislature adopted the United States Constitutional Amendment February 9, 1865. Male citizens, residents of the State one year and county thirty days, unless disqualified by rebellion, are entitled to vote.

WISCONSIN was settled at Green Bay, in 1669, by the French; was a part of the territory ceded by Virginia, and was set off from Michigan December 24, 1834, and was organized into a Territory April 30, 1836. Iowa was set off from it June 12, 1838, and acts were passed at various times setting its boundaries. March 3, 1847, an act for its admission into the Union was passed, to take effect on the issuing of a Proclamation by the President, and by act of May 29, 1848, it was admitted into the Union. Area 53,924 square miles, or 34,511,360 acres. Population in 1870, 1,055,501. It is an agricultural State, chiefly engaged in grain raising and wool growing. Citizens of the United States, or foreigners who have declared their intention to become citizens, are entitled to vote. Colored citizens were admitted to the franchise, by a decision of the Supreme Court, rendered the 27th day of March, 1866, holding that, whereas an election was held in 1849, under the provisions of chapter 137, of that year, at which election 5,265 votes were cast in favor of the extension of the right of suffrage to colored men, and 4,075 against such extension, therefore, the section of said law conferring such right had been constitutionally adopted and is the law of the land.

THE TERRITORIES,

THEIR BOUNDARIES, AREA, PHYSICAL FEATURES, ETC.

ALASKA, our new territory, recently purchased of Russia, comprehends all the north-west coast on the Pacific, and the adjacent islands north of the parallel of 50 degrees 40 minutes north, and the portion of the mainland west of the meridian (about 140° west) of Mount St. Elias. The area is computed at 481,276 square miles. The climate, although warmer than in the same latitude on the eastern coast, is too rigorous to admit of successful agricultural operations, and the chief value of the country and adjacent seas is derived from their fisheries and hunting grounds. The southern and central portions are mountainous; the northern portion along the Arctic ocean is quite flat, nowhere rising more than fifteen or twenty feet above the sea. The population is estimated at about 80,000, mostly Esquimeaux.

ARIZONA was organized by the Thirty-Seventh Congress, in the winter of 1863, out of the western half of New Mexico, the boundary between the two Territories being the 109th meridian (32d west from Washington,) and includes the greater portions of the valleys of Colorado and Gila, which two rivers drain its entire surface, with parts of Utah, New Mexico and Nevada, and yet convey, it is reported, a less volume of water to the sea than the Hudson at Albany. The fertile Messilla Valley was left with New Mexico. The Territory forms a block nearly square, and contains 126,141 square miles, or 80,730,240 acres. Its white population in 1870 was 9,658. For agricultural purposes it is probably the most worthless on the Continent, owing to the absence of rains, but it is reputed to abound in silver mines.

COLORADO was organized March 2, 1861, from parts of Kansas, Nebraska and Utah, and is situated on each side of the Rocky Mountains, between latitude 37° and 41°, and longitude 25° and 32° west from Washington. Area 104,500 square miles, or 66,880,000 acres. Population in 1870 was 39,706, besides numerous tribes of Indians. By an enabling act passed March 21, 1864, the people of the Territory were authorized to frame a State Constitution and organize a State Government, and a Convention accordingly met in 1865, and on the 12th of August adopted a Constitution, which was submitted to and adopted by the people September 5, and State officers elected November 14. A bill to admit the Territory as a State passed Congress, but was vetoed May 25, 1866. It is said to be a superior grazing and cattle producing region, with a healthy climate and rich soil. An extensive coal bed, and also gold, iron and other minerals abound.

COLUMBIA.—Originally the "*District of Columbia*" was ceded to the United States by Maryland and Virginia, in 1790, and became the seat of the National Government in 1800. It was orignally ten miles square, lying on both sides of the Potomac, thirty-six square miles having been taken from Virginia, and sixty-four square miles from Maryland. By an act of Congress in 1846, that portion taken from Virginia was retroceded to that State. The 41st Congress, 1870–71, erected the District into a Territory. Until this year the District was governed directly by the Congress of the United States, and its inhabitants had no representation and no voice in the Federal elections. The cities of the Territory are Washington and Georgetown. Population in 1870 was 131,706.

DAKOTA was first settled by employees of the Hudson Bay Company, but is now being peopled by emigrants from the Northern and Western States. It was set off from the western portion of Minnesota when that Territory became a State in 1857, and was organized March 2, 1861. Area 148,932 square miles, or 95,316,480 acres. Population in 1870 was 14,181 whites, besides the roving tribes of Indians.

IDAHO was organized by the Thirty-Seventh Congress, at its second session, in the winter of 1863. Its name means 'Bead of the Mountains,' and it embraces the whole breadth of the Rocky Mountain region, and has within its bounds the head waters of nearly all the great rivers that flow down its either slope, but the greater portion lies east of the mountains. Its southern boundary is the 41st, its northern the 46th parallel of latitude. It extends from the 104th meridian on the east to the 110th on the west. Area 326,378 square miles, or 208,870,720 acres. Population in 1870, 14,-998 besides the Indians. For agricultural purposes it is comparatively worthless, but abounds in gold and other valuable mines.

MONTANA was settled by emigrants from the Northern and Western States. Organized in 1864, with the following boundaries: Commencing at a point formed by the intersection of the 27° L. W. from Washington with the 45° N. L.; thence due west on said 45th degree to a point formed by its intersection with the 34th degree W. from Washington; thence due south along said 34th degree of longitude to its intersection with the 44th degree and 30 minutes of N. L.; thence due west along said 44th degree and 30 minutes of N. L. to a point formed by its intersection with the crest of the Rocky Mountains; thence following the crest of the Rocky Mountains northward till its intersection with the Bitter Root Mountains; thence northward along the crest of said Bitter Root Mountains to its intersection with the 39th degree of longitude W. from Washington; thence along said 39th degree of longitude northward to the boundary line of the British possessions; thence eastward along said boundary to the 27th degree of longitude W. from Washington; thence southward along said 27th degree to the place of beginning. This makes it the northermost Territory next the States east of the Missouri Valley. It is a good mining and agricultural region. The population in 1870 was 20,594.

NEW MEXICO was formed from a part of the territory ceded to the United States by Mexico, by the treaty of Guadaloupe Hidalgo, February 2, 1848, and was organized into a Territory September 9, 1850.— Area 121,201 square miles, or 77,568,640 acres. Population in 1870 was 91,789, besides large tribes of warlike Indians. The principal resource of the country is its minerals.

UTAH was settled by the Mormons, and was formed from a part of the territory ceded to the United States by Mexico, by the treaty of Guadaloupe Hidalgo, February 2, 1848, and was organized into a Territory, September 9, 1850. Area, 106,382 square miles, or 68,084,480 acres. Population in 1870 was 86,786. Brine, sulphureous and chalybeate springs abound; limestone, granite, sandstone and marble are found in large quantities; iron is abundant, and gold, silver, copper, lead and zinc have been found. Not one-fiftieth part of the soil is fit for tillage, but on that which is, abundant crops of grain and considerable cotton are raised. A Convention was held at Great Salt Lake City, January 22, 1862, and a State Constitution formed, but it has not been acted on by Congress.

WASHINGTON was settled by emigrants from the Northern and Western States, and was organized into a Territory, March 2, 1853, from the northern portion of Oregon, to which was added another portion from the eastern part when the latter Territory was admitted as a State, February 14, 1859. Area 69,994 square miles, or 48,636,800 acres. Population in 1870 was 23,901 besides numerous tribes of Indians.

WYOMING was organized in July 1868. It lies between the 27th and 34th meridians of longitude west from Washington, and between the 41st and 45th parallels of latitude. The Territory is rich in mineral wealth, having large quantities of iron, coal, gypsum and building stone, besides vast quantities of gold, silver and copper. Salt springs of great value are found within its limits. The western portion of the Territory embraces what is generally known as the "Sweet Water Mines." The climate is healthy, and the Territory is rapidly filling up with an enterprising and hardy population. The act of Congress organizing the Territory, provides that "There shall be no denial of the elective franchise or any other right, on account of color or race, and all persons shall be equal before the law." Population in 1870 was 9,118.

STAMP DUTIES.

Schedule of Duties on and after March 1, 1867, with amendments to take effect Oct. 1, 1870.
(See Note, at end of Schedule.)

	Stamp Duty.
Accidental injuries to persons, tickets, or contracts for insurance against,	exempt.
Affidavits,	exempt.
Agreement or contract not otherwise specified:	
For every sheet or piece of paper upon which either of the same shall be written,	$0 5
Agreement, renewal of, same stamp as original instrument.	
Appraisement of value or damage, or for any other purpose: For each sheet of paper on which it is written,	5
Assignment of a lease, same stamp as original, and additional stamp upon the value or consideration of transfer, according to the rates of stamps on deeds. (See Conveyance.)	
Assignment of policy of insurance, same stamp as original instrument. (See Insurance.)	
Assignment of mortgage,	exempt.
Bank check, draft or order for any sum of money drawn upon any bank, banker or trust compa-	

	Stamp Duty.
ny at sight or on demand,	2
When drawn upon any other person or persons, companies or corporations, for any sum exceeding $10, at sight or on demand,	2
Bill of exchange, (inland,) draft or order for the payment of any sum of money not exceeding $100, otherwise than at sight or on demand, or any memorandum, check, receipt, or other written or printed evidence of an amount of money to be paid on demand or at a time designated: For a sum not exceeding $100,	5
And for every additional $100 or fractional part thereof in excess of $100,	
Bill of exchange, (foreign,) or letter of credit drawn in, but payable out of, the United States: If drawn singly, same rates of duty as inland bills of exchange or promissory notes.	
If drawn in sets of three or more, for every bill of each set, where	

	Stamp Duty.
the sum made payable shall not exceed $100 or the equivalent thereof in any foreign currency	2
And for every additional $100, or fractional part thereof in excess of $100,	2
Bill of lading or receipt (other than charter party) for any goods, merchandise, or effects to be exported from a port or place in the United States to any foreign port or place,	10
Bill of lading to any port in British North America,	exempt.
Bill of lading, domestic or inland,	exempt.
Bill of sale by which any ship or vessel, or any part thereof, shall be conveyed to or vested in any other person or persons:	
When the consideration shall not exceed $500,	50
Exceeding $500, and not exceeding $1,000,	1 00
Exceeding $1,000, for every additional $500, or fractional part thereof,	50
Bond for indemnifying any person for the payment of any sum of money: When the money ultimately recoverable thereupon is $1,000 or less,	50
When in excess of $1,000, for each $1,000 or fraction,	50
Bond-administrator or guardian, when the value of the estate and effects, real and personal, does not exceed $1,000,	exempt.
Exceeding $1,000,	1 00
Bond for due execution or performance of duties of office,	1 00
Bond, personal, for security for the payment of money. (See Mortgage.)	
Bond of any description, other than such as may be required in legal proceedings, or used in connection with mortgage deeds, and not otherwise charged in this schedule,	25
Broker's notes. (See Contract.)	
Certificates of measurement or weight of animals, wood, coal or hay,	exempt.
Certificates of measurement of other articles,	5
Certificates of stock in any incorporated company,	25
Certificates of profits, or any certificate or memorandum showing an interest in the property or accumulations of any incorporated company: If for a sum not less than $10 and not exceeding $50,	10
Exceeding $50 and not exceeding $1,000,	25
Exceeding $1,000, for every additional $1,000 or fractional part thereof,	25
Certificate. Any certificate of damage or otherwise, and all other certificates or documents issued by any port warden, ma-	

	Stamp Duty.
rine surveyor, or other person acting as such,	25
Certificate of deposit of any sum of money in any bank or trust company, or with any banker or person acting as such: If for a sum not exceeding $100,	2
For a sum exceeding $100.	5
Certificate of any other description than those specified,	5
Charter, renewal of, same stamp as an original instrument.	
Charter party for the charter of any ship or vessel, or steamer, or any letter, memorandum, or other writing relating to the charter, or any renewal or transfer thereof: If the registered tonnage of such ship, vessel, or steamer does not exceed 150 tons,	1 00
Exceeding 150 tons, and not exceeding 300 tons,	3 00
Exceeding 300 tons, and not exceeding 600 tons,	5 00
Exceeding 600 tons,	10 00
Check. Bank check,	2
Contract. Broker's note, or memorandum of sale of any goods or merchandise, exchange, real estate, or property of any kind or description issued by brokers or persons acting as such: For each note or memorandum of sale.	10
Bill or memorandum of the sale or contract for the sale of stocks, bonds, gold or silver bullion, coin, promissory notes, or other securities made by brokers, banks, or bankers, either for the benefit of others or on their own account: For each hundred dollars, or fractional part thereof, of the amount of such sale or contract,	1
Bill or memorandum of the sale or contract for the sale of stocks, bonds, gold or silver bullion, coin, promissory notes, or other securities, not his or their own property, made by any person, firm, or company not paying a special tax as broker, bank or banker: For each hundred dollars, or fractional part thereof, of the amount of such sale or contract,	5
Contract. (See Agreement.)	
Contract, renewal of, same stamp as original instrument.	
Conveyance, deed, instrument or writing, whereby any lands, tenements, or other realty sold shall be granted, assigned, transferred, or otherwise conveyed to or vested in the purchaser or purchasers, or any other person or persons, by his, her or their direction, when the consideration or value does not exceed $500,	50

Stamp Duty.

When the consideration exceeds $500, and not to exceed $1,000,   1 00

And for every additional $500, or fractional part thereof, in excess of $1,000,   50

Conveyance. The acknowledgment of a deed, or proof by a witness,   exempt.

Conveyance. Certificate of record of a deed,   exempt.

Credit, letter of. Same as foreign bill of exchange.

Custom-house entry. (See Entry.)

Custom-house withdrawals. (See Entry.)

Deed.(See Conveyance Trust deed.)

Draft, payable at sight or on demand,   2

Draft, payable otherwise that at sight or on demand, for any sum not exceeding 100,   5

For every additional $100 or fractional part thereof in excess of $100,   5

Endorsement of any negotiable instrument,   exempt.

Entry of any goods, wares or merchandise at any custom-house, either for consumption or warehousing: Not exceeding $100 in value,   25

Exceeding $100, and not exceeding $500 in value,   50

Exceeding $500 in value,   1 00

Entry for the withdrawal of any goods or merchandise from bonded warehouse,   50

Gauger's returns,   exempt.

Indorsement upon a stamped obligation in acknowledgment of its fulfillment,   exempt.

Insurance (life) policy: When the amount insured shall not exceed $1,000,   25

Exceeding $1,000, and not exceeding $5,000,   50

Exceeding $5,000,   1 00

Insurance (marine, inland, and fire,) policies, or renewal of the same: If the premium does not exceed $10,   10

Exceeding $10, and not exceed ing $50,   25

Exceeding $50,   50

Insurance contracts or tickets against accidental injuries to persons,   exempt.

Lease, agreement, memorandum, or contract for the hire, use, or rent of any land, tenement, or portion thereof: Where the rent or rental value is $300 per annum or less,   50

Where the rent or rental value exceeds the sum of $300 per annum, for each additional $200, or fractional part thereof in excess of $300,   50

Legal documents:

Writ, or other original process, by which any suit, either criminal or civil, is commenced in any court, either of law or equity,   exempt.

Stamp Duty.

Confession of judgment or cognovit,   exempt.

Writs or other process on appeals from justice courts or other courts of inferior jurisdiction to a court of record.   exempt.

Warrant of distress.   exempt.

Letters of administration. (See Probate of will.)

Letters testamentary, when the value of the estate and effects, real and personal, does not exceed $1,000,   Exempt.

Exceeding $1,000,   5

Letters of credit. Same as bill of exchange, (foreign.)

Manifest for custom-house entry or clearance of the cargo of any ship, vessel, or steamer, for a foreign port:

If the registered tonnage of such ship. vessel, or steamer does not exceed 300 tons,   1 00

Exceeding 300 tons, and not exceeding 600 tons,   3 00

Exceeding 600 tons,   5 00

[These provisions do not apply to vessels or steamboats plying between ports of the United States and British North America.]

Measurers' returns,   exempt.

Memorandum of sale, or broker's note. (See Contract.)

Mortgage of lands, estate, or property, real or personal, heritable or movable, whatsoever, a trust deed in the nature of a mortgage, or any personal bond given as security for the payment of any definite or certain sum of money; exceeding $100, and not exceeding $500,   50

Exceeding $500, and not exceeding $1,000,   1 00

And for every additional $500, or fractional part thereof, in excess of $1,000,   50

Order for payment of money, if the amount is $10, or over,   2

Passage ticket on any vessel from a port in the United States to a foreign port, not exceeding $35,   50

Exceeding $35, and not exceeding $50,   1 00

And for every additonal $50, or fractional part thereof, in excess of $50,   1 00

Passage tickets to ports in British North America,   exempt.

Pawner's checks,   5

Power of attorney for the sale or transfer of any stock, bonds or scrip, or for the collection of any dividends or interest thereon,   25

Power of attorney, or proxy, for voting at any election for officers of any incorporated company or society, except religious, charitable, or literary societies, or public cemeteries,   10

Power of attorney to receive or collect rent,   25

Stamp Duty.

Power of attorney to sell and convey real estate, or to rent or lease the same, 1 00

Power of attorney for any other purpose, 50

Probate of will, or letters of administration; where the estate and effects for or in respect of which such probate or letters of administration applied for shall be sworn or declared not to exceed the value of $1,000, exempt.

Exceeding $1,000, and not exceeding $2,000, 1 00

Exceeding $2,000, for every additional $1,000, or fractional part thereof, in excess of $2,000, 50

Promissory note. For any sum less than $100, exempt.

For $100, and for each additional $100 or fractional part thereof, 5

Deposit note to mutual insurance companies, when policy is subject to duty, exempt.

Renewal of a note, subject to the same duty as an original note.

Protest of note, bill of exchange, acceptance, check, or draft, or any marine protest, 25

Quit-claim deed to be stamped as a conveyance, except when given as a release of a mortgage by the mortgagee to the mortgagor, in which case it is exempt; but if it contains covenants *may* be subject as an agreement or contract.

Receipts for satisfaction of any mortgage or judgment or decree of any court, exempt.

Receipts for any sum of money or debt due, or for a draft or other instrument given for the payment of money, exempt.

Receipts for the delivery of property, exempt.

Renewal of agreement, contract or charter, by letter or otherwise, same stamp as original instrument.

Sheriff's return on writ or other process, exempt.

Trust deed, made to secure a debt, to be stamped as a mortgage.

Warehouse receipts, exempt.

Warrant of attorney accompanying a bond or note, if the bond or note is stamped, exempt.

Weigher's returns, exempt.

Official documents, instruments, and papers issued by officers of the United States Government, exempt.

Official instruments, documents, and papers issued by the officers of any State, county, town, or other municipal corporation, in the exercise of functions strictly belonging to them in their ordinary governmental or municipal capacity, exempt.

Papers necessary to be used for

C

Stamp Duty.

the collection from the United States Government of claims by soldiers, or their legal representatives, for pensions, back pay, bounty, or for property lost in the service, exempt.

NOTE.—The last Congress passed an act, "That on and after the first day of October, 1870, the stamp tax imposed in Schedule B, on promissory notes for a less sum than one hundred dollars, and on receipts for any sum of money, or for the payment of any debt, and the stamp tax imposed in Schedule C, on canned and preserved fish, be, and the same are hereby repealed. And no stamp shall be required upon the transfer or assignment of a mortgage, where it or the instrument it secures has been once duly stamped."

CANCELLATION.

In all cases where an *adhesive* stamp is used for denoting the stamp duty upon an instrument, the person using or affixing the same must write or imprint thereupon *in ink* the initials of his name, and the date (the year, month, and day) on which the same is attached or used. Each stamp should be separately cancelled. When stamps are printed upon checks, &c., so that in filling up the instrument, the face of the stamp is and must necessarily be written across, no other cancellation will be required.

All cancellation must be distinct and legible, and except in the case of proprietary stamps from private dies, no method of cancellation which differs from that above described can be recognized as legal and sufficient.

PENALTIES.

A penalty of fifty dollars is imposed upon every person who makes, signs, or issues, or who causes to be made, signed, or issued, any paper of any kind or description whatever, or who accepts, negotiates, or pays, or causes to be accepted, negotiated, or paid, any bill of exchange, draft, or order, or promissory note, for the payment of money, without the same being duly stamped, or having thereupon an adhesive stamp for denoting the tax chargeable thereon, cancelled in the manner required by law, with intent to evade the provisions of the revenue act.

A penalty of two hundred dollars is imposed upon every person who pays, negotiates, or offers in payment, or receives or takes in payment, any bill of exchange or order for the payment of any sum of money drawn or purporting to be drawn in a foreign country, but payable in the United States, until the proper stamp has been affixed thereto.

A penalty of fifty dollars is imposed upon every person who fraudulently makes use of an adhesive stamp to denote the duty required by the revenue act, without effectually cancelling and obliterating the same in the manner required by law.

Attention is particularly called to the following extract from section 155, of the act of June 30, 1864, as amended by the act of July 13, 1866 :

"If any person shall wilfully remove or cause to be removed, alter or cause to be altered, the cancelling or defacing marks on any adhesive stamp, with intent to use the same, or to cause the use of the same, after it shall have been used once, or shall knowingly or wilfully sell or buy such washed or restored stamps, or offer the same for sale, or give or expose the same to any person for use, or knowingly use the same or prepare the same with intent for the further use thereof, or if any person shall knowingly and without lawful excuse (the proof whereof shall lie on the person accused) have in his possession any washed, restored, or altered stamps, which have been removed from any vellum, parchment, paper, instrument or writing ; then, and in every such case, every person so offending, and every person knowingly and wilfully aiding, abetting, or assisting in committing any such offence as aforesaid, shall, on conviction thereof, * * * be punished by a fine not exceeding one thousand dollars, or by imprisonment and confinement to hard labor not exceeding five years, or both, at the discretion of the court."

It is not lawful to record any instrument, document, or paper required by law to be stamped, or any copy thereof, unless a stamp or stamps of the proper amount have been affixed and cancelled in the manner required by law ; and such instrument or copy and the record thereof are utterly null and void, and cannot be used or admitted as evidence in any court until the defect has been cured as provided in section 158.

All wilful violations of the law should be reported to the United States District Attorney within and for the district where they are committed.

GENERAL REMARKS.

Revenue stamps may be used indiscriminately upon any of the matters or things enumerated in Schedule B, except proprietary and playing card stamps, for which a special use has been provided.

Postage stamps cannot be used in payment of the duty chargeable on instruments.

The law does not designate which of the parties to an instrument shall furnish the necessary stamp, nor does the Commissioner of Internal Revenue assume to determine that it shall be supplied by one party rather than by another ; but if an instrument subject to stamp duty is issued without having the necessary stamps affixed thereto, it cannot be recorded, or admitted, or used in evidence, in any court, until a legal stamp or stamps, denoting the amount of tax, shall have been affixed as prescribed by law, and the person who thus issues it is liable to a penalty, if he omits the stamps with an intent to evade the provisions of the internal revenue act.

The first act imposing a stamp tax upon certain specified instruments took effect, so far as said tax is concerned, October 1, 1862. The impression which seems to prevail to some extent, that no stamps are required upon any instruments issued in the States lately in insurrection, prior to the surrender, or prior to the establishment of collection districts there, is erroneous.

Instruments issued in those States since October 1, 1862, are subject to the same taxes as similar ones issued at the same time in the other States.

No stamp is necessary upon an instrument executed prior to October 1, 1862, to make it admissible in evidence, or to entitle it to record.

Certificates of loan in which there shall appear any written or printed evidence of an amount of money to be paid on demand, or at a time designated, are subject to stamp duty as "promissory notes."

When two or more persons join in the execution of an instrument, the stamp to which the instrument is liable under the law, may be affixed and cancelled by either of them ; and "when more than one signature is affixed to the same paper, one or more stamps may be affixed thereto, representing the whole amount of the stamp required for such signatures."

No stamp is required on any warrant of attorney accompanying a bond or note, when such bond or note has affixed thereto the stamp or stamps denoting the duty required ; and, whenever any bond or note is secured by mortgage, but one stamp duty is required on such papers—such stamp duty being the highest rate required for such instruments, or either of them. In such case a note or memorandum of the value or denomination of the stamp affixed should be made upon the margin or in the acknowledgement of the instrument which is not stamped.

Particular attention is called to the change in section 154, by striking out the words "or used ;" the exemption thereunder is thus restricted to documents, &c., *issued* by the officers therein named. Also to the changes in sections 152 and 158, by inserting the words "and cancelled in the manner required by law."

The acceptor or acceptors of any bill of exchange, or order for the payment of any sum of money, drawn or purporting to be drawn in any foreign country, but payable in the United States, must, before paying or accepting the same, place thereupon a stamp indicating the duty.

It is only upon conveyances of realty *sold* that conveyance stamps are necessary. A deed of real estate made without valuable consideration need not be stamped as a conveyance ; but if it contains covenants, such, for instance, as a covenant to warrant and defend the title, it should be stamped as an agreement or contract.

When a deed purporting to be a conveyance of realty sold, and stamped accordingly, is inoperative, a deed of confirmation, made simply to cure the defect, requires no stamp. In such case, the second deed should contain a recital of the facts, and should show the reasons for its execution.

Partition deeds between tenants in common, need not be stamped as conveyances, inasmuch as there is no sale of realty, but merely a marking out, or a defining, of the boundaries of the part belonging to each; but where money or other valuable consideration is paid by one co-tenant to another for equality of partition, there is a sale to the extent of such consideration, and the conveyance, by the party receiving it, should be stamped accordingly.

A conveyance of lands sold for unpaid taxes, issued since August 1, 1866, by the officers of any county, town, or other municipal corporation in the discharge of their strictly official duties, is exempt from stamp tax.

A conveyance of realty sold, subject to a mortgage, should be stamped according to the consideration, or the value of the property *unencumbered*. The consideration in such case is to be found by adding the amount paid for the equity of redemption to the mortgage debt. The fact that one part of the consideration is paid to the mortgagor and the other part to the mortgagee does not change the liability of the conveyance.

The stamp tax upon a mortgage is based upon the amount it is given to secure. The fact that the value of the property mortgaged is less than that amount, and that consequently the security is only partial, does not change the liability of the instrument. When, therefore, a second mortgage is given to secure the payment of a sum of money partially secured by a prior mortgage upon other property, or when two mortgages upon separate property are given at the same time to secure the payment of the same sum, each should be stamped as though it were the only one.

A mortgage given to secure a surety from loss, or given for any purpose whatever, other than as security for the payment of a definite and certain sum of money, is taxable only as an agreement or contract.

The stamp duty upon a lease, agreement, memorandum, or contract for the hire, use, or rent of any land, tenement, or portion thereof, is based upon the *annual* rent or rental value of the property leased, and the duty is the same whether the lease be for one year, for a term of years, or for the fractional part of a year only.

An assignment of a lease within the meaning and intent of Schedule B, is an assignment of the *leasehold*, or of some portion thereof, by the *lessee*, or by some person claiming by, from, or under him ; such an assignment as subrogates the assignee to the rights, or some portion of the rights, of the *lessee*, or of the person standing in his place. A transfer by the *lessor* of his part of a lease, neither giving nor purporting to give a claim to the leasehold, or to any part thereof, but simply a right to the rents, &c., is subject to stamp tax as a contract or agreement only.

The stamp tax upon a fire insurance policy is based upon the *premium*.

Deposit notes taken by a mutual fire insurance company, not as payment of premium nor as evidence of indebtedness therefor, but to be used simply as a basis upon which to make rateable assessments to meet the losses incurred by the company, should not be reckoned as premium in determining the amount of stamp taxes upon the policies.

When a policy of insurance properly stamped has been issued and lost, no stamp is necessary upon another issued by the same company to the same party, covering the same property, time, &c., and designed simply to supply the loss. The second policy should recite the loss of the first.

An instrument which operates as the renewal of a policy of insurance, is subject to the same stamp tax as the policy.

When a policy of insurance is issued for a certain time, whether it be for one year only or for a term of years, a receipt for premium, or any other instrument which has the legal effect to continue the contract and extend its operation *beyond that time*, requires the same amount of revenue stamps as the policy itself; but such a receipt as is usually given for the payment of the monthly, quarterly, or annual premium, is not a renewal within the meaning of the statute. The payment simply prevents the policy from expiring, by reason of non-performance of its conditions ; a receipt given for such a payment requires no stamp. When, however, the time of payment has passed, and a tender of the premium is not sufficient to bind the company, but a new policy or a new contract in some form, with the mutuality essential to every contract, becomes necessary between the insurer and the insured, the same amount of stamps should be used as that required upon the original policy.

A permit issued by a life insurance company changing the terms of a policy as to travel, residence, occupation, &c., should be stamped as a contract or agreement.

A bill single or a bill obligatory, i. e., an instrument in the form of a promissory note, *under seal*, is subject to stamp duty as written or printed evidence of an amount of money to be paid on demand or at a time designated, at the rate of five cents for each one hundred dollars or fractional part thereof.

A waiver of protest, or of demand and notice, written upon negotiable paper and signed by the indorser, is an agreement, and requires a five-cent stamp.

A stamp duty of twenty-five cents is imposed upon the "protest of every note, bill of exchange, check or draft," and upon every marine protest. If several notes, bills of exchange, drafts, &c., are protested at the same time and all attached to one and the same certificate, stamps should be affixed to the amount of twenty-five cents for each note, bill, draft, &c., thus protested.

When, as is generally the case, the caption to a deposition contains other certificates in addition to the jurat to the affidavit of the deponent, such as a certificate that the parties were or were not notified, that they did or did not appear, that they did or did not object, &c., it is subject to a stamp duty of five cents.

When an attested copy of a writ or other process is used by a sheriff or other person in making personal service, or in attaching property, a five-cent stamp should be affixed to the certificate of attestation.

A marriage certificate issued by the officiating clergyman or magistrate, to be returned to any officer of a State, county, city, town, or other municipal corporation, to constitute part of a public record, requires no stamp; but if it is to be retained by the parties, a five-cent stamp should be affixed.

The stamp tax upon a bill of sale, by which any ship or vessel, or any part thereof, is conveyed to or vested in any other person or persons, is at the same rate as that imposed upon conveyances of realty sold; a bill of sale of any other personal property should be stamped as a contract or agreement.

An assignment of real or personal property, or of both, for the benefit of creditors, should be stamped as an agreement or contract.

Written or printed assignments of agreements, bonds, notes not negotiable, and of all other instruments the assignments of which are not particularly specified in the foregoing schedule, should be stamped as agreements.

No stamp is necessary upon the registry of a judgment, even though the registry is such in its legal effect as to create a lien which operates as a mortgage upon the property of the judgment debtor.

When a "power of attorney or proxy for voting at any election for officers of any incorporated company or society, except religious, charitable, or literary societies, or public cemeteries," is signed by several stockholders, owning separate and distinct shares, it is, in its legal effect, the separate instrument of each, and requires stamps to the amount of ten cents for each and every signature; one or more stamps may be used representing the whole amount required.

A notice from landlord to tenant to quit possession of premises requires no stamp.

A stamp tax is imposed upon every "manifest for custom-house entry or clearance of the *cargo* of any ship, vessel, or steamer for a foreign port." The amount of this tax in each case depends upon the registered tonnage of the vessel.

If a vessel clears in ballast and has no cargo whatever, no stamp is necessary; but if she has any, however small the amount —a stamp should be used.

A bond to convey real estate requires stamps to the amount of twenty-five cents.

The stamp duty upon the probate of a will, or upon letters of administration, is based upon the sworn or declared value of all the estate and effects, real, personal, and mixed, undiminished by the debts of the estate for or in respect of which such probate or letters are applied for.

When the property belonging to the estate of a person deceased, lies under different jurisdictions and it becomes necessary to take out letters in two or more places, the letters should be stamped according to the value of all the property, real, personal, and mixed, for or in respect of which the particular letters in each case are issued.

Letters *de bonis non* should be stamped according to the amount of property remaining to be administered upon thereunder, regardless of the stamps upon the original letters.

A mere *copy* of an instrument is not subject to stamp duty unless it is a certified one, in which case a five-cent stamp should be affixed to the certificate of the person attesting it; but when the instrument is executed and issued in duplicate, triplicate, &c., as in the case of a lease of two or more parts, each part has the same legal effect as the other, and each should be stamped as an original.

POSTAL RATES AND REGULATIONS.

LETTERS.—The law requires postage on all letters (including those to foreign countries when prepaid), excepting those written to the President or Vice President, or members of Congress, or (on official business) to the chiefs of the executive departments of the Government, and the heads of bureaux and chief clerks, and others invested with the franking privilege, to be prepaid by stamps or stamped envelopes, prepayment in money being prohibited.

All drop-letters must be prepaid. The rate of postage on drop-letters, at offices where free delivery by carrier is established, is two cents per half ounce or fraction of a half ounce ; at offices where such free delivery is NOT established the rate is one cent.

The single rate of postage on all domestic mail letters throughout the United States, is three cents per half ounce, with an additional rate of three cents for each additional half ounce or fraction of a half ounce. The ten cent (Pacific) rate is abolished.

NEWSPAPERS, ETC.—Letter postage is to be charged on all handbills, circulars, or other printed matter which shall contain any manuscript writing whatever.

Daguerreotypes, when sent in the mail, are to be charged with letter postage by weight.

Photographs on cards, paper, and other flexible material, (not in cases), can be sent at the same rate as miscellaneous printed matter, viz., two cents for each four ounces or fraction thereof.

Photograph Albums are chargeable with book postage—four cents for each four ounces or fraction thereof.

NEWSPAPER POSTAGE.—Postage on daily papers to subscribers when prepaid quarterly or yearly in advance, either at the mailing office or office of delivery, per quarter (three months), 35 cts. ; six times per week, per quarter 30 cts. ; for tri-weekly, per quarter 15 cts. ; for semi-weekly, per quarter 10 cts.; for weekly, per quarter 5 cents.

Weekly newspapers (one copy only) sent by the publisher to actual subscribers within the county where printed and published, FREE.

Postage per quarter (to be paid quarterly or yearly in advance) on newspapers and periodicals issued less frequently than once a week, sent to actual subscribers in any part of the United States : Semi-monthly, not over 4 oz., 6 cts. ; over 4 oz. and not over 8 oz., 12 cts. ; over 8 oz. and not over 12 oz., 18 cts. ; monthly, not over 4 oz., 3 cts ; over 4 oz. and not over 8 oz., 6 cts. ; over 8 oz. and not over 12 oz., 9 cts.; quarterly, not over 4 oz., 1 cent; over 4 oz. and not over 8 oz., 2 cts. ; over 8 oz. and not over 12 oz., 3 cts.

TRANSIENT MATTER.—Books not over 4 oz. in weight, to one address, 4 cts. ; over 4 oz. and not over 8 oz., 8 cts. ; over 8 oz. and not over 12 oz., 12 cts. ; over 12 oz. and not over 16 oz., 16 cts.

Circulars not exceeding three in number to one address, 2 cts. ; over 3 and not over 6, 4 cts. ; over 6 and not over 9, 6 cts. ; over 9 and not exceeding 12, 8 cts.

On miscellaneous mailable matter, (embracing all pamphlets, occasional publications, transient newspapers, hand-bills and posters, book manuscripts and proof-sheets, whether corrected or not, maps, prints, engravings, sheet music, blanks, flexible patterns, samples, and sample cards, phonographic paper, letter envelopes, postal envelopes or wrappers, cards, paper, plain or ornamental, photographic representations of different types, seeds, cuttings, bulbs, roots and scions,) the postage to be pre-paid by stamps, is on one package, to one address, not over 4 oz. in weight, 2 cts. ; over 4 oz. and not over 8 oz., 4 cts. ; over 8 oz. and not over 12 oz., 6 cts. ; over 12 oz. and not over 16 oz., 8 cts. The weight of packages of seeds, cuttings, roots and scions, to be franked, is limited to thirty-two ounces.

Any word or communication, whether by printing, writing, marks or signs, upon the cover or wrapper of a newspaper, pamphlet, magazine, or other printed matter, other than the name or address of the person to whom it is to be sent, and the date when the subscription expires, subjects the package to letter postage.

Infallible Rules for Detecting Counterfeit or Spurious Bank Notes.

RULE 1st.—Examine the shading of the letters in title of Bank called LATHEWORK, which in genuine notes presents an even, straight, light and silky appearance, generally so fine and smooth as to appear to be all in one solid, pale body. In the counterfeit the lines are coarse and irregular, and in many of the longer lines breaks will be perceived, thus presenting a very inferior finish in comparison to genuine work.

2d.—Observe the dies, circles and ovals in the genuine; they are composed of a network of lines, which, by crossing each other at certain angles, produce an endless variety of figures; SEE THE ONE CENT STAMP ATTACHED. The fine line alone is the unit which enables you to detect spurious work. In the counterfeit, the REPRESENTED white lines are coarse, irregular, and cross each other in a confused, irregular manner, thus producing blurred and imperfect figures.

3d.—Examine the form and features of all human figures on the note. In the genuine, the texture of the skin is represented by fine dots and lines intermixed. In the eyes, the pupil is distinctly visible, and the white clearly seen; the nose, mouth and chin, well formed, natural and expressive; the lips are slightly pouting, and the chin well thrown out; and the delicate shading of the neck perfectly harmonizes with the rest of the figure. Observe the fingers and toes; they should be clearly and accurately defined. The hair of the head should show the fine strands and present a natural appearance. The folds of the drapery of human figures should lay natural and present a fine, finished appearance. In the counterfeit the female figure does not bear the natural prominence in outlines; observe, the eyes and shading surrounding does not present the lifelike appearance it should. The fingers and toes are not properly and proportionately defined; the hair does not bear that soft and finished appearance as in the genuine.

4th.—Examine the imprint or engraver's names in the evenness and shape of the fine letters. Counterfeits never bear the imprint perfect. This rule should be strictly observed, as it is infallible in detecting counterfeits.

5th.—In the genuine note the landscapes are well finished; trees and shrubs are neatly drawn; the limbs well proportioned, and the foliage presenting a fine natural appearance; clear sky is formed of fine parallel lines, and when clouds or heavy skies appear, they cross each other, and bear a soft, smooth and natural appearance. The perspective, showing a view of the surrounding country, is always clear and distinct. The small figures in the background are always plainly seen, and their outlines and general character recognized. Ships are well defined and the canvass has a clear texture; railroad cars are very accurately delineated; in examining a train observe carefully the car most distant. In the counterfeit the landscape is usually poorly executed; the leaves of trees poorly and unnaturally defined.— The lines representing still water are scratchy rather than parallel, the sky is represented generally in like manner, and where rolling clouds are to be seen, the unnatural effect is obvious. Domestic animals are generally poorly executed, particularly the head and limbs; the eyes are seldom clearly defined. Ships are poorly drawn, the texture of the canvass coarse and inferior in style of workmanship, thus giving an artificial appearance. Railroad cars are also poorly executed; the car farthest from the eye is usually the most imperfect. The perspective is always imperfect, the figures in the background can seldom be recognized.

6th.—Bills altered from a smaller to a higher denomination, can readily be detected by a close observer, in consequence of the striking difference between the parts which have been extracted and the rest of the note. This difference is readily perceived in the lack of color, body and finish of the dye; we have seen bills where the surrounding shading in altered dies was too dark, but from the back or finish of the white lines you have a sure test. Again observe particularly the words " Five " or " Ten Dollars " as the case may be, denoting the denomination of the note; the parallel outlines and shading (if any) are coarse and imperfect. Alterations are frequently made by pasting a greater denomination over a smaller, but by holding the bill up to the light, the fraud will be perceived. Another method resorted to is to cut out the figures in the dies as well as the words and shading, or the words two or three as the case may be, and with a sharp eraser, scrape down the ends and also the edges of the pieces to be inserted; when the pieces thus prepared are affixed they are hardly perceivable; but by passing the note through the hand, so as to feel the die both with the finger and thumb at the same time, the fraud will be detected by the stiffness of the outer edges, "occasioned by the gum or method adopted" in affixing the parts. The letter S should always be examined, as in many alterations it is pasted or stamped at the end of the word "dollar;" and even when stamped there, the carrying out of the outlines for its shading will readily show the fraud. Bills of broken banks are frequently altered by extracting the name of bank, state and town; they may readily be de-

tected by observing first the state, second the title or name of the bank, third the town or location.

GENERAL REMARKS IN REFERENCE TO COUNTERFEITS.—The paper on which they are printed is generally of a very inferior quality, with less body, finish and toughness than bank note paper has. The ink generally lacks the rich luster of the genuine; the red letters and figures are generally imperfect, and the ink does not present the vermillion hue as it should. The printing is generally inferior, usually exhibiting specks of white in the most prominent letters. The date and filling up, and the President's and Cashier's names are generally written by the same person, although in many instances they present a different appearance. There are bills in circulation bearing either genuine dies or vignettes; but upon close examination you will be enabled to detect any spurious bill, whether counterfeit or altered, by the instructions here given, if persevered in for a short time. We beg to suggest, if time will admit, the learner should examine minutely every bill he receives. A powerful pocket magnifying glass, which can be purchased for from fifty cents to one dollar at any of the opticians, will greatly enable you to see and comprehend the difference between genuine and spurious work.

HOW TO SUCCEED IN BUSINESS.

What will my readers give to know how to get rich? Now, I will not vouch that the following rules will enable every person who may read them to acquire wealth; but this I will answer for, that if ever a man does grow rich by honest means, and retains his wealth for any length of time, he must practice upon the principles laid down in the following essay. The remarks are not original with me, but I strongly commend them to the attention of every young man, at least as affording the true secret of success in attaining wealth. A single perusal of such an essay at an impressible moment, has sometimes a very wonderful effect upon the disposition and character.

Fortune, they say, is a fickle dame—full of her freaks and caprices; who blindly distributes her favors without the slightest discrimination. So inconstant, so wavering is she represented, that her most faithful votaries can place no reliance on her promises. Disappointment, they tell us, is the lot of those who make offerings at

her shrine. Now, all this is a vile slander upon the dear blind lady.

Although wealth often appears the result of mere accident, or a fortunate concurrence of favorable circumstances without any exertion of skill or foresight, yet any man of sound health and unimpaired mind may become wealthy, if he takes the proper steps.

Foremost in the list of requisites are honesty and strict integrity in every transaction of life. Let a man have the reputation of being fair and upright in his dealings, and he will possess the confidence of all who know him. Without these qualities every other merit will prove unavailing. Ask concerning a man, "Is he active and capable?" Yes. "Industrious, temperate and regular in his habits?"—Oh yes. "Is he honest? Is he trustworthy?" Why, as to that, I am sorry to say that he is not to be trusted; he needs watching; he is a little tricky, and will take an undue advantage, if he can. "Then I will have nothing to do with him," will be the invariable reply. Why, then, is honesty the best policy? Because, without it, you will get a bad name, and everybody will shun you.

A character for knavery will prove an insurmountable obstacle to success in almost every undertaking. It will be found that the straight line is, in business, as in geometry, the shortest. In a word, it is almost impossible for a dishonest man to acquire wealth by a regular process of business, because he is shunned as a depredator upon society.

Needy men are apt to deviate from the rule of integrity, under the plea that necessity knows no law; they might as well add that it knows no shame. The course is suicidal, and by destroying all confidence, ever keeps them immured in poverty, although they may possess every other quality for success in the world.

Punctuality, which is said to be the soul of business, is another important element in the art of money getting. The man known to be scrupulously exact in the fulfillment of his engagements, gains the confidence of all, and may command all the means he can use with advantage; whereas, a man careless and regardless of his promises in money matters will have every purse closed against him. Therefore be prompt in your payments.

Next, let us consider the advantages of a cautious circumspection in our intercourse with the world. Slowness of belief and a proper distrust are essential to success. The credulous and confiding are ever the dupes of knaves and impostors. Ask those who have lost their property how it happened, and you will find in most cases that it has been owing to misplaced confidence. One has lost by endorsing, another by crediting, another by false representations; all of which a little more foresight and a little more distrust would have prevented. In the affairs of this world men are not saved by faith, but by the want of it.

Judge of men by what they do, not by what they say. Believe in looks rather than words. Observe all their movements. Ascertain their motives and their ends. Notice what they say or do in their unguarded moments, when under the influence of excitement. The passions have been compared to tortures which force men to reveal their secrets. Before trusting a man, before putting it in his power to cause you a loss, possess yourself of every available information relative to him. Learn his history, his habits, inclinations and propensities; his reputation for honor, industry, frugality and punctuality; his prospects, resources, supports, advantages and disadvantages; his intentions and motives of action; who are his friends and enemies, and what are his good or bad qualities. You may learn a man's good qualities and advantages from his friends—his bad qualities and disadvantages from his enemies. Make due allowance for exaggeration in both. Finally, examine carefully before engaging in anything, and act with energy afterwards. Have the hundred eyes of Argus beforehand, and the hundred hands of Briarius afterwards.

Order and system in the management of business must not be neglected. Nothing contributes more to dispatch. Have a place for everything and everything in its place; a time for everything, and everything in its time. Do first what presses most, and having determined what is to be done, and how it is to be done, lose no time in doing it. Without this method all is hurry and confusion, little or nothing is accomplished, and business is attended to with neither pleasure nor profit.

A polite, affable deportment is recommended. Agreeable manners contribute powerfully to a man's success. Take two men, possessing equal advantages in every other respect, but let one be gentlemanly, kind, obliging and conciliating in his manners; the other harsh, rude and disobliging; and the one will become rich, while the other will starve.

We are now to consider a very important principle in the business of money-getting, namely—Industry—persevering, indefatigable attention to business. Persevering diligence is the Philosopher's stone, which turns everything to gold. Constant, regular, habitual and systematic application to business, must in time. if properly directed, produce great results. It must lead to wealth, with the same certainty that poverty follows in the train of idleness and inattention. It has been truly remarked that he who follows his amusements instead of his business, will, in a short time, have no business to follow.

The art of money-saving is an important part of the art of money-getting. Without frugality no one can become rich; with it, few would be poor. Those who consume as fast as they produce, are on the road to ruin. As most of the poverty we meet with grows out of idleness and extravagance, so most large fortunes have been the result of habitual industry and frugality. The practice of economy is as necessary in the expenditure of time as of money. They say if "we take care of the pence the pounds will take care of themselves." So, if we take care of the minutes, the days will take care of themselves.

The acquisition of wealth demands as much self-denial, and as many sacrifices of present gratification, as the practice of virtue itself. Vice and poverty proceed, in some degree, from the same sources, namely—the disposition to sacrifice the future to the present; the inability to forego a small present pleasure for great future advantages. Men fail of fortune in this world, as they fail of happiness in the world to come, simply because they are unwilling to deny themselves momentary enjoyments for the sake of permanent future happiness.

Every large city is filled with persons, who, in order to support the appearance of wealth, constantly live beyond their income, and make up the deficiency by contracting debts which are never paid. Others, there are, the mere drones of society, who pass their days in idleness, and subsist by pirating on the hives of the industrious. Many who run a short-lived career of splendid beggary, could they be but persuaded to adopt a system of rigid economy for a few years, might pass the remainder of their days in affluence. But no! They must keep up appearances, they must live like other folks.

Their debts accumulate; their credit fails; they are harassed by duns, and besieged by constables and sheriff. In this extremity, as a last resort, they submit to a shameful dependence, or engage in criminal practices which entail hopeless wretchedness and infamy on themselves and families.

Stick to the business in which you are regularly employed. Let speculators make thousands in a year or a day; mind your own regular trade, never turning from it to the right hand or to the left. If you are a merchant, a professional man, or a mechanic, never buy lots or stocks, unless you have surplus money which you wish to invest. Your own business you understand as well as other men; but other people's business you do not understand. Let your business be some one which is useful to the community. All such occupations possess the elements of profit in themselves.

How to Secure the Public Lands,

OR THE ENTRY OF THE SAME UNDER THE PRE-EMPTION AND HOMESTEAD LAWS.

The following circular gives all necessary information as to the procedure necessary in purchasing and securing the public lands:

DEPARTMENT OF THE INTERIOR, }
GEN'L LAND OFFICE, July 19, 1865. }

Numerous questions having arisen as to the mode of procedure to purchase public lands, or acquire title to the same by bounty land locations, by pre-emptions or by homestead, this circular is communicated for the information of all concerned.

In order to acquire title to public lands the following steps must be taken:

1. Application must be made to the Register of the district land office in which the land desired may be situated.

A list of all the land offices in the United States is furnished by the Department, with the seats of the different offices, where it is the duty of the Register and Receiver to be in attendance, and give proper facilities and information to persons desirous of obtaining lands.

The minimum price of ordinary public lands is $1,25 per acre. The even or reserved sections falling within railroad grants are increased to double the minimum price, being $2,50 per acre.

Lands once offered at public sale, and not afterwards kept out of market by reservation, or otherwise, so as to prevent free competition, may be entered or located.

2. By the applicant filing with the Register his written application describing the tract, with its area; the Register will then certify to the receiver whether the land is vacant, with its price; and when found to be so, the applicant must pay that price per acre, or may locate the same with land warrant, and thereafter the Receiver will give him a "duplicate receipt," which he is required to surrender previous to the delivery to him of the patent, which may be had either by application for it to the Register or to the General Land Office.

3. If the tract has not been offered at public sale it is not liable to ordinary private entry, but may be secured by a party legally qualified, upon his compliance with the requirements of the pre-emption laws of 4th September, 1841, and 3d March, 1843; and after such party shall have made actual settlement for such a length of time as will show he designs it for his permanent home, and is acting in good faith, building a house and residing therein, he may proceed to the district land office, establish his pre-emption claim according to law, by proving his actual residence and cultivation, and showing that he is otherwise within the purview of these acts.— Then he can enter the land at $1,25, either in cash or with bounty land warrant, unless the premises should be $2,50 acre lands. In that case the whole purchase-money can be paid in cash, or one-half in cash, the residue with a bounty land warrant.

4. But if parties legally qualified desire to obtain title under the Homestead Act of 20th May, 1862, they can do so on com

plying with the Department Circular, dated 30th October, 1862.

5. The law confines Homestead entries to surveyed lands; and although, in certain States and Territories noted in the subjoined list, pre-emptors may go on land before survey, yet they can only establish their claim after return of survey, but must file their pre-emption declaration within three months after receipt of official plat, at the local land-office where the settlement was made before survey. Where, however, it was made after survey, the claimant must file within three months after date of settlement; and where actual residence and cultivation have been long enough to show that the claimant has made the land his permanent home, he can establish his claim and pay for the same at any time before the date of the public sale of lands within the range in which his settlement may fall.

6. All unoffered surveyed lands not acquired under pre-emption, homestead, or otherwise, under express legal sanction, must be offered at public sale under the President's Proclamation, and struck off to the highest bidder, as required by act of April 24, 1820.

J. M. EDMUNDS,
Commissioner General Land Office.

LAW MAXIMS.

1. A promise of a debtor to give "satisfactory security" for the payment of a portion of his debt, is a sufficient consideration for a release of the residue by his creditor.

2. Administrators are liable to account for interest on funds in their hands, although no profit shall have been made upon them, unless the exigencies of the estate rendered it prudent that they should hold the funds thus uninvested.

3. Any person who voluntarily becomes an agent for another, and in that capacity obtains information to which as a stranger he could have had no access, is bound in subsequent dealing with his principal, as purchaser of the property that formed the subject of his agency, to communicate such information.

4. When a house is rendered untenantable in consequence of improvements made on the adjoining lot, the owner of such cannot recover damages, because it is presumed that he had knowledge of the approaching danger in time to protect himself from it.

5. When a merchant ship is abandoned by order of the master, for the purpose of saving life, and a part of the crew subsequently meet the vessel so abandoned and bring her safe into port, they will be entitled to salvage.

6. A person who has been led to sell goods by means of false pretenses, cannot recover them from one who has purchased them in good faith from the fraudulent vendor.

7. An agreement by the holder of a note to give the principal debtor time for payment, without depriving himself of the right to sue, does not discharge the surety.

8. A seller of goods who accepts, at the time of sale, the note of a third party, not endorsed by the buyer, in payment, cannot in case the note is not paid, hold the buyer responsible for the value of the goods.

9. A day-book copied from a "blotter" in which charges are first made, will not be received in evidence as a book of original entries.

10. Common carriers are not liable for extraordinary results of negligence that could not have been foreseen by ordinary skill and foresight.

11. A bidder at a Sheriff's sale may retract his bid at any time before the property is knocked down to him, whatever may be the conditions of the sale.

12. Acknowledgment of debt to a stranger does not preclude the operation of the statute.

13. The fruits and grass on the farm or garden of an intestate descend to the heir.

14. Agents are solely liable to their principals.

15. A deposit of money in bank by a husband, in the name of his wife, survives to her.

16. Money paid on Sunday contracts may be recovered.

17. A debtor may give preference to one creditor over another, unless fraud or special legislation can be proved.

18. A court cannot give judgment for a larger sum than that specified in the verdict.

19. Imbecility on the part of either husband or wife, invalidates the marriage.

20. An action for malicious prosecution will lie, though nothing further was done than suing out warrants.

21. An agreement not to continue the practice of a profession or business in any specified town, if the party so agreeing has received a consideration for the same, is valid.

22. When A consigns goods to B to sell on commission, and B delivers them to C, in payment of his own antecedent debts, A can recover their value.

23. A finder of property is compelled to make diligent inquiry for the owner thereof, and to restore the same. If, on finding such property, he attempts to conceal such fact, he may be prosecuted for larceny.

24. A private person may obtain an injunction to prevent a public mischief by which he is affected in common with others.

25. Any person interested may obtain an injunction to restrain the State or a municipal corporation from maintaining a nuisance on its lands.

26. A discharge under the insolvent laws of one State will not discharge the insolvent from a contract made with a citizen of another State.

27. To prosecute a party with any other motive than to bring him to justice, is malicious prosecution, and actionable as such.

28. Ministers of the gospel, residing in any incorporated town, are not exempt from jury, military, or fire service.

29. When a person contracts to build a house, and is prevented by sickness from finishing it, he can recover for the part performed, if such part is beneficial to the other party.

30. In a suit for enticing away a man's wife, actual proof of the marriage is not necessary. Cohabitation, reputation, and the admission of marriage by the parties, are sufficient.

31. Permanent erections and fixtures, made by a mortgagor after the execution of the mortgage upon land conveyed by it, become a part of the mortgaged premises.

32. When a marriage is denied, and plaintiff has given sufficient evidence to establish it, the defendant cannot examine the wife to disprove the marriage.

33. The amount of an express debt cannot be enlarged by application.

34. Contracts for advertisements in Sunday newspapers cannot be enforced.

35. A seller of goods, chattels, or other property, commits no fraud, in law, when he neglects to tell the purchaser of any flaws, defects, or unsoundness in the same.

36. The opinions of witnesses, as to the value of a dog that has been killed, are not admissible in evidence. The value of the animal is to be decided by the jury.

37. If any person puts a fence on or plows the land of another, he is liable for trespass whether the owner has sustained injury or not.

38. If a person, who is unable from illness to sign his will, has his hand guided in making his mark, the signature is valid.

39. When land trespassed upon is occupied by a tenant, he alone can bring the action.

40. To say of a person, "If he does not come and make terms with me, I will make a bankrupt of him and ruin him," or any such threatening language, is actionable, without proof of special damage.

41. In an action for slander, the party making the complaint must prove the words alleged; other words of like meaning will not suffice.

42. In a suit of damages for seduction, proof of pregnancy, and the birth of a child, is not essential. It is sufficient if the illness of the girl, whereby she was unable to labor, was produced by shame for the seduction; and this is such a loss of service as will sustain the action.

43. Addressing to a wife a letter containing matter defamatory to the character of her husband is a publication, and renders the writer amenable to damages.

44. A parent cannot sustain an action for any wrong done to a child, unless he has incurred some direct pecuniary injury therefrom in consequence of some loss of service or expenses necessarily consequent thereupon.

45. A master is responsible for an injury resulting from the negligence of his servant, whilst driving his cart or carriage, provided the servant is at the time engaged in his master's business, even though the accident happens in a place to which his master's business does not call him; but if the journey of a servant be solely for a purpose of his own, and undertaken without the knowledge and consent of his master, the latter is not responsible.

46. An emigrant depot is not a nuisance in law.

47. A railroad track through the streets is not a nuisance in law.

48. If an agreement upon which a party relies be oral only, it must be proved by evidence. But if the contract be reduced to writing, it proves itself; and now no evidence whatever is receivable for the purpose of varying the contract or affecting its obligations. The reasons are obvious. The law prefers written to oral evidence, from its greater precision and certainty, and because it is less open to fraud. And where parties have closed a negotiation and reduced the result to writing, it is presumed that they have written all they intended to agree to, and therefore, that what is omitted was finally rejected by them.— [PARSONS.

49. Delivery of a husband's goods by a wife to her adulterer, he having knowledge that she has taken them without her husband's authority, is sufficient to sustain an indictment for larceny against the adulterer.

50. The fact that the insurer was not informed of the existence of impending litigation, affecting the premises insured, at the time the insurance was effected, does not vitiate the policy.

51. The liability of an innkeeper is not confined to personal baggage, but extends to all the property of the guest that he consents to receive.

52. When a minor executes a contract, and pays money, or delivers property on the same, he cannot afterwards disaffirm such contract and recover the money, or property, unless he restores to the other party the consideration received from him for such money or property.

53. When a person has, by legal inquisition been found an habitual drunkard, he cannot, even in his sober intervals, make contracts to bind himself or his property, until the inquisition is removed.

54. Any person dealing with the representative of a deceased person, is presumed, in law, to be fully apprized of the extent of such representative's authority to act in behalf of such estate.

55. In an action against a railroad company, by a passenger, to recover damages for injuries sustained on the road, it is not compulsory upon the plaintiff to prove actual negligence in the defendants; but it is obligatory on the part of the latter to prove that the injury was not owing to any fault or negligence of theirs.

56. A guest is a competent witness, in an action between himself and an inn-keeper, to prove the character and value of lost personal baggage. Money in a trunk, not exceeding the amount reasonably required by the traveler to defray the expenses of the journey which he has undertaken, is a part of his baggage; and in case of its loss, while at any inn, the plaintiff may prove its amount by his own testimony.

57. The deed of a minor is not absolutely void. The court is authorized to judge, from the instrument, whether it is void or not, according to its terms being favorable or unfavorable to the interests of the minor.

58. A married woman can neither sue nor be sued on any contract made by her during her marriage, except in an action relating to her individual property. The action must be commenced either by or against her husband. It is only when an action is brought on a contract made by her before her marriage, that she is to be joined as a co-plaintiff, or defendant, with her husband.

59. Any contract made with a person judicially declared a lunatic is void.

60. Money paid voluntarily in any transaction, with a knowledge of the facts, cannot be recovered.

61. In all cases of specia. contract for services, except in the case of a minor, the plaintiff can recover only the amount stipulated in the contract.

62. A wife is a competent witness with her husband, to prove the contents of a lost trunk, or when a party.

63. A wife cannot be convicted of receiving stolen goods when she received them of her husband.

64. Insurance against fire, by lightning or otherwise, does not cover loss by lightning when there is no combustion.

65. Failure to prove plea of justification, in a case of slander, aggravates the offence.

66. It is the agreement of the parties to sell by sample that constitutes a sale by sample, not the mere exhibition of a specimen of the goods.

67. An agent is liable to his principals for loss caused by his misstatements, tho' unintentional.

68. Makers of promissory notes given in advance for premiums on policies of insurance, thereafter to be taken, are liable thereon.

69. An agreement to pay for procuring an appointment to office is void.

70. An attorney may plead the statute of limitations, when sued by a client for money which he has collected and failed to pay over.

71. Testimony given by a deceased witness on first trial, is not required to be repeated verbatim on the second.

72. A person entitling himself to a reward offered for lost property, has a lien upon the property for the reward; but only when a definite reward is offered.

73. Confession by a prisoner must be voluntarily made, to constitute evidence against him.

74. The defendant in a suit must be served with process; but service of such process upon his wife, even in his absence from the State, is not, in the absence of statutory provisions, sufficient.

75. The measure of damages in trespass for cutting timber, is its value as a chattel on the land where it was felled, and not the market price of the lumber manufactured.

76. To support an indictment for malicious mischief in killing an animal, malice towards its owner must be shown, not merely passion excited against the animal itself.

77. No action can be maintained against a sheriff for omitting to account for money obtained upon an execution within a reasonable time. He has till the return day to render such account.

78. An interest in the profits of an enterprise, as profits, renders the party holding it a partner in the enterprise, and makes him presumptively liable to share any loss.

79. Males can marry at fourteen, and females at twelve years of age.

80. All cattle found at large upon any public road, can be driven by any person to the public pound.

81. Any dog chasing, barking, or otherwise threatening a passer-by in any street, lane, road, or other public thoroughfare, may be lawfully killed for the same.

82. A written promise for the payment of such amount as may come into the hands of the promisor, is held to be an instrument in writing for the payment of money.

83. The declaration of an agent is not admissible to establish the fact of agency.— But when other proper evidence is given, tending to establish the fact of agency, it is not error to admit the declarations of the agent, accompanying acts, though tending to show the capacity in which he acted. When evidence is competent in one respect and incompetent in another, it is the duty of the court to admit it, and control its effects by suitable instructions to the jury.

84. The court has a general power to remove or suspend an attorney for such immoral conduct as rendered him unworthy of confidence in his official capacity.

85. Bankruptcy is pleadable in bar to all actions and in all courts, and this bar may be avoided whenever it is interposed, by showing fraud in the procurement of the discharge, or a violation of any of the provisions of the bankrupt act.

86. An instrument in the form of a deed, but limited to take effect at the termination of the grantor's natural life, is held to be a deed, not a will.

87. A sale will not be set aside as fraudulent, simply because the buyer was at the time unable to make the payment agreed upon, and knew his inability, and did not intend to pay.

88. No man is under an obligation to make known his circumstances when he is buying goods.

89. Contracting parties are bound to disclose material facts known to each, but of which either supposes the other to be ignorant, only when they stand in some special relation of trust and confidence in relation to the subject matter of the contract. But neither will be protected if he does anything, however slight, to mislead or deceive the other.

90. A contract negotiated by mail is formed when notice of acceptance of the offer is duly deposited in the post-office, properly addressed. This rule applies, although the party making the offer expressly requires that if it is accepted, speedy notice of acceptance shall be given him.

91. The date of an instrument is so far a material part of it, that an alteration of the date by the holder after execution, makes the instrument void.

92. A corporation may maintain an action for libel, for words published of them and relating to its trade or business, by which it has incurred special damages.

93. It is unprofessional for a lawyer who has abandoned his case without trying it, a term or two before trial, to claim a fee conditional upon the success of his client, although his client was successful.

94. Although a party obtaining damages for injuries received through the default of another, was himself guilty of negligence, yet that will not defeat his recovery, unless his negligence contributed to cause the injury.

95. A person may contract to labor for another during life, in consideration of receiving his support; but his creditors have the right to inquire into the intention with which such arrangement is made, and it will be set aside if entered into to deprive them of his future earnings.

96. A grantor may by express terms exclude the bed of a river, or a highway, mentioned as boundary; but if without language of exclusion a line is described as ' along,' or ' upon,' or as ' running to ' the highway or river, or as ' by,' or ' running to the bank of ' the river; these expressions carry the grantee to the center of the highway or river.

97. The court will take pains to construe the words used in a deed in such a way as to effect the intention of the parties, however unskillfully the instrument may be drawn. But a court of law cannot exchange an intelligible word plainly employed in a deed for another, however evident it may be that the word used was used by mistake for another.

98. One who has lost his memory and understanding is entitled to legal protection, whether such loss is occasioned by his own misconduct or by an act of Providence.

99. When a wife leaves her husband voluntarily, it must be shown, in order to make him liable for necessaries furnished to her, that she could not stay with safety. Personal violence, either threatened or inflicted, will be sufficient cause for such separation.

100. Necessaries of dress furnished to a discarded wife must correspond with the pecuniary circumstances of the husband, and be such articles as the wife, if prudent, would expect, and the husband should furnish, if the parties lived harmoniously together.

101. A fugitive from justice from one of the United States to another, may be arrested and detained in order to his surrender by authority of the latter, without a previous demand for his surrender by the executive of the State whence he fled.

102. A watch will not pass under a bequest of "wearing apparel," nor of "household furniture and articles for family use."

103. Money paid for the purpose of settling or compounding a prosecution for a supposed felony, cannot be recovered back by a party paying it.

104. An innkeeper is liable for the death of an animal in his possession, but may free himself from liability by showing that the death was not occasioned by negligence on his part.

105. Notice to the agent of a company is notice to the company.

106. An employer is not liable to one of his employes for an injury sustained by the latter in consequence of the neglect of others of his employes engaged in the same general business.

107. Where a purchaser at a Sheriff's sale has bid the full price of property under the erroneous belief that the sale would divest the property of all liens, it is the duty of the court to give relief by setting aside the sale.

108. When notice of protest is properly sent by mail, it may be sent by the mail of the day of the dishonor; if not, it must be mailed for the mail of the next day ; except that if there is none, or it closes at an unseasonably early hour, then notice must be mailed in season for the next possible mail.

109. A powder-house located in a populous part of a city, and containing large quantities of gunpowder, is a nuisance.

110. When the seller of goods accepts at the time of the sale, the note of a third person, unindorsed by the purchaser, in payment, the presumption is that the payment was intended to be absolute ; and though the note should be dishonored, the purchaser will not be liable for the value of the goods.

111. A man charged with crime before a committing magistrate, but discharged on his own recognizance, is not privileged from arrest on civil process while returning from the magistrate's office.

112. When one has been induced to sell goods by means of false pretenses, he cannot recover them from one who has bona fide purchased and obtained possession of them from the fraudulent vendor.

113. If the circumstances attendant upon a sale and delivery of personal property are such as usually and naturally accompany such a transaction, it cannot be declared a legal fraud upon creditors.

114. A stamp impressed upon an instrument by way of seal, is good as a seal, if it creates a durable impression in the texture of the paper.

115. If a party bound to make a payment use due diligence to make a tender, but through the payee's absence from home is unable to find him or any agent authorized to take payment for him, no forfeiture will be incurred through his failure to make a tender.

Government Land Measure.

A township, 36 sections, each a mile square.
A section, 640 acres.
A quarter section, half a mile square, 160 acres.
An eighth section, half a mile long, north and south, and a quarter of a mile wide, 80 acres.
A sixteenth section, a quarter of a mile square, 40 acres.
The sections are numbered from one to thirty-six, commencing at the northeast corner, thus:

6	5	4	3	2	n w / s w	n e / s e
7	8	9	10	11	12	
18	17	16	15	14	13	
19	20	21	22	23	24	
30	29	28	27	26	25	
31	32	33	34	35	36	

The sections are all divided in quarters, which are named by the cardinal points, as in section one. The quarters are divided in the same way. The description of a 40 acre lot would read: The south half of the west half of the southwest quarter of section 1 in township 24, north of range 7 west, or as the case might be; and sometimes will fall short, and sometimes overrun the number of acres it is supposed to contain.

THE DECIMAL SYSTEM

OF

WEIGHTS AND MEASURES.

As Authorized by Act of Congress--Approved July 28, 1866.

STANDARDS.

In every system of Weights and Measures it is necessary to have what are called " *Standards*," as the pound, yard, gallon, &c., to be divided and multiplied into smaller and larger parts and denominations. The definition and construction of these Standards involve philosophical and scientific principles of a somewhat abstruse character, and are made and procured by the legislative department of the government. The nominal Standards in the new system are the METER, the ARE, the LITER, and the GRAM. The only *real* Standard, the one by which all the other standards are measured, and from which the system derives its name of "Metric," is the METER.

THE METER

Is used for all measures of length, distance, breadth, depth, heighth, &c., and was intended to be, and is very nearly, one ten-millionth of the distance on the earth's surface from the equator to the pole. It is about 39⅜ inches, or 3 feet, 3 inches and 3 eighths, and is to be substituted for the yard.

THE ARE

Is a surface whose side is ten Meters, and is equal to 100 square Meters or about 4 square rods.

THE LITER

Is the unit for measuring solids and capacity, and is equal to the contents of a cube whose edge is one-tenth of a meter. It is about equal to 1 quart, and is a standard in cubic, dry and liquid measures.

☞ A cubic Meter (or Kiloliter) is called a *stere*, and is also used as a standard in certain cubic measures.

THE GRAM

Is the Unit of *weight*, and is the weight of a cube of pure water, each edge of the cube being one one-hundredth of a Meter. It is about equal to 15½ grains. It is intended as the Standard in *all* weights, and with its divisions and multiples, to supersede the use of what are now called Avoirdupois, Apothecaries and Troy Weights.

Each of the foregoing Standards is divided decimally, and larger units are also formed by multiples of 10, 100, &c. The successive subordinate parts are designated by the prefixes Deci, Centi and Milli; the successive multiples by Deka, Hecto, Kilo and Myria; each having its own numerical signification, as will be more clearly seen in the tables hereinafter given.

The terms used may, at first sight, have a formidable appearance, seem difficult to pronounce, and to retain in memory, and to be, therefore, objectionable; but with a little attention and use, the apprehended difficulty will be found more apparent than real, as has been abundantly proved by experience. The importance, also, of conformity in the use of commercial terms, on the part of the United States, with the practice of the many nations in which the system, *with its present nomenclature*, has already been adopted, must greatly overbalance the comparatively slight objection alluded to.

TABLES.

OLD.	MONEY.	NEW.

<table>
<tr><td>4 farthing make 1 penny.</td><td></td><td>10 mills make 1 cent.</td></tr>
<tr><td>12 pence   "   1 shilling.</td><td></td><td>10 cents   "   1 dime.</td></tr>
<tr><td>20 shillings   "   1 pound.</td><td></td><td>10 dimes   "   1 dollar.</td></tr>
</table>

LONG AND CLOTH MEASURE.—NEW.

10 millimeters	make	1 centimeter.
10 centimeters	"	1 decimeter.
10 decimeters	"	1 METER.
10 meters	"	1 dekameter.
10 dekameters	"	1 hectometer.
10 hectometers	"	1 kilometer.
10 kilometers	"	1 myriameter.

SQUARE MEASURE.—NEW.

100 square millimeters	make	1 square centimeter.
100 square centimeters	"	1 square decimeter.
100 square decimeters	"	1 square meter or CENTARE.
100 centares	"	1 ARE.
100 ares	"	1 hectare.

☞ The denominations less than the Are, including the Meter, are used in specifying the contents of surfaces of small extent; the terms *Centare*, *Are* and *Hectare*, in expressing quantities of land surveyed or measured.

The above table may, however, be continued beyond the Meter, thus:

100 square meters	make	1 square dekameter.
100 square dekameters	"	1 square hectometer.
100 square hectometers	"	1 square kilometer.
100 square kilometers	"	1 square myriameter.

CUBIC MEASURE.—NEW.

For Solids.

1000 cubic millimeters	make	1 cubic centimeter.
1000 cubic centimeters	"	1 cubic decimeter or liter.
1000 cubic decimeters	"	1 cubic meter or stere.
1000 cubic meters	"	1 cubic dekameter.
1000 cubic dekameters	"	1 cubic hectometer.
1000 cubic hectometers	"	1 cubic kilometer.
1000 cubic kilometers	"	1 cubic myriameter.

For Dry and Liquid Measures.

10 milliliters	make	1 centiliter.
10 centiliters	"	1 deciliter.
10 deciliters	"	1 LITER.
10 liters	"	1 dekaliter.
10 dekaliters	"	1 hectoliter.
10 hectoliters	"	1 kiloliter.
10 kiloliters	"	1 myrialiter.

[☞ A LITER, the standard of Measures of Capacity, usually in a cylindrical form, is equivalent to a cubic *Decimeter*, or the one-thousandth part of a cubic Meter, the contents of which are about one quart.]

The Kiloliter, or STERE, is a cubic Meter, and is used as a unit in measuring firewood and lumber.

10 decisteres	make	1 stere.
10 steres	"	1 dekastere.

ALL WEIGHTS.—NEW.

10 milligrams	make	1 centigram.
10 centigrams	"	1 decigram.
10 decigrams	"	1 GRAM.
10 grams	"	1 dekagram.
10 dekagrams	"	1 hectogram.
10 hectograms	"	1 kilogram.
10 kilograms	"	1 myriagram.
10 myriagrams	"	1 quintal.
10 quintals	"	1 millier or tonneau.

PRONUNCIATION OF TERMS.

TERMS.	ENGLISH.	TERMS.	ENGLISH.
Meter,	Mee-ter.	Stere,	Stare.
Millimeter.	Mill-e-mee-ter.	Are,	Are.
Centimeter,	Sent-e-mee-ter.	Centare,	Sent-are.
Decimeter,	Des-e-mee-ter.	Hectare,	Hect-are.
Dekameter,	Dek-a-mee-ter.	Gram,	Gram,
Hectometer,	Hec-to-mee-ter.	Milligram,	Mill-e-gram.
Kilometer,	Kill-o-mee-ter.	Centigram,	Sent-e-gram.
Myriameter,	Mir-e-a-mee-ter.	Decigram,	Des-e-gram.
Liter,	Li-ter.	Dekagram,	Dek-a-gram,
Milliliter,	Mill-e-li-ter.	Hectogram,	Hec-to-gram.
Centiliter,	Sent-e-li-ter.	Kilogram,	Kill-o-gram.
Deciliter,	Des-e-li-ter.	Myriagram,	Mir-e-a-gram.
Dekaliter,	Dek-a-li-ter.	Quintal,	Qnin-tal.
Hectoliter,	Hec-to-li-ter.	Millier,	Mill-i-er.
Kiloliter,	Kill-o-li-ter.	Tonneau,	Tun-no.
Myrialiter,	Mir-e-a-li-ter.		

Acts and Resolutions of Congress.

PUBLIC — No. 183.

AN ACT to authorize the use of the metric system of weights and measures.

Be it enacted by the Senate and House of Representatives of the United States of America in Congress assembled, That from and after the passage of this act, it shall be lawful throughout the United States of America to employ the weights and measures of the metric system ; and no contract or dealing, or pleading in any court, shall be deemed invalid or liable to objection, because the weights or measures expressed or referred to therein are weights or measures of the metric system.

SEC. 2. *And be it further enacted,* That the tables in the schedule hereto annexed, shall be recognized in the construction of contracts, and in all legal proceedings, as establishing, in terms of the weights and measures now in use in the United States, the equivalents of the weights and measures expressed therein in terms of the metric system ; and said tables may be lawfully used for computing, determining and expressing, in customary weights and measures, the weights and measures of the metric system.

MEASURES OF LENGTH.

METRIC DENOMINATIONS AND VALUES.		EQUIVALENTS IN DENOMINATIONS IN USE.
Myriametre, ...	10,000 metres,	6.2137 miles.
Kilometre, ...	1,000 metres,	0.62137 mile, or 2,280 feet and 10 inches.
Hectometre, ...	100 metres,	328 feet and one inch.
Dekametre, ...	10 metres,	393.7 inches.
Metre, ...	1 metre,	39.37 inches.
Decimetre, ...	1–10th of a metre,	3.937 inches.
Centimetre, ...	1–100th of a metre,	0.3937 inch.
Millimetre, ...	1–1000th of a metre,	0.0394 inch.

MEASURES OF SURFACE.

METRIC DENOMINATIONS AND VALUES.		EQUIVALENTS IN DENOMINATIONS IN USE.
Hectare, ...	10,000 square metres,	2.471 acres.
Are, ...	100 square metres,	119.6 square yards.
Centare, ...	1 square metre,	1.550 square inches.

D

MEASURES OF CAPACITY.

METRIC DENOMINATIONS AND VALUES.			EQUIVALENTS IN DENOMINATIONS	
Names.	No. of liters.	Cubic Measure.	Dry Measure.	Liquid or V
olitre or stere,.........	1000	1 cubic metre, ...	1.308 cubic yard,.........	264.17 ga
tolitre,....	100	.1 of a cubic metre,........	2 bus. and 3.35 pecks, ...	26.417 ga
alitre, ...	10	10 cubic decimetres, ...	9.08 quarts,.................	2.6417 ga
e, ...	1	1 cubic decimetre, ...	0.908 quart,.................	1.0567 qu
ilitre,.............. .	0.1	.1 of a cubic decimetre, ...	6.1022 cubic inches, ...	0.845 gill
tilitre,...............	0.01	10 cubic centimetres, ...	0.6102 cubic inch,...........	0.338 flui
llitre, ...	0.001	1 cubic centimetre, ...	0.061 cubic inch,...........	0.27 fluid

WEIGHTS.

Metric Denominations and Values.			Equivalents in Denominations in Use.
Names.	No. of grams.	Weight of what quantity of water at maximum density.	Avoirdupois weight.
Millier or tonneau,.	1000000	1 cubic metre,........	2204.6 pounds.
Quintal, ...	100000	1 hectolitre, ...	220.46 pounds.
Myriagram, ...	10000	10 litres, ...	22.046 pounds.
Kilogram, or kilo,....	1000	1 litre, ...	2.2046 pounds.
Hectogram, ;....	100	1 decilitre, ...	3.5274 ounces.
Dekagram, ...	10	10 cubic centimetres,........ .	0.3527 ounce.
Gram, ...	1	1 cubic centimetre, ...	15.432 grains.
Decigram, ...	1-10	.1 of a cubic centimetre.	0.5432 grain.
Centigram,..........	1-100	10 cubic millimetres,.........	0.1543 grain.
Milligram, ...	1-1000	1 cubic millimetre,..........	0.0154 grain.

INTEREST TABLE

At Seven per Cent. in Dollars and Cents, from $1 to $10,000.

AM'NT.	1 day.	7 days.	15 days.	1 mo.	3 mos.	6 mos.	12 mos.
$	$ C.	$ C.	$ C.	$ C.	$ C.	$ C.	$ C.
1	00	00	00¼	00½	01¾	03½	07
2	00	00¼	00½	01¼	03½	07	14
3	00	00½	00¾	01¾	05¼	10½	21
4	00	00½	01	02⅓	07	14	28
5	00	00¾	01½	03	08¾	17½	35
6	00	00¾	01¾	03½	10½	21	42
7	00	01	02	04	12¼	24½	49
8	00	01	02¼	04⅔	14	28	56
9	00	01¼	02½	05¼	15¾	31½	63
10	00¼	01¼	03	05¾	17½	35	70
20	00⅜	02¾	06	11⅔	35	70	1 40
30	00½	04	09	17½	52½	1 05	2 10
40	00¾	05½	12	23⅓	70	1 40	2 80
50	01	06¾	15	29¼	87½	1 75	3 50
100	02	13½	29	58⅓	1 75	3 50	7 00
200	04	27¼	58	1 16⅔	3 50	7 00	14 00
300	06	40¾	87½	1 75	5 25	10 50	21 00
400	08	54½	1 17	2 33⅓	7 00	14 00	28 00
500	10	68	1 46	2 91⅔	8 75	17 50	35 00
1000	19½	1 36	2 92	5 83⅓	17 50	35 00	70 00
2000	39	2 72¼	5 83	11 66⅔	35 00	70 00	140 00
3000	58	4 08¼	8 75	17 50	52 50	105 00	210 00
4000	78	5 44½	11 67	23 33⅓	70 00	140 00	280 00
5000	97	6 80½	14 58	29 16⅔	87 50	175 00	350 00
10000	1 94	13 61	29 17	58 33	175 00	350 00	700 00

Discount and Premium.

When a person buys an article for $1,00—20 per cent off, (or discount,) and sells it again for $1,00, he makes a profit of 25 per cent. on his investment. Thus: He pays 80 cents and sells for $1,00—a gain of 20 cents, or 25 per cent of 80 cents. And for any transaction where the sale or purchase of gold, silver, or currency is concerned, the following rules will apply in all cases.

RULE 1st.—To find premium when discount is given: Multiply 100 by rate of discount and divide by 100, less rate of discount.

RULE 2d.—To find discount when premium is given. Multiply the rate of interest by 100, and divide by 100, plus the rate of premium.

Suppose A has $140 in currency, which he wishes to exchange for gold, when gold is 27 per cent. premium, how much gold should he receive? In this case the premium is given, consequently we must find the discount on A's currency and subtract it from the $140, as per rule 2d, showing the discount to be a trifle more than 21 per cent. and that he should receive $110.60 in gold.

5 pr ct. Dis. allows	+5¼ pr ct. Pre. or profit		
10 "	"	"	+11 " " "
15 "	"	"	+17½ " " "
20 "	"	"	25 " " "
25 "	"	"	33⅓ " " "
30 "	"	"	*43 " " "
40 "	"	"	69⅔ " " "
50 "	"	"	100 " " "

☞ A dagger (†) denotes the profits to be a fraction more than specified. A (*) denotes profits to be a fraction less than specified.

Table of Weights of Grain, Seeds, &c.

ACCORDING TO THE LAWS OF NEW YORK.

Barley weighs	48 lb. per bushel.
Beans "	62 " "
Buckwheat"	48 " "
Clover Seed	60 " "
Corn weighs	58 " "
Flax Seed* "	55 " "
Oats "	32 " "
Peas "	60 " "
Potatoes "	60 " "
Rye "	56 " "
Timothy Seed	44 " "
Wheat	60 " "

*Flax Seed by cust'm weighs 56 lb. per bush.

Facts on Advertising.

The advertisements in an ordinary number of the London Times exceed 2,500. The annual advertising bills of one London firm are said to amount to $200,000; and three others are mentioned who each annually expend for the purpose $50,000. The expense for advertising the eight editions of the "Encyclopædia Britannia" is said to have been $15,000.

In large cities nothing is more common than to see large business establishments, which seem to have an immense advantage over all competitors, by the wealth, experience, and prestige they have acquired, drop gradually out of public view, and be succeeded by firms of a smaller capital, more energy, and more determined to have the fact that they sell such and such commodities known from one end ☞ of the land to the other. In other words, the establishments advertise; the old die of dignity.—The former are ravenous to pass out of obscurity into publicity; the latter believe that their publicity is so obvious that it cannot be obscured. The first understand that they must thrust themselves upon public attention, or be disregarded; the second, having once obtained public attention, suppose they have arrested it permanently; while, in fact, nothing is more characteristic of the world than the ease with which it forgets.

Stephen Girard, than whom no shrewder business man ever lived, used to say: I have always considered advertising liberally and long to be the great medium of success in business, and the prelude to wealth. And I have made it an invariable rule too, to advertise in the dullest times as well as the busiest; long experience having taught me that money thus spent is well laid out; as by keeping my business continually before the public it has secured me many sales that I would otherwise have lost.

Capacity of Cisterns or Wells.

Tabular view of the number of gallons contained in the clear, between the brick work for each ten inches of depth:

Diameter		Gallons.
2 feet equals		19
2½ "	"	30
3 "	"	44
3½ "	"	60
4 "	"	78
4½ "	"	97
5 "	"	122
5½ "	"	148
6 "	"	176
6½ "	"	207
7 "	"	240
7½ "	"	275
8 "	"	313
8½ "	"	353
9 "	"	396
9½ "	"	461
10 "	"	489
11 "	"	592
12 "	"	705
13 "	"	827
14 "	"	959
15 "	"	1101
20 "	"	1958
25 "	"	3059

Brilliant Whitewash.

Many have heard of the brilliant stucco whitewash on the east end of the President's house at Washington. The following is a recipe for it; it is gleaned from the National Intelligencer, with some additional improvements learned by experiments : Take half a bushel of nice unslacked lime, slack it with boiling water, cover it during the process to keep in the steam. Strain the liquid through a fine sieve or strainer, and add to it a peck of salt, previously well dissolved in warm water ; three pounds of ground rice, boiled to a thin paste, and stirred in boiling hot ; half a pound of powdered Spanish whiting, and a pound of clean glue, which has been previously dissolved by soaking it well, and then hanging it over a slow fire, in a small kettle within a large one filled with water. Add five gallons of hot water to the mixture, stir it well, and let it stand a few days covered from the dirt.

It should be put on right hot; for this purpose it can be kept in a kettle on a portable furnace. It is said that about a pint of this mixture will cover a square yard upon the outside of a house if properly applied. Brushes more or less small may be used according to the neatness of the job required. It answers as well as oil paint for wood, brick or stone, and is cheaper. It retains its brilliancy for many years. There is nothing of the kind that will compare with it, either for inside or outside walls.

Coloring matter may be put in and made of any shade you like. Spanish brown stirred in will make red pink, more or less deep according to the quantity. A delicate tinge of this is very pretty, for inside walls. Finely pulverized common clay, well mixed with Spanish brown, makes a reddish stone color. Yellow-ochre stirred in makes yellow wash, but chrome goes further, and makes a color generally esteemed prettier. In all these cases the darkness of the shades of course is determined by the quantity of coloring used. It is difficult to make rules, because tastes are different. It would be best to try experiments on a shingle and let it dry. We have been told that green must not be mixed with lime. The lime destroys the color, and the color has an effect on the whitewash, which makes it crack and peel. When walls have been badly smoked, and you wish to have them a clean white, it is well to squeeze indigo plentifully through a bag into the water you use, before it is stirred in the whole mixture. If a larger quantity than five gallons be wanted, the same proportion should be observed.

How to get a Horse out of a Fire.

The great difficulty of getting horses from a stable where surrounding buildings are in a state of conflagation, is well known.— The plan of covering their eyes with a blanket will not always succeed.

A gentleman whose horses have been in great peril from such a cause, having tried in vain to save them, hit upon the expedient of having them harnessed as though going to their usual work, when, to his astonishment, they were led from the stable without difficulty.

The Chemical Barometer.

Take a long narrow bottle, such as an old-fashioned Eau-de-Cologne bottle, and put into it two and a half drachms of camphor, and eleven drachms of spirits of wine ; when the camphor is dissolved, which it will readily do by slight agitation, add the following mixture : Take water, nine drachms ; nitrate of potash (saltpetre) thirty-eight grains ; and muriate of ammonia (sal ammoniac) thirty-eight grains. Dissolve these salts in the water prior to mixing with the camphorated spirit ; then shake the whole well together. Cork the bottle well, and wax the top, but afterwards make a very small aperture in the cork with a red-hot needle. The bottle may then be hung up, or placed in any stationary position. By observing the different appearances which the materials assume, as the weather changes, it becomes an excellent prognosticator of a coming storm or of a sunny sky.

Leech Barometer.

Take an eight ounce phial, and put in it three gills of water, and place in it a healthy leech, changing the water in summer once a week, and in winter once in a fortnight, and it will most accurately prognosticate the weather. If the weather is to be fine, the leech lies motionless at the bottom of the glass and coiled together in a spiral form ; if rain may be expected, it will creep up to the top of its lodgings and remain there till the weather is settled ; if we are to have wind, it will move through its habitation with amazing swiftness, and seldom goes to rest till it begins to blow hard ; if a remarkable storm of thunder and rain is to succeed, it will lodge for some days before almost continually out of the water, and discover great uneasiness in violent throes and convulsive-like motions ; in frost as in clear summer-like weather it lies constantly at the bottom ; and in snow as in rainy weather it pitches its dwelling in the very mouth of the phial. The top should be covered over with a piece of muslin.

To Measure Grain in a Bin.—Find the number of cubic feet, from which deduct *one-fifth.* The remainder is the number of bushels—allowing, however, one bushel extra to every 224. Thus in a remainder of 224 there would be 225 bushels. In a remainder of 448 there would be 450 bushels, &c.

VALUABLE RECIPES.

———•———

[The following recipes are vouched for by several who have tried them and proven their virtues. Many of them have been sold singly for more than the price of this book.—Pub.]

HORSES.

RING BONE AND SPAVIN.—2 oz. each of Spanish flies and Venice turpentine; 1 oz. each of aqua ammonia and euphorbium; ½ oz. red precipitate; ¼ oz. corrosive sublimate; 1½ lbs. lard. When thoroughly pulverized and mixed, heat carefully so as not to burn, and pour off free from sediment.

For ring-bone, rub in thoroughly, after removing hair, once in 48 hours. For spavin, once in 24 hours. Cleanse and press out the matter on each application.

POLL-EVIL.—Gum arabic ¼ oz; common potash ¼ oz; extract of belladonna ½ dr. Put the gum in just enough water to dissolve it. Pulverize the potash and mix with the dissolved gum, and then put in the extract of belladonna, and it will be ready for use. Use with a syringe after having cleansed with soap suds, and repeat once in two days till a cure is affected.

SCOURS.—Powdered tormentil root, given in milk, from 3 to 5 times daily till cured.

GREASE-HEEL AND SCRATCHES.—Sweet oil 6 ozs.; borax 2 ozs.; sugar of lead 2 ozs. Wash off with dish water, and, after it is dry, apply the mixture twice a day.

CHOLIC IN HORSES.—To ½ pt. of warm water add 1 oz. laudanum and 3 ozs. spirits of turpentine, and repeat the dose in about ¾ of an hour, adding ½ oz. powdered aloes, if not relieved.

BOTS.—Three doses. 1st. 2 qts milk and 1 of molasses. 2d. 15 minutes after, 2 qts. warm sage tea. 3d. After the expiration of 30 minutes, sufficient lard to physic.—Never fails.

MISCELLANEOUS.

PILES—PERFECTLY CURED.—Take flour of sulphur 1 oz., rosin 3 ozs., pulverize and mix well together. (Color with carmine or cochineal, if you like.) *Dose*—What will lie on a five cent piece, night and morning, washing the parts freely in cold water once or twice a day. This is a remedy of great value.

The cure will be materially hastened by taking a table-spoon of sulphur in a half pint of milk, daily, until the cure is affected.

SURE CURE FOR CORNS, WARTS AND CHILBLAINS.—Take of nitric and muriatic acids, blue vitriol and salts of tartar, 1 oz. each. Add the blue vitriol, pulverized, to either of the acids; add the salts of tartar in the same way; when done foaming, add the other acid, and in a few days it will be ready for use. For chilblains and corns apply it very lightly with a swab, and repeat in a day or two until cured. For warts, once a week, until they disappear.

HOOF-AIL IN SHEEP.—Mix 2 ozs. each of butter of antimony and muriatic acid with 1 oz. of pulverized white vitriol, and apply once or twice a week to the bottom of the foot.

COMMON RHEUMATISM.—Kerosene oil 2 ozs.; neats-foot oil 1 oz.; oil of organum ½ oz. Shake when used, and rub and heat in twice daily.

VERY FINE SOAP, QUICKLY AND CHEAPLY MADE.—Fourteen pounds of bar soap in a half a boiler of hot water; cut up fine; add three pounds of sal-soda made fine; one ounce of pulverized rosin; stir it often till all is dissolved; just as you take it off the fire, put in two table-spoonfuls of spirits of turpentine and one of ammonia; pour it in a barrel, and fill up with cold soft water; let it stand three or four days before using. It is an excellent soap for washing clothes, extracting the dirt readily, and not fading colored articles.

WATER PROOF FOR LEATHER.—Take linseed oil 1 pint, yellow wax and white turpentine each 2 ozs. Burgundy pitch 1 oz., melt and color with lampblack.

TO KEEP CIDER SWEET.—Put into each barrel, immediately after making, ½ lb. ground mustard, 2 oz. salt and 2 oz. pulverized chalk. Stir them in a little cider, pour them into the barrel, and shake up well.

AGUE CURE.—Procure 1½ table-spoons of fresh mandrake root juice, (by pounding) and mix with the same quantity of molasses, and take in three equal doses, 2 hours a part, the whole to be taken 1 hour before the chill comes on. Take a swallow of some good bitters before meals, for a couple of weeks after the chills are broken, and the cure will be permanent.

CURE FOR SALT RHEUM OR SCURVY.—Take of the pokeweed, any time in summer; pound it; press out the juice; strain it into a pewter dish; set it in the sun till it becomes a salve—then put it into an earthen mug; add to it fresh water and bees' wax sufficient to make an ointment of common consistency; simmer the whole over a fire till thoroughly mixed. When cold, rub the part affected. The patient will almost immediately experience its good effects, and the most obstinate cases will be cured in three or four months. Tested.—The juice of the ripe berries may be prepared in the same way.

SUPERIOR PAINT—FOR BRICK HOUSES.—To lime whitewash, add for a fastener, sulphate of zinc, and shade with any color you choose, as yellow ochre, Venetian red, etc. It outlasts oil paint.

FELONS.—Stir 1 oz. of Venice turpentine with ½ tea-spoonful of water, till it looks like candied honey, and apply by spreading upon cloth and wrapping around the finger. If not too long delayed will cure in 6 hours.

A poke root poultice is also said to be a sure remedy.

WATER-PROOF BLACKING AND HARNESS POLISH.—Take two and a half ounces gum shellac and half a pint of alcohol, and set in a warm place until dissolved; then add two and a half ounces Venice turpentine to neutralize the alcohol; add a tablespoonful of lampblack. Apply with a fine sponge. It will give a good polish over oil or grease.

MOSQUITOS.—To get rid of these tormentors, take a few hot coals on a shovel, or a chafing dish, and burn upon them some brown sugar in your bed-rooms and parlors, and you effectually banish or destroy every mosquito for the night.

CHEAP OUTSIDE PAINT.—Take two parts (in bulk) of water lime ground fine, one part (in bulk) of white lead ground in oil. Mix them thoroughly, by adding best boiled linseed oil, enough to prepare it to pass through a paint mill, after which temper with oil till it can be applied with a common paint brush. Make any color to suit. It will last three times as long as lead paint, and cost not one-fourth as much. IT IS SUPERIOR.

CURE FOR A COUGH.—A strong decoction of the leaves of the pine, sweetened with loaf sugar. Take a wine-glass warm on going to bed, and half an hour before eating three times a day. The above is sold as a cough syrup, and is doing wonderful cures, and it is sold at a great profit to the manufacturers.

How to Judge a Horse.

A correspondent, contrary to old maxims, undertakes to judge the character of a horse by outward appearances, and offers the following suggestions, the result of his close observation and long experience:

If the color be light sorrell, or chestnut, his feet, legs and face white, these are marks of kindness. If he is broad and full between the eyes, he may be depended on as a horse of good sense, and capable of being trained to anything.

As respects such horses, the more kindly you treat them the better you will be treated in return. Nor will a horse of this description stand a whip, if well fed.

If you want a safe horse, avoid one that is dish-faced. He may be so far gentle as not to scare; but he will have too much go-ahead in him to be safe with everybody.

If you want a fool, but a horse of great bottom, get a deep bay, with not a white hair about him. If his face is a little dished, so much the worse. Let no man ride such a horse that is not an adept in riding—they are always tricky and unsafe.

If you want one that will never give out, never buy a large, overgrown one.

A black horse cannot stand heat, nor a white one cold.

If you want a gentle horse, get one with more or less white about the head; the more the better. Many persons suppose the parti-colored horses belonging to the circuses, shows, &c., are selected for their oddity. But the selections thus made are on account of their great docility and gentleness.

Measurement of Hay in the Mow or Stack.

It is often desirable, where conveniences for weighing are not at hand, to purchase and sell hay by measurement. It is evident that no fixed rule will answer in all cases, as it would require more cubic feet at the top of a mow than at the bottom. The general rule adopted by those who have tested it, is that a cube, each side of which shall measure eight feet, of *solid* Timothy hay, as taken from mow or bottom of stack will weigh a *ton*. The rule may be varied for upper part of mow or stack according to pressure.

Almanac or Calendar for 20 Years.

CB	A	G	F	ED	C	B	A	GF	E
1864	1865	1866	1867	1868	1869	1870	1871	1872	1873
D	C	BA	G	F	E	DC	F	E	D
1874	1875	1876	1877	1878	1879	1880	1881	1882	1883

1	8	15	22	29	Sun.	Sat.	Frid'y.	Thurs.	Wed.	Tues.	Mon.
2	9	16	23	30	Mon.	Sun.	Sat.	Frid'y.	Thurs.	Wed.	Tues.
3	10	17	24	31	Tues.	Mon.	Sun.	Sat.	Frid'y.	Thurs.	Wed.
4	11	18	25	..	Wed.	Tues.	Mon.	Sun.	Sat.	Frid'y.	Thurs.
5	12	19	26	..	Thurs.	Wed.	Tues.	Mon.	Sun.	Sat.	Frid'y.
6	13	20	27	..	Frid'y.	Thurs.	Wed.	Tues.	Mon.	Sun.	Sat.
7	14	21	28	..	Sat.	Frid'y.	Thurs.	Wed.	Tues.	Mon.	Sun.

Jan. and Oct.	A	B	C	D	E	F	G
May.	B	C	D	E	F	G	A
August.	C	D	E	F	G	A	B
Feb., Mar., Nov.	D	E	F	G	A	B	C
June.	E	F	G	A	B	C	D
Sept. & Dec.	F	G	A	B	C	D	E
April & July.	G	A	B	C	D	E	F

EXPLANATION.—Find the Year and observe the Letter above it; then look for the Month, and in a line with it find the Letter of the Year; above the Letter find the Day; and the figures on the left, in the same line, are the days of the same name in the month.

Leap Years have two letters; the first is used till the end of February, the second during the remainder of the year.

OTSEGO COUNTY.

THIS COUNTY was formed from Montgomery, February 16, 1791, and embraced the two original towns of Otsego and Cherry Valley. A part of Schoharie was taken off in 1795, and a part of Delaware in 1797. It lies upon the highlands at the head of Susquehanna River, south-east of the center of the State. It is centrally distant 66 miles from Albany and contains 1,038 square miles. The surface is a hilly upland, divided into several ridges, separated by deep, broad valleys. The declivities are generally gradual, and the highest summits are from 400 to 700 feet above the valleys, and 1,700 to 2,000 feet above tide. The ridges have a general north-east and south-west direction. A high and rocky upland extends into the south-east corner from Delaware County, terminating upon Schenevus Creek, in an abrupt and wall-like declivity, 300 to 500 feet high. The other ridges of the County have a nearly uniform elevation, and generally terminate in steep declivities upon the valleys of the streams.

The principal streams are Unadilla River, forming the west boundary; Wharton and Butternut Creeks, its principal tributaries; Susquehanna River, Otego, Cherry Valley and Schenevus Creeks. Charlotte River forms a small portion of the south boundary. A large number of smaller streams are tributary to the above. A few small streams rise in the north-east corner and flow into the Mohawk. Otsego Lake, in the north-east part, is a fine sheet of water about eight miles long and one mile wide. It is 1,193 feet above tide and is surrounded by hills from 400 to 500 feet high. Its outlet forms the principal head branch of the Susquehanna. Schuyler Lake, situated a few miles north-west of Otsego, is about three and a half miles long. There are several other small ponds in the County.

The rocks in the north-east corner consist of the limestones of the Helderbergh division. The hills in the south part are composed of the shales of the Hamilton group and the shales and sandstones of the Portage and Chemung groups. The sum-

mits in the extreme south and south-east corner are crowned by
the red sandstone and shales of the Catskill group. Most of
the valuable quarries of the County are found in the limestone
region of the north-east. The soil in the north-east is a good
quality of gravelly and calcareous loam, but further south it is a
clay and shaly loam upon the hills, and a gravelly loam and alluvium in the valleys. The uplands are best adapted to grazing; the river intervales are well adapted to the cultivation of
grain. Stock raising and dairying furnish the principal employment of the people. Hops are extensively cultivated.
Manufacturing is limited, though there is an abundance of
water power.

The County Seat is located at Cooperstown, in the town of
Otsego, at the foot of Otsego Lake. The first Court House was
built in 1791; it was thirty feet square; the lower story was of
hewn logs and used as a Jail; the upper story was a frame and
used for the Courts. The Jury rooms were in a tavern occupied by the Jailor, and standing on the same lot at the south-
east corner of Main and Pioneer Streets. In 1806–7 a new
Court House was erected near the site of the present structure;
it was of brick and the lower story was used as a Jail. This
was burned December 17, 1840. The present structure was
erected in 1841; it is of stone, 46 by 56 feet. The Jail and
Sheriff's house are of stone and located a short distance west of
the Court House. The Clerk's office is of brick, two stories
high, and contains the Surrogate's office. It is located adjacent
to the Court House.

The first County officers were William Cooper, *First Judge;*
Jacob Morris, *County Clerk;* Richard B. Smith, *Sheriff;* and
James Cannon, *Surrogate.*

The County Poor House is located upon a farm of 160 acres,
in the town of Middlefield.

The Albany & Susquehanna Railroad extends along the val-
leys of the Susquehanna River and Schenevus Creek, through
Worcester, Maryland, Milford, Oneonta, Otego and Unadilla.
The Cooperstown & Susquehanna Valley Railroad connects with
the Albany & Susquehanna Railroad at Junction Station in the
town of Milford, and extends along the Susquehanna Valley
through Hartwick to Cooperstown. *The Utica, Chenango &
Susquehanna Valley R. R.*, connecting Utica with Richfield
Springs, passes through Plainfield and Richfield. *The Sharon
& Cherry Valley R. R.* extends from Cobleskill, on the A. & S.
R. R., to Cherry Valley. It is proposed to connect these roads
and it is also proposed to extend the Cooperstown road to some
point on the Utica road. Another road is in contemplation

from Oneonta to New Berlin, to connect with roads now in process of construction, making a direct line from New York to Syracuse.

There are ten weekly newspapers published in this County. The first paper published in the County, and the second in the State, west of Albany, was

The Otsego Herald or Western Advertiser, started at Cooperstown, April 3, 1795, by Elisha Phinney. Its motto was:

> "Historic truth our *Herald* shall proclaim,
> The law our guide, the public good our aim !"

Mr. Phinney continued its publication until his death in 1813. It was then published by his sons, H. & E. Phinney, until 1821, when it was discontinued.

The Impartial Observer was started at Cooperstown, October 22, 1808. It was owned by Judge Cooper and edited by Mr. Andrews. It soon after passed into the hands of John H. Prentiss, who changed the name to

The Cooperstown Federalist. As early as 1820 the name was changed to

THE FREEMAN'S JOURNAL. In 1849 it passed into the hands of Daniel Shaw and J. T. Titus. In 1851 Mr. Samuel M. Shaw, the present editor and proprietor, purchased the paper, enlarged and improved it, and has continued its publication to the present time.

The Otsego Republican was published at Cherry Valley in 1812 by Clark & Crandal.

The Switch was started March 11, 1809, at Cooperstown. It represented its editor's name as *Anthony Switchem.* It was short lived.

The Watch Tower was established at Cherry Valley in 1813. It was removed to Cooperstown in 1814, and published by Israel W. Clark until May 1817, when it passed into the hands of Edward B. Crandal, who continued its publication until 1831.

The Tocsin was commenced at Cooperstown in June 1829, by Dutton & Hewes. In 1831 the name was changed to

The Otsego Republican. It was published by Dutton & Hopkins about one year; by Hopkins, a year; by Hopkins & Clark, a year; by A. W. Clark, a year; and by Andrew M. Barber, four or five years. In 1840 it was issued by I. K. Williams & Co., and three years after it again passed into the hands of A. M. Barber, and was continued by him until his death in 1855. In October 1855 it was united with

The Otsego Democrat, which was commenced in 1847 by James I. Hendryx, by whom it was published until October 1855, when it was united with the *Republican* and the combined papers published as

THE REPUBLICAN AND DEMOCRAT, by James I. Hendryx & Co., until 1856. It was published by Hendryx & J. B Wood until May 1858, since which Mr. Hendryx has been the sole proprietor. Mr. Charles F. Hendryx, son of the proprietor, is now associated with his father as editor. It is a large paper, nine columns to the page, and a fitting representative of the enterprise of the publisher as well as of the flourishing village of Cooperstown.

The Otsego Examiner was commenced at Cooperstown in 1855 by Robert Shankland. B. W. Burditt soon after became the proprietor and continued its publication until 1857.

The Cherry Valley Gazette was started in October 1818, by William McLean, who continued its publication uutil 1832. It then passed into the hands of Charles McLean, who continued it until January 1, 1847, when A. S. Bottsford became the proprietor and continued it until 1851. Charles McLean again became the proprietor and, in 1853, sold to John B. King, who published it one year under the name of

The American Banner, when he sold to A. S. Bottsford, who changed the name back to

THE CHERRY VALLEY GAZETTE, under which title it has been published at intervals, by various parties, to the present time. It is now published by William A. Smith.

THE SAW BUCK is a monthly, published at Cherry Valley by John Fea.

The Otsego Farmer was published at Cherry Valley in 1841.

The Otsego County Courier was commenced at the village of Louisville, in the town of Morris, by Wm. H. S. Wynans, in 1845.

The Village Advertiser was commenced at the same place in 1851. It was a quarterly publication, conducted, in 1855, by A. S. Avery.

THE ONEONTA HERALD was commenced Feb. 9, 1853, at Oneonta Village, by L. P. Carpenter. In 1868 G. W. Reynolds became the publisher and continued it until 1870, when it passed into the hands of C. S. Carpenter, the present publisher.

THE OTSEGO DEMOCRAT was started July 31, 1868, by G. A. Dodge, at Oneonta, as

The Susquehanna Independent. It was published under this title until June 5, 1869, when the name was changed to

Home and Abroad. April 9, 1870, it received its present name. It is a large eight page sheet and published by G. A. Dodge.

The Unadilla Times was started in June 1856 by John Brown. It soon passed into the hands of E. S. Watson and subsequently to George B. Fellows. G. E. Beadle was the publisher for a time. In June 1869, G. A. Dodge purchased the paper and issued

HOME AND ABROAD, which is still continued.

The Unadilla Advertiser was published for a time.

THE SCHENEVUS MONITOR was started in September 1864, by J. J. Multer, as an independent paper. It soon after espoused the cause of the Democracy and is still published by him. J. J. & J. L. Multer are the editors.

The Otego Literary Record was started in 1868. It is now called THE OTEGO RECORD and is published by E. H. Orwen.

The Otsego Chronicle was started in 1866, at Morris, by Wm. A. Smith. In 1869 it passed into the hands L. P. Carpenter, who changed the name to

THE MORRIS CHRONICLE, and still continues to issue it under this title.

THE RICHFIELD SPRINGS MERCURY was started in July 1865. It is now published by C. Ackerman & Son.

The principal land Patents included in Otsego County were the following; one of 26,000 acres to Sir William Johnson and others, granted May 8, 1770; Banyar's Patent of 4,000 acres, granted April 14, 1753; Belvidere Patent, 100,000 acres, to George Croghan and others, partly in Schoharie County; Cherry Valley Patent, 7,000 acres, to John Lindsey and others; Croghan's Patent, 18,000 acres; Edmeston's Patents of 10,000 acres to Robert and William Edmeston; Franklin Patent, 9,000 acres, to Walter Franklin and others; Hartwick's Patent, 21,500 acres; Lispenard's Patent, 9,000 acres; Middlefield Patent, 29,000 acres, to Godfrey Miller and others; Nettlefield Patent, 13,-000 acres, to Richard Landon and others: Oothoudt's Patent, 13,000 acres; Otsego Patents, one of 69,000 acres to Charles Read and others, and one of 100,000 acres to George Croghan and 99 others; Schuyler's Patent of 43,000 acres; Springfield Patent of 17,000 acres; Upton's Patent of 20,000 acres; and Young's Patent of 20,000 acres, partly in Schoharie.

The first settlement of this County was made at Cherry Valley in 1740 by John Lindsay, who, in connection with Jacob Roseboom, Lendert Gansevoort and Sybrant Van Schaick, had in 1738 received a patent of 8000 acres, lying in the north-east corner of Otsego County and embracing a part of the village and town of Cherry Valley.

Mr. Lindsay subsequently obtained an assignment from the other three patentees, to himself and Governor Clark, made a survey of the patent in 1739, divided it into lots, and the next year made a settlement which he called *Lindsay's Bush.* He was a Scotch gentleman of some wealth and distinction, and the resemblance that this region bore to some portion of his native land, doubtless had some influence in making this selection. It abounded in game and was a favorite hunting ground of the Mohawk Indians, whose friendship Mr. Lindsay and the other early settlers found it important to cultivate. The first winter after the settlement, the snow fell to a great depth and all communication with the settlements upon the Mohawk was cut off. Sufficient preparation for such a winter had not been made, provisions were nearly exhausted and death by starvation awaited the whole settlement. At this critical time an Indian arrived on snow shoes and, on learning the condition of affairs, rendered them relief by going to the settlements and returning with provisions upon his back. This was continued at intervals until spring, and thus the lives of the first settlers were saved.

In New York, Mr. Lindsay became acquainted with Rev. Samuel Dunlap, upon whom he prevailed to visit his patent, offering him several hundred acres on condition that he would settle upon it and use his influence to induce his friends to accompany him. He was an Irishman by birth, but had been educated in Edinburgh and had spent several years in traveling through the American Colonies. Through his influence several families from Londonderry, N. H., were induced to settle at Cherry Valley in 1741. Among these were David Ramsay, William Galt, James Campbell, William Dickson, with their families, in all numbering about thirty persons. They had migrated from the north of Ireland several years previous, some of them having come originally from Scotland, being designated as *Scotch-Irish.*

For several years the most friendly relations existed between the Indians and settlers, but at length, through the intrigues of the French, the Indians in many instances came to look upon the settlers as intruders rather than friends. A war colony was sent out and established at Oquago in Broome County. It was composed chiefly of Mohawks who remained attached to the

English, paid their annual visits to Sir William Johnson and received presents from the English Government. Those who had violated the laws were not permitted to share with the others. A few of this class concerted a plan for destroying the settlement at Cherry Valley while the inhabitants were at church on the Sabbath, but being discovered, the settlers were on their guard, and the Indians withdrew and gave up the plan. Subsequently, owing to the danger arising from the defection of many of the western tribes and the threatenings of those in league with the French, a body of eight hundred Rangers was ordered to be raised for the defense of Tryon County, of which Otsego formed a part, and one company, under the command of Capt. McKean, was stationed at Cherry Valley. During the continuance of the French War the inhabitants were often called upon to repel the invasions of the French and Indians. During these troublesome times, small settlements had been established at various points in the County, in the present towns of Springfield, Richfield, Middlefield, Laurens and Otego. Rev. William Johnstone had established a colony on the east side of the Susquehanna, a short distance below the forks of the Unadilla. Previous to the Revolution, the territory now embraced in Otsego County formed a part of Canajoharie District, one of the five sub-divisions into which Tryon County was divided. Sir William Johnson had held almost unlimited sway over the Indians and exerted a vast influence over the white population of the County. He died just before active hostilities broke out, and his legal authority was transferred to his son, Sir John Johnson, and to his sons-in-law, Col. Guy Johnson and Col. Daniel Claus, all of whom espoused with great ardor the cause of the mother country. This operated unfavorably upon the patriots of Tryon County, as the influence of the Johnsons was such as to unite most of the Indians against the Colonists.

At a Court held in Johnstown in the spring of 1775, a declaration was drawn up and circulated by the loyalists of Tryon County, in which they avowed their opposition to the measures adopted by the Congress that had held its session the preceding year. Though this declaration was opposed, it was signed by nearly all of the Grand Jury and the Magistrates. The excitement increased, meetings were called in almost all the districts and precincts, and committees appointed to take into consideration the terrible state of affairs in the country. At Cherry Valley a meeting was called, the little church was filled with inhabitants of every age. "Parents took their children with them, that they might early breathe the air of freedom, and that their first lispings might be in favor of the liberties of their Country. Thomas Spencer, a resident of the place, and an Indian interpreter, addressed the meeting in a strain of rude though impassioned eloquence. The noblest efforts of a Henry or an Otis never wrought more sensibly upon the feelings of the respective congresses which they addressed, than did the harangue of this unlettered patriot upon that little assembly." The following is the article of association subscribed to by the patriots in various parts of the County:

Whereas the Grand Jury of this County and a number of Magistrates have signed a declaration declaring their disapprobation of the opposition made by the colonies to the oppressive and arbitrary acts of Parliament, the purport of which is evidently to entail slavery on America; and as the said declarati n may, in some measure, be looked upon as the sense of the County in general, if the same be passed over in silence, we the subscribers, freeholders and the inhabitants of the said County, inspired with a sincere love for our Country, and deeply interested in the common cause, do solemnly declare our fixed attachment and entire approbation of the proceedings of the grand Continental Congress held at Philadelphia last fall, and that we will strictly adhere to, and repose our confidence in the wisdom and integrity of the present Continental Congress; and that we will support the same to the u'most of our power, and that we will religiously and inviolably observe the regulations of that august body."

A meeting of the Committee of the County, chosen from the various districts, assembled June 2, 1775, among whose names we find that of Samuel Campbell of Cherry Valley. A correspondence was carried on between the Committee and the Johnsons as well as with Congress, and the people generally espoused the cause of the Colonies. In June 1777 Joseph Brant went to Unadilla with a party of seventy or eighty Indians and sent for the officers of the militia company and Rev. Mr. Johnstone. Brant informed them that the Indians were in want of provisions, and would take them by force if not by the consent of the citizens. The inhabitants let them have provisions, and after remaining two days they returned, taking with them cattle, sheep &c. The inhabitants friendly to the country immediately removed their families and effects to places of greater safety.

In July General Herkimer marched to Unadilla with 380 militia, and was met by Brant at the head of 130 warriors. To the question whether he would remain at peace if certain complaints which he made against the Colonies were rectified, Brant replied that the Indians were in concert with the King as their fathers and grandfathers had been; that the King's belts were lodged with them and they would not falsifiy their pledge. He declared that Gen. Herkimer and the rest had joined the Boston people against the King, but that he would subdue them. After making this declaration, Col. Cox said to Brant that if such was his determination, the matter was ended. Brant then turned to his men and, after a few words, they ran to their camp with a shout and, seizing their guns, raised the war-whoop, at the same time discharging several guns. Gen. Herkimer then assured Brant that the object of his interview was one of peace and urged him to prevent hostilities. A word from Brant hushed the storm that was raging in the breasts of his followers, but the interview was postponed until the next day. Previous to the meeting the next day, Gen. Herkimer selected four of his trusty soldiers and instructed them to be in readiness to shoot, at a given signal, Brant and three other chiefs, if the interview did not terminate peacefully. Fortunately the parties separated peacefully, Gen. Herkimer presenting to Brant several head of cattle which had just arrived, having been detained by obstructions in the outlet of Otsego Lake, down which they were transported. This is supposed to be the last interview that was held with any of the Six Nations, except the Oneidas, with a view to prevent their engaging in the war.

The Indians had for years been accustomed to receive their clothing and other necessaries from the English Government, and as they had received little from the Colonists, they joined the party offering the best prospect for pay. Oquago was a place of rendezvous for the Indians, from which place they had paths along the valleys of the main streams flowing into the eastern branch of the Susquehanna, thence to the Mohawk. One of these passes was through Cherry Valley. Every movement of the Indians about Oquago excited the liveliest apprehension on the part of the inhabitants, and when orders were given to remove Captain McKean's Company of Rangers, the following letter was written to the Committee by Rev. Mr. Dunlap, in behalf of the inhabitants. It was dated June 3, 1776:

"SIRS:—We the inhabitants of Cherry Valley, being assembled yesterday at a public town meeting, and among other things taking the present critical situation of affairs into consideration, look upon ourselves and the neighborhood around us, Springfield and Newtown-Martin, as a frontier, lying very open and unguarded, and very much exposed to the enemy, in case an Indian war should break out, or any party of the enemy should take it into their heads to come down upon us; and that it would be absolutely necessary to have a party of men stationed here among us, in order to keep a sharp look-out and to scout all around our frontiers; lest at any time we be taken by surprise. And therefore have appointed me to write to you to lay this matter warmly before the committee and earnestly to impress them with the absolute necessity of the thing, and to beg of them, that if Captain McKean and his company be removed from this place, that they would be pleased to send some others in his stead; that we may not lie together naked and exposed to the assaults of the enemy."

The Committee being unable to comply with this request, several of the inhabitants drew up and signed the following petition to the Provincial Congress of New York:

"The humble petition of the inhabitants of Cherry Valley, Newtown-Martin and Springfield, in the County of Tryon, humbly showeth :
E

"That we, the aforesaid inhabitants, from the most authentic intelligence we have received from our missionaries and Indian friends, learn that we are in imminent danger of being cut off by the savages, our enemies whom we understand are bribed by Sir John Johnson and Col. Butler to execute the same. Know also honorable gentlemen, that the spirit of our inhabitants has been such for the American cause, that out of the small and scattered bounds of Cherry Valley and Newton-Martin, no less than thirty-three have turned out for immediate service and good of their country, and thereby left us in a defenseless condition.

"We therefore, your humble petitioners, humbly pray you would forthwith take this, our deplorable condition, under your immediate consideration, and meditate some speedy relief for us, before it be too late; especially, as the inhabitants of the Old English and Unadilla, are daily flying into our settlement, so that we shall immediately, in all appearance, become an open, defenseless and unguarded frontier, and very much exposed to the insults of the enemy, especially scalping parties; and are at present without either ammunition or men any way sufficient to defend ourselves; and unless you, gentlemen, that can help us, will help us, by sending ammunition to the inhabitants, and a sufficient number of men, such as you may think proper, to guard our frontiers, we must expect to fall victims to the rage and fury of our merciless enemies. And therefore, must once more beg you may take this our deplorable circumstances under your consideration, and send us immediate relief, and your petitioners shall ever pray."

The petition was signed by Samuel Dunlap, Samuel Campbell, James Scott, Robert Wells, James Richey, James Moore and Samuel Clyde. Their request was now granted and a company of Rangers under Capt. Winn was ordered here. A company composed of those over sixty years of age or exempt from military duty, was formed in Cherry Valley to protect themselves and their families. In 1777 the house of Col. Samuel Campbell was fortified, a rude embankment of logs and earth inclosing the house and two large barns. Here the inhabitants assembled, bringing with them their most valuable effects. The doors and window shutters were made bullet-proof, and two small block houses were erected in the enclosure. No person was allowed to enter or leave the settlement without permission from the military authorities. Here they remained most of the summer, and in the fall returned to their habitations.

In the spring of 1778, Gen. LaFayette gave directions that a fort should be built at Cherry Valley, and the order was carried out, the inhabitants, during its erection, returning to the quarters occupied the previous summer.

In May, Brant came up from Oquago with a party of Indians for the purpose of making a raid on Cherry Valley. He posted them about a mile distant and, looking down upon the village and its little fortification through the intervening trees, and seeing troops parading on the green, decided to defer the attack. The soldiers which had so alarmed him, were boys with wooden guns.

The danger to which the inhabitants were exposed was so great, that they banded together and went about upon the different farms, some standing guard while others were at work.

In June of this year it was reported that Brant was fortifying at Unadilla and collecting large numbers of Indians and Tories around him. A reward was offered to any person who would gain satisfactory information relative to his plans. Captain McKean volunteered to go if five others would accompany him. The company was soon made up and the party started on their expedition. They arrived the first night at the house of a Quaker named Sleeper, in the town of Laurens. Sleeper informed them that Brant had been there the day before with fifty men, and would return there that night. He advised them to leave, as they would be killed or taken if Brant returned. McKean, seeing that the house was well built, and of logs, said: "Your house, friend Sleeper, shall be my fort to-night; I have with me five good marksmen, and I am not myself deficient in that qualification of a soldier." Sleeper remonstrated, as he wished to remain neutral, and would be involved in difficulty, and in all probability his property and life sacrificed. McKean finally withdrew to an unoccupied house a mile or two distant. He returned by way of the Susquehanna River, having taken two prisoners. He was pursued by the Indians and narrowly escaped being taken. On his return to Cherry Valley he found Capt. Ballard with a detachment of one hundred men belonging to Col. Alden's regiment of Continentals. The Colonel himself arrived in a few days. Stockades were placed around the church, and here Col. Alden took up his quarters.

On the 6th of November he received information that a large body of Indians under Col. Butler, were meditating an attack upon Cherry Valley. On receiving this information, the inhabitants requested permission to remove into the Fort or at least deposit their most valuable effects there; but Col. Alden, thinking the alarm needless, refused, saying he would keep out scouts who would apprise them in time to secure themselves in case of attack. The scout sent down the Susquehanna, kindled a fire on the night of the 9th, and all lay down to sleep. Just before daylight they were all made prisoners.

On the night of the 10th, the enemy encamped about a mile south-west of the Fort and, on the morning of the 11th, moved to the attack of the settlement. The officers of the garrison were stationed in private houses, and the forces of the enemy were so disposed that a party should surround every house in which an officer was lodged, nearly at the same time, while the main body would attack the Fort. Several inches of snow fell during the night, and in the morning it turned to rain, the air being thick and hazy. The assurances of Col. Alden had quieted the fears of the inhabitants and all were resting in fancied security as the savages came down upon them. Col. A. was one of the first victims. He and Lieut. Col. Stacia, with a small guard, lodged at the house of Mr. Robert Wells. At the first alarm Col. A. escaped from the house and fled towards the Fort, but was tomahawked and scalped. Stacia was taken prisoner and the guard were all killed or captured. The family of Mr. Wells were all massacred except one son who was in Schenectady at the time. Another party surrounded the house of Rev. Mr. Dunlap, whose wife was immediately killed. He was a feeble old man and released after a few days. A Mr. Mitchell was in the field and escaped, but his wife and four children were killed, and his house plundered and burnt. The party which surrounded the house of Col. Campbell, took Mrs. Campbell and four children prisoners. Col. C. was absent from home and returned in time to see his property destroyed, but did not learn the fate of his family. Many were killed, a few escaped and the remainder were taken prisoners. Thirty-two of the inhabitants, chiefly women and children, were killed, and sixteen Continental soldiers. The houses and barns, many of which were filled with grain, were burned, and thirty or forty prisoners were taken. The enemy with their prisoners and their booty encamped the first night about two miles south of the Fort. The night was cold and rainy and the prisoners suffered greatly. On the morning of the second day, the prisoners were collected together and it was decided to send back the women and children. Mrs. Campbell and her four children and Mrs. Moore and her children were retained because their husbands had been active partisans. They passed down the Susquehanna to Tioga Point, thence up the Chemung, across the Seneca Lake and down the east border of the lake to Kanadeseago, a village of the Senecas. The next day after the massacre, the mangled remains of those who had been murdered were buried, and those who had escaped to the woods came in. This was one of the most cold-blooded massacres of which history gives any account. The inhabitants abandoned the settlement, and the next summer the Fort was abandoned, the soldiers joining the troops of General James Clinton.

An expedition was fitted out under the command of General Sullivan, to march into the Indian country, destroy their settlements and lay waste their country. Gen. Sullivan's army assembled at Wyoming, on the Susquehanna, and on the 31st of July commenced their march for the Indian settlements. The stores and artillery were conveyed up the river in 156 boats.

At Tioga Point, Sullivan encamped to await the arrival of Gen. James Clinton, who had been ordered to join him by way of Canajoharie and Otsego Lake. For this purpose General Clinton opened a road from Canajoharie to Otsego Lake, and transported his boats thither in wagons. Passing down the lake to its outlet, he constructed a dam at this point, raising the water to such an extent that when the dam was removed, the increase of water in the outlet would bear his boats safely through. Gen. Clinton with his force joined the main army at Tioga, August 22, when the whole force proceeded up the river, laying waste the Indian towns, destroying their crops and taking from them their means of living. It is said that the Indians along the Susquehanna, witnessing the unusual rise of the water and seeing the troops descend in boats, were greatly alarmed and attributed the unusual rise of the water to some supernatural agency. While Gen. Clinton's forces were encamped on the present site of Cooperstown, two deserters were shot. It is said that 208 boats were required to transport the troops down the river.

The Otsego County Agricultural Society.—The first meeting in this County to organize an Agricultural Society, was held Jan. 1st, 1817. The first officers were: Jacob Morris, President; John H. Prentiss, Recording Secretary; James Cooper, Corresponding Secretary. The first Fair was held on the 14th of October, 1817, in the Presbyterian church. An address was delivered by Gen. Jacob Morris, and the premiums were declared by Elkanah Watson. A letter from Governor Clinton was also read. In 1841 the Society was organized under the act of the Legislature appropriating $8,000 among the different counties of the State for the encouragement of agriculture. The Fairs were held at Cooperstown annually until 1852, when it was held at Morris. In 1855 the Society was again re-organized, the first officers being Francis M. Rotch, of Morris, President; Alfred Clark, of Springfield, Vice-President; Jerome B. Wood, of Cooperstown, Secretary; G. Pomeroy Reese, of Cooperstown, Treasurer. A lot of land containing about eight acres was leased and fitted up for Fairs. The first Fair was held under this organization upon the new grounds in 1856. The success of this enterprise was so great that the Society proceeded to erect new buildings and make other additions as circumstances seemed to require. In 1861 their grounds were enlarged by leasing an adjoining lot, thereby nearly doubling its size. In 1871 a new lot containing twenty-seven acres, and situated a short distance from the village, was purchased, fenced, and will be in good order before the next annual Fair.

This County took an inportant part in the suppression of the great Rebellion. Cherry Valley, the oldest town in the County, was the first to respond to the call for men, after the fall of Sumter. A company was soon raised and their services tendered, but owing to what was known at Albany as skeleton regiments, their services were not accepted. After remaining in barracks for some time the Company was disbanded. Egbert Olcott and C. J. Campbell, the Lieutenants of the Company, afterwards enlisted as privates in the Forty-fourth Regiment, and by successive promotions became Colonels, the former of the One Hundred and Twenty-First, and the latter of the Twenty-Third United States colored troops, and Brevet Brig. General. During the summer of 1861, large numbers of young men in the County enlisted in various organizations. A recruiting station was established at Cherry Valley and three companies were raised for the Seventy-Sixth N. Y. V., and one Company of Berdan's Sharpshooters, most of the men being from that vicinity. Up to the time of the establishment of the senatorial or military districts, about one thousand men had been raised in the County. The 121st and 152d Regiments were largely raised in this County, nearly 1,500 men being furnished. About 2,500 men were raised before the first draft, most of whom were natives of the County. All the orders for drafts were cheerfully responded to and many of the soldiers sealed their devotion to their country with their blood

GAZETTEER OF TOWNS.

BURLINGTON was formed from Otsego, April 10, 1792. Pittsfield was taken off in 1797, and Edmeston in 1808. It is an interior town, lying north-west of the center of the County. The surface is a hilly upland, divided by three general ridges extending north and south. These ridges are about 400 feet above the valleys and are arable to their summits. The principal streams are Butternut Creek, flowing south through the center, and Wharton Creek, flowing south-west through the west part. The soil upon the hills is a slaty loam, in many places underlaid by hardpan; in the valleys it is a gravelly loam.

Burlington, (p. v.) known as Burlington Green, near the center of the town, contains two churches, a hotel, a store, a grist mill, two blacksmith shops, a shoe shop, a cheese factory and about 100 inhabitants.

Burlington Flats, (p. v.) north-west of the center, on Wharton Creek, contains two churches, a hotel, three stores, a grist mill, a saw mill, a tannery, a wagon shop, two shoe shops, two blacksmith shops, three milliner shops, a cheese factory, 33 dwellings and 129 inhabitants.

West Burlington, (p. v.) on Wharton Creek, in the west part of the town, contains two churches, a hotel, two stores, a blacksmith shop, a cheese factory, 25 dwellings and about 100 inhabitants.

The first settlement was commenced near West Burlington, in 1790, by Robert Garrat and Eber and Benjamin Harrington. Paul Gardner settled in 1792, and Benjamin Card, Miles Potter, Caleb Gardner, Alexander Parker, Ira Johnson, John Johnson, Lemuel Hubbell and Samuel Hubbard, settled about the same time in the vicinity of Burlington Flats. The first school was taught by Joseph Wright at Burlington Green. Paris Briggs and Willard Church kept the first inns, and Wal-

bridge & Co. the first store, at Burlington Flats. Augustus
and Adolphus Walbridge erected the first mill, at the same
place.

The First Baptist Church of Burlington, the first religious
society in the town, was organized in 1793 by James Southworth, the first pastor. The number of members at the organization was 30. The first house of worship was erected in 1804;
the present house in 1839, with a seating capacity of 200. The
present pastor is Rev. H. Steelman; the number of members is
37; the value of Church property is $3,000.

The Second Baptist Church, located at West Burlington, was
organized May 16, 1794, by a Council composed of members
from Springfield, Unadilla and the First Church of Burlington.
The number of members was 59 and the first pastor was Rev.
Ashbel Hosmer. The first house of worship was erected in
1803; the present house in 1841, with a seating capacity of 300.
The present pastor is Rev. E. G. Flint; the number of members is 16 and the value of Church property is $4,000. When
the Church was first organized, five brethren were chosen as
leaders, and the services of Elder Wm. Firman were secured to
administer the ordinances once in four weeks. Elder Hosmer
arrived about this time from Tolland, Connecticut, and subsequently became the pastor of the Church and continued until 1797, when he removed to Burlington Flats. The first
leading brethren were Martin Luther, Joseph Vaughn, Paul
Gardner and James Roberts. The Council which organized
the Church consisted of Elder Wm. Firman and Wm. Hill, of
Springfield; Rev. James Southworth and Wm. Goff, of the
First Church, Burlington; Solomon Hatch and Increase
Thurston, of Unadilla; and Josiah Mattison, Jonathan Pettit,
Stephen Taylor, David Sweet, Reuben Ellis and Abraham Bow-
dish, transient brethren.

Christ Church, (Episcopal,) at West Burlington, was organized in 1841 under the direction of Rev. J. V. Hughes, who
served the parish at intervals for several years. His successors
were E. N. Goddard and Joel Davis. For a time the Corporation owned a fourth interest in the Union Church at Burlington Flats, but sold it for $250, which amounted to about $1,000
in 1866. Bishop Onderdonk visited the parish once and con-
firmed several, and Bishop Potter visited it in 1858 for the same
purpose. In March 1865 West Burlington was made a station
of a circuit mission, and the next year the missionary became
resident here with only Garrattsville as additional care. Sept.
22, 1868, the corner stone of the Moss Memorial Church was
laid by the Rt. Rev. Daniel S. Tuttle, Bishop of Montana, Idaho

and Utah, assisted by Rev. J. V. Hughes, missionary in charge ; Rev. D. Hillhouse Buell, Cooperstown, and Rev. N. S. Rulison, Morris. In Sept. 1871, the Church was admitted into union with the Diocesan Convention. Services are held every alternate Sunday, in the morning and afternoon. The present number of communicants is 33 ; the pastor is Rev. E. H. Saunders, and the value of the Church property is about $4,200. Their house of worship will seat 250.

The Free Communion Baptist Church, at Burlington Flats, was organized March 9, 1825, by Revs. Hunt, Esterbrooks, Benjamin Roland, Phipps Lake, and Messrs. Hudson, Millican and Fitch, and consisted of 16 members. Rev. Wm. Hunt was the first pastor. The Church edifice was erected in 1829 at a cost of $1,100 and will seat 200. The present number of members is 30. The present pastor is Rev. S. S. Cady, and the present value of Church property is $2,000.

The Friends Meeting House, at Burlington, was organized in 1804 by Richard Emerson, Peleg Gifford and others. The first house of worship was erected in 1804; the present one, which will seat 200, in 1827. The original cost of the house of worship was $400 ; the present value of Church property is about $300. The present number of members is 13 or 14.

The population of the town in 1870 was 1,476, and its area 26,755 acres, with an assessed value of $358,675.

The number of school districts is 13, employing 13 teachers. The number of children of school age is 562 ; the number attending school, 452 ; the average attendance, 218 ; the value of school houses and sites, $5,770.

BUTTERNUTS was formed from Unadilla, February 5, 1796. Morris was taken off in 1849, and a part of Unadilla was annexed in 1857. It lies upon the west border of the County, south-west of the center. The surface is a hilly upland, divided by several ridges extending north and south. Unadilla River, forming its west boundary, is bordered by a narrow flat, from which the highlands arise in a series of steep bluffs to a hight of 500 to 600 feet. Butternut Creek flows south-west through a deep valley near the center of the town. A large number of smaller streams, tributaries to these, flow in deep valleys among the hills, dividing the ridges and giving to the region a peculiar broken appearance. The hills are arable to their summits and the soil is a good quality of red shale and sandy and gravelly loam.

Butternuts, (p. v.) known also as Gilbertsville, is situated near the center of the town and contains four churches, viz., Methodist, Baptist, Presbyterian and Episcopal; an academy, two sash and blind shops, three carriage shops, a marble shop, a flouring mill, two hotels, a number of stores and mechanic shops, and about 500 inhabitants. The village contains some fine residences and is surrounded by a fine farming region.

The Gilbertsville Academy is a substantial stone structure, occupying a prominent site in the village. The course of study pursued, embraces the branches usually taught in first-class academies.

Brookside Cemetery occupies a fine site and is being improved in a manner creditable to the taste of the managers.

The settlements were commenced about 1790, at Gilbertsville, by Gordon and Wyatt Chamberlin, and Abijah Gilbert. John Marsh, Joseph Cox and Daniel Eastwood, were among the first settlers in the west part of the town, and William Masson and Dr. John Burgess, in the south part. The first child born was William Shaw, and he is supposed to be the first one who died. The first marriage was that of Joseph Cox and Betsey Gilbert. The first school was taught by Levi Hallibert, at the house of Joseph Cox. Abijah Gilbert kept the first inn, and William Masson the first store, near Gilbertsville. The first mill was erected by Joseph Shaw and Abijah Gilbert.

The first town meeting was held in 1796, at which Hezekiah Dayton was chosen Town Clerk, and Lewis Franchot, Supervisor. In the Records of the town we find the following letter which explains itself:

"Butternuts, 15th June 1796.

" Mr. Hezekiah Dayton, Clerk of the town of Butternuts.

"Sir,

"Here inclosed I send you the certificate for the proportion of School money of the town of Butternuts. Also a bill of assessments for the ensuing year. Mr. Elisha Phinney of Cooperstown being Clerk of the board of supervisors, you may as soon as possible apply to him for to have the Laws of the State of New York for our Town, and make your application so as to have a complete set, last session included, it shall be paid for by the County. The Board of Supervisors have made it a part of their Clerk's duty to supply every year the towns with such Laws as may be in future enacted. Here followeth the account of poor money for the town of Butternuts, arising from the accounts given by the overseers of the poor of the old town of Unadilla, divided.

" 1 note given by Elisha Crow,...........................	£ 4	0 0
" Due by Azor Nash to the poor of this new Town,...	£ 1	4 0
" Cash received by myself,.....................................	£ 4	15 6
" Butternuts proportion of the old town poor money,...	£ 9	19 6
" For licenses granted by the Excise officers this present year in the town of Butternuts to John Marsh,..................	£ 2	0 0
" To Nathan Sull,...................	2	0 0
" To Sturges Bradley,..........	2	0 0
" To Russell Fairman,.................................	2	0 0
" Grand total of Butternuts poor money,...................	£17	19 6

" Paid by me into the hands of Alanson Moore, overseer of the
poor of this town,...£ 8 19 9
" To Deacon Shaw, overseer ditto,...............................£ 8 19 9

" Balance,...£17 19 6

" Which account you will please to put on record according to Law.

" It has been agreed by the Board of Supervisors that the Clark of the town of Butternuts shall be entitled to the sum of five dollars as a salary annexed to his office for this year. If you have any accounts against the town I wish you to send it to me. I hope you have provided yourself with a book to enter your records. I am Sir, your most

        obedient Servant, LEWIS FRANCHOT, Supervisor."

" The within is a true copy of the letter from the Supervisor & recorded by me.

        " HEZEKIAH DAYTON, Town Clerk."

Among those licensed to sell " strong liquor" in 1797, was Edward Thorp. He died a few years since after voting *seventy-one* consecutive years.

In 1800 the town voted to raise $50 for the support of the poor. In 1805 Sturgis Bradley, Aaron Aspenwall and John Marsh, were each licensed " to keep a public Inn or Tavern." In 1815 Azariah Metcalf, Oliver Judd, S. Elsworth, Isaac Hayes and Silas Crippen, each received 213 votes for member of Assembly, and Francis Henry, John C. Morris, Charles Mason, Billings Brown and William Campbell, each received 150 votes for the same office. Paschal Franchot, Alanson Moore and Richard D. Shepard, were the Inspectors of Election.

The following record indicates the existence of an institution from which our whole country is now free :

"Manumission of Joseph Jackson, Grace his wife and Jane & Flora.

" We the Overseers of the poor for the town of Butternuts in the county of Otsego and State of New York, do hereby certify that Joseph Jackson, Grace his wife and Jane and Flora their infant children, all people of color, and late the slaves of Jacob Morris of this town, and which the said Jacob Morris is now about to manumit, appear to us to be under the age of forty-five years. The said Joseph Jackson & Grace appear to us of sufficient ability to provide for themselves and are able and willing to maintain and provide for their said female children Jane & Flora.

" Given under our hand at Butternuts, this thirteenth day of April 1822.

        " WM JACKSON /
        " JARED LILLIE."

The following is another similar record :

"Stephen, slave of Jacob Morris of the town aforesaid appears to be under fifty years of age and of sufficient ability to provide for himself.

" Dated this tenth day of Nov. 1802.

        "PASCHAL FRANCHOT, one of
        the overseers of the Poor.
        "WM. MASSON, Poor Master."

The election returns in 1800 for member of Congress, show that Thomas Morris received 112 votes, and Wm. Stewart three votes. For Governor, Stephen Van Rensselaer received 69, and George Clinton 65 votes.

The Methodist Church of Butternuts was organized in 1831 by Wm. S. Bowdish, the first pastor, with ten members. The first house of worship was erected in 1832; the present house in 1862. It will seat 450. The present membership is 154; the pastor is Rev. A. M. Colgrove, and the value of Church property is $7,000.

The First Presbyterian Church of Butternuts was organized in 1795, with about twenty members. The first pastor was Rev. Isaac Garvin; the first house of worship was erected in 1795: the present house in 1832. The present membership is 225; the present value of Church property is $7,000. The Church edifice will seat about 450. Rev. Mr. Moore is the pastor.

The Baptist Church of Butternuts has a membership of 209. Their house of worship will seat 400. The value of Church property is $7,000. Rev. Samuel C. Moore is the pastor.

Christ Church, (Episcopal,) of Butternuts, was organized in 1833 by Rev. J. V. Hughes with 28 members. Their house of worship was erected in 1834, it will seat 300 and, with other Church property, is valued at $7,000. The present membership is 80, and the pastor is Rev. J. V. Hughes.

The population of the town in 1870 was 2,176, and its area 32,961 acres, with an assessed value of $530,891.

The number of school districts is 19, employing 16 teachers. The number of children of school age is 628; the number attending school, 445; the average attendance, 227; the value of school houses and sites, $6,810.

CHERRY VALLEY was formed from Canajoharie, (Montgomery Co.,) February 16, 1791. Middlefield, Springfield and Worcester, were taken off in 1797, and Roseboom in 1854. It is the north-east corner town in the County. The surface is a hilly and mountainous upland, some portion of which is too rough and rocky for cultivation. Mount Independence is a rocky eminence, situated south-east of the center, and is about 1,000 feet above the valleys and 2,000 above tide. It is the highest summit in the County. A range of highlands extends along the north-west boundary. The central and south parts of the town are drained by the head branches of the Susquehanna, and the north part by tributaries of the Mohawk. The soil upon the uplands is a slaty and gravelly loam, and in the valleys a fine quality of calcareous loam.

The Te-ka-ha-ra-wa Falls are upon a small creek of the same name in the north part of the town. The water flows over a limestone precipice 160 feet high, and down through a narrow ravine, thickly wooded on each side. Near the lower end of this ravine are several sulphur springs, unsurpassed in their medicinal qualities by any in the State. Pebbles, leaves and other substances, exposed to the action of the water, very soon become coated with sulphur. In the north-east corner are several salt springs from which salt was manufactured to a very limited extent at an early day. Bath-houses and other improvements have been made at the Sulphur Springs; and the picturesque scenery presents unusual attractions to summer tourists.

Cherry Valley, (p. v.) situated at the head of Cherry Valley Creek, near the center of the town, contains three churches, viz., Presbyterian, Methodist and Episcopal; a bank, a newspaper printing office, three hotels, seven stores, a melodeon factory, a sash and blind factory, a saw mill, a grist mill, a cheese factory and about 1,200 inhabitants.

The Cherry Valley Academy, which sustained so high a reputation for more than half a century, has been converted into a hotel. This village is the present terminus of the Sharon and Cherry Valley Railroad, which connects with the Albany and Susquehanna Railroad at Cobleskill. It is proposed to extend this road to Richfield Springs, thus opening direct communication with the New York Central at Utica. This village is becoming a resort for summer visitors; its streets are finely shaded, and the vicinity affords many fine drives amid scenery unsurpassed in beauty. The celebrated Sulpur Springs are only three miles distant. A monument erected to the memory of the soldiers who fell in their country's service, occupies a prominent site in the village. It is about twenty feet high, surmounted by a spread eagle. It contains the names of those to whose memory it was erected, and cost about $2,000.

Salt Springville, named from the salt springs in this vicinity, is a hamlet in the north-west part of the County, and contains a Methodist church, a hotel, a store, a grist mill, a saw mill, a blacksmith shop, a wagon shop, a cooper shop, a cheese factory and a school house.

The Cherry Valley Foundry of E. & J. Judd was first started as a brass foundry, in 1805, by Oliver Judd. The present proprietors have been running the foundry more than fifty years, turning out about fifty tons of light castings annually, and employing about half a dozen hands.

Center Valley, (p. v.) in the south-east part of the town, partly in Roseboom, contains two churches, viz., •Methodist and Lutheran ; a store, a blacksmith shop, a saw mill, a shoe shop, a cheese factory and about 100 inhabitants.

The Caloric Mill of James Rick, in the village of Cherry Valley, was started in 1871, for grinding feed. It is run by a caloric engine of three-horse power, and has a capacity for grinding 150 bushels per day.

The first settlement of this town was made by John Lindsay in 1740, at a place which he called *Lindsay's Bush.* The same farm has for many years been occupied by Mr. Joseph Phelon. In 1744 Mr. John Wells purchased this farm. In 1741 a colony of about thirty persons from Londonderry, New Hampshire, settled in the town. Among these were David Ramsay, Wm. Galt, James Campbell and William Dixon. They had previously emigrated from the north of Ireland and came to Cherry Valley under the advice of Rev. Samuel Dunlap, whom Mr. Lindsay had persuaded to take up his abode here. The place received its name from the abundance of wild cherry trees growing in the valley, and for many years it embraced a large extent of country, south and west.

Rev. Mr. Dunlap was an Irishman by birth, educated in Edinburgh, and had left Ireland under an engagemet of marriage with a young lady of that country. The engagement was conditional; if he did not return in seven years, she was at liberty to annul the contract. The time had nearly expired and she had heard nothing from him for some time. Another offered his hand, was accepted and the day appointed for the marriage. Mr. Dunlap arrived the day previous, was married and returned immediately to Cherry Valley with his bride, and entered upon the duties of pastor of the Church. In addition to this he opened a school for the instruction of boys who came from the settlements on the Mohawk, from Schenectady and Albany. This was the first grammar school in the State, west of Albany.

Mr. Dixon and Mr. Galt purchased farms in the south part of the Patent; Mr. Ramsay in the west part, and Mr. James Campbell purchased the farm now owned and occupied by his great-grandson, Hon. W. W. Campbell. Mr. Dunlap purchased the farm now occupied by Mr. Cox.

The settlement increased slowly, so that in 1752 there were only eight families in the settlement. In 1765 it had increased to forty families, and ten years after, at the commencement of the Revolution, the number did not probably exceed sixty families.

Most of the early settlers were members of the Christian Church, and they sought to inculcate the principles of an intelligent Christianity, believing that virtue and knowledge are the two great pillars of republican institutions. They were very strict in the observance of the Sabbath. They united their efforts with those of other patriots, when the Revolution broke out, and their Committee met with the Committee of Tryon County to devise means for the defense of their homes and their principles. The following letter gives an idea of the strictness with which the Sabbath was observed even in times of war:

"Cherry Valley, June 9th, 1775.

"Sirs,

"We received yours of yesterday, relative to the meeting of the Committee on Sunday, which surprised us not a little, inasmuch as it seems not to be on any alarming exigency; which, if it was, we should readily attend. But as that does not appear to us to be the case, we think it is very improper ; for unless the necessity of the Committee sitting super-exceed the duties to be performed in attending the public worship of God, we think it ought to be put off till another day ; and therefore we conclude not to give our attendance at this time, unless you adjourn the sitting of the Committee till Monday morning; and in that case, we will give our attendance as early as you please. But otherwise, we do not allow ourselves to be cut short of attending on the public worship, except the case be so necessitous as to exceed sacrifice. We conclude with wishing success to the common cause, and subscribe ourselves the free-born sons of liberty.

"JOHN MOORE.
"SAMUEL CLYDE.
"SAMUEL CAMPBELL.

"If you proceed to sit on the Sabbath, please to read this letter to the Committee, which we think will sufficiently assign our reasons for not attending."

This letter was sent to the County Committee.

Owing to the exposed position of Cherry Valley, in consequence of its lying in one of the routes of the Indians from the Susquehanna to the Mohawk, and the fact that nearly all of its inhabitants were ardent patriots, a company of Rangers were stationed there, under the command of Capt. Robert McKean, in 1776. Capt. McKean's company was soon after ordered away and another company, under Capt. Winn, was ordered there. Those exempt from military duty also formed a company for mutual protection. The next year the house of Col. Samuel Campbell was fortified by throwing up a rude embankment of logs and earth. In the spring of 1778 a fort was erected on the site of the Cemetery in the village. About two miles north of the village, near the road leading to the Mohawk, is the rock, behind which Brant was concealed when he shot Lieutenant Wormwood. It is still known as "Brant's Rock."

The destruction of the settlement and the massacre of the inhabitants on the 11th of November 1778, has already been noticed in another place. The acts of cruelty perpetrated by the Tories surpassed those of the Indians. A Tory boasted that he killed Mr. Robert Wells while at prayer. Mr. Wells was a son of Mr. John Wells, whose name has already been mentioned among the first settlers. Miss Jane Wells, who was distinguished for her amiable disposition and her acts of Christian benevolence, fled from the house to a pile of wood where she attempted to conceal herself. An Indian followed her and, deliberately wiping his bloody knife on his leggings, placed it in the sheath, and in spite of her entreaties and those of a Tory who had been a servant in the house of Mr. Wells, murdered her with his tomahawk. The party which surrounded the house of Col. Campbell, took Mrs. C. and four children prisoners. The wife of Col. Clyde, with her children, fled to the woods and, during that day and the following night, she lay with her children, one of whom was an infant, gathered around her and concealed under a large log. She could hear the yells of the savages as they prosecuted their bloody work, some of whom passed very near, and one so near that his gun trailed upon the log which concealed her. The next day a party from the Fort brought her in. Her oldest daughter, about ten years of age, became separated from her mother and concealed herself alone. Notwithstanding the exposure, all survived. About thirty or forty prisoners were taken. They encamped the first night about two miles south of the Fort. On the morning of the second day the women and children were sent back. Mrs. Campbell and her four children, and Mrs. Moore and her children were retained, as their husbands were active partisans. Mrs. Cannon, the mother of Mrs. Campbell, was killed the first day, being unable to travel on account of her age. Mrs. Campbell was driven along by the same Indian who had killed her mother, threatening her with the same fate if she should be unable to proceed on the journey. She carried in her arms a child about eighteen months old. They arrived at the Indian castle near Geneva about the last of November. Here all their children were taken from them and given to different Indian families. Mrs. Campbell was given to a family, to fill the place made vacant by death of one of its members. The family was composed of females, with the exception of one aged warrior. Mrs. C. made herself useful by instructing them in the arts of civilized life and making clothing for neighboring families, for which they returned corn and venison. She was under no restraint and her situation was as comfortable as could be in such a place. The next spring an arrangement was entered into, in accordance with which Mrs. C. was to be exchanged for Mrs. Butler, wife of Col. John Butler, who had remained in Tryon County after hostilities broke out. She was taken to Fort Niagara, where she arrived in June 1779, and a year after, with her children, was sent to Montreal, where she met Mrs. Butler and children, for whom she and her children had been exchanged. At Montreal they were detained several months and then sent to Crown Point and thence to Albany, where Mrs. Campbell was joined by her husband. They did not return to Cherry Valley until the spring of 1784.

At the close of the war, many of the surviving inhabitants of Cherry Valley returned to their former homes, houses were erected and the land that had been suffered to go to waste was again brought under cultivation.

On the 5th of April, 1785, a public meeting of the "ancient inhabitants of Cherry Valley" was held in the "meeting house yard," for the purpose of reorganizing a Presbyterian Church. Col. Samuel Clyde, John Campbell, Jr., and James Wilson, were chosen Trustees. James Cannon was appointed Clerk of the Board. The names of the electors were as sollows: Robert Shankland, William Thompson, Samuel Ferguson, James Moore, Jr., John Campbell, Jr. Hugh Mitchell, William Gault, James Cannon, Samuel Campbell, Jr., Samuel Clyde, Samuel Campbell, William Dickson, James Dickson, Daniel McCollum, John McKillip, Israel Wilson, Luther Rich, James Wilson, Thomas Whitaker, Benjamin Dickson and John Dunlap. Measures were soon after taken to build a church edifice, but it was not completed till some years after. Hon. W. W. Campbell, in his "Centennial Address," in 1840, speaks as follows of the meeting referred to:

"The meeting of the inhabitants of Cherry Valley on the 5th of April, 1785, is deserving of particular attention. The remnant of the *ancient* inhabitants, as they styled themselves, had returned to their former homes. They had returned, they say, from *exile*. The long and bloody war through which they had passed, had thinned their ranks and whitened the heads, and furrowed the cheeks of the survivors. They had once more a home, but it was again a forest home. The wild beast had made his lair amid the ruins of their former dwellings. The briar, the thistle and the sapling grew rank upon their garden spots. In the autumn of 1784 a few log huts had been built, but in the spring of 1785, when this meeting was called, there was no building in the settlement where the inhabitants could assemble together. They met, therefore, like their fathers, under the open heavens. The place where they gathered was hallowed ground. It had been set apart for the burial of their dead.

F

The graves of their kindred and friends were round about them. It was the place which had been consecrated by their patriotism, for there stood their little fort. On that same spot the inhabitants assembled together and organized anew, on the 5th of April 1785, that Presbyterian society which has continued to this day." The first settled pastor was Rev. Dr. Eliphalet Nott, for more than sixty years President of Union College.

An academy was established here in 1796, the first one west of Schenectady. Rev. Solomon Spaulding, the reputed author of the "Book of Mormon," was the first Principal. He was succeeded by Rev. Dr. Nott. The institution maintained a high reputation for more than sixty years, but has recently been converted into a hotel and boarding house.

Col. Samuel Campbell, the last survivor of the first settlers, died in 1824, at the age of 86. His wife died in 1836, at the age of 93. During the summer of 1784, Gen. Washington, Gov. George Clinton and several officers of the New York line, visited Cherry Valley, and were the guests of Col. and Mrs. Campbell, in the log house which they had just erected.

On the 4th of July, 1840, the centennial anniversary of the settlement of Cherry Valley was celebrated. A very large audience assembled to engage in the festivities of the occasion and listen to addresses by Hon. W. W. Campbell, Dr. Nott, Gov. Wm. H. Seward and others.

Among the distinguished men of this State, who were residents of Cherry Valley were John Mills, Esq., Hon. W. W. Campbell, author of "Annals of Tryon Co." and Judge of the Supreme Court; Rev. Eliphalet Nott, late President of Union College; Jabez D. Hammond, Esq., author of " Political History of New York;" Hon. Levi Beardsley, author of "Reminiscences of Otsego;" Alvin Stewart, Esq., James C. Morse, Esq. and others. Hon. W. W. Campbell, after several years residence in New York City, has returned to his native town, and the farm upon which his great-grandfather settled, and here he is enjoying the *otium cum dignitate* of an honorable and useful life.

On the 15th of December, 1860, the sixtieth anniversary of the wedding of James S. Campbell was celebrated at the old homestead. His eight children, after a separation of twenty-eight years, assembled at the place of their birth, and with the family circle unbroken, celebrated the diamond wedding of their parents. Among the speakers on this occasion were Hon. L. C. Turner, of Cooperstown, whose remarks were of some historical interest. He said:

"It is very seldom that a husband and wife celebrate the sixtieth anniversary of their wedding—scarcely ever has such an anniversary been observed at the same old homestead, where the party have spent sixty continuous years of wedded life; and never before, I apprehend, were their eight children present and participating—being all the children born unto the venerable wedded pair—present and participating in celebrating their parents' sixtieth wedding anniversary, and at the old homestead where they were all born and bred! Yes, at this old homestead, where Washington was a guest sixty-seven years ago—the same old homestead that is historically associated with the stirring events of the revolutionary days, and with the conflagrations, imprisonments, barbarities and massacres of Brant and his tory and savage allies, eighty-two years ago—the same old homestead of 200 acres, that is prominently distinguishable as never having been sold or demised—passing from father to son by gift, during the lifetime of the father, and the other children voluntarily and gratuitously releasing their prospective interest therein to the son—the same old homestead that has never been incumbered by mortgage, judgement or other lien, during the one hundred and twenty years it has been in the possession of the family! These are some of the reasons for saying, that this anniversary celebration is, personally and locally, distinguishable from any and all others of like kind, of which I have any knowledge."

When the tocsin of war was sounded in April 1861, the citizens of Cherry Valley rallied with a zeal worthy of their Revolutionary ancestors, and during the war, one hundred and twenty men were sent out of an agricultural population of 2,552. Eighty of these were from the village corporation. When peace was restored, the surviving citizens erected, in a conspicuous place in the village, a monument to the memory of the fallen. It is about twenty feet high, surmounted by a spread eagle, and cost about $2,000. The following are the names and inscriptions upon the monument, though not in the same order:

"Erected by the citizens of Cherry Valley in memory of their Patriot Dead, 1868."

"Second Bull Run, Petersburgh, Gettysburgh, Wilderness, Fredericksburg, Winchester, Antietam, Cold Harbor."

"These are the names of the men of Cherry Valley who died that their Country might live."

"6th N. Y. Cavalry, Sergt. Philo D. Chaddenden, Sergt. James H. Moore, Jacob Hardendorf, Samuel Bates, John Beaumont. 121st N. Y. Infantry, Sergt. John Daniels, Sergt. Edward Wales, James Sherman, Geo. N. L. Drake, Geo. G. Hardman, Wm. Harris, Chas. E. Hodge, Jabez D. Willson, Joseph B. Howe, John W. Bullard. U. S. N., Geo. P. Engell, Chas. P. Nichols. 1st U. S. Sharpshooters, Capt. Chas. D. McLean, Sergt. Wm. O. McLean, Dwight Reed, Chas. H. Gould, Henry T. Ferguson. 104th N. Y. Infantry, John Banker. 2d N. Y. H. Artillery, John H. Bush. 1st N. Y. Cavalry, John H. Botsford. 6th N. Y. H. Artillery, Salmon Drake. 152d N. Y. Infantry, George Nelson, Cornelius Hardendorf, Geo. Van De Bogart. 44th N. Y. Infantry, Corp. James H. Krake, John Wallace.

76th Infantry, Capt. Robert Story, 1st Lieut. Barnard Phenis, Thos. A. Leaning, Wm. Sterns, Bradford J. D. Fox. 8th N. Y. Cavalry, 1st Lieut. Wm. C. Crafts. Col. & Brig. Gen. Cleaveland J. Campbell."

General Campbell enlisted as a private in the 44th Regiment N. Y. V., and by successive promotions became Colonel of the 23d Regiment of United States colored troops and subsequently Brigadier-General.

The population of the town in 1870 was 2,338, and its area, 24,723 acres, with an assessed value of $419,990.

The number of school districts is 16; employing 13 teachers. The number of children of school age is 776; the number attending school, 572; the average attendance, 270; the value of school houses and sites, $6,055.

DECATUR, named in honor of Commodore Stephen Decatur, was formed from Worcester, March 25, 1808. It lies upon the east line of the County, south of the center. The surface is hilly and broken by the narrow valleys of several small streams. The hills generally have gradual slopes and rounded summits, and are elevated from 250 to 300 feet above the valleys. The town is drained south by Oak and Parker Creeks, flowing into the Schenevus. The soil is a sandy and gravelly loam.

Decatur, (p. v.) in the south-west part of the town, contains a church, a hotel, a store, a grist mill, a saw mill, two black-smith shops, a wagon shop and about 100 inhabitants.

The first settlements of this town were commenced about 1790, by Jacob Kinney, who was originally from New Milford, Connecticut. He located near the village of Decatur. Jacob Brown, John and Calvin Seward, and Oliver McIntyre, settled soon after. A man named Sloan, from Columbia County, settled near the village in 1797. Mr. Sloan opened the first tavern and the first store, north of the village. John Champion erected the first grist mill, and James Stewart, the first carding and fulling mill, about 1810. The first school was taught by Samuel Thurber in 1798. The first death is supposed to have been that of Mr. King, about 1797.

The First M. E. Church of Decatur was the first religious society organized in the town. It was organized about 1800 by Rev. John Cattin, the first pastor. A house of worship was erected in 1810 and repaired and improved in 1871. It will seat 350 and cost originally, about $1,500. The present membership is 130; the value of the Church property is $3,500; the pastor is Rev. S. H. Hill.

The population of the town in 1870 was 802, and its area, 13,-226 acres, with an assessed value of $156,500.

The number of school districts is 7, giving employment to 6 teachers. The number of children of school age is 238; the number attending school, 180,; the average attendance, 93; the value of school houses and sites $2,315.

EDMESTON was formed from Burlington, April 1, 1808. It lies on the west border of the County, north of the center. The surface is an elevated upland, broken by numerous irregular valleys. The highest elevations are from 400 to 500 feet above Unadilla River, which forms the west boundary. Wharton Creek flows across the south-east corner. Mill Creek and several other small streams take their rise in the town. Smith's Pond is a small sheet of water in the north-east corner. The soil is a sandy and clayey loam.

Edmeston, (p. v.) situated a little south of the center of the town, on Wharton Creek, contains three churches, viz., Methodist, Baptist and Universalist; two hotels, four stores, a tannery, two carpenter shops, a foundry, two blacksmith shops, a carriage shop, two tailoring establishments, a lodge of Odd Fellows, a lodge of Good Templars, a post of Grand Army of the Republic, a public hall and about 70 dwellings.

West Edmeston, (p. v.) in the north-west part, on the Unadilla River, contains a Seventh Day Baptist church, a hotel, two stores, a blacksmith shop, a carriage shop and about 30 dwellings.

South Edmeston, (p. v.) in the south-west part, contains a church, two stores, a hotel, a grist mill, a saw mill, a blacksmith shop, a carriage shop, a boot and shoe shop, a milliner shop and about 30 dwellings.

The first settlement of this town was made by Col. Edmeston, an officer of the English army, during the war with the French, in 1770. A tract of 10,000 acres lying in this town, was granted to him for his services, and Percifer Carr, a soldier who had served under him, was one of the first settlers. On the death of Col. Edmeston, the lands fell to heirs and minor children residing in England, from whom no safe title could be obtained for many years. This greatly retarded the settlement of the town. During the Revolutionary War the hired man of Mr. Carr was killed while at his work; his buildings were burned, his property destroyed and himself and family taken prisoners by the British and Indians, and detained until the close of the war. Abel DeForest and Gideon DeForest were among the early settlers on the Unadilla. Aden Deming and James Kenada settled at Edmeston, and Stephen Taylor, on Taylor Hill, where the first school was taught. Rufus Graves kept the first inn, and James Kenada erected the first grist mill, at Edmeston Center.

The Baptist Church was the first organized in the town, at Taylor Hill, March 8, 1794. Rev. Stephen Taylor was the first preacher.

The First Free Methodist Church, at Edmeston Center, was organized with 12 members, by Rev. Joseph Olney, the first pastor, January 1, 1862. The house of worship, which will seat 250, was erected in November 1868, at a cost of $900. The present value of Church property is $1,000. The present number of members is 48, and the present pastor, Rev. S. V. McVey.

The First Universalist Church, of Edmeston, was organized at Edmeston Center, Nov. 25, 1843, with 39 members. Rev. Z. Cook was the first pastor. Their house of worship was erected in 1844; it will seat 200 and cost originally $2,500. The present value of Church property is $3,000.

The Good Templars have an organization of 153 members.

The Grand Army of the Republic number 25 members. C. A. Payne, Assistant Inspector General, Otsego Division.

The population of the town in 1870 was 1,745, and its area, 27,280 acres, with an assessed value of $383,480.

The number of school districts is 13, employing 13 teachers. The number of children of school age is 560; the number attending school, 411; the average attendance, 228; the value of school houses and sites, $6,800.

EXETER was formed from Richfield, March 25, 1799. It is an interior town, lying north-west of the center of the County. The surface is hilly and broken, consisting mainly of elevated uplands. Angel Cliff and Town Cliff Hills, in the east part of the town, are from 400 to 500 feet above the valleys. The town is drained east by several small streams flowing into Schuyler Lake, and south by Butternut and Wharton Creeks, both of which rise in this town.   The soil is a clay and gravelly loam, well adapted to grazing.

Exeter, (p. v.) near the center of the town, contains two churches, viz., Congregationalist and Methodist; a town hall, a store, two blacksmith shops, a wagon shop, a shoe shop and about 20 dwellings.

Schuyler's Lake, (p. v.) in the east part of the town, contains two churches, viz., Baptist and Union ; two hotels, four stores, three shoe shops, three milliner shops, a harness shop, two blacksmith shops, a cheese factory, a cheese box factory, a steam saw and grist mill, a chair and cabinet shop, a tannery, a coufectionery store, 55 dwellings and 233 inhabitants. There is a flourishing lodge of Good Templars and one of Masons in this village.

The Cheese Box Factory of Israel L. Veber, is a two-story frame building, 26 by 40 feet, and is run by a six horse-power engine, giving employment to four hands and turning out 500 boxes per week.

The Cheese Factory of H. J. Baker, is a two-story frame building, 30 by 80 feet, has a capacity for making 24 cheeses a day, using the milk of 600 cows.

The Steam Saw and Grist Mill of William Rose, now in process of erection, is a two-story frame building, 24 by 64 feet, with two wings 22 by 24 and 17 by 14 feet. The mill will be run by a 40 horse-power engine.

West Exeter, (p. v.) on the west border, contains a Methodist church, two stores, a hotel, a blacksmith shop, two saw mills, a shoe shop, a cheese box factory and 100 inhabitants.

The first settlements were made by John Tunnicliff, near Schuyler's Lake, and William Angel, on Angel Hill, in 1789. About the same time Asa Williams settled in the south part of the town; Joshua and Caleb Angel, on Angel Hill; Seth Tubbs and Bethel Martin, at West Exeter, and M. Cushman, on the Rockdunga Creek. Eliphalet Brockway kept the first inn, at Schuyler's Lake, and C. Jones the first store, in 1810. John Hartshorne erected the first grist mill, on Herkimer Creek.

The first religious society organized was the *Presbyterian*, at Exeter Center, in 1800. Rev. T. W. Duncan was the first regular preacher.

The Baptist Church at Schuyler's Lake was organized in 1808 by Humphrey Palmer and others, with 45 members. The first pastor was Rev. D. Haskell. The first house of worship was erected in 1808; the present house in 1841. It will seat 240 and cost $2,300. The present membership is 43; the pastor is Rev. Henry Gorlock, and the value of Church property is $5,000.

The Union Church at Schuyler's Lake was erected in 1839 by the Methodists, Universalists, Free Will Baptists, Episcopalians and Christians. It will seat 260 and its present value is $2,500.

The Congregational Church of Exeter was organized in 1806 with 19 members. Rev. William Graves was the first pastor. The first house of worship was erected in 1808; the present house in 1861. It will seat 200, and the value of the Church property is $2,000. The present membership is 26.

The First M. E. Church of Exeter Center has a membership of 33. Their house of worship will seat 200 and the pastor is Rev. W. R. Cochrane.

The Second M. E. Church of West Exeter has a membership of 46. Their house of worship was erected in 1839; it will seat 250 and is valued at $3,000.

From the earliest records which we have been able to obtain, we find that in 1818 and 1820 the following names appear among the circuit preachers, viz., Revs. Abner Chase, George Gary, Charles Giles, B. G. Paddock, E. Whipple, Dan Barnes and Dana Fox.

The population of the town in 1870 was 1,256, and its area, 18,496 acres, with an assessed value of $273,644.

There are 8 school districts, employing 8 teachers. The number of children of school age is 395; the number attending school, 305; the average attendance, 160; the value of school houses and sites, $3,900.

HARTWICK, named in honor of Christopher Hartwick, the patentee of the Hartwick Patent, was formed from Otsego, March 30, 1802. Its north line was changed in 1803. It is the central town of the County. The surface is a hilly upland, the highest summits being from 200 to 350 feet above the valleys. The east part is drained by the Susquehanna, and the west part by Otsego Creek. The soil is chiefly a sandy and gravelly loam, with an occasional mixture of clay.

Hartwick, (p. v.) on Otego Creek, in the north-west part, contains 3 churches, 6 stores, 2 hotels, a grist mill, saw mill, 2 shingle mills, an iron foundry and wood shop, 2 carriage shops, 4 blacksmith shops, 2 shoe shops, 2 harness shops, an undertaker shop, cabinet shop and about 500 inhabitants.

Hartwick Seminary, (p. v.) in the east part, contains a church, (Evan. Luth,) the Hartwick Theological and Classical Seminary, and about 20 houses.

The Hartwick Theological and Classical Seminary was incorporated August 13, 1816, and endowed with a legacy of $80,000, by John Christopher Hartwick. The building has been recently remodeled at an expense of $23,000, and is one of the finest seminary buildings in the State. It is well supplied with philosophical apparatus, maps, libraries &c. The Classical Department is open to students of both sexes, and is extensively patronized.

South Hartwick, (p. v.) in the south-west part, on Otego Creek, contains a grist mill, saw mill, 2 stores, a shoe shop, a blacksmith shop and about a dozen dwellings.

Hyde Park, a hamlet, about a mile north of Hartwick Seminary, contains a hotel, store, shoe shop, 2 blacksmith shops, 2 carriage shops and about a dozen houses.

Toddsville, (p. v.) on Oaks Creek, in the north-east part, contains a church, cotton mill, paper mill, two stores, a carriage shop, blacksmith shop, jeweler's shop, shoe shop, saloon, chair and paint shop, and about 200 inhabitants.

Clintonville, a hamlet in the south-east part, on the Susquehanna River and C. & S. V. R. R., is the seat of the Clintonville Cotton Mills.

The Hartwick Patent, including the greater part of this town, was granted April 22, 1761. Settlements were commenced before the Revolution. Lot Crosby and Stephen Skiff were among the first settlers at Hartwick village; Elijah and Rufus Hawkins, and N. Lyon, settled in the north-east part of the town. James Butterfield kept the first inn, and Daniel Laurens the first store, at what is called *White House*, in the north-west part. The first mill was erected at Hartwick village by Samuel Mudge.

The first church organization was that of the Baptist, in 1795.

The Evangelical Lutheran Church of Hartwick, at Hartwick Seminary, was organized with 40 members, by Rev. J. D. Lawyer, the first pastor, in 1839. The house of worship, which will seat 300, was erected in 1840 at a cost of $1,600. The present value of Church property is $2,000. The present number of members is 25, and the pastor Rev. T. T. Titus. This Church is connected with Hartwick Seminary. Rev. G. B. Miller, D. D., was for many years the principal of the Seminary and pastor of the Church.

The Union Church (M. E.) at Toddsville was organized in 1865 by the Union Society with 25 members. The first pastor was Rev. H. V. Talbot. The house of worship was erected in 1865 at a cost of $2,300, and will seat 300. The present value of Church property is $2,400. The present number of members is 25, and the pastor is Rev. Geo. Parsons.

The Christian Church, near the north line of the town, was organized in 1820. The house of worship was erected in 1840 at a cost of $1,000, and will seat 150. The present value of Church property is $2,000. The pastorate is at present vacant.

The Christian Church at Hartwick was organized, with 46 members, February 1st, 1853, by Rev. S. B. Hayward, the first pastor. The house of worship, which will seat 300, was erected in 1853 at a cost of $2,500. The present value of Church property is $3,000. The present number of members is 199, and the pastor, Rev. N. Brown.

The Baptist Church at Hartwick was organized August 19, 1795, by Rev. James Bacon and John Bostwick, with 12 members. The first house of worship was erected in 1795; the present house, which will seat 350, in 1854–5, at a cost of $3,500. The present value of Church property is $6,000. The first pastor was Rev. John Bostwick. The present number of members is 102, and the pastor, Rev. Gould J. Travis. Since the organization of the Church the following pastors have successively officiated: Rev. Jno. Bostwick, Elder Robertson, Rev. Nathan Bundy, Rev. J. N. Adams, Rev. E. H. Bailey, Rev. J. B. Pixley, Rev. Jacob Grants, Rev. A. B. Earle, Rev. J. W. Hammond, Rev. Russell Spafford, Rev. A. Maynard, Rev. H. Fitch, Rev. H. H. Fisher, and the present incumbent. During the seventy-seven years the organization has been in existence, a large number of members have been added to the Church, which good results were brought about by the examples and exertions of the several pastors, seconded by Josiah Maples, Ziba Newland, Isaac Burch, and many other good and faithful men.

The population of the town in 1870 was 2,343, and its area, 25,978 acres, with an assessed value of $423,190.

The number of school districts is 17, employing the same number of teachers. The number of children of school age is 801; the number attending school, 579; the average attendance, 307; the value of school houses and sites is $6,090.

LAURENS was formed from Otsego, April 2, 1810. It is an interior town, lying south-west of the center of the County. The surface is high and hilly, with the exception of the broad valley of Otego Creek. It is drained south by Otego Creek and several tributaries, among which are Harrison and Wharton Creeks. The soil is a sandy and gravelly loam, in some parts slaty, and generally productive. About a mile and a half west of Laurens is a sulphur spring.

Laurens, (p. v.) pleasantly situated on Otego Creek, was incorporated April 22, 1834, and contains three churches, viz., Methodist, Presbyterian and Christian; a hotel, six stores, the Otsego Cotton Mills, a carriage factory, a grist and flouring mill, a saw mill, a planing mill, a cabinet shop, three blacksmith shops, two harness shops, three shoe shops, a wood turning shop, a tannery, two school houses, a lodge of Masons and one of Good Templars, and about 300 inhabitants.

The Otsego Cotton Mills were erected in 1847 and for several years manufactured sheetings, but all now run on paper cambric, having a capacity for making about 14,000 yards per week. The mills contain 72 looms, 2,700 spindles, and give employment to about 50 hands.

The Laurens Flouring and Custom Mill, erected in 1840, contains three runs of stones and has a capacity for grinding about 600 bushels per day. The mill is situated on the east side of Otego Creek and is owned by Lewis S. Elwell.

The Circular Saw Mill of Elwell & Allen has a capacity for sawing about 1,500,000 feet of lumber annually.

Mount Vision, (p. v.) situated in the north-east part of the town, on Otego Creek, contains two churches, viz., Methodist and Baptist; a select school, a hotel, five stores, a grist mill, a saw mill, a wagon shop, a shoe shop, four blacksmith shops, a harness shop and about 300 inhabitants.

West Laurens, (p. v.) in the west part of the town, on Harrison's Creek, is a hamlet.

The Steam Saw Mill of E. Tucker & Son, at West Laurens, has a capacity for sawing 6,000 feet of lumber per day. A lath, planing mill and matching machine are connected with the mill.

Butt's Corners, three miles west of Laurens, contains a saw mill, a tannery, a school house and 8 or 10 dwellings.

The first settlement of this town was made by Joseph Mayall, about a mile north-east of the village, in 1774. John Sleeper, a Quaker, from New Jersey, settled shortly after. Richard Smith and William Ferguson and his two sons, James and Thomas, settled within two years from the first settlement. Eastwood Allen and Samuel Gardner settled about the same time, having purchased one thousand acres about a mile south of the village.

Mr. Mayall was an Englishman by birth, but his sympathies were with the Colonies. After the close of the Revolution, while Mayall was engaged in hunting, he was accosted by three men who requested him to pilot them to the fording place on the Susquehanna. He did so, and the men then took his gun from him, and having taken off the lock, returned it, informing him, at the same time, that he must accompany them to Canada. He remonstrated, saying that peace had been declared and they had no right to take him prisoner. Finding all argument unavailing, he concluded to go with them and await an opportnity to escape. While crossing a branch of the Susquehanna, one of the party passed to the opposite side, another stationed himself in the middle of the stream, while the third was to accompany Mayall. Taking advantage of this, Mayall struck his companion over the head with his gun felling him to the ground, then quickly seizing his gun, discharged it at the one standing in the stream, wounding him. The third fired at Mayall and missed him, then fled. Mayall returned to Cherry Valley, bringing the guns of the two men and his own, which he deposited with Mr. Campbell. The barrel of Mayall's gun was bent almost to a semi-circle by the blow.

Just before the memorable massacre at Cherry Valley, Capt. Robert McKean and five others were on a scout and came to the house of Mr. Sleeper, who informed them that Brant had been at his house the day before with about fifty men, and was expected to return that night; and advised McKean and his party to leave, as they would surely be killed or taken prisoners in case Brant returned. McKean proposed to remain and make Sleeper's house his fortress, as it was a substantial log one; but as Sleeper wished to remain neutral and avoid all cause of complaint on the part of the enemy, McKean withdrew and took possession of a vacant house, a mile or two distant.

The day previous to the massacre of Cherry Valley, Mr. Sleeper started to return to New Jersey, leaving his family. At Cherry Valley some of his friends tried to induce him to remain, but being impressed to go on, he went to Bowman's Creek, seven miles distant, and thus escaped the destruction that fell upon that settlement. The next day a party of Indians passed through Laurens, robbing the family of Mr. Sleeper of all their personal property and destroying the buildings, allowing the family to escape with the clothes on their backs. Mr. Sleeper returned in 1784 with his family, rebuilt the mills which had been burned by the Indians and Tories, and again enjoyed the blessings of peace. He had been sent here to commence a settlement, preparatory to the arrival of a colony of Friends from England.

Erastus Crafts kept the first inn, about 1812; Erastus and Ezra Dean, the first store, and Daniel Johnson built the first factory.

Mr. Isaac Powell, the father of Erastus D. Powell, came to this town in 1800, with his father, who purchased the farm upon which Joseph Mayall settled, and which has ever since been in the possession of the family. Mr. P. is now 93 years of age and enjoys to a good degree the use of his mental and physical powers.

Smith Hall, now owned by Isaac G. Briggs, was commenced in 1775, by Richard Smith, one of the first settlers, and was the first framed building erected in the town. William Ferguson settled in 1774, where his grandson William now resides, about a mile and a half south of the village.

During the late Rebellion, Laurens sent out a noble band of patriots, twenty-five of whom sealed their devotion to their country with their lives. Of these, eight belonged to the 121st Regiment, viz., Samuel G. Snediker, killed at Spottsylvania, May 10, 1864; Richard Bennett, killed June 3, 1864, at Cold Harbor; James C. Gardner, killed May 10, 1864, at Spottsylvania; William Gardner, killed May 3, 1861, at Salem Church; James F. Hall, died of fever, December 23, 1862, near White Oak Church; Robinson F. Fox, killed May 3, 1863, near Fredericksburgh; Samuel A. Fenton, killed May 3, 1863, at Salem Church; Samuel A. Babcock, killed on skirmish line, near Winchester, Va., August 26, 1864. The five following were members of the 152d Regiment, viz., Galen H. Lull and Francis Ripley, died in Andersonville Prison in 1864; James Hubbard, killed on picket in 1864; Augustus Steere, died of sun stroke, May 4, 1864; Jacob H. Christman, died in New York City, May 13, 1863. The following four were members of the 2d New York Heavy Artillery, viz., James Haynes, died May 11, 1865; B. Erastus Brightman, wounded in battle at Deep Bottom, and died in November 1864; Henry Ackley, died from a wound, July 1864; Daniel Gile Smith, died at Alexandria, Va., June 17, 1864. Harvey Straight, accidentally killed by a member of his own company, in the second battle of Bull Run. He was a member of Co. E, 101st Regiment. Wm. Seward Hubbard and ——— Wright, of the 76th Regiment, killed; Willis Hillsinger, 43d Infantry, killed May 3, 1863, at Fredericksburgh, and John Herring, of the same, was killed in May 1864 in the battle of the Wilderness; Benjamin B. Comstock, Co. A, 12th Wisconsin, died July 16, 1862, in Tennesee. A son of Almon Y. Johnson was killed, and a son of Almanzo Green died of measles. Alonzo Jenks, Co. C, 61st Infantry, was killed at Fair Oaks, May 31, 1862.

The first religious organization in the town was that of the Friends, who erected a meeting house about 1800.

The Christian Church of Laurens was organized in 1836 by Rev. Charles I. Butler, the first pastor, with 36 members. Their house of worship will seat about 250 and is valued at $3,000. The present pastor is Rev. Henry Brown.

The First Presbyterian Church of Laurens was organized in 1844 by Rev. Horatio Pattengill. The first pastor was Rev. E. Vine Wales, and the first house of worship was erected in 1822, as a Union Church. It will seat 300 and is valued at $4,500. The present membership is 35.

The Baptist Church, located at Mount Vision, was organized in 1844 by Rev. Lemuel C. Pattengill, the first pastor, with 32 members. Their house was erected in 1844 and cost originally, $2,000; it is capable of seating 250. The present value of Church property is $4,000.

The population of the town in 1870 was 1,919, and its area, 26,027 acres, with an assessed value of $398,750.

There are 12 school districts, employing 13 teachers. The number of children of school age is 529; the number attending school, 429; the average attendance, 220; the value of school houses and sites, $3,140.

MARYLAND was formed from Worcester, March 25, 1808. It lies on the south line of the County, east of the center. The surface is a hilly upland, broken by the deep ravines of the streams. The principal stream is Schenevus Creek, which flows south-westerly through the south part of the County, receiving in its course several tributaries from the north and south. South Hill is a steep unbroken ridge, 350 to 500 feet above the valleys, and extends along the south bank of the creek, through the town. From its summit the surface spreads out into a rocky and broken upland, extending to the south border. The soil is chiefly a sandy loam and is best adapted to grazing. Grains of various kinds, hops and fruits, are raised extensively. There is a sulphur spring in the town. Lead was found by the Indians and one or two white men, but the place has never been made public. Traces of zinc and copper have been detected, and iron ore of various kinds is found. A specimen of magnetic ore, found near Crumhorn Lake, contained ninety per cent of iron.

Maryland (p. v.) is a station on the Albany & Susquehanna Railroad and contains two churches, two hotels, a dry goods store, a grocery and saloon, a grist mill, a steam saw mill, a school house, several mechanic shops of various kinds, and about 250 inhabitants.

Schenevus, (p. v.) incorporated in 1870, is a station on the A. & S. R. R., in the east part of the town, and contains two churches, two district schools, two select schools, a newspaper printing office, three hotels, seven dry goods stores, two hardware stores, two drug stores, two groceries, three saloons, two grist mills, a saw mill, a plaster mill, a sash, blind and door manufactory, a cheese factory, three carriage shops, four blacksmith shops, two cabinet shops, a marble shop, two undertakers, a bank, a tannery, various other mechanic shops and about 700 inhabitants. There are also Lodges of Good Templars, Odd Fellows and Masons.

The Schenevus Tannery, of Morse & Gleason, turns out about 14,000 sides of leather annually, using 12,000 cords of bark and giving employment to 22 men.

The Sash and Blind Manufactory of Lane & Hotchkin usually employ ten hands and use about 15,000 feet of lumber per month. The works are run by a fifteen horse-power engine.

The Grist Mill of Guy Brothers has three runs of stones, capable of grinding 450 bushels per day. The mill is run by a thirty horse-power engine, and last year ground 30,000 bushels.

The Feed and Plaster Mill of Mr. Ferry has three runs of stones and grinds about 200 tons of plaster annually.

The Marble Shop of Oscar P. Toombs is doing an extensive business in monuments, headstones &c.

The Schenevus Fair Grounds contain eighteen acres, well fenced and with suitable buildings.

Chaseville, (p. v.) about two miles west of Schenevus, contains a church, a flouring mill, a saw mill, a dry goods store, several mechanic shops and about 200 inhabitants.

Elk Creek, (p. v.) in the north part of the town, contains a church, a dry goods store and several mechanic shops.

In 1790, Israel, Eliphas and Phineas Spencer, and Elisha Chamberlin, from Columbia County, settled near Maryland Station. Nathaniel Rose, Eli Rose and Samuel Hotchkin, all from Columbia County, settled near the same place soon after. About 1791, Daniel Seaver, Josiah Chase, Edward Godard and Nathaniel Hazen, settled near the present site of Schenevus. About 1793, Col. J. Houghton, Caleb Byington, Wilder, Ezekiel and John Rice, and Jotham Houghton, settled near Chaseville, and Joseph Howe settled on Elk Creek. In 1794, Thomas and John Thompson, and J. Morehouse, from Columbia County, settled about a mile west of Maryland Station, near what has been called the "foot of Crumhorn."

The "Spencer Mills," erected by Israel Spencer, about 1794, were the first erected in the town. Jotham Houghton had an interest in the saw mill. Settlements were made in the east part of the town soon after. Phineas Spencer was the first stone mason, carpenter and joiner, cabinet and chair maker in town, and for many years made all coffins used for many miles around. He made plows also until cast iron plows came into use. The first tavern was kept by Josiah Chase at Schenevus; the first clothing mill was erected by Stephen G. Virgil. The first death was that of John Rice, who was killed by the fall of a tree near the present site of the Schenevus Depot. He was buried where the Schenevus Cemetery now is. The first marriage was that of Samuel Hotchkin and Polly Spencer, in January 1804. They were the parents of Ashley Hotchkin, Esq., of Schenevus. It is believed that Miss Spencer taught the first school, in 1802. The first post office was kept at the center of the town, and for several years Jared M. Chamberlin was the post master. The first building burned in the town was the blacksmith shop of Allen Ainsworth, and the first dwelling house destroyed by lightning was that of William Bowdish, about 1821. The first town officers were Edward Godard, Supervisor; John Chase, Town Clerk; D. Houghton, Justice of the Peace; J. Houghton and Heman Chamberlin, Commissioners of Highways.

The town embraces portions of several different tracts, among which are the "Crumhorn Mountain Tract" and Spencer's, Franklin's and Fitch's Patents. The first settlers, Eliphas and Israel Spencer, settled on Franklin's Patent, and Phineas Spencer on "States Land." Nathaniel Rose opened a tavern near Maryland Station, about 1806, and his brother Eli opened another near the same place. The remains of the first settlers and many of their descendants lie in the cemetery at this place.

The following incident shows the veneration of the early settlers for the dead. Samuel Chase's first wife, a step daughter of Phineas Spencer, after her death, was borne on a bier (team conveyance being considered sacrilegious,) seven miles, on a sweltering day, and deposited in this cemetery. One of the bearers is still living and over 91 years old.

Among the humorous incidents handed down from an early day is one that occurred at the raising of Israel Spencer's mill in 1793. One of the workmen, not overstocked with wisdom or the love of work, complained of thirst and kept up a continual cry for water. Phineas Spencer, a powerful man and ready for any emergency, seized the fellow by the nape of the neck and plunged him into the pond where the water was ten feet deep, with the sharp exclamation, " Get some water and be d——d."

A tavern was opened by Amos Spencer in 1802, about four miles west of Maryland village. Jerahamed Houghton started a distillery and a store at Chaseville about 1798. He also started a potash factory about the same time.

Philip Crippen, one of the oldest settlers of Maryland, is still living. He was the first white male child born in the town of Worcester, which included in its limits the present towns of Worcester, Westford, Maryland and Decatur. He is eighty-five years old, and retains to a remarkable degree his mental and physical powers. He never eats any fish or meat of any kind, and never uses tobacco or spirituous liquors. He is seldom sick and is as sprightly as a man of forty.

The First Baptist Church of Maryland, located at Chaseville, was organized Sept. 22d, 1808. Rev. Nathan D. Wright was for many years the pastor. Their house of worship was erected in 1834 at a cost of $1,500 and with a seating capacity of 450. The present value of the church is $3,000, and that of the parsonage, $1,000. The membership is 85 and the pastor is Rev. Hiram H. Fisher.

The First Baptist Church of Schenevus was organized in June 1871, by Rev. H. Martin, with 25 members. A church edifice, with a seating capacity of 250, was erected in 1868 at a cost of $4,000. The present membership is 40, and the pastor is Rev. H. W. Fisher.

The Methodist Church of Schenevus was organized more than fifty years ago, but the precise time is not known. Rev. Nathan Bangs was the first pastor, and the number of members was about a dozen. Their house of worship was erected in 1843 at a cost of about $2,500 and with a seating capacity of 400. The present membership is 140; the value of Church property is $4,500 and the pastor is Rev. J. V. Newell.

The Methodist Church of Elk Creek was organized about 1830, Rev. Lyman J. Martin being the first pastor. Their Church edifice was erected in 1857 at a cost of $800 and with a seating capacity of 300. The number of members is about 40; the value of the Church property is $2,000 and the pastor is Rev. John Filkinton.

The Methodist Church of Crumhorn Valley was organized about 1840 with about a dozen members. Their house of worship was erected in 1841 with a seating capacity of 300. It was repaired in 1867 and its present value is estimated at $2,000 The present membership is about half a dozen and the pastor is Rev. Wells Thompson.

Zion's Evangelical Lutheran Church of Maryland was organized in 1866 by Rev. Geo. W. Enders, the first pastor, with thirteen members. Their house of worship was erected in 1867 at a cost of $3,400 and with a seating capacity of 300. The present membership is 59.

G

The Methodist Church, located at Maryland Hill, was organized at an early day and has now a membership of 25. Their house of worship will seat 200 and is valued at $2,500. Rev. W. S. Winans is the present pastor.

The population of the town in 1870 was 2,402, and its area 30,164 acres, with an assessed value of $438,445.

The are 17 school districts, employing 16 teachers. The number of children of school age is 749; the number attending school, 599; the average attendance, 285; the value of school houses and sites, $7,405.

MIDDLEFIELD was formed from Cherry Valley, March 3, 1797. It is an interior town, lying north-east of the center of the County. The surface is a hilly upland, abruptly descending to Otsego Lake and Outlet, which form its west boundary. The summits of the hills are 400 to 600 feet above the valleys. Cherry Valley Creek flows south-west through the east part, and Red Creek through the west part. The soil is a sandy and gravelly loam.

Middlefield Center, (p. v.) situated in the north part of the town, contains a Presbyterian church, a store, a hotel, two boot and shoe shops, two blacksmith shops, a carriage and wagon shop, a last factory, a school house and about 600 inhabitants.

The Last Factory, at Middlefield Center, was erected in 1824, by Samuel and Mason C. Huntington. It was the first of the kind in the State, and the machine used is said to be the third one ever built. It turns out about 25,000 lasts annually and gives employment to three hands. It has been in the hands of the Huntington family since it was first started, and is now owned by S. G. Huntington.

The Cheese Factory of S. W. Barnum, about a mile south-west of Middlefield Center, was built in 1866, with a capacity for using the milk of 400 cows, making 10,000 pounds of cheese annually.

Lynchville is a hamlet about a mile and a half south-west of Middlefield Center, and contains a grist mill, a cider mill, a cheese-box factory, a carriage and wagon shop, a blacksmith shop and ten dwellings.

Middlefield, (p. v.) known also as "Clarksville," is situated on Cherry Valley Creek and contains two churches, viz., M. E. and Baptist; two hotels, three stores, three blacksmith shops, two wagon shops, a tailor shop, a milliner shop, a grist mill, a saw mill, a cheese-box factory, a graded school and about 300 inhabitants.

Bowers Town is situated on Red Creek, about a mile south-east of Cooperstown, and contains a Presbyterian church, a school house, a tannery, a saw mill, 22 dwellings and about 100 inhabitants.

Westville, (p. v.) in the south-east border of the town, partly in Westford, contains two churches, viz., Methodist and Baptist; two stores, two hotels, a blacksmith shop, a pump factory, a wagon shop and about 150 inhabitants.

Whey Corners is a hamlet about two miles north-east of Cooperstown, and contains a carriage and sleigh factory, a saw mill, a blacksmith shop, a school house and about a dozen dwellings.

Phœnix Mills (p. v.) is a hamlet in the south-west part of the town, on Susquehanna River, and contains a hotel, a store, a woolen factory, a saw mill, a grist mill, 15 dwellings and about 80 inhabitants.

The Phœnix Saw Mill was built in 1867 by W. H. Wood, and has one circular saw, capable of cutting 8,000 feet per day. A planing mill is connected with it.

The Phœnix Woolen Mill runs three sets of machinery, employs about 40 hands and works up about 100,000 pounds of wool annually.

The County Poor House is located in this town, on a farm of 160 acres, about three miles south of Cooperstown. The following statistics, which should properly have been given in connection with the general history of the County, but was received too late for insertion in that portion of the Gazetteer, we gather from the annual report of the Superintendent of the Poor, for the fiscal year, ending October 31, 1871:

The whole number of paupers received and supported at the Otsego County Poor House during the last fiscal year, was 228; of which 82 were county poor and 146 were town poor; 136 were males and 92 females. There were 5 births, 1 of county and 4 of town; 18 deaths; of county 6, of towns 12. Discharged 85, absconded 22, now at the Poor House 103. Insane 21—of county 5, of town 16. Idiocy 16—of county 3, of town 13. Mutes 1, of county.

The whole number of weeks board furnished at the County Poor House the past year for town paupers was.............................. 4,619
For county paupers... 2,178

Total... 6,797
The whole amount of money drawn from the Co. Treasurer
    the past year...$11,330 05

To be assessed on towns...................................... 7,699 00
To be assessed on county..................................... 2,631 05

The average weekly expenses of each pauper to be assessed upon the towns and county is 166 cents and 7 mills, amounting for 6,797 weeks and 5 days board to $11,330 05.

The whole number of weeks board furnished to the paupers at the County House, with the cost to be assessed upon the several towns and county, is as follows :

TOWNS.	Weeks.	Days	Cost of Support.
Burlington....................................	28	5	$ 47 88
Butternuts...................................	201	2	335 54
Cherry Valley...............................	171		285 06
Decatur.....................................	9	3	15 72
Edmeston...................................	52	1	86 92
Exeter......................................	107	6	179 81
Hartwick....................................	428	2	713 95
Laurens.....................................	5	5	9 54
Maryland...................................	330	5	551 31
Middlefield..................................	692	1	1153 80
Milford.....................................	260	5	434 62
Morris......................................	130	4	217 67
New Lisbon.................................	32	2	52 83
Oneonta....................................	107	1	178 61
Otego......................................	324	5	541 31
Otsego.....................................	555		925 18
Pittsfield...................................	153	6	256 50
Plainfield...................................	56	3	94 70
Richfield....................................	52	1	86 92
Roseboom..................................	128	4	214 34
Springfield..................................	302	1	503 67
Unadilla....................................	163		271 72
Westford...................................	168	3	280 77
Worcester..................................	156	5	261 26
	4619		7699 00
Otsego County.............................	2178	5	3631 05
	6797	5	$11330 05

I would further report that there is a surplus of about five thousand pounds of pork. There is also two hundred cords of wood cut and seasoned for the coming winter. The farm is in a good state of cultivation, and there are eight acres of rye sown which looks well.

STOCK ON FARM.

11 Cows, $40..	.$440 00
1 Yoke Oxen..	200 00
2 Horses...	250 00
8 Shotes...	80 00
	$970 00

PRODUCE ON FARM.

15 tons of Hay, at $15			$225 00
250 bushels of Oats			125 00
300	"	Corn	300 00
130	"	Rye	150 00
900	"	Potatoes	360 00
40	"	Apples	20 00
15	"	Onions	30 00
15	"	Turnips	6 00
10	"	Carrots	4 00
10	"	Beets	4 00
10 loads of Straw			40 00
25	"	of Corn Stalks	100 00
2200 pounds of Pork			132 00
1100	"	of Butter	330 00

$1,826 00

About two miles north of Clarksville is a rock, called *Niskayuna*, where various Indian tribes from the south were accustomed to meet the Mohawks in council. The rock was covered with hieroglyphics, but, from its scaly nature, they are now obliterated. The Indians encamped at this place on their retreat from Cherry Valley in November 1778.

The first settlement of the town was made about 1755, by immigrants originally from Ireland and Scotland. Among those who settled prior to the Revolutionary War, were Wm. Cook, Daniel, Benjamin and Reuben McCollum, Samuel and Andrew Wilson, Andrew Cochran, Andrew Cameron and a man named Hall, all of whom settled in the north part of the town. Among those who settled at a later date were Benjamin Gilbert in 1780; Reuben Beals, in the south part in 1786; William Campton, Bernard Temple, Stephen and Thomas Pratt, Whitney Juvil, Moses Rich and —— Rice, all of whom were from Massachusetts, and settled in 1787. William Temple, Daniel Moore and —— Dunham, from New England, settled in the south part of the town soon after. Hannah Hubbell taught the first school, about 1790. Alexander McCollum and Andrew Cameron kept the first inns, and Benjamin Johnson the first store, in 1790. Mr. McCollum built the first saw mill, before the war, and Moses Rich the first grist mill, in 1795.

John M. Bowers came from New York City in 1802, and set-in Cooperstown, where he remained until 1805, when he removed across the river into Middlefield. He was one of the largest landholders in the County, owning 18,000 acres of the "Bowers Tract" and 5,000 acres of the "Kettletas Tract." He died in 1846 at the age of 74 years. Mrs. M. M. S. Bowers, his widow, still resides at Lake Lands, a beautiful rural residence near Cooperstown. She is 93 years of age but retains her men-

tal faculties to a remarkable degree. She was the daughter of
Mrs. Martha Wilson, of Revolutionary memory, and the grand-
daughter of Col. Charles Stewart, Commissary General of the
army during the Revolution.

Mr. Orren Sibley came into this town in 1832 and settled at
what was known as "Bear's Swamp," about four miles from
Cooperstown. The place was a wilderness, and he built two
miles of road to open communication with the public highway.
Here he started a tannery and a saw mill. The latter has a
capacity for cutting 10,000 feet per day.

The First Baptist Church of Middlefield was organized in
1810 by Rev. Benjamin Sawin, the first pastor. Their house
of worship was erected in 1825 with a seating capacity of 500.
The present membership is 96; the pastor is Rev. D. F. Leach,
and the value of the Church property is $5,000.

The First Presbyterian Church of Middlefield Center was
organized Nov. 18, 1821, by Rev. Andrew Oliver, the first
pastor, with 14 members. The first house of worship was
erected in 1810; the present house in 1844. It will seat 225
and cost $1,500. The present membership is 60; the value of
the Church property is $2,500; the pastor is Rev. Philander
Griffin.

The Methodist Church of Middlefield erected a house of
worship in 1832. It will seat 300 and cost $2,000. The
present membership is 90; the value of the Church property
is $4,500; the pastor is Rev. Walter B. Thomas.

The population of the town in 1870 was 2,876, and its area
is 37,434 acres, with an assessed value of $567,547.

There are 19 school districts, employing the same number of
teachers. The number of children of school age is 886; the
number attending school, 654; the average attendance, 361;
the value of school houses and sites is $10,105.

MILFORD was formed from Unadilla, February 5, 1796,
as *Suffrage.* Its name was changed April 8, 1800. It is an
interior town, lying south of the center of the County. The
surface is a hilly upland, divided into two distinct ridges by
the Susquehanna River which flows south-west through the
town. The valley is deep and bordered by steep hillsides.
Crumhorn Mountain, on the east border, is about 600 feet
above the valleys, and the west hills are from 300 to 400 feet
high. Crumhorn Lake is a body of water about three miles in
circumference, on the summit of Crumhorn Mountain. The
soil is a sandy and gravelly loam.

Milford, (p. v.) in the north-east part, on the Cooperstown & Susquehanna Valley Railroad, contains 3 dry goods stores, 1 hardware store, 1 drug store, 2 tanneries, 1 hotel, 3 carriage shops, 2 blacksmith shops, 2 shoe shops, 2 banking institutions, 2 churches and about 375 inhabitants.

Portlandville, (p. v.) south of the center, on the C. & S. V. R. R. and the Susquehanna River, contains 3 churches, 2 stores, 1 grocery, 1 hotel, 3 carriage shops, 2 blacksmith shops, 1 grist mill, 2 saw mills, 1 planing mill, 1 shingle mill and about 250 inhabitants.

Colliersville, (p. v.) in the south, on the Susquehanna River, and A. & S. R. R., contains a store, shoe shop, hotel, sash and blind factory, blacksmith shop and several dwellings.

Milford Center is a hamlet.

Edson's Corners is a hamlet in the north part.

Junction is a station on the A. & S. R. R. and the southern terminus of the C. & S. V. R. R.

The first settlement was made on the Susquehanna River by a squatter named Carr, about 1770. The settlements made previous to the Revolution were broken up by the war, and little progress was made until peace was restored. Matthew Cully, from Cherry Valley, and George Mumford, settled near Milford Center in 1783. Abraham and Jacob Beals, and a family named Ford, all from Massachusetts, settled at and near Milford village in 1784. Henry Scott, from Ireland, settled a little north of the village in 1786. The first child born was Daniel Beals, in September 1786; the first marriage was that of James Brown and Rhoda Marvin, in 1788, and the first death was that of Mrs. Beals, about the same time. The first school was taught by Increase Niles, in 1790. Matthew Cully and Isaac Collier kept the first inn, below Milford village, and Isaac Edson the first store, at the village, in 1794. The first grist mill was erected by David Cully, in 1788, and the first saw mill by Matthew Cully, in 1792–3.

The first religious services were held by the Congregationalists, near Milford village, in 1793, by Rev. Mr. Reed.

The First Presbyterian Church of Milford was organized July 28, 1807, by Rev. Andrew Oliver, with eleven members. The first pastor was Rev. Alexander Conkey; the first house of worship was erected in 1805; it was repaired in 1843 and will seat 300. The present membership is 80; the value of the Church property is $10,000. Rev. William N. Schall, D. D., supplies the pulpit.

The Baptist Church of Milford Center was organized about 1805 with eight members. Rev. Josiah Morris was the first pastor. Their present house of worship was erected about 1820; it will seat 300 and cost about $2,000. The present membership is 181; the pastor is Rev. B. F. Williams. The present value of the Church property is about $5,000.

St. John's Episcopal Church, Portlandville, was organized in 1866 by Rev. Edward Pidsley, the first pastor, with ten members. Their house of worship was erected in 1866; it will seat 200 and cost $3,000. The present membership is 18; the pastor is Rev. Edward N. Goddard.

The Portlandville Christian Church was organized with six members, Dec. 29, 1838, by S. Soule, John Cook, Roberson Ellsworth, Hannah Smith, Harriet White and Minerva Windsor. Rev. Stephen Soule was the first pastor. The house of worship, which will seat 300, was erected in 1840, at a cost of $1,200. The Church property is at present valued at from $2,500 to $3,-000. The present number of members is 70, and the pastor Rev. D. M. Fuller.

The Methodist Church of Milford was organized in 1817 by Rev. Abner Chase, its first pastor. The first house of worship was erected in 1836. The present house, which will seat 350, in 1869, at a cost of $2,500. The present number of members is 122, and the pastor Rev. Wm. G. Queal. Rev. S. A. Eddy, of Cazenovia, was born in this town and had his first Church membership with this Church, of which he has also been the pastor. Hon. Levi Stewart, a former Judge of this County, was for a long time a leading member of this Church, and died in 1868. The present value of Church property is $10,000.

The Portlandville M. E. Church erected their first house of worship in 1848. The present house, which will seat 300, was erected in 1866 at a cost of $1,800. The present value of Church property is $5,000. The present number of members is 70, and the present pastor, Rev. W. G. Queal.

The population of the town in 1870 was 2,301, and its area, 28,402 acres, with an assessed value of $469,520.

The number of school districts is 14, employing the same number of teachers. The number of children of school age is 633; the number attending school, 528; the average attendance, 221; the value of school houses and sites is $8,318.

MORRIS, named after Gen. Jacob Morris, was formed from Butternuts, April 6, 1849. It lies upon the west border of the County, south of the center. The surface is a hilly upland, divided into two principal ridges by Butternut Creek, which flows south-west through the town, near the center. The west ridge terminates in a series of steep bluffs bordering on Unadilla River, which forms the west boundary of the town. The soil upon the uplands is composed of clay, gravel and disintegrated slate, and in the valleys it is a gravelly loam.

Morris, (p. v.) known also as "Louisville," on Butternut Creek, a little east of the center of the town, contains four churches, viz., Episcopal, Baptist, Methodist and Universalist; 3 hotels, 4 dry goods stores, 2 drug stores, a hardware store, jewelry store, 3 tailor shops, several mechanic shops and about 700 inhabitants. A short distance from the village are several manufactories, the most important of which are the *Cotton Mills* of W. F. & R. Leonard.

Maple Grove, (p. v.) near the south-east corner, is a hamlet, containing a blacksmith shop and about a dozen houses.

Elm Grove, about a mile and a half north-east of Morris, is a hamlet, containing a chair factory and about a dozen houses.

The citizens of this town have formed a Soldier's Monument Association, and are about to erect a monument in the Cemetery at Morris, in honor of those who went from this town and died in the service of their country during the late Rebellion. The following names are to be inscribed upon the monument: 121st Regiment, N. Y. V., Henry Tracy, killed at Salem Church, May 3d, 1863; Samuel Fenton, killed at Fredericksburg, May 3d, 1863; Edwin W. Loomis, killed at Sailor Creek, April 1865; Chancey Colton, killed at the Wilderness, 1864; Zepheniah Foot, died at White Creek Church, 1863; Chas. Camp, killed. 152d Regiment, N. Y. V., Lieut. Geo. Kidder, killed at the Wilderness, 1863; Chancey Kelsey, killed at Boynton Plank Road, Oct. 27, 1864; David F. Lewis, killed at Cold Harbor; Samuel G. Parcell, wounded and died, June 28, 1864; Alvin Kinney, wounded at Cold Harbor, and died, 1864; Daniel Miller, wounded and died at Washington, 1864; Levi McIntyre, killed; Abel Card, died in Andersonville, Jan. 22, 1864; Stanley G. Sergeant, died in Andersonville; Adelbred Eldred, died in Andersonville, 1864; Geo. Reeves, died in Andersonville; John Radley, missing at Deep Bottom; Millard Kirkland, died at Brandy Station, Jan. 12, 1864; James Kelsey, missing. U. S. N., C. L. Kenyon, died April 2d, 1865. 8th Regiment Cavalry, Wm. D. Adams, killed at Beverly Ford, June 9, 1863. 114th Regiment, N. Y. V., Ira A. Davis, died at New Orleans, July 8, 1863; Wallace W. Jackson, killed at Winchester, Sept. 19, 1864. 176th Regiment, N. Y. V., Alexis Goodrich, killed July 27, 1863;

Aaron A. Parcell. 2d Regiment, N. Y. V., Wm. E. Greene, died in Salisbury Prison, 1864; John S. Scudder; Geo. Davis, killed; Henry Rogers, died in Andersonville. Regiment not known, Henry Stockwell, killed, 1864.

The settlement of this town was commenced a short time previous to the Revolution. In 1772 Ebenezer Knapp and Increase Thurstin came from Dutchess County to the valley of Butternut Creek, 14 miles from its mouth, remained a few months making preliminary arrangements for a settlement, and returned home for the winter. In June 1773, they returned with their families. Mr. Knapp settled in the northeast part of the town, on the farm now owned by G. A. Yates, and built a cabin, about two and a half miles above Morris village. Mr. Thurstin settled a short distance from him, in the town of New Lisbon. Benjamin Lull, with his five sons, Benjamin, Jr., Joseph, Caleb, Nathan and William, and Jonathan Moore, from Dutchess County, came at the same time. Andre Renouard settled at Elm Grove, and Louis and Paschal Franchot, originally from France, settled near the village of Morris, in 1790. Quite a large family of Lulls settled near the northeast border of the town and in New Lisbon. Andrew Cathcart and Jacob Morris were among the early settlers. Ichabod Palmer and Elnathan Noble settled in 1778. The settlement was broken up during the war, some of the inhabitants being taken prisoners and others returning to their former homes. Previous to the massacre at Cherry Valley, some of the women and children of the Butternut settlement, passed through that place and were in hearing of the guns when the attack was made. In 1783 and the following years many of the settlers returned. Mr. Joseph Lull settled where D. Whitcomb now lives, near the school house in District No. 2. The first marriage was that of Joseph Lull and Martha Knapp in 1776, by a justice. The first inn was kept by Sturgess Bradley, and the first store by Louis and Paschal Franchot, at Morris village. The firm was known, after the death of Louis, as Franchot & Van Rensselaer, until 1814. Louis De Villier erected the first grist mill on Aldrich Creek, at a place called Elm Grove. The first cotton and woolen factory was carried on by a company, viz., A. G. Washburn, agent, Paschal Franchot, Volkert P. Van Rensselaer, John C. Morris, Benajah Davis, Captain Dan Smith, Luther Skidmore and others. The first deed granted in town was given to Benjamin Lull, Sen., in 1769, by Richard Wells. The first death was that of Mrs. Elizabeth Lull, wife of Benjamin Lull, Jr., and daughter of Ebenezer Knapp.

Joseph Lull was nineteen years of age when he married, and his wife, Martha Knapp, a little short of fourteen. She became the mother of sixteen children, eight sons and eight daughters. Soon after her marriage, and during the autumn months, accompanied with her sister and three children, one two years, one sixteen and one six months old, she went to Cherry Valley, a distance of thirty miles, on horseback. They followed a path leading through an unbroken forest guided only by marked trees. They rode alternately, thus relieving each other of their burden, and finally reached their place of destination. Added to the many hardships in this way suffered, was the want often of provisions. The cruelty and treachery of the Indian savage caused them to make this journey. It was with painful eye they beheld, as they departed, their rude dwellings enveloped in flames, and the spoiling of the fruits of their own self-denying toil; and when in after years they to their homes returned, it was with no cheering emotions they discerned the remaining marks of the red man's ruthless hand. In 1778, by reason of the war, Mr. and Mrs. Lull were driven to Dutchess Co. and there remained about six years. Mrs. Lull carried two children in her lap, on horseback, a distance of one hundred and sixty miles. She died in 1851, and had at her death ninety-nine grandchildren.

The following anecdote is related by Mr. Ezra Lull, son of Caleb Lull, and grandson of Benj. Lull, Sen., now a resident of the town. The year Cherry Valley was burned, a party of men had gathered together one evening for a husking. Seven of them, and several of them Mr. Benj. Lull's sons, were taken prisoners by fourteen Oneida Indians, who had been friendly to the Colonists, and they were taken to Fort Stanwix, (now Rome,) and reported there as Tories, ready to join the enemy. This was done merely to obtain liquor from the Continental commander of the Fort. While on their way to the jail, at Albany, they met a Continental Captain by the name of Winn, who knew them to be among the *neutrals*, as some were styled who had taken an oath to be neutral, and he obtained their release.

General Jacob Morris, who during the Revolution was on the staff of Major Gen. Charles Lee, settled in the south part of the town, near the site of the "Morris Memorial Chapel." About a mile north of this Chapel is a marble monument, upon one side of which is the following inscription, which needs no explanation :

" Sacred to the memory of Miss Hannah Cooper, Daughter of the Honble William Cooper and Elizabeth his wife. In the bloom of Youth, in perfect health, and surrounded with her Virtues; On the 10th day of Septembr 1800 she was instantly translated from this World. Thrown from her horse on the spot on which this monument is erected. Sensible, gentle, amiable. In life beloved, in death lamented by all who knew her. Unconscious of her own perfections, she was a stranger to all ambition but that of doing good. By her death, the tender joys of an affectionate father, the fond expectations of a delighted mother, in an instant were blasted. Passenger Stop! and for a moment reflect that neither accomplishments of Person, nor great improvements of mind, nor yet greater goodness of heart can arrest the hand of Death. But she was prepared for that immortality in which she believed and of which she was worthy. "To departed worth and excellence, this monument is erected, this tribute of affection is inscribed by a friend, this 1st day of January 1801."

Miss Cooper was a sister of J. Fenimore Cooper.

On the 5th of October 1871, Harry Fortune, a colored man, supposed to be 120 years old, died. He had been known for 65 years by some of the citizens of this town and was an old man at the first acquaintance. He was able to work some until within the last few years, and in 1870 voted the Republican ticket.

The Episcopal Church was organized about 1793. A house of worship was erected in 1801 and was known as *Harmony Church.* It was located on what is known as the "Church Burying Ground," and is supposed to have been the first Episcopal Church erected in the County. Rev. Daniel Nash was the first pastor. The present Church edifice was erected in 1818 under the direction of Jacob Morris, Paschal Franchot, Volkert P. Van Rensselaer, Martin Noble and Benjamin Davis. It is a stone structure, will seat 500, and cost $5,500. The name was then changed to *Zion Church,* which it still retains. In 1839 a parsonage was erected at a cost of $1,200. In 1867 Rev. Daniel S. Tuttle, rector of this Church, was elected Bishop of Montana, Utah and Idaho, and resigned the rectorship, May 1, 1867. The present rector is Rev. Thomas H. Cullen. The present number of members is 219. The present value of Church property is $20,000.

The Universalist Church was organized in 1843, by N. Stevenson and John W. Whitcomb, with 27 members. The first pastor was David Pickering. Their house of worship was erected in 1842; it will seat 300 and cost $1,200. The present membership is 51; the pastor is Rev. W. H. Harrington, and the value of the Church property is $5,000.

The Baptist Church of Morris was organized in Sept. 1793 with ten members, five male and five female. Their first services were held in private houses, in barns, in groves and in school houses after they were built. Rev. John Lawton was the first settled pastor. In 1798, when he was settled, the society "voted to raise for his support, one hundred dollars per annum, twenty to be paid in money and the balance in necessaries of life." In

1817 a house of worship was erected near the town line, in the north-east part. Uri Jackson, David Thurstin and Joseph Lull, were the Trustees. In 1841 a house was erected in the village; it was 36 by 40 feet and cost $800. Deacon Joseph Lull and his wife, Martha, were members of its organization to their death. Deacon Lull died in 1840, and Mrs. Lull in 1851. The present house of worship, which will seat 375, was erected in 1870 at a cost of $16,000. The present number of members is 142. The present pastor is Rev. Chas. Ayer. The present value of Church property is $18,000. The original members were in part the first settlers of Butternut Valley, and set up a prayer meeting here in 1773, when there were but two families on the ground, which has been continued till now, except as interupted by the Revolutionary War.

All Saints, Morris Memorial Chapel, located about three miles below Morrris village, is a beautiful stone structure, erected by the descendants of General Jacob Moris, one of the most distinguished of the early settlers and one of the first communicants of the Episcopal Church. It was erected in 1866, near the Morris family burying ground. It cost originally $5,000 and will seat 200. From a sermon of Rev. N. S. Rulison, former rector of Zion Parish, we extract the following notice of *Morris Memorial Chapel:* "The idea of this Chapel originated with two members of our Church, Mr. and Mrs. J. R. Morris. The expense of the work is borne by all the descendants of Gen. Jacob Morris, once one of the most distinguished citizens of this town. The objects had in view in building the Chapel, were to preserve and make sacred the Morris family burial grund, near which it stands, and to afford religious instruction to the families living near it." The Chapel is deeded in trust to the Vestry of Zion Church.

The population of the town in 1870 was 2,253, and its area, 24,057 acres, with an assessed value of $386,763.

There are 13 school districts, employing 14 teachers. The number of children of school age is 683 ; the number attending school, 579 ; the average attendance, 310; the value of school houses and sites is $8,550.

NEW LISBON was formed from Pittsfield, April 7, 1806, as *Lisbon.* Its name was changed April 6, 1808. It is an interior town, lying west of the center of the County. The surface is a hilly upland, divided into several ridges by the deep ravines of the streams. The highest summits are from 300 to 500 feet above the valleys. The principal streams are Butternut Creek, flowing south through the west part, and the west branch of the Otego Creek, through the east part. Gilbert's Lake is a small sheet of water on the south border. The soil upon the uplands is a clay and slaty loam, and in the valleys a gravelly loam.

Garrattsville (p.v.) in the north-west part, on Butternut Creek, about sixteen miles west of Cooperstown, contains two churches, one hotel, three dry goods and one grocery store, two wagon shops, three blacksmith shops, a shoe shop, tin shop, harness shop, two millinery shops, two physicians, two dress makers, a grist and cider mill, cheese box factory, saw mill, tailor shop, tannery, forty-two houses and about 175 inhabitants.

New Lisbon, (p. v.) known as "Noblesville," in the south-east corner, on Butternut Creek, contains one church, (union,) one hotel, one store, ten dwellings and about 35 inhabitants.

New Lisbon Center is a hamlet near the center of the town, and contains one church, (Baptist,) one shoe shop, nine dwellings and about 40 inhabitants.

Stetsonville, in the south-west part, near the line of Pittsfield, contains a wagon shop, blacksmith shop, two cooper shops and about 35 inhabitants.

The first settlement was made in 1773, in the south-west corner of the town, by Increase Thurstin and Benjamin Lull and his sons. Several of the sons settled in this town and some of them in Morris. Among the other early settlers were S. W. Park, Moses Thurston, Hughey Marks, O. Park, William Pierce, John Johnson, William and John Garratt, and —— Brook, all of whom settled in the vicinity of Garrattsville. Elnathan Nobles was among the first settlers at Noblesville, which took its name from him. Joseph Baldwin and John L. Stetson were the first settlers at Stetsonville. In 1778 the first settlers were driven off by the Indians and Tories, their buildings burned and their crops destroyed. After the close of the war, the former settlers returned. A haystack belonging to the Thurstins had been set on fire and burned over on the outside. On the return of the owners in 1783, they found the middle of the stack had been preserved in good order. Sally Thurstin was the first child born in town. The first school was taught by James Mc-Collum; the first inn was kept by Charles Eldredge, in the south part of the town. William Garratt kept the first store, at Garratsville. Louis DeVillier erected the first grist mill.

The first religious society organized was the *Baptist*, at New Lisbon Center, in 1804, by Elder S. Gregory. A Congregational Church was formed the same year by Rev. William Stone.

The M. E. Church of Garrattsville, was organized in 1840. Rev. M. French was the first pastor. The house of worship, which will seat 250, was erected in 1841, at a cost of $1,050, and repaired in 1870. The present value of Church property is $3,000. The present number of members is 25, and the present pastor, Rev. Wm. M. Hiller.

The First Congregational Church, at Noblesville, was organized with 11 members in April 21, 1805, by Rev. N. Stone, of Connecticut, its first pastor. The house of worship, which will seat 300, was erected in 1802 at a cost of $1,600, and repaired in 1861. The present value of Church property is $2,000, and the pastor is Rev. Evine Wales. Of the members of this Church, seven have become ordained ministers, and two (females) missionaries to foreign lands.

The population of the town in 1870 was 1,545, and its area, 26,779 acres, with an assessed value of $374,520.

The number of school districts is 16, employing 15 teachers. The number of children of school age is 472; the number attending school, 391; the average attendance, 211; the value of school houses and sites is $4,245.

ONEONTA was formed from Unadilla, February 5, 1796, as *Otego.* Its name was changed April 17, 1830. It is the central town on the south border of the County. The surface is a hilly upland, broken by the deep valley of the Susquehanna, which flows south-west through the south part. Otego and Oneonta Creeks flow into the Susquehanna from the north, and Charlotte River from the south. A range of hills 500 feet high extends along the south-east bank of the Susquehanna. The surface in the center and north part is hilly, broken by narrow and irregular valleys. The summits are from 150 to 300 feet above the valleys. The soil is a gravel, clay and slate, on the uplands, and gravelly loam and alluvium along the valley of the river.

Oneonta, (p. v.) situated in the south part of the town, is one of the principal stations on the A. & S. R. R., and contains five churches, three hotels, two newspaper printing offices, a large number of stores, several manufactories, among which are three foundries, a machine shop and agricultural works, sash and blind factory, a spoke factory, a saw mill, a grist mill, a manufactory of machines for cutting heading, two carriage shops, various other manufactories and a population of 1,383. The village is increasing rapidly in business and population, about 100 houses having been erected during the last season.

The Oneonta Agricultural Works of Ford Brothers, located near the railroad station, were started in 1866 by E. R. Ford and Henry Howe. They manufacture agricultural implements of various kinds and employ about twenty hands. The Works have been carried on by Ford Brothers since 1869.

West Oneonta (p. v.) contains a church, a hotel, a store, several mechanic shops and about twenty dwellings.

, *Emons,* in the east part, on the railroad, is a hamlet.

Oneonta Plains, about two miles west of Oneonta, is a small village.

The Indians had a camping ground on the flat, between the village and the river, and there was an old Indian orchard and a cemetery in the south-west part of the town, the former on the south side of the river, and the latter on the north.

Henry Scramblin and a man named Youngs, settled in the town previous to the Revolution. Aaron Brink, Frederick Brown and —— McDonald, were among the early settlers at Oneonta village. James Youngs settled at the mouth of Charlotte River; Baltus Himmel, north of the village. Abraham Houghtaling, Jacob Elias Brewer and Peter Swartz, settled in the north part of the town in 1786; and Josiah Peck, on Oneonta Creek.

The first birth was that of Abraham Houghtaling 2d, in 1786. Baltus Himmel kept the first inn, and Peter Dininey the first store. John Vanderwerker erected the first grist mill.

The first religious society organized was the Presbyterian, in 1786, at Oneonta village. Rev. Alexander Conkey was the settled pastor in 1816.

The population of the town in 1870 was 2,568, and its area, 22,498 acres, with an assessed value of $426,305.

The number of school districts is 15, employing 16 teachers. The number of children of school age is 924; the number attending school, 850; the average attendance, 389; the value of school houses and sites is $14,975.

OTEGO was formed from Franklin (Delaware Co.) and Unadilla, April 12, 1822, as *Huntsville.* A part of Milford was annexed and its name changed April 17, 1830. It lies on the south border of the County, west of the center.

The town is of uneven surface, the hills being in uneven ranges, nearly or quite parallel with the brooks which empty into the Susquehanna River. The range on the southerly side and along the valley of the river, is unbroken. The soil is a clay and sandy loam.

The Susquehanna River runs through the southerly side of the town for a distance of about seven miles. The brooks emptying into the river are four, Mill Creek, east and west branches of Ottawa Creek, Flax Creek and Center Brook, extending back from the river in a northerly and north-westerly direction, from five to eight miles.

These brooks pass through handsome valleys, with hill-sides well cleared and cultivated, the lands from the brooks to the tops of the hills being fertile and peculiarly adapted to grass growing and stock raising, growing also good crops of corn, oats, and the other grains cultivated in the region. These hills are generally easily accessible for the purposes of cultivation and use. The lands of this town are mostly devoted to dairying and stock raising.

Otego, (p. v.) is attractively situated on the Susquehanna River, in the south part of the town, and is an important station on the Albany & Susquehanna Rail Road. It contains 7 stores, 2 hotels, 5 churches, (Presb., Bap., M. E., Old School Bap. and Epis.) a sash and blind factory, several mechanic shops and about 600 inhabitants.

Otsdawa, (p. v.) on the creek of that name, in the north part, contains a church, (Free Will Baptist,) store, saw and grist mills, a wagon shop, harness shop, blacksmith shop, and about 100 inhabitants.

Settlements began in this town, along the Susquehanna, soon after the Revolution. The names of some of the first settlers are Peter Schramling, John Winn, John Vanderweriker, John Christian, Conrad Overhiser, Barnet Overhiser, John Hess and John Brimmer. John Youmans and others of Dutch extraction, from the counties of Albany, Schoharie, and along the Mohawk Valley. The residue of the first settlers were mostly from the New England States. Asahel Packard, —— Shepard, Philo Goodrich, Wm. French, Elijah Ferry &c., were from Massachusetts. Rowland Carr, Thurston Brown and Jonathan Weaver, were from Rhode Island. Anson Judson, Daniel Weller, Abram Blakely, Solomon Squires, Mareness Goodrich, Ransom Hunt and others, were from Vermont and Connecticut. Michael Birdsall and brothers, were from Dutchess County. Phineas and John Cook were from Connecticut. The Bundys were among the first settlers in town. Peter Bundy moved here from Montgomery Co. in 1780. He had eight sons and five daughters who settled in this town.

There was much jealousy and ill feeling, and often feuds, between the Dutch settlers and those designated as the *Yankees,* and they were very nearly equally divided in numbers for many

H

years. Disputes and often fighting occurred. At last the fighting feature of the trouble was nearly disposed of for all time
to come by a battle on Saw Mill Hill, after a saw mill raising,
between "Old John French" and David Schramling, the latter a Tory of the Revolution and an active partizan of the
Indians, in whose depredations and murders he was a wander-
ing participator during the greater part of the war. French
was the winner. They were the champions by arrangement.

The Indian chieftain Brant's encampment was still standing,
with its poles, crotches and covering, within the limits of
the present village of Otego, when the first settlers came in.
This encampment was made one of his resting places on his
way to the Cherry Valley massacre.

Very much of the business of the early settlers was that of
manufacturing pine lumber, which they "rafted" down the
Susquehanna River to the Chesepeake Bay. It was a stirring
and always a perilous business, this "rafting" upon a rapid and
tortuous river for about 350 miles, on its floods or "freshets."

The Baptist Church of Otego was organized in 1816, by Rev.
D. Robertson, the first pastor, with 32 members. The first
house of worship was erected in 1829, and repaired in 1855. The
present membership is 52, and the value of Church property is
$3,500.

The Christian Church of Otsdawa was organized in 1830 by
Rev. Joshua Hayward, the first pastor, with 13 members. Their
house of worship was erected in 1836, at a cost of $1,300 and
with a seating capacity of 400. The present membership is
92 ; the pastor is Rev. Wm. Case, and the value of the Church
property is $2,000.

The Second Christian Church, located in the north-west part
of the town, was organized in 1870, by Rev. Wm. Case, the
present pastor, with 19 members. Their house of worship was
erected the same year, at a cost of $1,800, and capable of seating
250. The present membership is 28.

The First Methodist Church of Otego was organized with about
40 or 50 members, and a house of worship was erected in 1848
or '49, at a cost of $1,400 and with a seating capacity of 300. The
first pastor was Rev. A. Queal ; the present pastor is Rev. J. W.
Merwin. The present membership is 130, and the value of the
Church property is $8,000.

Immanuel Church of Otego was organized in 1834 by Rev. J.
Messinger with 10 members. The first pastor was Rev. J.
Hughes. The first house of worship was erected in 1835 ; the
present house in 1866. It will seat seat 250 and cost $2,250.

The present membership is 60, and the value of Church property is $7,000.

The population of the town in 1870 was 2,052, and its area, 26,905 acres, with an assessed value of $421,151.

The number of school districts is 18, employing the same number of teachers. The number of children of school age is 582; the number attending school, 520; the average attendance, 270 ; the value of school houses and sites, $7,050.

OTSEGO was formed as a part of Montgomery County, March 7, 1788, and originally included the greater part of Otsego County. Burlington, Richmond and Unadilla were taken off in 1792, Hartwick in 1802, and Laurens in 1810. It is an interior town, lying upon the west bank of Otsego Lake, north of the center of the County. The surface is a hilly upland, lying between Otsego and Schuyler Lakes, and descending abruptly towards each. The summits are from 300 to 500 feet above the water. The uplands are divided into two ridges by Fly Creek, which flows south through the center. Oak Creek, the outlet of Schuyler Lake, flows south through the west part. The soil is a clay, sandy and gravelly loam.

Cooperstown, (p. v.) beautifully situated at the foot of Otsego Lake, was incorporated April 3, 1807, by the name of *Otsego.* The name was changed to Cooperstown, June 12, 1812. It contains the County buildings, six churches, viz., Presbyterian, Episcopal, Baptist, Methodist, Universalist and Roman Cotholic, three banks, six hotels, two first-class weekly newspapers, a union school, a saw mill, a grist mill, a sash and blind factory, a planing mill, a large number of stores, mechanic shops &c., and about 2,200 inhabitants. The sidewalks are well flagged, the streets are finely shaded with trees and lighted with gas. It is the present terminus of the Cooperstown & Susquehanna Valley Railroad, connecting with the A. & S. R. R. at Junction Station.

Lake Wood Cemetery, though not in this town, is an appendage of Cooperstown and as such may properly be described here. The association under whose control it is, was organized in 1856 with the following Board of Trustees: Samuel Nelson, Levi C. Turner, Frederick A. Lee, Ellery Cory, Theodore Keese, Joshua H. Story, John R. Worthington, Henry J. Bowers and Horace Lathrop, Jr. F. A. Lee was subsequently chosen President; Theodore Keese, Vice-President; Jerome B. Wood, Secre-

---

* *Otsego* was the original name of the Lake, from which the town and County were afterwards named. In the Indian language the place is said to signify a place of *friendly greeting.* At the foot of the lake was a place of general rendezvous for the Indians, and where traders were accustomed to meet them.

tary; Dorr Russell, Treasurer. The Cemetery is located near the
shore of the lake, about half a mile from the village, and contains twenty-four acres, the original cost of which was fifty
dollars an acre. It is tastefully laid out and contains some fine
monuments, among which the most prominent is that of J.
Fenimore Cooper, erected by his literary friends and admirers.
It is of Italian marble, resting on a granite base six feet square.
The shaft, including the base, die and cap, from which it rises,
is about 25 feet in hight and is surmounted by a richly carved
Corinthian capital. The four sides of the die are beautifully
sculptured in bold relief; the front with the name of J. Fenimore Cooper, surrounded by a wreath of palm and oak branches,
the latter with acorns, one falling and another fallen; the north
side with appropriate naval devices, viz., the anchor, oars
crossed, commander's sword and spy glass; the south side with
Indian emblems, such as bow and arrows, and quiver, lance with
scalp-locks attached, tomahawk and necklace of bears' claws.
On the east side are literary emblems, books and manuscript,
with the student's lamp just extinguished, an ink stand, the
pen from which has just been seized and borne aloft by an eagle.
On its capital stands the statuette of Leather Stocking, four
and a half feet high, representing him in the act of loading his
rifle and gazing intently in the direction of the game, while the
dog by his side, looks anxiously into his master's face, waiting
for permission to bound away. The monument stands near the
entrance to the Cemetery, and overlooks the lake, village and
surrounding country. It cost about $3,500.

The Union School of Cooperstown occupies a fine brick
edifice which was erected in 1868–9 at a cost of about $20,000.
The lot upon which it is located contains one and one-seventh
acres. Six teachers are employed and the average attendance
of pupils is about 300. J. G. Wright, A. M., is the principal.

Fly Creek, (p. v.) situated about three miles west of Cooperstown, contains three churches, a hotel, a store, a foundry and
machine shop, a manufactory of horse-powers, three blacksmith
shops, two wagon shops, a shoe shop, two millinery establishments, 67 dwellings and about 325 inhabitants. The Sons of
Temperance and the Good Templars have organizations here,
as well as the Grand Army of the Republic.

The Otsego Agricultural Works, at this place, were started in
1840 as the "Badger Horse-Power Works." In August 1871 Mr.
George H. Gross purchased the Works and changed the name
as indicated above. He manufactures threshers and cleaners,
horse-powers, churns, circular saws and fanning mills. The

works are driven by steam power and give employment to 8 or 10 hands.

The Fly Creek Valley Cheese Factory, about half a mile northeast of the village, has a capacity for making 600 pounds daily. H. E. Taylor is the proprietor.

Oaksville, (p. v.) situated on Oak Creek, about a mile northwest of Fly Creek, contains a hotel, a store, a cotton factory, a blacksmith shop, a saw mill, a grist mill, a carding mill, about 30 dwellings and 200 inhabitants.

The Otsego Iron Works, at Fly Creek, were started in 1812 and have been in successful operation ever since. Mr. Shepard, the present proprietor, became a partner in the business in 1869 and is now the sole proprietor. The works cover an area of two acres.

Toddsville (p. v.) is chiefly in the town of Hartwick.

The Otsego Paper Works at this place are owned by R. & I. Worthington, bankers, of Cooperstown. They were established about seventy years ago, give employment to eighteen hands and have a capacity for making 2,000 pounds of printing paper daily.

Hope Factory, about a mile south of Toddsville, on Oaks Creek, is a hamlet, containing sixteen houses, a cotton mill, a grist mill, a store, a school house and about 100 inhabitants. The grist mill contains four runs of stones, with a capacity for grinding 150 bushels per day.

The Hope Cotton Mills, in the south part of the town, owned by R. Steere, employ about seventy-five hands, make about 2,000 yards of print goods per week, using from 2,500 to 3,000 pounds of raw material.

The Cheese Factory of J. P. Kenney, in the west part of the town, has a capacity for making 600 pounds daily, using the milk of 250 cows.

Otsego Hill Cheese Factory, owned by Mr. Babbit, is about the same size.

Three Mile Point is a point of land jutting into the lake from the west shore, about three miles from Cooperstown. It is a place of resort for pleasure parties during the summer. It was originally the property of Judge Cooper and was willed to his descendants in common until 1850, after which it was to be the sole property of his youngest descendant bearing the name of William Cooper. The hotel of A. W. Thayer, near this place, affords all necessary accommodations.

Wild Rose Point is another place of resort near the one just mentioned.

The settlement of this town was commenced about 1785, though some slight improvements had previously been made and abandoned. In 1786 a permanent settlement was commenced at the village of Cooperstown by William Cooper, who had come into possession of a large tract of land in the vicinity. Among the first settlers were William Jarvis, William Ellison, Israel Guild, John Howard, Elisha Phinney, John Miller, Wm. Abbot and a widow named Johnson. The first framed house was erected on the site of the village, by Mrs. Johnson. Wm. Abbott settled on a farm about half a mile south of the village. Mr. Cooper, accompanied by his wife, arrived in the spring of 1787. They reached the head of the lake in a chaise, and came to the foot of the lake in a canoe. Mrs. Cooper did not remain, and she disliked the passage by boat so much that the chaise was brought down in two canoes. A bridge across the outlet was constructed of logs, and a road had been cut through the forest along the shore of the lake, but it was so difficult to pass, that when the chaise left the settlement, two men with ropes accompanied it to keep it from upsetting. In 1788 a village plat was laid out, including six streets extending in an east and west direction, and three crossing them at right angles. In 1788 Mr. Cooper erected a house on Main Street, opposite the head of Fair Street. It was of two stories, with two wings, and on some old maps is designated as the "Manor House." Here he was accustomed to entertain his visitors in a manner becoming his position. He did not bring his family to reside permanently until 1790. The first store was established in the winter of 1789–90, by Mr. Cooper, Mr. R. R. Smith having it in charge. At this time there were seven framed houses, three framed barns and thirty-five inhabitants in the village. This enumeration is supposed to have been made previous to the arrival of Mr. Cooper's family in October 1790, as that numbered in all, including children and servants, fifteen. The next year the first lawyers arrived and located in the village, one of whom was Abraham Ten Broeck, of New Jersey, and the other, Jacob G. Fonda, of Schenectady. The first physician was named Powers, and Dr. Fuller arrived in June 1791, and remained in practice for nearly fifty years. Dr. Powers was accused of mixing tartar emetic with the drink provided for the guests of a ball at the Red Lion Hotel. He was tried, convicted, put in the stocks and then banished. The first child born in the village was Nathan, son of John Howard, and the first death that of a son of Joseph Griffin, Oct. 11, 1792. The first child born on the Patent was William Cooper Jarvis, of Fly Creek. He was born in 1787 and received fifty acres of land from the proprietor after whom he was named. The first school was taught by Joshua Dewey. William Ellison kept the first inn, in 1786. James Averill was an early settler. In 1792 he exchanged his farm with Mr. Howard for a tannery, and afterwards became identified with that branch of business. Oliver Cary was the second school teacher in the town. In 1795 a plan was started for the erection of an academy, and about $1,500 were subscribed for that purpose. The building was raised September 18, 1795, by one hundred men selected for the purpose and superintended by E. Robbins. It was 65 by 32 feet, and two stories high, the upper story being all in one room. On the 28th of February, 1795, Mr. Elihu Phinney, from Connecticut, arrived in Cooperstown with the materials for printing a newspaper, and on the 3d of April appeared the first number of the *Otsego Herald or Western Advertiser*. It was the second paper in the State, published west of Albany. On the 9th of July of this year, a man named Porteus was flogged at the whipping post for stealing some pieces of ribbon. In 1799 the residence of Judge Cooper, known as 'Otsego Hall,' and subsequently occupied by J. Fenimore Cooper, was completed. For many years this was the finest private residence in the County. A new street has recently been laid out through the grounds.

Some idea of the facilities for traveling at this early day may be formed from the following incident: In 1795, Judge Cooper, with his wife and two children, left Cooperstown in his carriage, drawn by four horses. They dined at Middlefield Center and reached Cherry Valley a little before sunset. Leaving Cherry Valley early the next morning, they reached Canajoharie the same evening, and in two days from this time arrived in Albany, making the journey from Cooperstown in four days.

A post-office was established in this town in 1794 and the mail was received weekly. Joseph Griffin was the first postmaster. The place continued to increase in population, and in 1812 it contained 133 houses, 57 barns and 686 inhabitants. In 1809 a cotton factory was erected on Fly Creek, and manufacturing of various kinds was established in the village and in other parts of the town, causing an increase of population.

As already stated, the first inn was kept by William Ellison, near the outlet. The first one of any note was the "Red Lion," kept by Joseph Griffin. It stood on the corner of Main and Pioneer Streets.

"The second public house of any consequence, was the Blue Anchor, kept by William Cook on the corner diagonally opposite to the Red Lion; this house was in much request for many years among all the genteeler portion of the travelers. Its host was a man of singular humor, great heartiness of character and perfect integrity. He had been the steward of an English East Indiaman and enjoyed an enviable reputation in the village for his skill in mixing punch and flip. On holidays, a stranger would have been apt to mistake him for one of the magnates of the land, as he invariably appeared in a drab coat of the style of 1776 with buttons as large as dollars, breeches, striped stockings, buckles that covered half his foot, and a cocked hat large enough to extinguish him. The landlord of the Blue Anchor was a general favorite, his laugh and his pious oaths having become historical."—*Chronicles of Cooperstown.*

A large number of distinguished men have had their residence in the village of Cooperstown since its settlement. Among these were J. Fenimore Cooper, Gen. John A. Dix, Hon. Samuel Nelson, Hon. E. B. Morehouse, Hon. Schuyler Griffin and many others.

Hon. Elisha Phinney, the publisher of the first newspaper in the County and the proprietor of the first book store, came to Cooperstown in 1795, and continued to conduct the paper which he started until 1813. He was the father of H. & E. Phinney, who succeeded him in business and became extensive publishers as well as booksellers. In 1820 a stereotype foundry was established at which was cast a set of plates for a quarto family bible, from which 200,000 copies were manufactured. The business was carried on in Cooperstown until 1849, when the destruction of their establishment by fire caused their removal to Buffalo, where H. F. & E. Phinney, Jr., were members of the firm of Phinney & Co. Mr. H. F. Phinney was for several years a member of the firm of Ivison & Phinney, of New York City. He is now the largest real estate owner in Cooperstown and one of the most enterprising and public spirited of its citizens.

In 1813 an elephant was exhibited in Cooperstown. It was heralded by the following notice, which is in strong contrast with the flaming show bills and numerous menageries which exhibited in the village during the last season :

"Perhaps the present generation may never have an opportunity of seeing an elephant again, as this is the only one in the United States, and this is, perhaps the last visit to this place."

Cooperstown has suffered at various times from fires. The greatest conflagration was that of April 10, 1862, when about one-third of the business portion of the village was destroyed. On this occasion fifty-seven buildings were destroyed, valued at $48,850 ; the amount of insurance was $16,800. The loss of other property than buildings was estimated at $53,175, which was insured for $3,300. Another fire occurred the same year, destroying property to the amount of $10,000, with an insurance of $4,000.

The first religious society organized in the town was *The Presbyterian Church* of Cooperstown. In July 1795, a camp meeting was held in this vicinity by members of all denominations, and in August of the same year a call was issued for the formation of a Presbyterian Church. Before the society was organized, Rev. Mr. Mosely was employed to preach for six months. The legal society was organized Dec. 29, 1798, but the spiritual organization did not take place until June 16, 1800. Rev. Isaac Lewis was the first settled pastor. The services were held in the academy. The first house of worship was erected in 1807.

The Presbyterian Church, located at Fly Creek, was organized March 20, 1828, with twenty-one members. Rev. Samuel Manning was the first pastor. Their house of worship was erected in 1840 at a cost of $1,600, and capable of seating 200. The present membership is 40; the value of the Church property is $3,000, and the pastor is Rev. C. K. McHarg.

Christ Church (Episcopal) of Cooperstown was organized Jan. 1, 1811, by Rev. Daniel Nash, the first rector. The first services held in this town according to the rites of the Episcopal Church were at the funeral of Miss Hannah Cooper, who was killed by being thrown from a horse on the 10th day of September, 1800. The services were conducted by Rev. Daniel Nash, who was then a missionary in the County, and afterwards known as "Father Nash." Their Church edifice was erected in 1810. It has been enlarged and improved and is still occupied, having a seating capacity of 460. The number of communicants is 175; the present rector is Rev. D. Hillhouse Buel; the value of the Church property is $25,000.

The Methodist Church of Cooperstown was organized about 1816, and a house of worship was erected the next year. Their house of worship will seat 400 and is valued at $8,000. The number of members is 86; the pastor is Rev. H. M. Crydenwise. They have recently erected a parsonage which, with the lot, is worth about $3,000.

The Methodist Church at Fly Creek was organized about 1816 with seven members. Rev. Ralph Lanning was the first pastor. Their house of worship was erected in 1837 and has a capacity to seat 500. The present membership is 110; the value of the Church property is $5,000, and the pastor is Rev. George Parsons.

The First Baptist Church of Cooperstown was organized Jan. 21, 1834, and their house of worship was erected in 1835-6 at a cost of $3,000 and having a capacity to seat 275. The first pastor was Rev. Lewis Raymond. The present membership is 85 ; the pastor is Rev. Charles C. Smith, and the value of the Church property is $9,000.

St. Mary's Roman Catholic Church was organized about 1851, by Rev. Father Gilbride. The first house of worship was erected about 1855 ; the present house in 1867. It cost about $12,000 and will seat 300. The present membership is about 300; the pasor is Rev. M. C. Dewitt, and the value of the Church property is $25,000.

The First Universalist Church, (Christ Church) located at Fly Creek, was organized in 1805 and is the oldest Universalist Church in the State. The Church edifice was erected in 1820 and rebuilt in 1861. It will seat 250 and is valued at $5,000. There is a Parish Library connected with the society. The present membership is 40; the pastor is Rev. C. L. Wait. Services are held at 2 o'clock every Sunday afternoon.

The Second Universalist Church, (Church of the Messiah,) located at Cooperstown, was organized in 1831 by Rev. Jacob Potter, the first pastor. Their house of worship was erected in 1833 and remodeled in 1860. ' It cost $3,000 and will seat 300. The present membership is 40; the pastor is Rev. C. L. Wait, and the value of the Church property is $8,000.

The Thanksgiving Hospital, Cooperstown, was planned in April 1865, as a Thankoffering to Almighty God from the Christian people of Otsego, for the restoration of Peace and the preservation of the Union after the civil war. The necessary fund was raised and a suitable building was purchased and remodeled in 1867. On Thanksgiving day of the same year, the Hospital was solemnly dedicated by religious services. The institution was regularly incorporated in September 1868. The house and lot are valued at $5,000. The house can receive, if necessary, eighteen patients, though especially prepared for fifteen. The number of patients during the year 1871 was 35, many being severe chronic cases, remaining through the year. It is the expectation of the Trustees that a new building with thirty beds will be erected ere long in a favorable position. This institution is entirely free from debt. Many more applications are received than can be accommodated in the present building. The Trustees are E. Phinney, Horace Lathrop, M. D., Mrs. Harriet W. Way, Miss Susan Fenimore Cooper and F. G. Lee. The physicians are Dr. W. F. Bassett and Dr. M. L. Bassett.

The population of the town in 1870 was 4,605, and its area, 32,478 acres, with an assessed value of $884,144.

The number of school districts is 17, employing 22 teachers. The number of children of school age is 1,272; the number attending school is 886; the average attendance, 488; the value of school houses and sites, $26,815.

PITTSFIELD was formed from Burlington, March 24, 1797. New Lisbon was taken off in 1806. It is situated on the west line of the County, near the center. The surface is a hilly upland, terminating in abrupt declivities upon Unadilla River, which forms the west boundary. Wharton Creek flows across the north-west corner, and several small tributaries of Butternut Creek flow through the south part. The soil generally is a slaty and gravelly loam.

Pittsfield, (p. v.) locally known as "Pecktown," in the north part, contains a hotel, a store, a blacksmith shop, a carpenter shop, a saw mill, 14 dwelling houses and about 60 inhabitants.

Hoboken is a hamlet in the north-west part and contains a store, a cotton factory and several dwelling houses.

The first settlements were made in the valley of the Unadilla, about 1793, by Jacob Lull, Aaron Nobles, Hubbard Goodrich and Mathew Bennett. Seth Harrington and Benjamin Eddy settled in the east part of the town soon after the settlements on the Unadilla. The first school was taught by Benjamin Pendleton, at Richfield village. Mathew Bennett kept the first inn, in 1797, and Henry Randall, still residing in the town, the first store, in 1810. Benjamin Atwell built the first mill, and the Arkwright Manufacturing Company the first cotton factory, both of which were on the Unadilla.

The first religious organization in the town was the Baptist, in the south-east part. There are only two Church edifices in town, both union churches; one east of the center, built in 1849, and now occupied by the Methodists, which is the only religious organization in town; and the other in the south-west part, built about 1857.

The population of the town in 1870 was 1,468, and its area, 22,696 acres, with an assessed value of $268,088.

There are 12 school districts, employing 11 teachers. The number of children of school age is 485; the number attending school, 285; the average attendance, 182; the value of school houses and sites, $3,525.

PLAINFIELD was formed from Richfield, March 25, 1799. It is the north-west corner town of the County. The surface is a broken and hilly upland. Unadilla River forms the west boundary and is bordered by steep bluffs, rising to the hight of 400 to 600 feet. The soil is a clayey and sandy loam.

Unadilla Forks, (p. v.) in the west part of the town, at the junction of the east and west branches of the Unadilla, contains two churches, a hotel, a grist mill, a saw mill, a furniture manufactory, a planing mill, a carriage shop, three stores, a bedstead factory, a blacksmith shop, two boot and shoe shops and about 400 inhabitants.

Plainfield Center is a hamlet, containing a church and half a dozen houses.

Spooner's Corners is a post office in the north-east corner of the town.

Leonardsville, (p. v.) on the west border, chiefly in Madison Co., contains a foundry and blacksmith shop in this town.

The first settlement of this town was made at and near Plainfield Center, in 1793, by Ruggles Spooner, Elias Wright and John Kilbourne. Samuel Williams settled on the Unadilla, in the north part, and Benjamin and Abel Clark at the Forks, about the same time. The first school was taught at Spooner's Corners by James Robinson in 1797–8. William Lincoln kept the first inn, at Lloydville, and Luce & Woodward the first store. Caleb Brown built the first mill, in 1805, on the Unadilla.

The Baptist Church at Unadilla Forks was organized June 5, 1817, by a council composed of delegates as follows : from the First Baptist Church of Winfield, Jonathan Palmer, Jr.; from the Church in Edmeston, Elder Stephen Taylor, Nathan Wright, Chauncy Hopkins, Roger Southerland and Stephen W. Taylor; from the Second Church of Winfield, Elder Ebenezer Vining, Ethol Palmer, Jonathan Jones and Ebenezer Thayer ; from the Church in Brookfield, Elders Thomas Dye and Joshua Wells, Eleazer Brown, Luther Hinkley, Nathan Brown, 2d, and Daniel Main ; from the Church in Paris, Daniel Budlong, John Budlong, James Rhodes and John Davis. The number of members at the organization was 17, and the first pastor was Rev. Joshua Wells. Their house of worship was erected about 1830 at a cost of about $1,500 and with a seating capacity of 300. The present pastor is Rev. Jesse Evans; the number of members is 71, and the value of Church property is about $3,000.

The population of the town in 1870 was 1,248, and its area, 17,705 acres, with an assessed value of $268,140.

The number of school districts is 13, employing 11 teachers. The number of children of school age is 402; the number attending school, 298; the average attendance, 177; the value of school houses and sites is $5,045.

RICHFIELD was formed from Otsego, April 10, 1792. Exeter and Plainfield were taken off in 1799. It is the extreme northern town of the County. The surface is rolling and moderately hilly, with a mean elevation of 150 to 200 feet above Schuyler Lake. Nine Hill, on the west side of the head of the lake, rises to a hight of 300 to 400 feet. Schuyler Lake, in the south-east corner, occupies a deep valley and receives several small streams from the north and west. The soil is of a diversified character, consisting of gravel, slate, clay, and sandy loam, well cultivated and productive. Cheese is largely manufactured in the town.

Richfield Springs, (p. v.) in the north-east corner, near the head of Schuyler Lake, is pleasantly situated and contains four churches, viz., Presbyterian, Episcopal, Universalist and Roman Catholic, a newspaper office, a bank, two saw mills, a grist mill, a planing mill, a large number of hotels, stores, mechanic shops &c., and about 1,000 inhabitants. The village derives its name from the celebrated mineral springs, which are noted for their medicinal properties and are visited by a large number of invalids annually. The place is also a resort for summer tourists and is becoming one of the most frequented in the State. A railroad connects it with Utica, and it is proposed to extend it to Cherry Valley.

Monticello, (Richfield p. o.) near the center of the town, contains two churches, two stores, a hotel, a blacksmith shop, a shoe shop, a cheese factory, a saw mill, a cheese box factory, a cider mill, a wagon shop, a dress maker shop, a milliner shop, a seminary and about 200 inhabitants.

The Cheese Factory of H. C. Brockway, at Monticello, turned out about 20,000 pounds during the last season.

Brighton Corners is a hamlet in the north part and contains about 20 houses.

The settlement of the town was commenced before the Revolution, but it was broken up during the war. The first settlers after the war were John Kimball, Richard and William Pray, John Beardsley, Joseph Coats and Seth Allen, who came in about 1787. William Tunicliff, Daniel Hawks, John Hatch, Ebenezer Eaton and Joseph Rockwell, settled near Richfield Springs in 1789 ; and Obadiah Beardsley and Obadiah Beardsley, Jr., settled near Schuyler Lake in 1790.

From "Reminiscences of Otsego," by Hon. Levi Beardsley, we have gathered some interesting incidents connected with the early history of this town. Judge Beardsley was about four years old in 1790, when his grandfather, father and two brothers removed from Hoosick. They started with a cart and one or two wagons drawn by oxen and horses, and drove a few cattle, sheep and hogs. Judge B. and a sister two years old, were stowed away among the furniture, and the mother with a sick infant was left behind. They crossed the Mohawk near Fonda and went to Canajoharie, thence by the old Continental Road towards Springfield. At night they stopped at the house of Conradt Seeber. They were out of bread and could get none at Seeber's or of his neighbors, but were compelled to make a a meal of potatoes. The next day they went three miles with teams, and then left some of the wagons, as the roads were very bad. The Judge says; "My father put a saddle on one of the horses and on another packed a bed and bedding, on which the [servant] girl was to ride. I was placed on the horse behind him, on a pillow tied to the saddle, with a strap under my arms buckled around his waist to prevent me from falling off, and carrying my sister before him we proceeded on our journey, the girl riding the other horse on top of the bed and bedding, and a yearling colt tagging after." They proceeded to the foot of Schuyler's Lake, where they had hired the "Herkimer Farm," on which was a small clearing before the war, and two log huts. After planting corn, Mr. Beardsley returned for his wife, who came on horseback, on a man's saddle, and carried the child, Mr. B. walking beside them. During the summer they cut a road to their own land in Richfield and put up two log huts, a short distance apart, and covered them with poles and bark. The floors were of logs split and hewn, and the chimneys were of sticks and mud.

In 1791 William Tunicliff built a saw mill near Richfield Springs, and the next year a grist mill, near the same place. Judge Peck was the millwright.

It was no uncommon thing for ladies to walk two or three miles for an afternoon visit, returning in time for milking. Married and unmarried ladies were often seen walking with shoes and stockings in their hands, to avoid getting them soiled with mud, and putting them on just before entering the house. Carding and quilting bees were common. Spinning bees were meetings when they brought in the yarn spun from wool previously distributed. Wrestling, running, leaping &c., were the athletic sports indulged in by the men.

The first marriage in the town was that of Ebenezer Russell and Mrs. Moore, a sister of Judge Beardsley's mother. "Judge Cooper of Cooperstown was sent for, being the nearest magistrate, and came eighteen miles principally through the woods, to perform the ceremony. The neighbors were invited, the old pine table was in the middle of the room, on which I recollect was placed a large wooden bowl filled with fried cakes, (nut cakes or doughnuts as the country people call them.)   There might have been something else to constitute the marriage feast, but I do not recollect anything except a black junk bottle filled with rum, some maple sugar and water.   The Judge was in his long riding boots, covered with mud up to his knees; his horse was fed that he might be off when the ceremony was over. The parties presented themselves and were soon made man and wife as his 'Honor' officially announced. He then gave the bride a good hearty kiss, or rather a smack, remarking that he always claimed that as his fee; took a drink of rum, drank health, prosperity and long life to those married, ate a cake or two, declined staying even for supper, said he must be on his way home, and should go to the foot of the lake that night, refused any fee for his services, mounted his horse and was off; and thus was the first marriage celebrated."—*Reminiscences of Otsego.*

The first death was that of this same bride.   The first birth was that of Joseph Beardsley.   The first school house was built of logs and covered with bark, with a floor of logs, split and hewed.   Oiled paper supplied the place of glass, and a large fireplace daubed with mud, and a stick chimney, supplied the heating apparatus when cold weather arrived. The arrangements for recess were novel.   Only one scholar was to go out at a time, and to avoid the inconvenience of asking, a hole was bored in a log in which was placed a peg.   Any scholar was permitted to go quietly out, removing the peg at the same time, and on returning, replace it, when another was allowed the same privilege.

The Presbyterian Church of Richfield Springs, was organized in 1803.   Their house of worship was erected about 1825.   It will seat 250 and cost about $2,500.   The present membership is 50 ; the value of the Church property is about $10,000 ; the pastor is Rev. F. H. Seeley.

The First Universalist Church of Richfield Springs was organized in May 1835 by Rev. Job Potter, the first pastor, with 30 members.   Their first house of worship was erected in 1834; the present house in 1871, with a seating capacity of 300.   The society now numbers 100 members ; the value of Church property is $18,000 ; the pastor is Rev. S. R. Ward.

St. Joseph's Roman Catholic Church was organized in 1851 by Father Gilbride, the first pastor, with 15 members.   The present house of worship was erected in 1870, with a seating capacity of 250.   The membership is about 75 ; the value of the Church property is about $5,000 ; the pastor is Rev. M. O. Devitt.

The population of the town in 1870 was 1,831, and its area, 20,126 acres, with an assessed value of $432,400.

The number of school districts is 12, employing 11 teachers. The number of children of school age is 629; the number attending school, 417; the average attendance, 226; the value of school houses and sites is $9,360.

ROSEBOOM, named in honor of Abram Roseboom, one of the early settlers, was formed from Cherry Valley, Nov. 23, 1854. It lies on the east border of the County, north of the center. The surface is a hilly upland, broken by the valleys of several streams. The hills are generally rounded, and their summits elevated from 300 to 350 feet above the valleys. The soil is a gravelly loam.

Roseboom, (p. v.) in the north-west part, near the Middlefield line, on Cherry Valley Creek, contains two churches, two stores, a hotel, a wagon shop, two blacksmith shops, a grist mill, two saw mills, a cheese factory, a shoe shop, a millinery and dress making shop, a physician, planing mill and 225 inhabitants.

Pleasant Brook, (p. v.) situated west of the center, contains two churches, two stores, a hotel, a blacksmith and wagon shop, and about 200 inhabitants.

South Valley, (p. v.) situated a little south of the center, contains 2 churches, a store, hotel, harness shop, 3 wagon shops, 3 blacksmith shops, a shoe shop, a millinery shop, physician and 150 inhabitants.

South Valley Tannery, Geo. Barrett, prop., about one mile west of South Valley post office, employs five hands, consumes from 125 to 150 cords of hemlock bark, and from 100 to 125 cords of wood per annum, and turns out about 8,000 sides of leather annually. At this point there is also a grist and saw mill, and a rake manufactory.

Websters Corners is on the east border, partly in Schoharie County.

Center Valley is on the north border, partly in Cherry Valley.

The settlements were commenced about 1800. Abraham Roseboom erected the first saw mill, carding and fulling mill, in 1806, at Lodi. Daniel Antisdale kept the first inn and the first store, at the same place, in 1832. The first grist mill was erected by Cornelius Law in 1818.

The First Baptist Church of Cherry Valley, located at Roseboom, was organized about 1843 by Deacon Sherman with 18 members. The first pastor was Rev. Thomas P. Childs. The house of worship, which will seat 800, was erected in 1844 at a cost of $2,000. The present number of members is 28, and the pastor, Rev. Daniel Leach. The present value of Church property is $2,000.

The M. E. Church of Roseboom was organized in 1861 with 40 members. Elder Shank was the first pastor. The house of worship was erected in 1861 at a cost of $1,300, and will seat 300. The present value of Church property is $1,200. The present number of members is 30, and the pastor, Rev. W. B. Thomas.

First M. E. Church, Pleasant Brook. The first house of worship was erected in 1847. The present one, which will seat 200, was erected in 1866 and repaired in 1869. The present value of Church property is $3,000. The present number of members is about 75, and the pastor, Rev. W. B. Thomas.

The population of this town in 1870 was 1,590, and its area, 20,589 acres, with an assessed value of $212,285.

The number of school districts is 13, employing 11 teachers. The number of children of school age is 458; the number attending school, 382; the average attendance, 165; the value of school houses and sites is $3,890.

SPRINGFIELD was formed from Cherry Valley, March 3, 1797. It lies upon the north line of the County, east of the center. The surface is a rolling and moderately hilly upland, the hills generally rising about 200 feet above the valleys. Mount Wellington, east of the head of Otsego Lake, in the south part of the town, is about 400 feet high. Summit Lake, in the north part, lies so near the watershed that in high water it discharges its water both north and south. The streams are small brooks. In the north part is a deep sink, called the "The Chyle," into which a considerable stream of water runs and flows through a subterranean passage for some distance, and again comes to the surface. The sink is tunnel-shaped, about 240 feet in circumference and 15 feet deep. After heavy rains it is sometimes filled with water, which often moves around rapidly while being discharged through the orifice below. The soil is a black and yellow loam, resting upon limestone and slate. Hops are extensively raised in the town.

Springfield Center, (p. v.) situated about a mile from the head of Otsego Lake, contains 2 churches, 3 stores, 2 hotels, a wagon shop, 2 blacksmith shops, a grist mill, millinery shop, telegraph office, cooper shop, harness shop, shoe shop, machine shop, a physician and 225 inhabitants.

East Springfield, (p. v.) in the east part, on East Springfield Creek, contains a church, store, hotel, blacksmith and wagon shop, cabinet shop, shoe shop, millinery shop, a cheese factory,

I

a grist mill, a seminary, a cigar maker, a physician and 200 inhabitants.

Springfield, (p. v.) near the center, contains 2 churches, a store, blacksmith shop, cooper shop and 200 inhabitants.

In the summer of 1779, Col. William Butler was ordered to join the forces of General Clinton, and while at Springfield, assisting to open a wagon road from Canajoharie to the head of the Otsego Lake, for the transportation of boats, David Elerson, whose fame as a scout was widely extended, came near losing his life. He had obtained permission to go about a mile from camp, to a deserted house, and gather some mustard for greens. While engaged in this, he was surprised by about a dozen Indians who were advancing cautiously to capture him. He seized his rifle, which was standing against the house, several tomakawks being hurled at him at the same instant. The enemy cut off his flight to his friends, and in running in an opposite direction, he had to pass over a small clearing, the edge of which was covered with fallen trees, greatly obstructing his passage. Here the Indians discharged their rifles at him, but to no effect. After running for some time, and thinking he had escaped his pursuers, an Indian suddenly appeared before him. He raised his rifle to fire, just as the Indian sprang behind a tree, and a ball from the opposite direction entered his own body, making a severe wound just above the hip. He renewed his flight, and descending a hill into a valley, through which flowed a small stream, he became greatly exhausted. A draught of cool water revived him so that he reached the opposite hill with comparative ease. He had proceeded but a short distance when an Indian appeared in pursuit. A shot from his trusty rifle laid the savage in the dust. Scarcely had he reloaded his gun, when several others appeared in sight. As they gathered around their fallen comrade and began their death yell, Elerson darted off into the forest. Finding a large hollow tree, he crawled into it and heard no more of the Indians. The next morning he crawled out, and finding that it rained, and not knowing what direction to take, returned to his shelter. Here he remained three nights and two days without food. He then came out, cold, stiff and hungry, and directing his course by the sun he came out near Brown's Mills, in Cobleskill, about three miles from his place of concealment and about twenty-five from the place where he was first surprised. Here he fell among friends where he was kindly treated and removed to the Middle Fort, where he remained until his recovery.

The first settlements of this town were made in 1762 by John Kelly, Richard Ferguson and James Young, from Ireland, at

East Springfield; and Gustavus Klumph and Jacob Tygart, at the head of Otsego Lake. Most of these were driven off during the war. Mr. Tygart had two sons, John and Jacob, who were taken prisoners and carried to Canada during the war. Soon after the war, Elisha Dodge, Col. Herrick and Aaron Bigelow, from Connecticut, and Eli Parsons, Eliakim Sheldon and Isaac White, from Massachusetts, settled near the center of the town. Benjamin Rathbone, from Connecticut, settled in the east part in 1788. The first inn was kept by Eli Parsons, at East Springfield, and the first store by Thomas and Stacy Horner. Garrat Staats erected the first grist mill and saw mill, before the war.

The first church organized was the Baptist; Rev. Mr. Fairman was the first preacher.

The Universalist Church, at Springfield Center, was organized, with 15 members, in 1854, by O. Shipman, John Losee, D. Franklin and others. Rev Mr. Sage was the first pastor. The house of worship, which will seat 350, was erected in 1857 at a cost of $3,500. The present number of members is 5.

St. Paul's (Episcopal) *Church*, at East Springfield, was organized, with 25 members, January 25, 1871, by Rev. David L. Schwartz, the first pastor. A church site has been procured, valued at $350, but no house of worship has yet been erected. The present number of members is 25, and the pastor is Rev. E. Folsom Barker.

The population in 1870 was 2,022, and its area is 26,585 acres, with an assessed value of $499,225.

The number of school districts is 15, employing 14 teachers. The number of children of school age is 711; the number attending school, 505; the average attendance, 236; the value of school houses and sites is $5,680.

UNADILLA was formed from Otsego, April 10, 1792. Milford, under the name of *Suffrage*, was taken off in 1796, and Oneonta, under the name of *Otego*, was taken off the same year. A part of Otego was taken off in 1822, and a part of Butternuts in 1857. It lies at the junction of Unadilla and Susquehanna Rivers, in the south-west part of the County. The surface is a rolling and hilly upland, the highest summits being from 400 to 500 feet above the valleys. The principal streams are Unadilla River, which forms the west boundary, Susquehanna River, the east, and Sandy Hill Creek. The soil on the river bottoms is an alluvial loam, and on the uplands a slaty and gravelly loam.

Unadilla, (p. v.) incorporated April 2, 1827, and situated on the Susquehanna River, in the south part of the town, is a station on the Albany & Susquehanna Railroad, and contains four churches, two banks, a newspaper printing office, a union school, four hotels, two wagon shops, a cabinet shop, a saw mill, a grist mill, a paper mill, a spoke factory, a foundry and machine shop, a planing mill, several other manufactories, a large number of stores and about 1,200 inhabitants. The principal street is about a mile and a half in length, bordered by fine shade trees and good flagstone sidewalks.

Wells Bridge, (p. v.) in the south-east corner of the town, is a station on the A. & S. R. R. and contains two stores, a blacksmith shop, a cooper shop, a saloon and about a dozen dwellings. It was formerly called *East Unadilla.*

Unadilla Center, (p o.) in the north part, is a hamlet.

Sandy Hill, situated about a mile and a half from Wells Bridge, contains two churches and about a dozen dwellings.

Settlements were made along the valley of the Susquehanna River, previous to the Revolution, but we have no means of determining the precise date. A conference took place in this town, in 1777, between General Herkimer and Capt. Joseph Brant, which is described elsewhere. Among the early settlers were Daniel Bissel, Abijah Beach and Solomon Martin, at Unadilla; Peter Rogers and men named Bates and Morefield, at Unadilla Center, and Abel DeForest and Willis Buckley, in the east part of the town. Solomon Martin kept the first store, in 1800, and Sampson Conger built the first grist mill.

From the town records, to which we had access through the kindness of the Town Clerk, we have made some extracts. In 1796 the town meeting was held at the house of Daniel Bissell, at which the following officers were elected, viz., David Baits, Supervisor; Guidon Huntington, Town Clerk; Jonathan Spencer, William Hanna and Timothy Birdsall, Assessors; Nathan Tupper, Collector; Enos Yales and William Potter, Overseers of the Poor; David Francis, Enos Yales and Samuel Merriman, Commissioners of Highways; Nathan Tupper and Seth Scott, Constables; David Francis, Solomon Martin and Thomas Wilbur, School Commissioners. The same year we find the following record :

"Voted by majority, that Hogs which shall have on yoaks that are Eight Inches long above the neck, and four below, shall be allowed to run as free commoners."

"A Return of a highway laid out through the Town of Unadilla— Beginning at Abner Griffith's, on the River and running north to the Sand-hill Creek, where the Patent line crosses, then crossing the Creek, thence northerly through lot No. 119, until it runs 25 rods on the lot of Elisha Lathrop, then turning east unto the east line of lot No. 118, thence along said line and the east line of lots No. 117 and 116, thence by a line of marked trees to the north line of the Town. Also a road beginning near Samuel Merriman's house and running along the Patent line to the Indian Creek, then crossing the same, then on said Creek until it comes near Thomas Wilbur to Cranson's Road — Subject to straitning or altering where found necessary.

> "signed. "DAVID FRANCIS ⎫ Com.
> "ENOS YALE ⎬ of
> "SAMUUL MERRIMAN ⎭ Highways."

Among the *ear marks* recorded, is the following:

"Stephen Wilber's Mark. A swallows tail in the left ear with a half penny before it."

In 1797, "Voted That the Town will be at the expense of sending for Esq'r Scramblin or some other Magistrate to Qualify the Town officers."

The number of persons assessed in the town in 1797 was 106, and the town at this time included Butternuts, Oneonta and Otego. The total real and personal estate assessed, amounted to £2,409. The tax was £74 6 shillings. In 1799, Solomon Martin was appointed "Sealer of Weights and Measures," and the town voted to provide him with a standard of weights and measures. The Town Clerk was allowed five dollars for his services during the previous year. In 1800 the town voted to build two pounds, one to stand "not to exceed half a mile from Hubbel's Mill, so called, and the other, within half a mile of Yale's Ferry, so called." A commission was appointed to superintend the erection of the pounds, under the following instructions:

"Voted, That the 2 Pounds shall be built of logs rolled up in form or manner of a House and shall both be completed by the first day of July next, and the expense of both Pounds shall not exceed 30 dollars."

In 1804 the town meeting was held at the school house near Daniel Bissel's. In 1808, "Voted That hogs run free with yokes and rings." As this was not regarded sufficiently definite, the following was adopted:

"Voted, That hogs running on the commons shall be yoaked with yoaks, Eight Inches above the neck, four Inches below the neck and four Inches each side the neck—also that the rings above mentioned shall be put into the hogs noses."

Notwithstanding this "yoaking," the next year they were not allowed to run on the commons, under a penalty of twelve and a half cents for each offense.

The first church organization in the town was *St. Matthew's Episcopal Church*, organized in 1809, with seven members. The first wardens were Josiah Thatcher and Abijah H. Beach. The vestrymen were Israel Hayes, William Smith, Stephen Benton,

Abel Case, Solomon Martin, Curtis Noble, Nijah Cone and Sherman Page. Rev. Russell Wheeler was the first pastor. The first house of worship was commenced in 1810, and consecrated by Rt. Rev. John Henry Hobart, Sept. 11, 1814. The Church edifice was completed by a donation from Trinity Parish in 1813. The same year Goldsbrow Banyar donated a lot of land containing 116 acres, and lying about two miles west of the church. The land was subsequently cleared and became a valuable farm, which was sold in 1865, for $4,500, and in 1866 a parsonage was erected on a lot adjoining the church, costing $7,500. The present house of worship was erected in 1845, and enlarged in 1855, so as to seat 400. The present membership is 90; the pastor is Rev. M. Scofield; the value of the Church property is $15,000.

The Methodist Church at Unadilla has a membership of 100, and a house of worship that will seat 250. The present value of the Church property is $8,000, and the pastor is Rev. W. A. Wadsworth.

The Methodist Church at Unadilla Center was organized in 1830, and a house of worship was erected the same year at a cost of $500, and capable of seating 300. The present membership is 30; the pastor is Rev. W. A. Wadsworth, and the value of the Church property is $2,000.

The Presbyterian Church was organized in 1843, and their house of worship erected the next year. It will seat 300 and is valued at $3,000. The present membership is 75, and the pastor is Rev. Mr. Robinson.

The population of the town in 1870 was 2,555, and its area, 27,982 acres, with an assessed value of $444,500.

There are 19 school districts, employing 15 teachers. The number of children of school age is 797; the number attending school, 642; the average attendance, 319; the value of school houses and sites is $6,276.

WESTFORD was formed from Worcester, March 25, 1808. It is an interior town, lying south-east of the center of the County. The surface is hilly; the highest summits are from 400 to 500 feet above the valleys. It is drained south by Elk Creek, and west by tributaries of Cherry Valley Creek. The soil is a sandy loam of good quality.

Westford, (p. v.) situated on Elk Creek, near the center of the town, contains four churches, a hotel, two stores, a grocery, a grist mill, two blacksmith shops, two shoe shops, a wagon shop and about 200 inhabitants.

Westville, (p. v.) on the west line of the town, partly in Middlefield, contains 2 churches, viz., Methodist and Baptist; 2 stores, 2 hotels, a blacksmith shop, a pump factory, a wagon shop and about 150 inhabitants.

The first settlements were made about 1790, by Thomas Sawyer, Benjamin Chase, Oliver Salisbury, Alpheus Earl and father, Artemas, Moses and David Howe, and Ephraim Smith, all from Vermont. They settled in the south-east part of the town. Among the other early settlers were Luther Seaver and Samuel Babcock, from Massachusetts, about 1793. The first child born in the town was William Chase. Nathaniel Griggs kept the first inn, at Westford village, in 1795; and David Smith kept the first store about the same time. Captain Artemas Howe built the first grist mill, in 1794, and also the first saw mill.

The Congregational Church of Westford was organized in 1800 by J. Bushnell with eight members. The first pastor was Rev. G. Colton. The first house of worship was erected in 1809, and repaired in 1852, and has a seating capacity of 500. The present membership is 63, and the value of the Church property is $5,000.

The Baptist Church of Westville was organized in 1830 with 44 members. The first pastor was Rev. Benj. Sawin. The first house of worship was erected in 1829. The present house in 1871, with a seating capacity of 350. The present membership is 103. The value of Church property is $5,500. The pastor is Rev. James B. Grant.

The Methodist Church, located at Westville, was organized in 1851 by David Elliot, the first pastor. Their house of worship was erected the same year at a cost of $1,200 and with a seating capacity of about 400. It was repaired in 1870 and is valued at $5,500. The present membership is about 100, and the pastor is Rev. A. W. Thompson.

The Methodist Church of Westford was organized at a very early day, but we have no data to determine particulars. The present house of worship was erected in 1862 at a cost of about $2,500 and capable of seating 300. The present membership is 140; the pastor is Rev. John Pilkinton, and the value of the Church property is $5,000. A flourishing Sunday School is connected with the Church.

St. Timothy's Church of Westford was organized in 1838 by Rev. Timothy Minor, the first pastor. A house of worship was erected in 1840 and repaired in 1867, with a seating capacity of

200.   The number of members at its organization was 20; the present membership is 16.   The value of the Church property is $2,500.   The pastor is Rev. Edward Goddard.

The Baptist Church of Westford was organized in 1825 by Rev. Elijah Spafford, the first pastor, with 16 members.   The first house of worship was erected in 1835; the present house in 1860 at a cost of $1,000 and with a seating capacity of 300. The present membership is 50, and the value of Church property is $3,000.

The population of the town in 1870 was 1,300, and its area, 20,857 acres, with an assessed value of $259,300.

The number of school districts is 11, employing the same number of teachers.   The number of children of school age is 360; the number attending school, 300; the average attendance, 150; the value of school houses and sites is $3,620.

WORCESTER was formed from Cherry Valley, March 3, 1797.   Decatur, Maryland and Westford were taken off in 1808.   It is the south-east corner town of the County.   The surface is a hilly and broken upland.   The highlands, which occupy the south part of the town, descend towards the north by an abrupt declivity 350 to 400 feet high.   This declivity forms a continuous ridge, extending north-east and south-west through near the center of the town.   The principal streams are Charlotte River and its tributaries, and Schenevus Creek. The soil is a sandy loam.

Worcester, (p. v.) in the east part of the town, is a station on the Albany & Susquehanna Railroad, and contains three churches, viz., Methodist, Congregationalist and Baptist; a hotel, six stores, two milliner shops, two wagon shops, three blacksmith shops, a saloon, saw mill, a planing mill, a public school and 71 dwellings, with a population of 323.

East Worcester, (p. v.) in the north-east part of the town, is a station on the A. & S. R. R. and contains two churches, viz., Methodist and Baptist; a hotel, five stores, three blacksmith shops, two boot and shoe shops, a wagon and sleigh shop, four undertaking establishments, three milliner shops, a harness shop, a grist mill, a planing mill, a saw mill, a tailor shop, 85 dwellings and 393 inhabitants.

The East Worcester Woolen Mill, located a short distance north of the village, was erected about 1836.   The building is of wood, 30 by 60 feet, and two stories high besides the basement.   It gives employment to six or eight hands.

The East Worcester Rural Cemetery is located in the north part of the village and contains three acres laid out into 165 lots. It is a private enterprise and is owned by John M. Stever. It was laid out and opened in the spring of 1871, and compares favorably with other cemeteries in the County.

South Worcester, (p. v.) in the south part of the town, on Charlotte River, contains two churches, viz., Methodist and Lutheran; a bank, a hotel, two stores, a harness shop, a blacksmith shop, a wagon shop, a grist mill, a saw mill, 24 dwellings and 109 inhabitants.

Maple Grove Cemetery, located a little north of the village of Worcester, was organized June 7, 1865. It is well laid out and contains six acres. John Cook is the President, and W. H. Leonard the Secretary and Treasurer of the Association.

Tuscelan is about a mile west of the village of Worcester, and contains a grist mill, a saw mill and about a dozen dwellings.

The first settlements were made about 1788 and 1790, on Schenevus Creek. Among the early settlers were Silas Crippen and Henry Stever, from Columbia County; Solomon Hartwell, Uriah Bigelow and Nathaniel Todd, from Massachusetts; and Charles Wilder and Joseph Tainter, from Vermont. Philip Crippen, son of Silas Crippen, was the first child born in the town. The first school was taught by Joseph Tainter in 1798. Isaac Puffer kept the first inn, in 1793, and Aaron Kinney, the first store, in 1798. Silas Crippen built the first grist mill, in 1790, and the first saw mill about the same time. The first clothing and carding works was erected by Rufus Draper. Mr. Samuel Jaycox is the oldest man in this town, being 100 years old on the 24th day of December, 1871. He is a native of Dutchess County and has lived in this town about forty years. He remembers some of the scenes of the Revolution.

The Methodist Church of East Worcester was organized in 1836 by Rev. A. E. Daniels, the first pastor. The first house of worship was erected in 1838. It was repaired in 1866 and is capable of seating 350. The present membership is about 100; the value of the Church property is $5,000; the pastor is Rev. H. V. Talbot.

The Methodist Church of Worcester was organized in 1836 by Rev. A. E. Daniels. The first pastors were Revs. A. E. Daniels and Martin Marvin. The first house of worship was erected in 1840; the present house, in 1871, at a cost of $3,500 and with a seating capacity of 300. The number of members is about 40, and the pastor is Rev. H. V. Talbot.

The Methodist Church of South Worcester was organized by Rev. C. W. Lyon, with 26 members. Their house of worship was erected in 1868; it cost $2,500 and will seat 250. The present membership is 53; the value of the Church property is $3,000; the pastor is Rev. W. S. Winans.

The Congregational Church of Worcester erected a house of worship in 1822; it will seat 500 and is valued at $5,000. The present membership is 76; the pastor is Rev. J. Hallock Brown.

The Lutheran Church of South Worcester was organized in 1832 by Rev. J. Silmsen, the first pastor, with 30 members. The first house of worship was erected in 1839; the present house in 1867, at a cost of $2,000 and with a seating capacity of 400. The present membership is 136; the pastor is Rev. S. Bruce, and the value of the Church property is $3,500.

The Baptist Church of Worcester was organized March 30, 1841, by Rev. D. B. Collins, William Cork and others, with 39 members. Their house of worship was erected in 1841; it will seat 400 and its present value is $3,000. The present membership is 125; the pastor is Rev. H. Brotherton.

The population of the town in 1870 was 2,327, and its area, 28,364 acres, with an assessed value of $412,739.

There are 19 schools districts, employing 16 teachers. The number of children of school age is 791; the number attending school, 610; the average attendance, 349; the value of school houses and sites is $10,035.

OTSEGO COUNTY
BUSINESS DIRECTORY.

EXPLANATIONS TO DIRECTORY.

Directory is arranged as follows: 1. Name of individual or firm. 2. Post office address in parenthesis. 3. Business or occupation.

A Star (*) placed before a name, indicates an advertiser in this work. For such advertisement see Index.

Figures placed after the occupation of *farmers*, indicate the number of acres of land owned or leased by the parties.

Names set in CAPITALS indicate subscribers to this work.

The word *Street* is implied as regards directory for the villages.

For additions and corrections see Errata, following the Introduction.

BURLINGTON.
(Post Office Addresses in Parentheses.)

Ackerman, G. M., (Burlington,) cheese maker and painter.

ADAMS, BARNEY, (Burlington,) dairyman and farmer 90.

Ainslie, Wm., (Burlington,) farmer 131.

Alger, Margaret, (Hartwick,) farmer 60.

Arnold, Chas., (Burlington Flats,) dairyman and farmer 70.

ARNOLD, E. D., (Burlington Flats,) dairyman and farmer 76.

Arnold, E. Darwin, (Burlington Flats,) (*with Henry*,) farmer 76.

Arnold, Henry, (Burlington Flats,) (*with E. Darwin*,) farmer 76.

Arnold, H. B., (Burlington,) physician.

Arnold, H. P., (Burlington Flats,) watch maker and farmer 92.

Arnold, Welcome, (Burlington Flats,) farmer 70.

Austin, Jessie P., (West Burlington,) resident.

AUSTIN, SAMUEL J., (West Burlington,) egg dealer, hop raiser and farmer 127.

Aylsworth, Lyman, (Garrattsville,) farmer 100.

Bailey, Albert, (Burlington,) farmer leases of Edward Phillips, 130.

BAILEY, S. P., (West Burlington,) cooper.

BAKER, BENJAMIN, (Burlington,) farmer 40.

Balcom, Amasa N., (Hartwick,) hop raiser, dairyman and farmer 91.

Barber, Alanson, (Burlington Flats,) carpenter and farmer 41.

Baulch, Henry, (Burlington,) farmer 80.

Benjamin, Park, (Burlington Flats,) farmer 61.

Bennett, Alva, (West Burlington,) farmer 46.

Bilyea, Jefferson, (Hartwick,) farmer 33.

Bingham, O. H., (West Burlington,) wagon maker and blacksmith.

Bishop, Irving P., (Burlington Flats,) cheese maker and teacher.

Bishop, John, (Burlington Flats,) book agent, raiser of sage and farmer 50.

Boardman, Garus, (Burlington Flats,) farmer 27.

Bolton, Amos H., (Burlington,) butcher and farmer 149.

Bolton, A. P., (Burlington,) farmer leases of A. S., 90.

Bolton, A. S., (Burlington,) overseer of the poor, hop raiser and farmer 200.

Bolton, Chas. S., (Burlington,) (*with A. S.,*) farmer.

BOLTON, DANFORTH D., (Burlington,) dairyman and farmer 80.

Bolton, L. D., (Burlington,) farmer leases of A. S., 80.

Bolton, Morris, (Burlington,) dairyman and farmer 180.

Bolton, N. D., (Burlington,) hop raiser, dairyman and farmer 180.

Bolton, P., (Burlington,) farmer 50.

Bolton, R. E., (Burlington,) hop raiser and farmer 221.

BOWDISH, GEORGE N., (Garrattsville,) dairyman and farmer 118.

Brady, Anthony, (Burlington,) dairyman and farmer 96.

Brady, Anthony, (Burlington,) dairyman and farmer 82.

Brady, John, (Burlington,) farmer 60.

Brainerd, Jonathan, (Burlington Flats,) dairyman and farmer 132½.

BRAINERD, JUSTUS, (Burlington Flats,) (*with Jonathan,*) farmer.

Brainerd, Peter, (Burlington Flats,) dairyman and farmer 92.

Breese, H. L., (West Burlington,) general merchant.

Briggs, Caleb, (Burlington Flats,) farmer leases of Hart Mellis, 94.

Briggs, Lyman, (Garrattsville,) farmer.

BRIGGS, MELVIN D., (Burlington Flats,) hop raiser and farmer 36.

Bristoll, Chas., (Burlington,) farmer.

Bristoll, Ruth Ann, (Burlington,) farmer 150.

Brooks, Mrs. & Daughter, (Burlington Flats,) milliners and dress makers.

Buel, Henry, (Burlington,) hop raiser and farmer 42.

Burdick, Augustus, (Burlington Flats,) farmer 100.

BURDICK, CHARLES, (Burlington Flats,) dairyman and farmer 280.

Burdick, L. C., (Burlington Flats,) dairyman and farmer 61.

BURLINGTON FLATS HOTEL, (Burlington Flats,) Clark M. Huestis, prop.

BURLINGTON GREEN HOTEL, (Burlington,) M. W. Denmark, prop.

Burrett, Henry, (Burlington,) (*with Wm.,*) farmer.

Burrett, Wm., (Burlington,) dairyman and farmer 140.

Cane, John, (Hartwick,) hop raiser, dairyman and farmer 100.

Case, Bogardus, (West Burlington,) hop raiser and farmer 57½.

Case, Henry H., (West Burlington,) musician and farmer.

Caulkins, Nelson, (Burlington Flats,) hop raiser, dairyman and farmer 173.

CHAPIN, I. C., (Burlington Flats,) justice of the peace, shingle manuf., prop. of cheese box factory, saw and cider mill and farmer 30.

CHAPIN, J. H., (Burlington Flats,) farmer 50.

CHAPMAN, WM., (Burlington Flats,) dairyman and farmer 100.

CHASE, ALONZO W., (Burlington Flats,) dairyman and farmer 153.

Chase, Benjamin, Jr., (Burlington Flats,) dairyman and farmer 120.

Chase, Willet, (Garrattsville,) commissioner of highways and farmer 138.

Chisholm, George, (West Burlington,) dairyman and farmer 160.

Chisholm, R. D., (West Burlington,) farmer.

Church, Wm. Rev., (Burlington Flats,) clergyman and farmer 35.

Clark, Caleb, (Burlington,) commissioner of highways, hop raiser, dairyman and farmer 300.

Coleman, Alvin, (Garrattsville,) retired farmer 22.

Colgrove, Uri, (West Burlington,) dairyman and farmer 118.

Cook, H. S., (West Burlington,) farmer leases of A. A. Matteson, 157.

Cook, Pitman, (West Burlington,) house painter and farmer 35.

Coon, James, (Burlington,) shoemaker and farmer 3.

Cornell, Daniel, (West Burlington,) dairyman and farmer 275.

Cornell, Peleg, (West Burlington,) dairyman and farmer 110.

Cronk, Wallace, (Burlington Flats,) farmer 70.

Cronk, Wm., (West Burlington,) farmer 15.

Curry, Thomas, (Burlington,) hop raiser, dairyman and farmer 100.

CUSHMAN, DELOS, (Burlington,) hop raiser, dairyman and farmer 130.

Cushman, J. C., (Burlington,) dairyman and farmer 128.

Cushman, Orsemus, (Burlington,) carpenter.

Cutler, I. W., (Burlington Flats,) grist and saw mills.

Cutter, David, (Burlington Flats,) dairyman and farmer 112.

Dauchey, Daniel, (Burlington Flats,) farmer 110.

Day, Ira, (Burlington Flats,) town assessor, dairyman and farmer 127¼.

Day, Martha Mrs., (Burlington Flats,) milliner and dress maker.

DELONG, GEO. N., (Garrattsville,) (*with Orange,*) farmer.

Delong, Orange, (Garrattsville,) dairyman and farmer 140.

DENMARK, MARTIN W., (Burlington,) prop. of Burlington Green Hotel.

Dignan, David, (Burlington Flats,) hop raiser, dairyman and farmer 197.

Donaldson, John C., (Burlington,) farmer.

DONALDSON, WM. JR., (Burlington,) dairyman and farmer leases of H. Bush, 130.

DORAN, J. & D., (Burlington,) blacksmiths.

Dorsey, Daniel H. Jr., (Burlington Flats,) farmer 23.

Downing, Charles I., (Burlington Flats,) farmer 5.

Dye, David, (West Exeter,) farmer 90.

Dyer, H. L., (Burlington Flats,) rake manuf.

Dyer, Isaac, (West Burlington,) dairyman and farmer 250.

Dyer, Ziba, (Burlington Flats,) blacksmith and farmer 6.

Evans, Henry, (Burlington Flats,) farmer 70.

FAY, RUSSELL, (Burlington,) hop grower and farmer 215.

Fenton, George, (Burlington Flats,) dairyman and farmer 105.

FENTON, MILES A., (Burlington Flats,) dairyman and farmer 80.

Ferris, Jesse, (West Burlington,) retired farmer.

Ferris, Norman,(West Burlington,) farmer.

Firman, S. C., (Burlington Flats,) general merchant.

Fisk, David, (Burlington,) miller, mechanic and justice of the peace.

Fisk, W. C., (Burlington Flats,) local preacher.

Fitch, Jerome, (Burlington Flats,) prop. of brick yard, dairyman and farmer 120.

Fitch, Joseph, (Burlington Flats,) dairyman and farmer 168.

Fitch, O. H., (West Burlington,) harness maker.

Flinn, Patrick, (Burlington,) farmer 160.

Frater, John, (Burlington,) hop raiser, dairyman and farmer 130.

Freeman, Robert, (Garrattsville,) *(with Joel Porter,)* dairyman and farmer 112.

Gardner, Clark, (West Burlington,) retired farmer.

Gardner, David, (West Burlington,) saw mill, dairyman and farmer 390.

Gardner, Edward, (West Burlington,) dairyman and farmer 240.

Gardner, Orange, (West Burlington,) dairyman and farmer 270.

Gifford, D. M., (West Burlington,) carpenter.

Gorham, G. S., (Burlington,) lawyer and farmer 20.

Gnage, Henry, (West Burlington,) farmer 35.

Hall, E. W., (Burlington,) deputy sheriff, supervisor, hop raiser, dairyman and farmer 170.

Hall, James H., (Burlington,) *(Hall & Rutherford.)*

Hall, John, (Burlington,) hop raiser, dairyman and farmer 83.

HALL, MARK, (Burlington,) dairyman and farmer 163.

HALL, ROSWELL S., (Burlington,) farmer.

Hall & Rutherford, (Burlington,) *(James H. Hall and T. A. Rutherford,)* merchants.

Hall, Wm., (Hartwick,) hop raiser, dairyman and farmer 115.

HAND, AMOS H.,(Burlington,) egg dealer, dairyman and farmer 200.

HARRINGTON, ANDREW, (Burlington Flats,) dairyman and farmer 90.

Harrington, David, (West Burlington,) dairyman and farmer 171.

HARRINGTON, HULBERT, (Burlington,) farmer.

Harrington, John W., (Burlington Flats,) hop raiser, dairyman and farmer 100.

HARRINGTON, LEWIS, (Garrattsville,) *(with Lodewick,)* farmer.

HARRINGTON, LODEWICK, (Garrattsville,) farmer 64.

HAWKINS, SILAS K., (Burlington Flats,) *(V. R. Hawkins & Son.)*

HAWKINS, V. R. & SON, (Burlington Flats,) *(Silas K.,)* millwrights, manufs. of water wheels and farmers 20.

Higbee, John, (Burlington Flats,) farmer 32.

HIGGINS, SELDEN, (Burlington Flats,) farmer 77.

Hills, E. D., (Burlington Flats,) physician and surgeon.

Hitchcock, Morell, (Burlington,) prop. of hotel.

HOLCOMB, ASA F., (Burlington Flats,) shoe maker and farmer 12.

Holdridge, Artemus, (West Burlington,) patentee of rectangular cheese and curb, dairyman and farmer 300.

Holdridge, George, (West Burlington,) farmer 65.

Holdridge, Henry M., (West Burlington,) dairyman and farmer 96.

Holdridge, John A., (West Burlington,) dairyman and farmer 72.

Holdridge, Wm. M., (West Burlington,) farmer 55.

HOLLISTER, WM. H., (Burlington Flats,) dairyman and farmer 125.

HOLLOWAY, H. P., (Burlington Flats,) dairyman and farmer 44.

Hood, David, (Burlington,) farmer 123.

Horan, Daniel, (Burlington Flats,) farmer 100.

HOUSE, JAMES, (Burlington,) hop raiser, dairyman and farmer 115.

HUBBARD, LANGFORD T., (Burlington Flats,) farmer 76¾.

HUBBELL, I. C.,(Burlington Flats,) notary public and retired merchant.

Hubbell, L. F., (Burlington Flats,) dairyman and farmer 52.

HUESTIS, CLARK M., (Burlington Flats,) prop. of Burlington Flats Hotel, constable and farmer 24½.

Huestis, Giles, (Burlington Flats,) shoe maker.

Huestis, L. J. Mrs., (Burlington Flats,) farmer 40.

Hume, Robert, (West Burlington,) dairyman and farmer 100.

Irving, ——, (Burlington Flats,) town clerk.

Jacobs, Harvey, (West Burlington,) hotel keeper.

Jenks, Daniel, (Hartwick,) carpenter and farmer 13.

JENKS, HAWKINS, 2ND., (Burlington,) carpenter and joiner, and farmer 13.

Jenks, Peter, (Hartwick,) hop raiser, dairyman and farmer 100.

Jennings, David F., (West Burlington,) farmer 100.

JOHNSON, C. M., (West Burlington,) prop. of cheese factory.

Johnson, Elisha, (Burlington Flats,) farmer 90.

Johnson, Eri, (Burlington Flats,) dairyman and farmer 100.

Johnson, Ira, (Burlington Flats,) dairyman and farmer 120.

JOHNSON, L. D., (Burlington Flats,) commissioner of highways, cheese manuf. and farmer 235.

JOSLIN, NATHAN, (Burlington,) prop. of saw and cider mills, shingle maker, manuf of coffins and farmer 80.

Kellogg, Wm. H., (Burlington Flats,) shoemaker.

Klock, Lorenzo, (West Burlington,) hop raiser, dairyman and farmer 100.

KRILL, HIRAM, (Burlington Flats,) (*with Loren,*) farmer 180.

KRILL, LOREN F., (Burlington Flats,) (*with Hiram,*) farmer 180.

Ladd, Cyrus, (Garrattsville,) carpenter and blacksmith.

Ladd, Sylvenus, (Burlington,) carpenter.

LE VALLEY. LEVI, (Burlington Flats,) prop. of cheese factory.

Light, Dana, (Burlington Flats,) farmer 55.

Light, Devillo, (Burlington Flats,) farmer leases of Isaac, 113.

Light, Henry, (Burlington Flats,) farmer 53.

Light, Isaac, (Burlington Flats,) farmer 100.

Lines, Ferdinand, (West Burlington,) farmer.

Lines, Rufus, (West Burlington,) farmer 77.

Lines, Wm., (West Burlington,) town assessor and farmer leases of Roswell Kelsey, 200.

Loomis, Sydney, (Burlington.) (*with Henry L. Pierce,*) hop raiser, dairyman and farmer.

Low, Thomas, (Burlington,) farmer leases of Wm. Hall, 100.

Luce, Stephen, (Burlington Flats,) saw mill and farmer 20.

LYMES, D. F., (West Burlington,) farmer.

Mack, J. J., (Burlington Flats,) general merchant.

Main, Albert, (Burlington Flats,) dairyman and farmer leases 134.

Main, Madison, (Burlington Flats,) dairyman and farmer 134.

Marcey, Abraham, (Burlington Flats,) hop raiser, dairyman and farmer 125.

MARCY, NEWTON A., (Burlington Flats,) postmaster, general merchant and produce dealer.

Marian, Asahel, (Garrattsville,) farmer 50.

Mather, A. A., (Garrattsville,) breeder of Leicester sheep, dairyman and farmer 140.

MATHER, CHARLES C., (Burlington,) farmer 110.

Mather, Dan, (Garrattsville,) dairyman and farmer 78.

Mather, E. C., (Garrattsville,) dairyman and farmer 137.

Mather, Francis, (Hartwick,) saw mill and farmer 102.

Matterson, Harrison, (Burlington Flats,) farmer 224.

Matteson, A. Alonzo, (West Burlington,) farmer 8.

Maxson, C. A. Mrs., (Burlington Flats,) resident.

MAYNE, ALVA, (Burlington Flats,) dealer in eggs and poultry.

Mayne, Estelle Mrs., (Burlington Flats,) milliner and dressmaker.

Meacham, J. H., (Burlington,) farmer 100.

MEEKER, HIRAM G. Rev., (Burlington Flats,) minister, manuf. of wagons and sleighs, and farmer 10.

MEEKER, PHILO, (Burlington Flats,) mason and farmer 10.

Merville, Lora, (Burlington Flats,) farmer leases of Nathan W., 71½.

MILBERT, BERNARD, (Burlington Flats,) farmer 50.

Millis, Hart, (Burlington Flats,) farmer 23.

Millis, Wm., (Burlington Flats,) farmer 108.

Morey, Stephen V., (Garrattsville,) hop raiser and farmer 65.

Munroe, Wm. R., (Burlington,) farmer 80 and (*with John Prentice,*) 94.

Munson, Charles T., (Burlington Flats,) teacher and farmer 88.

Munson, George, (Burlington Flats,) farmer 80.

MYERS, M. L.,(Burlington,)town assessor, drover, hop raiser, dairyman and farmer 85.

Nearing, John, (Garrattsville,) farmer 100.

Norton, Chancey, (Burlington Flats,) (*with John,*) farmer 70.

Norton, John, (Burlington Flats,) (*with Chancey,*) farmer 70.

NORTON, WM., (Burlington Flats,) carpenter.

OLIVER, JAMES, (Burlington,) dairyman and farmer 257.

Ousterhout, Henry, (Burlington,) hop raiser, dairyman and farmer 110.

PALMER, ELIJAH, (Burlington,) farmer 127.

PALMER, WM. G., (Burlington Flats,) blacksmith and horse shoer.

Park, Avery, (Burlington,) farmer 200.

Park, Daniel A., (Burlington,) cheese manuf. and prop. of grist mill.

Parker, David, (West Burlington,) dairyman and farmer 330.

Parker, Harry, (Burlington,) farmer 100.

Parker, Henry, (Burlington Flats,)(*with Merrill,*) farmer 102.

Parker, Merrill, (Burlington Flats,) (*with Henry,*) farmer 102.

Pashley Brothers, (Garrattsville,) farmer 250

PASHLEY, ROBERT, (Burlington,) farmer 150.

PASHLEY, WM., (Burlington,) prop. of threshing machine and farmer 50.

PAYNE, JOHN, (Burlington,) farmer.

Perkins, Wm., (Burlington Flats,) dairyman and farmer 100.

Perry, Polly, (Burlington,) farmer 9.

Phillips, Edward, (Burlington,) farmer 126.

Pierce, Henry L., (Burlington,) (*with Sidney Loomis,*) hop raiser, dairyman and farmer.

Pierson, Delos, (West Burlington,) mason.

PIERSON, GEO. W., (Burlington Flats,) dairyman and farmer 96.

Pope, Stephen I., (West Burlington,) willow raiser and farmer 83.

Porter, Joel, (Garrattsville,) (*with Robert Freeman,*) dairyman and farmer 112.

Potter, Alfred, (Hartwick,) farmer 50.

Potter, James, (West Burlington,) general merchant.

Potter, Wm., (Hartwick,) farmer 75.

Powers, Patrick, (Burlington,) farmer 77½.

PRATT, HENRY, (Burlington,) prop. of saw mill, hop raiser, dairyman and farmer 400.

Pratt, Henry O., (Burlington,) hop raiser, dairyman and farmer 139.

Pratt, Ruel, (Hartwick,) farmer 174.

Pratt, Thomas, (Hartwick,) hop raiser and farmer 67.

Prentice, John, (Burlington,) (*with Wm. R. Munroe,*) farmer 94.

RATHBUN, I. P., (Burlington Flats,) farmer 54.

Rea, Wm., (Burlington,) blacksmith.

Reed, Calvin, (Garrattsville,) dairyman and farmer 125.

Reed, I. E., (Garrattsville,) dairyman and farmer 140.

Reynolds, Stephen, (Hartwick,) brick maker, hop raiser, dairyman and farmer 100.

Rice, John J., (West Burlington,) hop raiser, dairyman and farmer 235.

Ritter, Daniel B., (Burlington,) school teacher and (*with G. C.,*) farmer 146.

Ritter, G. C., (Burlington,) justice of the peace and (*with Daniel B.,*) farmer 146.

Robbinson, F. H.,(Burlington Flats,) traveling agent.

ROBINSON, J. M., (West Burlington,) justice of the peace, hop raiser, dairyman and farmer 161.

Rose, Alexander S., (West Exeter,) hop raiser, dairyman and farmer 126.

ROSE, JOSHUA J., (Burlington Flats,) hop raiser, dairyman and farmer leases of G. Munson, 80.

Rutherford, James, (Burlington,) farmer leases of L. B. Loomis, 135.

Rutherford, John, (Burlington,) farmer 275.

Rutherford, T. A., (Burlington,) (*Hall & Rutherford,*) post master.

SAUNDERS, ERASTUS H. REV., (West Burlington,) clergyman.

SHAUL, STEPHEN, (Burlington Flats,) dairyman and farmer 233.

Sheils, Patrick,(Burlington Flats,) hop raiser, dairyman and farmer 100.

Shield, Patrick, (Burlington Flats,) farmer 100.

Shipman, Burt, (Burlington Flats,) saw mill.

SILL, ABEL, (Burlington,) stock raiser, dairyman and farmer 140.

SILL, G. W., (Hartwick,) hop raiser, dairyman and farmer 170.

Simmons, George, (West Burlington,) mason.

Simmons, Myron, (Burlington Flats,) farmer 12.

Sits, Abram, (Burlington,) hop raiser and farmer 40.

Sloan, Joshua G., (Hartwick,) hop raiser, dairyman and farmer 209.

Smart, James, (Burlington,) (*with Thomas,*) hop grower, dairyman and farmer 127.

Smart, Thomas, (Burlington,)(*with James,*) hop grower, dairyman and farmer 127.

Smith, John, (Burlington Flats,) farmer 53.

Spencer, Ambrose, (West Burlington,) farmer.

SPRAGUE, CHARLES P., (Burlington,) farmer 70.

Sprague, W., (Burlington Flats,) farmer 90.

Stanhouse, George, (Burlington,) carpenter and farmer 140.

STEELMAN, HENRY,(Burlington,) pastor of First Baptist Church.

Summers, David E., (West Burlington,) hop raiser, dairyman and farmer 118.

Sweet, Timothy, (Burlington Flats,) wagon maker and farmer 11.

Talbot, Albert, (Burlington Flats,) farmer 100.

Talbot, Daniel, (Hartwick,) dairyman and farmer 100.

Talbot, Edwin, (Burlington Flats,) cooper and farmer 100.

Taylor, John B., (West Burlington,) wool manuf.

Teft, Samuel, (Burlington,) dairyman and farmer 110.

Telfer, James, (Burlington,) farmer 320 and leases 40.

Telfer, John, (Burlington,) farmer 94.

Telfer, Robert, (Burlington,) farmer.

Telfer, Samuel T., (Burlington,) farmer.

Telfer, Thomas. (Burlington,) farmer 105.

Telfer, Wm., (Burlington,) dairyman and farmer leases of J. Neff, 217.

Telfer, Wm. (Burlington,) farmer 222.

Telfer, Wm. J., (Burlington,) farmer leases of James, 140.

TELFOR, WALTER, (Burlington,) farmer.

THOMPSON, ELIHU, (Burlington Flats,) shoe maker.

THOMPSON, ELLIS C.,(Burlington Flats,) tanner and currier.

Thompson, Milo J., (Burlington Flats,) farmer leases 160.

Town, Whitman, (Burlington Flats,) dairyman and farmer 150.

Trewhit, James, (Burlington,) dairyman and farmer 150.

VAN FRADENBURGH, EDWARD REV., (Burlington Flats,) pastor of Baptist Church.

VAN WAGNER, MELVIN, (Burlington Flats,) farmer 24 and leases of Gilbert, 71.

WAGNER, ANDREW V., (Burlington Flats,) farmer leases of Gilbert, 85.

WALLING, WILBUR F., (Garrattsville,) hop raiser, dairyman and farmer 131.

Walling, Wm., (West Burlington,) hop raiser, dairyman and farmer 124.

Walworth, B. S., (Burlington,) dairyman and farmer 240.

WARD, W. H., (Garrattsville,) carriage maker.

Washburne, Clark J., (Burlington,) constable, collector and farmer 31.

Welch, Artemus, (West Burlington,) farmer 40.

WELCH, M. A., (West Burlington,) hop raiser, dairyman and farmer 240.

White, Andrew, (Garrattsville,) hop raiser, dairyman and farmer 75.

WHITMARSH, BENJAMIN. (Burlington,) dairyman and farmer leases 150.

Wightman, Dexter, (Burlington Flats,) blacksmith.

WINTERS, ANDREW T., (Garrattsville,) prop. of saw mill and threshing machine, and farmer 68¾.

Winters, Lauriston, (Garrattsville,) (*with Andrew,*) farmer.

WOOD, A., (West Burlington,) notary public and farmer 8.

Wood, George, (Burlington Flats,) shoe maker.

Wright, Emeline, (Burlington Flats,) farmer 71.

BUTTERNUTS.

(Post Office Addresses in Parentheses.)

Adam, Alvah, (Butternuts,) farmer 65.
Alslop, James. (Butternuts,) farmer leases of James Godsby, 125.
Babcock, W. D., (Butternuts,) merchant.
Bailey, Wm., (Butternuts,) farmer 197.
Ball, Martin B., (South New Berlin, Chenango Co.,) farmer 70.
Barnes, Abel, (Maple Grove,) farmer 60.
Barse, Alonzo, (Butternuts,) farmer leases 60.
Beardsley, Chauncey, (Butternuts,) farmer 100.
Beardsley, Erastus, (Butternuts,) farmer 90.
Beardsley, Wm., (Butternuts,) farmer leases of Harmon Norton, 100.
Bedient, Daniel, (Butternuts,) farmer 6.
Bedient, George C., (Butternuts,) (*Blackman & Bedient*.)
Bedient, J. W., (Butternuts,) farmer leases of Walter, 115.
Bedient, L. Mrs., (Butternuts,) farmer 65.
Benedict, F. B., (Butternuts,) farmer 100.
Bentley, W. C., (Butternuts,) lawyer.
Birdsell, Wm. H. Rev., (Butternuts,) Baptist minister and farmer 175.
Birdsell, Wm. O., (Butternuts,) farmer 80.
Bishop, Francis, (Butternuts,) farmer 123.
Bishop, Joseph, (Butternuts,) farmer 170.
Bishop, Joseph, (Butternuts,) farmer leases of Daniel White, 150.
Blackman & Bedient, (Butternuts,) (*Francis Blackman and Geo. C. Bedient*,) furniture dealers and undertakers.
Blackman, Francis,(Butternuts,)(*Blackman & Bedient*.)
Blackman, James R., (Butternuts,) farmer 190.
Blackman, J. R., (Butternuts,) (*with J. Mayne and J. Turner*,) saw mill.
Blore, Isaac, (Butternuts,) farmer 200.
Boraley, James, (Butternuts,) farmer 180.
Brewer, J. L., (Butternuts,) merchant.
Briggs, Andrew, (Butternuts,) farmer 42.
Bronson, Joseph, (South New Berlin, Chenango Co.,) farmer 100.
Brown, J. O., (South New Berlin, Chenango Co.,) farmer 150.
Bryant, Henry C., (Butternuts,) livery stable.
Bryant, Lewis, (Butternuts,) farmer 19.
Buckman, Horatio, (Butternuts,) farmer leases.
Bundy, Jerome, (Butternuts,) farmer 100.
Burgiss, Jeannette Mrs., (Butternuts,) farmer 100.
Burlingame, Otis E., (Butternuts,) farmer leases 75.

J

Burr, Edward, (South New Berlin, Chenango Co.,) carpenter and farmer 25.
Bushnell, H. C., (Butternuts,) sash, blind and door manuf.
Bushnell, Henry, (Butternuts,) barber.
Bushnell, Lucius. (Butternuts,) farmer 125.
Cady, Andrew, (Butternuts,) farmer 5.
Cady, C. C., (Butternuts,) farmer leases 180.
Cady, George, (Butternuts,) farmer leases of Asel Halbert, 180.
Calkins, Charles, (Butternuts,) farmer 126.
Calkins, Ezra, (Butternuts,) farmer 190.
Calkins, Wright, (Butternuts,) farmer 94.
Card, Luther, (Maple Grove,) farmer 200.
CARR, SAMUEL R., (Butternuts,) farmer 124.
Cass, Fred, (Butternuts,) harness manuf.
Chapel, John, (Butternuts,) farmer 60.
Chapin, Ezra O., (Butternuts,) farmer 69.
CHURCH, ISAAC D., (Butternuts,) wagon maker and farmer 58.
Clark, T. C., (Butternuts,) farmer 125.
Clinton, Dewitt, (Butternuts,) farmer 5.
Clinton, Eli R., (Butternuts,) retired farmer 130.
CLINTON, ELI R. JR.,(Butternuts,) school commissioner, 2d dist.
Clinton, Frederick, (Butternuts,) farmer 35.
Clinton, William Y., (Butternuts,) farmer 18.
CLINTON, WM. Y. JR., (Butternuts,) farmer 14.
Cobb, E N., (Butternuts,) post master.
Coe, H. N., (Butternuts,) farmer 131.
Cole, Henry, (South New Berlin, Chenango Co.,) farmer 127.
Cole, Wm. E., (Butternuts,) farmer 116.
Colgrove, A. M. Rev.,(Butternuts,) Methodist minister.
Collar, George, (Butternuts,) farmer 225.
Collar, Russell, (South New Berlin, Chenango Co.,) farmer 75.
Comstock, J., (Butternuts,) farmer 14.
Cone, Solomon, (Butternuts,) shoe maker.
Converse, Edward, (Mount Upton, Chenango Co.,) farmer 146.
Cook, John, (Butternuts,) farmer 70.
Cook, Scott, (Butternuts,) farmer 180.
Coon, Harmon, (Maple Grove,) farmer 74.
Coon, Hiram, (Mount Upton, Chenango Co.,) farmer 200.
Coon, Peter, (Mount Upton, Chenango Co.,) farmer leases 200.
Coon, Samuel, (Butternuts,) farmer leases 140.
Coon, W., (Butternuts,) farmer 65.

Cope, Edward Rev., (Butternuts,) Presbyterian clergyman and farmer 200.

Cornell, E. B., (Butternuts,) farmer 180.

COWAN, ANDREW J., (Butternuts,) farmer 50.

Cox, Richard, (Butternuts,) shoemaker and farmer 10.

Cox, Warren J., (South New Berlin, Chenango Co.,) farmer leases 50.

Cox, Wm., (Butternuts,) farmer 6.

Davis, John R., (South New Berlin, Chenango Co.,) farmer 156.

Dibble, Dan., (Butternuts,) (*with Oscar Gager*,) farmer 50.

Dibble, Geo. W., (Butternuts,) farmer leases of David S. Hurd, 70.

Dixon, A. J., (Butternuts,) blacksmith.

Donaldson, Chester, (Butternuts,) farmer 117.

Donaldson, E., (Butternuts,) carpenter.

Donaldson, H. D., (Butternuts,) supervisor.

Donaldson, Lewis, (Butternuts,) farmer 60.

Downing, W. A.,(Butternuts,) farmer leases 125.

Egleston, Rufus,(Butternuts,) farmer 250.

Emerson, Leander, (Butternuts,) farmer 50.

Emerson, Russell,(Maple Grove,) farmer 100

Fenno, John, (Mount Upton, Chenango Co.,) farmer 350.

Filer, Charles, (Butternuts,) farmer 137.

Fish, Wm. M., (Butternuts,) farmer 200.

Fisk, Amos, (Butternuts,) farmer.

Foster, George, (Butternuts,) farmer leases 84.

Frear, Thomas, (Butternuts,) farmer 525.

Freidhbenburg, Uri, (Maple Grove,) farmer 80.

Frone, Henry, (Butternuts,) farmer 100.

Frone. John, (Butternuts,) farmer 400.

Gadsby, John, (Butternuts,) farmer 80.

Gadsby, John H., (Butternuts,) tailor.

Gadsby, Wm., (Butternuts,) farmer works Geo. Gadsby estate, 250.

Gager, Alson W., (South New Berlin, Chenango Co.,) farmer 126.

Gager, Oscar, (Butternuts,) (*with Dan Dibble*,) farmer 50.

GARDNER, O. E., (Butternuts,) saloon and livery stable.

Gardner, W., (Butternuts,) prop. Empire House.

Getchel, Harvey, (Butternuts,) farmer 40.

Gibson, Abel, (Butternuts,) farmer 110.

Gibson, Geo., (Butternuts,) farmer 100.

Gibson, Lyman, (Butternuts,) farmer 1.

Gibson, S., (South New Berlin, Chenango Co.,) farmer 55.

Gilbert, Ebin S., (Butternuts,) farmer 32.

Gilbert, Geo., (Butternuts,) speculator.

Gilbert, J. L., (Butternuts,) retired merchant.

Gilbert, John, (Butternuts,) farmer leases 150.

Gilbert, John H., (Butternuts,) commission merchant and farmer 250.

Gilbert, Samuel, (Butternuts,) farmer 112.

Gilbert, Samuel C., (Butternuts,) exchange and farmer 4000.

Gilbertsville Academy and Collegiate Institute, (Butternuts,) Rev. Abel Wood, A. M., Mrs. S. P. Wood, Miss E. J. Hutchins and Miss M. E. Wood, teachers.

Goodsell, Lorenzo D., (Butternuts,) farmer leases 135.

GRAY, D. C.,(Butternuts,) restaurant, dealer in fruits, fish, oysters, clams &c.

Gray, Harvey, (Butternuts,) farmer 90.

Green, John R., (Butternuts,) carriage maker.

Greene, Arthur, (White's Store, Chenango Co.,) farmer 177.

Greene, Edwin R., (Mount Upton, Chenango Co.,) farmer 150.

Gregory, A. S., (Butternuts,) farmer 102.

Gregory, Henry, (Butternuts,) saloon.

GRIFFIN, EDWARD, (Butternuts,) harness manuf.

Griffin, Jehial, (Butternuts,) cooper.

Haines, George, (Butternuts,) farmer 300.

Hakes, Alonzo, (Butternuts,) farmer 120.

Hakes, Elihu, (Butternuts,) farmer 175.

Hakes, T. G., (Butternuts,) farmer 120.

Halbert, A., (Butternuts,) farmer 100.

Halbert, Emmitt, (Butternuts,) farmer 102.

Halbert, E. S., (Butternuts,) justice of the peace.

Hammond, Edgar W., (South New Berlin, Chenango Co.,) farmer 50.

Hanford, Benj. L., (Butternuts,) shoe maker and farmer 89.

Hanford, Bradley M., (Butternuts,) farmer 62.

Hartwell, A., (Butternuts,) grist mill.

Hartwell, David, (Butternuts,) farmer 14.

Hastings, Henry (Butternuts,) farmer leases 150.

Hastings, John, (Butternuts,) farmer 105.

Helsinger, Jacob, (Butternuts,) farmer.

Hendrix, Charles, (Maple Grove,) farmer 118.

Hendrix, Henry, (Butternuts,) farmer leases 120.

Heslup, John, (Butternuts,) farmer 200.

Houg, Stephen, (Butternuts,) farmer 142.

Holbert, Julius, (Butternuts,) farmer 35.

Hollis, Anthony B., (Butternuts,) farmer 160.

Hollis, R. S., (Butternuts,) blacksmith.

Holls, Robert, (Butternuts,) farmer leases 125.

Hood, Philip, (Butternuts,) farmer 164.

Hopkins, C. O., (Butternuts,) dairyman and farmer 240.

Howard, E. A., (Butternuts,) prop. of Central Hotel.

Howland, James, (Butternuts,) farmer 60.

Hughes, John V. Rev., (Butternuts,) Episcopal minister.

Hurd, D. N., (Butternuts,) (*Hurd & Shaw*.)

Hurd & Shaw, (Butternuts,) (*D. N. Hurd and F. Shaw*,) general merchants and produce dealers.

Hurlburt, David, (Butternuts,) farmer 200.

Hurlburt, John, (Butternuts,) farmer 160.

Hurlbut, Abram, (Butternuts,) farmer 95.

Hurlbutt, Elias, (Butternuts,) farmer 195.

Huson, N., (Butternuts,) farmer 175.

Hutchings, E. J. Miss,(Butternuts,) teacher Gilbertsville Academy and Collegiate Institute.

Hutchinson, Josiah, (Butternuts,) farmer leases 150.

Hutchinson, Josiah, (Butternuts,) meat market.

Isbel, Andrew, (White's Store, Chenango Co.,) farmer 8.

Jackson, Andrew, (Butternuts,) farmer leases 150.
Jackson, Thomas, (Butternuts,) farmer 204.
Jeffrey, John, (Butternuts,) farmer 100.
Jewel, F., (Butternuts,) farmer leases 198.
Johnson, Albert, (Butternuts,) farmer leases 175.
Jones, Ishmael, (Butternuts,) farmer 4.
Keen, Thomas, (Butternuts,) farmer 80.
Kellogg, John, (Butternuts,) painter.
Kellogg, John S., (Butternuts,) painter and farmer 6.
KINNE, JOHN J., (Butternuts,) farmer 102.
Kinne, Wm. R., (Butternuts,) farmer 157.
Lamphire, Lyman G. W., (Mount Upton, Chenango Co.,) cooper.
Leonard, Wm., (Butternuts,) farmer 200.
Lillie, Elisha, (South New Berlin, Chenango Co.,) farmer 150.
Lincoln, Johnson, (Butternuts,) saw mill and farmer 2.
Littlewood, Edward, (Butternuts,) farmer 12.
Lockwood, Joseph, (Butternuts,) farmer leases 120.
Lockwood, T. A., (Butternuts,) photographer.
Lyon, Otis, (Butternuts,) dairyman and farmer 161.
Mallory, Edward, (Butternuts,) farmer 200.
Mallory, Uri, (Butternuts,) farmer 100.
Marks, Matthew, (Butternuts,) farmer 105.
Marsh, Benjamin, (Butternuts,) farmer 14.
Marsh, Nelson, (Butternuts,) farmer 104.
Marsh, S., (Butternuts,) farmer 100.
Masters, Francis Mrs., (Mount Upton, Chenango Co.,) farmer 409.
Mayne, J., (Butternuts,) (with J. R. Blackman and J. Turner,) saw mill.
Mayne, John, (Butternuts,) foundry.
McCulloch, Alexander, (Butternuts,) (with John Woodlands,) farmer leases 125.
Merrick, Charles, (Butternuts,) farmer 160.
Millard, Henry, (Butternuts,) farmer 200.
Millard, John R., (Butternuts,) farmer 150.
Miller, E., (Butternuts,) farmer 66.
Miller, Riley, (South New Berlin, Chenango Co.,) farmer 32.
Moore, Samuel C. Rev., (Butternuts,) Baptist clergyman.
Morris, Adelaide Miss, (Mount Upton, Chenango Co.,) farmer 500.
Morris, Charles V., (Butternuts,) farmer 150.
Morrisey, John, (Butternuts,) carriage maker and blacksmith.
Morse, Arvin, (White's Store, Chenango Co.,) farmer 105.
Morse, Stephen, (Mount Upton, Chenango Co.,) farmer 150.
Morse, Stephen, Jr., (Mount Upton, Chenango Co.,) farmer 200.
Morton, H. P., (Butternuts,) farmer 550.
Moulton, Samuel,(Butternuts,) shoe maker.
Mussen, Benjamin, (Butternuts,) farmer 20.
Musson, Daniel, (Butternuts,) farmer 140.
Musson, James, (Butternuts,) farmer 90.
Musson, Judson, (Butternuts,) farmer 80.
Musson, R. H., (Butternuts,) farmer 132.
Musson, Theodore, (Butternuts,) farmer leases 160.
Musson, William, (Butternuts,) farmer 1.
Myrick, Albert, (Butternuts,) farmer 8.

Myrick, James, (Butternuts,) farmer 20.
Nearing, Ebenezer,(Butternuts,) farmer 116.
Nearing, Sylvester, (Butternuts,) farmer 100.
Neering, Hezekiah, (Butternuts,) farmer 50.
Nichols, Norman, (Mount Upton, Chenango Co.,) farmer 44.
Nichols, Norman, (Butternuts,) farmer 67.
Northcolt, John W., (Butternuts,) farmer leases 100.
Oliver, Henry,(Butternuts,) carriage shop.
Oliver,Wm.,(Butternuts,) general merchant.
Ollis, Clay, (Butternuts,) farmer 100.
Palmer, R. B., (Butternuts,) farmer leases 162.
Park, John M., (Butternuts,) fire and life insurance agent.
Park, L. W., (Butternuts,) shoe maker.
Patrick, Eliza Mrs., (Butternuts,) farmer 115.
Payne, Arthur, (South New Berlin, Chenango Co.,) cooper.
Peabody P., (Butternuts,) farmer 50.
Pearce, George, (Butternuts,) farmer 100.
Pearce, Ira, (Butternuts,) farmer 100.
Platt, David, (Butternuts,) farmer 15.
Polly, John, (Butternuts,) farmer 70.
Porter, Albert, (Butternuts,) farmer 140.
Porter, Ann Mrs., (Butternuts,) farmer 144.
Potter, Harvey, (South New Berlin, Chenango Co.,) farmer leases 165.
Powers, Alvin, (South New Berlin, Chenango Co.,) farmer leases 140.
Prentice, E., (Butternuts,) farmer 175.
Prentice, John R., (Mount Upton, Chenango Co.,) farmer leases 100.
Randall, N., (Butternuts,) farmer 14.
RAWLINGS, JOHN H., (Butternuts,) dairyman, cheese manuf. and farmer 265.
Raymond, Nathan, (Butternuts,) farmer 152.
Redman, James, (Butternuts,) (with Samuel,) farmer leases 150.
Redman, Samuel, (Butternuts,) (with Jas.,) farmer leases 150.
Reynolds, Sullivan, (Mount Upton, Chenango Co.,) farmer 200.
Rice, Augustus, (Butternuts,) farmer leases 200.
Richards, Lucius, (Butternuts,) farmer 120.
Richmond, Antoinette Mrs., (Mount Upton, Chenango Co.,) farmer 200.
Richmond, H. D. & G. A., (South New Berlin, Chenango Co.,) farmer 80.
Richmond, S. D., (Mount Upton, Chenango Co.,) retired farmer.
Robinson, Hiram, (Butternuts,) farmer leases 100.
Rockwell, G. A., (Butternuts,) dentist.
Rockwell, J. M., (Butternuts,) farmer 200.
Rockwell, S., (Butternuts,) tannery.
Rodman, Wm., (Butternuts,) farmer 2.
Rogers, Hiram, (Butternuts,) barber.
ROOT, C. P. Major, (Butternuts,) justice of the peace, dairyman and farmer 500.
Rowe, Benjamin, (Mount Upton, Chenango Co.,) farmer leases 190.
Rowe, Benj.,(Butternuts,) farmer leases 150.
Rowlstone, Wm., (Butternuts,) bowling alley.
Russell, David A., (Butternuts,) butcher.
Sage, Adelia Mrs., (South New Berlin, Chenango Co.,) farmer 96.

SAGE, GEORGE W., JR., (Butternuts,) farmer leases of H. Jenks, 170.
Sage, Wm., (South New Berlin, Chenango Co.,) farmer 77.
Sawyer, Charles, (Butternuts,) farmer 150.
Sawyer, Miles, (Butternuts,) farmer 112.
Sawyer, Wm., (Butternuts,) farmer 75.
Sergent, Charles, (South New Berlin, Chenango Co.,) farmer 125.
Sharts, Salmon, (Butternuts,) farmer leases 50.
Shaw, F., (Butternuts,) (Hurd & Shaw.)
Shaw, Lorenzo, (Butternuts,) farmer 80.
Shaw, Zadoc E., (Butternuts,) farmer 40.
Sherman, Perry, (South New Berlin, Chenango Co.,) farmer 125.
Sherwood, Clement, (Mount Upton, Chenango Co.,) farmer 60.
Sherwood, R., (Butternuts,) farmer leases 200.
Sherwood, Wm., (Butternuts,) farmer leases 200.
Sillie, G. W., (Butternuts,) general merchant.
Silvey, John, (Butternuts,) farmer 70.
Silvey, Samuel, (Butternuts,) farmer 30.
Slade, Henry R., (Butternuts,) sash, doors and blinds.
Slade, Orville, (Butternuts,) farmer works A. Slade estate. 75.
Smith, J. H., (Mount Upton, Chenango Co.,) farmer 118.
Smith, S., (Butternuts,) farmer 100.
Smith, Wm. R., (Butternuts,) jeweler.
Southard, Abram, (Butternuts,) farmer 20.
Spencer, Franklin, (Butternuts,) farmer 70.
Stebbins, Jesse M., (Butternuts,) farmer 62.
Stebbins, John, (Butternuts,) farmer 100.
Stebbins, Wm., (Butternuts,) farmer 170.
Stenson, Edward, (Butternuts,) farmer leases 175.
Stenson, John C., (Butternuts,) farmer 50.
Stenson, Robert Y., (Butternuts,) farmer leases of John S. Jackson, 230.
Stenson, Wm., (Butternuts,) farmer 65.
St. John, Lorin, (Butternuts,) farmer leases 140.
Stockwell, W. W., (Butternuts,) hardware.
Stoddard, George Z., (Butternuts,) town assessor and farmer 80.
Sturges, John A., (Butternuts,) farmer 93.
Sull, J., (Butternuts,) farmer leases 100.
Sutton, Merritt, (Butternuts,) mason.
Sweet, Ephraim, (Butternuts,) farmer 25 and leases 50.
Tanner, Alanson, (Butternuts,) farmer 20.
Thayer, John, (Butternuts,) saddle maker.
Thayer, Wm., (Mount Upton, Chenango Co.,) harness maker and farmer 10.
Thomas, Alfred, (Butternuts,) farmer 75.
Thompson, A. L., (Butternuts,) blacksmith.
Thompson, Charles, (Butternuts,) farmer leases 100.
Thorp, Henry, (Butternuts,) farmer 300.
Thorp, L. E., (Butternuts,) physician and surgeon.
Toles, H. P., (Butternuts,) (with M. W.,) farmer 240.

Toles, M. W., (Butternuts,) (with H. P.,) farmer 240.
Tolls, David, (Butternuts,) farmer 150.
Townsend, Israel, (Mount Upton, Chenango Co.,) farmer 14.
TRUAX, S. J., (Butternuts,) marble dealer.
Truesdell, Ransom, (Butternuts,) carpenter.
Truman, Nathan, (Butternuts,) farmer 130.
Tucker, Ansel, (Butternuts,) farmer 100.
Turner, Amos, (Butternuts,) farmer 50.
Turner, J., (Butternuts,) (with J. R. Blackman and J. Mayne,) saw mill.
Turney, Austin, (Butternuts,) farmer 150.
Tyler, Colonel, (Butternuts,) farmer 70.
Valentine, John G., (Butternuts,) dairyman and farmer 120.
Vanname, John, (Butternuts,) farmer 145.
Vanscoy, Hiram C., (Butternuts,) farmer leases 230.
Vanscoy, Stephen, (Butternuts,) farmer 15.
Walker, F., (Butternuts,) farmer 50.
Wallace, A. Mrs., (Butternuts,) milliner.
Wallace, Geo. W., (Butternuts,) painter.
Wallace, Homer, (Butternuts,) farmer leases of David Barritt, 100.
Walling, Theodore, (Butternuts,) farmer 200.
Walling, Wm., (Butternuts,) farmer 160.
Ward, Ira L., (Butternuts,) farmer 75.
Watkins, John, (Mount Upton, Chenango Co.,) farmer 92.
Webb, Jared, (Butternuts,) farmer 136.
Weston, Wm., (South New Berlin, Chenango Co.,) farmer 50.
White, Geo. A., (White's Store, Chenango Co.,) farmer 108.
White, John D., (Butternuts,) farmer leases of R. Turner, 60.
Whiting, John, (Butternuts,) shoemaker.
Whitmore, John, (Butternuts,) farmer 12.
Wickes, H. H., (Butternuts,) physician and surgeon.
WILBER, JACOB, (Butternuts,) wagon maker.
Wilbur, Wm., (Butternuts,) farmer leases 150.
Wilcox, Ephraim, (Butternuts,) farmer 110.
Wilde, Chester, (Butternuts,) farmer leases 825.
Williams, Asel, (Butternuts,) farmer 170.
Wood, Abel Rev., A. M., (Butternuts,) Gilbertsville Academy and Collegiate Institute.
Wood, Gilbert, (Butternuts,) farmer 110.
Wood, Irving, (Butternuts,) farmer 60.
Wood, Leonard, (Butternuts,) farmer 200.
Wood, M. E. Miss, (Butternuts,) teacher Gilbertsville Academy and Collegiate Institute.
Wood, S. P. Mrs., (Butternuts,) teacher Gilbertsville Academy and Collegiate Institute.
Wood, Walter L., (Butternuts,) farmer 105.
Wood, Wm., (Butternuts,) harness shop.
Wood, William H., (Butternuts,) carpenter and farmer 13.
Woodlands, John, (Butternuts,) (with Alex. McCulloch,) farmer leases 125.
Woodlands, John Jr., (Butternuts,) carpenter

CHERRY VALLEY.

(Post Office Addresses in Parentheses.)

Allen, Edward,(Sprout Brook, Montgomery Co.,) farmer 180.

Ashton, Thos., (Cherry Valley,) farmer 125.

Atinks, Clinton, (Sprout Brook, Montgomery Co.,) farmer leases of Harriet Garlick, 164.

Austen, Thomas, (Sprout Brook, Montgomery Co.,) farmer 10.

Austin, Wm., (Buel, Montgomery Co.,) farmer 13.

BALDWIN, WM. H., (Cherry Valley,) cashier National Central Bank and farmer 140, Montgomery.

Banker, Henry, (Cherry Valley,) farmer 223.

Barnum, J. W., (Cherry Valley,) lawyer, Main.

Barringer, Edward, (Cherry Valley,) farmer leases of John Gilday, 140.

Bartlett, R. H., (Cherry Valley,) conductor Cherry Valley Branch R. R.

Bastian, Wm. V. S., (Cherry Valley,) painter and grainer.

Bates, Davis W., (Cherry Valley,) lawyer and hop buyer, Lancaster.

Bates, Dewitt C., (Cherry Valley,) notary public, corner Main and Montgomery.

Bates, Wm. G., (Cherry Valley,) farmer 82¾.

Bates, W. H., (Cherry Valley,) lawyer, corner Main and Montgomery.

Baxter, Benjamin, (Cherry Valley,) farmer 100.

Baxter, Tobias, (Cherry Valley,) farmer 50.

Baxter, Urah, (Cherry Valley,) farmer 120.

Beaumont, Jane C. Mrs., (Cherry Valley,) ladies' furnishing goods, Main.

Bellman, Christopher, (Buel, Montgomery Co.,) farmer 80.

Berger, William, (Cherry Valley,) farmer 100.

Best, H. W., (Cherry Valley,) judge and farmer 26.

Best, J., (Cherry Valley,) farmer 103.

Bocock, John, (Cherry Valley,) farmer 2.

Botts, J., (Cherry Valley,) farmer 150.

Bowman, Obed, (Cherry Valley,) farmer 196.

Bradley, John W., (Cherry Valley,) harness maker, Main.

Bradley, Wm., (Center Valley,) farmer 50.

Brien, Thos., (Cherry Valley,) stoves and tinware, Main.

Bronson, C. W., (Cherry Valley,) dentist, Main.

Brown, Almon, (Cherry Valley,) marble dealer, Main.

Brown, Henry, (Cherry Valley,) farmer 144.

BURCH, WM., (Cherry Valley,) attorney at law, Harmony Row, Main.

Burger, C., (Cherry Valley,) farmer 106.

Burger, Horatio, (Cherry Valley,) farmer 50.

Bush, Elijah, (Cherry Valley,) farmer 100.

Campbell, A., (Cherry Valley,) farmer 100 and leases of George Clark, 100.

Campbell. Dewitt C., (Center Valley,) farmer 92.

Campbell, J. S.,(Cherry Valley,) farmer 140.

Campbell, Samuel Mrs., (Cherry Valley,) farmer 170.

CAMPBELL, WM. W., (Cherry Valley,) lawyer and farmer 230.

Cary, David, (Cherry Valley,) farmer.

*CHERRY VALLEY GAZETTE, (Cherry Valley,) Main St., Wm. A. Smith, prop.

Clark, George,(Cherry Valley,) post master, corner Main and Alden.

Clark, J. W., (Cherry Valley,) groceries and fancy goods, corner Main and Alden.

Clearwatter, Joseph, (East Springfield,) dry goods and groceries, Saltspringville.

Clyde, J. D., (Cherry Valley,) (*Clyde & Sharp.*)

Clyde & Sharp, (Cherry Valley,) (*J. D. Clyde and J. Sharp,*) physicians and druggists, Harmony Row.

Coats & Rudd, (Cherry Valley,) (*S. Coats and R. Rudd,*) butchers, Lancaster.

Coats, S., (Cherry Valley,) (*Coats & Rudd,*) farmer 44.

Coats, Solomon, (Cherry Valley,) farmer 40.

Coonradt, Jonas, (Cherry Valley,) farmer 124.

Coonradt, Joseph, (Cherry Valley,) cooper, Church.

Countryman, Hiram, (Cherry Valley,) farmer 85.

Cox, Abraham B.,(Cherry Valley,) farmer 240.

Cramers, James, (Cherry Valley,) farmer 70.

Crouch, Thos. J., (Cherry Valley,) mail carrier from Cherry Valley to Fort Plain, Genesee.

Culver, John, (Cherry Valley,) farmer leases of Harriet and Sophia Watson, 100.

DAKIN, GEO. W. B., (Cherry Valley,) assistant cashier National Central Bank, corner Main and Lancaster.

Dart. F. W., (Cherry Valley,) meat market, Genesee.

Davidson, Andrew, (Cherry Valley,) agent for Continental Life Insurance Co., Main.

Davidson, Robert, (Cherry Valley,) farmer 300.

Davis, Joseph, (Cherry Valley,) farmer 11.

Decker, ——, (Cherry Valley,) (*Spraker & Decker.*)

Delany, Henry, (Cherry Valley,) blacksmith, Main.

Diell, John K., (Cherry Valley,) barber and town clerk, Main.

Doran, Patrick, (Cherry Valley,) farmer leases of George Clark, 100.

Drake, Joel B., (Cherry Valley,) farmer 115.

Drain, Wm., (Cherry Valley,) organ maker, Montgomery.

Duffin, B. Mrs., (Cherry Valley,) farmer 60.

Dutcher, Geo. M., (Cherry Valley,) farmer 67.

Dutcher, Ransom, (Cherry Valley,) farmer 105.

Dutcher & Selmson, (Cherry Valley,) farmer 197.

Dutcher, W. (Cherry Valley,) farmer 50.

Dutton, E. G., (Cherry Valley,) saloon, Main.

Eckler, J. F., (Cherry Valley,) farmer 59.

Eckler, W. H., (Cherry Valley,) farmer 2.

ELDREDGE, O. H., (Cherry Valley,) manuf. organs and melodeons, Montgomery.

Engall, James, (Center Valley,) farmer leases of Adam Engell, 132.

Engell, Adam, (Center Valley,) farmer 208.

Farquherson, Robert, (Sprout Brook, Montgomery Co.,) farmer 120.

Fea, Alex., (Cherry Valley,) organ maker, Montgomery.

Fea, John, (Cherry Valley,) editor of *Saw Buck* and organ builder, Montgomery.

Fellows, E. E. Mrs., (Cherry Valley,) dress making and furnishing goods, Alden.

Fern, James, (Cherry Valley,) farmer.

Fields, Seth, (Cherry Valley,) farmer 112.

Fitzgerald, Alfred, (Cherry Valley,) wagon and sleigh maker, Main.

Fitzgerald, Arthur, (Cherry Valley,) wagon maker, Main.

Flint, Daniel, (East Springfield,) farmer 200, Saltspringsville.

FLINT, GEORGE J., (Cherry Valley,) attorney and counselor at law, Main.

Flint, Hiram, (Cherry Valley,) farmer 72.

Flint, John K., (Cherry Valley,) farmer 86.

Flint, Nelson, (Sprout Brook, Montgomery Co.,) farmer 27.

Foland, H., (Cherry Valley,) farmer 200.

Foland, Wm., (Cherry Valley,) farmer leases of Geo. Clark, 200.

Foland, Z., (Cherry Valley,) farmer 127.

Fonda, James J., (Cherry Valley,) boots and shoes, hats and caps, Alden.

Fuller, H. H., (Cherry Valley,) general merchant, Main.

Furmin, Walter, (Cherry Valley,) general merchant, Main.

Gales, Chancy, (Cherry Valley,) farmer 90.

Galt, John, (Cherry Valley,) farmer.

Galt, John S., (Cherry Valley,) farmer 4.

Galt, Wm., (Cherry Valley,) farmer 96.

George, Thos. Mrs., (Cherry Valley,) hotel keeper, corner Genesee and Railroad.

Gilbert, Delfonzo, (Cherry Valley,) farmer 223.

GILDAY, JOHN, (Cherry Valley,) carpenter and builder, and farmer 160, Genesee.

Gilday, Owen, (Cherry Valley,) carpenter.

Goodell, E., (Cherry Valley,) (*with Jacob,*) farmer 180.

Goodell, Jacob, (Cherry Valley,) (*with E.,*) farmer 180.

Gordon, S., (Cherry Valley,) farmer 140.

Gordon, Smith, (Cherry Valley,) farmer leases of J. C. Winnie, 100.

GRAND HOTEL, (Cherry Valley,) Alden, J. E. Robinson, prop.

Gross, Denison, (Cherry Valley,) last maker, Main.

Hall, Thos., (Cherry Valley,) farmer 97½.

Hamilton, L., (Cherry Valley,) saloon and mail carrier, Main.

Hawver, Andrew, (Cherry Valley,) farmer leases of Geo. Clark, 70.

Hawver, John, (Cherry Valley,) farmer 4.

Head, Albert, (Cherry Valley,) farmer.

Head, Delos, (Cherry Valley,) farmer leases of Geo. Clark.

Head, Geo., (Cherry Valley,) farmer 96.

Head, Hamilton, (Cherry Valley,) carpenter.

Herdman, Nelson, (Cherry Valley,) carpenter, Lancaster.

Herdman, Wm., (Cherry Valley,) farmer 240.

Hetherington, James, (Cherry Valley,) (*with J. E.,*) apiarian, Church.

Hetherington, J. E., (Cherry Valley,) (*with James,*) apiarian, Church.

HILLMAN, CALVIN, (Cherry Valley,) dealer in pianos, organs and melodeons, Lancaster.

Hone, Jacob, (Leesville, Schoharie Co.,) farmer 200.

Horning, Norman, (Sprout Brook, Montgomery Co.,) farmer 90.

Horning, R. G., (Sprout Brook, Montgomery Co.,) farmer 170.

Horton, Jacob, (Center Valley,) farmer 30.

Horton, James R., (Cherry Valley,) farmer 114.

Hubbard, J. F., (Cherry Valley,) restaurant, Genesee.

JUDD, EDWIN, (Cherry Valley,) (*E. & J. Judd.*)

JUDD, E. & J., (Cherry Valley,) (*Edwin and John,*) manufs. blind trimmings, Main.

JUDD, JOHN, (Cherry Valley,) (*E. & J. Judd,*) manuf. light iron castings, Main.

Keller, John, (Sprout Brook, Montgomery Co.,) farmer 200.

Kipple, James, (Cherry Valley,) farmer 50 and leases of Rachel and Catharine Rose, 100.

Kirby, Wm., (Cherry Valley,) farmer 200.

La Homadue, Isaac, (Cherry Valley,) carpenter and farmer 8.

Leaning, R. H., (Cherry Valley,) station agent, New.

Lettice, Stephen, (Sprout Brook, Montgomery Co.,) farmer 100.

Lewis, Charles H., (Cherry Valley,) farmer leases of Geo. Clark, 233.

Lewis, Theodore, (Sprout Brook, Montgomery Co.,) farmer 166.

Low, Henry, (Cherry Valley,) farmer 128.

Ludlam, Stephen, (Cherry Valley,) sash, blinds and doors, Wall.

Lumley, John Jr., (Cherry Valley,) farmer leases 170.

Lumley, John Sen., (Cherry Valley,) farmer 170.

Luscomb, D., (Cherry Valley,) farmer 17.

Lyke, Peter F., (Cherry Valley,) farmer.

Lynk, Edward,(Cherry Valley,) (*with Thos.*) farmer 160.
Lynk, Thomas, (Cherry Valley,) (*with Edward,*) farmer 160.
Mallett, Chas., (Cherry Valley,) farmer 400.
Mathias, John O., (Buel, Montgomery Co.,) farmer 97.
McFarran, Wm. E., (Cherry Valley,) cabinet maker and deputy sheriff.
McFee, Albert, (Cherry Valley,) farmer 4.
McFee, A. C., (Sprout Brook, Montgomery Co.,) farmer 62.
McFee, Geo., (Sprout Brook, Montgomery Co.,) farmer 100.
McFee, James,(Sprout Brook, Montgomery Co.,) farmer 163.
McFee, John, (Sprout Brook, Montgomery Co.,) farmer 40.
McFee, J. M., (Sprout Brook, Montgomery Co.,) farmer 50.
McFee, Melvin, (Cherry Valley,) farmer 60.
McFee, Norman, (Sprout Brook, Montgomery Co.,) farmer 62.
McKelley, Daniel, (Cherry Valley,) farmer 300.
McKelly, Joseph, (Cherry Valley,) farmer 100.
McLEAN, CHAS., (Cherry Valley,) justice of the peace and conveyancer, Harmony Row.
MERRITT, GEORGE, (Cherry Valley,) physician and surgeon, Main.
Michels, Philip, (Cherry Valley,) farmer 1.
Mills, Jacob, (Cherry Valley,) farmer 30.
Millson, John, (Cherry Valley,) farmer 120.
Millson, John, (Cherry Valley,) blacksmith, Main.
Millson, Samuel, (Cherry Valley,) prop. Harmony Row Saloon, Harmony Row.
Monheson, Wm., (Cherry Valley,) farmer leases of Geo. Clark, 130.
Moore, E., (Cherry Valley,) farmer 170.
Moore, John, (Cherry Valley,) farmer 2.
More, Augustus, (Cherry Valley,) farmer 64.
More, Philip, (Cherry Valley,) farmer 170.
Nash, David, (Cherry Valley,) merchant tailor, Main.
NATIONAL CENTRAL BANK, (Cherry Valley,) capital $200,000; Horatio J. Olcott, prest.; Wm. H. Baldwin, cashier; Geo. W. B. Dakin, asst. cashier; corner Main and Lancaster.
Nellis, Peter A., (Cherry Valley,) farmer 92.
Nelson, John, (Cherry Valley,) moulder.
Nestell, Geo., (East Springfield,) farmer 92, Saltspringville.
OLCOTT, HORATIO J., (Cherry Valley,) prest. National Central Bank, corner Main and Lancaster.
Oliver, Thos. (Cherry Valley,) saw mill and farmer 110.
Ough, Peter, (Cherry Valley,) farmer 125.
Palmer, H. P., (Cherry Valley,) prop. Palmer Hotel, Main.
Palmer, William, (Cherry Valley,) farmer leases of Hardy & Hues, 150.
Peaslee, Joseph B., (East Springfield,) farmer 175, Saltspringville.
Pegg, John, (Cherry Valley,) farmer.
Phelon, Joseph, (Cherry Valley,) farmer 260.
Pickard, Moses, (Cherry Valley,) farmer 75.

Pickard, Simeon, (Cherry Valley,) farmer 120.
Platner, C. H., (Cherry Valley,) farmer 164.
Platner, Jacob, (Cherry Valley,) farmer 297.
Platner, P. H., (Cherry Valley,) farmer 100.
Platner, Walter, (Cherry Valley,) farmer 35.
Platner, Wm., (Cherry Valley,) farmer 132.
Prime, John H., (East Springfield,) farmer 73, Saltspringville.
Prockter, Andrew, (Cherry Valley,) blacksmith.
RATHBUN, G. A., (Cherry Valley,) dealer in dry goods, groceries and crockery, corner Main and Montgomery.
Reynolds, Mary Miss, (Cherry Valley,) dress maker, Alden.
Rich, Washington, (Cherry Valley,) farmer 245.
RISK, JAMES, (Cherry Valley,) prop. Caloric Mill, Main.
Robbins, Wm., (Cherry Valley,) grist and saw mills, and farmer 12.
Roberts, George, (Cherry Valley,) farmer 98.
ROBINSON, J. E., (Cherry Valley,) prop. Grand Hotel, Alden.
Rose, David, (Cherry Valley,) agent Phœnix Mutual Life Insurance Co. of Hartford, Genesee.
Rowley, Ann Mrs., (Cherry Valley,) farmer 25.
Rudd, R., (Cherry Valley,) (*Coats & Rudd.*)
Rutt, Norman, (Cherry Valley,) farmer 14.
Salisbury, Joanna Mrs., (Cherry Valley,) millinery, Main.
Salsbury, Aaron, (Cherry Valley,) saloon, corner Main and Montgomery.
Sawyer, J. L., (Cherry Valley,) teacher select school, Montgomery.
Schwartz, D. L. Rev., (Cherry Valley,) rector of Grace Church, Montgomery.
Scism, Chas., (Cherry Valley,) farmer 112.
Scoot, E. C. Mrs., (Cherry Valley,) millinery, Main.
Scott, Chas. W., (Cherry Valley,) general agent for Empire State Life Insurance Co. for Otsego Co.
Scott, John, (Cherry Valley,) farmer 130.
Selmson, ——, (Cherry Valley,) (*Dutcher & Selmson.*)
Sharp, J., (Cherry Valley,) (*Clyde & Sharp.*)
Sharp, Jacob, (Cherry Valley,) merchant tailor, Harmony Row.
Shaul, Adam, (Cherry Valley,) farmer 159.
Shaul, John, (Cherry Valley,) farmer 178.
Shaul, Norman, (Cherry Valley,) farmer 100.
Shear, Pat. B., (Cherry Valley,) farmer 200.
Sheerar, J. B. Rev., (Cherry Valley,) pastor M. E. Church, Main.
Sherman, Geo., (Cherry Valley,) farmer 65.
Sherman, S. V., (Cherry Valley,) farmer 200.
Sherman, William, (Cherry Valley,) farmer 187.
Siber, Peter, (Cherry Valley,) hop buyer and farmer 590.
Sisum, James E., (Cherry Valley,) carpenter, Main.
Sisum, Oliver B., (Cherry Valley,) carpenter.
Smith, John, (Cherry Valley,) photographer, Lancaster.

*SMITH, WM. A., (Cherry Valley,) prop. *Cherry Valley Gazette*, Main.

Snow, George, (Cherry Valley,) farmer 8.

Snyder, Henry, (Cherry Valley,) (*with Venus*,) farmer 160.

Snyder, Isaac. (Cherry Valley,) farmer 80.

Snyder, Venus, (Cherry Valley,) (*with Henry*,) farmer 160.

Spencer, Wm., (Cherry Valley,) farmer 100.

Spraker & Decker, (Cherry Valley,) farmers lease of George Clark, 239.

Spraker, J., (Cherry Valley,) farmer 100.

Sternberg, J. H., (Cherry Valley,) physician and surgeon, Montgomery.

Sterns, Daniel, (Cherry Valley,) farmer 55.

Stiles, C. W., (Cherry Valley,) farmer leases 200.

Stringer, George, (Center Valley,) farmer 165.

Sutliff, J. R., (Cherry Valley,) farmer 200.

Suttliff, Edward H., (Cherry Valley,) farmer 144.

SWAN, A. L., (Cherry Valley,) undertaker, telegraph operator and prop. Swan Patent Door Bell Pull &c., Main.

Swift, Seth, (Cherry Valley,) farmer 175.

Swinnerton, H. U. Rev., (Cherry Valley,) pastor Presb. Church, Alden.

Talcott. H. W., (Cherry Valley,) marble worker, Main.

Teabout, Wm., (Cherry Valley,) barber, Harmony Row.

Thompson, A., (Cherry Valley,) farmer 108.

Thompson, Elijah, (Center Valley,) farmer 140.

Thompson, H. R., (Cherry Valley,) carpenter, Main.

Thompson, Jason, (Cherry Valley,) farmer 265.

Thompson, L. W., (Cherry Valley,) jeweler and agent for Singer Sewing Machines, Main.

Thompson, O., (Cherry Valley,) farmer 47.

Tucker, J. J., (Buel, Montgomery Co.,) farmer 140.

Ulman, Barrent, (Center Valley,) farmer 72.

Ulman, Benjamin, (Center Valley,) farmer 50.

Ulman, Frederick, (Center Valley,) farmer 129.

Van Alstine, Abram, (Cherry Valley,) farmer 50.

Van Alstine, Elias, (Cherry Valley,) farmer 59.

Van Derwerker, Peter, (Cherry Valley,) farmer 52.

Van Slyke, Adam, (Cherry Valley,) (*Van Slyke & Son*,)

Van Slyke, Lyman B., (Cherry Valley,) (*Van Slyke & Son*.)

Van Slyke & Son, (Cherry Valley,) (*Adam and Lyman B.*,) truss makers, Wall.

Van Valkenburg, George, (Center Valley,) farmer 93.

Van Valkenburgh, Henry B., (Cherry Valley,) farmer 97.

Voorhess, V., (Cherry Valley,) farmer 90.

Vosburg, Jacob, (East Springfield,) hotel.

Wales, Philip R., (Cherry Valley,) shoe maker, Lancaster.

Wales, Robert, (Cherry Valley,) sash, doors and blinds, Genesee.

Walrad, Jonas, (East Springfield,) farmer 50, Saltspringville.

Walradt, James, (East Springfield,) farmer 210, Saltspringville.

Walrath, L. C., (Cherry Valley,) farmer leases 200.

Wandell, Geo., (Cherry Valley,) farmer 52.

Waterhouse, J. B., (Cherry Valley,) shoe maker, Main.

Waterhouse, N. W., (Cherry Valley,) boots and shoes, Main.

Watrous, O., (Cherry Valley,) farmer 60.

Watrous, O. F., (Cherry Valley,) farmer 128.

Weller, Hiram, (East Springfield,) grist and saw mill, Saltspringville.

Wentworth, Chas. H., (Cherry Valley,) (*Wentworth & Son*.)

Wentworth, Henry, (Cherry Valley,) (*Wentworth & Son*.)

Wentworth, Seymour M., (Cherry Valley,) (*Wentworth & Son*.)

Wentworth & Son, (Cherry Valley,) (*Henry and Chas. H.*,) painters, Main.

Wentworth & Son, (Cherry Valley,) (*Henry and Seymour M.*,) photographers, Main.

Whitbeck, Albert, (Cherry Valley,) prop. of hotel.

White, J. M., (Cherry Valley,) physician and surgeon, Alden.

White, Willard D., (Sprout Brook, Montgomery Co.,) farmer 100.

Whiteman, John, (Cherry Valley,) farmer 150.

Wickwire, Amos F., (Cherry Valley,) farmer 150.

Wicoff, Truman, (Cherry Valley,) farmer 200.

Wiles, William, (Cherry Valley,) farmer 188.

Wilkins, C. M., (Cherry Valley,) blacksmith, Genesee.

WILLSON, WM. C., (Cherry Valley,) groceries, stoneware and woodenware.

Wils, Moses, (Sprout Brook, Montgomery Co.,) farmer 100.

Wilson, W. C., (Cherry Valley,) farmer 116.

Winne, A. & Co., (Cherry Valley,) (*J. C. Winne*,) boots, shoes, hats, caps and trunks, Harmony Row.

Winne, J. C., (Cherry Valley,) (*A. Winne & Co.*)

Winney, Adolphus, (Center Valley,) carpenter.

Winnie, Isaac, (Cherry Valley,) farmer 110.

Woodburn, R. R., (Cherry Valley,) farmer 57.

Woolcott, John, (Cherry Valley,) farmer 92.

Wyckoof, John, (Cherry Valley,) farmer 17.

Wykoff, John, (Cherry Valley,) farmer 68.

Wykoff, Thomas, (Cherry Valley,) farmer 50.

Yardon, Samuel, (Cherry Valley,) farmer 100.

Yindley, Francis, (Cherry Valley,) farmer 133.

Yordon, A., (Cherry Valley,) farmer 100.

Yordon, M., (Cherry Valley,) farmer 100.

Yordon, Peter D., (Cherry Valley,) farmer 115.

Youdon, Adam, (Buel, Montgomery Co.,) farmer 100.

Young, James, (Cherry Valley,) lawyer, corner Main and Montgomery.

Young, John, (Cherry Valley,) carpenter and farmer 243, Alden.

DECATUR.

(Post Office Addresses in Parentheses.)

Acley, Edward, (East Worcester,) carpenter.

Adams, Wm., (East Worcester,) farmer leases of James Bates, 90.

Babcock. Eli, (Decatur,) farmer 250.

Babcock, Elias, (East Worcester,) saw mill and farmer 107.

Babcock, Enos, (Worcester,) dairyman and farmer 110.

BABCOCK, ROBERT, (East Worcester,) (with Elias,) farmer.

Barnes, Rufus, (East Worcester,) dairyman and farmer 260.

Bentley, Cyrenius, (Decatur,) farmer.

Bishop, A. D., (Worcester,) gunsmith and farmer 98½.

Boorn, George M., (Decatur,) farmer 150.

Boorn, Isaac, (Decatur,) farmer 45.

BOORN, NAHUM T., (Decatur,) farmer 87.

Boorn, Stephen D., (Decatur,) farmer 87.

Bowen, Ansel, (East Worcester,) farmer leases of Hannah, 75.

Bowen, Ansel, (East Worcester,) farmer leases of John B. Dana, 50.

Bowen, Hannah, (East Worcester,) farmer 75.

Bowen, Warren L., (East Worcester,) teacher and farmer 80.

Brown, Barzilla, (Worcester,) hop raiser, dairyman and farmer 139.

Brown, B. R., (Decatur,) dairyman and farmer 144.

Brown, Squire, (Decatur,) farmer 55.

Brown, S. F., (Decatur,) hop raiser and farmer 55.

Buller, Alfred, (Decatur,) painter and farmer 14.

BUTLER, ALBERT, (Decatur,) justice of the peace, hop raiser and farmer 118.

Campbell, Alexander, (Decatur,) dairyman and farmer 156.

Campbell, Henry, (East Worcester,) hop raiser, dairyman and farmer 130.

Cass, Orsemus, (Worcester,) commissioner of highways, hop raiser, dairyman and farmer 130.

Chapin, Eliza, (Decatur,) farmer 24.

Chapman, Vincent, (East Worcester,) saw mill and farmer 75.

Cipperly, David, (Decatur,) teacher, town collector, constable and farmer 35.

Cooper, George, (Decatur,) farmer 62.

Cooper, Horace, (Decatur,) farmer 50.

Coss, Jacob, (East Worcester,) hop raiser and farmer 56.

Covey, Sylvanus, (East Worcester,) hop raiser, dairyman and farmer 83.

Crippen, David, (East Worcester,) town assessor, hop raiser, dairyman and farmer 120.

Crippin, Menzo, (Worcester,) butcher and farmer 12.

Daily, John, (Decatur,) farmer 78.

Daily, Peter, (East Worcester,) farmer 125.

Darling, Wm., (Decatur,) wagon maker and blacksmith.

Darling, Wm. H., (Decatur,) (with Wm.,) wagon maker and blacksmith.

Davis, Chalcey, (Decatur,) dairyman and farmer 215.

DAVIS, LORENZO D., (Decatur,) carriage maker, painter, trimmer and justice of the peace.

Day, Almer, (East Worcester,) blacksmith.

Day, Asa, (Worcester,) dairyman and farmer 148.

Day, Daniel, (Decatur,) postmaster and blacksmith.

Day, William H., (Decatur,) dairyman and farmer 165.

Devenbeck, George W., (Decatur,) hop raiser, dairyman and farmer 100.

Dodge, Isaac, (Decatur,) dairyman and farmer 104.

Dumont, Alonzo, (Decatur,) hop raiser and farmer 65.

Fern, Edmund, (Worcester,) hop raiser, dairyman and farmer 180.

FERN, JOHN, (Worcester,) president Schenevus Valley Agricultural Society, hop raiser, dairyman and farmer 800.

Fern, Wm., (Worcester,) (with Edmund,) farmer.

Ferris, Warren, (East Worcester,) justice of the peace, hop raiser, dairyman and farmer 191.

Flint, Valorus, (Decatur,) farmer 95.

Goodell, David, (Decatur,) farmer 124.

Goodell, John, (Decatur,) produce broker and town railroad commissioner.

Goodenough, Almon, (Decatur,) mason and farmer 63.

Goodenough, G. C., (Worcester,) saw mill, butter dealer and farmer 100.

Goodenough, Judson, (Decatur,) town assessor, mason and farmer 40.

Goodrich, Jay, (East Worcester,) farmer leases of Samuel Robbins, 184.

Granger, Byron, (East Worcester,) (with James Skinner,) farmer 100.

Griggs, Marvin, (East Worcester,) hop raiser and farmer 160.

GROFF, BOWMAN, (Decatur,) dealer in horses, prop. of saw and grist mills.

Groff, O. P., (Decatur,) agent for Advance Mowing Machine, dairyman and farmer 90.

Hartwell, Albert, (Decatur,) farmer 100.

Hartwell, Albert G., (East Worcester,) painter.

Hartwell, Anna, (East Worcester,) milliner.

Hartwell, Gibson, (Decatur,) merchant.

Hevenpeck, Sarah, (Decatur,) hop raiser, dairyman and farmer 60.

Hilsinger, Abram,(South Valley,) carpenter and farmer 57.

Hilsinger, Daniel, (South Valley,) (*with Solomon,*) farmer 114.

Hilsinger, Solomon, (South Valley,) (*with Daniel,*) farmer 114.

HOLMES, HENRY, (Decatur) dealer in hides and flour, and farmer 25.

Howland, Geo. H.,(South Valley,) farmer 40.

Hoyt, Gilbert, (Decatur,) (*with Horace,*) farmer.

Hoyt, Horace, (Decatur,) hop raiser, dairyman and farmer 200.

Kaple, Charles, (Decatur,) shoemaker and carpenter.

Kaple, Daniel,(Decatur,) town clerk, wagon maker and carpenter.

Knapp, Caroline, (Decatur,) farmer 17⅞.

Leonard, John, (East Worcester,) supervisor, physician, proprietor of saw and cider mills, dairyman and farmer 150.

LOWELL, MYRON H., (Decatur,) hop raiser, dairyman and farmer 140.

Lum, Barber, (East Worcester,) farmer 33.

Lum, Jonathan, (East Worcester,) farmer 118.

Lum, Wm., (South Valley,) farmer 65.

Markley, Daniel, (Decatur,) hop raiser and farmer 180.

Maybe, John,(Decatur,) thrashing machine and farmer 78.

Merchant, H. W., (Worcester,) farmer 106.

Mickle, Christopher, (East Worcester,) butcher and farmer 65.

Mickle, Henry, (East Worcester,) farmer 23.

Moak, Peter H., (Decatur,) dairyman and farmer 103.

Montgomery, Jacob, (East Worcester,) dairyman and farmer 90.

Munroe, Alfred, (Worcester,) farmer 3.

MURDOCK, DANIEL, (Decatur,) hotel keeper and carpenter.

Myers, Milard, (East Worcester,) saw mill and farmer 30.

Parker, George W., (Decatur,) hop raiser, dairyman and farmer 40.

Parker, Timothy, (Decatur,) hop raiser, dairyman and farmer 140.

Partman, James, (South Valley,) farmer 54.

Pierce, Edmund, (Decatur,) farmer 115.

Pitcher, Cornelius, (East Worcester,) hop raiser, dairyman and farmer 102.

Pitcher, John, (East Worcester,) farmer 30.

Potter, Horace B., (Decatur,) (*with H. S.,*) farmer.

Potter, H. S., (Decatur,) hop raiser, dairyman and farmer leases of Robert C. Lansing, 214.

Pratt, John, (East Worcester,) dairyman and farmer 150.

Putman, Lewis, (South Valley,) hop raiser, dairyman and farmer 123.

Putnam, David L., (East Worcester,) saw and turning mills, and farmer 17.

Rittou, Angevine, (East Worcester,) hop raiser, dairyman and farmer 125.

Rury, Frederick, (East Worcester,) farmer 75.

Rury, Levi, (East Worcester,) farmer 70.

Rury, Wm., (East Worcester,) saw mill, hop raiser, dairyman and farmer 125.

Salisbury, John H., (Decatur,) hop raiser, dairyman and farmer 107¾.

Salisbury, N. P., (Worcester,) mason and farmer 3.

Schutt, Horace, (Decatur,) apiarian, hop raiser, dairyman and farmer 248.

Seward, P., (Worcester,) (*with - - Van Allen,*) farmer leases of A. D. Bishop, 98½.

Shayes, C. B., (Decatur,) farmer 104.

Silman, George, (South Valley,) hop raiser, dairyman and farmer 220.

Simmons, Wm., (East Worcester,) farmer 100.

Skinner, James, (East Worcester,) (*with Byron Granger,*) farmer 100.

SKINNER, JARED, (East Worcester,) farmer leases of H. Smith, 100.

SMITH, AMOS, (Decatur,) farmer 103½ and leases of John Goodell, 100.

Snyder, Philip G., (South Valley,) hop raiser and farmer 63½.

Spafford, Wm., (Decatur,) farmer 104.

Starkweather George M., (Decatur,) justice of the peace, hop raiser and farmer 60.

Steward, Robert, (South Valley,) farmer 80.

Summers, W., (East Worcester,)farmer 175.

Summers, Wm., (East Worcester,) farmer 100.

Ten Eyck, Hannah, (East Worcester,) farmer 50.

Ten Eyck, John, (East Worcester,) farmer 70.

Thompson, Nahum, (Decatur,) dairyman, painter, paper hanger and farmer 260.

THOMPSON, SAMUEL, (East Worcester,) dairyman, farmer 111 and leases of Geo. Becker, 100.

Thompson, Selden, (East Worcester,) overseer of the poor, hop raiser, dairyman and farmer 63.

Treat, Barzilla, (Decatur,) farmer 80.

Treat, Elisha R., (Decatur,) farmer 51.

Treat, Russell, (Decatur,) farmer 80.

Umphrey, John, (Decatur,) farmer 70.

Van Allen, ——, (Worcester,) (*with P. Seward,*) farmer leases of A. D. Bishop, 98½.

Vanvorhis, Peter, (Decatur,) (*with Valorus Flint,*) farmer.

Van Voorhis, Samuel, (Decatur,) carpenter, hop raiser, dairyman and farmer 90.

Vroman, Wm. H., (East Worcester,) cattle dealer, hop raiser, dairyman and farmer 133.

Vrooman, Andrew, (East Worcester,) hop raiser, dairyman and farmer leases of John Skinner, 58.

Waldorf, Harvey, (East Worcester,) iron founder, carpenter, pattern maker, machinist and farmer 50.

WATERMAN, JOHN M., (Decatur,) physician and farmer 2.

Waterman, Perrin, (Decatur,) farmer 117.

Waterman, Russell, (Decatur,) insurance agent.

Winne, Mansfield W.. (East Worcester,) hop raiser, dairyman and farmer 83.

Winne, Peter F.. (South Valley,) commissioner of highways, hop raiser and farmer 80,

Winne, Wm. D., (Worcester,) dairyman and farmer 130.

Young, George, (East Worcester,) farmer 116.

YOUNG, JOHN W., (East Worcester,) mechanic.

EDMESTON.

(Post Office Addresses in Parentheses.)

Ackerman, Edwin R., (Edmeston,) painter, grainer, dairyman 3 cows, and farmer 20.

ACKERMAN, JAMES P., (Edmeston,) (*Ackerman & Son*,) dairyman, 5 cows, and farmer 50.

ACKERMAN, SAMUEL B., (Edmeston,) (*Ackerman & Son.*)

*ACKERMAN & SON, (Edmeston,) (*James P. and Samuel B.*,) builders, lumber dealers, manufs. of sash, blinds, doors and mouldings, and props. of cheese factory.

Adams, Thomas, (Edmeston,) tailor, dairyman, 2 cows, and farmer 100.

Allendorf, William P., (New Berlin, Chenango Co.,) commissioner of highways, dairyman, 9 cows, and farmer 86.

Anderson, John, (Burlington Flats,) farmer 82.

Andrews, Elias, (West Edmeston,) general merchant, postmaster and tailor.

Angel, David, (West Burlington,) dairyman, 10 cows, and farmer 123.

Angel, Edward W., (West Burlington,) dairyman, 5 cows, and farmer 60.

Arnold, Charles, (Edmeston,) farmer 25.

Arnold, David M.,(Burlington Flats,) dairyman, 10 cows, and farmer 104.

Arnold, Jessie, (Edmeston,) harness maker, dairyman, 10 cows, and farmer.

Arnold, Jesse L., (Edmeston,) harness maker, dairyman, 10 cows, and farmer 43.

Arnold, Sophia Mrs., (Edmeston,) dairy and farmer 76.

Arnold, T. Sheridan, (Edmeston,) school teacher.

Arnold, William M. B., (Burlington Flats,) farmer 6.

BANKS, LEVI B., (South Edmeston,) dairyman, 30 cows, and farmer 342.

Banks, Peter O., (New Berlin, Chenango Co.,) carpenter, dairyman, 5 cows, and farmer 42.

Barrett, Daniel R., (Edmeston,) farmer 21.

Barrett, Hiram, (Edmeston,) dairyman, 25 cows, and farmer 220.

Barrett, John, (Edmeston,) lumber dealer, dairyman, 12 cows, and farmer 100.

Barrett, Truman, (Edmeston,) dealer in live stock, dairyman, 10 cows, and farmer 126.

Barton, Samuel W., (Edmeston,) hotel prop. and farmer 68.

BASS, CHARLES H., (Leonardsville, Madison Co.,) dairyman, 19 cows, and farmer 175.

Bassett, Edgar, (Edmeston,) commission dealer in butter and cheese, dairyman, 17 cows, and farmer 125.

BASSETT, FLORUS C., (West Edmeston,) farmer.

Bean, James, (Edmeston,) dairyman, 6 cows, and farmer 60.

Bennet, Van Rensselær, (Burlington Flats,) farmer 51.

Bilyea Brothers, (Edmeston,) (*Foster H. and Homer*,) general merchants.

Bilyea, Foster H., (Edmeston,) (*Bilyea Brothers*,) town clerk.

Bilyea, Homer, (Edmeston,) (*Bilyea Bros.*)

Bilyea, Samuel C., (Edmeston,) carpenter.

Bingham, Barton M., (Edmeston,) physician and farmer 6.

Bingham, Henry, (Edmeston,) carriage maker.

Bootman, Edgar, (Edmeston,) general merchant and deputy postmaster.

Bootman, Truman, (Edmeston,) postmaster and provision safe manuf.

Boutwell, Henry. (Edmeston,) dairyman, 13 cows, and farmer 110.

Branch, Sanford, (Burlington Flats,) cooper and farmer 67.

Briggs, Hiram, (Edmeston,) dairyman, 12 cows, and farmer 103.

BROWN, JAMES O., (West Edmeston,) prop. Eagle Cheese Factory.

Brown, Joshua G., (Edmeston,) dairyman, 3 cows, and farmer 40.

BROWN, LEVI, (Edmeston,) blacksmith.

Brown, Ransom, (West Edmeston,) boots and shoes.

Brown, Samuel S., (Burlington Flats,) dairyman and farmer 25.

BURDICK, BALIUS, (Edmeston,) cooper and farmer works R. A. Perkins farm.

Burdick, Clark, (Burlington Flats,) dairyman, 3 cows, and farmer 36.

BURDICK, ICHABOD, (West Edmeston,) dairyman, 15 cows, and farmer 127.

Burdick, Wm., (Edmeston,) dairyman, 8 cows, and farmer 90.

Burdick, Wm. H., (West Edmeston,) carriage maker.

Burgess, Nathan, (Burlington Flats,) farmer 83.

Burlingham, Waterman, (Edmeston,) mason, dairyman, 21 cows, and farmer 193.

Burr Estate, (Burlington Flats,) (*Mrs. Harriet, Miss Mary, Selick, Miss Angeline M. and Ansel Burr, and Mrs. Elizabeth Angel,*) farmers 50.

Burr, Harriet Mrs., (Burlington Flats,) Burr estate.

Cady, Squire S. Rev., (South Edmeston,) pastor Free Will Baptist Church.

Cahoon, Ebenezer, (Burlington Flats,) dairyman, 27 cows, and farmer 230.

Carpenter, Gardner H., (South Edmeston,) dairyman, 17 cows, and farmer 180.

Caspius, Daniel, (Edmeston,) farmer 25.

CAULKINS, WILLIAM H., (South Edmeston,) dry goods, groceries, varieties &c., assistant postmaster, constable and collector.

Chace, Horace, (Edmeston,) saw and planing mills, manuf., of cheese boxes, dairyman, 10 cows, and farmer.

Chamberlain, Ely, (Edmeston,) general merchant.

Chambers, William B., (Edmeston,) physician and surgeon.

Champlin, Orson, (West Edmeston,) grocer.

Chapen, John, (Edmeston,) dairyman, 24 cows, and farmer 300.

CHAPEN, LAURENTINE, (West Burlington,) veterinary surgeon, dairyman, 9 cows, and farmer 50.

Chapin, Catherine Mrs., (New Berlin, Chenango Co.,) Chapin estate.

Chapin estate, (worked by James C. Moses,) (New Berlin, Chenango Co.,) dairy, 45 cows, and farmer 444.

Chase, Abner, (Edmeston,) dairyman, 16 cows, and farmer 22.

Chase, Anson, (Edmeston,) dairyman, 2 cows, and farmer 85.

Chase, Curren B., (West Edmeston,) dairyman, 10 cows, and farmer leases of Martha Gates, 88.

Chase, Erastus, (Edmeston,) dairyman, 8 cows, and farmer 84.

Chase, Freeman, (Edmeston,) dairyman and farmer.

Chase, Russell, (Edmeston,) dairyman, 16 cows, and farmer 16.

Chase, Warren, (West Edmeston,) cheese manuf., dairyman, 30 cows, and farmer 257.

Clark, Walter, (South Edmeston,) farmer 83.

Clarke, J. Bennett, (West Edmeston,) pastor of Seventh Day Baptist Church.

Coats, Charles W., (Edmeston,) farmer 40.

Coburn, Robert, (Edmeston,) dairyman, 10 cows, and farmer leases 100.

Cole, David B., (South Edmeston,) dairyman, wool grower and farmer 160.

COLE, HORACE C., (Burlington Flats,) dairyman, 13 cows, and farmer 186.

Colegrove, Almon R., (Edmeston,) farmer.

Colegrove, Asa I., (Edmeston,) agent for Singer Sewing Machine.

Colegrove, Daniel, (Edmeston,) minister, dairyman, 3 cows, and farmer 24.

COLEGROVE, DORR, (Burlington Flats,) dairyman, 10 cows, and farmer 114.

Colegrove, George A., (Edmeston,) minister, dairyman, 12 cows, and farmer 358.

COLEGROVE, ISRAEL, (Edmeston,) boot and shoe maker, minister, hop dealer, dairyman, 8 cows, and farmer 80.

Colegrove, Jeremiah, (Burlington Flats,) farmer 49.

COLEGROVE, JOHN D., (Edmeston,) dairyman, 15 cows, and farmer 120.

Colegrove, Warren, (Edmeston,) blacksmith and farmer 16.

COMAN, HENRY, (Edmeston,) dairyman, 31 cows, and farmer leases 220.

Coman, Phebe, (Edmeston,) farmer 96.

Comstock, Lucinda, (West Burlington,) dairy and farmer 20.

Coon, John S., (West Edmeston,) mechanic and farmer 10.

Coon, Murral, (West Edmeston,) dairyman, 22 cows, and farmer leases of Ezra Coon, 181½.

Cotton, Richard L., (Edmeston,) farmer.

Crandall, Sanders, (West Edmeston,) dairyman, 7 cows, and farmer 57.

CRANDALL, TRUMAN, (Edmeston,) dairyman, 15 cows, and farmer 115.

Crandall, Truman A., (West Edmeston,) blacksmith and justice of the peace.

Curry, Joseph B., (South Edmeston,) dairyman, 10 cows, and farmer 110.

Cushman, Pitt, (Edmeston,) prop. cheese factory, dairyman, 30 cows, and farmer 240.

Davis, Alvin, (Burlington Flats,) dairyman, 12 cows, and farmer 186.

Davis, John H., (Edmeston,) prop. Edmeston Center Hotel and carriage trimmer.

Davis, Simon, (Burlington Flats,) carpenter, cooper, dairyman, 4 cows, and farmer 34.

De Lancey, Oliver L., (South Edmeston,) farmer 60.

De Long, Mary B. Mrs., (South Edmeston,) millinery.

De Long, Willis, (South Edmeston,) miller, dairyman, 7 cows, and farmer 61.

Deming, Eri, (Edmeston,) farmer 40.

Deming, Lyman, (Edmeston,) lumber dealer, prop. of saw mill, dairyman, 15 cows, and farmer 300.

Deming, Warren, (Edmeston,) lumber dealer, dairyman, 9 cows, and farmer 80.

Denison, Stephen C., (Edmeston,) dairyman, 35 cows, and farmer 260.

Denison, Washington, (Edmeston,) dairyman, 16 cows, and farmer 216.

Digman, Jerome W., (Burlington Flats,) dairyman, 20 cows, and farmer 133.

Doolittle, Charles, (Edmeston,) farmer leases.

Doolittle, John, (Edmeston,) dairyman, 10 cows, and farmer 100.

Doolittle, John Jr., (Edmeston,) dairyman, 10 cows, and farmer 96.

Dresser, Franklin E., (West Edmeston,) dairyman, 15 cows, and farmer 130.
Dupee, James, (South Edmeston,) dairyman, 8 cows, and farmer 90.
Dupee, Wm. J., (South Edmeston,) cooper, assessor, dairyman, 6 cows, and farmer 59.
Dutcher, Andrus J., (South Edmeston,) blacksmith and veterinary surgeon.
Dutton, Alvin, (South Edmeston,) dairyman, 30 cows, and farmer 190.
Dutton, Elon G., (South Edmeston,) dairyman, 23 cows, and farmer 151.
Dutton, Julia Ann Miss, (Edmeston,) dairyman, 11 cows, and farmer 106.
DYE, JOHN L., (Leonardsville, Madison Co.,) farmer 58.
Dye, Russel, (Leonardsville, Madison Co.,) dairyman, 26 cows, and farmer 280.
DYE, SPENCER R., (Leonardsville, Madison Co.,) dairyman, 20 cows, and farmer 110.
DYE, WILLIAM G., (Leonardsville, Madison Co.,) dairyman, 18 cows, and farmer 151.
Dyer, Daniel A., (Burlington Flats,) dairyman, 11 cows, grain thrasher and farmer 150.
Dyer, Delos, (Edmeston,) dairyman, 11 cows, and farmer 109.
DYER, MORRIS W., (Burlington Flats,) grain thrasher, mechanic, dairyman and farmer 86.
EAGLE CHEESE FACTORY, (West Edmeston,) James O. Brown, prop.
Edwards, George T., (South Edmeston,) dairyman, 20 cows, and farmer 180.
Fasset, Adelbert C., (Edmeston,) cheese maker.
Felton, Gilbert, (West Edmeston,) dairyman, 26 cows, and farmer 210.
Flint, G. E. Rev., (Edmeston,) pastor Baptist Church.
Gaddis, John, (West Edmeston,) painter.
Gates, Avery T., (Edmeston,) dairyman and farmer 78.
Gates, W. Harrison, (Edmeston,) dairyman, 18 cows, and farmer 162.
Gazlay, Miles, (South Edmeston,) dairyman, 20 cows, and farmer 76.
Giles, Delos V., (Burlington Flats,) carpenter, dairyman, 10 cows, and farmer 67.
Gillmore, Moses, (South Edmeston,) butcher.
Glover, Emeline, (Edmeston,) farmer.
Goodrich, Charles F., (South Edmeston,) dairyman, 23 cows, and farmer 370.
Green, Lewis N., (Edmeston,) proprietor of wrought iron foundry.
Green, William, (Edmeston,) dairyman, 5 cows, and farmer 54.
HALL, HARVEY D., (Edmeston,) dairyman, 9 cows, and farmer 100.
HALL, JOHN A., (Edmeston,) dairyman, 15 cows, and farmer 150.
Harrington, John, (Edmeston,) farmer 10.
Hawkins, Andrew, (Edmeston,) saw mill, dairyman, 12 cows, and farmer 180.
Hecox, Andrew J., (Edmeston,) boots and shoes.
HICKLING, THOMAS, (Edmeston,) dairyman, 15 cows, and farmer 107.

HICOX, GEORGE W., (Edmeston,) manuf. of lumber and lath, prop. of cider mill and carpenter.
Hiller, William M. Rev., (Edmeston,) pastor M. E. Church.
Hinds, Reuben, (New Berlin, Chenango Co.,) dairyman 12 cows, and farmer 187.
HOOKER, ALONZO L., (South Edmeston.) (Hooker Brothers.)
HOOKER BROTHERS, (South Edmeston,) (Hiram C. and Alonzo L.,) carriage manufs.
Hooker, Charles D., (South Edmeston,) carpenter.
HOOKER, HENRY D., (South Edmeston,) carriage maker, butcher, dairyman, 10 cows, and farmer 87.
HOOKER, HIRAM C., (South Edmeston,) (Hooker Brothers.)
Hopkins, Charles H., (Burlington Flats,) dairyman, 10 cows, and farmer 115.
HOPKINS, EDWIN O., (Edmeston,) (Samuel Hopkins & Son,) dairyman and farmer 38.
HOPKINS, SAMUEL & SON, (Edmeston,) (Edwin O.,) blacksmiths, carriage and wagon manufs.
Hopkins, Truman L., (Edmeston,) stone mason.
Howard, Orin, (South Edmeston,) justice of the peace.
Hoxie, Samuel L., (South Edmeston,) dairyman, 40 cows, and farmer 210.
Hoxie, Solomon, (South Edmeston,) dairyman, 20 cows, and farmer 150.
Hubby, Milton, (South Edmeston,) farmer 115.
Hume, James, (South Edmeston,) dairyman, 10 cows, and farmer 128.
Hume, Walter, (West Burlington,) dairyman, 10 cows, and farmer 156.
Huntington, Franklin C., (West Edmeston,) dairyman, 30 cows, and farmer 186.
Johnson, Ira, (Burlington Flats,) cooper, dairyman, 8 cows, and farmer 79.
Jordan, David M., (Edmeston,) dairy, 17 cows, and farmer 145.
JOSLYN, WILLIAM, (Edmeston,) boots and shoes.
Keith, Kingsley, (Burlington Flats,) dairyman, 8 cows, and farmer 80.
Keith, Seth, (Burlington Flats,) carpenter.
Keith, Wm. M., (Edmeston,) dairyman, 8 cows, and farmer 77.
Kelsey, Andrew, (Edmeston,) dairyman, 25 cows, and farmer 237.
Kelsey, Daniel, (Edmeston,) dairyman and farmer 37.
Langworth, George, (West Edmeston,) dairyman, 22 cows, and farmer 150.
LANGWORTHY, HOLLUM, (West Edmeston,) apiarian, dairyman, 40 cows, and farmer 250.
Langworthy, Morgan, (West Edmeston,) dairyman, 11 cows, and farmer 142.
LUCUS, WM. H., (Edmeston,) blacksmith.
Main, Justus B., (Edmeston,) dairyman, 11 cows, and farmer 120.
Maine, Charles, (Burlington Flats,) dairyman, 6 cows, and farmer 64.
Manchester, Andrew J., (South Edmeston,) dairyman, 10 cows, and farmer 118.
Mather, Henry C., (Garrattsville,) dairyman, 10 cows, and farmer 180.

MATTERSON, NELSON W., (South Edmeston,) dry goods, groceries, varieties &c., postmaster, dairyman, 18 cows, and farmer 100.

Milliard, Jabez B., (West Edmeston,) farmer 130.

Mitchel, Charles, (Edmeston,) dairyman, 25 cows, and farmer 225.

Mitchel, Truman, (Edmeston,) carpenter, dairyman, 6 cows, and farmer 60.

Mitchell, Bera, (Edmeston,) carpenter, dairyman, 4 cows, and farmer 57.

Mitchell, Major, (Edmeston,) dairyman, 23 cows, and farmer 157.

Mitchell, Norman, (Edmeston,) farmer 36.

Moses, Henry, (South Edmeston,) dairyman, 22 cows, and farmer 165.

Moses, James C., (New Berlin, Chenango Co.,) carpenter, farmer 42, also works Chapin estate.

MOTT, JONATHAN, (West Edmeston,) dairyman, 40 cows, and farmer 259.

Mott, Sophia Mrs., (Leonardsville, Madison Co.,) dairy, 5 cows, and farmer 140.

Munro, Walter C., (Edmeston,) dairyman, 7 cows, and farmer 68.

Northup, William H., (Edmeston,) dairyman, 12 cows, and farmer 134.

Page, Horace, (South Edmeston,) dairyman, 11 cows, and farmer 65.

Page, Stephen, (South Edmeston,) dairyman, 12 cows, and farmer 107.

Page, Thomas A., (South Edmeston,) school teacher and farmer.

PALMER, GEORGE H., (Edmeston,) veterinary surgeon, house and sign painter.

Palmiter, William M., (West Edmeston,) blacksmith.

Pardee, Joseph Dwight, (West Edmeston,) cabinet maker.

Parker, Eri, (West Burlington,) dairyman, 40 cows, and farmer 404.

PARKER, IRA D., (Edmeston,) dairyman, 8 cows, and farmer 123.

PAYNE, C. ADELBERT, (Edmeston,) carpenter and joiner.

Payne, C. A. Mrs., (Edmeston,) millinery.

Peck, William S., (Burlington Flats,) blacksmith, dairyman, 8 cows, and farmer 92.

Peet, Silas, (Edmeston,) dairyman, 15 cows, and farmer 194.

Perkins, Amos, (Edmeston,) dairyman, 9 cows, and farmer.

Perkins, George, (Edmeston,) farmer 15.

PERKINS, OLIVER W., (Edmeston,) dairyman, 8 cows, and farmer 80.

Perkins, Ransom A., (Edmeston,) carpenter, dairyman, 8 cows, and farmer 88.

Perkins, Russell, (Edmeston,) dairyman and farmer.

Phelps, Charles, (South Edmeston,) dairyman, 19 cows, and farmer 90.

Phelps, Edgar, (Edmeston,) dairyman, 26 cows, and farmer 200.

Phelps, George W., (West Edmeston,) dairyman, 26 cows, and farmer leases of Gilbert Felton, 210.

Pitts, George M., (Edmeston,) grocer.

Pope, Charles H., (Edmeston,) express agent between Utica, Edmeston and New Berlin, and (with David B.,) dairyman, 10 cows, and farmer 113.

Pope, David B., (Edmeston,) (with Charles H.,) dairyman, 10 cows, and farmer 113.

Pope, Edwin M., (Edmeston,) agent for H. J. Wood, clothier, Utica, dairyman, 3 cows, and farmer 40.

Pope, Lloyd V., (South Edmeston,) blacksmith, dairyman, 6 cows, and farmer 50.

Pope, Marcus, (West Burlington,) dairyman, 3 cows, and farmer 24.

Pope, Perry, Jr., (Edmeston,) blacksmith, dairyman, 5 cows, and farmer 60.

Pope, Seth T., (Edmeston,) blacksmith, dealer in live stock, dairyman, 3 cows, and farmer 270.

Price, Leonard H., (West Burlington,) carpenter and farmer 7.

Raymond, Alfred G., (South Edmeston,) harness and carriage maker.

Reed, Douglass B., (Edmeston,) cabinet maker and farmer 30.

Richards, John T., (Edmeston,) (Smith & Richards.)

Robinson, Denzil, (West Burlington,) dairyman, 12 cows, and farmer 100.

Ross, David T., (Edmeston,) tannery.

Rutherford, George, (South Edmeston,) dairyman, 22 cows, and farmer 206.

Rutherford, Robert W., (South Edmeston,) dairyman, 30 cows, and farmer leases 190.

SCHERMERHORN, EDMUND J., (West Edmeston,) dairyman, 15 cows, and farmer leases 130.

SCHERMERHORN, SMITH, (South Edmeston,) dealer in live stock, dairyman, 4 cows, and farmer 51.

Simmons, Alburties, (Edmeston,) dairyman, 29 cows, and farmer 190.

Simmons, Chas., (Edmeston,) (with Geo.,) dairyman, 14 cows, and farmer 133.

SIMMONS, GEORGE, (Edmeston,) (with Chas.,) dairyman, 14 cows, and farmer 133.

Simmons, Henry, (Edmeston,) dairyman, 8 cows, and farmer 103.

SIMMONS, MARSHALL E., (Edmeston,) blacksmith and farmer 24.

Simmons, Roswell, (South Edmeston,) dairyman, 12 cows, and farmer 110.

SISSON, LUTHER S., (West Edmeston,) apiarian, patentee and manuf. of bee hives and honey emptying machines.

SITTS, DELOSS, (West Edmeston,) prop. hotel.

SMITH, DELOS, (Edmeston,) (with Jared,) dairyman, 20 cows, and farmer 200.

Smith, James, (Edmeston,) dairyman, 20 cows, and leases of A. W. Sutherland, 168.

SMITH, JARED, (Edmeston,) (with Delos,) dairyman, 20 cows, and farmer 200.

Smith, Oliver L., (Edmeston,) (Smith & Richards.)

Smith & Richards, (Edmeston,) (Oliver L. Smith and John T. Richards,) tinware and provision safes.

Southworth estate, heirs of, (Edmeston,) (Mrs. Thomas, Walter and Miss Julia,) dairy, 13 cows and farmers 90.

Spencer, Lewis, (Edmeston,) meat market.

Spencer, Wm. M., (Edmeston,) physician and surgeon.

C. W. SMITH & CO.,
BANKERS!

Iron Clad Building, Cooperstown, N. Y.

Interest paid on Deposits by special arrangement. **Government Bonds** and all First Class Securities bought and sold. **Loans** negotiated. **Drafts** for any sum drawn upon England, Ireland and prominent places in Europe. **Passage Tickets** to and from England, Ireland and the Continent. **Collections** made and remitted with utmost promptness.

New York Correspondent and Reference,....,.... First National Bank, New York.

Calvin Graves, E. M. Harris, A. A. Jarvis, C. W. Smith, and other Associates.

McINTOSH & HAYNES,
Attorneys and Counselors at Law,
Cooperstown, N. Y.

Particular attention given to business in Surrogate and Justices' Courts.

HINDS & PARSHALL,
BUTCHERS
AND
Meat Market,
Main Street, Cooperstown, N. Y.

Oscar N. Hinds.   *Israel A. Parshall.*

THREE MILE POINT HOUSE,
SITUATED
ON THE BANKS OF OTSEGO LAKE!
THREE MILES FROM COOPERSTOWN.

Otsego Bass and Trout, and Game Dinners,
SERVED AT ALL HOURS OF THE DAY.

A. W. THAYER, Proprietor.

Sprague, Asa W., (West Burlington,) dairyman, 4 cows, and farmer 19.

Spurr, John, (South Edmeston,) carpenter.

Stephens, James, (Edmeston,) dairyman, 12 cows, and farmer 130.

Stickney, Silas P., (Edmeston,) dairyman, 9 cows, and farmer 83.

Stillman, Amos S., (West Edmeston,) apiarian, dairyman, 15 cows, and farmer leases of Ichabod Burdick, 127.

Stillman, Ransom T., (West Edmeston,) harness maker and farmer.

ST. JOHN, DAVID B., (Edmeston,) justice of the peace, lawyer, civil engineer, dairyman, 10 cows, and farmer 138.

St, John, Solomon C., (Edmeston,) civil engineer, tin roofer and notary public.

SUTHERLAND, ALBERT, (Edmeston,) agent for Singer Sewing Machine, dairyman, 10 cows, and farmer.

Swayer, James, (Edmeston,) dairyman, 15 cows, and farmer 109.

Talbot, Arba C., (Burlington Flats,) dairyman, 9 cows, and farmer 85.

Talbot, Benjamin, (Burlington Flats,) dairyman, 8 cows, and farmer 230.

Talbot, David, (Edmeston,) dairyman, 4 cows, and farmer 30.

Talbot, Eric, (Burlington Flats,) dairyman, 5 cows, and farmer 70.

Talbot, Ira W., (Edmeston,) carpenter, dairyman, 25 cows, and farmer 230.

Talbot, Israel, (Edmeston,) carpenter, dairyman, 12 cows, and farmer 100.

TALBOT, JACOB, (Edmeston,) dealer in live stock, dairyman, 5 cows, and farmer 140.

Talbot, Joseph, (Edmeston,) dairyman, 35 cows, and farmer 333.

TALBOT, J. WELLINGTON, (Edmeston,) dealer in live stock, dairyman, 8 cows, and farmer 70.

Talbot, Newell, (Edmeston,) justice of the peace, dairyman, 20 cows, and farmer 195.

TALBOT, NEWEL N., (Burlington Flats,) commissioner of highways, constable, prop. of cheese factory, dairyman, 30 cows, and farmer 250.

Talbot, Norman, (Edmeston,) dairyman, 11 cows, and farmer 103.

Talbot, Perry, (Edmeston,) dairyman, 12 cows, and farmer 90.

Talbot, Sylvia Mrs., (Edmeston,) dairy, 6 cows, and farmer 45.

TALBOT, WILLIAM, (Edmeston,) assessor, dairyman, 15 cows, and farmer 122.

TALBOTT, ISAAC, (West Edmeston,) dairyman, 20 cows, and farmer 247.

Talbot, Phebe Miss, (Edmeston,) farmer 30.

Talcott, Hamilton G., (Edmeston,) cooper.

Taylor, Morris W., (New Berlin, Chenango Co.,) dairyman, 12 cows, and farmer 163.

Taylor, Solomon, (Burlington Flats,) farmer 28.

TAYLOR, SOLOMON JR., (Leonardsville, Madison Co.,) dairyman, 20 cows, and farmer 225.

Taylor, Truman, (Edmeston,) dairyman, 8 cows, and farmer 25.

Terry, Horace, (South Edmeston,) hotel prop.

Toles, Orson, (South Edmeston,) dairyman, 14 cows, and farmer 166.

Wait, Hiram S., (South Edmeston,) boots and shoes.

WALES, EDWARD, (Edmeston,) prop. of grist and saw mills, blacksmith and manuf. of lumber, lath and pickets.

WALLING, STEPHEN P., (South Edmeston,) prop. of saw, planing and grist mills, and millwright.

WATTERS, TRUMAN H., (South Edmeston,) carriage trimmer.

WELCH, ALVA, (West Edmeston,) dairyman, 16 cows, and farmer 134.

Welch, Charles M., (Edmeston,) dairyman, 21 cows, and farmer 180.

WELCH, DANIEL O., (Leonardsville, Madison Co.,) dairyman, 16 cows, and farmer leases of David, 134.

WELCH, DAVID C., (West Edmeston,) dairyman, 19 cows, and farmer 135.

Welch, Herman D., (West Edmeston,) dairyman, 13 cows, and farmer leases of Clarissa, 100.

Welch, Otis G., (Edmeston,) dairyman, 15 cows, and farmer 117.

Welch, William H., (Leonardsville, Madison Co.,) dealer in live stock, dairyman, 14 cows, and farmer 130.

West, Charles B., (Burlington Flats,) farmer 50.

WHEELER, EDWIN, (Edmeston,) dairyman, 6 cows, and farmer 50.

Wheeler, Ezra, (Edmeston,) mason.

White, Gideon, (Burlington Flats,) farmer 20.

White, John, (Burlington Flats,) cooper and farmer 38.

Whittemore, Mary Mrs., (Edmeston,) saw mill, dairy, 14 cows, and farmer 144.

WILLIAMS, HENRY C., (Edmeston,) dairyman, 25 cows, and farmer 216.

Winsor, Stephen, (Edmeston,) cooper.

Wright, Charles, (Burlington Flats,) dairyman, 20 cows, and farmer 184.

Wright, Charles P., (Burlington Flats,) farmer 25.

Wright, Hiram, (West Edmeston,) dairyman, 40 cows, and farmer 420.

Wright, Leander, (Burlington Flats,) dairyman, 5 cows, and farmer 35.

Wright, Nathan, (Burlington Flats,) dairyman, 17 cows, and farmer 140.

Yeaw, Chester, (West Edmeston,) dairyman and farmer 78.

K

EXETER.

(Post Office Addresses in Parentheses.)

Allen, David, (West Exeter,) blacksmith.
Anderson, Philander, (Schuyler's Lake,) (*with John Austick*,) farmer 14.
ANDERSON, WILLIAM, (Richfield,) farmer leases of Joseph Wilmarth, 300.
Angell, Byron P., (Exeter,) insurance agent and farmer 100.
Angell, David R., (Exeter,) farmer 125.
Angell, Henry J., (Exeter,) carpenter.
Angell, Jonathan, (Exeter,) farmer 160.
Angell, Joseph, (Exeter,) farmer 15.
Angell, Oscar E., (Exeter,) farmer 90.
Arnold, James, (West Exeter,) picture and frame peddler.
Austick, John, (Schuyler's Lake,) (*Austick & Mitchell*,) (*with Philander Anderson*,) farmer 14.
Austick & Mitchell, (Schuyler's Lake,) (*John Austick and D. W. Mitchell*,) general merchants.
Babcock, Almon, (Exeter,) farmer 130.
Baker, Henry J., (Schuyler's Lake,) cheese factory and farmer 18.
BALL, JOHN W., (Exeter,) notary public and farmer 100.
Bard, John A., (Schuyler's Lake,) farmer 114.
Barstow, George T., (West Exeter,) farmer 323.
Benjamin, Caleb F., (Exeter,) farmer 9.
BENJAMIN, RUDOLPH, (Exeter,) blacksmith and owns 2.
Bennett, Lewis J., (West Exeter,) farmer leases 165.
Bliss, Eunice A. Mrs., (Exeter,) farmer 60.
Bliss, John L., (Exeter,) farmer 120.
Bliss, Newel, (Exeter,) cooper and farmer 70.
Bliss, Seth L., (Schuyler's Lake,) farmer 11.
Bliss, Theodore, (Schuyler's Lake,) farmer 190.
Bowers, G. D., (Exeter,) (*with Russell*,) farmer 130.
Bowers, Russell, (Exeter,) (*with G. D.,*) farmer 130.
Brady, James, 1st, (Schuyler's Lake,) farmer 100.
Brady, James, 2nd, (Schuyler's Lake,) (*with John*,) farmer 180.
Brady, John, (Schuyler's Lake,) (*with James, 2nd.,*) farmer 180.
Brady, Thomas, (Schuyler's Lake,) farmer 80.
BROWN, WILLIAM G., (West Exeter,) farmer 110.
Bullion, George D., (Schuyler's Lake,) prop of Schuyler's Lake House.

CANEY, JOHN A., (Schuyler's Lake,) farmer 30.
Carson, James, (Schuyler's Lake,) farmer leases of J. J. Rider, 200.
CASS, JOHN T., (Exeter,) school teacher and farmer 92.
CASWELL, D. H., (Exeter,) school teacher.
Caswell, John R., (Exeter,) farmer 50 and leases of Banyer estate, 210.
Chappell, Charles, (Exeter,) physician and farmer 7.
Chappell, John, (Schuyler's Lake,) town clerk, tailor and farmer 15.
Clark, D. W., (Schuyler's Lake,) farmer 108.
Clark, John, (Exeter,) farmer 109.
Clark, John F., (Exeter,) farmer 97.
Clark, Joshua, (Exeter,) farmer 78.
Clark, Manville, (West Exeter,) farmer leases of John T. Barstow, 247.
Clark, Wayne, (Schuyler's Lake,) (*with Robert Wright*,) farmer 40.
CLARK, WILLIAM, (Exeter,) (*with John*.)
Clark, William D., (Exeter,) farmer leases 142.
Coats Brothers, (West Exeter,) (*Henry O. and Charles T.,*) general merchants.
Coats, Charles T., (West Exeter,) (*Coats Brothers*.)
Coats, Henry O., (West Exeter,) (*Coats Brothers*.)
Coats, Joseph, (West Exeter,) farmer 6.
Cochrane, William R. Rev., (West Exeter,) pastor of M. E. Church.
Coffin, William, (Exeter,) farmer 11.
Coleman, Murell, (Exeter,) farmer 140.
Counrod, Calvin, (Exeter,) farmer 80.
Counrod, George, (Exeter,) agent for A. B. Howe Sewing Machine.
Crumb, H., (West Eaton,) farmer 100.
Curley, Martin, (Exeter,) (*with Thomas*,) farmer 80.
Curley, Thomas, (Exeter,) (*with Martin*,) farmer 80.
Curtis, Charles, estate of, (Schuyler's Lake,) 228 acres.
Curtis, David, (Exeter,) farmer 56.
CURTISS, ALONZO, (Exeter,) wagon maker.
Daley, Moses, (Exeter,) farmer 115.
Darbey, Alonzo, (Exeter,) (*with Rufus*,) farmer 140.
Darby, Rufus, (Exeter,) (*with Alonzo*,) farmer 140.
Dauchy, Clark R., (Burlington Flats,) farmer 25.
Dauchy, George D., (Burlington Flats,) farmer 113.

Dauchy, George T., (Burlington Flats,) farmer 85.

Davenport, Richard, (Schuyler's Lake,) farmer 120.

Davis, Delos, (West Exeter,) deputy sheriff, constable and farmer leases of Harvey Hull, 106.

Devendorf. Nelson, (West Exeter,) prop. of West Exeter Hotel.

Doleman, James, (Exeter,) farmer leases 250.

Downs, James, (Schuyler's Lake,) farmer 6.

Durfy, John, (Schuyler's Lake,) (*J. & J. Durfy.*)

Durfy, Judson, (Schuyler's Lake,) (*J. & J. Durfy.*)

Durfy, J. & J., (Schuyler's Lake,) (*John and Judson*,) cabinet makers and undertakers.

Dyer, Henry, (West Exeter,) farmer 100.

Dyer, Philip, (West Exeter,) farmer 50.

Dygert, Daniel L., (Schuyler's Lake,) cooper, assessor and farmer 24.

Edick, Andrew M., (West Exeter,) farmer leases 96.

Edmonds, Amos, (Richfield,) resident.

EDMONDS, GEORGE P., (Richfield,) farmer 107.

Eygabroat, L. F., (Schuyler's Lake,) (*L. O. Veber & Co.*)

Fairchild, Lewis D., (West Exeter,) farmer 2.

Fay, Hiram, (Exeter,) farmer 64.

Fay, John, (Schuyler's Lake,) farmer 43.

Fearn, John, (Schuyler's Lake,) farmer 315.

FIRMAN, JAMES, (Schuyler's Lake,) wagon maker, blacksmith, painter and trimmer, owns 23.

Fitch, Lewis W., (Exeter.) farmer leases of Milo B. Robinson, 100.

Fitch, Nathan, (Schuyler's Lake,) farmer 71.

Flewellin, David A., (Schuyler's Lake,) farmer 100.

Garlick, Henry Rev., (Schuyler's Lake,) pastor of Baptist Church.

Gates, Alfred, (West Exeter,) (*with Lafayette*,) farmer 133.

Gates, Fernando C., (West Exeter,) farmer 220.

Gates, Hiram, (West Exeter,) resident.

Gates, Lafayette, (West Exeter,) (*with Alfred,*) farmer 133.

Gilmore, Cyrus A., (Schuyler's Lake,) farmer 80.

Gray, John F., (Schuyler's Lake,) farmer 7.

GREEN, THOMAS J., (Richfield,) farmer 268.

Hadsell, Jesse, (Schuyler's Lake,) farmer leases 80.

Hall, William, (West Exeter,) carpenter and farmer 4.

Henderson, A. W., (Schuyler's Lake,) produce dealer and farmer 60.

HENRY, LOWELL S., (Schuyler's Lake,) lawyer.

Herkimer, Nelson T., (Schuyler's Lake,) wagon maker and farmer 300.

Herkimer, Sarah Mrs., (Schuyler's Lake,) farmer 78.

Herkimer, Timothy, (Schuyler's Lake,) farmer 430.

Higbie, Delavan E., (Exeter,) farmer 35.

Higbie, Milton, (Exeter,) farmer 100.

Higgins, Levi, (Burlington Flats,) farmer 107.

Hills, L. H., (Schuyler's Lake,) physician and surgeon, and coroner.

Hinds, George W., (Richfield,) farmer 52.

Hinds, O. C., (Schuyler's Lake,) farmer 140.

Hinds, O. W., (Schuyler's Lake,) saw, grist and cider mills, and farmer 12.

Hollister, DeWitt C., (Burlington Flats,) farmer 107.

Horan, John, (Exeter,) farmer 120.

Horan, Patrick, (Exeter,) farmer 60.

Horton, Daniel, (Schuyler's Lake,) farmer 80.

Horton, John W.,(Schuyler's Lake,) farmer 54.

Hubbard, Deloss E., (Schuyler's Lake,) farmer.

Hubbard, Seth, (Schuyler's Lake,) farmer 168.

Hull, Harvey, (West Exeter,) farmer 106.

Huntley, C., (West Exeter,) farmer 200.

Huntley, Charles, (West Exeter,) farmer 140.

Huntley, D. C., (West Exeter,) farmer 110.

Huntley, Elisha, (West Exeter,) farmer 130.

Huntley, Starr D., (West Exeter,) farmer leases of Loring Huntley, 130.

Huntly, Loring, (West Exeter,) farmer 600.

Hurelle, J. T., (Schuyler's Lake,) shoe maker.

Huyck, Robert L., (Exeter,) farmer 93.

Huyck, Theodore C., (Schuyler's Lake,) farmer 30.

Jackson, Nathaniel B., (West Exeter,) farmer 168.

Joels, Hiram, (West Exeter,) shoemaker.

Johnson, Charles A.,(West Exeter,) (*W. A. & C. A. Johnson.*)

Johnson, Marquis D., (Exeter,) farmer 80.

Johnson, William,(West Exeter,) mechanic and farmer 5.

Johnson, W. Anson, (West Exeter,) (*W. A. & C. A. Johnson*,) wagon maker.

Johnson, W. A. & C. A., (West Exeter,) (*W. Anson and Charles A.*,) props. of saw mill and broom handle manufs.

Jones, John C., (West Exeter,) farmer leases 96.

JONES, SAMUEL, (Schuyler's Lake,) blacksmith.

JONES, WILLIAM P., (Exeter,) general merchant and post master.

Judd, L. C., (Schuyler's Lake,) farmer 150.

Judd, Mary A. Mrs., (Schuyler's Lake,) milliner.

Judd, Orrin A., (Schuyler's Lake,) farmer leases of Amelia Davenport, 96.

King, Constantine, (West Exeter,) farmer 306.

Lidell, Allen, (Schuyler's Lake,) farmer 200.

Lidell, B. W., (Schuyler's Lake,) supervisor and farmer 156.

Lidell, Jonas A., (Schuyler's Lake,) farmer 275.

LIDELL, PAUL A.,(Exeter,) cheese manuf.

Lipe, Joshua F., (Exeter,) farmer 93.

Mallory, Lucius S.,(Exeter,) shoemaker and farmer 80.

Matteson, Charles W., (West Exeter,) carpenter and farmer 8.

Matteson, Josiah, (West Exeter,) farmer 76.

MATTESON, MARVIN, (Exeter,) farmer leases of Jonathan Angell, 160.

Mattison, Peleg, (Richfield,) farmer 100.

May, Erastus, (Exeter,) blacksmith and farmer 5.

May, George, (Schuyler's Lake,) cheese maker.

McCrorie, James M., (Schuyler's Lake,) saw and cider mills, and farmer 16.

McDonough, John, (Schuyler's Lake,) farmer 100.

Minacuse, Matthias, (Exeter,) farmer 2.

Minor, William, (Schuyler's Lake,) farmer 30.

Mitchell, D. W.,(Schuyler's Lake,) (*Austick & Mitchell*.)

Mitchell, S. B. L., (Exeter,) farmer 350.

Monk, Daniel A., (West Exeter,) farmer 120.

Mooney, William, (Schuyler's Lake,) farmer 143.

Morey, George W., (Schuyler's Lake,) farmer 83.

Morey, Smith, (Schuyler's Lake,) farmer 65.

Mott, Robert C., (Exeter,) carpenter and farmer 76.

Mulvey, ——, (Schuyler's Lake,) farmer 13.

Newkirk, Charles H., (Schuyler's Lake,) cider mill and farmer 21.

Newkirk, William,(Schuyler's Lake,) blacksmith and farmer 105.

Newkirk, William S., (Schuyler's Lake,) (*with William*,) farmer.

Palmer, Ira, (Schuyler's Lake,) shoe maker.

Patrick, David W., (Schuyler's Lake,) physician and farmer 70.

Perkins, Lewis, (Schuyler's Lake,) farmer 100.

Phillips, Seth, (Exeter,) justice of the peace, farmer 33 and leases 150.

Phillips, W. Irving, (Exeter,) farmer 94 and leases 60.

Pickens, Philip, (Exeter,) shoe maker and farmer 6.

PLUMB, ORVILLE L., (Schuyler's Lake,) (*O. L. & V. Plumb*.)

PLUMB, O. L. & V., (Schuyler's Lake,) (*Orville L. and Volney*,) hotel props.

PLUMB, VOLNEY, (Schuyler's Lake,) (*O. L. & V. Plumb*.)

Pope, Joseph, (Exeter,) physician, commissioner of highways and farmer 150.

Pratt, George W., (Schuyler's Lake,) farmer 58½.

Pritchard, John E., (Schuyler's Lake,) farmer 132.

Purchase, Horace C., (Exeter,) cheese manuf.

Rider, J. J., (Schuyler's Lake,) cheese factory and farmer 300.

Roberts, Thomas, (West Exeter,) farmer 73.

ROBINSON, Barzilla, (Schuyler's Lake,) farmer 26.

Robinson, Henry C., (Schuyler's Lake,) farmer 209.

Robinson, Milo B., (Exeter,) farmer 100.

Robinson, Truman, (Schuyler's Lake,) farmer 54.

Rood, Elias, (West Exeter,) carpenter.

Rose, Benajah, (Schuyler's Lake,) farmer 140.

Rose, Dorre, (Schuyler's Lake,) carpenter and farmer 150.

Rose, George G., (West Exeter,) farmer 50.

Rose, Montgomery, (Schuyler's Lake,) carpenter and farmer 2.

Rose, Norman, (Schuyler's Lake,) farmer 131.

Rose, Samuel, (Schuyler's Lake,) farmer 75.

ROSE, WILLIAM, (Schuyler's Lake,) mechanic, prop. of steam saw and grist mills, justice of the peace and farmer 10.

Ruto, Luman B., (Exeter,) farmer 41.

Scott, George, (Schuyler's Lake,) dealer in butter and cheese.

Scott, Harriet Mrs., (Schuyler's Lake,) confectionery.

Seeber, Matilda Mrs., (Schuyler's Lake,) farmer 60.

Shumway, John W., (Schuyler's Lake,) carpenter and farmer 50.

Simmons, Frank, (Exeter,) farmer 200.

Simms, E. F., (West Exeter,) farmer 50.

Sloat, Irwin, (Schuyler's Lake,) farmer 27.

Smith, Philemon, (Schuyler's Lake,) cooper, carpenter and farmer 2.

Smith, Reuben D., (Schuyler's Lake,) harness maker.

Southworth, N. H., (West Exeter,) saw and grist mills, cheese box factory and feed mill, justice of the peace and farmer 18.

Southworth, William, (Schuyler's Lake,) general merchant and life insurance agent.

Stener, George, (Schuyler's Lake,) farmer leases of Daniel Peak, 300.

Sternberg, D. S., (Schuyler's Lake,) farmer 40.

Stewart, F. B., (West Exeter,) farmer 48.

Stone, Salmon, (Exeter,) carpenter and farmer 140.

Sumner, George B., (Exeter,) farmer 121.

SUTHERLAND, JOHN, (Schuyler's Lake,) farmer 531.

Sutherland, Orlando, (Schuyler's Lake,) general merchant.

Sweet, Mary Mrs., (Exeter,) farmer 2.

Taylor, Milton H., (Schuyler's Lake,) farmer 228.

Thompson, Charles F., (Schuyler's Lake,) school commissioner.

Town, Amos, (Schuyler's Lake,) farmer.

Turner, Caleb, (Schuyler's Lake,) farmer 84.

Turner, Syphera Mrs., (Exeter,) farmer 98.

Turner, William A., (Exeter,) (*with Mrs. Syphera*,) farmer.

Underwood, Amanda Mrs., (Schuyler's Lake,) farmer 13.

Underwood, Amos, (Schuyler's Lake,) prop. of Fish House and farmer 6.

Van Court, Daniel, (Schuyler's Lake,) farmer 113.

Van Court, Martin, (Schuyler's Lake,) farmer 50.

Van Court, Stephen, (Schuyler's Lake,) farmer 40.

Van Keuren, Charles, (Schuyler's Lake,) farmer leases 107.

Veber, Daniel, (Schuyler's Lake,) farmer 2.

Veber, Israel L., (Schuyler's Lake,) cheese box manuf.

Veber, John H., (Schuyler's Lake,) farmer 150.

Veber, Lucius O., (Schuyler's Lake,) (*L. O. Veber & Co.*,) postmaster.

Veber, L. O. & Co., (Schuyler's Lake,) (*Lucius O. Veber and L. F. Eygabroat*,) general merchants.

Walker, George G., (Exeter,) farmer.

Watson, Orlando, (Schuyler's Lake,) farmer 130.

West, John W., (West Exeter,) farmer 200.

West, Milton P., (West Exeter,) farmer 177.

Westcott, A. E. Miss, (Schuyler's Lake,) milliner and dressmaker.

WESTCOTT, T. M., (Schuyler's Lake,) boot and shoe maker, dealer in hides and pelts, and owns 3 acres.

Wheeler, Sanford, (Schuyler's Lake,) farmer leases 165.

Wilcox, O. H., (West Exeter,) postmaster and general merchant.

Williams, Sherman, (Exeter,) farmer 148.

Wilmarth, Joseph, (Richfield,) cheese factory and farmer 300.

Wood, Herman H., (Exeter,) farmer 196.

Wood, Jerome A., (Exeter,) farmer 110.

Wright, David, (Schuyler's Lake,) farmer 52.

Wright, Robert, (Schuyler's Lake,) (*with Wayne Clark*,) farmer 40.

Young, Henry G., (Exeter,) cheese factory and farmer 60.

HARTWICK.
(Post Office Addresses in Parentheses.)

Adams, Joshua, (Hartwick Seminary,) farmer 52.

Aldrich, Landrin, (South Hartwick,) farmer 84.

Alger, Obed, (South Hartwick,) farmer 15.

ALGER, WILLIAM C., (Hartwick,) undertaker, clock repairer and turner.

Angley, Thomas, (Hartwick,) farmer 100.

Aplin, George W., (Toddsville,) farmer 106.

Armstrong, John, (Hartwick Seminary,) farmer 40.

Arnold, Mason D., (Hartwick,) harness maker.

Ashcraft, Jedediah, (Hartwick,) cabinet maker.

Ashcroft, Orlando B., (Hartwick,) blacksmith.

Auger, Austin, (Hartwick,) farmer rents of George, 272.

Auger, Frederick, (Milford,) farmer 200.

Augur, Charles M., (Hartwick,) farmer 100.

Augur, George M., (Hartwick,) farmer 16.

Avery, Albert A., (Hartwick,) blacksmith.

Avery, Joanna Mrs., (Hartwick,) farmer 1½.

Barney, James H., (Hartwick,) farmer 29.

Beach, Frank, (South Hartwick,) farmer 1.

Beckley, Albert, (Milford,) farmer 60.

Beckley, Charles, (Hartwick Seminary,) farmer 8.

Beckley, Delos, (Milford,) farmer 92.

Beckley, Elijah, (Hartwick,) farmer 80.

Beckley, George, (Hartwick Seminary,) farmer 17.

Beckley, Horace, (Milford,) farmer 125.

BECKLEY, HORACE J., (Hartwick Seminary,) blacksmith.

Bilderbeck, Henry, (South Hartwick,) farmer 103.

Bishop, Andrew J., (Hartwick,) farmer 62.

Bishop, Delos, (Hartwick,) farmer 8.

Bishop, Oliver, (Hartwick,) veterinary surgeon and farmer 25.

Bissell, Edwin A., (Hartwick,) (*F. H. Bissell & Sons,*) farmer 25.

Bissell, Enoch, (South Hartwick,) farmer 50.

Bissell, Frederick H., (Hartwick,) (*F. H. Bissell & Sons,*) farmer 75.

Bissell, F. H. & Sons, (Hartwick,) (*Frederick H., Edwin A. and Theron E.,*) general merchants and harness makers.

Bissell, John, (Cooperstown,) blacksmith and farmer 90.

Bissell, Theron E., (Hartwick,) (*F. H. Bissell & Sons,*) farmer 16.

Bliss, Rensselaer, (Hartwick Seminary,) farmer 72.

Bolls, James W., (Toddsville,) carpenter.

Bolton, Daniel, (Toddsville,) farmer 22.

Bradley Hiram S., (Hartwick,) insurance agent, house painter and grainer.

Bradley, Horatio, (Hartwick,) farmer 60.

BRADLEY, ISAAC R., (Hartwick,) farmer 47.

Bradley, Oscar, (Milford,) farmer 180.

Branch, William H., (Hartwick,) tailor and farmer 117.

Brazee, David, (Hartwick Seminary,) farmer 240.

Brooks, Asahel, (Mount Vision,) farmer 125.

Brooks, Romanzo D., (Mount Vision,) farmer 20.

Brown, Henry Rev., (Hartwick,) pastor of Christian Church.

Brown, Julia Mrs., (Hartwick,) farmer 2.

Brownell, Erastus, (South Hartwick,) grist and saw mills, and farmer 2.

Brownell, Leonard, (Milford,) farmer 65.

Brownell, Samuel, (Milford,) farmer 164.

BUEL, CHAS. W., (Toddsville,) farmer 116.

Burch, Orlo, (Hartwick,) farmer 60.
Burdett, Adelbert, (South Hartwick,) farmer 128.
Burdick, Adelmer A., (South Hartwick,) farmer 128.
Burditt, William D., (Hartwick Seminary,) farmer leases of Luther I. Burditt, 125.
Burk, Gilbert, (Toddsville,) butcher.
BURLINGHAM, JAMES L., (Hartwick,) carriage maker.
Burlingham, Morell, (Milford,) farmer 60.
Butts, Elisha, (Toddsville,) paper maker.
Calkins, Selon, (Hartwick,) farmer 5.
Camp, James, (Toddsville,) farmer 96.
Campbel, Sylvenus, (Toddsville,) mason.
Card, Edward, (Hartwick,) farmer 50.
Card, Edward, Jr., (Hartwick,) farmer 114.
Card, Job, (South Hartwick,) ashery and farmer 80.
Card, John L., (Hartwick,) farmer 26.
Card, Jonathan, (South Hartwick,) shoemaker and farmer 36.
Carr, Arnold, (South Hartwick,) farmer 80.
Carr, Chester, (Toddsville,) farmer 56 and in Otsego, 81.
Carr, De Forest, (Toddsville,) farmer 88.
Carr, Edwin, (Toddsville,) farmer 75 and in Otsego, 25.
Carr, Samuel, (Hartwick Seminary,) farmer 87.
Carr, Samuel, (Toddsville,) farmer 85.
CASS, LEWIS, (Toddsville, farmer 68.
CHASE, ELIZABETH Mrs., (Cooperstown,) farmer 60.
CHASE, GEORGE W., (Hartwick Seminary,) (*Mercer, Son & Co.*)
Chase, Horace, (Hartwick,) farmer 140.
Chase, Hosea, (Cooperstown,) farmer 90.
Chase, Nathan, (Cooperstown,) farmer 160.
Chase, Reuben, (Hartwick,) farmer 50.
Chase, William, (Cooperstown,) saw mill and farmer leases 98.
CHILDS, JONATHAN, (Hartwick Seminary,) carriage maker and painter.
Clark, Francis, (Hartwick Seminary,) farmer 51.
Clinton, William, (Milford,) general agent of Clintonville Cotton Mill.
Conklin, John, (Hartwick,) farmer 200.
Conklin, Rufus S., (Hartwick,) horse breaker and farmer 13¼.
Conley, James M., (South Hartwick,) farmer 60.
Cook, Anson, (Hartwick,) farmer 100.
COOK, DANIEL, (South Hartwick,) carpenter and farmer 1¾.
Cook, Mordington, (Hartwick,) farmer 100.
Cook, Stephen, (Fly Creek,) farmer 92.
Curry, William, (Hartwick,) farmer 160.
Davis, William, (Hartwick,) attorney.
Davison, William, (Hartwick,) farmer 100.
Davison, William C., (Hartwick Seminary,) postmaster and farmer 120.
Dean, Abner, (Toddsville,) mason.
Dingman, Arminda Mrs., (Hartwick,) farmer 3.
DUNBAR, RENSSELAER H., (Hartwick,) (*Harrington & Co.*)
Edmons, Arnine, (Hartwick,) farmer 2¾.
Edmunds, Armon, (Hartwick,) cheese maker.
ELDRED, ANDREW M., (Hartwick,) (*R. & A. M. Eldred.*)

Eldred, Deloss, (South Hartwick,) farmer 66.
Eldred, Dexter H., (Hartwick Seminary,) cooper.
Eldred, Lucius F., (Toddsville,) carpenter and farmer 1.
ELDRED, RUSSEL, (Hartwick,) (*R. & A. M. Eldred.*)
ELDRED, R. & A. M., (Hartwick,) (*Russel and Andrew M.,*) props. of Eldred House.
EVANS, RANSOM, (Milford,) farmer leases of Samuel Harrison, 100.
EVANS, WILLIAM P., (Hartwick Seminary,) tutor Hartwick Theological and Classical Seminary.
Field, Delos T., (Hartwick,) farmer 178.
Field, Elisha, (Hartwick,) farmer 64.
Field, E. A., (Fly Creek,) farmer 6.
FIELD, GEORGE, (Hartwick,) farmer 488.
Field, Monroe H., (Hartwick,) farmer 62½.
Field, Orson, (Hartwick,) farmer 75.
FIELD, RILEY, (Toddsville,) farmer 85.
Fisk, Benjamin, (Cooperstown,) (*with Rufus,*) farmer 100.
Fisk, Rufus, (Cooperstown,) (*with Benjamin,*) farmer 100.
FITCH, CHANNING R., (South Hartwick,) woolen goods and groceries.
Fitch, James R., (South Hartwick,) farmer 80.
Fitch, Orrin, (Hartwick,) farmer 7.
Freeland, Peter, (South Hartwick,) farmer 1¼.
Fuller, Austin, (Hartwick,) farmer 80.
Gardner, Chauncey, (Hartwick,) farmer 83.
Gardner, David, (Hartwick,) farmer 18 and in New Lisbon, 90.
Gardner, Nelson B., (Mount Vision,) farmer 100.
GARDNER, ROBERT W., (Hartwick,) blacksmith and farmer 2.
Gardner, Samuel, (Hartwick,) farmer 8.
Gilbert, Addison, (Hartwick,) farmer 75.
Goewey, Henry, (Hartwick Seminary,) farmer 104.
Goewey, Robert E., (Hartwick,) farmer 100.
GOEWEY, THOMAS H., (South Hartwick,) farmer 118½.
Graves, Calvin, (Cooperstown,) farmer 10.
Green & Harrington, (Hartwick,) (*Merton Green and Nathan B. Harrington,*) props. of grist and saw mills, and farmers 9.
Green, Merton, (Hartwick,) (*Green & Harrington.*)
Hackley, Samuel N., (Hartwick,) farmer 150 and in Otsego, 40.
Hall, Lewis, (Cooperstown,) farmer 179.
HARRINGTON, ALFRED W., (Hartwick,) billiard saloon.
HARRINGTON, CHESTER L., (Hartwick,) (*Harrington & Co.*)
HARRINGTON & CO., (Hartwick,) (*Chester L. and Sheffield Harrington, and Rensselaer H. Dunbar,*) general merchants.
HARRINGTON, HASKEL, (Hartwick,) prop. of Hartwick Hotel.
Harrington, James K., (Hartwick,) farmer 10.
Harrington, Nathan B., (Hartwick,) (*Green & Harrington.*)

HARRINGTON, SHEFFIELD,(Hartwick,) (*Harrington & Co.*,) farmer 20.
HARTWICK HOTEL, (Hartwick,) Haskel Harrington, prop.
*HARTWICK THEOLOGICAL AND CLASSICAL SEMINARY, (Hartwick Seminary,) Rev. Timothy T. Titus, A. M., principal; Rev. James Pitcher, assistant; William P. Evans, tutor; Mrs. Helen E. Tilton, music teacher.
Head, Lavina Mrs., (Hartwick,) farmer 50.
Hinds, George L., (Cooperstown,) farmer 678.
HOLBROOK, CHESTER A., (Toddsville,) farmer leases 116.
HOLBROOK, DARIUS, (Toddsville,) (*with Harvey*,) farmer 130.
HOLBROOK, HARVEY, (Toddsville,) (*with Darius*,) farmer 130.
Holdridge, Harvey, (Hartwick,) farmer 82.
Hollister, George F., (Hartwick,) farmer 163¾.
Hoose, John, (Mount Vision,) farmer 100.
Hoose, Stephen, (South Hartwick,) farmer 100.
Houck, John M., (Toddsville,) carpenter and farmer 6.
House, George N., (Toddsville,) shoemaker and farmer 2.
House, Nelson, (Hartwick,) farmer leases 97½.
Howland, Asa, (Toddsville,) saloon keeper.
Hubbard, Henry R., (South Hartwick,) shoemaker and farmer 3.
HUBBARD, LASELLE L., (South Hartwick,) postmaster and grocer.
HUNGERFORD, ALLEN E., (Hartwick Seminary,) eclectic physician and farmer 11.
Hunter, William C., (South Hartwick,) farmer 115.
Hutchins, Martin, (South Hartwick,)farmer 40.
Hutchins, William, (Hartwick,) farmer 1.
HYDE, GEORGE, (Hartwick,) cooper.
Ingalls, Allen, (Cooperstown,) farmer 50.
Ingalls, Evander, (Cooperstown,) farmer 140.
Ingalls, Menzo, (Cooperstown,) farmer 70.
Ingalsbe, James, (Cooperstown,) farmer 105.
Ingalsbe, Jane Miss, (Hartwick,) dress maker.
Ingalsbe, Lorin, (Hartwick,) shoe maker.
Irish, Thomas S., (Toddsville,) farmer 97.
ISMOND, CEYLON E., (Hartwick,) homeo. physician.
JACKSON, ANDREW, (Toddsville,) carriage maker.
Jacobs, Chester, (South Hartwick,) farmer 144.
Jacobs, Horace, (Hartwick,) farmer 160.
Jacobs, Thomas, (South Hartwick,) farmer 121.
Jarvis, Frederick T., (Hartwick Seminary,) farmer 153.
Jeffrey, Thomas, (Hartwick Seminary,) farmer 93.
Jenks, Thomas, (Hartwick,) cooper.
Jones, Betsey Mrs., (South Hartwick,) farmer 15.
Jones, Jane E. Mrs., (Hartwick,) milliner.
Jones, Oscar H., (Toddsville,) farmer 100.

Jones, Rachel Mrs., (Hartwick Seminary,) farmer 200.
KENYON, AMOS, (Hartwick,) house and carriage painter.
King, Landin, (South Hartwick,) farmer 118.
Kinnie, Hiram, (Hartwick Seminary,) farmer 130.
Kinyon, Isaac, (Milford,) saw mill.
Kirby, George, (Hartwick Seminary,) farmer 87.
Knolton, Maria Mrs., (Hartwick,) farmer 50.
Knowlton, Elijah, (Toddsville,) farmer 21.
Lee, John, (Mount Vision,) farmer 98.
Lewis, George E., (Hartwick,) (*T. P. Lewis & Son*.)
Lewis, Theodore P., (Hartwick,) (*T. P. Lewis & Son*,) farmer 26 and in Otsego, 114.
Lewis, T. P. & Son, (Hartwick,) (*Theodore P. and George E.*,) general merchants and druggists.
Light, John G., (Milford,) blacksmith.
Linahen, Jeremiah, (Hartwick Seminary,) farmer 25.
Lineham, —— Mrs., (South Hartwick,) farmer 75.
Low, George, (Hartwick,) farmer 175.
LUCE, ADOLPHUS S., (Hartwick,) (*Luce Brothers*.)
LUCE BROTHERS, (Hartwick,) (*Rufus P. and Adolphus S.*,) general merchants and druggists.
LUCE, JOHN L., (Hartwick,) boot and shoe maker.
LUCE, RUFUS P., (Hartwick,) (*Luce Brothers.*)
LUTHER, ARTHUR A., (Hartwick,) farmer 98.
Luther, Marcus, (Milford,) farmer 200.
Luther, Margaret Mrs., (Milford,) farmer 72.
Luther, Walton, (Milford,) farmer 80.
Lyons, Alanson, (Hartwick,) farmer 100.
Mallory, William, (Toddsville,) farmer 30.
Manchester, Louisa Mrs , (Hartwick Seminary,) farmer 1.
Maples, Edwin, (Hartwick,) (*with Oscar,*) farmer 325.
Maples, Hannah E. Mrs., (Hartwick,) farmer 3.
Maples, Harvey, (Hartwick,) farmer 207.
Maples, Oscar, (Hartwick,) (*with Edwin,*) farmer 325.
Marsh, Hiram K., (Hartwick,) farmer 129.
Matteson, Henry, (South Hartwick,) farmer 72.
Mattison, Amos, (South Hartwick,) farmer 75.
Mattison, Leonard, (South Hartwick,) farmer 59.
McCabe, Michael, (Hartwick Seminary,) farmer 30.
MERCER, JAMES H., (Hartwick Seminary,) (*M. H. Mercer & Son*,) (*Mercer, Son & Co.*)
MERCER, MARSHAL H., (Hartwick Seminary,) (*M. H. Mercer & Son*,) (*Mercer, Son & Co.*)
MERCER, M. H. & SON, (Hartwick Seminary,) (*Marshal H. and James H.*,) groceries, boots and shoes.

MERCER, SON & CO., (Hartwick Seminary,) (*Marshal and James H. Mercer, and George W. Chase,*) blacksmiths.
METCALF, LUCIAN T., (Hartwick Seminary,) house painter and farmer 1.
Mickel, Philip, (Milford,) farmer 106.
Miller, James P., (Toddsville,) carpenter.
MILLS, ROBERT, (Hartwick,) farmer 70.
Monroe, Edwin M., (Toddsville,) jeweler.
Moon, James, (Hartwick Seminary,) farmer.
Morehouse, Gould, (Hartwick,) farmer 30.
Mott, Josiah, (Hartwick,) carpenter and farmer 8.
Munson, Abijah, (South Hartwick,) farmer 60.
Murdock, George, (Hartwick,) farmer 120.
Murdock, George M., (Toddsville,) carpenter and farmer 1.
Murdock, Harvey, (Hartwick,) farmer 80.
Murdock, Ira W., (Hartwick,) farmer 120.
MURDOCK, WHEELER, (South Hartwick,) farmer 132.
Murphy, John, (Hartwick,) farmer 9.
Murry, Charles H., (Hartwick,) farmer leases of George Hinds, 135.
Norton, Esli, (Hartwick,) tailor.
Norton, Theodore A., (Hartwick,) (*Wilcox & Norton.*)
Norton, Thomas, (Hartwick,) farmer 5.
Owen, Benjamin F., (Hartwick,) farmer 62½.
PAINE, EDWARD J., (Toddsville,) (*Paine & Wood.*)
Paine, John S., (Hartwick,) farmer 50.
PAINE & WOOD, (Toddsville,) (*Edward J. Paine and Wm. Wood,*) farmers 62.
PALMER, JOHN W., (Hartwick,) farmer 63.
Parshall, Orestes H., (Hartwick Seminary,) farmer 120.
Payne, Stephen W., (Toddsville,) machinist.
Pearse, Reuben, (South Hartwick,) farmer 50.
Pendel, David L. Rev., (Hartwick,) pastor of M. E. Church.
Perkins, L. P., (Hartwick Seminary,) farmer 168.
Perkins, Naaman, (Toddsville,) farmer 53.
Perry, Jonathan Rev., (Toddsville,) Lutheran clergyman.
Perry, Joshua G., (Milford,) farmer 165.
Perry, Mary A., (Milford,) farmer 116.
Pettengill, Deloss, (Mount Vision,) farmer 92.
Philips, Barney, (Hartwick,) farmer 125.
Philips, Frederick, (Hartwick,) farmer 142.
Pickens, Anson, (Hartwick,) farmer 50.
Pickens, Edwin, estate of, (Hartwick,) carriage and blacksmith shop, shingle and planing mill.
Pickens, Martin, (Hartwick,) farmer 100.
Pierce, Deleazon, (Hartwick,) farmer 60.
Pierce, Dewit, (Hartwick,) blacksmith.
PITCHER, JAMES Rev., (Hartwick Seminary,) assistant Hartwick Theological and Classical Seminary.
Pope, James, (South Hartwick,) farmer 116.
Potter, Ervin, (Hartwick,) butcher and farmer 8.
Potter, Rufus, (Hartwick,) farmer 60.
Prentice, John A., (Hartwick,) farmer 56.
Pride, Asa, (South Hartwick,) blacksmith.

Proctor, Leonard R., (Hartwick,) farmer 51.
Quackenbush, Granville J., (Toddsville,) overseer of cotton mill.
Reynolds, Laura and Rebecca, (Hartwick,) milliners.
Rich, Michael, (Milford,) farmer 80.
Richards, Welcome, (Hartwick,) carpenter.
Robinson, Charles, (Hartwick,) farmer 37.
Robinson, Delos, (Hartwick,) (*with Nelson T.,*) farmer 10.
ROBINSON, ELISHA, (Hartwick,) (*E. Robinson & Son,*) postmaster and farmer 26.
ROBINSON, E. & SON, (Hartwick,) (*Elisha and Henry D.,*) hardware.
Robinson, George F., (Hartwick,) farmer 249.
ROBINSON, GEORGE G., (Hartwick), farmer 122.
ROBINSON, HENRY D., (Hartwick,) (*E. Robinson & Son.*)
Robinson, Jared, (Hartwick,) farmer about 130.
Robinson, Melvin T., (Hartwick,) (*with Delos,*) farmer 10.
Robinson, Solomon L., (Hartwick,) allo. physician and farmer 35.
Rounds, Giles, (Mount Vision,) (*with John,*) farmer 86.
Rounds, John, (Mount Vision,) (*with Giles,*) farmer 86.
Rowland, Deloss, (Milford.)
Russel, David, (Toddsville,) farmer 125.
Russell, Charles, (Hartwick,) farmer 245.
Salesbury, Elmer, (Milford,) farmer leases of Edwin H. Tucker, 200.
Schermerhorn, Robert, (Toddsville,) blacksmith.
Seebort, Henry, (Hartwick,) farmer 22½.
SHAUL, JACOB D., (Hartwick,) horse broker.
Shepard, Asa J., (Hartwick,) farmer 65.
Shepard, Linus E., (South Hartwick,) farmer 50.
Sherman, James D., (Hartwick,) blacksmith.
Shillieto, Joseph, (Hartwick,) farmer 130.
Short, Cyrus, (Hartwick Seminary,) farmer 150.
Shove, Henry, (South Hartwick,) farmer 100.
Shove, John W., (Mount Vision,) farmer 110.
Shove, William H., (Mount Vision,) farmer 100.
Shumway, Allen D., (Toddsville,) foreman in machine shop.
Shumway, Sands, (Toddsville,) post master.
Shute, Orlands, (Toddsville,) general merchant and deputy postmaster.
Sitser, George W., (Hartwick,) carpenter.
SMITH, AUSTIN, (Mount Vision,) farmer 66.
Smith, Gerard R., (South Hartwick,) farmer 100.
Smith, Morell, (South Hartwick,) farmer 92.
SMITH, PETER S., (Hartwick,) allo. physician and farmer 15.
Spaulding, Hunt & Co., (Milford,) prop. Clintonville Cotton Mill and farmer 375.
Sperry, David, (South Hartwick,) farmer leases of Leroy Sergents, 111.

Stauton, John P., (South Hartwick,) farmer 80.

Steere, Delos, (Hartwick,) farmer 130.

Steere, Elizur, (Hartwick,) farmer 150.

STEERE, JEROME B., (Toddsville,) farmer 94.

STEERE, RUFUS, (Toddsville,) prop. of cotton mill, dry goods store and farmer 130; in Otsego, 2 cotton mills, 2 dry goods stores, one grist mill and 250 acres; in Middlefield, 50 acres.

Stewart, John, (Milford,) farmer 125.

Swackhammer, Susan, (Hartwick Seminary,) farmer 1.

Swartout, Cortland, (Hartwick Seminary,) farmer 200.

Swartout, Richard, (Hartwick Seminary,) farmer 175.

Sylvester, Joseph, (South Hartwick,) farmer leases of Abigail Murdock, 122.

Taylor, Chandler, (South Hartwick,) farmer 4.

Teachout, Cornelius, (Hartwick Seminary,) (*with Henry Winsor*,) farmer 125.

Teachout, Elkanah, (Hartwick Seminary,) carriage maker.

TEMPLE, EBEN M., (Hartwick Seminary,) farmer 13.

Thompson, Barzilla, (Hartwick,) farmer 3.

Tiffany, White, (Hartwick,) farmer 43.

TILTON, HELEN E. MRS., (Hartwick Seminary,) music teacher Hartwick Theological and Classical Seminary.

*TITUS, TIMOTHY T. REV., (Hartwick Seminary,) principal Hartwick Theological and Classical Seminary and pastor Lutheran Church.

TODD, ORANGE, (Hartwick Seminary,) farmer 133.

Todd, Samuel S., (Toddsville,) traveling agent for Rufus Steere.

Tompson, Barzillai, (Hartwick) carpenter.

Travis, Gould J. Rev., (Hartwick,) Baptist clergyman.

Tucker, Lucius G., (Hartwick,) farmer 85.

Van Buren, Martin, (South Hartwick,) farmer 110.

Vanlyke, Henry D., (Toddsville,) mason and farmer 12½.

Vanschaick, Samuel, (Hartwick,) farmer 100.

Vanslyck, Cypran, (Hartwick Seminary,) farmer 1½.

VAN SLYKE, NATHAN, (Milford,) general mason.

Vars, Anson, (South Hartwick,) farmer 60.

Vunk, Peter, (Hartwick Seminary,) shoemaker.

Walden, William P., (Hartwick,) farmer 25.

Walker, Ripley, (Hartwick,) farmer 22.

Walling, David, (South Hartwick,) saw, shingle and planing mills, and farmer 37.

Ward, Daniel, (Hartwick,) farmer 78.

Ward, Erastus, (Hartwick,) farmer 65.

Ward, Harvey, (Hartwick,) (*with Samuel*,) farmer 70.

Ward, Samuel, (Hartwick,) (*with Harvey*,) farmer 70.

Webb, Mary A. Mrs., (Hartwick,) farmer 125.

Wells, Amos F., (Toddsville,) farmer 96.

Weeks, Caroline Mrs., (Cooperstown,) farmer 50.

Weeks, Elisha, (Hartwick Seminary,) mason.

Weeks, Eve Mrs., (Hartwick,) farmer 144.

WEEKS, JABEZ R., (Toddsville,) boot and shoe maker.

Wells, Edwin A., (Hartwick,) farmer 50.

Wells, John, (Hartwick,) carpenter.

Wells, Stephen, (Hartwick,) farmer 218.

Wilcox, Frederick, (Hartwick,) (*Wilcox & Norton*,) farmer 5.

Wilcox & Norton, (Hartwick,) (*Frederick Wilcox and Theodore A. Norton*,) general merchants and produce dealers.

WILCOX, THOMAS, (South Hartwick,) dealer in butter and wool, and farmer 24.

WILLIAMS, MARLIN, (Hartwick,) farmer 135.

Williams, Palmer G., (Hartwick,) iron foundry.

Willis, Simon, (Hartwick,) farmer 15.

WILSON, JOHN T., (Toddsville,) chair maker and painter.

Wilson, William W., (Toddsville,) agent for paper mill.

WINDSOR, NATHAN E., (Toddsville,) farmer 16.

Winslow, James, (Milford,) farmer 38.

Winslow, Mary Miss, (Milford,) tailoress and dressmaker.

Winsor, Henry, (Hartwick Seminary,) (*with Cornelius Teachout*,) farmer 125.

Winsor, Hosea, (Hartwick,) farmer 130.

Wood, Walter, (Toddsville,) farmer 92.

WOOD, WILLIAM, (Toddsville,) (*Paine & Wood*.)

WOODCOCK, WILLIAM, (Hartwick,) carriage maker.

WRIGHT, ISAIAH D., (Mount Vision,) farmer 98.

WRIGHT, PORTER, (Hartwick Seminary,) hotel keeper and farmer 2.

LAURENS.

(Post Office Addresses in Parentheses.)

Ackley, Lemuel, (Mount Vision,) hop grower and farmer 96.

ACKLEY, WILLIS, (Laurens,) hop grower and farmer 140.

Allen, Aaron, (Laurens,) blacksmith and farmer 8.

Allen, Albert S., (Laurens,) (*Elwell & Allen.*)

Armstrong, Elisha, (Mount Vision,) farmer 40, Main.

Armstrong, Mary Mrs., (Mount Vision,) farmer 50.

Armstrong, Sylvester, (Mount Vision,) farmer 5.

Babcock, Hannah Mrs., (Oneonta,) farmer 100.

Babcock, Nathan W., (Laurens,) dairyman and farmer 75.

Baker, David, (West Oneonta,) saw mill, dairyman and farmer 88.

Baker, Oscar, (Laurens,) hop grower, dairyman and farmer 63.

Bard, Charles, (West Laurens,) farmer 50.

Barnard, Dennis, (Mount Vision,) justice of the peace, carriage maker and farmer 28, Main.

Barnard, John, (Mount Vision,) wholesale egg dealer, Main.

Barton, Almon, (Laurens,) farmer 108.

BARTON, PETER, (Laurens,) dairyman and farmer 160, Civil.

Bates, Roswell, (West Laurens,) blacksmith.

Beals, Edward E., (Mount Vision,) farmer 70.

BEERS, AMBROSE, (Laurens,) prop. upper leather tannery, shoe manuf. and farmer 9, Butts Corners.

Benedict, Albert, (Laurens,) shoemaker.

Bennett, Geo. G.,(West Oneonta,) farmer 76.

Bennett, Martha Mrs., (West Laurens,) farmer 50.

Bennett, Perry, (West Laurens,) retired farmer 5.

Bennett, Russell, (West Laurens,) produce buyer and farmer 16.

Benton, Smith, (Otsdawa,) farmer 50.

Betts, Rodney, (West Laurens,) farmer 60.

BIRDSELL, JACOB, (Mount Vision,) commissioner of highways, prop. Bloods Mills, feed, saw and planing mills, hop grower and farmer 18.

Bissell & Bunn, (Mount Vision,) (*Seth H. Bissell and Henry C. Bunn,*) general merchants and wholesale egg dealers.

Bissell, Seth H., (Mount Vision,) (*Bissell & Bunn,*) farmer 35.

Blanchard, Ezra, (West Laurens.)

Bowen, Amos, (West Oneonta,) farmer 111.

Bowen, Daniel H., (West Oneonta,) dairyman and farmer 115.

Bowen, Zebulon, (Laurens,) dairyman and farmer leases of Daniel Baker, 87.

Brewster, Daniel D., (West Oneonta,) grist, flouring, plaster and cider mills, and farmer 60.

Brewster, J. H., (Laurens,) butcher, Main.

Bridges, Eli, (Laurens,) farmer 93.

Bridges, E. W., (Laurens,) carpenter.

Bridges, Lyman, (Laurens,) hop grower, dairyman and farmer 117.

Briggs, Albert O., (Laurens,) dairyman and farmer 165.

BRIGGS, CHAS. I., (Laurens,) farmer 50 and occupies farm of Isaac G., 109.

Briggs, Godfrey, (West Laurens,) farmer 125.

Briggs, Howard, (West Laurens,) farmer 100.

Briggs, Isaac G., (Laurens,) farmer 260, Main.

Brightman, Chas., (Laurens,) farmer leases of Chas. Briggs, 50.

Brightman, Edward, (Laurens,) hop grower and farmer 25.

Brightman, Geo., (Laurens,) farmer 91.

Brown, Delos N., (New Lisbon,) farmer 156.

Brown, Henry, (West Laurens,) farmer leases 90.

Brown, Henry Rev., (Hartwick,) pastor Christian Church.

Brown, John, (West Laurens,) farmer 270.

Brown, Levi, (West Laurens,) farmer 73.

Brown, Levi, (West Laurens,) farmer 75.

Brown, Polly Mrs., (West Laurens,) farmer 90.

Brown, Wellington, (Laurens,) dairyman and farmer 275.

Brown, Wm., (Laurens,) farmer 62.

BUNN, HENRY C., (Mount Vision,) (*Bissell & Bunn.*)

BUNN, WM., (Mount Vision,) retired farmer 8, Main.

Burnside, Ephraim, (Mount Vision,) carpenter, Main.

Butts, Galen H., (West Laurens,) farmer 233.

Butts, Harvey, (Laurens,) farmer 280.

BUTTS, MORRIS, (Laurens,) dairyman and farmer 172.

Butts, Norris, (West Laurens,) saw mill and farmer 86.

BUTTS, SALMON H., (Laurens,) dairyman and farmer 70¼.

Camp, Geo. E., (Laurens,) butcher, Main.

Camp, James B., (Laurens,) farmer 160.

Carnrick, John, (Laurens,) cider mill and farmer 1.

CARR, ALFRED, (Laurens,) dairyman and farmer 180.

Carr, Daniel, (Laurens,) farmer 65.

Carr, Edmund, (Laurens,) (*with Roselpha A.,*) farmer 100.

Carr, Jonathan, (Laurens,) farmer 18.

Carr Roselpha A., (Laurens,) (*with Edmund,*) farmer 100.

Caulkins, Henry, (Mount Vision,) farmer 60.

Chamberlain, Jordan, (West Laurens,) farmer 82.

Charter, Chas. W., (Otsdawa,) farmer leases 11.

Chase, Nathan L., (Laurens,) farmer 113.

Cheney, Wm., (Mount Vision,) blacksmith, Main.

Clark, Justus T., (Laurens,) prop. Laurens Nursery and farmer 13, Butternut.

Clark, S. Andrew, (Laurens,) blacksmith, Main.

Clinton, Wm. M., (Clintondale, Ulster Co.,) agent Otsego Cotton Mill.

Cogshall, Isaac, (West Laurens,) farmer 64.

Cole, Wm. H., (Laurens,) (*Cook & Cole.*)

Coller, Robert, (West Laurens,) farmer 62½.

Comstock, D. Lansing, (Laurens,) hop grower and farmer 94.

Comstock, Wm., (Laurens,) farmer 660, Main.

Cook & Cole, (Laurens,) (*Nathan H. Cook and Wm. H. Cole,*) groceries and provisions, Main.

Cook, Hannah Mrs., (Laurens,) farmer 65.

Cook, John J., (West Oneonta,) dairyman and farmer 60.

Cook, Nathan H., (Laurens,) (*Cook & Cole,*) hop grower, dairyman and farmer 183.

Cooley, Adelia Mrs., (Laurens,) millinery, Main.

Cooley, Richard J., (Laurens,) dairyman and farmer 78, Main.

Cornell, Walter, (West Laurens,) farmer 200.

Couse, Peter, (Mount Vision,) blacksmith, Mount Vision St.

Crisman, Elizabeth Mrs., (Laurens,) farmer 14½.

CUTLER, JESSE K., (Mount Vision,) (*W. W. Cutler & Son.*)

Cutler, R. J., (Laurens,) farmer 96.

CUTLER, WILLARD W., (Mount Vision,) (*W. W. Cutler & Son.*)

CUTLER, W. W. & SON, (Mount Vision.) (*Willard W. and Jesse K.,*) manufs. and dealers in boots and shoes, Main.

Daley, Bennett, (Laurens,) farmer leases 160.

Davis, Adelbert G., (Laurens,) farmer leases 248.

Day, Addison, (West Oneonta,) (*with Wm. E.,*) farmer 50.

Day, P. W., (West Oneonta,) farmer 25.

Day, Wm. E., (West Oneonta,) (*with Addison,*) farmer 50.

Dean, Delos W., (Laurens,) (*Strong & Dean,*) farmer 60.

DECKER, EPHRAIM W., (Laurens,) carpenter and builder, Brook.

Decker, Philip, (Laurens,) carpenter.

De Forest, Abel, (West Oneonta,) farmer 150.

Dibble, Isaac B., (Oneonta,) blacksmith and farmer 8.

Dockstader, Jacob M., (West Laurens,) blacksmith and farmer 100.

Drew, H. N. & Co., (Laurens,) (*John A. Drew,*) general merchants, Main.

Drew, John A., (Laurens,) (*H. N. Drew & Co.*)

Dunbar, Delos W., (Laurens,) farmer 310.

Dunbar, Electa Mrs., (West Laurens,) farmer 2.

Dunbar, Jesse W., (Laurens,) hop grower, dairyman and farmer 230.

Eckerson, Mary R., (West Laurens,) farmer 30.

Edson, Barzilla, (Laurens,) carpenter and builder, Main.

Eldred, Aaron, (New Lisbon,) (*with Samuel,*) farmer 550.

Eldred, Alfred, (Laurens,) farmer 160.

Eldred, Harriet Mrs., (West Laurens,) farmer 50.

Eldred, Harvey, (Laurens,) farmer 191.

Eldred, Haskell, (West Laurens,) farmer 95.

Eldred, Samuel, (New Lisbon,) (*with Aaron,*) farmer 550.

ELWELL & ALLEN, (Laurens,) (*Lewis S. Elwell and Albert S. Allen,*) manufs. and dealers in lumber, shingles and lath.

ELWELL, LEWIS S., (Laurens,) (*Elwell & Allen,*) prop. Laurens Flouring and Custom Mills, and saw mill, manuf. and dealer in flour and feed.

Fairchild, Gideon J., (West Laurens,) carpenter and farmer 53.

Ferguson, Andrew, (Laurens,) hop grower and farmer leases 96.

Ferguson, Wm., (Laurens,) farmer 96.

Ferryl, James, (West Laurens,) farmer 60.

FIELD, HEZEKIAH, (Mount Vision,) dairyman and farmer 192.

Field, Rachel Mrs., (Mount Vision,) milliner, Main.

Field, Wm. C., (Laurens,) lawyer, Main.

Fields, Henry N., (West Laurens,) carpenter and farmer 25.

FISHER, ELISHA S., (Laurens,) (*Kidder & Fisher,*) town clerk.

FITCH, BUCKINGHAM, (Laurens,) (*Fitch & Richmond.*)

FITCH & RICHMOND, (Laurens,) (*Buckingham Fitch and Leonard P. Richmond,*) props. Laurens House, and Cooperstown and Oneonta stages.

Fletcher, Emeline Mrs., (West Oneonta,) farmer 50.

FOWLER, CHAS. A., (Mount Vision,) farmer 33, Main.

Fowlston, Geo. M., (Laurens,) farmer 183.

Fowlston, Joel L., (Laurens,) farmer 100.

Fuller, Chas., (Mount Vision,) farmer 80.

Fuller, James, (Laurens,) shoemaker, Maple.

Fuller, Jonathan, (Laurens,) farmer 270.

Gardner, Emilius, (Laurens,) dairyman and farmer 161.

Gardner, Horace, (West Laurens,) shoemaker.

Gardner, Nathaniel, (Laurens,) farmer 30.

Gardner, Seth A., (Mount Vision,) saw-mill and farmer 51, Main.

Garlick, John D., (West Laurens,) farmer 2.

Garlick, Rensselaer, (West Laurens,) farmer leases of Rensselaer L., 65.

GARLOCK, RUSH, (Mount Vision,) dairyman and farmer leases 77.

Georgia, Chas., (West Laurens,) farmer 76.

Georgia, Electa S., (Otsdawa,) farmer 11.

Gilbert, D. W., (West Laurens,) prop. West Laurens Hotel.

Gilbert, Levi, (Laurens,) farmer 200.

Gile, Cortland, (Laurens,) hop grower and farmer 81.

Gile, Edwin, (West Laurens,) farmer 50.

GILE, SYLVESTER, (Laurens,) manuf. boots and shoes, Main.

Gile, Wm., (Laurens,) horse dealer and farmer 100.

Grant, Warren, (Laurens,) farmer 100.

Green, Allen H., (West Oneonta,) (*with Ira*,) farmer 83.

Green, Erastus, (Laurens,) hop grower, dairyman and farmer 150.

Green, Ira, (West Oneonta,) (*with Allen H.*,) farmer 83.

Green, Lewis, (Laurens,) (*with Wheeler*,) farmer 40.

Green, Lyman, (Mount Vision,) farmer 50.

Green, Wheeler, (Laurens,) (*with Lewis*,) farmer 40.

Greene, Almanzo, (West Laurens,) farmer 52.

Greene, John W., (West Laurens,) farmer leases 52.

Gregory, Mathew, (Mount Vision,) farmer 150.

Griffith, Lorenzo, (Laurens,) farmer 145.

GROVER, HENRY C., (Laurens,) hop grower, dairyman and farmer 80.

GURNEY, MILTON, (Laurens,) (*Gurney & Tucker*,) postmaster and justice of the peace.

GURNEY & TUCKER, (Laurens,) (*Milton Gurney and Le Roy Tucker*,) dry goods, groceries, boots, shoes, hats, caps, and manufs. and dealers in clothing.

Haight, Lewis, (Otsdawa,) farmer 105.

HALL, NATHAN G., (Mount Vision,) carpenter and builder, Main.

Hall, Roswell, (Laurens,) harness maker, Main.

HARRINGTON, ELLEN MRS., (Laurens,) millinery, Main.

Harrington, Samuel H., (Laurens,) lawyer, Main.

HARRINGTON, WM,, ((Laurens,) prop. billiard saloon and dealer in groceries, Main.

Harris, Henry T., (Laurens,) druggist, physician and surgeon, Maple.

Harrison, Delos, (Mount Vision,) (*with Samuel*,) farmer.

Harrison, James, (Laurens,) farmer 50.

Harrison, Samuel, (Mount Vision,) farmer 684.

Harrison, Wm. H., (Laurens,) farmer 123.

Hathaway, James, (Otsdawa,) (*with heirs of Jonathan*,) farmer 190.

Hathaway, King J., (Otsdawa,) farmer 67.

Hathaway, Le Grand U., (Otsdawa,) farmer 133.

Hathaway, Warren, (Otsdawa,) (*with Willard*,) farmer 88.

Hathaway, Willard, (Otsdawa,) (*with Warren*,) farmer 88.

Hayward, Allen Rev., (West Laurens,) pastor Christian Church, physician and surgeon.

Herring, John, (Laurens,) farmer 96.

Herring, Louisa Mrs., (Laurens,) farmer 116.

Herring, Mary Mrs., (Laurens,) farmer 33.

Herrington, Abel, (West Laurens,) farmer 78.

Hillsinger, John, (West Oneonta,) farmer 100.

Hoag, Ira, (Laurens,) wagon maker, Main.

Hoose, Thos., (Mount Vision,) farmer leases of Cornelius Lane, 150.

Hopkins, Eliza A. Mrs., (Laurens,) farmer 80.

Hopkins, Henry, (West Oneonta,) dairyman and farmer 155.

Hopkins, Samuel, (Laurens,) farmer 87.

Hopkins, Willard, (West Oneonta,) farmer 50.

Hopkins, Willis, (West Laurens,) farmer 50 and leases 100.

Hopkins, Wm. L., (Laurens,) dairyman and farmer 270.

Howe, Henry Mrs., (Laurens,) farmer 117.

Howe, William, (Laurens,) carpenter and builder, Maple.

HUDSON, HORACE, (Laurens,) (*S. T. & H. Hudson*.)

HUDSON, STEPHEN T., (Laurens,) (*S. T. & H. Hudson*.)

HUDSON, S. T. & H., (Laurens,) (*Stephen T. and Horace*,) dealers in stoves and hardware, and manufs. tin, sheet iron and copper ware, Main.

Hull, M. A. Mrs., (Laurens,) dressmaker, Main.

Hunt, G. Darwin, (West Oneonta,) dairyman and farmer 155.

HUNT, JAMES, (Mount Vision,) carpenter and joiner.

Hurlbert, Chas., (Otsdawa,) farmer 70.

Hurlbert, Geo., (Otsdawa,) farmer 105.

Hurlbert, Julia Mrs., (Laurens,) millinery, Main.

Jenks, M. S., (Laurens,) house painter, Civil.

Jenks, Sylvester, (Laurens,) farmer 100.

Jewell, Henry C., (Mount Vision,) farmer 20.

Johnson, Amos, (New Lisbon,) farmer 125.

JOHNSON, MENZO, (Laurens,) dairyman and farmer 75, head of Main.

Jones, Jennie C., (Mount Vision,) milliner, Main.

Kenyon, Brenton, (Mount Vision,) farmer 45.

Kenyon, Catharine, (Mount Vision,) farmer 23, Mount Vision St.

Kenyon, James H., (Mount Vision,) retired farmer 15, Main.

Keyes, Harvey, (Mount Vision,) farmer 34.

KEYES, JOSIAH D., (Mount Vision,) wholesale dealer in eggs, hop grower, dairyman and farmer 83.

Keyes, Melville, (Mount Vision and Oneonta,) lawyer.

Keyes, Omar, (Mount Vision,) saw mill, dealer in lumber, lath &c., hop grower, dairyman and farmer 115.

KEYES, WASHINGTON T., (Mount Vision,) dealer in dry goods, groceries, crockery, hardware, boots, shoes, hats, caps, ready-made clothing, drugs, medicines, paints, oils, dyestuffs &c., Main, also farmer 5.

KIDDER & FISHER, (Laurens,) (*John S. Kidder and Elisha S. Fisher*,) carriage and cutter manufs., also dealers in paints, oils, varnish &c., Main.

KIDDER, JOHN S., (Laurens,) (*Kidder & Fisher*,) farmer 16.

Lake, Spencer, (Mount Vision,) farmer leases of Henry Arver, 80.

Lane, Cornelius, (Mount Vision,) farmer 164, Main.

Lane, Cornelius E., (Mount Vision,) farms estate of Elihu, 224.

Lane, Elihu, estate of, (Mount Vision,) 224 acres, Cornelius E. Lane, manager.

Lasher, Jacob A., (New Lisbon,) farmer 175.

LAURENS FLOURING AND CUSTOM MILLS, (Laurens,) Lewis S. Elwell, prop.

LAURENS HOUSE, (Laurens,) Main, Fitch & Richmond, props.

Lent, Isaac, (Laurens,) hop grower and farmer 90.

Loomis, Daniel C., (Oneonta,) dairyman and farmer 54.

Lull, Mianda, (West Laurens,) farmer 12.

Mackey, Le Roy, (West Laurens,) farmer 176.

MacMinn, George, (West Laurens,) farmer 16.

Manchester, Josephus, (Mount Vision,) carpenter and farmer 1.

Mann, Abel, (Mount Vision,) hop grower and farmer 119.

Mann, Clark, (Mount Vision,) farmer leases 119.

Mann, Ezra, (Mount Vision,) hop grower, dairyman and farmer 75.

Marlet, Menzo, (Mount Vision,) farmer 50.

Marlett, Ezra, (Mount Vision,) farmer 215, Main.

Marlett, Geo. W., (Mount Vision,) retired farmer 6, Main.

Marlett, Menzo, (Mount Vision,) dairyman and farmer 57.

Marlett, Silas, (Mount Vision,) retired farmer, Main.

Marlett, Simon S., (Laurens,) farmer 203 and leases 80, Main.

Martindale, James, (West Laurens,) veterinary surgeon.

Matteson, David S., (West Oneonta,) farmer 61.

MAYNARD, WM., (Laurens,) overseer weaving department Otsego Cotton Mills.

McCleland, Wm., (Laurens,) farmer 130.

McDOUGAL, EZRA, M. D., (Mount Vision,) physician and surgeon, Main.

MEAD, CHAS. H., (Mount Vision,) hop grower and farmer 52.

Mead, Damon H., (Laurens,) blacksmith, Main.

Mead, James N., (Laurens,) hop grower and farmer 64.

Mead M. C., (Laurens,) blacksmith, Main.

Merrill, Nelson, (Laurens,) shoemaker.

Mickel, Chas., (West Laurens,) farmer 20.

Miller, Elijah B., (Laurens,) farmer leases 150.

Miller, Samuel B., (Laurens,) surveyor and farmer 150.

Mills, Daniel, (West Laurens,) postmaster, general merchant and harness maker.

Morton, Porter, (West Laurens,) blacksmith.

Mulkins, Albert, (Laurens,) farmer 43.

Mulkins, Clarence, (Laurens,) planing mill.

Mulkins, Ezekiel, (Laurens,) wood turner and farmer 5.

Mulkins, Wm., (Laurens,) carpenter, Main.

Murdock, Hiram J., (Mount Vision,) farmer 22, Main.

MURPHY, WM., (Laurens,) mason and farmer leases of Hiram Fritts, 100.

Myers, Chas. P., (Laurens,) farmer 310.

Naylor, Geo., (New Lisbon,) saw mill and farmer 104.

Nearing, Richard, (Mount Vision,) farmer leases 70.

Nichols, Abram D., (Laurens,) carpenter.

Northrup, Morgan S., (Mount Vision,) supt. County Poor House and farmer 77.

Pattengill, Samuel, (Mount Vision,) cabinet maker.

Peck, Isaac B., (Mount Vision,) blacksmith, West.

PECK, WM. F., (Laurens,) dairyman and farmer leases of Wm. H. Peck, 118.

Pendell, D. L. Rev., (Mount Vision,) pastor M. E. Church, Main.

Perkins, Seymour, (West Laurens,) farmer 100.

Perry, Raymond, (Laurens,) farmer 100.

PHILLIPS, EDWARD, (Oneonta,) hop grower, dairyman, farmer 126 and leases 170.

Phillips, John R., (West Laurens,) farmer 112.

PIXLEY, ANDREW J., (Laurens,) carpenter and joiner, Maple.

Pixley, Lewis L., (Laurens,) sawyer.

Potter, Orman, (Laurens,) cutter for Gurney & Tucker.

Powell, Erastus D., (Laurens,) farmer 160, Main.

Pratt, Wm. H., (Mount Vision,) patent right dealer, stationer and farmer 35.

Randall, Geo. W., (Laurens,) grocer.

Rathbun, James D., (Laurens,) farmer 140.

Rathbun, Jonathan F., (Laurens,) farmer 170.

Rathbun, Stephen C., (Mount Vision,) farmer 294.

Richards, Enoch K., (West Oneonta,) farmer 85.

Richardson, Egbert, (Oneonta,) dairyman and farmer 70.

Richardson, Jacob, (Laurens,) hop grower, dairyman and farmer 230.

RICHARDSON, JUSTUS G., (Laurens,) hop grower and farmer 170.

Richmond, K. V., (Laurens,) cabinet maker and undertaker, Main.

RICHMOND, LEONARD P., (Laurens,) (*Fitch & Richmond.*)

ROBERTS, JOHN N., (Laurens,) supt. Otsego Cotton Mills.

ROBINSON, ADDISON T., (Mount Vision,) (*Tiffany & Robinson.*)

Robinson, Levitt Mrs., (Morris,) farmer 130.

Robinson, Silas F., (Mount Vision,) dairyman and farmer 100.

ROBINSON, WM. W., (Mount Vision,) dairyman and farmer 157.

Rockwell, John, (Laurens,) carpenter.

Root, Sylvester, (Mount Vision,) dairyman and farmer 60.

Rous, Albert, (West Oneonta,) farmer 60.

Rous, Erastus C., (West Oneonta,) saw mill and farmer 100.

Scofield, Eben, (Laurens,) farmer 150.

SERGENT, L. R., (Mount Vision,) speculator and farmer 262.

Shaw, Mary A., (Laurens,) farmer 11.

SHERMAN, SYLVESTER, (Mount Vision,) egg dealer and carpenter, Main.

Shoudy, Geo., (Mount Vision,) prop. Jacksonville Mills.

Shove, Brice, (Mount Vision,) farmer 44.

SHOVE, HENRY, (Mount Vision,) dairyman, farmer 229 and leases of Banyer heirs, 100.

Shovel, John B., (Laurens,) harness &c.

Shutters, Jerry, (Mount Vision,) farmer 1.

SLEEPER, HUDSON, (Laurens,) hop grower and farmer 250.

Smith, Horton, (West Laurens,) farmer leases 16.

Smith, James, (Laurens,) hop grower, dairyman and farmer 136.

Smith, John, (Laurens,) farmer 248.

Smith, John G., (West Oneonta,) dairyman and farmer 100.

Smith, Lewis D., (West Laurens,) farmer 212.

Smith, Robert, (Mount Vision,) spinner and farmer 2.

Smith, Wm. Mrs., (Laurens,) farmer 50.

SODEN, JOHN, (West Laurens,) justice of the peace and farmer 250.

Stafford, Rowland, (West Laurens,) farmer 200.

Stanton, Jeremiah, (Laurens,) farmer 50.

Stanton, Thos. E., (Laurens,) farmer 150.

Stenson, Richard, (West Laurens,) farmer 207.

Stevens, Gilbert, (Mount Vision,) farmer 41, Main.

St. John, Chas., (Mount Vision,) butcher.

St. John, Erastus, (Mount Vision,) (*St. John & Wilber.*)

St. John & Wilber, (Mount Vision,) (*Erastus St. John and M. J. Wilber,*) groceries, provisions &c., Main.

Straight, Austin F., (Laurens,) farmer.

STRAIGHT, JEREMIAH B., (Laurens,) carpenter and builder, and manuf. and dealer in cabinet ware.

Straight, Job, (Laurens,) farmer 10.

Straight, Nancy Mrs., (Laurens,) farmer 125.

Straight, Samuel, (West Laurens,) farmer 100.

Straight, Stephen F., (Laurens,) carpenter, Main.

Straight, Wm., (Laurens,) farmer 204.

STRONG, A. P., M. D., (Laurens,) physician and surgeon, Main.

Strong & Dean, (Laurens,) (*Harvey Strong and Delos W. Dean,*) general merchants, Maple.

Strong, Harvey, (Laurens,) (*Strong & Dean,*) farmer 60.

Strong, Wm. A., (Laurens,) justice of the peace and farmer 388, Main.

Sullivan, David, (Mount Vision,) farmer 9.

Sweet, Jane E.,(Mount Vision,) farmer 100.

Taylor, Wm., (Laurens,) farmer 62.

Tentor, Elijah, (West Laurens,) farmer 36.

Thayer, John, (Laurens,) farmer 46.

Thord, David, (West Laurens,) farmer 60.

Thurston, Mary Miss, (Mount Vision,) dressmaker, Main.

TIFFANY & ROBINSON, (Mount Vision,) (*Thos. Tiffany and Addison T. Robinson,*) dealers in hardware and stoves and manufs. and dealers in tin, sheet iron and copper ware, Main.

TIFFANY, THOS., (Mount Vision,) (*Tiffany & Robinson.*)

Tinnie, Silas, (Laurens,) farmer leases of Wm. Comstock, 270.

TUCKER, CHAUNCEY L., (West Laurens) (*E. Tucker & Son,*) dealer in hops and butter at Morris village, and farmer 11.

TUCKER, ERIE, (West Laurens,) (*E. Tucker & Son,*) farmer 126.

TUCKER, E, & SON, (West Laurens,) (*Erie and Chauncey L.,*) manufs. and dealers in dressed and undressed lumber and lath.

TUCKER, EZRA, (West Laurens,) manuf. and dealer in lumber, and farmer 86.

TUCKER, J. LEE Hon., (West Laurens,) justice of the peace and conveyancer.

TUCKER, LE ROY, (Laurens,) (*Gurney & Tucker,*) supervisor.

Van Buren, Abram, (Mount Vision,) farmer 236.

Van Buren, Cornelius, (Mount Vision,) farmer 57, Main.

Van Deusen, H. N. Rev., (Laurens,) pastor M. E. Church.

Verry, Geo. H., (New Lisbon,) egg dealer and farmer 25.

Walby, Delos, (Mount Vision,) farmer 3.

Ward, Abraham, (West Oneonta,) farmer 21.

WARD, JARVIS, (Laurens,) architect and builder, Main.

Ward, Jarvis Mrs., (Laurens,) farmer 24.

Washbon, Wm. G., (Laurens,) farmer 3.

Washburn, David, (West Laurens,) farmer 30.

Weatherby, Samuel, (West Laurens,) farmer 2 and leases 40.

Weatherly, Anson, (West Laurens,) carpenter and farmer 95.

Weatherly, Eliza Mrs., (West Laurens,) farmer 80.

Weatherly, Henry, (West Laurens,) farmer 76.

Weatherly, Hiram, (Otsdawa,) farmer 50.

Weatherly, Hiram, (West Laurens,) farmer 112.

Weatherly, Warren, (West Laurens,) carpenter.

Webb, Benjamin, (Mount Vision,) cooper and farmer 8, Main.

Webster, Hannon, (West Laurens,) farmer 50.

Wellman, Geo. P., (Mount Vision,) harness maker, Main.
Wentworth, Chester L., (Mount Vision,) (*D. Wentworth & Son.*)
Wentworth, David S., (Mount Vision,) (*D. Wentworth & Son,*) farmer 20.
Wentworth, D. & Son, (Mount Vision,) (*David S. and Chester L.,*) blacksmiths, Main.
WEST, E. M., (Mount Vision,) physician and surgeon, and farmer 1½, Main.
WHITEMAN, JOSEPH, (Laurens,) farmer 16½ and leases of Robert White, 35.
Wilber, M. J., (Mount Vision,) (*St. John & Wilber.*)
Wilcox, Orrin, (Mount Vision,) farmer 8.
Windsor, L. H., (Laurens,) tannery, Main.
Wing, Asa, (West Laurens,) farmer 225.
Wing, J., (West Laurens,) grocer and farmer 7½.

Wing, W. C., (West Laurens,) farmer 150.
Winsor, Amos, (Laurens, (*with Lemuel E.*) dairyman and farmer 160.
Winsor, Lemuel E., (Laurens,) (*with Amos,*) dairyman and farmer 160.
WOOLHOUSE, CORNELIUS, (Laurens,) farmer leases of Simon Marlett, 200.
Wright, Chas., (Laurens,) cooper and farmer 1.
WRIGHT, CHAUNCEY, (Mount Vision,) post master and dealer in dry goods, groceries, crockery, hardware, boots, shoes &c., Main, also farmer 10.
Wright, Giles, (Laurens,) farmer leases of heirs of Chas. Brightman, 105.
WRIGHT, HARLAN A., (Mount Vision,) wholesale egg dealer, hop grower, dairyman and farmer 183.
Zuller, Daniel, (West Laurens,) farmer occupies farm of Delos W. Dunbar, 310.

MARYLAND.

(Post Office Addresses in Parentheses.)

Albert, Alfred, (Schenevus,) farmer 75.
Albert, Andrew, (Schenevus,) marble worker, Mill.
Allen, Jane Mrs., (Schenevus,) farmer 40.
Allen, Timothy, (Chaseville,) farmer.
Allen, Timothy B., (Chaseville,) farmer 100.
Babcock, Richardson, (Schenevus,) carpenter.
Bailey, Sumner, (Chaseville,) farmer 130.
Bailey, S. J., (Chaseville,) farmer 100.
Baldwin, Jennie, (Schenevus,) dressmaker, Main.
Baldwin, Solomon, (Schenevus,) farmer 100, Main.
Ball, Ogilvie D., (Schenevus,) allo. physician and surgeon, Main.
Bauner, Hiram, (Schenevus,) farmer 131.
BARNES, JERRY P., (Colliersville,) farmer 75.
Barnes, Jutson, (Schenevus,) farmer 130.
Barnes, Pendell, (Colliersville,) saw mill &c.
Barnes, Philip, (Colliersville,) farmer 125.
Bates, Alexander J., (Schenevus,) groceries and provisions, near Depot.
Beers, D., (Schenevus,) farmer 70.
Benedict, George A., (Schenevus,) farmer 40.
BENEDICT, PHILOR, (Schenevus,) (*Ferrey & Benedict.*)
Bennett, Aaron W., (Schenevus,) farmer 216.
Bennett, Ansel, (Schenevus,) farmer 125.
Bennett, Ellis L., (Schenevus,) farmer 175.
Bennett, George H., (Schenevus,) farmer 200.

L

Bennett, John C., (Schenevus,) farmer 119.
Bennett, M. & W., (Schenevus,) farmer 160.
Bennett, Simeon, (Schenevus,) farmer 100.
Bennett, William, (Schenevus,) farmer 100.
Bennett, William H., (Schenevus,) merchant tailor and clothier, Main.
Bice, Henry, (Schenevus,) sawyer, Mill.
Blanchard, Joseph G., (Maryland,) practical engineer and machinist, and (*with Mary,*) saw mill and farmer 215.
Blanchard, Morey, (Maryland,) (*with Joseph G.,*) saw mill and farmer 215.
Bliven, Green, (Schenevus,) farmer 55.
Bliven, William, (Schenevus,) farmer 102.
Boardman, Levi, (Schenevus,) farmer 720.
Boorn, Henry W., (Colliersville,) allo. physician.
*BORDEN, GEORGE W., (Schenevus,) dealer in fine watches and jewelry, Main.
Bostwick, David, (Colliersville,) sash and blind maker.
Bostwick, Hiram, (Schenevus,) farmer 50.
Bostwick, Orran, (Maryland,) carpenter and farmer 1½.
Bostwick, William, (Schenevus,) marble worker.
Brady, Peter J., (Schenevus,) cooper, Main.
Bresee, Julian, (Schenevus,) farmer 40.
Bronk, Catharine E. Mrs., (Schenevus,) farmer 120, Main.
Brown, Amos H. Hon., (Schenevus,) farmer 140.

BROWN, C. & H. W., (Schenevus,) farmer 566.

Brown, F. H., (Schenevus,) marble worker, East.

Brown, Loren T., (Schenevus,) (*Brown & Mills.*)

Brown, Mary C. Mrs., (Maryland,) farmer 84½.

Brown & Mills, (Schenevus,) (*Loren T. Brown and William O. Mills*,) carriage manufacturers, Main.

Brown, P. W., (Schenevus,) wagon manuf., Race.

Brown, Sanford, (Schenevus,) assessor and farmer 200.

BROWN, THADDEUS C., (Schenevus,) farmer 192.

Brownell, Alfred, (Schenevus,) farmer 85.

Brownell, Charles, (Elk Creek,) farmer 150.

Brownell, Daniel, (Elk Creek,) farmer 100.

Bulson, Myron, (Schenevus,) farmer 50.

Bulson, William H., (Schenevus,) farmer 140.

Burnside, Byron S., (Maryland,) (*Burnside & Sons.*)

Burnside, Dewitt, (Maryland,) farmer 100.

Burnside, E. S., (Maryland,) (*Burnside & Sons.*)

Burnside, Horace L., (Maryland,) (*Burnside & Sons.*)

Burnside, James C., (Colliersville,) refused information.

Burnside, John P., (Maryland,) farmer 145.

Burnside, Lester, (Maryland,) assessor and farmer 175.

Burnside, Nelson, (Colliersville,) farmer.

Burnside & Sons, (Maryland,) (*E. S., Byron S. and Horace L.*,) saw mill, lath machine and farmers 450.

Burnside, Tyler, (Maryland,) farmer 140.

Bush, Augustus, (Schenevus,) farmer 100.

Bush, Clark T., (Schenevus,) dealer in patent rights, Main.

Bush, John H., (Schenevus,) farmer 150.

Bush, Jonas, (Maryland,) farmer 1.

Bush, Peter, (Chaseville,) farmer 140.

BUTLER, L. E., (Maryland,) (*Butler & Van Zandt.*)

Butler, Stewart E., (Maryland,) farmer 109.

BUTLER & VAN ZANDT, (Maryland,) (*L. E. Butler and B. F. Van Zandt,*) lumber dealers and farmers 135.

Butler, William S. Rev., (Schenevus,) Christian clergyman.

Butts, Jacob, (Schenevus,) farmer.

Butts, Jacob A., (Schenevus,) furniture dealer and undertaker, Main.

Cady, John M., (Maryland,) farmer 274.

Cady, William, (Maryland,) resident.

Campbell, Addison, (Maryland,) farmer leases of James McKeown.

Carpenter, Ira E., (Schenevus,) wagon maker, Main.

Carven, —— Mrs., (Maryland,) dress maker.

Carvin, L. F., (Maryland,) shoemaker.

Cass, Byron W., (Schenevus,) farmer 200.

Chamberlain, Dewitt, (Schenevus,) physician.

Chamberlain, Harvey, (Maryland,) farmer 185.

Chamberlain, Henry, (Chaseville,) farmer.

Chamberlain, John, (Schenevus,) carpenter.

Chamberlain, Maria Mrs., (Chaseville,) farmer 4.

Chamberlain, Mary Mrs., (Schenevus,) resident, Main.

Chamberlain, Mary A., (Schenevus,) saloon keeper, billiard rooms, dealer in fish, oysters, fruits and confectionery, Main.

Chamberlain, Salley A. Mrs., (Maryland,) farmer 2.

Chamberlain, W. H., (Elk Creek,) farmer leases 130.

Chase, Azro, (Chaseville,) farmer 800.

Chase, Brazil, (Chaseville,) carpenter.

Chase, Charles, (Schenevus,) mason.

Chase, Cyrus, (Elk Creek,) teamster.

Chase, Jerry, (Schenevus,) farmer 50.

Chase, John, (Schenevus,) carpenter, East.

Chase, Mary Ann Mrs., (Chaseville,) resident.

Chase & Mills, (Schenevus,) (*Samuel T. Chase and John Mills,*)hardware,stoves, coal, lime, cement, carriage trimmings &c., Main.

Chase, Milo, (Schenevus,) farmer 1.

Chase, Samuel G., (Schenevus,) farmer 90.

Chase, Samuel T., (Schenevus,) (*Chase & Mills.*)

Chauncey, William R., (Colliersville,) justice of the peace and farmer 55.

Chester, H., (Schenevus,) cashier Thompson, Chester Co.'s Bank, Main.

Clark, John, (Elk Creek,) farmer 20.

Clark, William H., (Schenevus,) keeper of boarding house for Morss and Gleason, Main.

Cole, Schuyler, (Schenevus,) farmer 130.

Colyer, Wesley, (Schenevus,) restaurant and billiard rooms, Main.

Cook, Harvey W., (Schenevus,) retired farmer, Main.

Cook, James W., (Schenevus,) farmer 27.

Cooley, Hannah C. Mrs., (Schenevus,) tailoress, Main.

Cornish, T. E., (Chaseville,) shoemaker.

Crippen, Amos H., (Schenevus,) painter, Main.

Crippen Bros., (Chaseville,) (*P. and C. H.,*) grain, flour, feed and lumber.

Crippen, Egbert, (Schenevus,) miller, Main.

Crippen, Joseph G., (Maryland,) harness maker.

Crippen, Philip, (Schenevus,) farmer 7, Main.

Crippen, Wellington E., (Schenevus,) farmer 110 and leases 25, Main.

Cross, Isaac, (Maryland,) farmer 92.

Cunningham, John, (Schenevus,) resident.

Cyphers, Caroline Mrs., (Schenevus,) resident, Main.

Davis, Eugene, (Schenevus,) wagon maker, Main.

Davis, Jeremiah, (Chaseville,) constable.

Davis, John, (Colliersville,) teaming and farmer leases of Azro Chase, 100.

DeLong, Alanson C., (Schenevus,) farmer 12, Main.

Demmens, Chester, (Schenevus,)farmer 50.

Demming, John, (Chaseville,) mason.

Demmings, H., (Schenevus,) farmer 100.

Denoyelles, Edward, (Schenevus,) (*with Ransom,*) farmer 175.

Denoyelles, Ransom, (Schenevus,) (*with Edward,*) farmer 175.

Doolittle, Wilber S., (Schenevus,) millwright and carpenter.

Draper, Lysander, (Maryland,) postmaster, hardware and groceries.

DUMONT, CYRUS, (Schenevus,) watch maker and jeweler, Main.

Dunham, Samuel H., (Schenevus,) resident, Race.

Dutcher, William, (Schenevus,) blacksmith.

Eldridge, Daniel, (Schenevus,) farmer.

Ellis, Norman, (Elk Creek,) farmer 30.

Ellsworth, Alonzo, (Maryland,) resident.

Emerson, William S., (Maryland,) cabinet maker.

Ennies, T. W., (Schenevus,) barber, Main.

Evans, Ransom M., (Schenevus,) carpenter, East.

Fagan, Patrick H., (Schenevus,) wagon maker and painter, and blacksmith, Main.

FAIRCHILD, PHILIP W., (Schenevus,) farmer 60.

Fellows, William, (Schenevus,) farmer 16.

FERREY & BENEDICT, (Schenevus,) (*Hon. E. E. Ferrey and Philor Benedict*,) attorneys.

FERREY, ELIJAH E. Hon., (Schenevus,) (*Ferrey & Benedict*,) prop. of plaster and feed mills, planing factory, cider and saw mills, and farmer 320.

Ferrey, Julian, (Schenevus,) agent for Hon. E. E. Ferrey.

Ferris, Hattie Mrs., (Schenevus,) dressmaker, Main.

Fields, John, (Schenevus,) farmer, Main.

Fink, John, (Schenevus,) pedler.

Fisher, Hiram H. Rev., (Maryland,) Baptist clergyman.

Follett, Ashley C., (Schenevus,) physician and druggist, Main.

Follett, Halsey, (Schenevus,) blacksmith, Main.

Follett, Henry, (Schenevus,) dentist, Main.

Fox, George, agent, (Maryland,) farmer 125.

Fuller, Salmon, (Schenevus,) farmer 80.

GARVIN, DANIEL M., (Schenevus,) track master.

Gilland, A. Delilah, (Schenevus,) milliner, Main.

Glazier, Loren, (Schenevus,) (*Glazier & Waterman*,) town clerk.

Glazier & Waterman, (Schenevus,) (*Loren Glazier and Lester Waterman*,) harness makers, Main.

Gleason, Frank, (Schenevus,) agent for Morss & Gleason.

Goddard, Diana Mrs., (Schenevus,) farmer 1.

Gove, Eliza Ann, (Elk Creek,) farmer 9.

Graham, Charles H. (Schenevus,) attorney, Main.

Graney, John O., (Schenevus,) agent for Gernon & Lynch, saloon keepers, near Depot.

Grassfield, Lewis, (Maryland,) wagon maker.

Green, Don D., (Schenevus,) farmer 52.

Gridley, Lyman, (Maryland,) farmer 5.

Gunn, George D. (Colliersville,) constable, carpenter and farmer 5.

Gurney, Chester, (Schenevus,) expressman, Race.

Gurney, David S., (Maryland,) farmer 232.

Gurney, Jesse, (Maryland,) lumbering and farmer 143.

Gurney, John J., (Maryland,) farmer 72.

Gurney, Sanders, (Schenevus,) express carrier, Main.

GURNEY, S. H., (Schenevus,) general merchant, postmaster and justice of the peace, Main.

Guy Brothers, (Schenevus,) (*Harry and George,*) grist mill.

Guy, George, (Schenevus,) (*Guy Brothers.*)

Guy, Harry, (Schenevus,) (*Guy Brothers.*)

Haith, Dennis, (Schenevus,) farmer 52.

Hall, Thomas, (Schenevus,) farmer.

Halleck, Daniel, (Schenevus,) resident.

Ham, Kate Mrs., (Schenevus,) tailoress, Main.

Hammond, Robert, (Maryland,) farmer 100.

HAMMOND, ROBERT W., (Maryland,) farmer 110.

Hand, Isaac, (Maryland,) variety pedler.

Hanor, E. B., (Schenevus,) farmer 200.

Hanor, William A., (Maryland,) farmer 130.

Haswell, Edward, (Schenevus,) bridge carpenter, Mill.

Hathaway, Christopher, (Schenevus,) clock repairer and farmer 1.

Haynes, Levi, (Schenevus,) farmer leases 300.

Haynor, Harvey M., (Schenevus,) saw mill and farmer 375.

Haynor, John, (Schenevus,) farmer 90.

Hazen, Levi, (Schenevus,) farmer 80.

Holbrook, Ziba, (Schenevus,) farmer 100.

Holdridge & Hubbard, (Schenevus,) (*R. Holdridge and J. Hubbard*,) hardware, Race.

Holdridge, R., (Schenevus,) (*Holdridge & Hubbard.*)

Hooker, E., (Maryland,) farmer 180.

HOOKER, R., (Maryland,) (*Van Zandt & Hooker.*) farmer 90.

Hoose, Laura, (Maryland,) farmer 47.

Hotchkin, Ashley, (Schenevus,) resident.

HOTCHKIN, WILLIAM S., (Schenevus,) (*Lane & Hotchkin.*)

Houck, Peter, (Schenevus,) farmer 100.

Houghton, Daniel D., (Chaseville,) cooper and farmer 18.

Houghton, Eliphalet E., (Schenevus,) allo. physician, Main.

House, Daniel, (Maryland,) farmer 160.

House, Joseph, (Maryland,) blacksmith.

Howland, Henry, (Schenevus,) farmer 80, Main.

Hoyt, Andrew, (Schenevus,) farmer leases of Levi Boardman, 100.

Hubbard, Edward, (Maryland,) farmer 130.

Hubbard, Ezra, (Elk Creek,) farmer 114.

Hubbard, J., (Schenevus,) (*Holdridge & Hubbard.*)

Hubbard, Oliver B., (Schenevus,) farmer 21.

Hubbard, Samuel, (Schenevus,) farmer 200.

Hull, Hobart B., (Schenevus,) carpenter and farmer 100, Mill.

Isman, ——, (Schenevus,) farmer 100.

Jackson, Lemuel, (Maryland,) farmer 1.

Johnson, Brocksannia Mrs., (Maryland,) saw mill and farmer 15.

Johnson, William, (Maryland,) blacksmith.

Jones, James J., (Schenevus,) carpenter and farmer 20.

Kelley, Edmund, (Elk Creek,) postmaster and farmer 50.

Kelley, Thomas, (Elk Creek,) painter.

Kelly, Daniel, (Elk Creek,) farmer 5.

Kelly, Hugh, (Elk Creek,) farmer 30.
Kelly, Levi, (Maryland,) farmer 30.
Kelly, Lewis, (Schenevus,) livery stables, Main.
Kelly, Mary A., (Schenevus,) dressmaker, Main.
Kenyon, Darius, (Maryland,) farmer 100.
Ketchum, Lorenzo, (Schenevus,) farmer 50.
Kingsley, Kate Mrs., (Elk Creek,) resident.
Knough, Casper, (Maryland,) (*with Alonzo Stalker*,) farmer leaves of J. Leonard.
Knough, Martin, (Maryland,) farmer leases of John Knough, 156.
Lake, Isaac V., (Schenevus,) farmer 100.
LAMPHERE, ARNOLD S., (Schenevus,) farmer 110.
LAMPHERE, ASENATH Mrs., (Schenevus,) farmer 20.
Lamphere, Orin, (Schenevus,) carpenter.
LANE & HOTCHKIN, (Schenevus,) (*Oscar F. Lane and William S. Hotchkin*,) steam sash and blind manufactory. Main.
Lane, Jane Mrs., (Schenevus,) resident.
Lane, Nelson, (Schenevus,) resident, Main.
LANE, OSCAR F., (Schenevus,) (*Lane & Hotchkin*.)
Lason, James W., (Maryland,) lumberman, prop. grist mill and farmer 520.
Lason, Joel, (Schenevus,) farmer 140.
Livingston, Jacob, (Schenevus,) farmer 20.
Loveland, Benjamin, (Schenevus,) painter.
Magee, Israel, (Maryland,) farmer 86.
Mallett, William W., (Schenevus,) farmer 112.
Mallory, Harvey, (Schenevus,) farmer 50.
Manzer, Benjamin, (Schenevus,) (*Manzer & Young*.)
Manzer, Silas, (Chaseville,) farmer 75.
Manzer & Young, (Schenevus,) (*Benjamin Manzer and Perry Young*,) photographers, Main.
Marble, Banner, (Maryland,) farmer 80.
Marble, Henry L., (Maryland,) farmer 213.
Martin, Albert Rev., (Schenevus,) Baptist clergyman, Main.
Martin, Page, (Schenevus,) farmer 100.
MARYLAND HOUSE, (Maryland,) Henry Wilson, keeper.
McHarg, J. Jr., (Schenevus,) general merchant, Main.
McIntyre, J. H., (Schenevus,) sawyer.
McKeown, Gilbert, (Maryland,) farmer 101.
McKown, James, (Maryland,) farmer 813.
Merrihew, William, (Schenevus,) painter and farmer 1, Monitor.
Milligan, Robert, (Schenevus,) farmer 140.
Mills, John, (Schenevus,) (*Chase & Mills*.)
Mills, William O., (Schenevus,) (*Brown & Mills*.)
Morehouse, Betsy S., (Schenevus,) milliner, Main.
Morss & Gleason, (Schenevus,) props. Schenevus Tannery, Main, and farmers 270.
Mull, Barney, (Schenevus,) mason.
MULTER, JACOB J., (Schenevus,) (*J. J. & J. L. Multer*.)
*MULTER, J. J. & J. L., (Schenevus,) (*Jacob J. and J. Leslie*,) editors and proprietors *Schenevus Monitor*.
MULTER, J. LESLIE, (Schenevus,) (*J. J. & J. L. Multer*.)
Nellis, Abram, (Schenevus,) farmer 5.

Nellis, David, (Chaseville,) farmer leases of Andrew Chase, 600.
Nellis, George W., (Schenevus,) carpenter.
Nellis, William, (Schenevus,) farmer 164.
Newell, John V. Rev., (Schenevus,) M. E. clergyman, Main.
NOONAN, DENNIS, (Schenevus,) (*with John*,) farmer 200.
NOONAN, JOHN, (Schenevus,) (*with Dennis*,) farmer 200.
O'Brien, Michael, (Schenevus,) blacksmith, Main.
Odell, Daniel B., (Maryland,) cooper.
Olmstead, William, (Schenevus,) lime burner.
Packer, James W., (Maryland,) carpenter.
Page, John, (Elk Creek,) cooper.
Palmatier, James, (Schenevus,) farmer 8.
Palmer, David A., (Elk Creek,) farmer 100.
Palmer, Henry, (Elk Creek,) farmer 92.
Parsons, Timothy, (Schenevus,) resident.
Patrick, Barley, (Schenevus,) (*with Thomas*,) farmer 150 in town of Westford.
Patrick, Thos., (Schenevus,) (*with Barley*,) farmer 150 in Westford.
Pechtel, Jacob, (Maryland,) (*with John W.*,) farmer 140.
Pechtel, John H., (Maryland,) farmer leases.
Pechtel, John W., (Maryland,) (*with Jacob*,) farmer 140.
Peck, John, (Chaseville,) miller.
Peebles, Hugh, (Schenevus,) farmer 420.
Peebles, John E., (Schenevus,) carpenter and farmer 5.
Pendell, George M., (Colliersville,) farmer 45.
Perry, David, (Elk Creek,) wagon maker and farmer 130.
Perry, Flavel W., (Elk Creek,) farmer 90.
Perry, Hannah, (Elk Creek,) farmer 6.
Perry, Milton F., (Schenevus,) dry goods, groceries, drugs and medicines, Main.
Pierce, Jefferson, (Schenevus,) farmer 180.
Pierce, William, (Schenevus,) farmer 100.
Place, William A., (Schenevus,) prop. of Place's Hotel, Main.
Platt, Andrew H., (Maryland,) farmer 230.
Platt, Merlin J., (Maryland,) farmer leases 230.
PLUMB, JAMES M., (Maryland,) farmer leases of David Wilber, 255.
Pratt, Daniel, (Maryland,) farmer leases of John M. Cady, 105.
Preston, Julius E., (Schenevus,) telegraph operator, Schenevus Station.
Price, Tryphena Mrs., (Chaseville,) resident.
Prindle, John H., (Elk Creek,) farmer 35.
Rathbone, Amos H., (Schenevus,) constable and farmer 100, Monitor.
Rathbone, Elizabeth, (Schenevus,) tailoress, Monitor.
Ray, Frederick, (Maryland,) (*Ray & Son*.)
Ray & Son, (Maryland,) (*William and Frederick*,) planing and saw mills, and rake factory.
Ray, William, (Maryland,) (*Ray & Son*.)
Reynolds, Halsey, (Chaseville,) farmer 210.
Rich, Henry W., (Maryland,) liquor agent.
Rider, John, (Maryland,) painter.
Rider, Silas, (Maryland,) farmer 22.
Ritch, Mary A., (Maryland,) milliner.
Robinson, Frederick G., (Maryland,) leases woodland of J. Leonard.

Robinson, Rensselaer W., (Schenevus,) overseer of the poor and butcher, Main.

Robison, Joseph B., (Schenevus,) mason and farmer 15.

Rose, Ithamer, (Maryland,) *(with James,)* farmer 100.

Rose, James, (Maryland,) *(with Ithamer,)* farmer 100.

Rose, John J., (Maryland,) commissioner of highways and farmer 6.

Rury, Frederick B., (Schenevus,) carpenter, Mill.

Russell, H. & R., (Maryland,) farmers 100.

Russell, Isaac, (Maryland,) farmer 40.

SCHENEVUS MARBLE WORKS, (Schenevus,) Oscar P. Toombs, prop.

*SCHENEVUS MONITOR, (Schenevus,) J. J. & J. L. Multer, editors and proprietors, Monitor.

Schermerhorn, Jasper, (Elk Creek,) farmer 30.

Schermerhorn, Philip, (Colliersville,) blacksmith.

Seaver, Zenas, (Schenevus,) *(with Philor D.,)* farmer 80.

Seward, John E., (Elk Creek,) blacksmith and farmer 1¼.

Seward, Porter, (Chaseville,) farmer 25.

Shaver, Eliza Mrs., (Chaseville,) resident.

Shelly, George, (Schenevus,) marble worker, Race.

Shelly, George, (Schenevus,) farmer 100.

Shutts, George A., (Chaseville,) carpenter.

Shutts, John, (Chaseville,) farmer 3½.

Shutts, Simon, (Chaseville,) resident.

Sibley, Jared, (Maryland,) farmer 100.

Sides, George W., (Elk Creek,) cooper.

Simmons, Peter, (Schenevus,) eclectic physician and general merchant, Main, also produce commission dealer in New York City.

SKINNER, THOMAS J., (Maryland,) general merchant.

Slater, Dexter C., (Maryland,) blacksmith.

Slater, Henry, (Schenevus,) prop. of Railroad House, Main.

Slingerland, Isaac, (Schenevus,) general merchant and farmer 72, Main.

Slingerland, Stephen R., (Schenevus,) farmer 150, Main.

Smallin, Abram, (Maryland,) farmer 72.

Smallin, Edgar, (Maryland,) farmer 49.

Smallin, John, (Schenevus,) resident.

Smallin, John J., (Maryland,) farmer 9½.

Smallin, Martin T., (Maryland,) farmer 114.

Smith, Gilbert, (Schenevus,) resident.

Smith, Jesse, (Schenevus,) shoemaker, Mill.

Smith, J. W., (Schenevus,) butcher.

Smith, Shubal, (Maryland,) farmer 14.

Snyder, Frederick, (Schenevus,) farmer 6, Main.

Snyder, S., (Schenevus,) farmer 70.

Somerville, Joseph, (Maryland,) farmer 70.

Sornberger, G., (Schenevus,) farmer 100.

Soule, Mira Mrs., (Schenevus,) resident, Main.

Spafford, Amos, (Schenevus,) farmer 11, Main.

Spencer, Amos D., (Colliersville,) farmer 200.

Spencer, Eugene W., (Maryland,) farmer 25.

Spencer, George, (Schenevus,) shoemaker and farmer.

Spencer, Horace D., (Colliersville,) farmer 550.

Spencer, Israel, (Maryland,) *(with Uriah, Philip D. and Joseph,)* saw mill and farmer 300.

Spencer, Joseph, (Maryland,) *(with Uriah, Philip D. and Israel,)* saw mill and farmer 300.

Spencer, Philip D., (Maryland,) *(with Uriah, Israel and Joseph,)* saw mill and farmer 300.

Spencer, Uriah, (Maryland,) *(with Philip D., Israel and Joseph,)* saw mill and farmer 300.

Spencer, William C., (Maryland,) farmer 98.

Sperry, Alanson, (Schenevus,) farmer 30.

Sperry, Alvin, (Schenevus,) farmer 190.

Sperry, Robert E., (Maryland,) station agent and telegraph operator.

Spurbeck, Frank, (Schenevus,) farmer 100.

Stalker, Alonzo, (Maryland,) *(with Caspar Knough,)* farmer leases of J. Leonard.

Stevenson, Irving, (Schenevus,) books, stationery and confectionery, Main.

Stever, Charles, (Schenevus,) farmer 140, Main.

Stever, C. H., (Maryland,) wagon maker.

Stever, Delos W., (Schenevus,) life and fire insurance agent, and farmer 130, Main.

Strain, Milton, (Schenevus,) farmer 70.

Strauss, Samuel, (Schenevus,) dry goods and clothing, Main.

Streter, Casper, (Maryland,) farmer leases of Hugh Peebles, 200.

Stuart, Thomas, (Maryland,) farmer 116.

Swackhammer, Isaiah, (Schenevus,) farmer 4.

Swartout, Joseph, (Chaseville,) grocer.

Swift, Jerome, (Maryland,) farmer 220.

Swift, Stephen G., (Maryland,) farmer 72.

Swift, Zaccheus, (Maryland,) mason.

TABER, WILLIAM L., (Schenevus,) prop. of Taber House, farmer 40 and in Broome Co., 114¾.

Tallmadge, Adelbert, (Maryland,) carpenter.

Tallmadge, John M., (Schenevus,) farmer 100.

Tallmadge, —— Mrs., (Maryland,) farmer 2.

Tator, George, (Schenevus,) farmer 35.

Tator, Rose M., (Schenevus,) milliner.

Thompson, Augustus G., (Chaseville,) blacksmith.

Thompson, D. S., (Elk Creek,) wagon maker and farmer 3.

Thompson, James D., (Elk Creek,) shoemaker.

Thompson, James M., (Schenevus,) supervisor.

Thompson, John, (Elk Creek,) brick maker, auctioneer and farmer 121.

Thompson, Julius R., (Schenevus,) attorney, Main.

Thompson, J. T., (Schenevus,) general merchant, president of Thompson, Chester & Co.'s Bank and farmer 600, Main.

Thompson, Niram C., (Maryland,) farmer 1.

Tipple, Charles E., (Chaseville,) farmer leases of Henry Howland, 85.

Tompkins, Austin, (Schenevus,) baggage man, Race.

Tompkins, John, (Schenevus,) mason, Main.

Tompkins, Robert, (Schenevus,) farmer 20.

Tompkins, Samuel, (Schenevus,) farmer 120.

TOOMBS, OSCAR P., (Schenevus,) prop. Schenevus Marble Works, Monitor.

Tubbs, Amos, (Maryland,) farmer leases of Hugh Peebles, 100.

Tubbs, Chester, (Maryland,) (*with John and Melvin*,) farmer 109.

Tubbs, George, (Colliersville,) sash and blind maker.

Tubbs John, (Maryland,) (*with Chester and Melvin*,) farmer 109.

Tubbs, Melvin, (Maryland,) (*with John and Chester*,) farmer 109.

Tyler, James E., (Schenevus,) speculator, Main.

Utter, Augustus, (Maryland,) mason and farmer 2.

Vanderboe, Orlando, (Schenevus,) shoemaker.

VAN ZANDT, B. F., (Maryland,) (*Butler & Van Zandt*,) (*Van Zandt & Hooker*,) justice of the peace.

VAN ZANDT & HOOKER, (Maryland,) (*B. F. Van Zandt and R. Hooker*,) lumber dealers and farmers 25.

Van Zandt, Joseph, (Schenevus,) farmer 2.

Van Zant, Betsy Mrs., (Schenevus,) farmer 300.

Vincent, Edward, (Maryland,) farmer leases of David Wilber, 160.

Vincent, Henry, (Maryland,) farmer leases of David Wilber, 342.

Wagar, M. A., (Maryland,) grocery and saloon.

Wagar, Philip J., (Maryland,) farmer 100.

Wager, Delevan, (Maryland,) farmer 120.

Wager, Hamilton, (Maryland,) farmer 120.

Wager, Morell, (Maryland,) refused information.

Wager, Truman, (Schenevus,) farmer 6.

Walker, A. D., (Schenevus,) furniture dealer and undertaker.

Walker, Fanny, (Chaseville,) farmer 70.

Walling, Milton, (Chaseville,) justice of the peace and farmer 100.

Warner, Henry, (Schenevus,) farmer 50.

Warner, J., (Schenevus,) marble worker.

Warner, Joel T., (Maryland,) blacksmith.

Warner, Samuel H., (Maryland,) prop. of Maryland House.

Waterman, Lester, (Schenevus,) (*Glazier & Waterman*.)

Waterman, Samuel, (Elk Creek,) farmer 50.

Waters, E. & L., (Maryland,) farmers 209.

Wayman, Moses, (Schenevus,) farmer 100.

Webster, D. M., (Schenevus,) farmer 200.

Webster, Ebenezer, (Maryland,) farmer 150.

Webster, John, (Maryland,) farmer leases of James Lason, 130.

Webster, Michael, (Elk Creek,) farmer 110.

Webster, Myron N., Jr., (Schenevus,) school teacher and farmer 100.

Webster, Myron N., Sen., (Schenevus,) farmer 45 and in town of Westford, 100.

Webster, Samuel, (Elk Creek,) assessor, prop. of saw mill and farmer 8.

White, Hiram, (Schenevus,) drover, Main.

Wickham, Shepherd, (Schenevus,) farmer 190.

Wickham, Thaddeus, (Schenevus,) farmer 130.

Wightman, Bennet, (Maryland,) stone mason.

Wightman, Melvin, (Maryland,) farmer leases of William, 130.

Wightman, Oliver, (Maryland,) farmer 170.

Wightman, Paul, (Maryland,) carpenter and farmer 30.

Wilber, Elizabeth, (Maryland,) farmer 60.

Wilber, Samuel M., (Schenevus,) carpenter and farmer 1.

Wilber, Smith, (Schenevus,) retired merchant, Main.

Wilber, Elijah J., (Schenevus,) lumbering and farmer 183.

Wilbur, Lewis, (Maryland,) farmer 35.

Wilcox, Albert E., (Schenevus,) tinsmith, Race.

Wilcox, Henry, (Schenevus,) shoemaker.

Wilsey, James, (Elk Creek,) resident.

WILSON, HENRY, (Maryland,) keeper Maryland House.

Wilson, Richard C., (Schenevus,) farmer 160, Main.

Wilson, Simon B., (Chaseville,) general merchant, postmaster and farmer 4½.

Wilson, William, (Elk Creek,) farmer 18.

Wilson, Wilsey, (Elk Creek,) farmer 100.

Wilson, ——, (Schenevus,) farmer leases of Hobart Hull, 100.

Winnie, Rensselaer, (Maryland,) farmer 160.

Winnie, Samuel, (Schenevus,) commission merchant, New York City.

Witt, George L., (Schenevus,) carpenter and farmer 200, Mill.

Wood, Charles G. Rev., (Schenevus,) M. E. clergyman, Main.

Woodcock, Delos, (Maryland,) farmer 2.

Woodcock, Gilbert, (Chaseville,) farmer 2½.

Wright, German, (Schenevus,) railroad contractor, carpenter and farmer 90.

Wright, German Mrs., (Schenevus,) milliner, Main.

Wright, John, (Schenevus,) carpenter, wagon maker and painter, Race.

Wright, Milton, (Schenevus,) carpenter, Main.

Wright, William E., (Schenevus,) carpenter, Monitor.

Young, J. Edward, (Schenevus,) printer, Main.

Young, Perry, (Schenevus,) (*Manzer & Young*.)

MIDDLEFIELD.

(Post Office Addresses in Parentheses.)

Adams, Harry, (Cooperstown,) farmer 24.
Aldridge, Smith, (Middlefield,) saw mill, threshing machine and farmer 40.
Allen, Frederick, (Middlefield,) manuf. of wagons and sleighs.
Allen, James J., (Middlefield,) blacksmith and farmer 15¾.
ALLER, HIRAM, (Phœnix Mills,) farmer.
Aller, James, (Phœnix Mills,) farmer 120.
Allison, Andrew, (Middlefield,) farmer 100.
AMERICAN HOTEL, (Middlefield,) Albert Palmer, prop.
Andrews, Henry, (Middlefield Center,) butcher and farmer 51.
Andrews, James, (Middlefield Center,) farmer leases of Stephen Judson, 150.
Andrews, N., (Middlefield,) farmer 60.
Aney, George, (Roseboom,) (*with Adolphus Lewis*,) farmer leases of Henry Aney, 255.
ANTISDEL, ARTHUR, (Middlefield,) agent for American Lightning Rod Co.
Baldwin, Henry A., (Westville,) farmer 75.
BALDWIN, PHILO, (Westville,) farmer 82.
BARNUM, H. G., (Middlefield Center,) farmer 177 and leases of T. J. Barnum, 124.
BARNUM, S. W., (Middlefield Center,) prop. of cheese factory and farmer 169.
Bates, A. T., (Westville,) cooper and farmer 8.
Bates, Catharine Mrs., (Westville,) farmer 4.
Bates, Nelson J., (Westville,) prop. of grist and cider mills and mason.
Bates, Reuben H., (Cooperstown,) farmer.
Bates, Samuel, (Westville,) saw mill and farmer 118.
Bates, T. I., (Westville,) farmer 125.
Beach, Nelson, (Middlefield Center,) physician and surgeon, and farmer 10.
Becker, Morgan, (Cooperstown,) farmer.
BELL, EDWIN, (Cooperstown,) supt. and keeper of Lake Wood Cemetery.
Bell, Lysander W., (Phœnix Mills,) spinner and farmer.
Bice, Jacob, (Westville,) farmer 60.
Blair, Cassius H., (Middlefield,) farmer leases of Robert Blair, 93.
Blair, David, (Middlefield Center,) farmer 120.
Blair, Robert, (Middlefield,) farmer 108.
Borst, David I., (Cooperstown,) farmer 105.
Bowen, Levi H., (Middlefield Center,) farmer 220.
Bowers, G. J., (Middlefield Center,) carriage maker.

BOWERS, MARTHA S. Miss, (Cooperstown,) resident.
Bowers, M. M. S. Mrs., (Cooperstown,) farmer 109.
Bowers, Peter, (Middlefield Center,) farmer 150.
Bowne, Lucian, (Cooperstown,) farmer 150.
BRADLEY, JAMES, (Cooperstown,) general agent for Cherry Valley Organ Co., prop. saw and shingle mills, and farmer 34.
Briggs, Alanson, (Middlefield,) machinist.
Briggs, E. C., (Middlefield,) saw and grist mills, and farmer 115.
Brimmer, Andrew J., (Phœnix Mills,) furnaces and tinware.
BROOKS, WILLIAM, (Cooperstown,) dealer in eggs and farmer 334.
Brown, Aaron C., (Cooperstown,) farmer leases 102.
Brown, Adelbert, (Middlefield,) (*with Robert*,) farmer 200.
Brown, A. G., (Middlefield,) farmer 86.
Brown, Joseph, (Cooperstown,) mason and farmer 2.
Brown, Moses R., (Middlefield,) farmer 280.
Brown, R., (Middlefield,) farmer 96.
Brown, Robert, (Middlefield,) (*with Adelbert*,) farmer 200.
Buel, Ira, (Middlefield,) farmer 100.
Bunday, Grandille, (Milford,) farmer leases of Wm. Clinton, 224.
Burlon, J. H., (Middlefield,) farmer 60.
BURNS, CYRUS H., (Middlefield Center,) carriage, wagon and sleigh maker.
Burton, Charles, (Middlefield,)(*with Jerome Head*,) farmer leases of Geo. Clark, 350.
Burton, Daniel, (Middlefield Center,) farmer 170.
Burton, Samuel, (Middlefield Center,) farmer 50.
Butler, Benjamin N., (Middlefield,) farmer.
Butler, Rensselaer, (Middlefield,) farmer 100.
Camp, Henry, (Westville,) saw and cider mills, and farmer 30.
Camp, John, (Middlefield Center,) farmer 112.
Camp, Lot, (Milford,) farmer 154.
Campbell, George, (Westville,) farmer leases of Geo. Clark, 200.
CANNEFF, WILLIAM T., (Middlefield Center,) farmer leases of Mrs. M. J. Wood, 235.
Celnen, John, (Middlefield Center,) farmer leases of George Clark, 400.
CENTRAL HOTEL, (Middlefield Center,) Henry Wilson, prop.

HENRY BAYER,

MERCHANT TAILOR,

AND DEALER IN

Gentlemen's Furnishing Goods,

In J. H. Story's New Building,

North Main Street,

COOPERSTOWN, N. Y.

O. J. & J. WALRATH,

COOPERSTOWN, N. Y.,

JOBBERS AND BUILDERS

AND DEALERS IN

Ready Made Houses,

Are prepared to do all kinds of Jobbing and to furnish Building Materials to parties desiring them.

Office Near the Railroad Crossing.

CHANCEY WILLIAMS,

COOPERSTOWN, N. Y.,

PROPRIETOR OF

Saw Mill, Shingle Mill

AND

Cider Mill.

LUMBER AND SHINGLES, in any quantity, on hand or manufactured to order. Special attention paid to

SAW GUMING.

CIDER manufactured to order.

Located on Willow Brook, one-fourth of a mile west of Depot.

Chapel, John, (Middlefield Center,) (*with Joseph,*) farmer 54.

Chapel, Joseph, (Middlefield Center,) (*with John,*) farmer 54.

Chappell, John, (Middlefield Center,) farmer 50.

Chase, David H., (Middlefield Center,) farmer 108.

Chase, Henry, (Cooperstown,) farmer 10.

Chase, William P., (Westville,) butcher.

Cheles, Joseph, (Middlefield,) farmer 60.

Clark, Denison, (Cooperstown,) (*with Henry,*) farmer 280.

Clark, Henry, (Cooperstown,) (*with Denison,*) farmer 280.

Clark, Isaac, (Westville,) farmer leases of Albert Burt, 200.

Claxton, John, (Middlefield,) farmer 60.

Clayton, John, (Middlefield,) farmer 100.

Cloxton, George, (Roseboom,) farmer leases of Henry Roseboom, 70.

Clyde, Joseph L., (Middlefield Center,) farmer leases of D. C. Clyde, 140.

COFFIN, A. D., (Middlefield,) farmer 150.

COFFIN, CHARLES G., (Middlefield,) farmer 361.

Coffin, Jerome, (Middlefield,) farmer leases of Charles, 260.

Conklin, Alonzo, (Cooperstown,) farmer 39.

Connolly, Thomas O., (Roseboom,) farmer leases of Henry Roseboom, 150.

Cook, Garvin, (Middlefield.)

Cook, John, (Cooperstown,) farmer 73.

Cook, John, (Middlefield,) farmer 240.

Coonrod, Ann O. Mrs., (Cooperstown,) milliner and dressmaker.

Coonrod, John H., (Cooperstown,) prop. of saw mill, manuf. of cheese boxes, painter, wagon maker and farmer 10.

COOPER, ALEXANDER H., (Milford,) dealer in clover and timothy seed, and farmer 67.

Cooper, Jacob W., (Middlefield Center,) carpenter and builder.

Cooper, William, (Milford,) farmer.

Cornish, A. B., (Westville,) farmer 130.

CORNISH, HIRAM N., (Westville,) farmer leases of Ira Howland, 165.

Cornish, Judson, (Westville,) farmer 100.

Cornish, L. P., (Westville,) farmer 90.

Cornwell, John E., (Middlefield,) school teacher.

Coss, John A., (Phœnix Mills,) carpenter and builder.

CRANDALL, JOSEPH, (Westville,) manuf. of pumps and wagons, and farmer 30.

Crandell, Levi, (Middlefield,) harness maker.

Crunan, Daniel, (Middlefield Center,) farmer 104.

Cummings, Daniel, (Middlefield,) farmer 65.

Cummings, Schuyler, (Middlefield,) hop raiser and farmer 320.

Daniels, Thomas, (Middlefield,) farmer 11.

Davidson, James W., (Middlefield Center,) farmer leases of N. L. Mason, 250.

Davis, Peter, (Middlefield,) farmer 8.

Davis, William W., (Middlefield,) school teacher.

Dean, Egbert, (Middlefield,) farmer.

Denton, B. A., (Westville,) dealer in eggs.

Denton, Joel, (Westville,) carpenter and farmer 4.

Devoe, William, (Phœnix Mills,) farmer leases of Mrs. Betsey Banister, 80.

Dockstader, George, (Middlefield Center,) farmer 100.

Dodge, Timothy, (Phœnix Mills,) farmer 6.

Doolittle, Porter, (Westville,) mason and farmer 9.

Dusenbury, George, (Middlefield,) shoemaker.

Dutcher, Oliver A., (Middlefield Center,) farmer 43.

Dutcher, Parchall, (Middlefield Center,) farmer 107.

Dutcher, Peter, (Middlefield Center,) farmer 36.

Dutton, William, (Westville,) farmer 80.

Easton, George, (Cooperstown,) farmer 65.

Eckler, Charles, (Middlefield,) hop raiser and farmer 146.

Eckler, Elson P., (Middlefield,) farmer 75.

Eckler, Josiah, (Cooperstown,) farmer 85.

Eckler, Lorenzo, (Westville,) hop raiser and farmer 97½.

Eckler, Martin, (Middlefield Center,) saw mill and farmer 220.

Eckler, Mary J. Mrs., (Middlefield,) farmer 146.

Eckler, Nelson, (Cooperstown,) farmer 167.

EGGLESTON, EUGENE, (Milford,) farmer 100.

Eggleston, James, (Westville,) farmer 156.

Eggleston, Niles, (Milford,) farmer 63.

EGGLESTON, NILES B., (Westville,) farmer 77.

Eggleston, Raymond W., (Cooperstown,) farmer 116.

Eggleston, Wm., (Westville,) farmer 109.

Ellsworth, Hiram, (Phœnix Mills,) farmer.

Ernst, George W., (Phœnix Mills,) (*Scott, Ernst & Co.*)

Ernst, Theodore, (Phœnix Mills,) (*Scott, Ernst & Co.*)

Fay, P., (Middlefield Center,) farmer leases of R. Swetzy, 100.

Ferris, W. H., (Westville,) wagon and sleigh maker.

Finley, William, (Cooperstown,) farmer 35.

Fling, Abram, (Middlefield Center,) farmer 96.

Fling, Charles, (Middlefield Center,) farmer 127.

Follett, J. C., (Middlefield,) justice of the peace, blacksmith and farmer 10.

Foster, Thomas, (Middlefield,) farmer 10.

Fowler, J. G., (Middlefield Center,) prop. of saw mill and farmer 114.

Francis, Samuel, (Phœnix Mills,) supt. for Scott, Ernst & Co.

FRITTS, VALENTINE, (Milford,) farmer leases of Geo. Sweet, 167.

Galer, Martin, (Middlefield,) farmer 70.

Gano, Philip, (Westville,) farmer 70.

GANO, THOMAS P., (Westville,) farmer 104.

Gates, Benjamin, (Middlefield Center,) farmer 160.

Gates, Darius, (Middlefield Center,) farmer 100.

GATES, MARTIN E., (Cooperstown,) carpenter and builder.

Gaylord, Henry, (Phœnix Mills,) sawyer.

Gilbert, B. M., (Middlefield,) surveyor.

Gilbert, Fred. A., (Middlefield,) farmer leases of Mrs. George Parshall, 150.

GILBERT, FAYETTE L., (Middlefield,) dry goods and groceries, agent for Singer Sewing Machines and farmer 43.

Gildersheaves, Peter, (Middlefield,) farmer.

Gillett, Russell, (Middlefield,) farmer 108.

Gridley, George S., (Middlefield,) (*Warner & Gridley*.)

Griffin, David M., (Phœnix Mills,) farmer 4.

Griffin, Geo. W., (Middlefield,) farmer 120.

Griffin, Philander Rev., (Middlefield Center,) pastor of First Presbyterian Church.

Griffin, Willard, (Cooperstown,) farmer 205.

Hampson, Thomas, (Hartwick Seminary,) spinner.

HAND, RICHARD C., (Westville,) town constable, mechanic and farmer.

HANNAH, WILLIAM, (Middlefield Center,) blacksmith.

Hanor, Ira S., (Cooperstown,) farmer 108.

Haskins, William, (Middlefield,) farmer leases of Geo. Clark, 20.

Head, Jerome, (Middlefield,) (*with Charles Burton,*) farmer leases of Geo. Clark, 350.

Hearn, George, (Middlefield,) tailor and farmer 10.

HEARN, THOMAS H., (Middlefield,) tailor.

Herdman, George G., (Middlefield,) harness maker.

Hicks, M. B., (Middlefield,) agent for American Lightning Rod Co.

Hinds, Lucian, (Milford,) farmer leases of Geo. Clark, 700.

Hinman, George D., (Cooperstown,) tanner and farmer 20.

Hinman, Julius, (Middlefield,) farmer.

HOGAN, MICHAEL, (Middlefield,) farmer 100.

Holiday, John, (Middlefield,) farmer 152.

Hollenbeck, Francis, (Middlefield,) farmer 60.

Hopkins, Orville M., (Middlefield,) farmer 107.

Hoyt, Joseph, (Middlefield Center,) farmer leases of Geo. Clark, 234.

Hubbard, Charles H., (Cooperstown,) farmer for Leonard.

Hubbard, Harrison, (Cooperstown,) farmer leases 100.

Hubbard, Leonard, (Cooperstown,) farmer 125.

Hubbell, Abigail Mrs., (Middlefield,) farmer 120.

Hubbell, E. F., (Middlefield,) farmer 50.

Hubbell, F., (Middlefield,) farmer 50.

Hubbell, M. G., (Westville,) farmer 125.

Hubbell, P. L., (Middlefield,) farmer 92.

Hunter, Dilora M., (Middlefield Center,) farmer 125.

Hunter, Elizabeth Mrs., (Cooperstown,) farmer 50.

Hunter, George, (Cooperstown,) (*with Henry,*) farmer 100.

Hunter, Henry, (Cooperstown,) (*with Geo.,*) farmer 100.

Hunter, S. W., (Cooperstown,) farmer.

HUNTINGTON, SAMUEL G., (Middlefield Center,) manuf. of shoe lasts and farmer 30.

HUTCHINGS, JOHN, (Cooperstown,) farmer 100.

HUTCHINGS, WILLIAM, (Phœnix Mills,) prop. of Phœnix Hotel and store.

Ingalls, Alanson, (Milford,) farmer 140.

Ingalls, Ralph, (Middlefield,) farmer 90.

Ingals, William, (Middlefield,) farmer 60.

Irish, David, (Middlefield,) farmer 73.

Irish, John, (Middlefield,) farmer 95.

ISMOND, BELA, (Middlefield,) farmer.

Ismond, James, (Cooperstown,) farmer 102.

ISMOND, JAMES M., (Middlefield,) farmer 144.

Jewell, Paschal A., (Westville,) farmer 100.

Jones, George C., (Middlefield,) cider mill.

Jones, Henry, (Cooperstown,) blacksmith.

Jones, J. E. Mrs., (Middlefield,) milliner.

Jones, Sanders, (Middlefield,) farmer 157.

Jones, William, (Phœnix Mills,) farmer 75.

Judson, J. V., (Cooperstown,) farmer 9.

Kaple, John D., (Middlefield,) school teacher.

KELLER, DAVID, (Middlefield Center,) shoemaker and farmer 25¾.

Keller, D. H., (Middlefield Center,) shoemaker and agent for Warrior Mower and Reaper.

Kelley, Jeremiah, (Middlefield Center,) dry goods and groceries.

Kelley, J. C., (Middlefield,) farmer 222.

Killey, Thomas, (Middlefield Center,) farmer 112.

Kitts, Adam, (Milford,) farmer 10.

Kiuyon, Thomas, (Middlefield Center,) farmer 8.

Knapp, Austin, (Cooperstown,) tanner.

Knapp, Edward, (Middlefield,) farmer 60.

Kraham, James, (Rooseboom,) farmer leases of Thomas Vickers, 125.

Lane, James, (Middlefield,) farmer 100.

Lawler, Peter, (Middlefield,) blacksmith.

LEONARD, D. H., (Middlefield,) farmer 86 and leases of Geo. Clark, 610.

Lettis, Lester, (Middlefield,) farmer leases of Mrs. H. Darling, 85.

Lettis, Olive Mrs., (Middlefield,) farmer 8.

Lewis, Adolphus, (Rooseboom,) (*with Geo. Aney,*) farmer leases of Henry Aney, 255.

Ludlam, Henry, (Rooseboom,) farmer 110.

Lynes, William H., (Cooperstown,) farmer 150.

Mackey, Anson, (Cooperstown,) farmer 59.

Manchester, T. G., (Cooperstown,) farmer 50.

MARKS, EGBERT, (Middlefield,) (*Parshall & Marks,*) supervisor.

Mason, Linus S., (Middlefield Center,) farmer 275.

Mason, Norman L., (Middlefield Center,) wagon maker and farmer leases of L. S. Mason, 252.

McCabe, Patrick, (Cooperstown,) mason and farmer leases 23.

McCarthy, Charles, (Middlefield Center,) farmer 133.

McCollister, Timothy, (Westville,) farmer 18.

McDonald, James, (Middlefield Center,) (*with Thomas,*) farmer 216.

McDonald, Thomas, (Middlefield Center,) (*with James*,) farmer 216.

McDonald, William, (Middlefield Center,) farmer 92.

McEwen, David, (Phœnix Mills,) farmer.

McGowen, Elias, (Middlefield Center,) farmer 66.

McKELLIP, DANIEL, (Middlefield,) farmer 93.

McLean, Andrew, (Milford,) farmer leases of Geo. Clark, 200.

McNallon, Peter, (Cooperstown,) mason and farmer 50.

Molloy, Michael, (Middlefield Center,) farmer 172.

Murphy, A. S., (Middlefield,) farmer 100.

Murphy, Norman, (Cooperstown,) farmer 100.

Murphy, S. T., (Middlefield,) farmer 100.

Neal, W. J., (Roseboom,) farmer 110.

Newell, N., (Cooperstown,) farmer 105.

Newton, Avery, (Milford,) farmer.

Newton, E. A., (Westville,) farmer 53.

North, Aaron, (Middlefield,) farmer.

North, A. B., (Middlefield,) (*with Thomas*,) farmer 275.

North, Harrison, (Middlefield,) dealer in hops and wool.

North, Harry, (Middlefield,) (*Yager & North*.)

North, Hiram, (Middlefield,) (*with James*,) farmer.

North, James, (Middlefield,) (*with Hiram*,) farmer.

North, Mary J. Mrs., (Middlefield,) farmer 70.

North, Thomas, (Middlefield,) (*with A. B.*,) farmer 275.

Northrup, Morgan, (Phœnix Mills,) keeper of poor house.

Olendorf, Peter, (Cooperstown,) farmer 200.

Olive, John, (Cooperstown,) farmer 5.

Osborn, Benjamin, (Westville,) farmer 95.

Ottaway, Henry N., (Cooperstown,) farmer 50.

Ottaway, John, (Cooperstown,) farmer 50.

Ottaway, Robert, (Cooperstown,) farmer 60.

PALMER, ALBERT, (Middlefield,) prop. of American Hotel.

PALMER, ALMON D., (Westville,) farmer 76.

Palmer, Biram, (Westville,) farmer 180.

Palmer, Byron, (Westville,) mechanic, grafter of trees, hop grower and farmer 182.

Palmer, Charles, (Westville,) farmer.

Palmer, Elon, (Westville,) physician.

Palmer, Everitt, (Cooperstown,) farmer 45.

Palmer, Rensselaer, (Middlefield,) dealer in wool, hops and butter.

PALMER, WILSON N., (Westville,) farmer.

Parshall, Adriel, (Cooperstown,) carriage maker and farmer 5.

Parshall, A. C., (Middlefield,) (*Parshall & Marks*.)

Parshall, Albert O., (Cooperstown,) cider mill and farmer 185.

Parshall, Daniel, (Middlefield,) (*with Levi*,) farmer 240.

PARSHALL, ELIAS H., (Cooperstown,) farmer 65.

Parshall, G. W., (Cooperstown,) farmer 80.

Parshall, Levi, (Middlefield,) (*with Daniel*,) farmer 240.

Parshall & Marks, (Middlefield,) (*A. C. Parshall and Egbert Marks*,) dry goods and groceries.

Parshall, Peter, (Cooperstown,) saw mill and farmer 275.

Parshall, Anson C., (Middlefield,) (*with Jonas P. Vanhuzon*,) farmer 120.

Paschell, C. D., (Middlefield,) auctioneer.

Patten, Thomas, (Phœnix Mills,) (*with William*,) farmer 185.

Patten, Wm., (Phœnix Mills,) (*with Thos.*,) farmer 185.

PAY, HENRY, (Westville,) farmer leases 100.

Peake, Hiram, (Cooperstown,) farmer 160.

Perkins, Arthur, (Middlefield Center,) farmer 100.

PHŒNIX HOTEL, (Phœnix Mills,) Wm. Hutchings, prop.

Pickins, Charles, (Phœnix Mills,) farmer leases of H. Sherman, 35.

PIER, G. A., (Phœnix Mills,) (*with Isaac*,) hop raiser and farmer 100.

PIER, ISAAC, (Phœnix Mills,) (*with G. A.*,) hop raiser and farmer 100.

Pier, Timothy, (Cooperstown,) farmer leases of Mrs. A. Jones, 100.

Pierce, Horace M., (Cooperstown,) farmer 76 and leases 168.

Pierce. O. I., (Cooperstown,) tanner and farmer 7.

Pitts, Catherine Mrs., (Middlefield,) farmer 96.

Pitts, Thomas H., (Middlefield,) farmer 125.

POPE, JAMES H., (Middlefield,) manuf. of cheese boxes and cider.

Post, John, (Westville,) postmaster, prop. of hotel and tin shop.

Pratt, A. J., (Westville,) blacksmith.

Pratt, D. E., (Westville,) (*with Thomas*,) blacksmith and farmer 4.

Pratt, George, (Middlefield,) farmer 65 and leases of Coffin estate, 300.

PRATT, JEREMIAH, (Westville,) farmer 125.

Pratt, R. D., (Westville,) farmer 80.

Pratt, Thomas, (Westville,) (*with D. E.*,) blacksmith and farmer 4.

Preston, S., (Middlefield,) farmer leases of Geo. Clark, 160.

Putman, John, (Middlefield,) farmer 145.

Reynolds, Eugene, (Westville,) farmer 77½.

Reynolds, E. W., (Cooperstown,) farmer 90.

Reynolds, Israel, (Middlefield,) farmer 50.

Reynolds, James, (Middlefield Center,) farmer 140 and leases of Geo. Clark, 200.

Reynolds, William, (Middlefield,) farmer 55.

Rich, Morgan, (Westville,) farmer 60.

Risendorf, John, (Middlefield,) farmer leases of Geo. Clark, 160.

ROBBINS, HARRY, (Middlefield,) prop'r. of grist mill.

ROBERT, E., (Middlefield,) butcher.

ROBERTS, HENRY C., (Middlefield,) farmer leases 205.

ROBINSON, JOHN, (Phœnix Mills,) prop. of saw and planing mills.

ROGERS, BARTLETT, (Cooperstown,) farmer 105.

ROGERS, CALVIN, (Cooperstown,) farmer 157.

Rolland, Joel, (Middlefield,) wagon maker.

Rouse, Robert, (Cooperstown,) farmer 105.

Russell, Door, (Cooperstown,) banker, New York City, and farmer 200.

Ryan, William, (Middlefield Center,) farmer leases 100.

Saxton, James, (Westville,) farmer 80.

SAXTON, STEPHEN, (Westville,) farmer 50.

Scott, Ernst & Co., (Phœnix Mills,) (*John F. Scott, George W. and Theodore Ernst.*) woolen mills.

Scott, John F., (Phœnix Mills,) (*Scott, Ernst & Co.*)

Secor, Levi M., (Middlefield,) painter, grainer and frescoer.

Sherman, Ansel, (Cooperstown,) farmer 50 and leases 200.

Shipway, Ann Mrs., (Middlefield Center,) farmer 150.

Short, Joshua, (Cooperstown,) farmer 11½.

Short, William S., (Cooperstown,) farmer 3.

SHUMWAY, URI, (Westville,) carpenter, mason and farmer 38.

Sibley, James, (Cooperstown,) farmer 75.

SIBLEY, ORRIN, (Cooperstown,) saw mill and farmer 234.

Silenbeck, Arnold, (Westville,) farmer 60½.

SIMMONS, A. M., (Westville,) physician and surgeon.

Sittel, William, (Cooperstown,) farmer 50.

Smith, Alfred, (Middlefield Center,) farmer 102.

Smith, Caroline Mrs., (Middlefield Center,) farmer 210.

Smith, Caroline A. Mrs., (Cooperstown,) farmer 110.

Smith, Clark, (Middlefield Center,) farmer 103.

Smith, Francis C., (Cooperstown,) farmer 145.

Smith, Jerome, (Middlefield Center,) farmer 137.

Smith, Lorenzo, (Middlefield Center,) farmer 50.

SMITH, NATHAN, (Middlefield,) physician and surgeon.

Smith, Russell, (Cooperstown,) farmer 80.

Smith, Warren C., (Cooperstown,) farmer 16.

Smith, William, (Milford,) farmer 56.

SMITH, WM. B., (Cooperstown,) assistant supt. and conductor C. S. V. R. R.

SNYDER, CHAUNCELAER, (Westville,) carpenter and builder, undertaker and farmer 100.

Steere, Amasa S., (Cooperstown,) farmer 96.

Stowell, Anson D., (Cooperstown,) farmer leases 50.

Stowell, Henry M., (Cooperstown,) farmer 30.

Stowell, Royal, Cooperstown,) farmer 175.

Stowell, Winfield S., (Cooperstown,) farmer leases 75.

Sutherland, N. H., (Westville,) shoemaker.

Swezey, Richard, (Roseboom,) farmer leases of A. & J. Snell, 270.

Tabor, William, (Middlefield,) farmer 92.

TALBOT, EBEN, (Phœnix Mills,) farmer leases 10.

Tarpenning, George, (Cooperstown,) farmer leases of Seth J. Temple, 80.

Tarpenning, John, (Cooperstown,) farmer leases of Eben M. Temple, 214.

Taylor, Daniel, (Middlefield Center,) farmer 150.

TEMPLE, WILLIAM, (Cooperstown,) farmer 200.

THAYER, CALEB B., (Cooperstown,) farmer for Wm. Brooks.

Thayer, John, (Cooperstown,) farmer 172.

Thomas, Walter B. Rev., (Middlefield,) pastor of M. E. Church.

Tripp, E. R., (Middlefield Center,) blacksmith.

TRIPP, HENRY, (Middlefield,) farmer leases of John Eddy, 152¾.

Tumber, John, (Cooperstown,) farmer 40.

Upham, Byron M., (Cooperstown,) shoemaker and farmer 53.

Van Buskark, Morris, (Cooperstown,) farmer 235.

Van Buskark, W. H., (Cooperstown,) farmer.

Vandee, Wm., (Milford,) farmer 27.

Van Deusen, William, (Middlefield Center,) farmer 160.

Van Duzen, W. H., (Middlefield Center,) farmer 100.

Van Duzsen, Harry, (Middlefield Center,) farmer 170.

Van Huzon, Delose, (Middlefield,) blacksmith.

Van Huzon, Harry, (Middlefield,) blacksmith and farmer 17.

Vanhuzon, Jonas P., (Middlefield,) (*with Anson C. Parshell,*) farmer 120.

VANNORT, ADAM, (Cooperstown,) gardener for John F. Scott.

Van Patten, Abram, (Middlefield Center,) farmer 94½.

Van Patten, Henry, (Westville,) farmer 80.

Ventress, Joseph S., (Middlefield Center,) (*Ventress & Weeks.*)

Ventress & Weeks, (Middlefield Center,) (*Joseph S. Ventress and James G. Weeks,*) blacksmiths.

Vickers Dan., (Roseboom,) farmer 97½.

Vunk, Francis, (Middlefield Center,) farmer 40.

Wait, Daniel W., (Middlefield Center,) agt. for Champion Mower, Wood's Mower and Reaper, low wheel horse rake and tedder, and farmer 24.

Walker, Chester, (Middlefield,) farmer 50.

Warner, Charles, (Middlefield,) (*Warner & Gridley.*)

Warner & Gridley, (Middlefield,) (*Charles Warner and George S. Gridley,*) prop'rs of hotel and farmers lease of George Clark, 61½.

Warren, Barditt, (Middlefield,) W. U. telegraph operator.

WARREN, E. B., M. D., (Middlefield,) physician and surgeon.

Webb, Joseph, (Roseboom,) farmer 99.

Webb, J. H. Jr., (Roseboom,) farmer 99.

Webb, William, (Middlefield Center,) farmer 128.

Weeks, James G., (Middlefield Center,) (*Ventress & Weeks.*)

Westcott, E. R., (Phœnix Mills,) farmer 190.

White, James, (Cooperstown,) farmer 2.

White, Jerome, (Cooperstown,) farmer 50.
White, S. Miss, (Middlefield Center,) farmer 36.
White, William, (Cooperstown,) farmer 56.
Whiteman, Gara, (Roseboom,) farmer 240.
Wicks, Henry, (Middlefield,) blacksmith.
Wicks, William L., (Middlefield Center,) prop. of grist and cider mills, turner and cheese box maker.
Wickwire, Amos C., (Middlefield Center,) farmer 115.
Wigby, William, Jr., (Roseboom,) farmer 245.
Wilber, John, (Westville,) farmer 28.
Wilber, John I., (Westville,) farmer 18.
Wilber, Menzo, (Westville,) farmer 75.
Wilbor, H., (Middlefield,) farmer leases of O. Wilbor, 50.
Wilbor, R. W., (Middlefield,) farmer 30.

WILSON, HENRY, (Middlefield Center,) prop. of Central Hotel.
Winegar, Oren, (Cooperstown,) farmer 80.
Wood, Henry, (Cooperstown,) farmer 100.
Wood, James C., (Cooperstown,) farmer 50.
Wood, John T., (Cooperstown,) farmer 117.
Wood, Nelson, (Middlefield Center,) shoemaker.
Wood, Oliver, (Middlefield Center,) farmer leases of William Wood, 100.
Wood, Robert, (Cooperstown,) farmer.
Wood, William H., (Phœnix Mills,) farmer 80.
Yager, Chancey, (Middlefield,) (*Yager & North.*)
Yager & North, (Middlefield,) (*Chancey Yager and Harry North,*) hardware and tinware.

MILFORD.

(Post Office Addresses in Parentheses.)

Ackley, Eli, (Colliersville,) farmer 70.
ACKLEY, GEORGE W., (Colliersville,) farmer 110.
Ackley, Seth, (Portlandville,) farmer 58.
ADAMS, GEORGE W., (Milford,) general merchant.
Adams, Noah W., (Portlandville,) farmer 10.
ADAMS, ORVILLE J., (Milford,) furniture.
Ailesworth, Floyd, (Portlandville,) farmer 57.
ALLEN, ABRAHAM, (Milford,) shingle maker.
Allen, Judson, (Milford,) farmer leases of David Wilber, 150.
Aplin, Samuel C., (Portlandville,) dentist.
Avery, Alonzo B., (Colliersville,) (*Avery & Platt.*)
Avery & Platt, (Colliersville,) (*Alonzo B. Avery and G. Platt,*) saloon and grocery.
Aylesworth, Frelin, (Portlandville,) farmer 170.
Aylesworth, George, (Portlandville,) farmer 63.
Aylesworth, Luzerne, (Portlandville,) farmer 65.
BABCOCK, ALEXANDER H., (Portlandville,) farmer 1.
BAKER, JAMES O., (Milford,) farmer 100.
Baker, Jerome E., (Milford,) carpenter.
Baker, Warren L., (Portlandville,) farmer 178.
Barnes, Ansell, (Colliersville,) farmer 150.
Barnes & Fox, (Colliersville,) sash, doors and blinds, and lumber dealers.

Barney, Daniel, (Milford,) carriage maker and farmer 35.
BARNEY, ELERY H., (Milford,) farmer.
Barney, John, (Portlandville,) farmer 130.
Bartlett, Deloss, (Portlandville,) farmer 11 and in Oneonta, 64.
Bates, Byron, (Milford,) farmer 186.
BATES, HENRY, (Milford,) farmer 164 and in Hartwick, 10.
Bates, Henry Z., (Milford,) house painter.
Beals, George W., (Milford,) farmer 30.
Beam, George, (Colliersville,) farmer leases of Abram Cuck, 160.
Bissell, Amos, (Milford,) farmer 185 and in Hartwick, 20.
Bliss, William, (Portlandville,) farmer leases of George Clark, 125.
Boorn, L. Mrs., (Milford,) tailoress.
BOORN, STEPHEN C., (Milford,) currier for W. E. Stickney.
BOWE, SENECA, (Colliersville,) farmer 50.
Brady, Thomas, (Portlandville,) stone mason and farmer 1½.
BROOKS & HALL, (Milford,) (*Orson M. Brooks and George Hall,*) blacksmiths.
BROOKS, ORSON M., (Milford,) (*Brooks & Hall.*)
BROWER, PETER O., (Portlandville,) prop. Milford Center House, grocery and farmer 3.
BROWN, GEORGE W., (Milford,) farm laborer.
Brown, James, (Laurens,) farmer 80.
Brownell, Walter W., (Milford,) farmer 120.
Bullis, Albert, (Colliersville,) painter and glazier.

Bunn, William A., (Oneonta,) farmer 200.

Burk, Ira, (Portlandville,) farmer 40.

Burnett, Isaac, (Milford,) allo. physician.

Burns, Robert, (Colliersville,) farmer 3.

Burnside, Alfred, (Milford,) farmer 112.

Burnside, Andrew, (Colliersville,) farmer 102.

Burnside, Washington, (Maryland,) farmer 100 and in Maryland, 77.

Bush, George, (Portlandville,) farmer 73.

Butler, Daniel E., (Portlandville,) farmer 200.

Cady, Frederick J., (Maryland,) farmer 128 and in Maryland, 62.

Carpenter, Azel, (Portlandville,) farmer 80.

Carvin, David, (Colliersville,) farmer 5.

Carvin, Porter, (Colliersville,) farmer 30.

CEPERLEY, CHAUNCEY, (Colliersville,) farmer 95.

Chase, Isaac, (Portlandville,) blacksmith and farmer 30.

CHASE, OLIVER T., (Portlandville,) farmer 129.

Chauncey, Edwin, (Portlandville,) blacksmith and farmer 20.

CHAUNCEY, EDWIN, (Portlandville,) (*Chauncey, Squires & Co.,*) (*Chauncey & Morgan,*) farmer 61½.

Chauncey & Morgan, (Portlandville,) (*Edwin Chauncey and Henry H. Morgan,*) undertakers.

CHAUNCEY, SQUIRES & CO., (Portlandville,) (*Edwin Chauncey, Asa D. Squires, Marcus Eliott and —— Rowley,*) prop'rs of saw mill and lath mill, and farmers in Middlefield, 205.

Clark, Elihu W., (Portlandville,) works farm of heirs of Wm. L. Wright.

CLINE, HIRAM C., (Milford,) deputy sheriff, farmer 208 and in Hartwick, 68.

Clough, Eli D., (Milford,) carpenter and farmer 2½.

Cole, Cornelius, (Mount Vision,) farmer 6.

Collier, Isaac, (Portlandville,) farmer 6½.

Cooke, Morey S., (Portlandville,) attorney.

Coon, George H., (Colliersville,) farmer 200.

Coxhead, Henry, (Milford,) carpenter.

Crandall, Timothy, (Portlandville,) farmer 146.

Crandall, Timothy, (Portlandville,) farmer 140.

CRANDELL, JUSTUS, (Portlandville,) farmer 250.

Cronkhite, Ebenezer, (Milford,) carriage maker.

CRONKHITE, ELIZABETH A. MRS., (Portlandville,) tailoress and dress maker.

CRONKITE & DENISON, (Portlandville,) (*James W. Cronkite and Samuel Denison,*) carriage makers.

CRONKITE, JAMES W., (Portlandville,) (*Cronkite & Denison.*)

Cronkite, Marsavan, (Laurens,) farmer leases of Mrs. Adelia Cronkite, 15.

Cronkite, Nelson, (Portlandville,) carriage and sleigh maker, blacksmith and manuf. of Cronkite's patent wheelbarrow.

Crouch, William, (Milford,) farmer 125.

Crowford, Henry, (Portlandville,) farmer 100.

Cumming, James, (Milford,) farmer 100.

Cummings, Egbert, (Milford,) farmer leases of James Brown, 4.

Dailey, Morris, (Milford,) farmer 6.

Daniels, Emily Mrs., (Mount Vision,) farmer 130.

Dayton, Gideon M., (Colliersville,) saw mill.

DENISON, SAMUEL, (Portlandville,) (*Cronkite & Denison.*)

Deuel, Egbert, (Portlandville,) carpenter and farmer 24.

Diefendorf, Abram, (Colliersville,) general merchant and post-master.

Dingman, Jacob, (Portlandville,) farmer 75.

Drew, Harris B., (Portlandville,) farmer leases of Mrs. Adelia Cronkhite, 60.

Dunham, Dwight, (Milford,) rents tannery of John Eddy.

EDDY, JOHN, (Milford,) (*Eddy & Reige,*) banker, tannery, saw mill and coal dealer.

Eddy & Reige, (Milford,) (*John Eddy and E. A. Reige, of New York,*) dealers in hops, malt and barley.

EDSON, DAMON, (Portlandville,) farmer 150.

Edson, Elijah, (Portlandville,) farmer 135.

Edson, Eugene, (Portlandville,) farmer leases of Barzilia Edson, 270.

EDSON, JOSEPH, (Portlandville,) farmer 130.

Edson, Reuel, (Portlandville,) farmer 260.

EKERSON, JOHN, (Milford,) foreman in tannery for Walton E. Stickney.

ELIOT, ISAAC, (Milford,) boot and shoe maker.

ELIOTT, MARCUS, (Portlandville,) (*Chauncey, Squires & Co.*)

Elliot, Marcus A., (Milford,) farmer 107.

Ellis, Lewis, (Portlandville,) farmer leases 162.

ELWELL, JULIUS, (Portlandville,) prop. grist mill, saw mill, shingle machine, planing mill and lath mill, and farmer 2.

Empie, Daniel, (Milford,) farmer 91.

Epes, George, (Portlandville,) farmer 50.

FAY, WILLIAM L., (Milford,) farmer.

Ferguson, James, (Portlandville,) farmer 130.

FERN, JAMES, (Colliersville,) farmer 47.

Finch, Elmer, (Colliersville,) (*with Hamilton J. Lane,*) farmer rents of George Clark, 260.

Finch, Henry, (Portlandville,) farmer leases of Mrs. Mary Lane, 35¾.

Fox, Gilbert A., (Milford,) harness maker and farmer 1¼.

GAGE, JAMES B., (Portlandville,) farmer rents of Samuel Preston, 138, and of K. Wilber, 48.

GAGE, WILLIAM, (Maryland,) farmer 60 and in Maryland, 36.

Gammet, Solomon, (Portlandville,) farmer leases of Simon Green, 258.

Garlock, Elbert C., (Portlandville,) farmer leases of Henry C. Miller.

Garlock, George S., (Portlandville,) farmer 70.

Gaylord, Elijah D., (Portlandville,) blacksmith.

GEORGIA, ORIN N., (Milford,) farmer 90.

Georgia, Orin N., (Portlandville,) farmer 90.

Gifford, Elihu, (Oneonta,) farmer 150.

Gifford, Nathaniel, (Portlandville,) farmer 104.

Gillett, Lester, (Portlandville,) farmer 75.

Goodenough, Artemas, (Colliersville,) farmer 60.

Goodrich, Chauncey, (Milford,) farmer 39½.

GOODYEAR HOUSE, (Colliersville,) Horace F. Jencks, prop.

Goodyear, Jared, (Portlandville,) grist mill, saw mill, cider mill and plaster mill, and farmer 2124.

GREEN, CHUYLER, (Colliersville,) manuf. of laths and pickets, and turning lathe.

Green, Daniel, (Colliersville,) farmer 142.

GREEN, MARVIN, (Colliersville,) farmer 115.

Gurnay, William H., (Portlandville,) grocer.

Gurney, Abram D., (Portlandville,) farmer 75½.

Hall, Frank H., (Milford,) butcher.

HALL, GEORGE, (Milford,) (*Brooks & Hall.*)

Hall, George Mrs., (Milford,) milliner,

Hall, Thomas, (Portlandville,) farmer 103.

Hanes, Menzo, (Colliersville,) farmer 64.

HARDY, ALBERT, (Milford,) attorney.

HARDY, WILLIAM H., (Milford,) farmer leases of Wm. R. Hardy, 100.

HARDY, WILLIAM R., (Milford,) farmer 108.

HART, ISAAC J., (Portlandville,) farmer.

Hawver, Boyce W., (Milford,) (*Hawver & Lidell.*)

Hawver, John V., (Milford,) carpenter.

Hawver & Lidell, (Milford,) (*Boyce W. Hawver and John H. Lidell,*) general merchants.

HAYNER, GEORGE, (Milford,) boot and shoe maker and farmer 4½.

Haynor, Erastus, (Milford,) farmer leases of Geo. Clark, 300.

HILSINGER, ELIAS, (Colliersville,) blacksmith and farmer 1½.

Hoag, George D., (Milford,) farmer 200.

Hollister, Leroy, (Milford,) farmer 60.

Howel, David, (Milford,) tailor.

HOUSE, CHAUNCEY, (Milford,) farmer leases of Jacob Seeber, 120.

Howland, Egbert A., (Milford or Portlandville,) farmer 104.

Hubbard, Augustus, (Portlandville,) farmer 135.

Huested, James, (Colliersville,) mason.

Humphrey, Fanny Mrs., (Milford,) farmer 2.

Hungerford, Hannah Mrs., (Colliersville,) farmer 20.

Hungerford, James, (Colliersville,) farmer leases of Sylvester Lyman, 70.

HUNT, WILLIAM, (Milford,) carpenter.

Huntington, Solon, (Colliersville,) farmer 100.

HYNEY, ABRAM H., (Portlandville,) farmer rents of George Goodrich, 80.

JENCKS, HORACE F., (Colliersville,) prop. of Goodyear House.

JUDD, FRED., (Milford,) cooper.

Kieth, Elijah R., (Portlandville,) farmer 120.

KIMBELL, HENRY, (Colliersville,) farmer leases of Jared Goodyear, 110.

KIMBELL, LEMUEL, (Colliersville,) blacksmith and farmer 18.

Kingman, Nehemiah W., (Mount Vision,) farmer 95.

Knapp, Anson C., (Milford,) farmer 200.

Knapp, Levi S., (Milford,) farmer 50 and in Westford, 37.

Kniskern, Gilbert, (Milford,) prop. of Milford House.

Lane, Hamilton J., (Colliersville,) (*with Elmer Finch,*) farmer rents of George Clark, 260.

Lane, William, (Portlandville,) farmer 30.

Lawyer, Philetus, (Colliersville,) saw mill, cider mill and farmer 22.

LEANING, JOHN, (Portlandville,) farmer 155.

Leaning, Mary Mrs., (Portlandville,) farmer 5.

LEE, MORTIMER M., (Milford,) general merchant.

Lidell, John H., (Milford,) (*Hawver & Lidell.*)

Low, John, (Milford,) farmer 201.

Low, Joseph M., (Portlandville,) dealer in patent portable gas works and farmer 130.

LUTHER, ALBERT, (Milford,) dentist and farmer 1½.

LYON, ALONZO, (Portlandville,) farmer leases of John M. Low, 130.

Lyon, Alvin, (Milford,) prop. of saw mill and farmer 120.

Lyon, Harry, (Portlandville,) farmer 40.

Lyon, Rebecca Mrs., (Mount Vision,) farmer 50.

Lyon, Warren, (Milford,) farmer 90.

Manchester, George, (Portlandville,) farmer leases of B. Alesworth, 104.

Manning, Joseph H., (Portlandville,) boots and shoes and carpenter.

Marble, John, (Portlandville,) mason.

Martin, Albert M., (Milford,) farmer 498.

Maryhew, David, (Mount Vision,) farmer 5.

McAuliff, John, (Portlandville,) farmer rents of Aaron Wilber, 200.

McKown, Patrick, (Milford,) farmer 100.

McLaury, John H., (Milford,) farmer leases of George Clark, 300.

Meckevoy, Patrick, (Milford,) farmer 4.

MILFORD CENTER HOUSE, (Portlandville,) Peter O. Brower, prop'r.

Miller, Henry C., (Portlandville,) farmer 4.

MILLER, PETER, (Portlandville,) farmer 130.

MILLER, WILLIAM H., (Portlandville,) carpenter and farmer 3½.

Millett, Abram, (Colliersville,) boot and shoe maker.

More, Andrew, (Milford,) farmer 110.

Morgan, Henry H., (Portlandville,) (*Chauncey & Morgan,*) carriage maker.

MORRIS, ADOLPHUS G., (Portlandville,) farmer 192.

Morris, David E., (Portlandville,) farmer 105.

Morris, Richard R., (Portlandville,) farmer 16½.

Mosher, Alfred, (Portlandville,) farmer 164.

Mott, John A., (Portlandville,) farmer 100.

MUMFORD, ALBERT A., (Portlandville,) farmer.

Mumford, Alfred, (Portlandville,) farmer 130.

Mumford, Hiram, (Oneonta,) farmer 130.

Mumford, Roberson, (Portlandville,) carpenter and farmer.

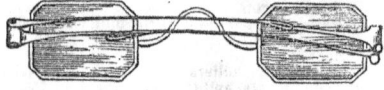

MUMFORD, THOMAS G., (Portlandville,) farmer 37.
Murdock, Ellory, (Milford,) farmer leases of David Wilber, 65.
Murry, Freeman, (Milford,) farmer 134.
Murry, William, (Portlandville,) farmer 40.
Newell, John F., (Milford,) house painter.
NEWMAN, LESTER G. W., (Mount Vision,) farmer 42.
Osburn, Chester, (Portlandville,) farmer 3½.
OSTERHOUDT, HIRAM, (Colliersville,) farmer 60.
Packer, David, (Portlandville,) blacksmith.
Packer, David, (Portlandville,) farmer 83.
PACKER, DEMMON, (Portlandville,) farmer 63.
Packer, Mary Mrs., (Portlandville,) farmer 1.
PACKER, OSBORN, (Portlandville,) farmer.
Packer, Oscar, (Portlandville,) farmer 63.
Packer, William, (Portlandville,) farmer 261.
Palmer, Ruth Miss, (Portlandville,) Yankee notions.
Parshall, Elias, heirs of, (Milford,) farmers 80.
PARSHALL, JAMES E., (Milford,) general merchant.
PARSHALL, JAMES N., (Milford,) tailor.
Patrick, George, (Milford,) farmer 57.
PEASLEE, ROBERT, (Milford,) farmer 1½.
Peck, Alfred W., (Milford,) farmer leases 125.
Pepper, Cary B., (Milford,) clerk in Wilber's Bank.
PHILLIPS, FREDERICK, (Milford,) blacksmith.
Phillips, George W., (Milford,) carriage maker and (*with John*) farmer 122.
Phillips, John, (Milford,) (*with George W.,*) farmer 122.
Pitts, John B., (Milford,) farmer leases of George Clark, 300.
Platt, Deloss D., (Portlandville,) farmer 64.
Platt, G., (Colliersville,) (*Avery & Platt.*)
Platt, Garret, (Mount Vision,) farmer 190.
PORTLANDVILLE HOUSE, (Portlandville,) John G. Sickler, prop.
POTTER, EMERY, (Portlandville,) laborer.
Potter, Horace, (Portlandville,) farmer 85.
POTTER, JOHN, (Portlandville,) carpenter.
Potter, Leroy, (Portlandville,) farmer 1.
POTTER, RICHMAN H., (Mount Vision,) farmer leases of Ezra Marlett, 205.
Pratt, Spencer T., (Milford,) produce dealer.
Pride, Hebbard, (Milford,) farmer 132½.
QUACKENBUSH, EGBERT M., (Portlandville,) farmer 114.
Quackenbush, Jacob I., (Portlandville,) farmer 104.
Quackenbush, James, (Colliersville,) farmer 116.
QUACKENBUSH, MILTON, (Colliersville,) farmer 144.
Queal, William G. Rev., (Milford,) pastor M. E. Church.
Ray, Alonzo, (Milford,) farmer 163.
M

REYNOLDS, AMOS A., (Portlandville,) farmer 47½.
Reynolds, George N., (Portlandville,) farmer 50.
Rice, Abram, (Colliersville,) carpenter.
Richards, Rebecca Mrs., (Portlandville,) farmer 1½.
Robinson, Henry, (Milford,) farmer 100.
Rose, Eli, (Portlandville,) dealer in hops and butter, and farmer 176.
ROSE, EUGENE K., (Portlandville,) farmer 120.
Rose, Nathan W., (Portlandville,) farmer 180.
Rose, Robert M., (Portlandville,) farmer 130.
Rowland, Ezra, (Portlandville,) farmer leases of Seth Rowland, 150.
Rowland, Humphrey, (Portlandville,) farmer 40.
ROWLAND, LEWIS, (Portlandville,) farmer leases of George Rose, 85.
Rowland, Seth, (Portlandville,) farmer 215.
Rowley, Daymon L., (Milford,) farmer leases 220.
ROWLEY, ——, (Portlandville,) (*Chauncey, Squires & Co.*)
RYNESS, GEORGE, (Portlandville,) mason.
Safford, Ezra W., (Portlandville,) allo. physician.
SALISBURY, ANDREW, (Milford,) prop. of saw mill and cider mill and farmer 5.
SALISBURY, JOHN, (Milford,) farmer 65.
Sargenes, Job R., (Milford,) meat market, farmer 2 and in Hartwick, 50.
Sargents, Solomon, (Milford,) farmer 50.
SCHERMEHORN, NICHOLAS, (Milford,) farmer 184.
Schermehorn, Peter, (Milford,) farmer 65.
Schermehorn, George H., (Portlandville,) farmer 16½.
Scholl, William N. Rev., (Milford,) pastor of Presbyterian Church.
Scott, Charles, (Portlandville,) farmer 60.
SCOTT, EGBERT L., (Milford,) farmer 54 and in Hartwick, 87.
Scott, William, (Milford,) farmer 100 and in Hartwick, 25.
SCRAMLING, EGBERT A., (Portlandville,) (*Van Etten & Scramling,*) postmaster.
SEBOLT, ORLANDO, (Milford,) blacksmith.
Seeber, Abram S., (Milford,) allo. physician.
Seeger, Edward, (Portlandville,) farmer 60.
Seger, Dudley, (Colliersville,) farmer 164.
Seger, William H., (Colliersville,) saw mill and cider mill and farmer 175.
Shafer, Peter T., (Milford,) farmer 4.
Sherman, Adelbert, (Mount Vision,) farmer 132.
Shute, John, (Milford,) farmer 63.
SICKLER, JOHN G., (Portlandville,) prop. of Portlandville House and meat market.
Silleman, Asa, (Colliersville,) farmer 105.
Silleman, Francis B., (Colliersville,) farmer 40.
Siver, Adam, (Portlandville,) farmer 75.
Siver, George, (Portlandville,) farmer 2.
Siver, John, (Portlandville,) farmer leases of George Siver, 50.

SMITH, EDWARD H., (Portlandville,) farmer 113.
SMITH, HIRAM, (Portlandville,) farmer leases 90.
SMITH, JOHN W., (Milford,) ticket, express, freight and mail agent, and farmer 40½.
SMITH, MARTIN L., (Colliersville,) ticket, freight and express agent, and telegraph operator.
Smith, Sullivan, (Milford,) hardware and tinware, and farmer 16.
SNOOK, ELIZA Mrs., (Colliersville,) farmer 50.
SOMERS, GEORGE A., (Portlandville,) ticket, freight and express agent.
SOULE, ERASTUS, (Milford,) carpenter.
Southworth, Ithamer, (Portlandville,) farmer 104.
SOUTHWORTH, MARTIN G., (Portlandville,) saw mill and farmer leases of David Wilber, 3.
Southworth, Peter, (Portlandville,) farmer 104½.
SOUTHWORTH, SANFORD L., (Portlandville,) farm laborer.
Spencer, Andrew, (Milford,) farmer 150.
SQUIRE, ISRAEL, (Portlandville,) farmer 31.
Squire, William, (Portlandville,) farmer 47.
SQUIRES, ASA D., (Portlandville,)(Chauncey, Squires & Co.,) farmer 80.
Stephens, Ezra, (Portlandville,) farmer 200.
Stickney, Walton E., (Milford,) tannery and feed mill, farmer 62 and in Middlefield, 13¼.
Still, Joseph, (Portlandville,) farmer 61¼.
STOCKING, OTIS I., (Maryland,) carpenter.
Stocking, William S., (Maryland,) farmer 109.
Stone, Norman, (Portlandville,) farmer 1¼.
STOUTENBURGH, CHARLES H., (Milford,) farm laborer.
Swartwout, James, (Colliersville,) hotel proprietor.
Sweet, Emilius B., (Milford,) farmer occupies estate of Amos Sweet, 93.
TARBOX, LEVI B., (Colliersville,) farmer 124.
Tarbox, William A., (Portlandville,) house painter.
Teel, George, (Milford,) farmer 80.
Thayer, William T., (Portlandville,) farmer 60.
Thorn, Denison R., (Portlandville,) carpenter.
THORN, JOEL, (Portlandville,) eclectic physician.
THORN, LEWIS D., (Portlandville,) boot and shoe maker, and farmer 53.
Thorn, Loren, (Colliersville,) farmer 1¼.
Thorn, Lucinda Mrs., (Portlandville,) dress maker.
THORN, STEPHEN W., (Portlandville,) carpenter, prop. of saw mill and farmer 5.
THURSTON, RICHARD C., (Milford,) farmer 80.
Tillapaugh, Charles, (Maryland,) farmer 80.
Tobias, Jonathan, (Milford,) blacksmith.
Townsend, Charlotte Mrs., (Portlandville,) farmer 57.

Townsend, Edward, (Portlandville,) carpenter and farmer 4.
Townsend, John J. and Enoc, (Portlandville,) farmer 415.
Townsend, Robert M., (Portlandville,) attorney.
Van Buren, Ann Eliza Mrs., (Mount Vision,) farmer 140.
Vanburen, Henry, (Mount Vision,) farmer 50.
VAN ETTEN, ELI, (Portlandville,) (Van Etten & Scramling.)
Van Etten, Eli, (Portlandville,) farmer.
VAN ETTEN & SCRAMLING, (Portlandville,) (Eli Van Etten and Egbert A. Scramling,) general merchants.
Vanvlack, Jesse, (Portlandville,) farmer 60.
Vescelius, William A., (Milford,) jeweler and watch repairer.
Wakefield, Thomas L., (Portlandville,) harness maker.
Walker, Isaac, (Portlandville,) farmer 110.
WALLACE, HARLEM, (Portlandville,) farm laborer.
Ward, Henry B., (Portlandville,) farmer leases of David Wilbur, 210.
Waters, Amos F., (Milford,) farmer 165.
Waters, Russel, (Milford,) farmer 173.
Weatherly, Philo, (Portlandville,) farmer 3.
Wellman, Alfred, (Milford,) farmer 124.
Wellman, Alfred E., (Mount Vision,) farmer 190.
Wellman, Alonzo, (Portlandville,) farmer 44.
Wellman, Harrison, (Portlandville,) farmer 250.
WELLMAN, MARTIN B., (Milford,) farmer 131.
Wells, Peter, (Colliersville,) farmer 25.
Wescot, Orlando, (Portlandville,) farmer 100.
Westcott, Daniel H., (Colliersville,) farmer 20.
WESTCOTT, GEORGE, (Milford,) farmer 158.
Westcott, Hosea, (Milford,) farmer 175.
Westcott, James C., (Portlandville,) carpenter.
Westcott, Luzerne, (Portlandville,) farmer 125.
WESTCOTT, OTIS, (Portlandville,) farmer 274.
WESTCOTT, O. W., (Milford,) druggist and assistant postmaster.
Whitford, Samantha A. Miss, (Portlandville,) milliner.
Whitney, Orason, (Portlandville,) carriage painter and farmer 2.
Wilber, Aaron, (Milford,) farmer 1¾.
Wilber, Briggs, (Portlandville,) billiard saloon.
WILBER, DAVID, (Milford,) (D. Wilber & Son,) banker, postmaster, farmer 25 and in Maryland, 200.
WILBER, D. & SON, (Milford,) (David and George J.,) dealers in hops.
WILBER, GEORGE I., (Milford,) (D. Wilber & Son,) cashier Wilber's Bank.
Wilcox, George M., (Milford,) farmer 196.
Wilcox, Henry, (Milford,) farmer 176.
Wilcox, Menzo, (Milford,) farmer 72.
Williams, Benjamin F. Rev., (Portlandville,) pastor Milford Baptist Church.

Willman, Horace, (Milford,) farmer leases of David Wilber, 300.

Winsor, Daniel, (Portlandville,) farmer 51.

Wood, Julia Miss, (Milford,) milliner.

WOODBECK, JASPER, (Colliersville,) farmer 149½.

Woodcock, James B., (Colliersville,) farmer 24.

Wright, Daniel, (Portlandville,) farmer 13.

WRIGHT, E. HARRIS, (Colliersville,) miller.

Wright, Walter, (Portlandville,) carpenter and farmer 3.

YAGER, BYRON, (Portlandville,) general merchant.

YAGER, ELBERT, (Milford,) farm laborer.

Yager, Philetus, (Portlandville,) house painter.

Yeoumans, John, (Portlandville,) farmer 50.

Youman, Anthony, (Portlandville,) farmer 20.

Youmans, Benjamin, (Portlandville,) farmer 23.

Youmans, Catharine Mrs., (Portlandville,) farmer 80.

Youmans, Nathan, (Portlandville,) farmer 90.

MORRIS.

(Post Office Addresses in Parentheses.)

Adams, Geo., (Morris,) teamster.

Adams, O. Mrs., (Morris,) milliner and farmer 330, Main.

Aldrich, Dennis J., (Morris,) farmer leases 56.

Aldrich, Job, (Morris,) hop raiser and farmer 56.

Aldrich, Sylvester, (Morris,) carpenter and farmer leases 65.

ALLEN, BENJ. T., (Morris,) assessor, prop. saw mill, general speculator and farmer 113.

Angell, James R., (Morris,) retired farmer, Main.

Angell, Jonathan, (Morris,) farmer.

Aplin, Alanson, (Morris,) hop raiser, dairyman and farmer 100.

Applin, Geo., (Morris,) farmer leases 70.

Arnold, Chas., (Morris,) farmer 50.

Arries, Alex., (Morris,) farmer leases 112.

Avery, Asahel, (Morris,) retired cabinet maker, Main.

Avery, Asahel S., (Morris,) photographer, Main.

Avery, Nelson, (New Berlin Center, Chenango Co.,) farmer.

AYER, CHAS. REV., (Morris,) pastor Baptist Church.

Babcock, Lucy Mrs., (Morris,) resident.

Bagg Bros., (New Berlin Center, Chenango Co.,) (*Wm. H. and Stanley,*) farmers lease 196.

Bagg, Gamaliel, (Morris,) farmer 76.

Bagg, Henry, (New Berlin Center, Chenango Co.,) hop raiser, dairyman and farmer 196.

Bagg, Nathaniel B., (South New Berlin, Chenango Co.,) manuf. hand sleighs.

Bagg, Stanley, (New Berlin Center, Chenango Co.,) (*Bagg Bros.,*) inspector of elections.

Bagg, Wm. H., (New Berlin Center, Chenango Co.,) (*Bagg Bros.*)

Bailey, Caleb, (South New Berlin, Chenango Co.,) hop raiser and farmer 70.

Bailey, Chas., (South New Berlin, Chenango Co.,) carpenter.

Bailey, Jared, (South New Berlin, Chenango Co.,) farmer 30 and leases 93.

Bailey, Legrand, (Morris,) saw mill and farmer.

Bailey, Leray, (New Berlin Center, Chenango Co.,) farmer 120.

Bailey, Squire, (South New Berlin, Chenango Co.,) inspector of elections and farmer leases 80.

Bailey, Stephen, (South New Berlin, Chenango Co.,) dairyman and retired farmer 80.

Baldwin, Lewis, (Morris,) farmer 7.

Baldwin, Milo, (Morris,) dairyman and farmer 90.

Baldwin, Wm., (Maple Grove,) dairyman and farmer 158.

Barker, Loring, (Maple Grove,) postmaster, manuf. agricultural implements and farmer 9.

Barr, H. H., (South New Berlin, Chenango Co.,) farmer leases 40.

Barr, Wm. M., (South New Berlin, Chenango Co.,) farmer.

Barrett, Geo. M., (Morris,) wooden manuf. and farmer 56.

Barrett, James H., (Morris,) manuf. wooden ware, Broad.

Barrett, Samuel E., (Morris,) blacksmith.

Bassett, L. D., (Morris,) dentist, Main.

Bauff, Edward, (Morris,) farmer 100.

Beadman, John, (South New Berlin, Chenango Co.,) farmer 16.

Becker, Eugene, (Morris,) butcher and wooden ware manuf., Hargrave.

Beekman, David, (Morris,) (*Beekman & Ward.*)
Beekman & Ward, (Morris,) (*David Beekman and John A. Ward,*) dry goods, groceries and ready-made clothing, Main.
Beers, Oliver, (Morris,) farmer 100.
Beers, Wm., (Morris,) farmer occupies 87.
Bell, Geo., (Morris,) hop raiser and farmer 60.
Belmelly, Chas., (Morris,) farmer 2½.
Bemiss, Thompson, (Morris,) farmer 109¾.
Benjamin, Andrew, (Morris,) chair maker and farmer 1.
BENJAMIN, GEORGE, (Morris,) prop. chair and cabinet ware manufactory, and farmer 9.
BIDWELL, HORACE, (Morris,) farmer.
Bill, J. C., (Morris,) saw mill and manuf. of brackets, mouldings &c.
Bishop, Ann Mrs., (Morris,) occupies 6 acres.
Bishop, Chas. H., (Morris,) dairyman, farmer 6 and leases 100.
Bishop, Lewis C., (Morris,) wooden ware manuf. and farmer 12.
Bourne, Cyrus, (Morris,) hop raiser and farmer leases 50.
Bourne, Danford, (Morris,) dairyman, farmer 150 and (*with John Colvin*) cheese factory.
Bourne, Hosea, (Morris,) farmer 50.
Bourne, Philo, (Morris,) farmer 29.
BOWNE BROS., (Morris,) (*Charles A. and John*) dairymen and farmers 250.
BOWNE, CHARLES A., (Morris,) (*Bowne Bros.,*) attorney and counselor at law.
Bowne, Isaac L., (Morris,) carpenter.
BOWNE, JOHN, (Morris,) (*Bowne Bros.*)
Braley, Jesse P., (Maple Grove,) carpenter and farmer 3½.
Braley, Olney, (Butternuts,) farmer leases 102.
Breed, Henry O., (Butternuts,) farmer leases 5.
Breffle, Gordon, (Morris,) carpenter and farmer.
Breffle, Spencer, (Morris,) farmer.
Breffle, Wm. F., (Morris,) farmer 112.
Bresee, Daniel J.,(Morris,) (*Breses & Harris.*)
Bresee & Harris, (Morris,) (*Daniel J. Bresee and Chancey S. Harris,*) undertakers and cabinet makers, Broad.
Bridges, Nathan, (Morris,) lawyer and justice of the peace, Main.
Briggs, Nathan H., (Morris,) carpenter, Hargrave.
Brooks, Lyman, (Morris,) farmer 5, Main.
Brooks, Wm. R., (Morris,) farmer 67.
Brown, Steven M., (Morris,) carpenter.
BROWN, WM., (Butternuts,) farmer leases 50.
Brownel, David, (Morris,) retired farmer.
Brownell, Hiram, (Morris,) farmer 25.
Bugby, Lyman T., (Morris,) farmer 106, Water.
Bundy, Hosea, (Morris,) farmer 250.
Bunn, A. C., (Morris,) physician, surgeon and coroner, Main.
Bunn, W. E. & Co., (Morris,) (*Walter H. Bunn,*) hardware, stoves and tinware, Main.

Bunn, Walter H., (Morris,) (*W. E. Bunn & Co.*)
Bunnell, Samuel H., (Morris,) carpenter and farmer 2¾.
Burdick, Nelson, (Morris,) farmer 50.
Burgess, Albert, (Morris,) carpenter.
Burgess, Hiram, (Morris,) farmer.
Burlingame, Tracy, (Morris,) saw and cider mills, and farmer 5.
Busby, Richard, (Morris,) farmer 66.
Butler, Edwin, (Morris,) wooden ware manuf.
Butler, Francis, (Morris,) wooden ware manuf.
Buzzell, John D., (Morris,) blacksmith and farmer 50, Broad.
Camp, Chas., (New Berlin Center, Chenango Co.,) farmer 60.
Camp, Harrison, (New Berlin Center, Chenango Co.,) carpenter, farmer 80 and (*with A. Skinner,*) cheese box factory, grist and saw mills.
Camp, Henry, (New Berlin Center, Chenango Co.,) farmer.
Card, Stephen, (Morris,) farmer.
Card, W. P., (Morris,) carriage maker, Broad.
*CARPENTER, S. P., (Morris,) editor of *Morris Chronicle,* Main.
Casler, John, (South New Berlin, Chenango Co.,) farmer.
Caswell, John B., (Morris,) chair maker and farmer 2¾.
Chaffee, Henry, (Morris,) farmer.
Chaffee, J. D., (Morris,) hop raiser, dairyman and farmer 114.
Chapin, Almon, (Morris,) carriage maker.
CHASE, HENRY, (Morris,) mule spinner.
Chase, Jothan D., (Morris,) dairyman and farmer 76.
Chase, Newell H., (Morris,) farmer 2¾.
Church, Ervin, (Morris,) farmer 67¾.
Churchill, Geo., (Morris,) miller.
Churchill, James, (Morris,) farmer leases 140.
Churchill, Richard M., (Morris,) farmer.
Churchill, Wm., (Morris,) farmer leases 90.
Clark, Burt, (South New Berlin, Chenango Co.,) farmer.
Cogshall, Jacob, (Morris,) farmer 72.
Colburn, Elijah, (Morris,) farmer leases 140.
Cole, John, (Morris,) farmer 70.
Cole, Richard, (Butternuts,) dairyman and farmer 200.
Collar, Aaron B., (Morris,) hop raiser and farmer 114.
Collar, Duane, (Morris,) hop raiser and farmer 50.
Collar, Edmund, (Morris,) farmer.
Collins, Jabez, (Morris,) farmer 40, West.
Colvin,Christopher, (Morris,) wooden ware manuf. and farmer 49.
Colvin, Geo. I., (Morris,) hop grower, dairyman and farmer 100.
Colvin, Geo. M., (Morris,) farmer.
Colvin, John, (Morris,) (*with D. Bourne,*) cheese factory, dairyman and farmer 145.
Cook, Harvey G., (Morris,) (*Pope & Cook.*)
Cook, Harvey W., (Morris,) dairyman, hop raiser and farmer 148.
COOK, J. E., (Morris,) (*A. G. Moore & Co.*)
Cook, Samuel T., (Morris,) farmer 13.

Cooley, Richard, (Morris,) jewelry, fancy goods, musical instruments &c., Main.
Cooper, James C., (Morris,) tailor, Main.
COYLE, JAMES, (Morris,) mule spinner in cotton factory.
Cramer, S. A. Mrs., (Morris,) milliner and dress maker, Main.
Crawford, Lewis, (Morris,) farmer.
Creedon, Timothy, (South New Berlin, Chenango Co.,) dairyman and farmer leases 180.
Cristman, Catharine Mrs., (Morris,) (*with heirs,*) farmer 50.
Cristman, Urias, (Morris,) hop grower, farmer 100 and leases 50.
Cruttenden, Albert, (Morris,) farmer leases 146½.
Cruttenden, Hopestill, (Morris,) farmer 146½.
Cullen, Thos. Rev., (Morris,) rector Zion's Church.
Culver, Thos., (Morris,) hop raiser and farmer 100.
Curtis, Chas. W., (Butternuts,) mason and farmer 10.
DANIELS, A. E. REV., (Morris,) M. E. clergyman, Main.
Daniels, John N., (Morris,) dairyman and farmer 84.
Davenport, Lucius, (Morris,) saw mill and farmer 40.
Davis, Geo. B., (South New Berlin, Chenango Co.,) farmer 5.
Davis, Jonah Mrs., (Morris,) farmer 100, Church.
Davis, Luther J., (Morris,) blacksmith, Grove.
Davis, Nelson B., (South New Berlin, Chenango Co.,) farmer 56.
Davis, Samuel, (South New Berlin, Chenango Co.,) farmer 5.
Davis, Wm. J., (Morris,) dairyman and farmer 150.
Deming, Daniel T., (South New Berlin, Chenango Co.,) farmer 28.
Denning, Chas. L., (Morris,) hop grower and farmer 80.
Denning, Samuel, (Morris,) hop grower and farmer 56.
Dixson, Henry J., (South New Berlin, Chenango Co.,) constable and farmer 80.
Dixson, Samuel R., (Morris,) commissioner of highways, dairyman and farmer 80.
Dolman, R., (Morris,) carpenter and machinist.
Draper, Samuel C., (Morris,) dairyman and farmer 128.
Duroe, Collingwood, (Morris,) dairyman and farmer leases 140.
Dye, David D., (Morris,) paper maker and farmer 75.
Edwards, Orville, (Morris,) cooper.
Edwards, Wm., (Morris,) farmer.
Ehle, David W., (Morris,) butcher, Main.
Eldred, Andrew, (Morris,) dairyman and farmer 110.
Eldred, John, (Morris,) hop raiser and farmer 200.
Elliot, Geo., (Morris,) hop raiser, dairyman and farmer 196.
Falls, Chas., (Morris,) farmer.
Falls, Richard, (Morris,) dairyman and farmer 100.

Falls, Scott, (Morris,) farmer.
Fenton, M. W. D., (Morris,) printer, Third.
Flagg, Deloss L., (Morris,) carpenter, corner Church and High.
Flagg, James H., (Morris,) (*Flagg & Son.*)
Flagg, Jonathan, (Morris,) (*Flagg & Son.*)
Flagg, Orson, (Morris,) farmer 1, Main.
Flagg & Son, (Morris,) (*James H. and Jonathan,*) hop raisers and farmers 70.
Fleming, Benjamin, (Maple Grove,) farmer 40.
Fleming, Wm., (Morris,) cattle dealer and farmer 50.
Folts, Jacob, (Morris,) retired farmer 70.
Folts, Spelman, (Morris,) hop raiser, dairyman and farmer 240.
Folts, Thurlow, (Morris,) dairyman and farmer 113.
Foot, Albert, (Morris,) mechanic and farmer.
Foot, Daniel, (Morris,) farmer 62.
Foot, Reuben, (Morris,) hop raiser and farmer 1.
Foot, Sedate, (Morris,) farmer 84.
FOOTE, LUCIUS, (Morris,) farmer 26.
Ford, Albert H., (South New Berlin, Chenango Co.,) dairyman and farmer 200.
Ford, E. J., (Morris,) carriage maker.
Ford, Geo., (South New Berlin, Chenango Co.,) farmer.
Fox, C. W., (Morris,) (*Fox & Matteson.*)
Fox, David, (Morris,) cooper, dairyman and farmer 118.
Fox & Matteson, (Morris,) (*C. W. Fox and Merritt Matteson,*) physicians, Main.
Franchot, Elizabeth Mrs., (Morris,) resident, Church.
FRANCHOT, J. A. MISS, (Morris,) resident, Church.
Furbush, John, (Morris,) hop raiser and farmer 58.
Gage, Chas., (South New Berlin, Chenango Co.,) shingle manuf.
Gage, Wm., (South New Berlin, Chenango Co.,) blacksmith.
Gardner, Chas. B., (Morris,) dairyman, farmer 73½ and leases 225.
Gazlay, J. H., (Morris,) cheese manuf.
Genung, Benj., (Morris,) farmer.
George, George, (Morris,) farmer 60.
Gifford, Christopher, (Morris,) watch repairer.
Gifford, Jefferson, (Morris,) farmer 8.
Gifford, William, (Morris,) wooden ware manuf., Lake.
Gilbert, Butler, (Morris,) dairyman and farmer 200.
Gilbert, Morris, (Morris,) dairyman and farmer 173.
Goodrich, George N., (Morris,) farmer 60.
Goodrich, Lucius, (Morris,) farmer.
Goodrich, Menzo D., (Morris,) butcher.
Goodwin, Aner L., (South New Berlin, Chenango Co.,) farmer 130.
Goodwin, Charles, (South New Berlin, Chenango Co.,) farmer leases 130.
GRAFTON, EDWIN, (Morris,) carriage and ornamental painter, Broad.
Gray, Albert Jr., (Morris,) principal Union School.
Green, Nelson, (Butternuts,) farmer 40.
Greene, Reuben, (Morris,) farmer 3.
Greene, Wm. P., (Morris,) hop raiser and farmer 60.

Greig, Orlando H., (Morris,) shoemaker.
Griffin, Chas., (Morris,) painter and farmer 2.
Griffin, Wm., (Morris,) machinist and farmer 5.
Haight, David, (Morris,) farmer 17.
Haines, Geo., (Morris,) carpenter and farmer 15.
HALL, A. L., (Morris,) wooden ware and cabinet manuf., and produce dealer, West.
Hall, Geo., (Morris,) carpenter, Water.
Hall, Geo. W., (Morris,) saw mill, carpenter, hop raiser and farmer 116.
Hammond, Henry, (South New Berlin, Chenango Co.,) farmer 95.
Hargrave, James R., (Morris,) shoemaker.
Hargrave, William, (Morris,) shoemaker, Broad.
Harrington, E. M., (Morris,) tinsmith.
Harrington, W. H. Rev., (Morris,) pastor Universalist Church.
Harris, Albert A., (Morris,) carpenter.
Harris, Chauncey S., (Morris,) (*Bresee & Harris.*)
Harris, Leonard, (Morris,) farmer 45.
Harris, Reuben, (Morris,) farmer 103.
Harris, Wm., (Morris,) farmer 98.
Harris, Zalmon, (Morris,) dairyman and farmer 160.
Harrison, Horace, (Morris,) retired farmer 146, Main.
Hathaway, Hiram, (Morris,) hop raiser and farmer 25.
Hathaway, Orlando, (Morris,) farmer 130.
Hawkins, Uriah, (Morris,) carpenter.
HAWVER, R. J., (Morris,) grist mill, Lake.
Hay, John D., (Morris,) dairyman and farmer 225.
Hay, John T., (Morris,) teacher.
Hay, Walter S., (Morris,) teacher and farmer leases 225.
Henderson, Cyrel, (South New Berlin, Chenango Co.,) farmer 100.
Hendrix, Adelbert, (Morris,) farmer 45.
Hewel, M. J. Mrs., (Morris,) seamstress and laundress, Main.
Hickok, Horace J., (Morris,) farmer 50 and leases 500.
Hoffman, John C., (Morris,) tanner and currier.
Hoke, Jonas, (Morris,) farmer.
HOLCOMB, EDGAR, (Morris,) manuf. croquet and wooden ware.
Holden, Alpheus, (South New Berlin, Chenango Co.,) retired farmer.
Holdredge, J. E., (Morris,) tailor, Main.
Holiday, Chas., (Morris,) dairyman and farmer 133.
Hopkins, Abram C., (Morris,) farmer leases 61.
Hopkins, C. J., (Butternuts,) dairyman and farmer leases 200.
Hopkins, Leonard, (Morris,) farmer 61.
Hopson, E. A., (South New Berlin, Chenango Co.,) carpenter.
Houghtailing, Abram B., (Morris,) farmer 80.
Houghtailing, Geo., (South New Berlin, Chenango Co.,) carpenter and farmer 30.
Houghtaling, Peter, (Morris,) hop grower, dairyman and farmer 150.
Howland, Albert, (Morris,) farmer.

Howland, Wm., (Morris,) wheelwright.
Hull, Clark B., (Maple Grove,) farmer.
Hull, Josiah B., (Maple Grove,) farmer 52.
Hurlbutt, Abraham E., (Morris,) dairyman and farmer 175.
Hurlbutt, E. F., (Morris,) farmer leases 175.
Hurlbutt, Harvey, (Morris,) farmer 109.
Hurlbutt, Wm. H., (Morris,) farmer 107.
Jackson, Daniel, (Morris,) farmer 100.
Jaquish, Daniel H., (Morris,) blacksmith.
Jaquish, E. R., (Morris,) carriage maker and farmer 8.
Jaycox, Margaret A., (Morris,) saw mill and farmer 5.
Jacox, Thos., (Morris,) saw mill and farmer 37.
Jacox, Wm., (Morris,) physician and farmer 415.
Johnson, Frederick, (Morris,) dairyman, hop raiser and farmer 109.
Johnson, Israel R., (Morris,) farmer.
Johnson, Moses T., (Morris,) farmer.
Johnson, Perry, (Morris,) farmer.
Johnson, Rha, (Morris,) retired farmer, Grove.
Keith, Horace, (Morris,) farmer 45.
KELLER, JOHN N., (Morris,) farmer leases 260.
KELLOGG, EZRA, (Morris,) farmer 50.
Kellogg, Joel, (Morris,) farmer.
Kenyon, J. P., (Morris,) druggist, Main.
Kidder, Edward P., (Morris,) mason.
Kidder, Major H. P., (Morris,) carpenter.
Killkennie, Dennis, (Morris,) dresser tender in cotton factory.
Kinney, C. G., (Morris,) farmer, Main.
Kinney, Chas. P., (Morris,) hop raiser and farmer 40.
Kinney, Oliver P., (Morris,) farmer, High.
Kirkland, Wm., (Morris,) farmer 6.
LAKE, CHARLES, (Morris,) farmer.
Laurence, D. I., (Morris,) drugs, groceries and fancy goods, Main.
Laurence, John, (Morris,) farmer 105.
Lawrence, Chas. H., (Morris,) wooden ware manuf.
Lee, R. H., (Morris,((*Lee & Yates.*)
Lee & Yates, (Morris,) (*R. H. Lee and W. H. Yates,*) carriage makers and dealers in springs, axles, iron &c. Broad.
Leggett, Isaac, (Morris,) farmer 104.
LEONARD, RUSSELL, (Morris,) prop. cotton factory in Pittsfield, dairyman, farmer 230 and (*with W. F.,*) prop. cheese factory, Broad.
LEONARD, W. F., (Morris,) (*with Russell,*) cheese factory.
Leonard, W. T., (Morris,) prop. cotton factory, saw mill, grist mill, general store and farmer 600.
Lewis, Israel P., (South New Berlin, Chenango Co.,) farmer 23.
Lewis Nelson, (South New Berlin, Chenango Co.,) carriage makers.
Lewis, Sarah Mrs., (Morris,) farmer 1.
Light Bros., (Maple Grove,) (*John and Chas.*) farmers lease 65.
Light, Chas., (Maple Grove,) (*Light Bros.*)
Light, John, (Maple Grove,) (*Light Bros.,*) farmer 200.
Light, Wm. B., (Maple Grove,) printer, hop grower and farmer 65.
Little, James, (Morris,) merchant tailor, Main.

Lucus, John, (South New Berlin, Chenango Co.,) shingle manuf. and farmer 1.
Lull, Abigail, (Morris,) farmer 65.
Lull, A. B., (Morris,) carpenter, dairyman and farmer 200.
LULL, EDWARD W., (Morris,) farmer 25 and leases 100.
Lull, Ezra, (Morris,) farmer 150.
Lull, Ezra, Jr., (Morris,) farmer leases 150.
Lull, Henry J., (Morris,) woolen factory and farmer 15.
Lull, Jacob K., (Morris,) retired tanner, boot and shoe dealer and farmer 4.
LULL, J. M., (Morris,) dealer in dry goods and groceries, pres't. Soldiers' Monument Association, and Pres't. Hillington Cemetery, Main.
Lull, Nathan, (Morris,) carder, dairyman and farmer 140.
Lull, Oliver T., (Morris,) farmer 260.
Luther, Moses H., (Morris,) stone cutter, wagon and sleigh repairer, Grove.
Lynch, S. A. Mrs.,(Morris,) resident, Third.
MANN, CHANCELLER, (Morris,) prop. of Morris Hotel, Main.
Manning, John P., (Morris,) carpenter, corner Broad and Lake.
Mansfield, Isaac, (Morris,) supervisor and farmer 78.
Matterson, Andrew P., (Morris,) farmer 96.
Matterson, Edward, (Morris,) farmer 52.
Matteson, Benj. H., (Morris,) hop raiser, dairyman and farmer 150.
Matteson, Henry S., (Morris,) sealer of weights and measures and farmer leases 150.
Matteson, Joshua D., (Morris,) retired manuf. and farmer 5, Church.
Matteson, K. C., (Morris,) saw mill, carpenter and farmer 31¼.
Matteson, Merritt, (Morris,) (*Fox & Matteson*.)
Matteson, Otis B., (Morris,) prop. Holmesville Tannery and dealer in produce, wooden ware &c.
Matteson, S. S.,(Morris,) general merchant.
Matthews, Henrietta and Marietta Misses, (Morris,) farmers 6, Main.
Maxum, C. H., (Morris,) harness maker, Third.
Maxum, Charles H., (Morris,) carpenter, Water.
McCard, Jesse, (Morris,) farmer.
McIntier, Parley, (Morris,) farmer, West.
McINTYRE, HENRY,(Butternuts,) farmer.
McNitt, Nelson, (Morris,) dairyman and farmer 210.
MERRIMAN, ISAAC, (New Berlin Center, Chenango Co.,) dairyman and farmer 110.
Merriman, R. R., (New Berlin Center, Chenango Co.,) dairyman and farmer 53.
MICKEL, ARTEMUS, (Butternuts,) farmer 18.
Mickle, Ira H., (Morris,) hop raiser and farmer 80.
Millard, Nathan, (Morris,) farmer 50.
Millard, Thos., (Morris,) farmer leases 50.
Miller, Alvin, (Maple Grove,) hop raiser and farmer 87.
Miller, Benj., (South New Berlin, Chenango Co.,) farmer.
Miller, Josiah, (South New Berlin, Chenango Co.,) dairyman and farmer 150.

Minor, Clinton, (Morris,) farmer leases 280.
Mitchel, Joseph, (Morris,) farmer.
Moffeit, Wesley, (Morris,) wooden ware manuf. and farmer 53.
Moffet, Richmond, (Morris,) saw mill and farmer 42.
Monroe, Hiram, (Morris,) mason and farmer.
Moody, Lucius, (Maple Grove,) blacksmith.
Moore, A. C., (Morris,) retired farmer, Broad.
MOORE, A. G. & CO., (Morris,) (*J. E. Cook*,) bankers, Main.
Moore, Chester, (Morris,) farmer 133.
Moore, Nathaniel, (Morris,) (*Moore & Thurston*,) farmer 173.
Moore, Orrin H., (Morris,) dairyman and farmer 100.
Moore & Thurston, (Morris,) (*Nathaniel Moore and Alfred Thurston*,) general merchants, Main.
*MORRIS CHRONICLE, (Morris,) Main, S. P. Carpenter, editor.
MORRIS HOTEL, (Morris,) Main, Chanceller Mann, prop.
Morris, J. R., (Morris,) dairyman and farmer 150.
*MORRIS LIVERY STABLE, (Morris,) J. W. Still, prop.
Mott, Joseph, (Morris,) expressman, Water.
Mudge, Ransom, (Morris,) farmer.
Murdock, S. W., (Morris,) dry goods, hats, caps, boots and shoes, Main.
Myrick, Orlando, (Morris,) retired carpenter.
Newton, Horatio P., (Morris,) farmer 50.
Nooning, Alanson, (Morris,) farmer 2.
Osborn, Asel, (Morris,) dresser tender in cotton factory and farmer 1¼.
OTSEGO HOUSE, (Morris,) E. L. Payne, prop., Main.
Ott, Michael, (Morris,) hop raiser and farmer 60.
Palmater, Amos, (Morris,) carpenter and wooden ware manuf.
Palmater, Wm., (Morris,) manuf. wooden ware, Water.
Palmer, A. P., (Morris,) (*Palmer Bros*.)
Palmer Bros., (Morris,) (*W. H. and A. P.*,) (with heirs,) farmers 225.
Palmer, W. H., (Morris,) (*Palmer Bros*.)
Parcell, A. L.,(Morris,)hand sleigh manuf., Water.
Parcell, Isaac R., (Morris,) farmer 10.
Parcell, P. J. Mrs., (Morris,) farmer 5¼.
Patrick, John J., (Morris,) farmer 180.
PAYNE, E. L., (Morris,) prop. of Otsego House and farmer 14, Main.
Payne, Helen Miss, (Morris,) milliner and dress maker, Main.
Pearsall, Mary Mrs., (Morris,) hop raiser and farmer 126.
Pearsall, Nelson B., (Morris,) hop raiser, dairyman and farmer 140.
Perine, Peter S., (Morris,) carpenter.
Perkins, Willis, (Morris,) hop raiser and farmer 100.
PERRY, H. M., (Morris,) farmer 4.
Perry, James, (Morris,) dairyman and farmer 522.
PERSONS, PETER, (Morris,) carpenter and joiner.
Phelps, James, (South New Berlin, Chenango Co.,) farmer 62.

Philips, Reuben W., (South New Berlin, Chenango Co.,) farmer 99.
Place, Gilbert, (Morris,) blacksmith.
Platt, Chas. G., (Maple Grove,) farmer 1.
Pope & Cook, (Morris,) (*James Pope and Harvey G. Cook,*) boots and shoes, Main.
Pope, Hamilton, (Morris,) flour and feed, Main.
Pope, James, (Morris,) (*Pope & Cook.*)
Porter, Jacob G., (Butternuts,) hop raiser and farmer 120.
PORTER, V. D., (New Berlin Center, Chenango Co.,) farmer 10.
POTTER, GILBERT, (Morris,) general speculator, Hargrave.
Potter, O. R., (Morris,) general speculator.
Potter, Royal, (Morris,) farmer, High.
Potter, W. M., (Morris,) prop. of Louisville House, Main.
Quinby, Thomas, (Morris,) carpenter.
Radley, Aaron, (Morris,) hop raiser and farmer 50.
Ramsdell, Nehemiah, (Morris,) wooden ware manuf.
Rawlins, Alpheus, (Butternuts,) farmer leases 180.
Reave, Ellis, (Morris,) farmer 107.
Ridley, T. A., (Morris,) cabinet maker and wooden ware manuf., West.
Ripley, Benj. P., (Morris,) printer, High.
Rockwell, Harvey W., (Morris,) farmer leases 133.
Rood, Martha Mrs., (Morris,) retired farmer.
Root, Wm. G., (Morris,) farmer.
ROSE, ADAM, (Morris,) farmer.
Rotch, Francis, (Morris,) farmer occupies 150.
Rowe, Thos., (Morris,) cooper and farmer.
Sage, Deborah Mrs., (South New Berlin, Chenango Co.,) (*with heirs,*) farmer 1.
Sample, Wm., (Morris,) cotton spinner, Lake.
Sanderson, Leroy, (Morris,) machinist.
Sanderson, Rufus, (Morris,) farmer 7, Lake.
Scribner, John M., (Morris,) farmer occupies 6.
Scudder, Edwin L., (Morris,) shoemaker.
Seely, John F., (Morris,) carpenter and farmer 15.
Sergeant, H., (Morris,) postmaster, Main.
Sergeants, Ira M., (South New Berlin, Chenango Co.,) dairyman and farmer leases 200.
Sergeant, Isabel Mrs., (South New Berlin, Chenango Co.,) farmer 50.
Shaw, John, (Morris,) dairyman and farmer occupies 150.
SHAW, LEWIS N., (Morris,) carder in cotton factory.
Shaw, Peter, (Morris,) dairyman and farmer 133½.
SHAW, WM. W., (Morris,) farmer.
Sheff, Albert, (Morris,) farmer leases 50.
Sheff, Charles, (Morris,) carpenter.
Sheff, George, (Morris,) dairyman and farmer 62½.
Sheff, George H., (Morris,) blacksmith.
Sheff, Russel M., (Morris,) farmer 52.
Shelland, James C. Rev., (Morris,) pastor M. E. Church, Broad.
Sherborne, F. W., (South New Berlin, Chenango Co.,) dairyman and farmer 103.

Sherman, S. Miss, (Morris,) dress maker, corner Third and West.
SHOLES, ANDREW J., (South New Berlin, Chenango Co.,) farmer 55 and leases 156.
Skinner, A., (New Berlin Center, Chenango Co.,) (*with Harrison Camp,*) cheese box factory, grist and saw mills.
Smith, Benj., (Morris,) carpenter and farmer 12.
Smith, Chas. J., (Morris,) farmer 51.
SMITH, DAVID D., (Maple Grove,) farmer 100.
Smith, F. A., (Morris,) overseer of weaving in cotton factory.
SMITH, IRA, (Morris,) teacher.
SMITH, JACOB, (New Berlin Center, Chenango Co.,) farmer.
Smith, Jacob, (Morris,) retired tanner.
SMITH, SILAS, (Butternuts,) farmer 17.
Smith, Silas S., (Morris,) farmer leases 126.
Smith, Wm., (Morris,) farmer 100, Broad.
SNOW, NEWTON, (Morris,) supt. cotton factory.
Southern, James, (Morris,) hop raiser and farmer 50.
SPAFFORD, ANSON, (Morris,) (*Wenmoth & Spafford,*) farmer 3½.
Spear, H. S., (Morris,) farmer occupies 175.
Starr, Bera, (Morris,) (*Starr Bros.*)
Starr Bros., (Morris,) (*Geo. and Bera,*) hop raisers and farmers 130.
Starr, David, (Maple Grove,) farmer 50.
Starr, Geo., (Morris,) (*Starr Bros.*)
Starr, Gould, (Morris,) farmer.
Starr, Henry, (Maple Grove,) hop raiser and farmer 47.
Starr, Samuel S., (Maple Grove,) retired farmer.
Stenson, Francis F., (South New Berlin, Chenango Co.,) carpenter.
Stenson, Richard, (Morris,) carpenter, hop grower and farmer 56.
Stevens, John H., (Morris,) farmer 6½.
Stewart, T. E., (Morris,) overseer of spinning in cotton factory.
Stewart, Wm., (Morris,) farmer 5.
Stewart, Wm. J., (Morris,) machinist and farmer 27.
Stewart, Wm. J., Jr., (Morris,) machinist and farmer.
*STILL, JOHN W., (Morris,) physician and surgeon, and prop. Morris Livery Stable, Broad.
St. Mary, M., (Morris,) chair maker.
Stone, E. M. Mrs., (Morris,) tailoress.
Stone, Wm. J., (Morris,) painter and farmer.
Stranahan, James W., (Morris,) retired farmer 25.
Sutherland, A. R., (Morris,) teacher and farmer 30.
Sutherland, Reuben, (Morris,) farmer.
Sweet, Elijah P., (Morris,) mechanic and farmer.
SWIFT, H. M., (Maple Grove,) general speculator.
Tanner, Doolittle, (Morris,) farmer.
Taylor, Wm., (Morris,) farmer leases 230.
Terry, Leroy, (Morris,) farmer 27.
Thomas, Alex., (Morris,) farmer, Third.
Thomas, James, (Morris,) farmer 20.
Thomas, James S., (Morris,) farmer 40.

Thomas, John, (Morris,) hop raiser and farmer 12.
Thresher, Edwin, (Morris,) farmer.
Thresher, Nathan, (Morris,) dairyman, hop raiser and farmer 170.
Thurston, Alfred, (Morris,) (*Moore & Thurston.*)
Thurston, A. E., (Morris,) painter and paper hanger, Third.
Thurston, D. Wesley, (Morris,) mason, Third.
Thurston, Elijah, (Morris,) carpenter, Third.
Thurston, Elijah, (Morris,) farmer 35.
Thurston, Elisha, (Morris,) mason, Third.
Tilley, C., (Morris,) cooper and farmer 50.
Tillson, Albert, (Morris,) farmer.
Tillson, Asa, (Morris,) saw mill, hop raiser, dairyman and farmer 200.
Tillson, A. H., (Maple Grove,) dairyman and farmer 280.
Tillson, Cephas S., (Maple Grove,) dairyman and farmer 162.
Tillson, Chas. B., (Maple Grove,) farmer 52.
Tillson, Sidney M., (Morris,) farmer 82½.
Tipple, John, (Morris,) retired farmer.
Tobey, Albert, (Morris,) carpenter.
Tobey, Edward, (Morris,) farmer 53.
Tobey, Elisha, (Morris,) dairyman and farmer 120.
Tobey, Joseph E., (Morris,) farmer leases 120.
Tobey, Stephen, (Morris,) dairyman and farmer 65.
Tobey, Zaccheus, (Morris,) dairyman and farmer 250.
Tobey, Zaccheus, Jr., (Morris,) dairyman and farmer 150.
Tobias, D. C., (Morris,) farmer 16.
Toles, Nelson, (Morris,) dairyman and farmer 150.
Tracy, Alonzo, (Morris,) farmer.
Tracy, Elijah, (Morris,) farmer.
Tucker, C. L., (Morris,) lumber dealer, prop. saw mill in Laurens, and farmer 25.
Tucker, Robert, (Morris,) farmer 3.
Tucker, Robert, (Morris,) farmer 50.
Turner, Albert, (Morris,) painter.
Turner Bros., (Morris,) (*Thos. and Leroy,*) hop raisers, dairymen and farmers 109.
Turner, Francis G., (Morris,) farmer 60 and occupies 30.
Turner, Jonathan, (Morris,) dairyman and farmer 130.
Turner, Leroy, (Morris,) (*Turner Bros.*)
Turner, Thos., (Morris,) (*Turner Bros.*)
Turner, Wm., (Butternuts,) dairyman and farmer leases 130.
Turner, Wm., (Morris,) shoemaker.
TURNEY, C. H., (Morris,) prop. billiard and dining rooms, Broad.
Tyler, Samuel, (South New Berlin, Chenango Co.,) retired farmer 40.
Valentine, Henry, (Morris,) farmer 60.
Van Deusen, Henry H., (Morris,) carpenter and farmer 11, Broad.
Van Deusen, John, (Maple Grove,) carpenter.
Van Rensselaer, R. H., (Morris,) farmer 200, Main.
Vrooman, Wm., (Morris,) teamster.
Wade, Isaac, (Morris,) farmer 35.
Wakefield, Hezekiah, (South New Berlin, Chenango Co.,) farmer leases 150.

Wanzer, D. C., (Morris,) farmer 80.
Wanzer, Wm., (Morris,) farmer 50.
Ward, John A., (Morris,) (*Beekman & Ward.*)
Ward, W. F., (Butternuts,) dairyman and farmer 110.
Washbon, H. R., (Morris,) lawyer and farmer 200, Main.
Washbon, John G., (Morris,) dairyman and farmer 240.
WATERS, BENJAMIN, (Morris,) farmer.
Weatherley, Daniel, (Morris,) farmer 50.
Webster, Edwin, (Morris,) dairyman and farmer 100.
Weeden, Peleg, (Morris,) (*S. G. Weeden & Co.,*) farmer 15.
Weeden, Samuel G., (Morris,) (*S. G. Weeden & Co.,*) farmer 14.
Weeden, S. G. & Co., (Morris,) (*Samuel G. and Peleg Weeden,*) harness manufs. and dealers, Main.
Wellman, Jesse, (Morris,) retired farmer.
WENMOTH & SPAFFORD, (Morris,) (*Wm. H. Wenmoth and Anson Spafford,*) carriage and sleigh makers, props. planing mill, scroll sawing and turning, also dealers in and manufs. of brackets, mouldings and bendings of every kind, Grove.
WENMOTH, WM. H., (Morris,) (*Wenmoth & Spafford.*)
Wheaton, John E., (South New Berlin, Chenango Co.,) teacher of school and practical penmanship.
WHEELER, EDSON, (South New Berlin, Chenango Co.,) justice of the peace, hop raiser, dairyman and farmer 130.
Wheeler, N. H., (South New Berlin, Chenango Co.,) carpenter.
Whitcomb, Chas. L., (Morris,) farmer leases 167.
Whitcomb, David E., (Morris,) dairyman and farmer 167.
Whitcomb, Edwin G., (Morris,) farmer.
Wickham, Daniel, (Morris,) retired blacksmith and farmer.
Wickham, German, (Morris,) farmer 86.
Wightman, Adelbert, (South New Berlin, Chenango Co.,) painter.
Wightman, Athlina, (South New Berlin, Chenango Co.,) farmer.
Wightman, Sidney R., (Morris,) teacher and farmer 77.
Wilcox, Monroe, (Morris,) retired farmer.
Wilcox, Stephen, (Morris,) retired farmer.
Wing, Elizabeth Mrs., (Morris,) (*with heirs,*) farmer 40, Main.
Wing, Stephen D., (Morris,) farmer leases 40, Main.
Wing, Stephen H., (Morris,) retired farmer 225.
Wing, Walter A., (Morris,) farmer 40.
Winsor, E. E., (Morris,) retired insurance agent.
WINTER, LORENZO, (Morris,) farmer 28.
Winton, Amasa A., (Morris,) farmer 50.
WINTON, D. C., (Morris,) wooden ware manuf. and justice of the peace, Hargrave.
Winton, John, (Morris,) expressman.
Winton, Zar, (Morris,) farmer 50.
Withey, Josiah, (Morris,) cabinet maker and farmer 1¾.

Wood, Erastus T., (South New Berlin, Chenango Co.,) painter.

Wood, Noah, (Morris,) carding mill, dairyman and farmer 115.

Yates, E. W., (Morris,) retired hotel keeper and farmer 3, West.

Yates, Geo. A., (Morris,) farmer 250.

Yates, W. H., (Morris,) (*Lee & Yates.*)

Youmans, Levi, (Morris,) farmer.

Young, Chas., (Morris,) farmer 3½.

YOUNG, MOSES, (Morris,) farmer.

NEW LISBON.

(Post Office Addresses in Parentheses.)

ADAMS, JOSEPH C., (Hartwick,) carpenter, sleigh maker, prop. of cider mill and farmer 50.

Adams, Luzerne, (Hartwick,) farmer occupies 50 owned by J. C. Adams.

Adams, Rocena, (Mount Vision,) tailoress.

Ainslie, Walter, (Hartwick,) hop raiser, carpenter and farmer 40.

Aldrich, Emerson, (Hartwick,) hop raiser, dairyman and farmer 240.

Aldrich, Mumford, (Hartwick,) (*with Emerson,*) farmer.

Alger, Isaac, (Hartwick,) hop raiser, dairyman 7 cows and farmer 75.

Alger, Rodolphus, (Hartwick,) justice of the peace and farmer 95.

Alger, Wm., (Hartwick,) retired farmer.

Allen, E. J., Jr., (New Lisbon,) farmer.

Avery, Daniel S., (Garrattsville,) miller and constable, (*with O. G.*)

Avery, O. G., (Garrattsville,) grist and planing mills, cheese box factory and cider mill, also dealer in flour and feed.

Babcock, Loren, (Garrattsville,) carriage manuf. and farmer 43¾.

Babcock, Sydney, (Garrattsville,) shoe maker.

Ballard, George, (Garrattsville,) hop raiser and farmer 70.

Ballard, John, (Garrattsville,) shoemaker and farmer 32.

Baresee, Geo., (Mount Vision,) farmer occupies 115 owned by Mrs. E. Ballard.

Barton, Amasa, (New Lisbon,) grist and saw mills and farmer 50.

Barton, Amos, (Mount Vision,) farmer 120.

Barton, Betsey, (Mount Vision,) farmer.

Barton, Mary, (Hartwick,) farmer 50.

Barton, Porter, (New Lisbon,) farmer.

Barton, S., (New Lisbon,) saw mill and farmer 112.

Bassett, J., (Garrattsville,) dairyman 13 cows and farmer 200.

Beach, Mary, (Mount Vision,) farmer 25.

Beach, Thomas, (Mount Vision,) farmer occupies 25 owned by Mary Beach.

Beers, James, (New Lisbon,) cooper and farmer 15.

Bell, Benj., (Garrattsville,) commissioner of highways and (*with Wm.,*) farmer 170.

Bell, James, (Garrattsville,) farmer occupies 135 owned by C. Bell.

Bell, John M., (Garrattsville,) retired farmer.

Bell, Wm., (Garrattsville,) (*with Benj.,*) farmer 170.

BENINGTON, ROBERT & SON, (Garrattsville,) dairymen 16 cows and farmer 160.

BENINGTON, ROBERT H., (Garrattsville,) dairyman and farmer 130.

Benjamin, John, (Garrattsville,) dairyman 9 cows and farmer 96.

Benjamin, Wm., (Garrattsville,) dairyman and farmer 96.

Bennett, David H., (New Lisbon,) minister of Friends' Society at Morris.

Bennett, Lewis, (Garrattsville,) farmer.

BENNINGTON, CHARLES, (Garrattsville,) cheese and butter manuf.

Bennington, Henry, (Garrattsville,) farmer 20.

Bennington, Henry G., (Garrattsville,) farmer.

BINGHAM, C. D., (Garrattsville,) carriage maker.

BINGHAM, F. O., (Garrattsville,) supervisor, dairyman 10 cows and farmer 100.

Bishop, Samuel, (Hartwick,) farmer 14.

Blanchard, Washburne, (New Lisbon,) farmer 30.

Bresee, Edgar, (Mount Vision,) dairyman 10 cows and farmer 110.

Briggs, Garrison, (New Lisbon,) farmer 15.

Briggs, Lewis, (Mount Vision,) dairyman 8 cows and farmer 77.

Briggs, Spencer, (Garrattsville,) farmer 50.

Brimmer, Albert, (New Lisbon,) farmer 67.

BROOKS, REUBEN, (Hartwick,) charcoal burner and farmer 120.

Brooks, Samuel, (Hartwick,) dairyman 6 cows and farmer 75.

Brown, Andrew, (Garrattsville,) farmer 20.

Brown, Damon, (Garrattsville,) farmer leases 7.

Brownell, Van Buren, (Laurens,) hop raiser, dairyman and farmer 500.

BUCK, H. C., (New Lisbon,) justice of the peace, dealer in pianos and organs and farmer 100.
Bundy, Chas. H., (Garrattsville,) carpenter and farmer 80.
Bundy, Elias G., (Garrattsville,) farmer.
BUNDY, ELON, (Garrattsville,) farmer 75.
Bundy, Herbert F., (Garrattsville,) mechanic.
Bundy, Horace, (New Lisbon,) farmer 44.
BUNDY, WM., (Garrattsville,) justice of the peace, hop raiser, dairyman and farmer 235.
Butts, J. K., (Mount Vision,) mason and farmer leases 48.
Butts, Marble, (Mount Vision,) hop raiser and farmer 100.
Campbell, Joseph Rev., (Garrattsville,) clergyman.
Card, Peter, (Garrattsville,) cooper and (with Wm. H.,) saw mill and farmer 154.
Card, Wm. H., (Garrattsville,) (with Peter,) saw mill and farmer 154.
Carlton, Ziba, (Hartwick,) farmer 50.
Cary, Joshua, (New Lisbon,) farmer 6.
Chapin, George M., (New Lisbon,) farmer.
Chapin, Linus N., (New Lisbon,) farmer 115.
Chase, A. B., (Garrattsville,) tanner, shoemaker and farmer 10.
Chase, Adelbert L., (Garrattsville,) shoe maker.
CHASE, GEORGE, (Garrattsville,) dairyman 10 cows and farmer 90.
Chase, Wm., (Garrattsville,) dairyman 7 cows and farmer 50.
Church, Isaac, (Garrattsville,) town assessor and farmer 40.
Clark, J. L., (Garrattsville,) (with Ezra D. Hoag,) produce broker.
Connor, John, (New Lisbon,) farmer 3.
Cook, George, (Garrattsville,) farmer occupies 125 owned by Isaac Gregory.
Cope, Henry, (New Lisbon,) dairyman 11 cows and farmer 114.
Coy, Brayton, (New Lisbon,) dairyman and farmer 50.
COY, ELI O., (Garrattsville,) carpenter.
Cummings, Leman, (Garrattsville,) farmer 145.
CUMMINGS, M. D., (Garrattsville,) farmer 15.
Daniels, Chas., (Hartwick,) farmer.
Daniels, M., (Hartwick,) farmer 83.
Davis, George, (New Lisbon,) farmer occupies 40 owned by P. Clark.
DEAN, H. M. Rev., (Garrattsville,) pastor of New Lisbon Center Baptist Church.
Drum, Stephen H., (Mount Vision,) farmer 84.
DUROE, FRANCIS J. Mrs., (New Lisbon,) hop raiser, dairyman 23 cows and farmer 214.
EATON, JAMES, (Garrattsville,) hop raiser, dairyman and farmer 150.
Edgerton, Erastus, (New Lisbon,) civil engineer.
Edmunds, A. J., (Garrattsville,) town assessor and farmer 101.
Eldred, Charles, (New Lisbon,) hop raiser, dairyman 15 cows and farmer 200.
Elliott James, (New Lisbon,) drover and farmer 53.

Elliott, James, (Garrattsville,) farmer 75.
Elliott, John, (Garrattsville,) dairyman and farmer 156.
ELLIOTT, J. H., (Garrattsville,) (with James,) farmer.
ELLIOTT, JOHN H., (Garrattsville,) general merchant.
Emmerson, Richard, (Garrattsville,) hop raiser and farmer 115.
Emmerson, Thomas R., (Garrattsville,) threshing machine, hop raiser, dairyman and farmer 115.
Emmons, Levi, (New Lisbon,) farmer.
Estes, Benj., (Garrattsville,) butcher.
ESTES, WILBUR, (Garrattsville,) produce dealer and farmer 106.
Field, Ira, (Mount Vision,) farmer 15.
Fitch, Edgar, (Mount Vision,) dairyman, 8 cows, and farmer 115.
Follett, Dwight, (New Lisbon,) hop raiser, dairyman, 10 cows, and farmer 190.
Follett, Francis, (New Lisbon,) (with Dwight,) farmer.
Foote, Alva E., (Garrattsville,) farmer.
Foote, John, (Garrattsville,) farmer 114.
Foote, Ransom A., (Garrattsville,) farmer and school teacher.
Foote, Wm., (Garrattsville,) dairyman 10 cows and farmer 108.
Fowler, Horace, (Garrattsville,) dairyman 10 cows and farmer 114.
Fowlston, George, (Garrattsville,) (with John,) hop raiser, dairyman and farmer 200.
Fowlston, G. B., (Garrattsville,) farmer.
Fowlston, John, (Mount Vision,) farmer 30 and occupies 54 owned by Polly Fowlston.
Fowlston, John, (Garrattsville,) (with Geo.,) hop raiser, dairyman and farmer 200.
Fox, Elias, (New Lisbon,) farmer 202.
Fox, Lucas, (New Lisbon,) refused to give information.
Fuller, Ansell, (Hartwick,) carpenter.
Fuller, Daniel, (Hartwick,) farmer 59.
Fuller, Thomas R., (Garrattsville,) hop raiser, dairyman 8 cows and farmer 132.
Fuller, Wm., (Hartwick,) (with Daniel,) farmer.
Gardner, Allen, (New Lisbon,) farmer 200.
Gardner, Amanda, (Mount Vision,) farmer 75.
Gardner, Benjamin, (Mount Vision,) farmer 27.
Gardner, Benjamin, (New Lisbon,) farmer 310.
Gardner, Clark, (Mount Vision,) farmer 30.
Gardner, David, (New Lisbon,) dairyman 9 cows and farmer 150.
Gardner, H. C., (Garrattsville,) hop raiser, dairyman 9 cows and farmer 100.
Gardner, M., (Hartwick,) farmer 12.
Gardner, Martin, (New Lisbon,) hotel keeper.
Gardner, Samuel, (Mount Vision,) saw mill, hop raiser, dairyman, 5 cows, and farmer 53.
Gardner, Samuel B., (Mount Vision,) stone mason and farmer 2½.
Gardner, W., (Mount Vision,) cider mill, dairyman, 8 cows, and farmer 110.
Gaylord, Edwin, (Garrattsville,) blacksmith.

George, Florense, (Mount Vision,) mechanic.

George, John, (New Lisbon,) farmer.

George, Samuel, (New Lisbon,) farmer 21.

Gilbert, John, (New Lisbon,) cooper and (*with Wm.*,) farmer 90.

Gilbert, Wm., (New Lisbon,) (*with John*,) farmer 90.

Gillett, E. D., (New Lisbon,) cooper.

Gillett, Israel, (Garrattsville,) dairyman 7 cows and farmer 100.

Gillett, Myron, (Garrattsville,) dairyman 15 cows and farmer 100.

Gledhill, I. N., (Garrattsville,) carpenter and farmer 127.

Gledhill, J. L., (Garrattsville,) butcher, dairyman 18 cows and farmer 130.

Gledhill, Lora J., (Garrattsville,) house painter.

Gorton, Joseph, (Garrattsville,) millwright and prop. saw mill.

Green, Benjamin, (Mount Vision,) (*with Thomas*,) hop raiser, dairyman and farmer 100.

Green, J. W., (Garrattsville,) farmer 4.

Green, Thomas, (Mount Vision,) (*with Benjamin*,) hop raiser, dairyman and farmer 100.

Greene, John, (Mount Vision,) cooper and farmer 55.

Greene, Thomas Mrs., (Mount Vision,) farmer 45.

Gregory, Andrew, (Garrattsville,) cheese manuf. and farmer 116.

Gregory, Angel, (Garrattsville,) mason and farmer 70.

Gregory, Anson, (Garrattsville,) dairyman 14 cows and farmer 160.

Gregory, Clayton, (Garrattsville,) farmer.

GREGORY, E., (Garrattsville,) prop. of Garrattsville Hotel and farmer 3.

Gregory, E. D., (New Lisbon,) farmer 80.

Gregory, E. & E. Misses, (Garrattsville,) dairy and farmers 125.

Gregory, Henry, (Garrattsville,) farmer.

Gregory, Hezekiah, (Garrattsville,) dairyman 8 cows and farmer 117.

Gregory, Isaac, (Mount Vision,) farmer 380.

Gregory, Joseph, (Garrattsville,) retired farmer.

GREGORY, K. P., (Garrattsville,) tin, iron and stoves.

Gregory, N. Mrs., (Garrattsville,) farmer 15.

Gregory, Smith, (Garrattsville,) dairyman 14 cows and farmer 150.

Gregory, S. C., (Garrattsville,) dairyman 15 cows and farmer 150.

Gregory, Wm., (Garrattsville,) dairyman and farmer 123.

Grey, Simon, (Garrattsville,) retired farmer.

Griffin, John, (New Lisbon,) farmer 85.

Gross, Ellis, (Garrattsville,) farmer 11.

Grover, Ruth Ann, (New Lisbon,) farmer 11½.

Harington, Caleb, (New Lisbon,) carpenter and farmer 4.

Harington, Francis, (New Lisbon,) dealer in hides and pelts, and farmer 70.

Harington, George, (Garrattsville,) farmer 50.

Harington, Hamilton A., (Garrattsville,) farmer 123.

Harington, Horace, (New Lisbon,) carpenter and joiner.

Harrington, Aaron, (Hartwick,) farmer 54½.

Harrington, Caleb B., (New Lisbon,) dairyman 6 cows and farmer 44.

Harrington, Dana F., (Hartwick,) hop raiser and farmer 116.

Harrington, E., (Mount Vision,) farmer 85.

Harrington, Harvey, (Mount Vision,) farmer occupies 40 owned by Charles Williams.

Harrington, John, (Laurens,) farmer 75.

Harrington, Lansing, (Laurens,) farmer 50.

Harrington, M. J., (New Lisbon,) farmer 10.

Harris, Albert, (Garrattsville,) dairyman and farmer 136.

Herrick, Stephen, (Garrattsville,) retired.

HICKLING, CHARLES H., (Garrattsville,) farmer.

Hickling, George, (Garrattsville,) farmer.

Hickling, Wm., (Garrattsville,) hop raiser, dairyman 8 cows and farmer 104.

Hickling, Wm. J., (Garrattsville,) farmer.

Hinman, George, (Mount Vision,) (*with Nelson*,) farmer.

Hinman, Meriba, (New Lisbon,) farmer 60.

Hinman, Miles, (New Lisbon,) dairyman 15 cows and farmer 120.

Hinman, Nelson, (Mount Vision,) hop raiser, dairyman 7 cows and farmer 75.

Hoag, Chas. M., (Garrattsville,) farmer 40.

Hoag, Edward S., (Garrattsville,) harness maker, grocer and postmaster.

Hoag, Ezra D., (Garrattsville,) produce broker and farmer 14.

Hoag, M. J., (Garrattsville,) farmer 20¾.

Holdridge, A. M., (Garrattsville,) farmer 36.

Holister, J., (New Lisbon,) egg dealer and farmer 60.

Holt, O. C., (Garrattsville,) photographer.

Huckaboon, Simeon, (Mount Vision,) farmer 60.

Hume, John, (Garrattsville,) dairyman and farmer 95.

Hume, Robert B., (Garrattsville,) hop raiser, dairyman and farmer 290.

Hume, Thomas, (Garrattsville,) hop raiser, dairyman and farmer 125.

Hunt, Charles, (Mount Vision,) cooper.

Jackson, Amasa A., (Garrattsville,) dairyman 12 cows and farmer 161.

Jackson, Charles A., (Garrattsville,) farmer 60.

Jackson, D. D., (Garrattsville,) school teacher, dairyman 10 cows and farmer 85.

Jackson, James, (Garrattsville,) hop raiser, dairyman and farmer 125.

Jacobs, David, (Hartwick,) farmer 53.

Jacobs, Norton, (Hartwick,) hop raiser and farmer 150.

Jenks, Ahab, (Garrattsville,) farmer leases of Jacob Seaver, 100.

JOHNSON, DAVID L., (New Lisbon,) farmer 1.

Johnson, Elvira, (Garrattsville,) dairyman 12 cows and farmer 150.

Johnson, Jason, (Hartwick,) farmer 50.

Johnson, Jonathan, (Laurens,) hop raiser, dairyman 11 cows and farmer 133½.

Johnson, Robert, (Mount Vision,) dairyman 7 cows and farmer 58.

Johnson, Solomon, (New Lisbon,) farmer 93.

Johnson, W. R., (Laurens,) agent for Sanborn Churn and Butter Worker Combined, and farmer.

JONES, JAMES, (New Lisbon,) hop raiser, dairyman 10 cows and farmer 200.

Jones, M. C., (Garrattsville,) hop raiser, dairyman 10 cows and farmer 120.

Keith, Amos, (Hartwick,) shoemaker and farmer 44.

KELLOGG, WM. J., (Garrattsville,) notary public, mechanic, and secretary of Garrattsville Agricultural Society.

Kembell, Isaac C., (Mount Vision,) hop raiser, dairyman and farmer 300.

Knochs, Nicholas, (Garrattsville,) farmer 75.

Laidler, John, (Garrattsville,) farmer 47.

Laidler, Thomas, (Garrattsville,) (*with Wm.,*) farmer 170.

Laidler, Wm., (Garrattsville,) president of Garrattsville Agricultural Society and (*with Thomas,*) farmer 170.

Lake, Wm., (Mount Vision,) farmer 52.

Lasher, George V., (New Lisbon,) hop raiser, dairyman and farmer 140.

LASHER, JOSIAH, (New Lisbon,) hop raiser, dairyman and farmer 112.

Lasher, W. S., (New Lisbon,) threshing machine, hop raiser, dairyman and farmer 104.

Lont, Killeon, (Garrattsville,) farmer 10.

Lull, Albert, (New Lisbon,) (*with David C.,*) carriage maker.

Lull, Alexis, (New Lisbon,) farmer.

Lull, Ansel, (New Lisbon,) cooper.

LULL, DAVID C., (New Lisbon,) carriage manuf. and farmer 17.

Lunn, Wm., (Garrattsville,) dairyman 22 cows and farmer 120.

Mack, D. H., (Hartwick,) dairyman 10 cows and farmer 170.

Martin, John, (Mount Vision,) farmer 25.

Mather, Ezra Mrs.,(Garrattsville,) resident.

Mather, G. C., (Garrattsville,) farmer 160.

MATHER, JOHN F., (Garrattsville,) general merchant and notary public.

Matteson, Hiram A., (Garrattsville,) dairyman 18 cows and farmer 159.

McCollom, Alvah, (New Lisbon,) dairyman 12 cows and farmer 110.

McCollom, James T., (New Lisbon,) school teacher.

Miller, Garret, (Garrattsville,) farmer 71.

Miller, Samuel M., (New Lisbon,) farmer 45.

Millis, Samuel I., (Garrattsville,) farmer 56.

Mills, La Fayette, (Garrattsville,) dairyman 10 cows and farmer 136.

Morehouse, Benjamin, (Hartwick,) hop raiser, dairyman 10 cows and farmer 133.

MORSE, J. D., (Garrattsville,) carriage maker and blacksmith.

Morse, Merlin, (New Lisbon,) farmer 50.

Morse, Rensselaer, (New Lisbon,) farmer 130.

Morse, Wm., (New Lisbon,) cooper and farmer 65.

Myers, Orson, (New Lisbon,) carpenter and farmer 7.

Nearing, Asa, (Garrattsville,) farmer 87.

NEARING, A. G., (Garrattsville,) hop raiser, dairyman and farmer 150.

NEARING, EDWIN A., (New Lisbon,) stock raiser and farmer 50, occupies 90 owned by John Nearing.

Nearing, H. D., (Garrattsville,) farmer 75.

Nearing, John, (New Lisbon,) farmer 90.

NEARING, O. B., (New Lisbon,) dairyman 6 cows and farmer 80.

NEARING, W. B., (New Lisbon,) dairyman 7 cows and farmer 75.

Nearing, W. G., (New Lisbon,) dairyman 12 cows and farmer 93.

Neff, Jno. W., (Garrattsville,) farmer 185.

Neff, Joseph, (Garrattsville,) farmer 11.

NICHOLS, CHARLES, (New Lisbon,) dealer in glass and wooden ware, and town collector.

Oakley, J. M., (Garrattsville,) farmer 5.

Oakly, Hannah E. Mrs., (Garrattsville,) milliner.

Olendorf, Delancey, (Mount Vision,) hop raiser and farmer 56.

PACKER, JAMES W., (Mount Vision,) dairyman and farmer leases of Isaiah Wright, 175.

Paine, L. B., (Garrattsville,) general merchant.

Paine, O. H., (Garrattsville,) blacksmith.

Parker, Elisha, (Garrattsville,) dairyman and farmer 330.

Parr, Wm., (Hartwick,) farmer 80.

Pattengill, Daniel, (Hartwick,) hop raiser, commissioner of highways, dairyman and farmer 250.

Pattengill, Wm., (Hartwick,) dairyman and farmer 202.

PECK, G. CLAYTON, (New Lisbon,) town clerk and (*with G. I. Peck,*) merchant.

Peck, G. I., (New Lisbon,) postmaster, merchant and farmer 55.

PERKINS, JAMES S., (Hartwick,) hop raiser and farmer 220.

Perry, Albe, (Hartwick,) dairyman 9 cows and farmer 215.

Perry, James, (Garrattsville,) dairyman 12 cows and farmer 245.

Pickens, Samuel M., (Hartwick,) hop raiser, dairyman 7 cows and farmer 108.

Pope, C. D., (Garrattsville,) dairyman and farmer 60.

Porter, Alberto, (Garrattsville,) dairyman 10 cows and farmer 94.

Porter, Elijah H., (Garrattsville,) dairyman 6 cows and farmer 50.

Porter, J. P., (Hartwick,) dairyman 8 cows and farmer 100.

Potter, Alonzo, (Hartwick,) refused to give information.

Potter, C., (New Lisbon,) hop raiser and farmer 50.

Potter, Caleb, (Hartwick,) hop raiser, dairyman 15 cows and farmer 220.

Potter, C. A., (Hartwick,) farmer 85.

POTTER, DELOS, (Hartwick,) (*with Caleb,*) farmer.

Potter, Edwin D., (Hartwick,) farmer 76.

POTTER, HIRAM C., (Garrattsville,) cheese manuf. and farmer 36.

Potter, Rodolphus, (Hartwick,) dairyman 5 cows and farmer 82.

Potter, R. W. & Son, (Hartwick,) farmers 184.

Price, Parmer, (New Lisbon,) dairyman 5 cows and farmer 40.

PURPLE, DAVID C., (Garrattsville,) shoemaker.

Reed, R. L. Mrs., (Garrattsville,) dressmaker.

Reed, Wm., (Garrattsville,) farmer 14.

Renwick, Wm., (Garrattsville,) hop raiser and farmer 110.

Reynolds, Wm. P., (Hartwick,) dairyman 15 cows and farmer 230.

RICHARDS, MILTON, (Hartwick,) carpenter, prop. of saw mill and threshing machine, and farmer 30.

Robinson, Geo., (Mount Vision,) farmer.

Robinson, George C., (Garrattsville,) dairyman and farmer 131.

ROBINSON, MATTHEW, (Mount Vision,) dairyman 14 cows and farmer 150.

Rockwell, Abner, (Hartwick,) dairyman and farmer 115.

Rockwell, D. C., (Garrattsville,) dairyman and farmer 100.

Rockwell, George, (Mount Vision,) farmer 75.

Rockwell, Leander T., (Hartwick,) hop raiser, dairyman 8 cows and farmer 62½.

Rockwell, W. R., (Garrattsville,) hop raiser, dairyman 9 cows and farmer 100.

Russell, Frederick W., (Garrattsville,) dairyman 35 cows and farmer 300.

Rutherford, Thomas, (Garrattsville,) dairyman 8 cows and farmer 87.

Sawyer, Henry, (New Lisbon,) drover and cooper.

Sawyer, N. D., (New Lisbon,) dealer in flour and firkins, hop raiser, dairyman 8 cows and farmer 5.

Seaman, Benjamin, (New Lisbon,) carpenter and farmer 80.

Sewell, D. I., (Garrattsville,) carpenter.

Sewell, Joseph R., (Garrattsville,) carpenter, cooper and farmer occupies 30 owned by Mrs. Mary Ballard.

Shepherd, Francis, (Mount Vision,) farmer 55.

Sherman, Charles, (Mount Vision,) farmer 50.

Sherman, E. J., (Garrattsville,) saw mill and farmer 100.

Sherman, John, (Mount Vision,) farmer 150.

Simons, Clarissa Mrs., (New Lisbon,) farmer 140.

Smith, Albert, (New Lisbon,) farmer 90.

SMITH, AMARIAH, (New Lisbon,) dairyman 9 cows and farmer 148.

Smith, Frank, (Garrattsville,) mason.

Smith, John, (Garrattsville,) cooper and farmer 17½.

Smith, Philetus, (New Lisbon,) farmer 41.

Smith, Samuel, (Garrattsville,) tailor.

Southworth, Joseph, (Garrattsville,) blacksmith and farmer 32.

Southworth, Robert S., (New Lisbon,) blacksmith.

Spencer, Wm., (Hartwick,) farmer 60.

Starr, Ira, (New Lisbon,) cooper.

Stevens, Edgar, (Garrattsville,) farmer 60.

Stevens, Simon, (Garrattsville,) hop raiser, dairyman 9 cows and farmer 150.

Stow, Isaac, (New Lisbon,) farmer 80.

SUTHERLAND, L. B., (New Lisbon,) carpenter and joiner, and school teacher.

Talbot, Isaac N., (Hartwick,) farmer.

Talbut, Reuben, (Hartwick,) dairyman 7 cows and farmer 145.

TEAL, D. E., (New Lisbon,) inventor and farmer 103.

Telfer, Andrew, (Hartwick,) cattle dealer, hop raiser, dairyman and farmer 175.

Telfer, Andrew, Jr.,(Hartwick,) farmer 100.

Telfer, Wm., (Hartwick,) farmer.

THAYER, THOMAS W., (Garrattsville,) commissioner of highways, hop raiser, dairyman 8 cows and farmer 90.

Thorp, E. S., (Garrattsville,) dairyman 7 cows and farmer 134.

Thurston, Ganes, (New Lisbon,) retired.

Thurston, James, (New Lisbon,) cheese manuf. and farmer 18¾.

Thurston, Joel, (New Lisbon,) farmer 125.

Tilley, Alonzo, (Mount Vision,) cooper and farmer.

Tilley, Charles, (Mount Vision,) cooper.

Tilley, Ellis, (Mount Vision,) cooper, hop raiser, dairyman 7 cows and farmer 80.

Turnabull, J. George, (Garrattsville,) farmer 133.

Van Steenbergh, William, (Garrattsville,) (*with Alvah*,) dairyman 8 cows and farmer leases 80.

Van Steenburgh, Alvah, (Garrattsville,) (*with William*,) dairyman 8 cows and farmer leases 80.

WALLACE, HENRY, (Garrattsville,) (*with Hiram*,) hop grower, dairyman and farmer 125.

WALLACE, HIRAM, (Garrattsville,) (*with Henry*,) hop raiser, dairyman and farmer 125.

Walter, Michael, (New Lisbon,) dairyman 11 cows and farmer 96.

WARD, WM. HENRY, (New Lisbon,) carriage maker.

Warren, Harrison, (New Lisbon,) farmer 100.

Warren, Stephen, (Garrattsville,) dairyman 10 cows and farmer 80.

Watkins, Jasper, (New Lisbon,) farmer 40.

Wellman, Cyrus, (Hartwick,) hop raiser and farmer 60.

Wheeler, G. W. P.,(Garrattsville,) physician and surgeon, and farmer 10.

Wheeler, John P., (Garrattsville,) agent for Warrior Mower and Reaper, justice of the peace, hop raiser, dairyman and farmer 236.

Whipple, John, (Garrattsville,) farmer 20.

Whipple, Lewis J., (Laurens,) hop raiser, dairyman 6 cows and farmer 80.

WHITE, WM. H., (Garrattsville,) carpenter and joiner.

Whitford, James,(Garrattsville,) hop raiser, dairyman and farmer 300.

Wickes, Peter, (Mount Vision,) mason and farmer 10.

WING, ALBERT H., (New Lisbon,) carpenter.

Winsor, Wm. E. D., (Garrattsville,) shoemaker.

WOOD, H. R., (New Lisbon,) grafter of fruit trees and cooper.

Yale, D. C., (New Lisbon,) carriage painter.

Yates, George A., (New Lisbon,) (*with Trevor*,) farmer.

Yates, Trevor, (New Lisbon,) dairyman 17 cows and farmer 162.

YOUNG, ALEXANDER,(Hartwick,) dairyman 10 cows and farmer 170.

Young, Robert, (Garrattsville,) mason, hop raiser, dairyman 11 cows and farmer 186.

Young, Robert, Jr., (Garrattsville,) farmer.

ONEONTA.

(Post Office Addresses in Parentheses.)

Ackley, Mitchell, (Oneonta,) farmer 12.

Alger, David, (Oneonta,) farmer 1.

Alger, Delos, (Oneonta,) farmer 100.

Alger, George, (Oneonta,) farmer 3.

Alger, Hiram N., (West Oneonta,) blacksmith.

Allen, George, (Oneonta) (*Tourjee & Allen.*)

Allen, H. H. Rev., (Oneonta,) Presbyterian minister.

Allsap, John, (Oneonta,) farmer 160.

Alton, W. W., (Oneonta,) (*Tobey, Alton & Co.*)

Amsden, John M., (Oneonta,) blacksmith, Main.

Anable, Alfred, (Oneonta,) farmer 31.

Arnold, Francis, (Oneonta,) farmer 94.

Babcock, Seymour, (Oneonta,) saw mill and farmer 100.

Baker, Daniel, (West Oneonta,) farmer 156.

Baker, Harvey, (Oneonta,) carpenter, Main.

Baker, Luther, (Oneonta,) farmer 65.

Baker, Spencer, (West Oneonta,) farmer 139.

Ballard & Lewis, (Oneonta,) (*S. M. Ballard and A. C. Lewis,*) props. Susquehanna House, Main corner Chestnut.

Ballard, N., (Oneonta,) (*Ballard & Pardoe.*)

Ballard & Pardoe, (Oneonta,) (*N. Ballard and W. Pardoe,*) billiard hall and restaurant, Main, up stairs.

Ballard, S. M., (Oneonta,) (*Ballard & Lewis.*)

Barnes, Ira, (Oneonta,) farmer 1.

Barr, Catharine Mrs., (Oneonta,) farmer 14.

Bates, Jonathan, (West Oneonta,) farmer 75.

Bates, Justice, (Oneonta,) farmer 50.

Beach, Chancellor, (Oneonta,) commissioner of highways.

Beach, Noah, (Oneonta,) mason and farmer 9, Chestnut.

Beach, Oren N., (Oneonta,) (*Miles & Beach.*)

Beams, Dewitt, (Oneonta,) farmer 49.

Beams, Jacob, (Oneonta,) farmer 100.

Beams, John, (Oneonta,) farmer 21.

Beams, Phebe, (Oneonta,) farmer 80.

Beams, Wm., (Oneonta,) farmer 20.

Beman, Wm., (West Oneonta,) farmer 1.

Bentley, Webster, (West Oneonta,) farmer 50.

Bergen, W. J., (West Oneonta,) cooper.

Betts & Culver, (West Oneonta,) (*F. M. Betts and Benj. Culver,*) general merchants.

Betts, F. M., (West Oneonta,) (*Betts & Culver.*)

Bingham, Anson, (Oneonta,) farmer leases 120.

Bissell, F. A., (Oneonta,) (*Bunn & Bissell.*)

Bissell, W. D., (Oneonta,) (*Bissell & Yager.*)

Bissell & Yager, (Oneonta,) (*W. D. Bissell and D. J. Yager,*) coal dealers, near A. & S. Depot.

Bixby, Charles W., (Oneonta,) (*Ford & Bixby.*)

Blakely, Jerusha, (Oneonta,) farmer 20.

Blanchard, Erastus, (Oneonta,) farmer 120.

Blanchard, William, (Oneonta,) farmer 50.

Blend, Abram, (Oneonta,) farmer 183.

Blend, Esick, (Oneonta,) farmer 60.

Blend, G. W., (Oneonta,) physician and druggist, Main.

Blend, George W., (Oneonta,) farmer 120.

Blend, John A., (Oneonta,) hop grower and farmer leases 60.

BLEND, L. H., (Oneonta,) architect and builder, manuf. of mouldings, brackets, newels,store fronts, pickets, &c., Broad near Depot.

Bornt, Frederick, (Oneonta,) farmer 250 and (*with Adelbert Champlin,*) 200.

Botsford, Wm. Mc., (West Oneonta,) general merchant.

Bowen, Darius, (West Oneonta,) farmer 106.

Bowen, J. W., (Oneonta,) liquors, Main.

Brewer, Hiram, (Oneonta,) (*Brewer & McDonald.*)

Brewer, Hiram J., (Oneonta,) carpenter and farmer 15.

Brewer, Isaac, (Oneonta,) farmer 5.

Brewer, Jonathan, (Oneonta,) farmer 129.

Brewer & McDonald, (Oneonta,) (*Hiram Brewer and J. McDonald,*) carpenters and builders, Main.

Brewer, S. F., (Oneonta,) mason.

Brightman, Delos, (Oneonta,) farmer 57.

Brightman, Joseph, (Oneonta,) farmer 125.

Brightman, Wm., (Oneonta,) farmer 57.

Brisack, Anson B.,(Oneonta,) mechanic and farmer 8.

Brisack, Joseph, estate of, (Oneonta,) 17 acres.

Bronson, Herbert M., (Oneonta,) carpenter.

Brown, A., (Oneonta,) farmer 2.

Brown, Wm. D., (Oneonta,) farmer 173.

Brownson, L. E., (West Oneonta,) general merchant.

Brownson, Seymour, (Oneonta,) insurance agent and town clerk, Main.

Hull, Henry, (West Oneonta.) farmer 93.
Bull, Joseph, (West Oneonta,) farmer 96.
Bull, N. N., (Oneonta,) principal Oneonta Free School.
Bundy, E. C. & J. H., (Oneonta,) bakery, confectionery, groceries, toys, &c., Main.
Bundy, L. L., (Oneonta,) (*Bundy & Scramling.*)
Bundy & Scramling, (Oneonta,) (*L. L. Bundy and George Scramling,*) attorneys, Main.
Bunn & Bissell, (Oneonta,) (*C. E. Bunn and F. A. Bissell,*) wholesale and retail dealers in meats, fish, oysters, produce &c., Main.
Bunn, C. E., (Oneonta,) (*Bunn & Bissell.*)
Burnside, G. R. Rev., (Oneonta,) Baptist minister, Main.
BURNSIDE, S. S., (Oneonta,) lawyer and notary public, Main.
Burton & Co., (Oneonta,) (*P. C. Burton, T. J. Gildersleeve and L. Goldsmith,*) own 9 acres.
Burton, P. C., (Oneonta,) (*Burton & Co.,*) watches and jewelry, Main.
Bush, Peter, (Oneonta,) mechanic.
Butler, Ervin E., (West Oneonta,) merchant tailor.
Butler, E. S. Mrs., (West Oneonta,) milliner and dressmaker.
Butts, Chas. H., (Oneonta,) freight receiver A. & S. R. R. Depot.
Campbell, Gilbert P., (Oneonta,) farmer.
Carr, A. E., (West Oneonta,) carriage maker.
Carver, E. M., (Oneonta,) cashier First National Bank of Oneonta.
Case, S. H., (Oneonta,) physician and farmer 8.
Ceperley, David, (Oneonta,) farmer 58.
Champlin, Adelbert, (Oneonta,) (*with Frederick Bornt,*) farmer 200.
Champlin, Benj., (Oneonta,) farmer 161.
Christian, William, (Oneonta,) farmer 5.
Ciperly, Francis, (Oneonta,) farmer 4.
Clark, John L., (Oneonta,) farmer 27.
Coates, L. T., (Oneonta,) (*Pardee & Coates.*)
Cobb, W. N. Rev., (Oneonta,) presiding elder M. E. Church.
Cohn, Jacob, (Oneonta,) merchant tailor, hats, caps and gents' furnishing goods, Main.
Cook, Chauncey, (West Oneonta,) farmer 100.
Cook, Robert S., (West Oneonta,) farmer 40.
Cook, Seth, (West Oneonta,) farmer leases 150.
Cook, Wm. S., (West Oneonta,) farmer 32 and leases 66.
Cooley, Morris, (Oneonta,) farmer 120.
Cooley, Wm., (Oneonta,) hop raiser, farmer 62 and leases 60.
Cope, James, (Oneonta,) (*J. Cope & Co.*)
Cope, John, (Oneonta,) (*J. Cope & Co.,*) president First National Bank of Oneonta, and supervisor.
Cope, J. & Co., (Oneonta,) (*John and James Cope,*) dry goods, groceries and building materials, Main corner Broad.
Couse, Anthony, (Oneonta,) farmer 103.
Couse, E. D., (Oneonta,) farmer 125.
Couse, Henry, (Oneonta,) farmer 118.
Couse, James W., (Oneonta,) farmer 125.

N

COUSE, JARED, (Oneonta,) carpenter and farmer 12½.
Couse, Wm. H., (Oneonta,) farmer 125.
Crandall, ——, (Oneonta,) farmer 80.
Culver, Benj., (West Oneonta,) (*Betts & Culver,*) postmaster and constable.
Culver, Freeman, (West Oneonta,) manuf. agricultural implements and farmer 70.
Cummings, H. J., (Oneonta,) groceries, Main.
CURTISS, E. G., (Oneonta,) tobacco, cigars, pipes, and all kinds of smokers' goods, Main.
Dean, Milo, (West Oneonta,) farmer 37.
Dean, Paulina, (Oneonta,) farmer 6.
Deyo, Simeon, (Oneonta,) gents' furnishing goods, farmer 264 and in Cobleskill, 206, Main.
Dillenbeck, A., (Oneonta,) billiard rooms.
*DODGE, G. A., (Oneonta,) publisher of Otsego Democrat.
Douglass, Elizabeth A. Mrs., (Oneonta,) farmer 25.
DRIGGS, SETH B., (Oneonta,) sash and blind manuf., Chestnut.
Durfee, Samuel, (West Oneonta,) resident.
DYE, A. D., (Oneonta,) books, stationery and music, Main.
Dye, Jonathan, (Oneonta,) farmer 90.
Edmunds, Nathaniel, (Oneonta,) farmer 250.
Elwell, M. N., (Oneonta,) custom miller, grain dealer and lumber manuf., Main.
Emmons, Carleton, (Oneonta,) farmer 560.
Enos, Ariel, (Oneonta,) farmer 25.
Farrington, Jacob, (Oneonta,) general merchant, Broad.
Fern, E. D., (Oneonta,) miller, Main.
Ferrell, J. M., (Oneonta,) deputy sheriff and agent for Phœnix Life Insurance Co., Main.
Figger, Wm. H., (Oneonta,) farmer 11.
First National Bank of Oneonta, (Oneonta,) John Cope, president; E. M. Carver, cashier, Main.
Fisher, Joseph, (Oneonta,) gate tender, Charlotte Turnpike.
Ford & Bixby, (Oneonta,) (*N. I. Ford and Charles W. Bixby,*) drugs, medicines, paints, oils, paper hangings &c., Main.
*FORD BROTHERS, (Oneonta,) (*D. W. and C. E.,*) manufs. of cultivators, plows, scrapers, head cutters &c., Mechanic, near A. & S. Depot.
FORD, C. E., (Oneonta,) (*Ford Brothers.*)
FORD, D. W., (Oneonta,) (*Ford Brothers.*)
Ford, E. R., (Oneonta,) director of A. & S. R. R. and farmer 240.
Ford, N. I., (Oneonta,) (*Ford & Bixby.*)
FOX, R. L., (Oneonta,) (*Osborn & Fox.*)
Francis, Levi, (West Oneonta,) shoemaker and farmer 1.
Francis, Wm., (West Oneonta,) mechanic.
Freiot, C. J., (Oneonta,) photographer, Main.
Fritts, Benjamin, (Oneonta,) farmer 118.
Gallup, David, (Oneonta,) farmer 109.
Gamut, Henry M., (Oneonta,) farmer 30.
Gates, A. J., (Oneonta,) (*Gates & Spaulding.*)
Gates & Spaulding, (Oneonta,) (*A. J. Gates and William Spaulding,*) carriage makers, Main.
Gaylor, James, (West Oneonta,) carpenter.

Gifford, Daniel, (Oneonta,) farmer 206.
Gifford, Daniel, (Oneonta,) farmer 180.
Gifford, Daniel E., (Oneonta,) farmer 70.
Gifford, Henry, (Oneonta,) farmer 100.
Gifford, H. R., (Oneonta,) assessor, prop. saw mill and farmer 15.
Gifford, James H., (Oneonta,) farmer 100.
Gifford, R. C., (Oneonta,) (with Daniel,) speculator.
Gildersleeve, T. J., (Oneonta,) (Burton & Co.)
Gile, Alvin, (Oneonta,) farmer 115.
Gile, Edward, (Oneonta,) farmer 50.
Gile, Erastas, (Oneonta,) farmer 89.
Gile, Lydia J. Mrs., (Oneonta,) farmer 141.
Gile, S. J., (Oneonta,) marble works, Main.
Godsell, John, (Oneonta,) farmer 32.
GOLDSMITH, L., (Oneonta,) (Burton & Co.,) millinery, silks, fancy and dry goods, Main.
Goodyear, Jared, (Oneonta,) farmer 101.
Gould, Hanson, (Oneonta,) farmer.
Gowey, John A., (Oneonta,) farmer 130.
Green, Betsey Mrs., (West Oneonta,) resident.
Green, Clark, (West Oneonta,) (with Ezra,) farmer 75.
Green, Ezra, (West Oneonta,) (with Clark,) farmer 75.
Green, Rha, (West Oneonta,) farmer 75.
Green, Simon, (Oneonta,) farmer 218.
Gregory, J., (Oneonta,) harness maker, Main.
Griffin, Austin Rev., (Oneonta,) M. E. minister.
Hackett, John, (Oneonta,) farmer 130.
Hackett, William, (Oneonta,) farmer 232.
Haines, ——, (Oneonta,) farmer leases of Emery Quackenbush, 150.
Hamilton, H. A., (Oneonta,) physician, Main.
Hand, Alex., (Oneonta,) farmer 14.
Harrington, A. G., (West Oneonta,) blacksmith.
Hathaway, Al., (Oneonta,) constable and clerk Eagle Hotel.
Hathaway, L., (Oneonta,) prop. Eagle Hotel, Broad near Depot.
Hemstreet, Nathan, (Oneonta,) (Hemstreet & Young.)
Hemstreet & Young, (Oneonta,) (Nathan Hemstreet and George Young,) wholesale and retail dealers in flour, feed, plaster, salt, seeds &c., White Store, near A. & S. Depot.
Henniker, Henry, (Oneonta,) farmer leases 35.
Hoag, Wilson, (West Oneonta,) farmer 70.
Hodge, Andrew E., (West Oneonta,) assessor and farmer 56.
Hodge, Daniel, (West Oneonta,) farmer 186.
Hodge, E. C. Rev., (Oneonta,) Free Will Baptist minister and farmer 100.
Holmes, Isaac, (West Oneonta,) farmer 108.
Holmes, Willis, (Oneonta,) farmer 2.
Houghtaling, Jane Mrs., (Oneonta,) farmer 60.
Howard, Charles, (Oneonta,) mason and musician, south side river.
Hudson, Silas, (Oneonta,) farmer 54.
Hummell, Aaron, (Oneonta,) farmer 60.
Hummell, Nicholas, (Oneonta,) farmer 120.
Humphrey, R. V., (Oneonta,) billiard room, Main.

Hungerford, George, (Oneonta,) farmer 40.
Hunt, John L., (Oneonta,) farmer 22.
Huntington, Solon, (Oneonta,) farmer 175.
INGALLS, GEO. W., (Oneonta,) carpenter, Chestnut.
Ingalls, John C., (Oneonta,) stone cutter, Chestnut.
Jay, Wm., (Oneonta,) prop. East Oneonta Hotel and farmer 2.
Jencks, Andrew J., (Oneonta,) farmer 5.
Jencks, Jas. W., (Oneonta,) farmer 70.
Jenks, Devear, (West Oneonta,) farmer leases 60.
Jenks, Patience Mrs., (West Oneonta,) farmer 6.
Jenks, Willard, (Oneonta,) farmer 60.
Johnson, Alex. H., (Oneonta,) farmer 143.
Johnston, William, (Oneonta,) merchant tailor, gents' furnishing goods, &c., Main.
Keenan, M., (Oneonta,) blacksmith, Main.
Keyes, J. H. & M., (Oneonta,) attorneys and notaries public, Main.
Kibbe, T. V., (Oneonta,) meat market, Main.
Kilbourne, Seymour, (Oneonta,) farmer 106.
King, Oren, (West Oneonta,) farmer 84.
Knapp, Seth, (Oneonta,) farmer 10.
Lakin, Wm., (Oneonta,) barber, Main.
Lewis, A. C., (Oneonta,) (Ballard & Lewis.)
Lewis, C. W., (Oneonta,) prop. Oneonta Rail Road House, Main corner Chestnut.
Losee, Joel, (Oneonta,) farmer 47½.
Luther, E., (Oneonta,) (Wing & Luther.)
Madison, Palmer, (West Oneonta,) farmer 3.
Martin, Andrew, (Oneonta,) resident.
McCrum, William, (Oneonta,) furniture dealer and undertaker, Main.
McDonald, J., (Oneonta,) (Brewer & McDonald.)
MEAGHER, THOMAS F., (Oneonta,) dining saloon, Main.
Mendel, Andrew, (Oneonta,) (A. Mendel & Bros.)
Mendel, A. & Bros., (Oneonta,) (Andrew, Samuel and Benedict,) ready made clothing, dry goods, hats, caps, boots, shoes &c., Main.
Mendel, Benedict, (Oneonta,) (A. Mendel & Bros.)
Mendel, Samuel, (Oneonta,) (A. Mendel & Bros.)
Michael, C. L., (Oneonta,) agent for Washington Life Insurance Co. and real estate agent, Main.
Miles, Abel S., (Oneonta,) (Miles & Beach.)
Miles & Beach, (Oneonta,) (Abel S. Miles and Oren N. Beach,) livery and exchange stables, Chestnut.
Miller, Cornelius, (Oneonta,) farmer 50.
Miller, D. M., (Oneonta,) farmer 99.
Miller, D. M., (Oneonta,) produce commission merchant, Main.
Miller, John E., (Oneonta,) farmer 32.
Miller, Reuben W., (Oneonta,) tailor, Main.
Miner, John, (Oneonta,) farmer 22.
Moffatt, Ransom, (Oneonta,) farmer 83.
Moody, A. C., (Oneonta,) (Moody & Vosburgh.)

Moody & Vosburgh, (Oneonta,) (*A. C. Moody and E. M. Vosburgh,*) wholesale and retail dealers in stoves, tinware &c., agents for the Buckeye Mower and Reaper, Main.

Morell, Isaac, (Oneonta,) farmer 45.

Morell, Jacob, (Oneonta,) farmer 61.

Morenus, J. T., (Oneonta,) farmer 45.

Morgan, E. J.,(Oneonta,) physician dentist, Brick Block.

Morris, Albert,(Oneonta,)(*Morris Brothers.*)

Morris Brothers, (Oneonta,) (*Albert and Wm. H.,*) flour, salt, feed, grain, cheese &c., wholesale and retail, Chestnut.

Morris, Wm. H., (Oneonta,) (*Morris Bros.*)

Morrison, A. B., (Oneonta,) wholesale and retail dealers in groceries, wines and liquors, Brick Block, Main.

Mosher, Joshua, (Oneonta,) (*T. K. Mosher & Bros.*)

Mosher, T. K. & Bros., (Oneonta,) (*Joshua and Wm. H.,*) carriage and spoke makers, Main.

Mosher, Wm. H., (Oneonta,) (*T, K. Mosher & Bros.*)

Moulton, O. T. Rev., (Oneonta,) Free Will Baptist minister.

Nash, Henry, (Oneonta,) farmer 140.

Niles, Hanson, (West Oneonta,) farmer 150.

Niles, Henry, (West Oneonta,) brick maker and (*with Nathaniel,*) farmer 96.

Niles, Nathaniel, (West Oneonta,) (*with Henry,*) farmer 96.

Northrup, Betsey Mrs., (West Oneonta,) resident.

Northrup, Isaac, (West Oneonta,) farmer.

Olin, J. M., (West Oneonta,) wagon maker and painter.

Olin, Polly Mrs., (West Oneonta,) resident.

Olin, S. M., (West Oneonta,) justice of the peace and farmer 20.

Orr, David, (Oneonta,) farmer 139.

OSBORN & FOX, (Oneonta,) (*L. S. Osborn and R. L. Fox,*) wholesale and retail dealers in dry goods, groceries, drugs, medicines &c., Main.

OSBORN, L. S., (Oneonta,) (*Osborn & Fox,*) farmer 75.

Osborn, Luman S., (Oneonta,) farmer 62.

Osterhout, Abram, (Oneonta,) farmer 75.

Osterhout, Ann, (Oneonta,) prop. Susquehanna Valley Hotel and farmer 70.

*OTSEGO DEMOCRAT, (Oneonta,) G. A. Dodge, publisher.

Ottman, John W., (Oneonta,) hack driver, Chestnut.

Packard, Melissa, (Oneonta,) farmer 2½.

Pardee & Coates, (Oneonta,) (*H. S. Pardee and L. T. Coates,*) boots and shoes, Main.

Pardee, H. S., (Oneonta,) (*Pardee & Coates.*)

PARDOE, EDWARD B., (Oneonta,) house, sign, banner and ornamental painting, done with neatness and dispatch, Chestnut.

PARDOE, JOHN, (Oneonta,) house, sign and ornamental painter, Chestnut.

Pardoe, W., (Oneonta,) (*Ballard & Pardoe.*)

Parish, Ephraim, (Oneonta,) farmer 250.

Parish, George, (Oneonta,) farmer 125.

Parish, Huntington, (Oneonta,) farmer 95.

Parish, Stephen, (Oneonta,) farmer 66.

Parr, Geo., (Oneonta,) poultry dealer and farmer 2, Chestnut.

Peet, Elizabeth, (Oneonta,) farmer 5.

Peet, James, (Oneonta,) farmer 77.

Peet, John F., (Oneonta,) farmer 114.

Peet, Solomon, (Oneonta,) farmer 150.

Perry, Jesse V., (West Oneonta,) commissioner of highways and farmer 50.

Perry, John, (Oneonta,) carpenter.

Peters, Isaac H., (Oneonta,) boots, shoes, leather and hides, Main.

Peters, John, (Oneonta,) farmer 80.

Phillips, John, (Oneonta,) farmer 60.

Pope, C. D., (Oneonta,) flour, feed, grain, seeds &c., Main.

Pope. E. D. Mrs., (Oneonta,) physician, Dietz.

Quackenbush, Clinton, (Oneonta,) farmer 100.

Quackenbush, David, (Oneonta,) resident.

Quackenbush, Emery, (Oneonta,) (*Strait & Quackenbush.*)

Quackenbush, Jacob, (Oneonta,) farmer 40.

Ramsey, George H., (Oneonta,) groceries, fruits, oysters &c., Main.

Ray, James Mrs., (Oneonta,) millinery and fancy goods, Main.

Reynolds, E. A., (Oneonta,) agent D. & H. C. Express Co.

*REYNOLDS, G. W., (Oneonta,) postmaster and publisher.

Reynolds, Reuben, (Oneonta,) (*Ruland & Reynolds.*)

Richards, S. & A., (Oneonta,) brick makers and farmers 33.

Richards, Samuel N., (Oneonta,) farmer 134.

Richardson, Jonathan, (Oneonta,) commissioner of highways and farmer 120.

Richardson, Sally Mrs., (Oneonta,) farmer 154.

Roberts, James, (Oneonta,) groceries and provisions, Main.

Roberts, John B., (Oneonta,) groceries, provisions, crockery, glass ware, wall paper &c., Main.

Roberts, William, (Oneonta,) farmer 9.

Rood, William, (Oneonta,) farmer 47.

Roundy, ——. (Oneonta,) station agent, Emmons Station.

Rowe, H. N., (Oneonta,) farmer 170.

Rowe, Jacob, (Oneonta,) tin peddler.

Ruland, John, (Oneonta,) (*Ruland & Reynolds.*)

Ruland & Reynolds, (Oneonta,) (*John Ruland and Reuben Reynolds,*) flour, seeds and groceries, Main.

Sabin, Egbert, (Oneonta,) (*T. Sabin & Son.*)

Sabin, T., (Oneonta,) (*T. Sabin & Son,*) farmer 10.

Sabin, Timothy, (Oneonta,) cheese factory and creamery.

Sabin, T. & Son, (Oneonta,) (*Egbert,*) butter, cheese and wool, Main.

Sage, Harvey, (Oneonta,) farmer 100.

Schermerhorn, John, (Oneonta,) farmer 80.

Scramlin, Allen, (Oneonta,) farmer.

Scramlin, John, (Oneonta,) farmer 3.

Scramlin, Peter Rev., (Oneonta,) Free Will Baptist clergyman and farmer 31.

Scramling, Allen, (Oneonta,) farmer 570.

Scramling, George, (Oneonta,) (*Bundy & Scramling.*)

Seperly, David, (Oneonta,) farmer 60.

Sessions, Horace, (Oneonta,) farmer 3.

Sheldon, James, (Oneonta,) farmer.

Shellman, W. H., (Oneonta,) wagon maker, Chestnut.

Shepard, Erastus, (Oneonta,) farmer 100.

Shepard, Isaac, (Oneonta,) farmer 197.

Shepard, Sanford, (Oneonta,) farmer 51.

Sickler, John, (Oneonta,) farmer 12.

Sickler, J. G., (Oneonta,) farmer 13.

Silvernail, L. C., (Oneonta,) eclectic physician and surgeon, Main.

Slade, Hiram, estate of, (Oneonta,) 4 acres.

Slade, James & H. L., (Oneonta,) farmers 254.

Slade, Sherman, (Oneonta,) farmer 163.

Sleeper, Ephraim, estate of, (West Oneonta,) 25 acres.

Smith, Jane Mrs., (Oneonta,) farmer 22.

Smith, Katie, (West Oneonta,) resident.

Smith, Samuel, (Oneonta,) farmer 4.

Smith, —— Mrs., (Oneonta,) farmer 20.

Snow, William W. Hon., (Oneonta,) farmer 50, Chestnut.

Spaulding, William, (Oneonta,) (*Gates & Spaulding.*)

Stanton, Mary Mrs., (West Oneonta,) resident.

Steere, Irving, (Oneonta,) farmer 61.

Stewart, ——, (Oneonta,) wagon maker.

Stowell, J. D., (Oneonta,) boots, shoes, leather and findings, Main.

Strait, Alvinza, (West Oneonta,) farmer 90.

Strait, Andrew, (West Oneonta,) watch repairer.

Strait, Burton, (West Oneonta,) farmer 19.

Strait, Geo., estate of, (West Oneonta,) 26 acres.

Strait & Quackenbush, (Oneonta,) (*William Strait and Emery Quackenbush,*) practical machinists and props. Oneonta Iron Works, near A. & S. Depot.

Strait, Rufus, (West Oneonta,) farmer 25.

Strait, William, (Oneonta,) (*Strait & Quackenbush.*)

Swart, Ascenath Mrs., (Oneonta,) farmer 40.

Swart, Elkanah, (Oneonta,) farmer 109.

Swart, George, (Oneonta,) farmer 188.

Taber, Joseph, (West Oneonta,) saw mill and farmer 130.

Taber, J. N., (West Oneonta,) farmer 175.

Terry, Isaac, (Oneonta,) mason and farmer 1.

Thayer, Asa, (West Oneonta,) (*with Geo. W.,*) prop. West Oneonta Hotel.

Thayer, Enos, (West Oneonta,) farmer 150.

Thayer, Geo. W., (West Oneonta,) (*with Asa,*) prop. West Oneonta Hotel.

Tobey, A. B., (Oneonta,) (*Tobey, Alton & Co.*)

Tobey, Alton & Co., (Oneonta,) (*H. M. Tobey, W. W. Alton and A. B. Tobey,*) general merchants, Main.

Tobey, H. M., (Oneonta,) (*Tobey, Alton & Co.*)

Tourjee & Allen, (Oneonta,) (*George Tourjee and George Allen,*) planing and feed mills, Main.

Tourjee, George, (Oneonta,) (*Tourjee & Allen.*)

Treadwell, Lyman, (Oneonta,) farmer 4½.

Tucker, Jay, (Oneonta,) telegraph operator A. & S. R. R. Depot.

Tyler, John N., (Oneonta,) farmer 120.

Van Luvan, Jonas, (West Oneonta,) resident.

Van Wie, A., (Oneonta,) (*Van Wie Bros.*)

Van Wie Bros., (Oneonta,) (*D. A. and A.*) stoves, tinware, hardware, paints, oils &c., Brick Block, Main.

Van Wie, D. A., (Oneonta,) (*Van Wie Bros.*)

Van Woert, Andrew, (Oneonta,) farmer 356.

Van Woert, James S., (Oneonta,) farmer 80.

Van Woert, J. P., (Oneonta,) constable and collector, Main.

Van Woert, Peter, (Oneonta,) farmer 12.

Van Woert, S. P., (Oneonta,) farmer 189.

VILLOZ, A. L., (Oneonta,) fashionable hair dresser, Main. Particular attention paid to children's hair cutting.

Vosburgh, E. M., (Oneonta,) (*Moody & Vosburgh.*)

Wadsworth, Paul, (Oneonta,) station agent A. & S. R. R. Depot.

Wales, E. V. Rev., (Oneonta,) Presbyterian clergyman, Main.

Walling, Alonzo, (Oneonta,) farmer leases of Samuel, 140.

Walling, Erastus, (Oneonta,) farmer 300.

Walling, J. R. L., (Oneonta,) surveyor and farmer 141.

Walling, Ransom, (Oneonta,) farmer 66.

Warner, Hezekiah, (Oneonta,) farmer 92.

Watkins, Hezekiah, (Oneonta,) farmer 23.

Watkins, John M., (Oneonta,) farmer 42.

Wells, J. L. Rev., (Oneonta,) M. E. clergyman.

White, Anthony, (Oneonta,) carpenter and farmer 24.

White, Ezra, (Oneonta,) farmer 153.

White, Horace, (West Oneonta,) farmer 144.

WHITE, RANSOM, (Oneonta,) carpenter and joiner, Academy.

Whitman, Geo. R., (West Oneonta,) farmer 265.

Whitman, Henry C., (West Oneonta,) farmer 90.

Whitmarsh, Berlinda, (Oneonta,) farmer 80.

Whitney, Delos, (Oneonta,) farmer leases 88.

Whitney, Geo. R., (Oneonta,) carpenter and farmer 5.

Whitney, Roswell, (West Oneonta,) shoemaker.

Whitney, Wm., (Oneonta,) physician.

Wickham, A. G., (Oneonta,) farmer 130.

Wickham, H., (Oneonta,) coopering, staves, hoop poles, lime, plaster and cement, Broad.

Wickham, Henry, (Oneonta,) farmer 19.

Wickham, Henry, (Oneonta,) cooper and farmer 21.

Wilcox, Henry, (Oneonta,) farmer 75.

Wilde, Lavina, (West Oneonta,) resident.

Williams, Francis J., (West Oneonta,) farmer 38.

Williams, Thoms, (Oneonta,) barber, Main.

Winans, Judson, (West Oneonta,) carpenter.

Wing, A. F., (Oneonta,) (*Wing & Luther.*)

Wing & Luther, (Oneonta,) (*A. F. Wing and E. Luther,*) furniture dealers and undertakers, Chestnut.

Winne, David, (Oneonta,) farmer 104.

Winne, John, (Oneonta,) farmer 100.
Winne, Robert, (Oneonta,) farmer 50.
Wolf, Conrad, (Oneonta,) farmer 88.
Wood, Alonzo, (Oneonta,) baggageman, A. & S. R. R. Depot.
WOOD, DAVID, (Oneonta,) carpenter, Main.
Wood, Seeley, (Oneonta,) farmer 75.
Woodbeck, Freeman, (Oneonta.) farmer 63.
Woodin, Henry, (Oneonta,) carpenter.
Yager, Burton C., (Oneonta,) farmer 83 and leases of Freelove Gould, 42.
Yager, David, (Oneonta,) resident.
Yager, David J., (Oneonta,) (*Bissell & Yager,*) justice of the peace and farmer 6.

Yager, Delos, (Oneonta,) farmer.
Yager, Geo. H., (Oneonta,) farmer 48.
Yager, Harmon D., (Oneonta,) resident.
Yager, Henry, (Oneonta,) farmer 50.
Yager, Jacob, estate of, (Oneonta,) 123 acres.
Yager, John, (Oneonta,) farmer 130.
Yager, Peter, (Oneonta,) farmer 200.
Yager, Solomon, (Oneonta,) hop grower and farmer 170.
Yager, Theodore, (Oneonta,) farmer 121.
Young, George, (Oneonta,) (*Hemstreet & Young.*)
Youngman, John, (Oneonta,) farmer 144.
Youngs, John, (Oneonta,) farmer 120.

OTEGO.

(Post Office Addresses in Parentheses.)

ALDRICH, S. K., (Otego,) furniture manuf. and dealer, and undertaker, Main.
Allen, Justin, (Otego,) farmer 165.
Apley, Edwin, (Otego,)(*with Philip Hodge,*) farmer 140.
Aplin, B., (Otego,) farmer 40.
Arnold, Alfred, (Otego,) stone quarryman and farmer 140.
Arnold, Wm. E., (Otego,) farmer 75.
Arris, Sallie, (Otego,) farmer 2½.
Atkins, Charles G. W., (Otego,) barber.
Austin, Harvey, (Otego,) farmer 36.
Baker, W. H., (Otego,) farmer 150.
Baldwin, E. J., (Otego,) agent for Guardian Mutual Life Insurance Co., Main.
BALDWIN, HIRAM, (Otego,) (*Goodman, Baldwin & Packard.*)
Baldwin, John, (Otego,) blacksmith.
Baldwin, Salmon, (Otego,) farmer 108.
Baldwin, Wm., (Otego,) blacksmith.
Bank of Otego, (Otego,) S. R. Follett, president.
Barney, Wm., (Otego,) carpenter.
Barton, Geo., (Otego,) farmer 105.
Bedient, Lewis, (Wells' Bridge,) hop raiser and farmer leases of Lorin Dodge, 150.
Beeman, W. A., (Otsdawa,) shoemaker.
Birdsall, David, (Otego,) farmer 178.
Birdsall, Edwin, (Otego,) farmer.
Birdsall, Geo., (Otego,) farmer 20.
Birdsall, Henry, (Otego,) carriage manuf.
Birdsall, Homer, (Otego,) (*with Jefferson Ferrey,*) farmer leases 160.
Birdsall, T. A., (Otego,) farmer.
Birdsell, William, (Otego,) lumber dealer and farmer 230.
Bissel, Fitch, (Otego,) (*with Silas,*) farmer 118.

Bissel, Silas, (Otego,) (*with Fitch,*) farmer 118.
BLAKELY, EBENEZER, (Otego,) lawyer.
Bliss, Wm., (Otego,) farmer 100.
Borden, J. W., (Otego,) jeweler, Main.
Bowe, L. E., (Otego,) attorney, Main.
Bowen, Edward E., (Otego,) carriage trimmer.
Brand, Abner, (Otego,) blacksmith and farmer 1.
Briggs, Martin, (Otego,) farms Briggs' estate, 160.
Briggs, Theo., (Otego,) carpenter.
Brink, Ephraim, (Otego,) farmer 43.
Brink, Moses, (Otego,) farmer 75.
Bristol, Sylvester, (Otego,) farmer 150.
Broadfoot, Wm. T., (Otego,) farmer 16.
Brown, Alfred, (Otego,) farmer 265.
Brown, Andrew, (Otsdawa,) farmer 117.
Brown, Ezra, (Otego,) farmer 2.
Brown, Geo., (Otego,) farmer 90.
Brown Geo. R., (Otego,) stock dealer and farmer 46.
Brown, James, (Otego,) farmer 75 and (*with Thurston,*) 150.
Brown, John H., (Otego,) farmer 122½.
Brown, Nancy, (Otego,) farmer 115.
Brown, Thurston, (Otego,) (*with James,*) farmer 150.
Brown, Wm., (Otego,) farmer leases 175.
BROWN, WILLIS C., (Otego,) farmer 25.
Bugbee, D., (Otego,) farmer 50.
Bugbee, Dexter, (Otego,) farmer 12.
Bugbee, M., (Otego,) farmer 12.
Bugbee, Oliver, (Otego,) farmer 20.
Bugbee, Stephen, (Otego,) farmer 75.
Bundy, B., (Otego,) retired farmer.
Bundy, Edgar, (Otego,) farmer.
Bundy, Elisha, (Otego,) farmer 30.

Bundy, Henry J., (Otego,) farmer 46.
Bundy, I. Mrs., (Otego,) farmer 7.
Bundy, Martin E., (Otego,) farmer 120.
Bundy, Oscar A., (Otego,) farmer works estate of James Bundy, 140.
*BUNDY, PETER, (Otego,) prop. of stone quarry and farmer 110.
Bundy, Willard, (Otego,) farmer 40.
Burdick, A., (Otego,) farmer 100.
BURDICK, EZEKIEL, (Otego,) farmer 103.
Burdick, Geo., (Otego,) farmer 200.
Burdick, Jared, (Otego,) farmer 290.
Burdick, Jared, (Otego,) (*Burdick & Rathbone*,)
Burdick & Rathbone, (Otego,) (*Jared Burdick and Robert E. Rathbone,*) variety store, Main.
Burdick, Z., (Otego,) (*with Henry,*) farmer 80.
Burgin, Charles,(West Oneonta,) farmer 30.
Burnside, Delmer, (Wells' Bridge,) (*with Thos.,*) hop grower and farmer 200.
Burnside, Thomas, (Wells' Bridge,) (*with Delmer,*) hop raiser and farmer 200.
Burnside, Wm., (Otego,) farmer 75.
Burrall, Hiram, (Otego,) farmer 35.
Case, John, (Otego,) farmer.
Case, Joseph, (Otego,) farmer 57.
Case, William Rev., (Otego,) Christian clergyman and farmer 7.
Castle, Abner, (Otego,) farmer 75.
Castle, Lyman, (Otego,) farmer 108.
CENTER BROOK CHEESE FACTORY, (Otego,) James C. Emmons, prop.
Chamberlain, G. A., (Otsdawa,) (*Chamberlain & Son,*) post master.
Chamberlain, Jordan, (Otsdawa,) (*Chamberlain & Son.*)
Chamberlain & Son, (Otsdawa,) (*G. A. and Jordan,*) general merchants and farmer 84.
Chittenden, James, (Otego,) farmer 17.
Church, Addison, (Otego,) farmer.
Church, Harvey, (Otego,) farmer 21.
Church, Jefferson, (Otego,) farmer 120.
Clark, Henry E., (Otego,) (*Clark & Olmsted.*)
Clark & Olmsted, (Otego,) (*Henry E. Clark and S. B. Olmsted,*) hardware, Main.
CLEGG, SAMUEL, (Otego,) dairyman and farmer 128.
COBINE, JOHN W., (Otego,) farmer 280.
COBURN, L. & CO., (Otego,) (*Wm. M. Whitney,*) manufs. of saddles, harness, trunks, boots and shoes, Main.
Cole, James, (Otego,) farmer 100.
Cole, N., (Otego,) farmer 60.
Colgrove, Orrin, (Otego,) farmer 7.
Collar, Morris, (Otsdawa,) farmer 100.
Cook, Alex., (Otego,) farmer.
Cook, H., (West Oneonta,) farmer 60.
Cook, J. A., (Otego,) farmer 600.
Cook, Lee, (Otego,) farmer 75.
Cook, Otis, (Otego,) farmer 50.
Cook, Robert, (Otsdawa,) farmer 66.
Cook, Wm. P., (West Oneonta,) farmer 60.
Cook, Wyman, (Otego,) farmer 12½.
Cooke, Berosus, (Otego,) (*Cooke & Parker.*)
Cooke, G. W., (Otego,) physician and surgeon, Main.
Cooke & Parker, (Otego,) (*Berosus Cooke and W. H. Parker,*) drugs, medicines, dry goods &c., Main.
Corey, B., (Otego,) shoemaker.

Corey, Leroy, (Otego,) shoemaker.
Cornell, Isaac, (Otego,) farmer 150.
Cossaart, A. B., (Otego,) homeo. physician, office Susquehanna House.
Coye, G. W., (Otego,) dentist, Main.
Crandall, David, (Otego,) farmer 100.
Davis, Joseph D., (Otsdawa,) farmer 90.
Davis, Robert, (Otego,) grocer, Main.
Day, Rensselaer, (Otego,) farmer 312.
Decker, Thomas, (Otsdawa,) (*Smith & Decker.*)
Dodge, L. C., (Otego,) farmer.
Doolittle, Henry, (Otego,) farmer 188.
Duncle, Jerry, (Otego,) barber, Main.
Eckert, M. H., (Otego,) mechanic.
Edson, F. W., (Otego,) farmer.
Edson, Henry, (Otego,) farmer.
Edson, Martin A., (Otego,) farmer 100.
Edwards, Daniel, (Otego,) farmer 135.
EDWARDS, DANIEL M., (Otego,) farmer.
Edwards, N. G., (Otego,) farmer.
Eldridge, Solomon, (Otsdawa,) farmer 80.
Emerson, Dudley, (Otego,) farmer 30.
Emerson, Ensign, (Otego,) farmer 130.
Emerson, Russell, (Otsdawa,) farmer 55.
Emerson, Samuel, (Otego,) farmer 175.
Emmons, Carson, (West Oneonta,) farmer 157.
EMMONS, JAMES C., (Otego,) prop. Center Brook Cheese Factory and farmer 176.
Fairchild, L., (Otsdawa,) farmer 30.
Fancher, Charles G., (Otego,) farmer 7½.
Ferrey, Abner, (Otego,) farmer 30.
Ferry, Jefferson, (Otego,) (*with Homer Birdsall,*) farmer leases 150.
Finch, Perry G., (Otego,) farmer 112.
Fink, Henry, (Otego,) (*with Willis T.,*) farmer 160.
Fish, L. C. B., (Otego,) farmer 150.
Fisk, Rufus, (Otego,) farmer 55.
Fitzgerald, John H. Rev., (Otego,) Episcopal clergyman.
Flint, A. O., (Otego,) overseer of the poor, hop raiser, dairyman and farmer 50.
Follett, S. R., (Otego,) president of Bank of Otego.
*FOOTE, ALPHEUS S., (Otego,) editor and prop. of *Otsego Recorder.*
Ford, Abijah T., (West Oneonta,) mason.
Ford, John, (West Oneonta,) farmer 58.
Fosdike, Mark, (Otego,) farmer 68.
Fowler, Frederick H., (Otego,) blacksmith.
Fowler, Wm. B., (Otego,) farmer 100.
French, Dennis, (Otego,) farmer.
French, M., (Otego,) farmer 70.
French, W. D., (Otego,) farmer 100.
French, W. H., (Otego,) blacksmith.
Frink, Willis T., (Otego,) (*with Henry,*) farmer 160.
Fuller, J. B., (Otego,) farmer 128.
Gates, A. A., (Otego,) farmer 150.
Goddard, S. & W. J., (Otego,) farmer 118.
GOODMAN, BALDWIN & PACKARD, (Otego,) (*George H. Goodman, Hiram Baldwin and H. O. Packard,*) carriage manufs.
GOODMAN, GEORGE H., (Otego,) (*Goodman, Baldwin & Packard.*)
Goodrich, C. Miss, (Otego,) tailoress.
Goodrich, Helen M. Miss, (Otego,) milliner.
Goodrich, S. & A., (Otego,) sash and blind manufs. and farmers 12.
Gould, Sylvenus, (Otego,) farmer 75.

Gray, J. C., (Otego,) painter.
Green, Adoniram, (Otego,) farmer 24.
Green, Geo., (Wells' Bridge,) farmer 80.
Green, Samuel, (Wells' Bridge,) farmer leases 100.
Gummon, D. N. Rev., (Otego,) Presbyterian clergyman.
Haight, Willis T., (Otego,) farmer 10.
Haines, John J., (Otego,) farmer 1.
Hallocker, Henry, (Otego,) farmer 75.
Harris, William, (Otego,) farmer 110.
Haskins, Russell J., (Otego,) farmer 7.
Hathway, Cyrus, (Otsdawa,) farmer 90.
Hathaway, Irenas, (Otego,) farmer 130.
Hathaway, Julius, (Otsdawa,) farmer 120.
Hathaway, Lysander, (Otsdawa,) farmer 100.
Haynes, Thomas, (Otego,) farmer 142.
Head, C. W., (Otego,) telegraph operator.
HENDRIX, HORACE, (Otsdawa,) blacksmith.
HENDRIX, S. W., (Otego,) justice of the peace and farmer 40.
Hess, S. J., (Otego,) farmer 146.
Hillsinger, Jacob, (Otego,) farmer 60.
Hoag, Ira J., (Otego,) druggist, Main,
Hodge, Philip, (Otego,) (*with Edwin Apley*,) farmer 140.
Holbrook Bros., (Otsdawa,) (*Otis and H. R.*,) harness makers.
Holbrook, H. R., (Otsdawa,) (*Holbrook Bros.*)
Holbrook, Otis, (Otsdawa,) (*Holbrook Bros.*)
Holden, Luther, (Otsdawa,) farmer leases 50.
Hopkins, Clark, (Otego,) farmer 160.
Hopkins, Lucy, (Otego,) farmer 6.
Hopkins, Nathan, (Otego,) farmer.
Horton, Adam, (Otego,) farmer 290.
Horton, Gilbert, (Otego,) farmer 125.
Horton, Theron, (Otego,) farmer 140.
Horton, W. L., (Otego,) livery, sale and exchange stable, River.
Hughston, Harriet, (Otego,) teacher.
Hulbert, Edward L., (Otsdawa,) farmer 85.
Hunt, Cyrus, (Otego,) farmer 15.
Hunt, Harvey, (Otego,) lawyer.
Hunt, John, (Otego,) farmer 170.
HUNT, S. E., (Otego,) (*M. Wilcox & Co.*)
Hunt, W. D., (Otego,) farmer 105.
Hunt, Wm. D., (Otego,) farmer leases of James Cole, 100.
Hurlburt, H. D., (Otego,) farmer 135.
Hurlbut, Amos, (West Oneonta,) farmer 28.
Hyatt, Geo. (Otsdawa,) farmer 21.
Hyatt, Isaac, (Otsdawa,) farmer 26.
HYATT, JOHN, (Otego,) farmer 50.
Hyde, Albert, (Otego,) carpenter.
Ivingston, Peter, (Otego,) farmer leases 92.
Jenks, Elmore, (Otsdawa,) farmer 190.
Jenks, J. L., (Otego,) farmer 50.
JENNINGS, A., (Otego,) prop. Susquehanna Valley Mill.
Jester, Daniel, (Otego,) farmer 12.
Jester, John, (Otego,) farmer 32.
Judd, Abel, (Otego,) farmer leases 335.
Judson, Russel, (Otego,) farmer 25.
Keller, Jacob, (Otego,) farmer leases of Edmond Emmons, 97.
Knapp, Theodore, (Otego,) farmer 50.
Lamb, Asa W., (Otego,) farmer 12.
Lamb, William C., (Otego,) farmer 125.

Laraway, Marvin J., (Otego,) wagon maker.
Lathrop, Morell, (Otego,) farmer leases 125.
Lent, James, (Otego,) farmer 25.
Lent, Lorenzo, (Otsdawa,) farmer works estate of Ezra Gates, 167.
Lewis, Morgan, (Otego,) farmer 100.
Livingston, Wm., (Otego,) farmer 145.
Livingston, William Jr., (Otego,) farmer 36.
Loomis, Jacob, (Otego,) farmer 2.
LOVELAND, J. S., (Otego,) prop. of Otego House.
Luther, Samuel B., (Otsdawa,) farmer 10.
Madison, David D., (West Oneonta,) farmer leases 65.
Madison, Pascal, (West Oneonta,) farmer 78.
Makham, Quartus, (Otego,) farmer 60.
Marble, F., (Otego,) farmer 97.
Marble, Thornton, (West Oneonta,) farmer 12.
Martin, Dewitt C., (Otego,) town assessor and farmer 130.
Martin, Elliott, (Otego,) hop raiser and farmer 90.
Martin, Geo., (Otego,) saw mill and farmer 267.
Martin, Theodore J., (Otego,) farmer 160.
Martin, Wallace, (Otego,) farmer.
MARTIN, WILLIAM W., (Otego,) commissioner of highways and farmer 100.
McCall, James, (Otego,) farmer 40.
McKever, Wilson, (Otego,) farmer leases 112.
MERITHEW, WM., (Otego,) prop. South Otsdawa Mill and farmer 107.
Merrick, Perry, (Otego,) billiard saloon.
Mevis, J. W. Rev., (Otego,) Methodist clergyman.
Miles, Harlow, (Otego,) farmer.
Miles, Timon, (Otego,) farmer 40.
MILLER, GILBERT, (Otego,) blacksmith.
Miller, H., (Otego,) photographer.
Miller, John, (Otsdawa,) farmer 65.
Moak, Jacob, (Wells' Bridge,) farmer 75.
Moak, James D., (West Oneonta,) farmer 140.
Mudge, Ed., (Otsdawa,) farmer.
Mudge, Rufus, (Otsdawa,) farmer 100.
Mumford, D., (West Oneonta,) farmer 60.
Myors, James, (Otego,) farmer 2.
Newland, Lester, (Otego,) farmer 19.
Newman, Joshua, (West Oneonta,) farmer 45.
Niles, D. Mrs., (Otego,) milliner.
Niles, J. H., (Otego,) justice of the peace.
Northrup, Samuel, (Otego,) farmer 130.
Northup, Robert, (Otego,) (*with Stephen D.*,) farmer 160.
Northup, Stephen D., (Otego,) (*with Robert*,) farmer 160.
Olmsted, C., (Otego,) farmer 125.
Olmsted, S. B., (Otego,) (*Clark & Olmsted.*)
OTEGO HOUSE, (Otego,) J. S. Loveland, prop.
*OTEGO RECORD, (Otego,) Alpheus S. Foote, editor and prop.
PACKARD, H. O., (Otego,) (*Goodman, Baldwin & Packard.*)
Parish, Asbury, (Otego,) farmer.
Parker, W. H., (Otego,) (*Cooks & Parker,*) town clerk.

Pearce, Leander, (Otego,) farmer 130.
Perry, Jane Mrs., (West Oneonta,) farmer 20.
Perry, John, (Otego,) carpenter.
PERRY, JOSIAH A., (West Oneonta,) farmer 85.
Perry, Marlow F., (West Oneonta,) farmer 185.
Phelps, Alfred, (Otego,) cooper.
Place, Gilbert, (Otego,) carpenter and farmer 85.
Place, Levi, (Otego,) farmer 70.
Place, Morgan, (Otego,) farmer leases 100.
Place, W. M., (Otego,) farmer leases 50.
Potter, Robert, (Otego,) farmer 105.
Price, Joseph, (Otego,) dry goods, clothing and millinery.
Quackenbush, Orlando, (Otego,) farmer 200.
Qualkenbush, Orrin, (Otego,) farmer.
RAILROAD HOUSE, (Otego,) Abram Rockwell, prop.
Randall, Hiram, (Otego,) farmer 56.
Rathbone, John, (Otego,) farmer.
Rathbone, Robert E., (Otego,) (Burdick & Rathbone.)
Rathbun, Emmet J., (Otego,) farmer 100.
Redington, Edgar, (Otego,) farmer 60.
Reed, William, (Otego,) farmer 50.
Reid, Platt, (Otego,) drover and farmer 50.
Reynolds, Jacob, (Otsdawa,) farmer 86.
Richardson, Jefferson, (Otego,) farmer.
Robbins, E. H., (Wells' Bridge,) agent for Elias Howe Sewing Machine and musical instruments, and farmer 100.
ROCKWELL, ABRAM, (Otego,) prop. Railroad House and farmer 75.
Root, Edward, (Otego,) (with Willard,) farmer 125.
Root, Lafayette, (Otego,) town assessor and farmer 150.
Root, Willard, (Otego,) (with Edward,) farmer 125.
Russell, J. E.,(Otego,) (Shepard & Russell.)
SAUNDERS, ELISHA S., (Otego,) physician and surgeon, Main.
SCRAMBLING, G. D., (Otego,) pianos, organs and musical merchandise, also life and fire insurance agent, Main.
SCRAMLING, CELESTIA Mrs., (Otego,) dairy and farmer 260.
Sheldon, Albert H., (Otego,) farmer.
Sheldon, Barber B., (Otego,) farmer 2.
Sheldon, Timothy, (Otego,) farmer 115.
Shepard, Charles A., (Otego,) speculator.
Shepard, F. E., (Otego,) (Shepard & Russell.)
Shepard, Geo., (Otego,) fruit dealer.
Shepard & Russell, (Otego,) (F. E. Shepard and J. E. Russell,) flour, grain &c.
Shepard, Wm. H., (Otego,) dairyman and farmer 110.
Shepherd, Augustus, (Otego,) dairyman and farmer 146.
Shepherd, Royal, (Otego,) farmer 60.
Sherman, Geo., (Otego,) meat market.
Shumway, F. D., (Otego,) principal of Otego Union School.
Sipley, Alonzo, (West Oneonta,) farmer 82½.
Sloan, S. S., (Otego,) station agent.
Smith, Alva, (Otego,) farmer 12.
Smith, A. D., (Otego,) merchant tailor, Main.

SMITH, CHARLES S., (Otego,) civil engineer and farmer 115.
Smith, Chauncy, (Otego,) farmer 350.
Smith & Decker, (Otsdawa,) (John J. Smith and Thomas Decker,) saw mill, grist mill and wagon shop.
Smith, Edward, (Otego,) farmer 110.
Smith, John Rev., (Otego,) Baptist minister and farmer 20.
Smith, John J., (Otsdawa,) (Smith & Decker.)
Smith, John V., (Otego,) farmer 100.
Smith, Thomas D., (Otego,) retired surveyor and farmer.
Smith, William O., (Otego,) dentist.
Snyder, Daniel, (Otego,) farmer 25.
SOUTH OTSDAWA MILL, (Otego,) Wm. Merithew, prop.
Southard, James, (Otego,) farmer 150.
Spencer, Wm., (Otego,) farmer 30.
Stanton, Chauncy, (West Oneonta,) farmer 4.
Starr, David O., (Otego,) farmer 106.
Starr, Edgar, (Otego,) (with Eli and Jesse,) farmer 175.
Starr, Eli, (Otego,) (with Jesse and Edgar,) farmer 175.
Starr, Jesse, (Otego,) (with Eli and Edgar,) farmer 175.
Stiles, Samuel, (Otego,) farmer leases 80.
Stilson, Charles, (Otego,) merchant.
Strait, James, (Otego,) farmer 1.
Strong, D. S., (Otego,) groceries and fruit.
Stuart, William, (Otego,) farmer 335.
Sullivan, Walter, (Otego,) farmer 140.
SUSQUEHANNA VALLEY MILL,(Otego,) A. Jennings, prop.
Tallmadge, Jerome H., (Otego,) drover and farmer 127½.
Taylor, S. W., (Otsdawa,) farmer 56.
TERPENING, JACOB, (Otego,) farmer 80.
Terry, Charles, (Otego,) farmer 184.
Terry, James, (Otego,) farmer 41.
Terry, James, (Otego,) hunter and farmer 7.
Thayer, Alfred, (West Oneonta,) farmer 60.
Thayer, Wm., (Otego,) farmer leases 36.
THOMAS, ALANSON REV., (Otego,) Baptist clergyman and farmer 200.
Thomas, William, (Otego,) farmer 110.
Thorp, Charles T., (Otego,) farmer 90.
Thorp, J. R., (Otego,) farmer 50.
Thorp, Orrin, (Otego,) farmer 40.
Thorp, Rutson, (Otego,) farmer.
Trask, Austin W., (Otego,) farmer 100.
Trask, Elisha A., (Otego,) farmer.
Trask, Henry S., (Otego,) farmer 58.
Trask, Justus L., (Otego,) farmer 95.
Trask, W., (Otego,) farmer 65.
Truman, Charles, (Otego,) farmer 80.
Utter, George, (Otego,) farmer 56.
Vandusen, Henry, (Otego,) farmer 30.
Vandusen, Tobias, (Otego,) farmer 44.
Vannamee, Wm., (Otego,) farmer 200.
Wait, Stephen, (Otego,) farmer 110.
Waite, E. F., (Otego,) farmer 90.
Walker, Dora N., (Otego,) preceptress Otego Union School.
Ward, Amasa, (West Oneonta,) farmer 25.
WARD, AMASA H., (West Oneonta,) agent for Kennedy's Revolving Mould Board Plow and farmer 82½.
Ward, Ansel, (Otego,) farmer 90.
Weatherly, B., (Otsdawa,) farmer 100.
Westcott, George, (Otego,) farmer 117.

WHEELER, E. R., (Otego,) carpenter and joiner, and farmer 2½.
Wheeler, John, (Otego,) farmer 70.
WHEELER, JOHN H., (Otego,) gunsmith.
White, W. D., (Wells' Bridge,) farmer 120.
Whitney, Henry, (Otego,) farmer 38.
WHITNEY, WM. M., (Otego,) (*L. Coburn & Co.*)
Wicks, L. D., (Otego,) shoemaker.
Wilbur, Johnson, (Otego,) farmer 80.
WILCOX, M., (Otego,) (*M. Wilcox & Co.*,) postmaster.
WILCOX, M. & CO., (Otego,) (*S. E. Hunt,*) general merchants, Main.

WILLIAMS, JOHN, (Otego,) farmer 25.
Williams, W. S., (Otego,) prop. Susquehanna House, Main.
Wilsey, Orville, (Otego,) farmer 400.
WILSEY, STEPHEN, (Otego,) farmer 140.
Wood, L., (Otego,) farmer.
Wood, Zelotus, (Otego,) farmer 150.
Wyckes, Joseph B., (Otego,) farmer 200.
Wyman, J. W., (Otego,) farmer 60.
Wyman, William, (Otego,) farmer 88.
YOUMANS, E. B., (Otego,) attorney and counselor at law, Main.
YOUNG, FITZ HENRY, (West Oneonta,) farmer 67.
Youngs, J. C., (Otsdawa,) farmer 20.

OTSEGO.

(Post Office Addresses in Parentheses.)

Adams, Eli B., (Fly Creek,) farmer 100.
Adams, John, (Toddsville,) farmer 2.
ADSIT, JAMES F., (Cooperstown,) head miller in Johnston's grist mill.
Alden, G. R. Rev., (Cooperstown,) pastor of Presbyterian Church.
Alger, Mary Miss, (Fly Creek,) millinery and fancy goods.
Alger, Silas W., (Fly Creek,) postmaster and wagon maker.
Allen, James, (Cooperstown,) farmer 115.
Allen, Shubael, (Oaksville,) farmer 120.
ALMY, E. J. MRS., (Toddsville,) (*with heirs,*) farmer 49 and leases 35.
Andrews, Anna Mrs., (Fly Creek,) (*with heirs,*) farmer 60.
Angell, Samuel, (Cooperstown,) groceries, provisions, flour and feed, Chestnut.
Archer, Alfred, (Hartwick,) carpenter.
Armstrong, Bradley A., (Cooperstown,) painter and prop. of livery stable, Chestnut.
Armstrong, Geo., Jr., (Oaksville,) farmer 48¼.
Augur, John W., (Phœnix Mills,) coal dealer and farmer 70.
Averell, Wm. H., (Cooperstown,) retired.
AVERY, D. A., (Cooperstown,) director Second National Bank of Cooperstown.
Babbett, Daniel, (Fly Creek,) shoemaker and farmer 93.
Babbit, Chester, (Fly Creek,) cheese factory and farmer 240.
Babcock, Abram, (Schuyler's Lake,) farmer 100.
BABCOCK, BINGHAM, (Schuyler's Lake,) (*with Norman,*) farmer 104.
BABCOCK, NORMAN, (Schuyler's Lake,) (*with Bingham,*) farmer 104.
Bailey, Charles, (Fly Creek,) farmer 90.

BAILEY, ERWIN H., (Cooperstown,) (*Bassett & Bailey.*)
BAILEY, JOHN S., (Cooperstown,) manuf. of shaved shingles and fanning mill sieves.
Bailey, Samuel C., (Fly Creek,) farmer 94.
Bailey & Thompson, (Cooperstown,) (*Wm. C. Bailey and Samuel K. Thompson,*) boots and shoes, Main.
Bailey, Wm. C., (Cooperstown,) (*Bailey & Thompson.*)
BALDWIN, LEONARD W., (Oaksville,) machinist and farmer 10.
Ball, Martha A. Miss, (Cooperstown,) teacher Cooperstown Union Free School.
Barnum, Abijah, (Cooperstown,) farmer 136.
Barton, Alpha, (Hartwick,) farmer.
Barton, Hiram, (Hartwick,) farmer 393.
*BASSETT & BAILEY, (Cooperstown,) (*Liston B. Bassett and Erwin H. Bailey,*) druggists, Main.
BASSETT, LISTON B., (Cooperstown,) (*Bassett & Bailey.*)
*BASSETT, MARY A. MRS., (Cooperstown,) physician, office in Russel Block.
*BASSETT, WILSON F., (Cooperstown,) physician and surgeon, office in Russel Block.
Bates, Albert, (Cooperstown,) farmer leases 100.
BATES, C. P., (Schuyler's Lake,) farmer 150.
Bates, Horace, (Cooperstown,) blacksmith.
*BAYER, HENRY, (Cooperstown,) merchant tailor and dealer in gents' furnishing goods, Main.
Beadle, Benj. F., (Cooperstown,) (*Beadle & Soule.*)

Beadle, B. F. Mrs., (Cooperstown,) boarding house.

Beadle, Erastus, (Cooperstown,) publisher of Beadle Dime Novels, New York.

Beadle, Geo. E., (Cooperstown,) farmer 64.

Beadle, Orville, (Cooperstown,) mechanic and farmer 3.

Beadle & Soule, (Cooperstown,) (*Benj. F. Beadle and Silas A. Soule*,) boots and shoes, corner Main and Pioneer.

Beattie, John A., (Oaksville,) farmer 2.

Becker, Peter, (Cooperstown,) president of village corporation.

BELL, EDWIN, (Cooperstown,) supt. and keeper of Lake Wood Cemetery.

Bellinger, Jacob A., (Cooperstown,) carpenter.

Benjamin, Rodolphus, (Fly Creek,) farmer 68.

Benjamin, Smith, (Oaksville,) farmer 47½.

BENTON, ORRIN, (Cooperstown,) cooperage, Lake.

BEST, PETER, (Oaksville,) blacksmith.

Bice, Ellen Miss, (Cooperstown,) dress maker.

Birge, Delos L., (Cooperstown,) ale brewery, River.

Bishop, Asel, (Hartwick,) farmer 60.

Bixby, Orris S., (Cooperstown,) (*Bixby & Stevens*.)

Bixby & Stevens, (Cooperstown,) (*Orrin S. Bixby and Ira W. Stevens*,) manufs. of artificial teeth and dealers in dental goods, corner Main and Pioneer.

Bliss, Henry, (Fly Creek,) retired farmer.

Bliss, S. T., (Cooperstown,) deputy post master.

Blodgett, Thomas S., (Cooperstown,) physician and surgeon, and postmaster.

Blunk, Jacob, (Schuyler's Lake,) farmer leases of A. Shaw, 132.

BODEN, DANIEL B., (Cooperstown,) groceries and liquors, prop. steamer *Mary Boden* and row and sail boats.

Boman, Abram, (Oaksville,) farmer 162.

Bourne, Menzo, (Cooperstown,) farmer 100.

BOURNE, ORLANDO, (Richfield Springs,) farmer leases 200.

Bowen, Eleazer, (Fly Creek,) farmer 80.

BOWEN, SAMUEL A., (Cooperstown,) attorney and counselor at law, Main.

*BOWES, JAMES, (Cooperstown,) plumber, steam and gas fitter, wholesale and retail dealer in wrought iron and lead pipe.

Bradford, Geo. S., (Cooperstown,) (*Story & Co.*)

BRADLEY, ANDREW J., (Cooperstown,) carpenter.

Brainard, Hobart A., (Schuyler's Lake,) farmer.

Brainard, Jared, (Cooperstown,) farmer 50.

Brainard, Jesse A., (Schuyler's Lake,) farmer.

BRAINARD, SHELDEN, (Schuyler's Lake,) farmer 181.

BRAUNSDORF & HECOX, (Cooperstown,) (*Robert L. Braunsdorf and Danford Hecox*.) contractors and builders.

BRAUNSDORF, ROBERT L., (Cooperstown,) (*Braunsdorf & Hecox*.)

Bristol, Sherman, (Hartwick,) farmer 100.

Brockway, Albert, (Cooperstown,) shoemaker, Main.

Brooks, Abel A., (Fly Creek,) blacksmith.

Brooks, Abram S., (Fly Creek,) blacksmith.

Brooks, Delos, (Fly Creek,) carriage maker.

Brooks, Geo., (Cooperstown,) (*Burditt & Brooks*,) notary public.

BROWN, LOREN, (Cooperstown,) blacksmith, Pioneer.

Brownell, Russel, (Fly Creek,) surveyor and farmer 70.

Browning & Hooker, (Cooperstown,) (*Stephen G. Browning and Horace M. Hooker*,) wholesale and retail dealers in coal, flour, feed, salt, &c., Main, near Depot.

Browning, Stephen G., (Cooperstown,) (*Browning & Hooker*.)

Buel, D. Hillhouse Rev., (Cooperstown,) rector of Christ Church.

Bullis, James, (Cooperstown,) house and sign painter, paper hanging &c.

BURCH, CHARLES R., (Cooperstown,) watches, clocks and jewelry, also treasurer village corporation, Main.

Burditt & Brooks, (Cooperstown,) (*Luther I. Burditt and Geo. Brooks*,) lawyers, 1st door west of 2d National Bank.

Burditt, L. I. (Cooperstown,) (*Burditt & Brooks*.)

Burnham, Alfred, (Oaksville,) deputy post master.

Butler, M. J., (Cooperstown,) principal stock holder Cooperstown Gas Light Works.

Butler, O. R., (Cooperstown,) supt. Cooperstown Gas Light Works.

BUTTERFIELD, HORACE, (Cooperstown,) supt. of Hope Factory.

Butts, Elijah, (Fly Creek,) (*Veber & Butts*.)

BYARD, BROS., (Oaksville,) (*James J. and John S.*,) cattle dealers and farmers 350.

BYARD, JAMES J., (Oaksville,) (*Byard Bros*.)

BYARD, JOHN S., (Oaksville,) (*Byard Bros*.)

Byram, Eliab P., (Cooperstown,) dentist, Fair.

CADY, B. M., (Cooperstown,) asst. cashier Second National Bank of Cooperstown.

CALAHAN, PATRICK, (Oaksville,) farmer 10.

Cane, John, (Fly Creek,) farmer leases of J. Hinds, 380.

Carpenter, Daniel, (Fly Creek,) mason and farmer 186.

CARR HOTEL, (Cooperstown,) Main, Wm. H. Scott, prop.

CARROLL, FRANK, (Cooperstown,) (*Carroll & Jarvis*.)

CARROLL & JARVIS, (Cooperstown,) (*Frank Carroll and Kent Jarvis*,) painters and decorators, Main.

Carter, Amos, (Cooperstown,) (*Persons & Carter*.)

CENTRAL HOTEL, (Cooperstown,) Main, Keyes & Son, props.

Chamberlin, Edward, (Cooperstown,) farmer 11½.

Chamberlin, ———, (Cooperstown,) (*Elwood & Chamberlin*.)

Chapman, Gilbert, (Hartwick,) farmer 100.

Chapman, Lewis, (Oaksville,) farmer 59½.

Chapman, Mason, (Schuyler's Lake,) farmer 50.

Chapman, Thomas, (Schuyler's Lake,) farmer 16.

Cheesebrough, Mary W. Mrs., (Oaksville,) farmer 31.

Cheesebrough, Stephen E., (Oaksville,) farmer 30.

Cheney, Charles H., (Fly Creek,) farmer works 100.

Cheney, Joseph A., (Fly Creek,) book agent.

Cheney, Stephen P., (Fly Creek,) farmer 84½.

Cheney, S. Wilson, (Fly Creek,) farmer 197½.

CHILDS, CHARLES, (Oaksville,) produce dealer and farmer 210.

CLARK, ALEXANDER H. Mrs., (Cooperstown,) (*with heirs*,) farmer 148.

CLARK, FRANK A., (Cooperstown,) hair dresser, basement Iron Clad Building, Main.

Clark, James F., (Cooperstown,) horse dealer and farmer leases 148.

Clark, Nancy Mrs., (Cooperstown,) (*with heirs*,) farmer 75.

Clark, Ruby A. Miss, (Cooperstown,) dress maker.

COATS, ALONZO B., (Fly Creek,) boot and shoe maker.

COATS, MARTIN, (Schuyler's Lake,) farmer 120.

Coats, Orlando, (Fly Creek,) farmer 85.

Cole, Gilbert A.,(Cooperstown,) farmer 112.

COLE & GRAY, (Cooperstown,) (*Nathan W. Cole and Noah D. Gray*,) groceries, provisions, flour and feed, agent for Danforth's non-explosive fluid, corner Main and Chestnut.

Cole, Martin H., (Cooperstown,) farmer leases of Gilbert A., 112.

COLE, NATHAN W., (Cooperstown,) (*Cole & Gray*.)

Coleman, Edward, (Oaksville,) farmer 100.

COLEMAN & MAXWELL, (Cooperstown,) (*Wm. B. Coleman and Albert Maxwell*,) props. of Cooper House, near Depot.

COLEMAN, WM. B., (Cooperstown,) (*Coleman & Maxwell*.)

COLLINS, THOMAS, (Cooperstown,) carpenter and joiner.

COLMAN, DEWITT C., (Cooperstown,) head sawyer with Johnston Brothers.

Colman, Lester, (Cooperstown,) farmer 60.

Comstock, Benajah, (Oaksville,) carding mill.

Comstock, Benajah, (Oaksville,) clothier and farmer 170.

Comstock, Deloss, (Oaksville,) farmer.

Connor, Michael, (Oaksville,) farmer 140.

CONRAD, HOMER A., (Schuyler's Lake,) farmer 145 and leases 85.

COOPER HOUSE, (Cooperstown,) near the Depot, Coleman & Maxwell, props.

Cooper, Peter P., (Cooperstown,) boat livery and fisherman.

COOPERSTOWN UNION FREE SCHOOL, (Cooperstown,) John G. Wight, principal; Charles P. Thompson, Miss Martha A. Ball, Miss Maggie K. Gaylord, Miss Sarah Shipway, Miss E. I. Reed, teachers.

Corwin, Thomas, (Cooperstown,) tailor, Pioneer.

Cory, Ellery, (Cooperstown,) (*Geo. Jarvis & Co.*)

Cory, Henry W., (Cooperstown,) town clerk, notary public and attorney, Iron Clad Building, Main.

Cory, Wm. E., (Cooperstown,) hardware, Main.

Counrod, Hiram, (Schuyler's Lake,) farmer 84.

Countryman, Edwin, (Cooperstown,) attorney, Main.

COYLE, MATHEW, (Cooperstown,)watchman in Hope Factory.

Crandall, Edward W., (Cooperstown,) book bindery, Pioneer.

Crippen, C. Schuyler, (Cooperstown,) (*Lake & Crippen*.)

CRIPPEN, SCHUYLER, (Cooperstown,) attorney and counselor at law, ex-judge of the Supreme Court, Main.

Cross, Aaron, (Schuyler's Lake,) blacksmith and farmer 6.

CRYDENWISE, H. M. REV., (Cooperstown,) pastor M. E. Church.

Curry, Thomas N., (Hartwick,) (*with Wm.*,) farmer 127.

Curry, Wm., (Hartwick,) (*with Thomas N.*,) farmer 127.

Dalphin, Margaret Mrs., (Cooperstown,) (*with heirs*,) farmer 13.

Dalphin, Robert G., (Cooperstown,) farmer 87.

Davidson, Frank, (Oaksville,) farmer 120.

DAVIDSON, LEWIS, (Fly Creek,) farmer 150.

Davidson, Nancy T., (Fly Creek,) farmer 30.

DAVIDSON, RICHARD, (Fly Creek,) ¾ interest in saw mill and farmer 217.

Davis, Robert, (Cooperstown,) groceries and provisions, corner Pioneer and Main.

DeLONG, DAMON H., (Richfield Springs,) farmer 134.

Denton, Theron, (Toddsville,) farmer 50.

DEVITT, M. C. REV., (Cooperstown,) pastor of Catholic Church at Cooperstown and Richfield Springs.

Doane, F. S., (Oaksville,) farmer 62½.

Doubleday, Emily W. Miss, (Cooperstown,) organist and music teacher, Pioneer.

Dubleday, Rufus C., (Fly Creek,) machinist.

Doubleday, Theodore N., (Fly Creek,) carpenter.

Doubleday, Wm. A., (Cooperstown,) farmer 150.

Drake, Chauncey N., (Cooperstown,) farmer 50 and leases of Ovid Drake, 77.

DRAKE, DANIEL W., (Cooperstown,) farmer 68.

Drake, Francis, (Oaksville,) farmer.

DRAKE, H. CLINTON, (Oaksville,) farmer 240.

Drake, Ovid, (Cooperstown,) farmer 77.

DUGGLEBY, HENRY H., (Cooperstown,) farmer 150.

DULEY, JAMES & SON, (Cooperstown,) leases grist mill, flour and custom mill.

Dunigan, Helen Mrs., (Cooperstown,) (*Dunigan & Hinman*.)

Dunigan & Hinman, (Cooperstown,) (*Mrs. Helen Dunigan and Mrs. Anna A. Hinman,*) millinery and ladies' furnishing goods, Main.

Eddy, Ransom, (Cooperstown,) farmer 119.

Edget, Peter, (Fly Creek,) farmer 110.

Edick, Samuel S., (Cooperstown,) notary public and county judge, Iron Clad Building.

EDWARDS, EDWARD, (agent,) (Cooperstown,) cabinet and chair dealer, Main.

Egleston, Ebenezer, (Oaksville,) farmer 53.

Eldred, T. W., (Cooperstown,) sewing machine agent, corner Main and Pioneer.

Eldred, Thomas, (Cooperstown,) sewing machine agent.

Eldridge, Truman, (Hartwick,) farmer 200.

Ellsworth, Anna Mrs., (Schuyler's Lake,) (*with heirs,*) farmer 400.

ELLSWORTH, SYLVESTER, (Schuyler's Lake,) farmer.

Elward, John, (Fly Creek,) farmer 10.

Elwood & Chamberlin, (Cooperstown,) props. of the W. U. telegraph line from Cooperstown to Richfield Springs.

ERNST, GEO. W., (Cooperstown,) (*C. W. Smith & Co.*)

Fellows, Chester, (Cooperstown,) harness manuf., Main.

Fern, John, (Fly Creek,) information refused.

Ferns, James, (Fly Creek,) farmer 140.

Field, Marcus, (Cooperstown,) (*Johnson & Field.*)

FING, PETER, (Richfield Springs,) (*with Philip,*) farmer 729.

FING, PHILIP, (Richfield Springs,) (*with Peter,*) farmer 729.

First National Bank of Cooperstown, (Cooperstown,) Calvin Graves, president; Fred. L. Palmer, cashier.

FISH, JEROME, (Cooperstown,) carriage maker and blacksmith, Pioneer.

FITCH, BUCKINGHAM, (Cooperstown,) farmer 102.

FIVE MILE POINT HOUSE, (Cooperstown,) John D. Tunnicliff, prop.

FLANSBURGH, ASA, (Cooperstown,) overseer in card room, Hope factory.

Fogarty, Michael, (Fly Creek,) farmer 3.

FRANKLIN, DANIEL, (Cooperstown,) sheriff and farmer 140, office Main.

FREEMAN, OLIVER, (Cooperstown,) farmer 100.

*FREEMAN'S JOURNAL, (Cooperstown,) S. M. Shaw, editor and prop.

Gardner, Albert, (Cooperstown,) farmer leases of J. Brainard, 50.

Gardner, Elisha P., (Cooperstown,) farmer 200.

Garlick, Zebulon G., (Cooperstown,) mechanic and farmer, superintends E. Phinney's farm.

Gaylord, Maggie K. Miss, (Cooperstown,) teacher Cooperstown Union Free School.

GEYVITS, ABRAM, (Richfield Springs,) farmer 100.

Gibbs, Elisha, (Fly Creek,) (*with Francis G. Jarvis,*) farmer 144½.

GIBBS, HENRY & SON, (Fly Creek,) (*Milo H.,*) farmers 91.

GIBBS, MILO H., (Fly Creek,) (*Henry Gibbs & Son.*)

Goffe, Frederick A., (Cooperstown,) treasurer and secretary of C. & S. V. R. R., office Main.

GOODENOUGH, JAMES C., (Cooperstown,) mason and builder.

GOODRICH, LUTHER, (Oaksville,) carpenter and joiner, and boarding house keeper.

Gould, John, (Cooperstown,) farmer.

GRAHAM, THOMAS, (Oaksville,) overseer of the mule room, Oaksville Cotton Mill.

Grant & Co., (Cooperstown,) (*Geo. M. Grant and Benj. F. Kipp,*) fancy goods, groceries &c., Main.

Grant, Geo. M., (Cooperstown,) (*Grant & Co.*)

Graves, Calvin, (Cooperstown,) president First National Bank of Cooperstown.

GRAVES, CALVIN, (Cooperstown,) (*C. W. Smith & Co.*)

GRAY, LEVI, (Cooperstown,) (*Gray & Shaw.*)

GRAY, NOAH D., (Cooperstown,) (*Cole & Gray.*)

GRAY & SHAW, (Cooperstown,) (*Levi Gray and George Shaw.*) house, carriage and sign painters, Main.

GRISWOLD, EDWARD N., (Cooperstown,) (*Griswold & White.*)

GRISWOLD & WHITE, (Cooperstown,) (*Edward N. Griswold and Geo. L. White,*) groceries, flour, feed, plaster, coal &c., Main St., main office near Depot.

Groat, Harmon, (Cooperstown,) prop. American Hotel, Pioneer.

*GROSS, G. H., (Fly Creek,) manuf. of horse powers, fanning mills, threshers and cleaners, &c.

Hadsell, David P., (Schuyler's Lake,) farmer leases of A. Shaw, 80.

Hannan, John, (Richfield Springs,) farmer 40.

HARPER, SAMUEL, (Cooperstown,) cabinet ware, chairs, chamber sets &c., Main.

HARRIS, E. M., (Cooperstown,) lawyer, Iron Clad Building, Main.

HARRIS, E. M., (Cooperstown,) (*C. W. Smith & Co.*)

Hartson, C. R., (Cooperstown,) Arbor Billiard Rooms, Pioneer.

Haswell, Betsey Mrs., (Cooperstown,) milliner, Elm.

HAYNES, S. IRVIN, (Cooperstown,) (*McIntosh & Haynes.*)

HECOX, DANFORD, (Cooperstown,) (*Braunsdorf & Hecox.*)

Hecox, Francis, (Oaksville,) farmer 240.

*HENDRYX, CHAS. F., (Cooperstown,) editor *Republican and Democrat.*

*HENDRYX, JAMES I., (Cooperstown,) editor and prop. *Republican and Democrat.*

HERDMAN, NORMAN W., (Cooperstown,) deputy county clerk, Main, house Eagle.

HERRICK, ELMAN C., (Oaksville,) deputy sheriff and miller leases grist mill of P. Johnson & Sons.

Herrick, Geo., (Schuyler's Lake,) farmer 60.

Hewes, Susan M. Miss, (Cooperstown,) milliner, Main.

HIGBY, BEECHER, (Oaksville,) farmer 100.

Higby, Thomas T., (Fly Creek,) overseer of the poor, dealer in agricultural implements and farmer 95.

HILLS, E. DELAVAN, (Cooperstown,) County Clerk, Main, house Eagle near Elm.

Hinds, Charles, (Cooperstown,) (*with Lewis,*) farmer 300.

HINDS, FAYETTE, (Fly Creek,) supervisor and farmer 350.

Hinds, Henry C., (Cooperstown,) farmer.

HINDS, JAMES, (Schuyler's Lake,) cattle dealer and farmer 137½.

HINDS, JOHN, (Schuyler's Lake,) farmer 65.

HINDS, LEWIS, (Cooperstown,) justice of the peace and (*with Charles,*) farmer 300.

HINDS, NEHEMIAH E., (Cooperstown,) farmer 100.

HINDS, OSCAR N.,(Cooperstown,) (*Hinds & Parshall.*)

*HINDS & PARSHALL, (Cooperstown,) (*Oscar N. Hinds and Israel Parshall,*) butchers and meat market, Main.

Hinman, Anna A. Mrs., (Cooperstown,) (*Dunigan & Hinman.*)

Hinman, G. D., (Cooperstown,) (*Tyley & Hinman.*)

Hoke Bros., (Cooperstown,) (*Menzo and Isaac,*) props. of cheese factory and farmers 300.

HOKE, ELIZABETH Mrs.,(Cooperstown,) resident.

Hoke, Isaac, (Cooperstown,) (*Hoke Bros.*)

Hoke, Menzo, (Cooperstown,) (*Hoke Bros.*)

HOKE, PHILIP J., (Cooperstown,) dairyman and farmer 270.

Holmes, Geo. W., (Cooperstown,) blacksmith, Lake.

HOMES, ERASTUS, (Oaksville,) Oaksville Cotton Mill.

HOOKER & Co., (Cooperstown,) (*H. M. Hooker, D. I. McCown and M. H. Lippitt,*) hardware, cutlery, stoves and tinware, Main.

Hooker, Horace, (Fly Creek,) mason.

HOOKER, HORACE M., (Cooperstown,) (*Hooker & Co.,*) (*Browning & Hooker,*) (*C. W. Smith & Co.*)

Hooker & Jarvis, (Cooperstown,) (*John B. Hooker and Henry K. Jarvis,*) insurance agents, Iron Clad Building, Main.

Hooker, John B., (Cooperstown,) (*Hooker & Jarvis.*)

Hooker, John B., (Fly Creek,) U. S. assessor for Otsego Co., fire and life insurance agent and farmer 105.

HOOSE & MOONEY, (Cooperstown,) (*Stephen H. Hoose and Thomas E. Mooney,*) carpenters and jobbers, corner Chestnut and Beaver.

HOOSE, STEPHEN H., (Cooperstown,) (*Hoose & Mooney.*)

Horn, Michael, (Schuyler's Lake,) farmer 100.

HOUSE, ALONZO, (Fly Creek,) farmer 71.

HOUSE, MENZO, (Richfield Springs,) farmer 125.

HOWES, ERASTUS, (Oaksville,) overseer of the weaving department, Oaksville Cotton Mill.

Hubbell, Elijah, (Cooperstown,) farmer works 80.

Hughs, Patrick, (Cooperstown,) blacksmith.

Hull, Alonzo, (Fly Creek,) farmer 6.

Hull, Geo., (Fly Creek,) farmer 91.

Hull, Irving D., (Fly Creek,) (*Randall & Hull.*)

Hull, Stephen, (Fly Creek,) farmer 28.

Hyde, Eli, (Cooperstown,) farmer 76½.

HYDE, GEO. D., (Cooperstown,) chief clerk in R. Steere's store at Hope Mills.

Hyde, Lucy Miss, (Fly Creek,) farmer 26.

INGHAM, JOHN, (Cooperstown,) boss weaver, Hope Factory.

JACKSON, JOHN H., (Cooperstown,) hair dresser, Main.

JARVIS, A. A., (Cooperstown,) (*C. W. Smith & Co.*)

Jarvis, Francis G., (Fly Creek,) (*with Elisha Gibbs,*) farmer 144½.

Jarvis, Geo. & Co., (Cooperstown,) (*Ellery Cory,*) undertakers, Main.

Jarvis, Henry K., (Cooperstown,) (*Hooker & Jarvis.*)

JARVIS, KENT, (Cooperstown,) (*Carroll & Jarvis,*) drugs, medicines, groceries, paints, oils &c., Main.

Jarvis, Lorenzo, (Schuyler's Lake,) farmer 160.

Jarvis, Lorenzo T., (Schuyler's Lake,) farmer 134.

Jarvis, Rufus P., (Schuyler's Lake,) farmer 50.

JOHNSON, DANIEL A., (Cooperstown,) butcher.

Johnson & Field, (Cooperstown,) (*Thomas Johnson and Marcus Field,*) merchant tailors, Main.

Johnson, James B., (Cooperstown,) (*Van Deusen & Johnson.*)

Johnson, James H., (Fly Creek,) farmer 200.

Johnson, Parley, (Oaksville,) (*Johnson & Son.*)

JOHNSON, P. E., M. D., (Cooperstown,) physician and lumber dealer.

Johnson, Richard P., (Oaksville,) (*Johnson & Son.*)

Johnson & Son, (Oaksville,) (*Parley and Richard P.,*) grist and saw mills, and farmers 100.

Johnson, Thomas, (Cooperstown,) (*Johnson & Field.*)

JOHNSTON BROTHERS, (Cooperstown,) (*F. U. and L. M.,*) props. of Otsego Mills, grist saw and planing, dealers in lumber, flour, feed and grain.

JOHNSTON, F. U., (Cooperstown,) (*Johnston Brothers,*) physician.

JOHNSTON, L. M., (Cooperstown,) (*Johnston Brothers.*)

JUDD, CHAUNCEY P., (Oaksville,) farmer 103¼.

KEESE, C. POMEROY, (Cooperstown,) vice president Second National Bank of Cooperstown.

KEESE, G. POMEROY, (Cooperstown,) president of Otsego Co. Agricultural Society and farmer 250.

Kelley, James, (Cooperstown,) farmer 34½.

KELLOGG, ALBERT, (Cooperstown,) farmer 65.

KELLOGG, GARRIT B., (Cooperstown,) boat builder.

Kellogg, Tracy, (Cooperstown,) farmer 66.

Kelsey, Asa, (Schuyler's Lake,) farmer 250.

Keyes, Daniel L., (Cooperstown,) prop. of St. James Hotel, Main.

KEYES & SON, (Cooperstown,) (*Webster C. and Squire W.,*) props. Central Hotel, Main.

KEYES, SQUIRE W., (Cooperstown,) (*Keyes & Son.*)

KEYES, WEBSTER C., (Cooperstown,) (*Keyes & Son.*)

KING, PETER, (Fly Creek,) farmer.

Kinney, D. D., (Schuyler's Lake,) road commissioner and farmer.

KINNEY, EPHRAIM F., (Oaksville,) farmer 118 and leases 62.

Kinney, Joseph P., (Schuyler's Lake,) cheese factory and farmer 200.

KINNEY, NANCY L., (Oaksville,) resident.

Kinney, Samuel, (Schuyler's Lake,) farmer 60.

KINNEY, SAMUEL K., (Schuyler's Lake,) farmer 121.

Kinney, Wm., (Schuyler's Lake,) farmer 100.

Kipp, Benj. F., (Cooperstown,) (*Grant & Co.*)

Knapp, Orsemus, (Cooperstown,) (*Wood & Knapp.*)

KNOWLTON, ACKLEY, (Fly Creek,) farmer 50.

KNOWLTON, SANFORD G., (Oaksville,) farmer 101½.

Kyser, Michael, (Schuyler's Lake,) farmer 14.

Lake & Crippen, (Cooperstown,) (*Nathaniel H. Lake and C. Schuyler Crippen,*) clothing, gents' furnishing goods, hats, caps &c., Main.

Lake, Edwin D., (Oaksville,) farmer 76.

Lake, Nathaniel H., (Cooperstown,) (*Lake & Crippen.*)

Lathrop, Horace, (Cooperstown,) physician.

LEANING, J. K., (Fly Creek,) physician and surgeon, justice of the peace and notary public.

LEE, F. A. & F. G., (Cooperstown,) insurance and real estate agents, Phinney Block.

LEE, F. G., (Cooperstown,) (*F. A. & F. G. Lee,*) cashier Second National Bank of Cooperstown.

Leg, E. J. Mrs., (Toddsville,) millinery.

LEWIS, EVAN D., (Cooperstown,) bank note printer with American Banking Co., New York.

Lewis, Evan D. Jr., (Cooperstown,) farmer.

LEWIS, JOHN, (Cooperstown,) clerk of Surrogate Court, lawyer and justice of the peace, Main.

LEWIS, SARAH W. Mrs., (Cooperstown,) farmer 88.

Linday, David, (Fly Creek,) farmer 113.

Lindsay, Geo., (Fly Creek,) farmer 116.

LIPPITT, M. H., (Cooperstown,) (*Hooker & Co.*)

Loper, R. F. Miss, (Cooperstown,) millinery and fancy goods, Main.

Lough, Geo. Jr., (Cooperstown,) farmer leases 62.

LOUGH, LOTTIE Mrs., (Cooperstown,) resident.

Low, Vital E., (Fly Creek,) farmer leases of T. P. Lewis, 100.

LUMLEY, CHRISTOPHER, (Fly Creek,) butcher.

Lumley, John, heirs of, (Fly Creek,) (*Mary Jane, Lydia and Melissa Lumley, and Mrs. E. Philips,*) farmers 258.

LYNES, JAMES A., (Cooperstown,) attorney and counselor at law, Main.

Mackey, John V., (Cooperstown,) farmer leases of Peter Sales, 133.

MARKEL, CHARLES N., (Cooperstown,) butcher.

MARVIN, THEODORE, (Fly Creek,) dealer in agricultural implements and farmer 114.

Marvin, T. Mrs., (Fly Creek,) millinery and fancy goods.

Masters, Burdett, (Cooperstown,) farmer 81.

Matteson, Wanton G., (Fly Creek,) carpenter.

MAXWELL, ALBERT, (Cooperstown,) (*Coleman & Maxwell.*)

McCABE BROTHERS, (Cooperstown,) (*Owen, Michael, Lawrence and Peter,*) stone dealers, masons and jobbers.

McCABE, LAWRENCE, (Cooperstown,) (*McCabe Brothers.*)

McCABE, MICHAEL, (Cooperstown,) (*McCabe Brothers.*)

McCABE, OWEN, (Cooperstown,) (*McCabe Brothers,*) farmer 18.

McCABE, PETER, (Cooperstown,) (*McCabe Bros.*)

McChesney, John, (Cooperstown,) blacksmith.

McCOWN, D. I., (Cooperstown,) (*Hooker & Co.*)

McDonald, Timothy, (Cooperstown,) marble works, Chestnut,

McEwan, Thomas, (Cooperstown,) farmer 152.

McEWEN, DAVID, (Cooperstown,) cheese maker, Hickory Grove Factory.

McEwen, John, (Cooperstown,) thresher and farmer 152.

McEWEN, JOHN A., (Cooperstown,) farmer 100.

McFarland, Reuben W., (Fly Creek,) farmer 77½.

McGuire, P. H., (Cooperstown,) billiard saloon, corner Main and Pioneer.

*McINTOSH & HAYNES, (Cooperstown,) (*Thomas McIntosh and S. Irvin Haynes,*) attorneys and counselors at law.

McINTOSH, THOMAS, (Cooperstown,) (*McIntosh & Haynes.*)

McNallay, Andrew, (Cooperstown,) farmer 60.

McRORIE, CHESTER, (Springfield Center,) farmer 96.

McRORIE PETER Jr., (Cooperstown,) farmer 96.

Merchant, Wm. H., (Cooperstown,) (*Story & Co.*)

Merrels, Wm., (Fly Creek,) cheese maker and farmer 54.

Merrit, Daniel, (Fly Creek,) (*with Hiram Pierce,*) farmer 44 and leases of C. Thayer, 75.

MERVIN, PETER JR., (Cooperstown,) farmer.

Metcalf, A. & A. W., (Fly Creek,) farmers 110.

MILLARD, DANIEL, (Oaksville,) overseer of carding and spinning department, Oaksville Cotton Mills.

Millis, Malvin M., (Cooperstown,) tin ware, stoves &c., Main.

Mills, H., (Cooperstown,) medical electrician.

Miner, Erastus, (Cooperstown,) farmer 16.

MOONEY, THOMAS E., (Cooperstown,) (*Hoose & Mooney.*)

MURDOCK, B. F., (Cooperstown,) (*Murdock & Bro.*)

*MURDOCK & BRO., (Cooperstown,) (*B. F. and H. K.*,) dry goods, crockery, groceries &c., Main.

MURDOCK, H. K., (Cooperstown,) (*Murdock & Bro.*)

NELSON, SAMUEL SEN., HON., (Cooperstown,) justice of the U. S. Supreme Court.

Nelson, S. Williams, (Cooperstown,) farmer 301.

NEWELL, C. A., (Cooperstown,) (*Newell & Pank.*)

*NEWELL & PANK, (Cooperstown,) (*C. A. Newell and John Pank, H. F. Phinney, special partner,*) builders and jobbers, manufs. of sash, blinds, doors, mouldings &c., opposite Depot.

NEWKIRK, GEO., (Cooperstown,) farmer.

Niles, J. L. Miss, (Cooperstown,) dress maker, Lake.

Niles, Oscar, (Fly Creek,) carpenter.

Northrup, E. B., (Hartwick,) farmer 120.

Northrup, Wm., (Oaksville,) farmer 60.

Palmer, Fred. L., (Cooperstown,) cashier First National Bank of Cooperstown.

OLENDORF, E. A., (Fly Creek,) prop. of hotel and deputy U. S. marshall.

Olendorf, Morris, (Fly Creek,) manuf. of horse rakes.

OTSEGO MILLS, (Cooperstown,) grist, saw and planing, Johnston Bros., props.

PANK, JOHN, (Cooperstown,) (*Newell & Pank.*)

PARMELEE, EDWARD C., (Fly Creek,) carpenter.

PARSHALL, ISRAEL, (Cooperstown,) (*Hinds & Parshall.*)

Parsons, George Rev., (Fly Creek,) pastor of M. E. Church.

Pashley, Joseph, (Hartwick,) farmer 46.

Pashley, Samuel, (Hartwick,) farmer 130.

PATTEN, MERRICK R., (Fly Creek,) lumberman and farmer 140.

Paul, Caleb J., (Cooperstown,) wagon maker, Chestnut.

Pearsall, Simon, (Fly Creek,) machinist.

Pearson, John, (Cooperstown,) farmer 50.

PEARSON, JOHN K., (Cooperstown,) farmer.

Peck, Daniel, (Cooperstown,) prop. of Clinton Hotel, Pioneer.

Peck, Wm., (Oaksville,) farmer 65.

Perkins, Orrin Rev., (Cooperstown,) Universalist minister.

PERKINS, PHILO W., (Oaksville,) farmer 64.

PERSE, ROBERT, (Cooperstown,) (*Smith & Co.*)

Persons & Carter, (Cooperstown,) (*Wm. C. Persons and Amos Carter,*) saloon, Main.

Persons, Wm. C., (Cooperstown,) (*Persons & Carter.*)

PETRIE, DAVID, (Cooperstown,) macinist, Hope Factory.

PETRIE, IRVING, (Cooperstown,) boss mule spinner, Hope Factory.

Phinney, Alucia, (Schuyler's Lake,) berries and small fruit 2.

PHINNEY, ELIHU, (Cooperstown,) originally of the firm of Phinney & Co., Buffalo, subsequently of Phinney, Blakeman & Mason, New York, book publishers, now retired, owns 450 acres.

PHINNEY, H. F., (Cooperstown,) (*Newell & Pank.*)

PICKENS, IRVING, (Richfield Springs,) farmer 50.

PIERCE, ELIZUR, (Fly Creek,) farmer 93.

Pierce, Frederick, (Fly Creek,) moulder and farmer 12½.

Pierce, Hiram, (Fly Creek,) (*with Daniel Merrit,*) farmer 44 and leases of C. Thayer, 75.

PLATTS, A. I., (Cooperstown,) carpenter and joiner.

Plumb, Leander, (Oaksville,) retired clothier and farmer 26.

Potter, Colonel A., (Fly Creek,) marble works.

POTTER, PHILIP H., (Cooperstown,) brick yard and farmer 200.

POTTS BROTHERS, (Cooperstown,) (*John and Thomas,*) props. of hotel at Oaksville, farmers 175 and lease of Geo. Potts, 125.

Potts, George, (Cooperstown,) farmer 125.

POTTS, JOHN, (Cooperstown,) (*Potts Brothers.*)

POTTS, THOMAS, (Cooperstown,) (*Potts Brothers.*)

Preston, Alson, (Oaksville,) farmer 50.

Preston, Rufus, (Oaksville,) farmer 400.

Prosser, Napoleon, (Fly Creek,) farmer 100.

Quaip, Robert, (Cooperstown,) hop dealer.

QUAIS, SAMUEL, (Fly Creek,) farmer 80 and leases of F. Taylor, 140.

Randall, Daniel B., (Fly Creek,) (*Randall & Hull.*)

Randall & Hull, (Fly Creek,) (*Daniel B. Randall and Irving D. Hull,*) props. of saw, grist and shingle mills.

Redfern, James, (Hartwick,) farmer 53.

Reed, E. I. Miss, (Cooperstown,) teacher Cooperstown Union Free School.

Reed, Hiram, (Cooperstown,) farmer 62.

*REPUBLICAN AND DEMOCRAT, (Cooperstown,) Jas. I. Hendryx, prop., James I. and Chas. F. Hendryx, editors, Pioneer.

Richards, Daniel, (Hartwick,) farmer 65.

Risedorph, Carrie Miss, (Cooperstown,) millinery and ladies' furnishing goods, Main.

Roberts, Frederick, (Oaksville,) (*with J. P. and Homer,*) farmer 315.

Roberts, Homer, (Oaksville,) (*with J. P. and Frederick,*) farmer 315.

Roberts, J. P., (Oaksville,) town assessor and (*with Frederick and Homer,*) farmer 315.

Robinson, F. M. & Co., (Cooperstown,) hardware, stoves &c., Main.

Rockwell, Anson Mrs., (Cooperstown,) weaver and farmer 11.

ROOT, CHARLES L., (Cooperstown,) carpenter and builder.

ROSE, ORTON G., (Schuyler's Lake,) farmer 212.

Rosenthal, Morris, (Cooperstown,) merchant tailor, Main.

RUGGLES, WM. H., (Cooperstown,) bookseller and stationer, Pioneer.

RUSSELL, LEVI N., (Cooperstown,) farmer 158.

Russell, Lucian G., (Cooperstown,) school teacher.

RUSSELL, PARDON H., (Fly Creek,) farmer leases 88.

RUSSELL, RICHARD, (Oaksville,) farmer 200.

*RUSSELL, ROBERT & CO., (Cooperstown,) (*Wm, H. Russell,*) Central Cash Store, dry goods, groceries &c., Main.

RUSSELL, WM. H., (Cooperstown,) (*Robert Russell & Co.*)

Ryan, Andrew, (Fly Creek,) farmer 4.

SAVAGE, MARY MRS., (Cooperstown,) dress maker, Main.

SCOFIELD, BYRON J., (Cooperstown,) lawyer and surrogate.

Schrom, Jasper A., (Cooperstown,) watch repairer and jeweler, Main.

SCOTT, JOHN F., (Cooperstown,) hop merchant, office Main.

SCOTT, WM. H., (Cooperstown,) prop. of Carr Hotel, Main.

Scribner, Geo. D., (Fly Creek,) farmer 47.

SECOND NATIONAL BANK OF COOPERSTOWN, (Cooperstown,) capital $300,000; Jedediah P. Sill, president; C. Pomeroy Keese, vice-president; F. G. Lee, cashier; B. M. Cady, asst. cashier.

Seeber, Jacob, (Oaksville,) horse and cattle dealer, and farmer 917.

SEYMOUR, MARGARET MISS, (Cooperstown,) agent for A. B. Howe Sewing Machine, Main.

SHAW, ANDREW, (Cooperstown,) hop and wool merchant, established 1852, Main.

Shaw, Charlotte M., (Cooperstown,) cheese maker.

SHAW, GEORGE, (Cooperstown,) (*Gray & Shaw.*)

Shaw, James, (Hartwick,) farmer 130.

*SHAW, SAMUEL M., (Cooperstown,) editor and prop. of *Freeman's Journal.*

Shaw, Thomas, (Cooperstown,) blacksmith, Chestnut.

Shaw, Wm., (Schuyler's Lake,) butcher and farmer 196.

SHAW, WM. W., (Oaksville,) supt. of Oaksville Cotton Mill.

Shepard, Emily Mrs., (Cooperstown,) farmer 32.

Shepard, Francis, (Cooperstown,) farmer 42.

Shepard, Tracy G., (Cooperstown,) carpenter and farmer 56.

Shepard, T. & W., (Cooperstown,) farmers 184.

Shepherd, James E., (Fly Creek,) machinist.

*SHEPHERD, WM., (Fly Creek,) manuf. of stationary and portable steam engines, circular saw mills, flour mills and castings of all kinds.

Shipway, Sarah Miss, (Cooperstown,) teacher Cooperstown Free School.

Sholes, George W., (Cooperstown,) dry goods and groceries, Main.

Shumway, Allen, (Toddsville,) farmer 3.

SILL, JEDEDIAH P., (Cooperstown,) president Second National Bank of Cooperstown.

SILVERNAIL, LEVI, (Cooperstown,) boss of spinning room, Hope Factory.

Sitts, Wm., (Cooperstown,) farmer 160.

Siver, Datus E., (Cooperstown,) dentist, corner Main and Pioneer.

Small, Frederick, (Cooperstown,) farmer leases of Mrs. A. A. Winsor, 190.

Smith, Alexander W., (Cooperstown,) farmer 110.

Smith, Charles C. Rev., (Cooperstown,) pastor of Baptist Church.

SMITH & CO., (Cooperstown,) (*Nelson Smith and Robert Perse,*) butchers and meat market, Pioneer.

*SMITH, C.W. & CO., (Cooperstown,) (*Calvin Graves, E. M. Harris, A. A. Jarvis, Geo. W. Ernst, H. M. Hooker and other associates,*) bankers.

Smith, Ezra, (Cooperstown,) attorney, Iron Clad Building, Main.

Smith, F. Scott, (Cooperstown,) express agent and telegraph operator, Main.

SMITH, G., (Cooperstown,) (*R. H. & J. C. Smith & Co.*)

SMITH, HENRY, (Cooperstown,) carpenter and joiner.

SMITH, JOHN C., (Cooperstown,) mason.

Smith, Miller, (Cooperstown,) farmer 68.

SMITH, NELSON, (Cooperstown,) (*Smith & Co.*)

SMITH, R. H. & J. C. & CO., (Cooperstown,) (*G. Smith,*) master masons, contractors and builders.

Smith, Thomas B., (Cooperstown,) allo. physician and surgeon, Main.

SMITH, WASHINGTON G., (Cooperstown,) photographer, Main.

Scott, Samuel, (Fly Creek,) farmer 60.

Soule, Silas A., (Cooperstown,) (*Beadle & Soule,*) boarding house, corner Main and Chestnut.

Southerland, Ira, (Schuyler's Lake,) farmer 144.

Sprague, Hezekiah B., (Cooperstown,) farmer 90.

SPRAGUE, JENKS S., (Cooperstown,) farmer.

SQUIER, J. J. MRS., (Cooperstown,) (*with heirs,*) farmer 200.

STAFFORD, JAMES, (Fly Creek,) farmer leases of C. Childs, 90.

STEERE, J. H., (Oaksville,) (*J. H. & R. Steere,*) postmaster.

STEERE, J. H. & R., (Oaksville,) merchants.

Steere, R., (Cooperstown,) prop. of three cotton mills, grist mill and two stores, also a store and cotton mill in town of Hartwick.

Stephens, Carloss, (Toddsville,) carpenter.

Stephens, Roswell, (Oaksville,) farmer 16.

Stevens, Ira W., (Cooperstown,) (*Bixby & Stevens.*)

O

STEVENS, WM B.,(Cooperstown,) manuf. and dealer in ready made boots and shoes, Main.

Stickle, Robert, (Cooperstown,) butcher and farmer leases of G. Niles, 22.

Story & Co., (Cooperstown,) (Joshua H. Story, George S. Bradford and Wm. H. Merchant,) dry goods, Main.

Story, Joshua H., (Cooperstown,) (Story & Co.)

Stowell, Harvey, (Richfield Springs,) farmer 250.

Sturges, Hezekiah, (Cooperstown,) attorney, Main.

Taft, Thomas, (Cooperstown,) mason and farmer 120.

TANNER, FRED. P., (Cooperstown,) (Tanner & Son.)

Tanner, Mary Ann Mrs., (Cooperstown,) (with heirs,) farmer 73.

TANNER, PERRY G., (Cooperstown,) (Tanner & Son.)

*TANNER & SON, (Cooperstown,) (Perry G. and Fred. P.,) watch makers and jewelers, Main.

Taylor, Alexander, (Fly Creek,) farmer 130.

TAYLOR, ALLEN, (Fly Creek,) farmer 170.

Taylor, Chester, (Fly Creek,) nurseryman and farmer 88.

TAYLOR, FRANCIS, (Fly Creek,) one-fourth interest in saw mill and farmer 160.

TAYLOR, HORACE E., (Fly Creek,) prop. of Fly Creek Valley Cheese Factory and farmer 38.

TAYLOR, LANCELOT, (Fly Creek,) estate of late Horace Taylor, commissioner of highways and farmer 118.

Taylor, Lester, (Fly Creek,) farmer 275.

TAYLOR, THOMAS, (Fly Creek,) farmer 182.

Temple, Geo. A., (Cooperstown,) school teacher.

*THAYER, ALMOND W., (Cooperstown,) prop. of Three Mile Point House, (summer resort,) and farmer 30.

Thompson, Charles P., (Cooperstown,) teacher Cooperstown Union Free School.

Thompson, Samuel K., (Cooperstown,) (Bailey & Thompson.)

THORN, CALVIN C., (Cooperstown,) carpenter and joiner.

Thorp, Earl P., (Oaksville,) farmer leases of Mrs. E. D. Preston, 103.

THREE MILE POINT HOUSE, (Cooperstown,) (summer resort,) Almond W. Thayer, prop.

Thurston, Elias, (Schuyler's Lake,) farmer 70.

Thurston, John, (Cooperstown,) farmer 24.

Thyer, Caleb, (Cooperstown,) farmer 140.

Tompson, Benj., (Fly Creek,) farmer 31.

Tral, Wm., (Cooperstown,) boss dresser, Hope Factory.

Truax, A. Mrs.,(Cooperstown,) (with heirs,) farmer 100.

Tunecliff, Walter, (Oaksville,) farmer 180.

TUNNICLIFF, JOHN D., (Cooperstown,) prop. of Five Mile Point House and farmer 30.

Turner, Sumner E., (Fly Creek,) teamster.

Tyley, G., (Cooperstown,) (Tyley & Hinman.)

Tyley & Hinman, (Cooperstown,) (G. Tyley and G. D. Hinman,) merchants, Main.

Underwood, Orlo C., (Richfield Springs,) farmer 50.

Van Benschoten, Elias, (Cooperstown,) farmer 62.

Van Court, Daniel P., (Fly Creek,) merchant.

Vanderwerken, J. D., (Cooperstown,) wholesale dealer in liquors.

Van Deusen, Charles M., (Cooperstown,) (Van Deusen & Johnson.)

Van Deusen & Johnson, (Cooperstown,) (Charles M. Van Deusen and James B. Johnson,) marble works, Pioneer.

Van Horn, Abram C., (Cooperstown,) farmer 88.

Van Horn, Albert, (Cooperstown,) farmer 70.

Van Horn, Abram T., (Cooperstown,) farmer 183.

VAN HORN, ALBERT T., (Cooperstown,) school teacher and farmer.

Van Horn, Cornelius, (Schuyler's Lake,) farmer 143.

Van Horn, Cornelius, (Schuyler's Lake,) farmer 60.

VAN HORNE, RICHARD, (Cooperstown,) farmer 221.

VAN HORNE, WALTER, (Cooperstown,) farmer 206.

VAN VALKENBURG, CEYLON, (Schuyler's Lake,) farmer.

Van Valkenburgh, Peter, (Schuyler's Lake,) farmer 196.

Veber & Butts, (Fly Creek,) (Jerome Veber and Elijah Butts,) blacksmiths.

Veber, Jerome, (Fly Creek,) (Veber & Butts.)

WADSWORTH, CHESTER I., (Cooperstown,) dentist, Main.

Waldby, Wm., (Cooperstown,) grist mill.

Wale, Edward, (Cooperstown,) W. U. telegraph operator, Main.

Wallace, M. Miss, (Cooperstown,) school teacher.

Wallace, Spencer A., (Cooperstown,) school teacher.

WALRADT, DELOS, (Cooperstown,) carpenter, jobber and builder.

*WALRATH BROTHERS, (Cooperstown,) (O. J. and J.,) jobbers and builders.

Walrath, James, (Schuyler's Lake,) farmer leases of A. Shaw, 70.

WALRATH, J., (Cooperstown,) (Walrath Brothers.)

WALRATH, O. J., (Cooperstown,) (Walrath Brothers.)

Walrath, Oliver, (Cooperstown,) farmer 80.

Warren, Charlotte, (Cooperstown,) resident.

Warren, Cyrenus,(Cooperstown,) farmer 35.

Warren, Erastus, (Cooperstown,) farmer 120.

Warren, Joseph, (Cooperstown,) farmer 50.

WARREN, JULIUS, (Cooperstown,) farmer leases of Erastus Warren. 120.

WARREN, RUSSEL, (Cooperstown,) farmer 155.

WARREN, WM. K., (Cooperstown,) farmer 125.

Watkins, A. H., (Cooperstown,) general ticket and passenger agent C. & S. V. R. R., and prop. of steamer *Nattie Bumps.*

Wedderspoon, David, (Cooperstown,) farmer 120.

Wedderspoon, Geo., (Cooperstown,) dairyman, farmer 122 and leases of Abram T. Van Horn, 100.

WEDDERSPOON, JAMES, (Cooperstown,) farmer 71.

WEDDERSPOON, MORTIMER H., (Cooperstown,) cheese manuf., Metcalf Hill Factory.

Weeks, Lewis, (Hartwick,) farmer 140.

WELDEN, LEANDER, (Cooperstown,) constable and farmer 150.

Welden, Nicholas, (Richfield Springs,) farmer leases of H. Stowell, 250.

WELLMAN, GEO. B., (Cooperstown,) blacksmith and wagon maker, corner Main and Chestnut.

WHEELER, DANIEL, (Toddsville,) carpenter and builder, and farmer 410.

WHIPPLE, FENIMORE C., (Cooperstown,) farmer 76.

Whipple, James M., (Cooperstown,) farmer 150.

WHITE, GEO. L., (Cooperstown,) (*Griswold & White,*) captain engine No. 1.

White, Joel G., (Cooperstown,) harness maker and carriage trimmer, Main.

Whitwell, Thomas, (Cooperstown,) farmer 62.

WIGHT, JOHN G., (Cooperstown,) principal Cooperstown Union Free School.

Wikoff, Rufus, (Cooperstown,) farmer 225.

Wilcox, Alfred, (Fly Creek,) farmer 35.

Wiles, John, (Oaksville,) farmer 275.

Wiley, Jane Mrs., (Oaksville,) (*with heirs,*) farmer 60.

*WILLIAMS, CHANCEY, (Cooperstown,) prop. of saw mill, cider mill and shingle mill, lath maker, saw gummer and farmer 14.

Williams, Daniel, (Fly Creek,) prop. of grist and saw mill, carpenter and farmer 12.

WILLIAMS, HARVEY, (Cooperstown,) patentee of the Self-Feeding Feed Cutter, patented Sept. 24, 1867, and farmer 114.

Williams, H. Mrs., (Cooperstown,) (*with heirs,*) farmer 94.

Williams, John C., (Fly Creek,) prop. of cider mill and farmer 99.

Williams, Justin, (Cooperstown,) farmer 3.

Williams, Sherman, (Fly Creek,) farmer 79.

Williams, Silas R., (Fly Creek,) sawyer and farmer 64.

Williams, William, (Fly Creek,) retired farmer.

Wilsie, Lothe Miss, (Cooperstown,) dress maker.

Wilson, John, (Hartwick,) wall layer and farmer 30.

Wilson, Washington, (Cooperstown,) justice of the peace, ticket and freight agent C. & S. V. R. R.

WILSON, WM. W., (Toddsville,) supt. of Otsego Paper Works.

Wiltse, Adolphus, (Richfield Springs,) farmer 130.

Wiltse, H., (Richfield Springs,) farmer 144.

WOOD, JOHN, (Cooperstown,) butcher and meat market, Main.

Wood & Knapp, (Cooperstown,) (*Walter Wood and Orsemus Knapp,*) props. Central Livery, Main.

Wood, Lewis G., (Hartwick,) farmer 155.

Wood, Walter, (Cooperstown,) (*Wood & Knapp.*)

Woolsey, ———, (Toddsville,) carpenter.

Worthington Bank, (Cooperstown,) J. R. Worthington, president; John Worthington, cashier; Main.

Worthington, John, (Cooperstown,) cashier Worthington Bank, Main.

Worthington, J. R., (Cooperstown,) president Worthington Bank, Main.

WRIGHT, IRA, (Oaksville,) overseer of dressing department, Oaksville Cotton Mill.

YATES, JOHN W., (Richfield Springs,) saw mill, cheese box manuf. and farmer 28.

Young Men's Association, (Cooperstown,) Elihu Phinney, president; Samuel A. Bowler, corresponding secretary; Iron Clad Building.

Youngs, Henry, (Richfield Springs,) farmer leases 103.

Youngs, Lewis P., (Schuyler's Lake,) farmer 100.

PITTSFIELD.

(Post Office Addresses in Parentheses.)

ALLEN, HENRY, (Pittsfield,) farmer.
Ames, Sett, (New Berlin, Chenango Co.) farmer 15.
Angel, Ansel, (New Berlin, Chenango Co.,) farmer 100.
Angell, Jonathan, (New Berlin, Chenango Co.,) hop raiser and farmer 100.
Atwell, Amos, (Morris,) farmer 70.
ATWELL, JASON, (Pittsfield,) farmer.
Austin, John, (New Berlin, Chenango Co.,) hop raiser and farmer 70.
Aylesworth, Henry, (New Berlin, Chenango Co.,) carpenter.
Aylesworth, Robinson, (New Berlin, Chenango Co.,) farmer occupies 175.
Aylesworth, Samuel, (New Berlin, Chenango Co.,) farmer 175.
Babcock, Delos, (New Berlin, Chenango Co.,) farmer 112.
BACKUS, GEO. N., (New Berlin, Chenango Co.,) farmer.
Backus, Heman, (New Berlin, Chenango Co.,) farmer 77.
Backus, Leonard, (New Berlin, Chenango Co.,) farmer 57.
Backus, Solomon, (Morris,) assessor, hop raiser, dairyman and farmer 150.
Bailey, Alvah, (New Berlin, Chenango Co.,) farmer 72.
Ball, Thomas, (Morris,) rope maker.
Barber, Hiram, (Morris,) farmer occupies 50.
Barber, Mary, (Morris,) farmer 50.
Barber, Palmer, (Morris,) farmer 90½.
Barber, Richard, (Garrattsville,) carpenter and farmer 55.
Bard, Edwin M., (Morris,) farmer 75.
Bartholomew, James, (New Berlin, Chenango Co.,) farmer 88.
BASSETT, W. C., (Pittsfield,) carpenter.
Beardslee, Charles, (New Berlin, Chenango Co.,) farmer 105.
Beardslee, Cyrel, (New Berlin, Chenango Co.,) farmer 109 and owns in Texas, 16,000.
Beardslee, Jesse, (New Berlin, Chenango Co.,) justice of the peace, hop raiser, dairyman and farmer 681.
Beardslee, Reoloff T., (New Berlin, Chenango Co.,) farmer 165.
Beatty, John, (New Berlin, Chenango Co.,) farmer 42.
Beatty, Robert, (New Berlin, Chenango Co.,) farmer 84.
BECKWITH, ANDREW, (Pittsfield,) farmer.
Bemis, Julia A., (Morris,) farmer 25.

BEMIS, ORIN, (Morris,) prop. of saw mill, dealer in lumber, sash, blinds &c., and farmer 136.
Benjamin, John A., (Pittsfield,) dairyman and farmer leases 100.
Bennett, Calvin. (Garrattsville,) farmer 52.
BENNETT, EZRA, (New Berlin, Chenango Co.,) farmer.
Bennett, Richard, (Pittsfield,) farmer 128.
BENNETT, SOLOMON, (Pittsfield,) farmer.
Billings, Hiram R., (New Berlin, Chenango Co.,) farmer 53.
Blackwell, Evert, (New Lisbon,) physician.
Boardman, Spencer, (Pittsfield,) farmer 54.
Bolls, Frederick, (Morris,) rope manuf. and farmer 64.
Bourne, Richard, (New Berlin, Chenango Co,) farmer 157.
Brace, Joseph, (Pittsfield,) farmer 6.
Briggs, Francis, (Pittsfield,) farmer 105.
Briggs, Wm., (Pittsfield,) farmer 98.
Brown, Jonathan, (Morris,) retired farmer 89.
Brownel, Wm. H., (New Berlin, Chenango Co.,) farmer 37.
Bruce, Daniel, (Morris,) dairyman and farmer 100.
BRUCE, ERVIN J., (Morris,) drover and farmer 80.
Bruce, Julius, (Pittsfield,) farmer 7½.
BUNDY, SETH, (Pittsfield,) farmer.
BURDICK, LEWIS, (Pittsfield,) teacher.
Burlingame, Isaac, (New Berlin, Chenango Co.,) farmer 31.
Button, Lucy, (Morris,) farmer 63.
Cady, Anna E.,(New Berlin, Chenango Co.,) (*with heirs*,) farmer 160.
Cady, Edwin H., (New Berlin, Chenango Co.,) dairyman and farmer leases 160.
CADY, PERKINS, (New Berlin, Chenango Co.,) farmer.
Cady, Willis, (New Berlin, Chenango Co.,) farmer.
Card, Chester, (Pittsfield,) postmaster and farmer 130.
Card, Francis, (Morris,) farmer 50.
Card, Job, (Pittsfield,) farmer 170.
CARD, REUBEN, (Pittsfield,) farmer.
Carpenter, Levi, (Pittsfield,) farmer.
Carr, Green, (Morris,) farmer 65.
Carr, Richard, (Morris,) farmer.
Chapin, Ezekiel, (Pittsfield,) farmer 222.
Chapin, John T., (Pittsfield,) dairyman, hop raiser and farmer 160.
Chase, Amasa, (Pittsfield,) farmer 55.
Chase, Ambrose, (Morris,) farmer 18.

Chase, Daniel, Morris,) farmer 142.
Chase, Daniel B., (Pittsfield,) farmer 100.
Chase, Eliakim. (Pittsfield,) farmer 123.
Chase, John, (Morris,) cooper and farmer 47.
Chase, Joseph, (Pittsfield,) farmer 291.
Chase, Joseph L., (Pittsfield,) farmer 77.
Chase, Polly Mrs., (Pittsfield,) (with heirs,) farmer 30.
Chase, Ruth D., (Pittsfield,) farmer 31.
Church, Wm. H., (Pittsfield,) farmer 146.
Clark, James, (New Berlin, Chenango Co.,) farmer 4.
Clark, Orsemus, (Pittsfield,) farmer 50.
Coats, Silas A., (Pittsfield,) assessor and farmer 159.
Cogshall, Curtis, (Morris,) farmer 50.
Collier, Mortimer, (Pittsfield,) farmer 84.
Conkey, Wm. F., (New Berlin, Chenango Co.,) farmer 95.
Conner, John O., (Pittsfield,) farmer 10.
Cook, Harvey M., (Garrattsville,) farmer.
Cook, Milton, (Garrattsville,) farmer 100.
Couse, Abram B., (Morris,) blacksmith and farmer 50.
Crawford, Effa, (New Berlin, Chenango Co.,) farmer 2.
Davis, Ezra, (Pittsfield,) farmer 80.
Davis, John H., (Morris,) farmer 90.
DeForest, Elson, (New Berlin, Chenango Co.,) carpenter and toll gate keeper.
Deming, Wm. N., (Pittsfield,) supervisor and farmer 40.
Denison, Spencer, (Morris,) farmer 44.
Dennison, Nelson, (Pittsfield,) farmer 160.
Denton, John R., (Edmeston,) farmer 90.
Dilworth, John, (Pittsfield,) farmer 16 and leases 100.
Doane, Arvilla Miss, (New Lisbon,) teacher and (with Sarah,) farmer 50.
Doane, Sarah Miss, (New Lisbon,) (with Arvilla,) farmer 50.
Downning, S., (Morris,) farmer 73.
Eddy, Benjamin, (Pittsfield,) farmer 63.
Eddy, David R., (Pittsfield,) farmer 2.
Eddy, John, (Pittsfield,) carpenter and farmer 4.
Edwards, LeRoy, (New Berlin, Chenango Co.,) farmer leases 80.
Elliot, Walter, (Morris,) farmer 65.
ELLIOTT, JOHN, (Garrattsville,) (with William,) dairyman, farmer 260 and leases 30.
Elliott, Walter, (New Lisbon,) farmer 50.
ELLIOTT, WILLIAM, (Garrattsville,) (with John,) dairyman, farmer 260 and leases 30.
Ferguson, James, (Pittsfield,) dairyman and farmer 88½.
Finks, Alberto, (New Berlin, Chenango Co.,) saw mill and farmer 9.
Fitch, Ferdinand, (Pittsfield,) general merchant.
FOSTER, EZEKIEL, (Pittsfield,) farmer.
FREEMAN, AMASA, (Pittsfield,) farmer.
FROST, ISAAC, (New Berlin, Chenango Co.,) farmer.
Fuller, Albert, (Morris,) farmer.
FULLER, J. B., (Morris,) shoe maker, constable, hop raiser and farmer 53.
Fuller, Thomas W., (New Berlin, Chenango Co.,) dairyman and farmer leases 320.
Fuller, Wm., (Morris,) hop raiser and farmer 73.

Furgeson, John, (Morris,) farmer 25.
Gafner, John, (New Berlin, Chenango Co.,) farmer 50.
Gailop, Nathaniel, (Pittsfield,) farmer 9½.
Genung, Charles, (Morris,) farmer leases 2.
Genung, John W., (New Berlin, Chenango Co.,) farmer 125.
Gibson, Cyrus, (Morris,) hop raiser and farmer 25.
Gibson, Cyrus L., (Morris,) farmer 98.
Gibson, Thomas, (Morris,) farmer 50.
Gibson, Wm. R., (Morris,) farmer.
Gill, John, (Morris,) dairyman and farmer 97.
Goodfellow, Wm. H., (New Lisbon,) hop raiser, dairyman and farmer 123.
Goodspeed, Artimitia, (Morris,) farmer 132.
Gorton, Simon, (New Berlin, Chenango Co.,) dairyman and farmer leases 205.
Greenleaf, Manville T., (New Berlin, Chenango Co.,) farmer leases 150.
Gregory, Hannah, (Pittsfield,) farmer.
Gregory, Z. A., (Morris,) hop raiser, dairyman and farmer leases 150.
Grey, Wm., (Pittsfield,) farmer 173.
Gross, Seth, (Pittsfield,) farmer 56.
Haight, Benjamin, (New Berlin, Chenango Co.,) farmer 7.
Hall, Caleb G., (Pittsfield,) dairyman and farmer 140.
Hall, Henry, (New Berlin, Chenango Co.,) farmer 72.
Hall, Lyman P., (Pittsfield,) farmer 162.
Hall, Orimel, (Pittsfield,) farmer 337.
Hall, Wm. G., (Pittsfield,) farmer 124.
Hamilton, Thomas, (New Berlin, Chenango Co.,) farmer 2.
Harrington, Charles, (Pittsfield,) farmer 85.
HARRINGTON, DAVID, (Pittsfield,) farmer.
Harrington, Eber, (New Berlin, Chenango Co.,) farmer 98.
Harrington, Henry, (Garrattsville,) (with Mylena A. Holt,) farmer 47.
Harrington, Job, (Pittsfield,) farmer 98.
Harrington, Morris S., (New Berlin, Chenango Co.,) dairyman and farmer 150.
Harrington, Seth, (Pittsfield,) farmer 150.
Harrington, Sidney, (Pittsfield,) farmer 10.
Harrington, Smith, (New Berlin, Chenango Co.,) farmer 150.
Harrington, Solomon, (New Berlin, Chenango Co.,) dairyman and farmer 99.
Harrington, Wm. R., (Morris,) farmer 30.
Havins, Charles, (New Berlin, Chenango Co.,) farmer 158.
Hawkins, Ann, (Pittsfield,) farmer 160.
Hawkins, Ansel, (Pittsfield,) farmer 5.
Hawkins, Elijah, (Pittsfield,) farmer 33.
Hawkins, Reuben M., (Pittsfield,) saw mill, carpenter and farmer 122.
Hawks, Augustus C., (Morris,) farmer.
Hawks, Harvey, (Morris,) dairyman and farmer 140.
Hide, John, (New Berlin, Chenango Co.,) farmer 14.
Hill, Arnold, (New Berlin, Chenango Co.,) shingle maker.
Hill, Barnett, (New Berlin, Chenango Co.,) farmer 125.
Hill, Catherine, (New Berlin, Chenango Co.,) farmer 3.

Hill, Lewis, (New Berlin, Chenango Co.,) farmer 154.
Hill, Wm., (New Berlin, Chenango Co.,) farmer 1.
Holmes, Tollivin, (Pittsfield,) farmer 10.
Holt, Mylena A., (Garrattsville,) (with Henry Harrington,) farmer 47.
Hooper, Laratta, (New Berlin, Chenango Co.,) farmer 106.
Howe, Betsey, (Morris,) farmer 26.
Howe, Charles, (Morris,) farmer 25.
Howe, Stephen, (Morris,) farmer occupies 26.
Howe, Stephen, (Pittsfield,) farmer 51.
Hurlbutt, Leland, (New Lisbon,) farmer 75.
Hurlbutt, Samuel, (Garrattsville,) farmer 50.
Jaquish, Lorenzo, (New Berlin, Chenango Co.,) farmer 114.
Jaycox, Anthony, (Pittsfield,) farmer 13.
Jenison, Ceylum, (Morris,) hop raiser and farmer 67½.
Johnson, Sylvester, (New Berlin, Chenanga Co.,) farmer 113.
KEITH, GEORGE, (New Berlin, Chenango Co.,) carpenter.
Kellogg, Mary A., (New Berlin, Chenango Co.,) farmer 140.
Kidder, John, (Morris,) farmer 64.
Knich, Henry, (Morris,) farmer 60.
LEWIS, HENRY, (Pittsfield,) farmer.
Light, Andrew, (New Berlin, Chenango Co.,) machinist.
LIGHT, SAMUEL, (Pittsfield,) farmer.
Lindsley, Joseph, (New Berlin, Chenango Co.,) farmer leases 266.
MALCOMB, HOSEA, (Pittsfield,) farmer.
Marsh, Minerva, (Morris,) farmer 20.
Matteson, Cela J., (New Berlin, Chenango Co.,) farmer 142.
Matteson, Charles, (Pittsfield,) farmer 24.
Matteson, Harriet L., (Pittsfield,) farmer 78.
Matteson, Hezekiah, (New Berlin, Chenango Co.,) hop raiser and farmer 100.
Matteson, Josiah, (New Berlin, Chenango Co.,) farmer 142.
Matteson, Josiah Jr., (New Berlin, Chenango Co.,) farmer 60.
McCormick, John, (New Berlin, Chenango Co.,) farmer 8.
McIntyre, Ansel, (Pittsfield,) farmer 3.
McIntyre, Polly, (New Berlin, Chenango Co.,) farmer 18.
McINTYRE, W. V., (New Berlin, Chenango Co.,) farmer.
Miller, George, (New Berlin, Chenango Co.,) farmer 38.
Miller, Isaac, (New Berlin, Chenango Co.,) dairyman and farmer 295.
Miller, John, (New Berlin, Chenango Co.,) farmer 48.
Miller, John H., (New Berlin, Chenango Co.,) farmer 112.
Moore, Arthur L., (Garrattsville,) commissioner of highways and farmer 76½.
Moore, Horace, (Pittsfield,) farmer 22.
Moore, John, (New Berlin, Chenango Co.,) farmer 12.
Moore, Thomas, (New Berlin, Chenango Co.,) farmer 12.
Morse, Timothy P., (Pittsfield,) farmer 184.
Morten, Wm., (Pittsfield,) farmer leases 160.
Mumbulo, Joseph, (Morris,) farmer 125.

Murdock, Chester, (New Berlin, Chenango Co.,) farmer 69.
Noch, Henry, (Morris,) farmer 60.
Northrop, John, (Pittsfield,) farmer 132.
Olin, Wm. A., (Pittsfield,) constable.
Ouls, Spencer, (Morris,) farmer 8.
Parish, Francis, (Morris,) farmer 32.
Parish, George, (Morris,) farmer 16.
PARISH, ISAAC, (Morris,) farmer.
Parish, James, (Morris,) farmer 25.
Parish, John, (Morris,) farmer 16.
Parish, Nerus, (Morris,) farmer 20.
Parish, Prime, (Morris,) farmer 20.
Patrick, Alfred, (Morris,) dairyman and farmer 100.
Patrick, Isaac, (Morris,) farmer 50.
Patrick, Jesse S., (Pittsfield,) farmer leases 62.
Patrick, Lyman C., (Pittsfield,) farmer 62.
Patrick, Richard, (Pittsfield,) dairyman and farmer 92.
Peck, Alvin, (Pittsfield,) prop. of hotel and town clerk.
Peck, Lyman Z., (New Berlin, Chenango Co.,) farmer 142.
Perkins, Eri, (Edmeston,) farmer 2 and (with Harvey,) dairyman and farmer 150.
Perkins, Harvey, (Edmeston,) (with Eri,) dairyman and farmer 150.
Persons, Phineas, (New Berlin, Chenango Co.,) farmer 65.
Place, Leonard, (New Berlin, Chenango Co.,) mule spinner in cotton factory and farmer 40.
Place, R. D., (New Berlin, Chenango Co.,) farmer 50.
Pope, Allen, (Morris,) retired farmer.
Pope, Charles L., (Morris,) hop raiser and farmer 30.
Pope, Dana, (New Lisbon,) hop raiser and farmer 45.
Potter, Cyrus, (New Berlin, Chenango Co.,) farmer 20.
Potter, Horace, (New Berlin, Chenango Co.,) shingle maker.
Potter, Samuel, (New Berlin, Chenango Co.,) farmer 20.
Potter, Wm., (New Berlin, Chenango Co.,) farmer 50.
Pudney, Andrew, (New Berlin, Chenango Co.,) farmer 50.
Purdy, Wm., (New Berlin, Chenango Co.,) farmer 1.
Radley, Charles, (Morris,) hop raiser and farmer 63.
Radley, James, (Morris,) farmer 25.
Radley, Wm., (Morris,) dairyman and farmer 78.
Randall, Henry, (Pittsfield,) farmer 28.
Rathbun, Sarah M. and Phebe E. Misses, (Morris,) farmers 47.
ROOD, ABNER, (Pittsfield,) farmer.
Russell, Hiram, (Pittsfield,) farmer 62.
Sarle, Henry, (New Berlin, Chenango Co.,) assessor and farmer 63.
Sarle, Solomon, (New Berlin, Chenango Co.,) farmer 51.
Schism, Martha, (Pittsfield,) farmer 9.
Scott, Any, (Pittsfield,) farmer 1.
Searl, S. S., (Morris,) farmer 51.
Shipman, Stephen, (Pittsfield,) farmer 34.
Simmons, James F., (New Berlin, Chenango Co.,) farmer.

Skinner, David, (New Berlin, Chenango Co.,) farmer 38.
SMALL, IRA, (New Berlin, Chenango Co.,) teacher.
Smith, David S., (New Lisbon,) justice of the peace and farmer 160.
Smith, Harmon, (New Berlin, Chenango Co.,) farmer 10.
SMITH, JOEL, (Morris,) farmer.
SMITH, JOSEPH, (Pittsfield,) farmer.
Smith, Kate A. Miss, (Morris,) teacher.
Smith, Richard, (Morris,) farmer leases 10.
Smith, Seth, (Morris,) farmer 45 and leases 85.
Smith, Thomas, (Morris,) farmer 50.
Smith, Uriah, (Morris,) farmer 61.
SNOW, CYRUS, (Morris,) painter.
SNOW, GEORGE, (Morris,) farmer 84.
Spafford, Asa, (Pittsfield,) farmer 7.
Spafford, Harlem, (Pittsfield,) farmer 62.
Spafford, Harvey, (New Berlin, Chenango Co.,) farmer 100.
Spafford, Henry, (Pittsfield,) farmer 41.
Spafford, Lewis, (Pittsfield,) farmer 242.
Spafford, Parley B., (Pittsfield,) farmer 13.
Spafford, Truman, (Pittsfield,) farmer 40.
Spencer, David J., (Pittsfield,) blacksmith.
Stanton, Catherine, (Morris,) farmer 34.
Stevens, Joshua, (New Berlin, Chenango Co.,) farmer 60.
Swarthout, Andrew, (Morris,) farmer 7½.
Sweet, Caleb, (Pittsfield,) farmer.
Sweet, Erastus, (Pittsfield,) farmer leases 50.
Talman, Seneca, (Pittsfield,) farmer 50.
Taylor, Robert, (Morris,) farmer.
Taylor, Stephen, (Morris,) dairyman and farmer 216.
Thayer, Enos, (Pittsfield,) farmer 119.
Thayer, Levi, (Pittsfield,) farmer 110.

Thayer, Nelson, (New Berlin, Chenango Co.,) farmer 45.
Thayer, Orin, (New Berlin, Chenango Co.,) farmer 1.
Tilley, A. D., (Edmeston,) teacher and farmer 62½.
Tilley, Wm. F., (Pittsfield,) farmer 42.
Tinker, Charles, (New Berlin, Chenango Co.,) farmer 10.
TITUS, NATHAN, (New Berlin, Chenango Co.,) farmer.
Titus, Wm., (New Berlin, Chenango Co.,) farmer 1.
Tolland, Robert, (Garrattsville,) farmer 50.
Turner, Edwin, (Morris,) farmer 28.
Weaver, Joshua, (Morris,) farmer 5.
Wicks, Miles, (Pittsfield,) farmer 1.
Wighman, Wm., (Morris,) dairyman and farmer 180.
Williams, Giles G., (New Berlin, Chenanco Co.,) (*with Halsey H.,*) dairyman and farmer leases 100.
Williams, Halsey H., (New Berlin, Chenango Co.,) (*with Giles G.,*) dairyman and farmer leases 100.
Wilson, Austin, (Morris,) farmer.
Wilson, Charles, (Morris,) cooper and farmer 27.
Wilson, George, (Morris,) farmer 44.
Wilson, Joseph, (Morris,) blacksmith.
Wilson, Samuel, (Garrattsville,) farmer 50.
Wilson, William, (Morris,) farmer 150.
Wood, Carrie A. Miss, (Morris,) teacher.
WOOD, DAVID, (Morris,) farmer.
Wood, Russell, (Morris,) dairyman and farmer 114.
Woodard, John S., (Pittsfield,) justice of the peace and farmer 95.
Wormwood, Obadiah, (New Berlin, Chenango Co.,) farmer.

PLAINFIELD.

(Post Office Addresses in Parentheses.)

Adams, John S., (Leonardsville, Madison Co.,) dairyman, 12 cows, and farmer 119.

Anderson, Menzo, (Burlington Flats,) dairyman, 10 cows, and farmer 143.

ANTHONY, MYRON, (Leonardsville, Madison Co.,) (*Williamson, Anthony & Co.*)

ARMLING, JAMES, (Unadilla Forks,) dairyman, 25 cows, and farmer leases of Charles B. Brown, 185.

Armstrong, Chas. H., (Unadilla Forks,) (*with David M. and Mowry W.,*) dealer in live stock, dairyman and farmer 500.

Armstrong, David M., (Unadilla Forks,) supervisor and (*with Mowry W. and Charles H.,*) dealer in live stock, dairyman and farmer 500.

Armstrong, Hopestile, (West Exeter,) justice of the peace, dairyman, 16 cows, and farmer 114.

ARMSTRONG, MOWRY W., (Unadilla Forks,) (*with David M. and Charles H.,*) dealer in live stock, dairyman and farmer 500.

ARMSTRONG, SOLOMON, (Spooner's Corners,) prest. Plainfield Union Cheese Manuf. Co., poor master, butcher, dairyman, 12 cows, and farmer 182.

BABCOCK, GIDEON H., (Leonardsville, Madison Co.,) farmer 50.

Babcock, Henry D., (Leonardsville, Madison Co.,) (*St. John & Babcock.*)

Babcock, J. Franklin, (Unadilla Forks,) dairyman and farmer 100.

Bass, Delos E., (Leonardsville, Madison Co.,) dairyman, 19 cows, and farmer 158.

Bass, Ebenezer, (Leonardsville, Madison Co.,) dairyman, 11 cows, and farmer 80.

Bassett, Orin, (Leonardsville, Madison Co.,) dairyman, 8 cows, and farmer leases of Permelia Wilcox, 100.

Bassett, William, (Leonardsville, Madison Co.,) dairyman, 4 cows, and farmer 100.

BASSETT, WILLIAM L., (Unadilla Forks,) general merchant.

Bassinger, Henry B., (Leonardsville, Madison Co.,) dairyman, 18 cows, and farmer leases 140.

Baum, John, (West Winfield, Herkimer Co.,) farmer 10.

Beach, David R., (West Exeter,) dairyman, 6 cows, and farmer 56.

Bevin, Isaac, (Unadilla Forks,) (*with Samuel,*) dealer in live stock, dairyman and farmer 120.

Bevin, Julius, (Unadilla Forks,) patentee of churn scraper, dairyman, 6 cows, and farmer 90.

Bevin, Samuel, (Unadilla Forks,) (*with Isaac,*) dealer in live stock, dairyman and farmer 120.

BEVIN, WILLIAM, (Unadilla Forks,) dairyman, 4 cows, and farmer 88.

Bliss, Charles Jr., (West Exeter,) dairyman, 15 cows, and farmer 110.

Bostwick, L. Williard, (Bridgewater, Oneida Co.,) commissioner of highways, cigar manuf., dairyman, 15 cows, and farmer 91.

BROWN, ALONZO W., (Unadilla Forks,) (*Daggett & Brown.*)

Brown, Ann Mrs., (Unadilla Forks,) dairy, 4 cows, and farmer 50.

BROWN, CYRUS, (Unadilla Forks,) cooper and notary public.

Brown, L. Kellogg, (Unadilla Forks,) carpenter.

Brown, Samuel A., (Leonardsville, Madison Co.,) deputy sheriff, dairyman, 18 cows, and farmer 140.

BROWN, WILLIAM L., (Unadilla Forks,) cheese manuf., dairyman, 33 cows, and farmer 160.

Buel, Egbert, (Burlington Flats,) dairy, 5 cows, and farmer 62.

Burdick, Elisha S., (Unadilla Forks,) dairyman, 9 cows, and farmer 96.

Burgess, Nathan, (West Exeter,) butcher, constable and farmer 10.

Burmingham, Michael, (West Winfield, Herkimer Co.,) dairyman, 3 cows, and farmer 18.

Burns, John, (Bridgewater, Oneida Co.,) stone mason and farmer 9.

Chapman, Pembroke A., (Unadilla Forks,) dairyman, 24 cows, and farmer leases of Stephen, 150.

CHARLES, LEWIS A., (West Exeter,) dairyman, 12 cows, and farmer 95.

Clapson, Silas, (West Winfield, Herkimer Co.,) dairyman, 9 cows, and farmer 80.

Clark, Alvin, (Leonardsville, Madison Co.,) agent for agricultural implements, dairyman, 5 cows, and farmer 50.

Clark, Amos L., (Unadilla Forks,) dairyman, 17 cows, and farmer 150.

Clark, Lewis, (Leonardsville, Madison Co.,) dairyman, 4 cows, and farmer 40.

Clark, Nelson, (Unadilla Forks,) dairyman, 21 cows, and farmer 169.

CLARK, SAMUEL, (Unadilla Forks,) boots and shoes.

CLARKE, FRANCIS O., (Unadilla Forks,) patentee of Clarke's Turbine King Water Wheel, machinist.

Clarke, Jared, (Unadilla Forks,) manuf. of furniture and horse rakes, also undertaker.

Colburn, Edward, (Burlington Flats,) dairyman, 11 cows, and farmer 125.

Coon, George, (Unadilla Forks,) dairyman, 20 cows, and farmer leases 100.

Crandall, Avery C.,(Leonardsville, Madison Co.,) dairyman, 11 cows, and farmer 120.

CRANDALL, STEPHEN H., (Leonardsville, Madison Co.,) polisher and farmer.

Crumb, Albert B., (Unadilla Forks,) (*A. B. & E. F. Crumb*,) postmaster.

Crumb, A. B. & E. F., (Unadilla Forks,) (*Albert B. and Everett F.*,) general merchants.

Crumb, Delos, (West Winfield, Herkimer Co.,) dairyman, 14 cows, and farmer 125.

Crumb, Everett F.,(Unadilla Forks,) (*A. B. & E. F. Crumb*,) deputy postmaster.

CRUMB, FRANCIS, (Unadilla Forks,) dairyman, 16 cows, and farmer 100.

Crumb, Franklin H., (Leonardsville, Madison Co.,) mechanic and farmer 26.

CRUMB, JOSEPH O., (Leonardsville, Madison Co.,) dairyman, 14 cows, farmer 206 and leases 300.

Crumb, Nathaniel, (Unadilla Forks,) dairyman, 30 cows, and farmer 200.

DAGGETT, ADELBERT W., (Unadilla Forks,) (*Daggett & Brown*,) station agent D. D. and W. R. R., dealer in coal.

DAGGETT & BROWN, (Unadilla Forks,) (*Adelbert W. Daggett and Alonzo W. Brown*,) dealers in coal.

Daggett, Rufus, (Unadilla Forks,) tinware, stoves &c.

Davis, Becky Mrs., (Unadilla Forks,) dairy, 7 cows, and farmer 100.

Davis, David, (Burlington Flats,) dairyman, 15 cows, and farmer 115.

Davis, John L., (Spooner's Corners,) dairyman, 16 cows, and farmer 100.

DAVIS, JOHN T., (Spooner's Corners,) dairyman, 14 cows, and farmer 99.

Davis, Richard W., (West Exeter,) dairyman, 21 cows, and farmer 136.

Davis, Thomas N., (Unadilla Forks,) carpenter and farmer.

Day, Almond, (Bridgewater, Oneida Co.,) dairyman, 10 cows, and farmer 64.

Dewey, Dennis A., (Spooner's Corners,) teacher, dairyman, 30 cows, and farmer 200.

Dye, Charles A., (Leonardsville, Madison Co.,) dairyman, 12 cows, and farmer 120.

Dye, Daniel D., (Leonardsville, Madison Co.,) dairyman, 18 cows, and farmer 164.

Dye, Job, (Leonardsville, Madison Co.,) dairyman, 22 cows, and farmer 425.

Dye, Joseph L., (Leonardsville, Madison Co.,) dairyman, 9 cows, and farmer 100.

Dye, William, (Leonardsville, Madison Co.,) dairyman and farmer 50.

Edwards, David L., (West Winfield, Herkimer Co.,) dairyman, 10 cows, and farmer leases of David Richards, 65.

Edwards, Lewis, (West Winfield, Herkimer Co.,) farmer leases 65.

Edwards, Thomas R., (West Exeter,) dairyman, 15 cows, and farmer 130.

Elliott, Henry, (West Winfield, Herkimer Co.,) dairyman, 31 cows, and farmer 200.

Ellsworth, John, (Leonardsville, Madison Co.,) dairyman, 7 cows, and farmer.

Enos, Sheffield, (Unadilla Forks,) carding works.

Evans, Henry, (West Exeter,) dairyman, 20 cows, and farmer 220.

Evans, Jesse Rev.,(Unadilla Forks,) pastor Baptist Church.

Evans, John, (West Exeter,) dairyman, 15 cows, and farmer 115.

Evans, Robert, (West Winfield, Herkimer Co.,) dairyman, 19 cows, and farmer 121.

FIRMAN, ALBERT P., (Bridgewater, Oneida Co.,) dairyman, 11 cows, and farmer leases of Horace, 64.

Firman, Horace, (Bridgewater, Oneida Co.,) dairyman, 11 cows, and farmer 64.

FIRMAN, LORIN, (Leonardsville, Madison Co.,) dairyman, 24 cows, and farmer leases 206.

Fisk, Amos, (Unadilla Forks,) saw mill.

Fitch, Charles H., (Bridgewater, Oneida Co.,) dairyman, 7 cows, and farmer 57.

Fitch, E. Peabody, (Bridgewater, Oneida Co.,) dairyman, 8 cows, and farmer 56.

Frost, Amos S.,(Spooner's Corners,) dairyman, 6 cows, and farmer 90.

GARDNER, WM. R., (Leonardsville, Madison Co.,) blacksmith, patentee of Gardner's Hinged Cup Anatomical Uterine Pessary.

Gates, I. Palmer, (Spooner's Corners,) dairyman, 18 cows, and farmer 114.

GATES, JAMES M., (Unadilla Forks,) livery, prop. of Unadilla Forks and New Berlin Stage Line.

Gates, Nathaniel H., (Unadilla Forks,) dairyman, 43 cows, and farmer 300.

Gaughram, Peter, (Unadilla Forks,) shoe maker.

Gordon, Jedediah, (Unadilla Forks,) dairyman, 10 cows, and farmer 100.

Griffis, Edmund W., (Burlington Flats,) dairyman, 12 cows, and farmer 120.

Griffis, Hugh, (West Exeter,) dairyman, 7 cows, and farmer 30.

Griffis, Peter, (Spooner's Corners,) dairyman, 25 cows, and farmer 180.

GRIFFIS, RICHARD C., (Leonardsville, Madison Co.,) cheese manuf.

Griffis, Thomas, (Spooner's Corners,) dairyman, 8 cows, and farmer 50.

Griffis, William S., (Unadilla Forks,) dairyman, 18 cows, and farmer 130.

GRIFFITH, FRANCIS G.,(Unadilla Forks,) dairyman, 24 cows, and farmer 178.

GRIFFITH, J. C., (Unadilla Forks.)

Hackley, A. H., (Bridgewater, Oneida Co.,) dairyman, 4 cows, and farmer 40.

Hackley, Salinus, (Bridgewater, Oneida Co.,) dairyman, 9 cows, and farmer 88.

Hackley, Salinus H., (Bridgewater, Oneida Co.,) farmer.

HALL, SIMEON, (Unadilla Forks,) prop. Unadilla Forks Hotel.

Hanan, Anthony, (Spooner's Corners,) dairyman, 10 cows, and farmer 68.

Hayes, John M., (Unadilla Forks,) foreman for Jared Clarke, cabinet maker.

HOLDREDGE, WILLIAM P., (Unadilla Forks,) dairyman and farmer 175.

HOTCHKISS, EDGAR F., (Unadilla Forks,) prop. grist and flour mill, dealer in flour, feed &c.

HOXIE, JOHN, (Unadilla Forks,) dealer in live stock, prop. of cheese factory, dairyman, 22 cows, and farmer 230.

Hughes, Thomas, (Leonardsville, Madison Co.,) dairyman, 12 cows, and farmer leases of David Prichard, 100.

Huntley, Albert P., (West Exeter,) dairyman, 15 cows, and farmer 80.

Jones, David O., (Leonardsville, Madison Co.,) dairyman, 20 cows, and farmer 149.

Jones, Edward, (Spooner's Corners,) dairyman, 20 cows, and farmer 160.

JONES, OWEN, (Spooner's Corners,) dairyman, 21 cows, and farmer 174.

JONES, ROBERT, (Spooner's Corners,) dealer in live stock, dairyman, 27 cows, and farmer 130.

Jones, Rowland T., (Leonardsville, Madison Co.,) dairyman, 9 cows, and farmer 54.

JOSLYN, DELOS R., (West Exeter,) dairyman, 50 cows, and farmer 265.

KEHRER, GEORGE JACOB, (Unadilla Forks,) cigar maker, dairyman, 6 cows, and farmer 47.

Kilbourn, Francis S., (Spooner's Corners,) dairyman, 23 cows, and farmer 170.

King, Erastus, (Unadilla Forks,) physician and surgeon.

King, Mary Mrs., (Spooner's Corners,) cheese maker, Plainfield Union Cheese Manufacturing Co.

Larabee, Richard S., (Leonardsville, Madison Co.,) dairyman, 10 cows, and farmer leases of Thomas W. Stearns.

Lewis, William U., (Unadilla Forks,) constable and huckster.

LLOYD, DAVID L., (Unadilla Forks,) dairyman, 13 cows, and farmer 110.

Mallard, Joseph, (West Exeter,) dairyman, 10 cows, and farmer 63.

Mallory, Albert, (Spooner's Corners,) dairyman, 29 cows, and farmer 250.

Mason, Charles L., (Leonardsville, Madison Co.,) dairyman, 6 cows, and farmer 40.

Mason, John D., (West Exeter,) dairyman, 8 cows, and farmer 95.

McFARLAND, LEVI P., (Spooner's Corners,) treasurer Plainfield Union Cheese Manuf. Co., dairyman, 23 cows, and farmer 191.

McLaughlin, John W., (West Exeter,) dairyman, 19 cows, and farmer 140.

McLaughlin, Solomon, (West Exeter,) dairyman, 14 cows, and farmer 90.

MEEKER, ORSON C., (Spooner's Corners,) dairyman, 11 cows, and farmer 109.

Morris, Edward L., (West Exeter,) dairyman, 18 cows, and farmer 114.

Murray, James B., (Bridgewater, Oneida Co.,) dairyman, 5 cows, and farmer.

NYE, ABEL & SON, (West Exeter,) (*Wm. H.*,) dairymen, 15 cows, and farmers 123.

NYE, WM. H., (West Exeter,) (*Abel Nye & Son*.)

Oatley, Jonathan, (Unadilla Forks,) farmer 10.

Owens, ——, (Unadilla Forks,) dairyman and farmer.

Pearsall, Edwin R., (West Exeter,) dairyman, 15 cows, and farmer 107.

Penny, Alva, (Unadilla Forks,) dairyman, 15 cows, and farmer 197.

Perkins, Criton M., (Unadilla Forks,) cabinet manuf.

Perkins, Wells W., (Unadilla Forks,) physician and surgeon.

PHILLIPS, PARLEY, (Unadilla Forks,) dairyman, 30 cows, and farmer 175.

Plainfield Union Cheese Manuf. Co., (Spooner's Corners,) Solomon Armstrong, president; A. J. Sanders, secretary; L. P. McFarland, treasurer.

Pollock, James, (Unadilla Forks,) dairyman and farmer leases of Alfred Moore, 170.

PUGH, WILLIAM, (Unadilla Forks,) dairyman, 20 cows, and farmer 160.

Richards, Job J., (Burlington Flats,) dairyman, 8 cows, and farmer 60.

Richards, Morris, (Burlington Flats,) dairyman, 8 cows, and farmer 112.

Richards, Richard C., (Unadilla Forks,) dairyman, 20 cows, and farmer 140.

RICHARDS, ROBERT J., (West Exeter,) dairyman, 32 cows, and farmer 207.

RICHARDS, WILLIAM C., (Unadilla Forks,) dealer in live stock, assessor, dairyman, 40 cows, and farmer 230.

Roberts, John R., (West Winfield, Herkimer Co.,) dairyman, 5 cows, and farmer 66.

ROBERTS, RICHARD, (Unadilla Forks,) dairyman, 18 cows, and farmer 120.

Rogers, Charles W., (Leonardsville, Madison Co.,) dealer in hides, dairyman, 22 cows, and farmer 160.

ROGERS, DENISON, (Unadilla Forks,) dairyman, 20 cows, and farmer 175.

Rooney, Patrick, (Spooner's Corners,) dairyman, 3 cows, and farmer 14.

SANDERS, ANDREW J., (Spooner's Corners,) secretary Plainfield Union Cheese Manuf. Co., carpenter, justice of the peace, dairyman, 6 cows, and farmer 50.

Saunders, Clark, (Leonardsville, Madison Co.,) overseer of the poor, dairyman, 10 cows, and farmer 100.

SHOLES, RODERICK, (West Winfield, Herkimer Co.,) dairyman, 24 cows, and farmer 200.

Smith, Alonzo, (Unadilla Forks,) tailor.

Smith, Benjamin & Son, (Spooner's Corners,) (*Francis B.*,) cheese manuf., dairymen, 40 cows, and farmers 385.

Smith, Francis B., (Spooner's Corners,) (*Benjamin Smith & Son*,) post master.

SMITH, GOULD P., (Unadilla Forks,) carriage, sign and ornamental painter.

SMITH, HENRY D., (West Exeter,) (*Smith & Wilber*,) dairyman, 30 cows, and farmer 196.

SMITH & WILBER, (West Exeter,) (*Henry D. Smith and William Wilber*,) cheese manufs.

Southworth, Oscar L., (Leonardsville, Madison Co.,) physician and surgeon.

SPICER, E. HENRY, (West Exeter,) layer of water lime and aqueduct pipe, blacksmith, dairyman, 21 cows, and farmer 153.

Spicer, Elizabeth Mrs., (Unadilla Forks,) dairy, 4 cows, and farmer 38.

Spicer, Henry A., (West Exeter,) dairyman, 32 cows, and farmer leases 186.

Stevens, A. B. Mrs., (Unadilla Forks,) tailoress and dress maker.

Stillman, George C., (Leonardsville, Madison Co.,) dairyman, 3 cows, and farmer 50.

St. John & Babcock, (Leonardsville, Madison Co.,) (Milton W. St. John and Henry D. Babcock,) iron founders and machinists, and manufs. of Kinney's Adjustable Fork Press.

ST. JOHN, HENRY C., (Leonardsville, Madison Co.,) dentist and machinist.

St. John, Milton W., (Leonardsville, Madison Co.,) (St. John & Babcock.)

Tailor, N. D., (West Winfield, Herkimer Co.,) farmer 60.

Tarball, J. Franklin, (Unadilla Forks,) carriage manuf.

TAYLOR, JOHN, (Leonardsville, Madison Co.,) cheese manuf., assessor, dairyman, 30 cows, and farmer 225.

Thomas, William L., (West Exeter,) carpenter.

Todd, Lewis E., (Unadilla Forks,) cabinet maker.

Tool, Peter, (Unadilla Forks,) dairyman, 3 cows, and farmer 20.

Tooly, Reuben O., (Spooner's Corners,) assistant postmaster and farmer 20.

UNADILLA FORKS HOTEL, (Unadilla Forks,) Simeon Hall, prop.

Warddell, Isaac, (Unadilla Forks,) dairyman and farmer.

Watkins, John J., (West Exeter,) commissioner of highways, dairyman, 28 cows, and farmer 200.

Webster, Dorr J., (West Exeter,) dairyman, 23 cows, and farmer leases 158.

WELLS, JOHN B., (Leonardsville, Madison Co.,) dealer in live stock, dairyman, 10 cows, and farmer 136.

WELLS, LUTHER H., (Leonardsville, Madison Co.,) surveyor and farmer 12.

WHEELER, BENJAMIN F., (Unadilla Forks,) blacksmith and carriage ironer.

WHITE, DAVID S., (Leonardsville, Madison Co.,) dairyman, 12 cows, and farmer 115.

Whitford, Clark, (Leonardsville, Madison Co.,) (with Samuel D.,) dairyman, 17 cows, and farmer 117.

WHITFORD, HAMILTON J., (Leonardsville, Madison Co.,) (Williamson, Anthony & Co.)

Whitford, Samuel D., (Leonardsville, Madison Co.,) (with Clark,) dairyman, 17 cows, and farmer 117.

WILBER, WILLIAM, (West Exeter,) (Smith & Wilber.)

Wilcox, Asa D., (Unadilla Forks,) carriage maker.

Wilcox, Franklin H., (Unadilla Forks,) harness and carriage trimmer.

Wilcox, Henry, (Unadilla Forks,) carriage manuf.

Wilcox, Pamelia Mrs., (Unadilla Forks,) dairy, 10 cows, and farmer 74.

Wilcox, William H., (Unadilla Forks,) dealer in live stock and farmer 114.

Williams, Hugh R. Rev., (Spooner's Corners,) pastor of Congregational Church.

Williams, John, (Leonardsville, Madison Co.,) dairyman, 24 cows, and farmer 189.

Williams, John J., (West Exeter,) dairyman, 25 cows, and farmer 150.

Williams, John W., (West Exeter,) dairyman, 14 cows, and farmer 100.

Williams, Morris O., (Spooner's Corners,) dairyman, 10 cows, and farmer.

WILLIAMSON, ANTHONY & CO., (Leonardsville, Madison Co.,) (Charles H. Williamson, Myron Anthony and Hamilton J. Whitford,) grist and saw mills.

WILLIAMSON, CHARLES H., (Leonardsville, Madison Co.,) (Williamson, Anthony & Co.,) justice of the peace, carriage and horse-rake maker, dairyman, 32 cows, and farmer 300.

Wing, Leander J., (Unadilla Forks,) cheese manuf.

Witter, Delos, (Bridgewater, Oneida Co.,) dairyman, 14 cows, and farmer leases of Henry D., 76.

WOOD, ALFRED, (West Exeter,) dairyman, 35 cows, and farmer 192.

WOOD, JOHN, (Burlington Flats,) dairyman, 9 cows, and farmer leases of John Shaw, 86.

RICHFIELD.

(Post Office Addresses in Parentheses.)

*ACKERMAN, C. & SON, (Richfield Springs,) publisher *Richfield Springs Mercury*, Main.

Allen, A. & Son, (Richfield Springs,) blacksmith, James.

Allen, Henry H., (Richfield Springs,) farmer 75.

Allen, Jordan, (Richfield,) farmer 60.

Allen, Norman, (Richfield,) farmer 10.

AMERICAN HOTEL, (Richfield Springs,) Mrs. Julia A. Johnson, prop., Main opposite the Sulphur Spring.

AMES, ABNER, (Richfield,) farmer 140.

Ames, Charles, (Richfield,) farmer 66 and leases 146.

Ames, Daniel W., (Richfield,) farmer 114.

Ames, David, (Richfield Springs,) farmer 120.

Ames, Jerome, (Richfield Springs,) farmer 161.

Ames, John S., (Richfield,) farmer 113.

AMES, LUCIUS, (Richfield Springs,) farmer.

AMES, MARIETTA E. MRS., (Richfield,) farmer 132.

Ames, Nathan, (Richfield Springs,) school teacher.

Ames, Otis, (Richfield,) farmer 246.

Andrews, David, (Richfield,) mechanic.

Andrus, Elbert E., (Richfield,) (*with Wm. Henry,*) thresher and farmer 46.

Andrus, Wm. Henry, (Richfield,) (*with Elbert E.,*) thresher and farmer 46.

Austin, Wm., (Richfield,) farmer 4.

Backus, Henry, (Winfield, Herkimer Co.,) farmer 133.

Backus, John, (Richfield Springs,) prop. of steam saw mill and lumber yard, and speculator in real estate.

Badger, Dewitt C., (Richfield Springs,) assistant freight and ticket agent.

BADGER, EZRA W., (Richfield Springs,) freight and ticket agent D. L. & W. R. R., and farmer 88.

Bailey, Geo., (Richfield Springs,) farmer 202.

Bailey, Wm. T., (Richfield Springs,) dentist.

Baker, Jonathan, (Schuyler's Lake,) farmer 25.

Baker, Norman R., (Schuyler's Lake,) commissioner of highways and farmer 232.

Bargey, Francis, (Richfield,) farmer 43¾.

Bargey, Reuben, (Richfield,) farmer 121.

Barker, Alfred, (Richfield Springs,) carriage manuf., River.

Barrus, A., (Richfield Springs,) prop. of National Hotel, Main.

Barstow, A. E., (Winfield, Herkimer Co.,) hop buyer.

Barstow, Elias, (Winfield, Herkimer Co.,) farmer 244.

Barstow, Floyd, (Winfield, Herkimer Co.,) farmer.

Barstow, James, (Winfield, Herkimer Co.,) farmer 144.

Bates, John J., (Richfield Springs,) farmer 291.

Beard, Samuel, (Richfield Springs,) retired farmer 5.

Bennett, Elijah, (Richfield Springs,) farmer 184.

Bennett, Orma, (Richfield Springs,) carpenter and farmer.

Bigelow, Alonzo, (Richfield,) farmer 87.

Black, James, (Richfield Springs,) farmer 121.

BLISS, JAMES D., (Winfield, Herkimer Co.,) farmer 250.

Bloomfield, Allen, (Richfield Springs,) farmer 90.

BOWDISH, N. S., (Richfield Springs,) photographer and patentee of photographic posing chair, Main.

Brainard, Minoris S., (Richfield Springs,) dealer in real estate and farmer 31.

BROCKWAY, HIRAM C., (Richfield,) prop. of cheese factory, poormaster, farmer 25 and, in Exeter, 220.

Bronner, Frederick, (Richfield Springs,) (*Getman & Bronner*.)

Brooks, Thomas, (Richfield Springs,) farmer 42.

Brown, Almon, (Richfield Springs,) (*with Norman,*) farmer 112.

Brown, Charles, (Richfield Springs,) (*Vroman & Brown*.)

Brown, Charles H., (Cedarville, Herkimer Co.,) (*with Milo H.,*) cheese factory and farmer 121.

BROWN, JUDSON C., (Richfield,) farmer 275.

Brown, Lafayette, (Richfield,) farmer 150.

Brown, Milo H.,(Cedarville, Herkimer Co.,) (*with Charles H.,*) cheese factory and farmer 121.

Brown, Morgan L., (Richfield,) farmer 65.

Brown, Norman, (Richfield Springs,) (*with Almon,*) farmer 112.

BRYAN, MORGAN, (Richfield Springs,) (*Bryan & Ransom*.)

BRYAN & RANSOM, (Richfield Springs,) (*Morgan Bryan and Norman K. Ransom,*) props. of Spring House and private bankers, corner Main and Church.

Buchanan, Robert, (Richfield Springs,) tin and hardware, Main.

Bullion, William, (Richfield Springs,) cattle dealer, speculator and farmer 200.

Builions, John, (Richfield Springs,) farmer 187.

Bunnell, Abel, (Richfield Springs,) head miller with John Dana.

Bunnell, Charles A.,(Richfield,) shoe maker.

Bunnell, Edward R., (Richfield Springs,) farmer 130.

BURGESS, HIRAM, (Winfield, Herkimer Co.,) dairyman, 50 cows, farmer 460 and leases 140.

BURLINGAME, E. A., (Richfield Springs,) carriage maker, James.

Burnes, Bartlet, (Richfield,) farmer 4.

BUSH, ISAAC, (Richfield,) farmer 182½.

BUSH, PETER C., (Richfield Springs,) cheese factory and farmer 100.

CALWELL, JOHN, (Richfield Springs,) bakery, corner James and Center.

Calwell, Alfred, (Richfield,) farmer 30.

Caney, Geo., (Richfield Springs,) carpenter and farmer 75.

Caney, Richard F., (Richfield Springs,) merchant tailor and gents' furnishing goods, corner Main and Lake.

CAREY, EZRA L., (Richfield,) blacksmith.

Carey, Geo. B. & Son, (Richfield Springs,) boarding house, Main.

Carpenter, Luke H., (Richfield Springs,) farmer leases.

Cary, James C., (Richfield Springs,) undertaker and furniture dealer, Main.

Catbin, Russell, (Richfield Springs,) retired farmer 140.

CHAMBERLIN, ALFRED HON., (Richfield Springs,) member of Assembly and farmer 200.

CHAMBERLIN, C. C., (Richfield Springs,) justice of the peace, boarding house keeper and farmer 216.

CHAMBERLIN, JAMES P., (Richfield Springs,) farmer 230.

CHAMPION, ISAAC, (Winfield, Herkimer Co.,) farmer 139.

CHURCHILL, E. M. MISS., (Richfield,) teacher select school.

Clapsaddle, Stephen, (Schuyler's Lake,) farmer 123.

Coats, Alfred, (Richfield,) farmer 12.

COLE & BROTHER, (Richfield,) (James and Franklin,) props. of saw mill, cider mill and cheese box factory.

Cole, Byron, (Winfield, Herkimer Co.,) farmer 57.

COLE, CHARLES, (Richfield Springs,) farmer 142.

Cole, Eseck, (Richfield,) town assessor and farmer 78.

COLE, FRANKLIN, (Richfield,) (Cole & Brother.)

COLE, JAMES,(Richfield,)(Cole & Brother,) farmer 66.

Cole, John, (Richfield,) farmer 214.

COLE, LINOUS, (Richfield Springs,) cheese factory and farmer 42.

Cole, Mercy Mrs.,(Richfield Springs,) (with heirs,) farmer 118.

COLE, VEEDER, (Richfield Springs,) (with Sylvester J. McRorie,) farmer 10.

Colman, Hamilton, (Richfield Springs,) retired farmer 47.

Colman, Lester, (Richfield Springs,) farmer leases 47.

Colwell, James M., (Richfield,) farmer 110.

Colwell, John L., (Richfield,) wagon maker.

Colwell, Martha A. Mrs., (Richfield,) milliner.

*COMSTOCK, JAY L., (Richfield Springs,) justice of the peace, surveyor and conveyancer.

*COMSTOCK, M. E. MISS, (Richfield Springs,) millinery, Church.

CONKLIN, HENRY, (Schuyler's Lake,) farmer 130.

CONVERSE, J. M., (Richfield Springs,) fashionable clothing and furnishing store, corner Main and Center.

Corbin, Benj. F., (Richfield,) town assessor and farmer 220.

Crain, Wm. B., (Richfield Springs,) physician and surgeon, corner Main and Lake.

Dager, Dennis, (Cedarville, Herkimer Co.,) farmer 91.

Dana, John, (Richfield Springs,) grist mill, Main.

DARROW, WM. E., (Richfield Springs,) (Tunnecliff & Darrow,) prop. International Hotel, on the European plan, Lake.

DAVENPORT HOUSE,(Richfield Springs,) Main opposite the spring, James S. Davenport, prop.

DAVENPORT, JAMES S., (Richfield Springs,) (Davenport & Young,) prop. of Davenport House, Main.

DAVENPORT & YOUNG, (Richfield Springs,) (James S. Davenport and John W. Young,) attorneys and counselors at law, Johnson Block, corner Main and Lake.

DAVIES, H. L., (Richfield Springs,) cheese manuf. at Bush Cheese Factory.

DAYGER, IRA, (Cedarville, Herkimer Co.,) farmer 180.

Deck, John H., (Richfield,) (with Eli Shimel,) farmer 160.

Delong, Isaiah, (Richfield Springs,) town assessor.

Derthick, James M., (Richfield Springs,) summer boarding house.

Derthick, John, (Richfield Springs,) boarding house, Main.

Derthick, John, (Richfield Springs,) farmer 212.

Ducher, Rulus, (Richfield Springs,) blacksmith.

Ealy, Lorenzo S., (Winfield, Herkimer Co.,) farmer 120.

Eason, Otis, (Richfield Springs,) farmer.

Eaton, Elizabeth Miss, (Richfield,) tailoress.

Eaton, Elizabeth Mrs., (Richfield,) farmer 9.

Eaton, Harriet, (Richfield,) tailoress.

EDICK, JOHN J., (Richfield Springs,) retired farmer.

Edick, Wm., (Richfield Springs,) farmer leases 140.

Elwood, Augustus R., (Richfield,) (Elwood & Tuller.)

Elwood & Tuller, (Richfield,) (Augustus R. Elwood and Melvin Tuller,) dry goods and groceries, corner Lake and Main.

ELY, DANIEL D., (Richfield,) farmer 121.

ELY, LUCIA MRS., (Winfield, Herkimer Co.,) resident.

FAY, PARKER D., (Richfield Springs,) attorney and counselor at law.

Fenton, Gilbert, (Richfield Springs,) gardener 15.

Fentou, Joel, (Richfield,) farmer 350.

Firman, Albert, (Richfield,) carpenter and farmer.

Firman, Geo., (Richfield,) carpenter and farmer 12.

Firman, John, (Richfield,) cooper and farmer 48.

Firman, Nelson, (Richfield,) farmer 74 and, in Exeter, 36.

Firman, Otis, (Richfield,) cooper and farmer 10.

Ford, Sylvester, (Richfield,) farmer 96.

Fort, Peter A., (Richfield Springs,) teamster and farmer 3.

Freudenberg Brothers, (Richfield Springs,) (*Henry J. and Gottlieb C.,*) carriage manufs., Main.

Freudenberg, Gottlieb C., (Richfield Springs,) (*Freudenberg Brothers.*)

Freudenberg, Henry J., (Richfield Springs,) (*Freudenberg Brothers.*)

*FULLER, CHAUNCEY B., (Richfield Springs,) manuf. harness and saddles, dealer in trunks and upholstering of all kinds, Main.

Gano, Garrett B., (Richfield Springs,) retired farmer 4.

Gano, James H., (Richfield Springs,) commissioner of highways and farmer 70.

Getman, Alonzo, (Richfield Springs,) (*Getman & Shimel.*)

Getman & Bronner, (Richfield Springs,) (*John F. Getman and Frederick Bronner,*) druggists, Main.

Getman, Frederick, (Richfield Springs,) (*with Ansley Locke,*) farmer leases 92.

Getman, John F., (Richfield Springs,) (*Getman & Bronner.*)

GETMAN, NORMAN, (Richfield Springs,) homeo. physician and surgeon, and supervisor.

Getman & Shimel, (Richfield Springs,) (*Alonzo Getman and E. Shimel,*) groceries &c., Main.

Gillet, Wm. H., (Richfield Springs,) book keeper.

GOODALE, AMOS A., (Richfield Springs,) express agent and stage prop., stages leave daily for Little Falls and Cooperstown station.

Goodale, Charles, (Richfield Springs,) grocery, meat market and express office.

Griffin, Orlando, (Richfield,) farmer 60.

Griffin, Peter, (Richfield,) farmer 105.

Hall, Robert, (Richfield,) farmer 114.

Hannahs, John N., (Richfield Springs,) blacksmith and livery stable, River.

Harding, Curtis, (Cedarville, Herkimer Co.,) farmer 80.

Harrington, Daniel, (Richfield,) retired farmer 44.

Harrington, Daniel D., (Richfield,) farmer leases 44.

Harte, L. A. Miss, (Cedarville, Herkimer Co.,) school teacher.

Harter, Levi, (Cedarville, Herkimer Co.,) shoemaker and farmer 3.

Haskall, Wm., (Richfield Springs,) farmer for Lewis Jones.

Hayward, Thomas, (Richfield,) farmer 60.

Hendrix, Erastus R., (Richfield Springs,) foreman in J. Backus' mill.

Hicks, Warren, (Richfield Springs,) farmer leases of C. C. Chamberlin, 210.

Hinds, Eugene A., (Richfield Springs,) general merchant, postmaster and notary public, Main.

Hitchings, Wm. T., (Winfield, Herkimer Co.,) farmer 66.

HOPKINS, P. K., (Richfield Springs,) farmer 90.

Hopkinson, Wm., (Richfield Springs,) farmer 5.

Hosford, Matthew K., (Richfield Springs,) private boarding house, Main.

HOUSE, LAFAYETTE, (Cedarville, Herkimer Co.,) farmer leases of James Arnold, 162.

Hull, Jerome, (Richfield,) farmer leases of Jared Green, 250.

Hull, Lewis B., (Winfield, Herkimer Co.,) farmer 2.

Hull, Sturgis B., (Richfield,) general merchant.

Huntley, Isaac, (Richfield,) farmer 20.

HYDE, JOSEPH M., (Richfield,) merchant, post master, justice of the peace and farmer 69.

Ingalls, Daniel D., (Schuyler's Lake,) farmer leases 127.

Ingalls, Harriet Mrs., (Schuyler's Lake,) milliner.

Ingalls, Henry F., (Schuyler's Lake,) farmer 22.

INTERNATIONAL HOTEL, (Richfield Springs,) on the European plan, Wm. E. Darrow, prop., Lake.

Jacobson, A. A., (Richfield,) prop. of Monticello House.

Johnson, James B., (Richfield Springs,) farmer 167.

JOHNSON, JULIA A. Mrs., (Richfield Springs,) prop. of American Hotel, Main, opposite the Sulphur Spring.

Johnson, William, (Richfield Springs,) farmer 40.

Jones, Damon, (Richfield Springs,) musician and farmer 40.

Jones, Griffith, (Winfield, Herkimer Co.,) farmer 202.

Jones, John B., (Richfield Springs,) farmer 60.

Jordan, James, (Richfield,) farmer 27.

Joshlyn, James C., (Winfield, Herkimer Co.,) farmer 370.

Keene, Albert E., (Richfield Springs,) shoe maker, Main.

KELLER, SANDUSKY, (Richfield Springs,) prop. of Richfield Hotel.

King, Ellen Mrs., (Richfield,) millinery and fancy goods, Main.

Kinne, Guy, (Richfield Springs,) boots, shoes, trunks &c., corner Main and Lake.

Kling, —— Mrs., (Richfield Springs,) millinery, Elm.

KNAPP, ORRA, (Richfield Springs,) merchant tailor, corner Lake and James.

Langdon, Patrick, (Richfield Springs,) butcher and farmer 42.

Laning, Sylvester, (Richfield,) farmer 47.

Layten, Harvey, (Richfield Springs,) farmer 160.

Leary, John, (Richfield,) farmer 5.

Lewis, Wm. H., (Richfield Springs,) prop. of Lake House.
Locke, Ansley, (Richfield Springs,) *(with Frederick Getman,)* farmer leases 92.
LOCKE, DAVID, (Richfield,) farmer 151.
Loomis, Ann Mrs., (Richfield,) dress maker.
Loomis, Edwin, (Richfield,) dairyman, 50 cows, and farmer 410.
Loomis, Sibyl Mrs., (Richfield,) *(with heirs,)* farmer 136 and leases 66.
Manley, Horace, (Richfield Springs,) physician and surgeon, Main.
*MARTIN, M. DeV., (Richfield,) cabinet ware, upholstery and undertaker, James.
McCredy Brothers, (Richfield Springs,) *(John and Lewis,)* hardware, groceries and produce, Main.
McCredy, Charles W., (Richfield Springs,) farmer 108½.
McCredy, John, (Richfield Springs,) *(McCredy Brothers.)*
McCredy, Lewis, (Richfield Springs,) *(McCredy Brothers.)*
McRorie, Alfred, (Richfield Springs,) farmer 96.
McRORIE, CHARLES, (Richfield,) farmer.
McRorie, George, (Richfield,) farmer 126.
McRORIE, SYLVESTER J., (Richfield Springs,) *(with Veeder Cole,)* farmer 10.
Morgan, Nelson, (Richfield Springs,) justice of the peace and farmer 40.
Moxley, Wm., (Richfield Springs,) blacksmith.
Mulligan, —— Mrs., (Winfield, Herkimer Co.,) farmer leases of A. More, 220.
Norton, Alpheus, (Schuyler's Lake,) farmer 23.
Oltever, Peter, (Richfield Springs,) carpenter.
Orendorff, Alson, (Richfield Springs,) farmer 52.
Orendorff, C. Mrs., (Richfield Springs,) farmer 17.
Orendorff, O. C., (Richfield Springs,) physician and surgeon, Main.
Osborne, Wm., (Richfield Springs,) farmer leases of E. Bennett, 184.
Owen, Robert, (Winfield, Herkimer Co.,) farmer 400.
Palmer, Damon, (Richfield Springs,) physician and surgeon, and farmer 80.
Palmer, Humphrey, (Richfield Springs,) saw filer.
Perkins, Thomas B., (Richfield,) farmer 25.
Perkins, Willis, (Richfield,) farmer 230.
Pierce, J. R. Rev., (Richfield Springs,) pastor of Episcopal Church.
PORTER, DUDLEY, (Richfield Springs,) farmer 40.
Purchase, Alvin A., (Cedarville, Herkimer Co.,) farmer leases 95.
Purchase, DeWitt, (Cedarville, Herkimer Co.,) farmer 200.
Purchase, R. C., (Cedarville, Herkimer Co.,) farmer leases 108.
RANSOM, NORMAN K., (Richfield Springs,) *(Bryan & Ransom.)*
Rathbun, Elizabeth Mrs., (Richfield Springs,) boarding house, Main.
Reed, Christopher, (Richfield,) farmer 200.
Richardson, Almor, (Richfield,) *(with Dexter,)* farmer 75.

Richardson, Dexter, (Richfield,) *(with Almor,)* farmer 75.
RICHFIELD HOTEL, (Richfield Springs,) Sandurky Keller, prop.
*RICHFIELD SPRINGS MERCURY, (Richfield Springs,) C. Ackerman & Son, publishers and proprietors, Main.
ROBERTS, HENRY C., (Richfield Springs,) *(Norman C. Roberts & Son.)*
ROBERTS, NORMAN C. & SON, (Richfield Springs,) *(Henry C.)* props. of saw, cider and planing mills.
Robinson, Elizabeth Mrs., (Richfield,) *(with heirs,)* farmer 364.
Robinson, John, (Winfield, Herkimer Co.,) farmer 170.
Robinson, J. G. & A. D., (Richfield Springs,) farmer 175.
Robinson, Luther J., (Winfield, Herkimer Co.,) farmer leases 170.
Rooker, Leander P., (Richfield Springs,) farmer 25.
Rose, Homer, (Richfield Springs,) farmer 46.
Seaman, Abram, (Richfield,) *(with Albert,)* farmer 111.
Seaman, Albert, (Richfield,) *(with Abram,)* farmer 111.
Seckner, Francis A., (Cedarville, Herkimer Co.,) *(with Phineas G.,)* farmer leases 240.
Seckner, Phineas G., (Cedarville, Herkimer Co.,) *(with Francis A.,)* farmer leases 240.
Seeber, Mattie Miss, (Richfield Springs,) *(Stitts & Co.,)* librarian Ladies' Circulating Library Association.
Seeley, F. H. Rev., (Richfield Springs,) pastor of Presbyterian Church.
Shaul, Cornelius, (Richfield Springs,) cattle broker and farmer 142.
Shepard, Kate Miss, (Richfield,) music teacher.
Shimel, Amelia Miss, (Richfield Springs,) dressmaker.
Shimel, E., (Richfield Springs,) *(Getman & Shimel.)*
Shimel, Eli, (Richfield,) *(with John H. Deck,)* farmer 160.
Shoemaker, David, (Richfield Springs,) billiards and dining rooms, Union Hall.
Shwitzer, John, (Richfield Springs,) blacksmith.
Sitts, Anson, (Richfield Springs,) farmer 174.
Sloan, W. Mrs., (Richfield,) farmer 37.
Smith, A. J. & Son, (Richfield Springs,) druggists, Main.
Smith, Gamaliel, (Richfield Springs,) farmer 4.
Smith, Michael, (Richfield,) farmer leases of Nelson Denman, 150.
Snyder, Horace, (Richfield,) physician and surgeon.
Sommers, Wm., (Richfield Springs,) farmer 3.
SPRING HOUSE, (Richfield Springs,) Bryan & Ransom, props., corner Main and Church.
Stanton, Frederick, (Richfield,) refused information.
STARKWEATHER, IRA, (Richfield Springs,) house painter in all its branches.

STARR, JAMES, (Richfield Springs,) farmer 130.

Starr, James P., (Richfield Springs,) farmer.

Starr, Wallace, (Richfield Springs,) farmer.

Sternburg, Peter, (Richfield Springs,) refuses information.

STILLMAN, WILLETT D., (Richfield Springs,) dentist, Main, 3d floor Water's Block.

Stitts & Co., (Richfield Springs,) (*Miss Libbie Stitts and Miss Mattie Seeber,*) ladies' furnishing goods, Main.

Stitts, Libbie Miss, (Richfield Springs,) (*Stitts & Co.*)

STITTS, THOMAS, (Richfield Springs,) carpenter and joiner.

St. John, Newton, (Richfield Springs,) farmer 124.

St. John, Samuel, (Richfield Springs,) farmer 40.

Storer, James A.,(Richfield Springs,) books, stationery, fancy goods &c., telegraph operator and town clerk.

Swift, A. D., (Schuyler's Lake,) information refused.

Taylor, ——, (Richfield Springs,) (*Youngs & Taylor.*)

Terpening, Valentine, (Richfield,) farmer leases of A. Crandal, 230.

THOMPSON, G. S., (Richfield Springs,) hair dresser,American Hotel and Spring House.

Town, Rufus, (Richfield,) farmer 85.

Tuller, Melvin, (Richfield,) (*Elwood & Tuller.*)

TUNNECLIFF, C. C., (Richfield Springs,) (*Tunnecliff & Darrow.*)

Tunnecliff, Cornelia E. Miss, (Richfield,) (*C. E. & M. M. Tunnecliff.*)

Tunnecliff, C. E. & M. M., (Richfield,) (*Miss Cornelia E. and Miss Mary M.,*) boarding house, Main.

TUNNECLIFF & DARROW, (Richfield Springs,) (*C. C. Tunnecliff and Wm. E. Darrow,*) props. of livery, office at International Hotel, Lake.

Tunnecliff, Mary M. Miss, (Richfield,) (*C. E. & M. M. Tunnecliff.*)

Tuttle, Charles, (Richfield,) farmer 126.

Tuttle, Jared, (Richfield,) farmer leases of O. Tuttle, 126.

Vancuren, Wm., (Richfield Springs,) summer hotel and farmer 167.

Vanderwerken, Emma Miss, (Richfield Springs,) milliner and pattern dealer, Main.

Vroman & Brown, (Richfield Springs,) (*Nicholas Vroman and Charles Brown,*) butchers, props. meat market and farmers lease 80.

Vroman, Nicholas, (Richfield Springs,) (*Vroman & Brown.*)

WAGNER, JOHN F., (Richfield Springs,) carpenter and joiner.

Walker, Henry, (Richfield Springs,) farmer 194.

Walker, Lucius, (Richfield,) farmer 98.

Walker, Wm., (Richfield,) farmer 126.

Walker, —— Mrs.,(Richfield Springs,) dress maker.

*WALTER, J. & H. C., (Richfield Springs,) watches, jewelry, silver ware &c., Main.

Ward, Ephraim, (Richfield,) farmer 130.

Ward, Ephraim, (Richfield,) farmer 122.

Ward, S. R. Rev., (Richfield Springs,) pastor Universalist Church.

WARD, WM. B., (Richfield Springs,) dealer in lumber, flour and feed, Lake near Depot.

Wheeler, Harvey,(Winfield, Herkimer Co.,) farmer 190.

Whithan, Charles, (Richfield Springs,) painter and grainer.

WIKOFF, GARRETT, (Richfield Springs,) farmer 220.

Wilder, Geo., (Richfield Springs,) farmer 60.

Winnie, Jay, (Richfield Springs,) boots and shoes, corner Lake and James.

Woodbert, John, (Richfield,) farmer 25.

WOODBURY, DANIEL H., (Richfield,) rail road commissioner and farmer 100.

Wright, John, (Cedarville, Herkimer Co.,) farmer 72.

Wright, Sarajah, (Cedarville, Herkimer Co.,) farmer.

YOUNG, JOHN W., (Richfield Springs,) (*Davenport & Young.*)

YOUNG, N. & S. R., (Cedarville, Herkimer Co.,) farmers 80.

Youngs & Taylor, (Richfield Springs,) house, sign, carriage and ornamental painters.

P

ROSEBOOM.

(Post Office Addresses in Parentheses.)

ALLEN, ANDREW D., (South Valley,) agent for agricultural implements and farmer 137.

Allen, David, (Seward,) farmer leases of Andrew, 50.

Allen, Isaac H., (South Valley,) thrashing machine and farmer 46.

Allen, Menzo, (South Valley,) farmer 100.

Allen, ——, (Middlefield,) farmer 100.

Amy, Henry, (Pleasant Brook,) farmer 40.

Aney, Jeremiah, (Pleasant Brook,) farmer leases of Geo. Clark, 250.

Aney, John, (Seward,) farmer 140.

Aney, Menzo, (South Valley,) farmer 290.

Aney, Wm. H., (South Valley,) farmer 200.

Antisdel, George, (Roseboom,) carriage manuf.

Armstrong, John, (South Valley,) farmer 4.

Arrey, Henry, (Pleasant Brook,) farmer 40.

Bailey, Aaron, (Pleasant Brook,) farmer 60.

BAILEY, DAVID W., (Roseboom,) shoemaker.

Bailey, Wm. H., (Roseboom,) shoemaker.

BARNARD, ETHELBERT D., (Pleasant Brook,) teacher.

BARRETT, GEORGE, (South Valley,) tanner and farmer 30.

Barrett, Jacob, (Pleasant Brook,) carpenter and millwright.

Barter, John, (Center Valley,) farmer 100.

Barton, Wm., (Middlefield,) farmer 250.

Baxter, David V., (Pleasant Brook,) farmer 111.

Baxter, D. & O., (South Valley,) farmer 120.

Baxter, John, (Pleasant Brook,) farmer 171.

Baxter, —— Mrs., (South Valley,) farmer 200.

Becker, A. H.,(Pleasant Brook,) farmer 154.

BECKER, ISAAC, (Pleasant Brook,) painter and agent for Warrior Mowing Machine.

Bell, John, (South Valley,) farmer 6¼.

Blythe, John H., (Roseboom,) miller.

BLYTHE, STEPHEN, (Roseboom,) leases grist mill.

BOTSFORD, GEO. Y., (Pleasant Brook,) resident.

Bowen, Hiram L. Rev., (South Valley,) pastor of Methodist Church.

Boyce, German, (Roseboom,) farmer 84.

Boyce, James, (Roseboom,) farmer 130.

Bradley, Christopher, (Center Valley,) farmer 20.

BRIGGS, G. & E., (South Valley,) wagon makers, blacksmiths and farmers 18.

Brown, Abram I., (Pleasant Brook,) (with *John A. Eldred*,) farmer 94.

Brown, A. N., (Roseboom,) (with *Thomas I.*,) farmer 141.

BROWN, DANIEL G., (Pleasant Brook,) farmer 88.

Brown, Joseph R., (Pleasant Brook,) farmer 70.

Brown, Thomas I., (Roseboom,) (with *A. N.*,) farmer 141.

Brozie, Wm., (Pleasant Brook,) shoemaker.

Bullis, Avery P., (Roseboom,) farmer 5.

BUSH, GEO. P., (South Valley,) farmer 4.

BUTLER, JOHN L., (South Valley,) (with *Wm.*)

Butler, John N., (South Valley,) farmer 122.

Butler, Seth, (South Valley,) farmer 65.

Butler, Watson, (South Valley,) farmer 160.

Butler, Wm., (South Valley,) farmer 108.

Campbell, Leonard, (Roseboom,) farmer 68.

CAREY, EDWARD B., (Seward,) farmer.

Chamberlain, John, (Pleasant Brook,) farmer 119.

Chamberlain, Wm., (Pleasant Brook,) farmer 15.

CHAMBERLIN, CYRUS,(Pleasant Brook,) farmer leases of L. Hoose, 260.

Chambers, James, (South Valley,) farmer leases of Thomas Folmsbee, 100.

Chambers, William, (South Valley,) farmer 100.

Coats, Lester, (Roseboom,) farmer 220.

Coats, Orvel, (Roseboom,) butcher.

Cole, John D., (Pleasant Brook,) farmer.

Conrad, Daniel, (Pleasant Brook,) farmer 77.

Conrad, Henry, (Pleasant Brook,) farmer 75.

Contryman, John, (Center Valley,) farmer 90.

Cornell, Peter, (South Valley,) farmer leases of Geo. Antisdale, 112.

Coulter, Wm., (Pleasant Brook,) farmer leases of George Clark, 100.

Countryman, Alexander, (Pleasant Brook,) farmer 140.

Countryman, Jeremiah, (Pleasant Brook,) farmer 72.

COUNTRYMAN, MARTIN, (Pleasant Brook,) constable and farmer 132.

Crippen, Matilda, (South Valley,) farmer 64.

Cross, Charles, (Center Valley,) farmer 25.

CROSS, CHESTER G., (Roseboom,) carpenter and farmer 48.

Cross, Norman, (Center Valley,) farmer 144.
CROUNSE, LEVI, (Pleasant Brook,) farmer leases 35.
Crounse, Margaret, (Pleasant Brook,) farmer 30.
Dailey, Henry, (South Valley,) poor master and farmer 150.
Davis, George, (Pleasant Brook,) farmer 50.
Davis, Hiram, (Pleasant Brook,) farmer leases 40.
Davis, Leman, (Pleasant Brook,) farmer 40.
DEAN, VALENTINE, (Pleasant Brook,) farmer 106.
DECKER, FRIENDAY Mrs., (Center Valley,) carpet weaver and farmer 2.
Degraff, Morris, (Cherry Valley,) farmer 122.
Degraff, Richard, (South Valley,) farmer 50.
Diefendorf, Berlin, (Center Valley,) farmer 4.
Diefendorf, William, (Center Valley,) farmer 97.
Dingman, John A., (Cherry Valley,) farmer 125.
Divendorf, Daniel G., (Pleasant Brook,) farmer 90.
Doningburgh, Henry, (Pleasant Brook,) farmer 30.
Doningburgh, Wm., (Pleasant Brook,) farmer 2.
Eckerson, James, (Pleasant Brook,) inspector of elections and farmer 80.
Eckerson, Ozias, (Pleasant Brook,) farmer 80.
ECKERSON, ZEPHANIAH, (South Valley,) shoemaker and farmer 84.
ELDRED, CHAS., (Pleasant Brook,) (O. Low & Co.)
Eldred, Daniel, (Pleasant Brook,) retired farmer.
Eldred, John A., (Pleasant Brook,) (with Abram I. Brown,) farmer 94.
ELWELL, FREDERICK A., (Roseboom,) overseer of the poor, prop. of grist and saw mills, and farmer 50.
Empie, Delos, (South Valley,) farmer 150.
Farwell, Lanson, (Roseboom,) farmer 91.
FINCH, D. A., (South Valley,) post master, dry goods and groceries.
Finch, John, (Pleasant Brook,) farmer leases of William Adams, 16.
Finch, Stephen, (South Valley,) wagon maker.
Fœlensbee, Thomas, (South Valley,) farmer 35.
Folan, Levi, (South Valley,) farmer 80.
Foland, James, (Center Valley,) farmer leases 100.
Foland, John H., (South Valley,) farmer 90.
Foland, Levi, (South Valley,) farmer 100.
Foland, Z., (Center Valley,) farmer 100.
Folmesbee, Dempster, (Pleasant Brook,) farmer 86.
Folmsbee, John, (South Valley,) farmer 208.
Fratts, Henry, (South Valley,) mason and farmer 15.
Fredenburgh, Benjamin, (South Valley,) farmer 5.
Frink, Henry, (Roseboom,) farmer 6.
Gage, Allerton P., (Roseboom,) farmer 96.
GAGE, HENRY B., (Roseboom,) farmer leases of Oliver Gage, 50.

Gage, Oliver, (Roseboom,) farmer 50.
Gage, Oscar F., (South Valley,) carpenter.
Gage, S. T., (Roseboom,) carpenter and farmer 5.
Galer, Emerson, (Roseboom,) farmer leases of I. Shafer, 125.
GARDNER, ISAAC, (Seward,) carpenter and farmer 13.
GARDNER, JEREMIAH W., (Pleasant Brook,) blacksmith and wagon maker.
GARDNER, PELEG E., (South Valley,) hotel keeper and farmer 5.
GILLETT, ALBERT, (South Valley,) dealer in live stock and produce.
GILLETT, CULVER, (Pleasant Brook,) (C. & L. M. Gillett,) justice of the peace.
GILLETT, C. & L. M., (Pleasant Brook,) (Culver and Lewis M.,) merchants.
GILLETT, LEWIS M., (Pleasant Brook,) (C. & L. M. Gillett,) farmer 70.
Gillett, Robert, (Pleasant Brook,) farmer leases of A. H. Becker, 150.
Granger, John, (South Valley,) farmer leases of Newell, 107.
Green, Daniel N., (Middlefield,) farmer 48.
GRIFFEN, EDWARD, (South Valley,) justice of the peace, cradle manuf. and farmer 12.
GRIFFIN, HENRY, (South Valley,) manuf. of cradles and rakes, and farmer 25.
Griffin, Jehial, (Pleasant Brook,) saw mill and farmer 123.
Hadsell, Elijah, (South Valley,) farmer 9.
HANSON, NICHOLAS, (South Valley,) farmer 104.
Hanson, Nicholas, (South Valley,) farmer 104.
Hartom, Daniel, (South Valley,) blacksmith.
Hartom, John, (Pleasant Brook,) carpenter.
Hartom, Michael, (Pleasant Brook,) farmer 10.
HILL, HIRAM, (South Valley,) farmer 2.
HILLSINGER, DELEVAN, (South Valley,) laborer.
HOOSE, LINARD, (South Valley,) commissioner of highways and farmer 260.
Howland, Harmon, (Roseboom,) farmer 60.
Howland, Isaac, (South Valley,) carpenter.
HOWLAND, WM., (Roseboom,) saw mill and cabinet shop.
Hubbard, Wm., (Pleasant Brook,) farmer 60.
Hubleson, William, (Roseboom,) liquor agent.
Hunt, Edward, (Middlefield,) farmer leases 131.
Hyney, Sylvester, (Pleasant Brook,) saw mill, wool carding and farmer 21.
Jorden, Nelson, (Center Valley,) farmer 125.
Karner, Solomon, (Pleasant Brook,) farmer 50.
KELLER, FRANK, (South Valley,) farmer.
Keller, Peter, (South Valley,) carpenter and farmer 100.
Kinsman, Nicholas, (South Valley,) farmer 15.
Kinsman, Nicholas, (South Valley,) farmer 8.
Kneskern, Lyman, (Roseboom,) tailor.
Korn, John, (Pleasant Brook,) farmer 70.
Lovejoy, D., (Pleasant Brook,) farmer 25.

Low, Alfred, (South Valley,) farmer 87.

LOW, CHARLES E., (Roseboom,) sewing machine agent.

Low, David, (Roseboom,) farmer 152.

Low, Edward, (Roseboom,) sewing machine agent.

LOW, HIRAM L., (Roseboom,) (*with David*,) farmer.

LOW, O'THELBERT, (Pleasant Brook,) (*O. Low & Co.*,) town clerk and postmaster.

LOW, O. &. CO., (Pleasant Brook,) (*Othelbert Low and Chas. Eldred*,) dry goods and groceries.

Lowell, Floyd, (Seward,) teacher and farmer 60.

MABIE, A. O., (South Valley,) assessor and farmer 180.

MABIE, DAVID A., (South Valley,) farmer 93.

Mabie, Washington, (South Valley,) farmer 76.

MABIE, WM. H., (South Valley,) farmer 182.

MARKS, DANIEL C., (Pleasant Brook,) farmer leases of M. Marks, 92.

Marks, Lawrence, (South Valley,) mason.

Marks, Leroy, (Roseboom,) farmer 132.

Marks, Pamelia H. Mrs., (Pleasant Brook,) farmer 18.

Mattice, Conrad, (South Valley,) farmer 68.

McFee, Geo., (South Valley,) farmer leases of A. Allen, 70.

McKay, John H., (Roseboom,) farmer 160.

Miller, Anna, (Roseboom,) milliner and dressmaker.

Miller, A. J., (Roseboom,) carpenter.

Miller, Garrie, (South Valley,) blacksmith.

MILLER, HENRY G., (South Valley,) blacksmith and carriage manuf.

Miller, S. K. Mrs., (South Valley,) milliner.

Murdock, C. L., (Pleasant Brook,) farmer leases of D. Devendorf, 115.

Nelson, Henry, (Roseboom,) hotel keeper.

Oaks, Eli, (Roseboom,) farmer 103.

Oaks, Lucinda, (Roseboom,) farmer 77.

Ochampaugh, James, (South Valley,) farmer 75.

Parson, Sumner, (Pleasant Brook,) cooper and farmer 90.

PEARSON, EDWARD, (Pleasant Brook,) farmer 192.

PEARSON, SAWYER F., (Pleasant Valley,) (*Pearson & Whittleton*,) post master.

PEARSON & WHITTLETON, (Center Valley,) (*Sawyer F. Pearson and Edward Whittleton*,) fruit and ornamental trees.

Peeso, Austin E., (Roseboom,) wagon maker.

Peeso, Joseph, (Roseboom,) farmer 10.

PEESO, WM. D., (Pleasant Brook,) shoe maker.

Phillips, Daniel, (South Valley,) saw mill and farmer 14.

Pickerd, Charles A., (Cherry Valley,) carpenter and farmer 100.

Pierce, Martin, (Roseboom,) carpenter.

PITCHER, PETER H., (Pleasant Brook,) farmer 20.

Pitcher, Ranson, (Pleasant Brook,) farmer 30.

Pixley, Myron J., (Pleasant Brook,) farmer 117.

Platts, Peter, (South Valley,) farmer 83.

POPE, LEVI, (Roseboom,) general merchant, supervisor, prop. cheese factory, farmer 130 and leases 200.

Pramer, Henry, (Seward,) farmer 186.

PRESTON, JAMES E., (Pleasant Brook,) farmer 40.

PRESTON, SAMUEL E., (Pleasant Brook,) lumberman.

Putnam, Abram, (Pleasant Brook,) farmer 86.

Putnam, Albert, (South Valley,) farmer 63.

Putnam, John F., (South Valley,) farmer 10.

Race, Andrew, (Center Valley,) (*with John*,) farmer.

Race, Cortland, (Center Valley,) (*with John*,) farmer.

Race, John, (Center Valley,) farmer 229.

Race, Peter, (Center Valley,) (*with John*,) farmer.

REUREY, WM. M., (Roseboom,) farmer leases of Geo. Clark, 177.

Reury, James M., (Pleasant Brook,) (*with Josiah H.*,) farmer 150.

Reury, Josiah H., (Pleasant Brook,) (*with James M.*,) farmer 150.

Rhines, Garner, (Roseboom,) saw mill.

Rhines, Wandal, (Pleasant Brook,) deputy sheriff.

Ring, John, Jr., (South Valley,) tanner and farmer 75.

ROSEBOOM, HENRY, (Roseboom,) farmer 1,800.

Schemerhorn, George, (South Valley,) farmer 120.

SCOTT, GEO., (Roseboom,) blacksmith and assessor.

SEEBER, ADAM, (South Valley,) farmer 23.

Seeber, James W., (South Valley,) farmer 27.

Seever, James W., (South Valley,) pump manuf. and farmer 30.

Shafer & Son, (Roseboom,) dry goods and groceries, and farmer 135.

Sherman, Caroline, (Cherry Valley,) farmer 11.

Sherman, Eli, (Roseboom,) farmer 77.

Sherman, Joseph A., (Cherry Valley,) farmer 41 and leases of Mrs. Hicks, 30.

Sherman, Russell, (Roseboom,) farmer 125.

Sillman, George, (South Valley,) farmer 40.

SIMMONS, PETER, (South Valley,) farmer 87.

Sisum, Joseph, (Pleasant Brook,) painter and farmer 17.

Sisum, Wm., (Pleasant Brook,) farmer 158.

Sisum, Wm. H., (Westford,) farmer 228.

Skinner, Wm., (South Valley,) farmer 150.

Slocum, Harris, (Center Valley,) farmer 40.

Smith, Gilbert, (Center Valley,) saw mill and farmer 65.

Smith, James, (Seward,) farmer 50.

Smith, James H., (South Valley,) farmer 56.

Smith, John, (Pleasant Brook,) farmer 74.

Smith, Moses, (Pleasant Brook,) farmer 5.

Smith, Robert H., (Pleasant Brook,) carpenter.

Smith, Samuel, (South Valley,) saw mill.

Smith, Thomas, (Roseboom,) farmer 11.
Smith, Wesley, (Middlefield,) farmer 63.
Snyder, Duane, (South Valley,) farmer 100.
SNYDER, HENRY, (Pleasant Brook,) (*with Nicholas*,) retired farmer 207.
SNYDER, NICHOLAS, (Pleasant Brook,) (*with Henry*,) farmer 207.
Snyder, Philo, (Roseboom,) saw mill and farmer 154.
Sommers, Peter, (South Valley,) farmer 275.
Spangler, John, (South Valley,) farmer 176.
Stephens, John R., (Roseboom,) apiarian.
STERRICKER, JOHN W., M. D., (Roseboom,) physician and surgeon, postmaster and farmer 30.
Strael, Peter J., (Seward,) farmer 18.
SULLIVAN, DAVID E., (South Valley,) harness maker, jeweler and sewing machine agent.
Sutphen, Wm. H., (Roseboom,) insurance agent and farmer 105.
Thrall, Oliver P., (South Valley,) farmer 125.
Thrall, Oliver P., (Seward,) farmer 120.
Tillapaugh, Geo. H., (South Valley,) (*with Martin*,) farmer 185.
TILLAPAUGH, MARTIN, (South Valley,) (*with Geo. H.*,) farmer 185.
Tompson, Hiram, (Roseboom,) farmer 29.
Treat, Eisha, (Westford,) farmer 4.
Treat, John, (Westford,) farmer 70.
TUCKER, ISAAC, (Roseboom,) justice of the peace and farmer 131.
Tuller, D. M. Rev., (South Valley,) pastor Christian Church.
Ulman, John F., (South Valley,) farmer 150.
Ulman, Mathew, (South Valley,) farmer 85.
Van Alstine, Wm., (South Valley,) farmer leases of Henry Pramer, 50.
Vanalstyne, Wm., (Roseboom,) farmer 73.
Van Derwerker, Peter, (Pleasant Brook,) saw mill and farmer 134.
Vandeusen, E. G., (Westford,) farmer 124.
Van Patten, Menzo, (Center Valley,) farmer 100.
Vanvakengburgh, Christopher, (Center Valley,) farmer 4.
Vickers, Edward, (Roseboom,) farmer leases of William Francis, 260.
Waldorf, David, (Seward,) farmer 50.
Waldorf, David H., (Seward,) farmer 130.
WALDORFF, DAVID, (South Valley,) farmer 50.
Waldorff, John, (Pleasant Brook,) painter and farmer 4.

Waldroff, David H., (South Valley,) farmer 150.
WALKER, D. N., M. D., (South Valley,) physician and surgeon.
Ward, John E., (Seward,) carpenter.
WARREN, CHARLES, (Pleasant Brook,) hotel keeper.
Weaton, Peter, (South Valley,) saw mill and farmer 22.
WEBER, JOHN, (Seward,) farmer 130.
Webster, G. T., (Pleasant Brook,) saw mill and farmer 14.
Welch, Harris, (South Valley,) farmer 50.
Welch, James, (South Valley,) grist and saw mills, and farmer 25.
WELCH, OLIVER P., (South Valley,) miller.
WHITTLETON, EDWARD, (Center Valley,) (*Pearson & Whittleton*.)
Wilber, Osey, (Middlefield,) farmer 57.
Willeby, Samuel, (South Valley,) farmer 75.
Willis, Wm., (Roseboom,) farmer leases of Geo. Clark, 200.
Wilson, Charles R., (Pleasant Brook,) farmer leases of Peter Vanderwerker, 40.
WINNE, DAVID, (South Valley,) farmer 85.
Winne, Eliza Miss, (Middlefield,) farmer 14.
Winne, Harris, (Pleasant Brook,) farmer 80.
WINNE, ISAAC, (South Valley,) farmer 125.
WINNE, JOHN H., (South Valley,) farmer 110.
WINNE, LEONARD, (Pleasant Brook,) assessor and farmer 120.
Winne, Leonard P., (Pleasant Brook,) mason and farmer 110.
Winne, Levi, (Center Valley,) (*with Wm. F.*,) farmer 45.
Winne, Mathew, (Center Valley,) farmer 3.
Winne, Wm. F., (Center Valley,) saw mill, farmer 50 and (*with Levi*,) 45.
Winney, Angevine, (Pleasant Brook,) farmer.
Winney, Ozias, (Roseboom,) farmer 100.
Winnie, Harris, (Pleasant Brook,) farmer leases 110.
Wright, John, (Pleasant Brook,) farmer 44.
Wright, Martin, (South Valley,) farmer 164.
Wright, Sarah Mrs., (Middlefield,) farmer 40.
Wrin, Redman, (Roseboom,) farmer 65.
Yenley, Francis, (Roseboom,) farmer 91.
Yenley, Francis, Jr., (Roseboom,) farmer 6.

SPRINGFIELD.

(Post Office Addresses in Parentheses.)

Ackler, Peter P.,(Richfield Springs,) farmer 51.

Allen, Benjamin, (Richfield Springs,) farmer 170 and leases of Hiram L. Fay, 150.

Allen, Geo. E., (Richfield Springs,) (*with Jacob*,) farmer.

Allen, Jacob, (Richfield Springs,) hop dealer and farmer 340.

ALLEN, JAMES A., (Richfield Springs,) farmer 165.

Armstrong, Levi, (Springfield Center,) farmer 85.

Armstrong, Rufus C., (Springfield Center,) tinsmith.

Armstrong, William, (Van Hornesville, Herkimer Co.,) farmer 124.

Ayres, J. L., (Springfield Center,) farmer 11.

Backus, Daniel, (Springfield,) farmer leases of John, 105.

Backus, John, (Springfield,) farmer 105.

Baird, David, (Springfield Center,) horse dealer and overseer for Geo. Clark.

Barenger, Eliza, (East Springfield,) farmer 157.

Barenger, Moses, (East Springfield,) farmer 232.

BARKER & STEWART, (Springfield Center,) (*S. P. Barker and Stephen R. Stewart*,) insurance agents.

BARKER, S. P., (Springfield Center,) (*Barker & Stewart*.)

Bates, Joseph, (East Springfield,) farmer 131.

Batson, John, (East Springfield,) farmer 100.

BEACH, E. O., (East Springfield,) farmer 265.

Bennett, Marvin, (Springfield Center,) farmer 190.

Bennett, Royal, (Springfield Center,) farmer 100.

Bradley, Patrick, (Springfield,) farmer 103.

BRANCH, B. D., (East Springfield,) (*with G. W.*) farmer 152.

BRANCH, G. W., (East Springfield,) carpenter and (*with B. D.*,) farmer 152.

Brando, Worthing,(Van Hornesville, Herkimer Co.,) farmer 52.

Brezee, Calvin, (Springfield Center,) farmer leases of Henry S. Shaul, 175.

BREZEE, JOHN W., (Richfield Springs,) farm laborer.

Bringloe, Robert, (Springfield Center,) merchant tailor.

BROOKS, ORLANDO D., (Springfield Center,) blacksmith.

Burley, Daniel, (East Springfield,) farmer 92.

Burlingame, Billings G., (East Springfield,) farmer leases 125.

Burlingame, Thomas, (East Springfield,) farmer 130.

Burnham, R. O., (Springfield Center,) blacksmith.

BURST, JOHN N., (Springfield,) farm laborer.

Cam, Henry, (Springfield Center,) farmer leases of Peter McRorie, 73.

Campbell, Anna, (Springfield Center,) milliner.

Campbell, Theodore, (Springfield Center,) telegraph operator and town collector.

Cary, H. R., (Springfield Center,) farmer 95.

Casler, Levi, (Springfield,) farmer 26.

CHILSON, LEONARD, (Springfield Center,) farm laborer.

Christey, John, (Springfield Center,) farmer leases 160.

Clark, George, (East Springfield,) farmer 900.

CONGDON, ARTHUR W., (Richfield Springs,) (*with John*.)

CONGDON, CHARLES, (Richfield Springs,) farmer leases 126.

Congdon John, (Richfield Springs,) farmer 128.

Conklin, Wm., (Richfield Springs,) farmer 100.

Cook, Alvin, (East Springfield,) farmer 58.

Cook, James H., (East Springfield,) farmer leases of P. & D. Cook, 65.

Cook, Nison, (Van Hornesville, Herkimer Co.,) farmer 68.

COOKE & CURTIS, (Springfield Center,) (*Stewart E. Cooke and Damon C. Curtis*,) dry goods and groceries.

COOKE, STEWART E., (Springfield Center,) (*Cooke & Curtis*.)

Cotton, Erasmus D., (Springfield Center,) butcher.

Cross, Thomas, (Springfield Center,) farmer 115.

CURTIS, DAMON C., (Springfield Center,) (*Cooke & Curtis*.)

Davy, Henry A., (East Springfield,) justice of the peace and farmer 96.

Davy, Henry H., (East Springfield,) justice of the peace and farmer 105.

Davy, James, (East Springfield,) farmer 100.

Davy, Jeremiah, (East Springfield,) farmer 95.

Devoe, William, (Springfield,) farmer 5.

Dingman, Erin, (Van Hornesville, Herkimer Co.,) farmer 225.

Douglass, William, (Springfield Center,) carpenter.

Druse, Lyman, (Springfield Center,) farmer 200.

DRYDEN, WM., (Springfield Center,) farm laborer.

Dunckel, Ira T., (East Springfield,) farmer leases of Ephraim Gray, 10.

Durfey, James N., (Springfield,) blacksmith and farmer 18.

DUTCHER, C., (East Springfield,) farmer 133.

ECKLER, THOMAS, (Springfield Center,) farmer leases of Alfred Clark, 268.

Eckler, Thomas, (Springfield,) farmer 41.

Elwood, Joseph, (Van Hornesville, Herkimer Co.,) wagon maker and farmer 32.

Ely, Smith, (Springfield,) farmer leases 167.

ENDRES, JOHN P., (East Springfield,) cigar manuf.

Engell, Giles H., (Springfield Center,) saw mill, turning shop and farmer 13.

Engell, Joshua, (Springfield Center,) farmer 76.

English, Henry, (Springfield Center,) farmer leases of Jacob Hoke, 184.

Fake, Joseph, (Springfield Center,) farmer 145.

FAY, JAMES, (Richfield Springs,) cheese factory.

Fort, John, (East Springfield,) farmer 60.

FOWLER, G. HENRY, (East Springfield,) general merchant.

Fowler, George R., (East Springfield,) post master and farmer 12.

FRANCIS, E. S., (East Springfield,) carriage maker and farmer 8.

Franklin, Henry, (East Springfield,) farmer 90.

Frisbie, T. W., (East Springfield,) physician and surgeon.

Frost, Gilbert, (East Springfield,) farmer 230.

Furgessor, James R., (East Springfield,) farmer 100.

Gayler, Martin J., (Springfield Center,) painter.

Genter, Alvin, (East Springfield,) farmer leases of George Clark, 225.

GENTER, ALVIN Jr., (East Springfield,) (with Alvin,) farmer.

Genter, Clark, (East Springfield,) farmer 115.

Genter, Nicholas, (East Springfield,) farmer 112.

GETMAN, WM., (Springfield Center,) farmer 170.

GILCHRIST, ANDREW F., (Springfield Center,) farmer 180.

GILLETT, ABNER, (Springfield Center,) farm laborer.

Gilthrist, Daniel, (East Springfield,) farmer 150.

Grant, I. W., (East Springfield,) hotel keeper.

Gray, Charles, (East Springfield,) grist mill, saw mill and turning shop.

GRAY, CHARLES, (East Springfield,) farmer 291.

Gray, Daniel W., (East Springfield,) farmer 300.

Griggs, A. G., (Springfield,) farmer 130.

GRIGGS, JAMES A., (Springfield,) farmer 96.

Grinner, John, (Richfield Springs,) shoe maker.

Hahn, John, (Springfield,) farmer 25.

HALL, MYRON A., (Springfield Center,) hotel keeper.

HANCOCK, CORNELIUS A., (Richfield Springs,) farmer 100.

Hancock, John, (Springfield Center,) basket and shoemaker.

Hardy, John, (East Springfield,) farmer 122.

Hardy, Wm. E., (East Springfield,) farmer 40.

Harris, John, (East Springfield,) farmer 121.

Hewes, A. M., (Springfield Center,) farmer leases of G. H. Snyder, 101.

Hines, John W., (Richfield Springs,) farmer 120.

HITCHCOCK, HENRY W., (Springfield Center,) carpenter and joiner.

HOKE, JAMES W., (Springfield Center,) farmer 49.

Holmes, John, (East Springfield,) farmer 71.

Hood, James, (Springfield Center,) farmer 210.

HORNING, LAWRENCE, (Springfield Center,) harness maker and carriage trimmer.

Hoyer, Alonzo, (East Springfield,) farmer 120.

Hoyer, Wm., (East Springfield,) farmer 145.

Ingals, S. M., (Springfield,) farmer 202.

Kinder, Richard P., (Van Hornesville, Herkimer Co.,) farmer 85.

King, Edward, (East Springfield,) farmer leases of Geo. Clark, 350.

King, Philip P., (Springfield Center,) farmer 100.

King, Thomas, (Springfield Center,) farmer 100.

Lay, Zina E., (Springfield,) merchant and postmaster.

LENEGER, IRA A., (Springfield Center,) shoemaker.

LEWIS, MOSES P., (Springfield Center,) butcher.

Lewis, N. L., (Springfield,) cooper and carpenter.

LOSEE, JOHN, (Springfield Center,) postmaster, hop dealer and farmer 4.

MANLEY, THOMAS S., (Richfield Springs,) farmer leases of Horace, 100.

Manzer, James, (Springfield,) farmer 40.

Markell, Oliver S., (Springfield Center,) carpenter.

Marks, Herbert, (East Springfield,) (with Wm.,) farmer.

MARKS, WM., (East Springfield,) farmer 112.

Marshal, John, (Springfield Center,) farmer 130.

McAdams, James, (Springfield Center,) cheese maker.

McCarthy, Patrick, (East Springfield,) farmer leases of Geo. Clark, 300.

McDough, Michael, (Springfield Center,) farmer 2.

McRoice, Peter, (Springfield Center,) farmer 193½.

McRorie, Daniel, (Springfield Center,) assessor and farmer 105.

McRorie, Geo. A., (Springfield Center,) farmer 50.

McRorie, John, (Springfield Center,) farmer 50.

Monigan, Philip, (Springfield Center,) farmer leases of Geo. Clark, 50.

MORSE, HALL A., (Springfield Center,) ornamental plaster.

O'Halon, Michael, (East Springfield,) farmer leases of Geo. Clark, 400.

OLIVE, JOHN, (Springfield Center,) blacksmith.

Oliver, Robert, (East Springfield,) farmer 175.

Oliver, Robert O., (East Springfield,) farmer 140.

OLIVER, WM. M., (East Springfield,) attorney and justice of the peace.

Ostrander, John, (Springfield,) farmer 126.

Ostrander, Wm., (East Springfield,) farmer 206.

Ostrander, Wm.,(Springfield Center,) (*with Mrs. James Thayer*,) farmer 7.

OUGH, JOHN P., (Springfield Center,) farmer 50.

Peck, Aaron, (Springfield Center,) farmer 7½.

PECK, ISAAC, (Springfield Center,) resident.

Permelie, R. J. A. Mrs., (Springfield,) farmer 19.

Person, Geo. E., (Springfield Center,) wagon maker and painter.

PICKENS, HORACE T., (Richfield Springs,) farmer 100.

PIERCE, ALFRED K., (Richfield Springs,) farmer leases of John Wilsey, 100.

PITCHER, MENZO A., (Springfield Center,) farmer.

Rathbun, George, (Springfield Center,) farmer 109.

RATHBUN, JACOB C., (Springfield Center,) saw and cider mills, and farmer 170.

Rathbun, John A., (Springfield Center,) farmer 109.

RATHBUN, L. W., (East Springfield,) grist and saw mills, supervisor of town and farmer 201.

Rickert, Henry, (Van Hornesville, Herkimer Co.,) farmer leases of C. J. Canine, 104.

Riley, Nicholas, (Springfield Center,) farmer 40.

Robinson, Louis Mrs., (Springfield Center,) farmer 25.

Root, John, (Springfield Center,) farmer 270.

Runolds, Daniel, (Richfield Springs,) farmer 6.

Schofield, James, (Springfield Center,) farmer 100.

Scollard, David, (East Springfield,) farmer 120.

Scollard, John, (East Springfield,) farmer leases 120.

Seeber, Warren, (Richfield Springs,) farmer 168.

Seward, Seneca, (East Springfield,) blacksmith.

Shaul, John D., (East Springfield,) farmer 400.

Shaul, Wm. H., (Van Hornesville, Herkimer Co.,) farmer 135.

Sheldon, John B., (Springfield,) farmer 115.

Sheldon, Samuel, (Springfield,) farmer 60.

Sherdon, Barney, (Richfield Springs.)

Shipman, Alvin N., (Springfield Center,) farmer 140.

Simmons, E. Mrs., (Springfield,) farmer 90.

Sitts, Menzo, (Springfield Center,) farmer leases 100.

Sliter, Horace, (Richfield Springs,) farmer 200.

Sliter, Octavia Mrs., (Richfield Springs,) farmer 180.

Slone, John, (East Springfield,) farmer 87.

Small, Charles, (Springfield Center,) farmer leases of Peter McRorie, 100.

Small, Herbert, (Springfield Center,) farmer leases of Martin Springer, 155.

Smith, Calvin P., (Springfield,) farmer 77.

Smith, C. P., (East Springfield,) farmer 290.

Smith, Daniel, (Springfield,) farmer 146.

Smith, Samuel, (Van Hornesville, Herkimer Co.,) farmer 137.

Snyder, George, (Springfield Center,) farmer 226.

Snyder, Thomas, (East Springfield,) farmer 60.

Springer, Daniel, (Van Hornesville, Herkimer Co.,) farmer 225.

Stanbury, Frederick, (Springfield Center,) farmer 2.

Stansil, Wm., (East Springfield,) farmer 64.

STEWART, STEPHEN R., (Springfield Center,) (*Barker & Stewart*,) justice of the peace, butcher and farmer 50.

STOCKING, CHARLES R., (Springfield Center,) cider mill and farmer leases of J. Wood, 10.

STOCKING, M. D., (Springfield Center,) saw mill, cheese box factory and farmer 26½.

Summers, Allen, (Springfield Center,) farmer 60.

Taylor, David, (Springfield,) farmer 104.

Taylor, D. M., (Springfield,) teacher.

Teneyck, Lindell, (Springfield Center,) farmer 121.

Thayer, James Mrs., (Springfield Center,) (*with Wm. Ostrander*,) farmer 7.

Thayer, Stephen D., (Springfield Center,) farmer 200.

Theyer, Wm., Jr., (Springfield Center.)

Thursting, Job, (Springfield Center,) farmer 152.

THURSTON, LUCIOUS, (Springfield Center,) (*with Job*,) farmer.

Tompson, Alfred, (Springfield Center,) carpenter.

Tompson, Peter, (East Springfield,) farmer 16.

TORRY, JOHN L., (Richfield Springs,) farmer leases of Levi Ackler, 225.

Tumbler, George, (Springfield,) farmer leases.

TUNNICLIFF, GEORGE, (Springfield Center,) grist mill, carriage manuf. and farmer 44.

Tutty, Joseph, (Richfield Springs,) farmer 23.

Van Aucan, John, (Springfield Center,) farmer 100.

Van Aukin, John, (East Springfield,) farmer 135.

Van Buren, Tobias, (East Springfield,) farmer 2.

VAN DEVEER, G. W., (Springfield Center,) hardware, stoves and agricultural implements, manuf. of tin, sheet iron and copper ware, also town clerk.
Vandewacker, Wm., (East Springfield,) farmer 2.
Van Horn, A., (Springfield Center,) physician and surgeon.
VAN HORN, FREDERICK, (Richfield Springs,) farmer 120.
Van Horn, Lyman, (East Springfield,) farmer 126.
Van Horn, R. T. E., (Van Hornesville, Herkimer Co.,) farmer 160.
Vedder, Mattison, (Springfield,) farmer 200.
Vedder, Richard, (Springfield,) farmer 188.
Vibbard, Loren, (Springfield Center,) farmer 8.
Waer, John, (Springfield Center.)
Waffle, John, (East Springfield,) farmer 123.
Walrath, Jacob, (East Springfield,) farmer 193.
Way, Martin, (Springfield Center,) farmer 130.
Way, Wm. S., (Springfield Center,) physician.
WEBB, SEYMOUR, (Springfield Center,) harness maker and farmer 35.
Whipple, Ezra, (Springfield Center,) farmer 185.
Whipple, Jeannette, (Springfield Center,) farmer 110.
WHIPPLE, JOSEPH S., (Springfield Center,) farmer 81.
Whipple, Lewis, (East Springfield,) farmer 43.
White, Granville T., (Springfield Center,) farmer.
White, Jacob J., (Springfield Center,) dealer in fish, fur and poultry, and commissioner of highways.

White, John, (Springfield Center,) farmer 2.
WHITE, MARY D. Mrs., (Springfield Center,) farmer 96.
White, Theresa M. Miss, (Springfield Center,) farmer 24.
Wikoff, James, (Springfield Center,) farmer 200.
Wikoff, Wm., (Springfield Center,) retired farmer.
Wiles, Levi, (Van Hornesville, Herkimer Co.,) justice of the peace and farmer 130.
Wiles, Sabrina Mrs., (Van Hornesville, Herkimer Co.,) farmer 115.
Willis, P., (East Springfield,) farmer 168.
Winslow, James, (East Springfield,) mason.
WOLCOTT, THEO. E., (Springfield Center,) farmer.
Woleben, A., (Springfield,) farmer leases of Geo. Clark, 330.
WOOD, GANSEVOORT, (Springfield Center,) farm laborer.
Wood, H. R., (Springfield Center,) general merchant and dealer in hops.
Wood, Joseph, (Springfield Center,) farmer 180.
Wood, Robert, (Springfield Center,) saw and cider mills, and farmer 40.
Wykoff, Garrett, (East Springfield,) farmer 25.
Yong, John R., (East Springfield,) hop dealer and farmer 180.
Yong, Sheldon A., (Springfield,) (*with John R.*,) farmer.
Yongs, Lewis, (Van Hornesville, Herkimer Co.,) farmer 140.
Young, Andrew, (East Springfield,) farmer 265.
YOUNG, HERBERT M., (East Springfield,) (*with Andrew*,) farmer.

UNADILLA.

(Post Office Addresses in Parentheses.)

Aikins, David, (Unadilla,) farmer 50.
Albright, A., (Unadilla,) tailor, Main.
Amsden, A. T., (Unadilla,) carriage maker.
Arms, C. S., (Unadilla,) lawyer, Main.
Arms, Sylvester, (Unadilla,) farmer 80.
Arnold, Frank B., (Unadilla,) attorney, Main.
Avery, Melvin, (Unadilla,) miller.
Badger, Joseph, (Sidney Plains, Delaware Co.,) farmer 30.
BAILEY, HORACE E., (Unadilla,) (*Bailey & Robinson.*)
BAILEY & ROBINSON, (Unadilla,) (*Horace E. Bailey and Marshall Robinson,*) dry goods, drugs, medicines and manufs. of clothing, corner Main and Clifton.
Barnard, G. A., (Unadilla,) (*M. W. Duley & Co.*)
Barnes, Edwin J., (Unadilla,) farmer leases of Wm. Fritts, 150.
Barnes, Eunice Mrs., (Unadilla,) farmer.
Bartholomew, Chas., (East Guilford, Chenango Co.,) farmer 75.
Batterson, Ezekiel W., (Rockdale, Chenango Co.,) farmer 110.
Beardsley, James F., (Wells' Bridge,) farmer 125.
Beers, Edwin, (Wells' Bridge,) hop grower and farmer 117.
Bellknap, E. C., (Unadilla,) attorney, Main.
Benedict, Alex. N., (Unadilla,) farmer 113.
Benedict, Hiel E., (Unadilla,) tailor, Main.
Bennett, Nelson, (Unadilla,) shingle mill and farmer 22.
Bennett, P. O., (Unadilla,) carpenter and farmer 25.
Billings, Sally A., (Unadilla,) farmer 15.
Birdsel, Ira, (Unadilla Center,) farmer 65.
Birdsel, Night Mrs., (Unadilla,) farmer 110.
BISHOP, CHARLES, (Unadilla,) prop. Brick Hotel.
Bishop, John, (Wells' Bridge,) farmer 100.
Blakely, John, (Unadilla,) farmer 75.
Blanchard, Ebenezer R., (Wells' Bridge,) justice of the peace and farmer 68.
Blanchard, Edward J., (Wells' Bridge,) overseer of the poor and farmer 70.
Blanchard, Larkin H., (Wells' Bridge,) farmer 105.
Bolles, Frederick A., (Unadilla,) (*Cone & Bolles.*)
Boorn, C. A., (Unadilla,) (*Halsey & Boorn.*)
Breed, Abel, (Unadilla,) farmer 70.
BRICK HOTEL, (Unadilla,) Chas. Bishop, prop.
Brown, Alex., (Rockdale, Chenango Co.,) farmer 25.

Brown, D. M., (Rockdale, Chenango Co.,) farmer 100.
Brown, Harvey, (Wells' Bridge,) farmer 65.
Buckley, Arthur M., (Unadilla,) lawyer.
Buckley, Judson, (Wells' Bridge,) farmer leases 9.
Buckley, Oliver E., (Unadilla Center,) farmer 200.
Buckley, Orman H., (Wells' Bridge,) carpenter and farmer 4.
Buckley, Wm., (Wells' Bridge,) farmer 18.
Bundy, James, (Sidney Plains, Delaware Co.,) farmer 120.
Burdick, Alden, (Unadilla Center,) farmer 50.
Burdick, Thos., (Unadilla,) farmer 96.
Burgin, Geo. M., (Unadilla,) boots, shoes, leather &c., Main.
Burris, Duane, (Rockdale, Chenango Co.,) farmer 10.
Butler, Francis D., (Unadilla Center,) farmer 80.
Butler, Lanman A., (Unadilla,) farmer leases of Ezra Hemingway.
Card, Nathan, (Unadilla Center,) mason.
Carr, Benj., (Wells' Bridge,) drover and farmer 170.
Carr, Hezekiah, (Wells' Bridge,) mechanic and farmer 4.
Carver, Egbert M., (Unadilla,) (*Carver & Wendall.*)
Carver & Wendall, (Unadilla,) (*Egbert M. Carver and Wm. Wendall,*) bankers, Main corner Depot.
Chaffin, Samuel H., (Unadilla Center,) farmer 100.
Chapin, Wm., (Unadilla,) stock dealer and farmer 323.
Chapman, Porter D., (Unadilla,) farmer 150.
CHURCH, GAYLORD L., (Wells' Bridge,) cooper.
Cohn, Aaron, (Unadilla,) (*Cohn Bros.*)
Cohn Bros., (Unadilla,) (*Aaron and Wolfe,*) fancy goods and ready made clothing, Main.
Cohn, Wolfe, (Unadilla,) (*Cohn Bros.*)
Cole, Hiram, (Unadilla Center,) postmaster.
Collins, Henry, (Wells' Bridge,) farmer 100.
Collins, Leroy S., (Unadilla,) farmer leases 50.
Collins, Rufus S., (Wells' Bridge,) farmer 165.
Cone & Bolles, (Unadilla,) (*Lewis G. Cone and Frederick A. Bolles,*) hardware, Main.
Cone, Lewis G., (Unadilla,) (*Cone & Bolles.*)

Cone, Salmon G., (Unadilla,) farmer 116.
Connelly, Charley M., (Unadilla Center,) farmer 110.
Connelly, Thos. N., (Wells' Bridge,) farmer 67.
Copley, E. J., (Unadilla,) farmer 110.
Copley, Wm., (Wells' Bridge,) hop grower and farmer 20.
Corbett, David, (Unadilla,) carpenter and farmer 20.
Crandal, Geo., (Unadilla,) farmer.
Crandal. Hial, (Unadilla,) cigar manuf., Main.
Crimby, Robert, (Unadilla,) farmer 33.
Cunningham, Solomon, (Wells' Bridge,) farmer 150.
Curtis, Lysander, (Unadilla,) farmer 200.
Cutler, Ralph B., (Unadilla,) farmer 130.
Dag, Walter, (Unadilla,) farmer 180.
Daggett, Geo. W., (Wells' Bridge,) farmer 21.
DAVIS, ANTHONY J., (Unadilla,) farmer leases 76½.
Davis, Anthony J. Mrs., (Unadilla,) farmer 76½.
Davis, Thos. J., (Wells' Bridge,) farmer 100.
Day, Albert, (Rockdale, Chenango Co.,) farmer leases of E. Brainard, 100.
Day, Oren W., (Unadilla,) prop. of Unadilla Livery Stable, Depot.
Deforest, Arthur, (Unadilla,) farmer 40.
Deforest, Geo., (Unadilla,) farmer 100.
Deforest, Isaac, (Unadilla,) farmer 145.
Deforest, John N., (Unadilla,) farmer 70.
Deforest, Lafayette, (Unadilla,) farmer 165.
Deforest, L. H., (Unadilla,) ready-made clothing and furnishing goods, Main.
Deforest, Mary Mrs., (Unadilla,) farmer 100.
Deforest, Wm., (Unadilla,) farmer 285.
Deforrest, W. E., (Unadilla,) grocery, Main.
DELAP, HIRAM E., (Unadilla,) farmer.
DeVol, Silas, (Wells' Bridge,) farmer 125.
Dibble, Tustin, (Unadilla,) (Smith & Dibble.)
*DODGE, G. A., (Unadilla,) prop. Home and Abroad, Main corner Bridge.
Duley, M. W. & Co., (Unadilla,) (G. A. Barnard,) grist, saw and planing mills.
Dunham, A. C., (Rockdale, Chenango Co.,) farmer 200.
Dunlap, David, (Rockdale, Chenango Co.,) farmer 150.
Dunlap, John, (Rockdale, Chenango Co.,) farmer 100.
Earl, John H., (Wells' Bridge,) farmer 200.
Ellsworth, Ransom, (Unadilla,) farmer 56.
Emery & Son, (Unadilla,) (W. H. and W. P.,) groceries, Main.
Emery, W. H., (Unadilla,) (Emery & Son.)
Emery, W. P., (Unadilla,) (Emery & Son.)
Fairbank, Henry F., (Unadilla Center,) shoemaker and farmer 25.
Fancher, Selleck H., (Unadilla,) boots and shoes, Main.
Faulkner, Freddie Miss, (Unadilla,) millinery, Main.
Fellows, Christopher D., (Unadilla,) (C. D. Fellows & Son.)
Fellows, C. D. & Son, (Unadilla,) (Christopher D. and George B.,) general merchants, corner Main and Bridge.
Fellows, Geo. B., (Unadilla,) (C. D. Fellows & Son.)

Finch, David, (Unadilla,) prop. of Empire House, Main.
Fisher, Margaret, (Unadilla,) farmer 67.
Fisher, Oren W., (Unadilla,) farmer 10.
Fisk, Albert, (Unadilla Center,) farmer 21.
Fisk, Geo. L., (Unadilla,) farmer 36.
Fisk, Hiram, (Unadilla,) farmer 112.
Fisk, Hiram Jr., (Unadilla,) farmer 50.
Fitch, Rensselaer, (Unadilla,) prop. Rogers Hollow Saw Mill and farmer 11½.
Fitzgerald, John, (Wells' Bridge,) farmer 12.
Flint, Wm. L., (Wells' Bridge,) farmer 3.
Foot, Hyatt, (Unadilla,) farmer 120.
Foster, Henry, (Unadilla,) farmer 100.
Foster, Norman, (Unadilla,) farmer 125.
Fox, Samuel, (Unadilla,) farmer 120.
FULLER, CHARLES, (Unadilla,) (Fuller & Lehrberg,)
FULLER & LEHRBERG, (Unadilla,)(Chas. Fuller and Mendel Lehrberg,)dry goods, millinery and fancy goods, agents for Elias Howe Sewing Machine, Main.
Gage, Walter, (Unadilla,) agent for Albany Coffee and Spice Mills, and farmer 23.
Gates, Jehiel, (Unadilla,) farmer 172.
Gates, Wm., (Unadilla,) farmer 116.
GOLDSMITH & HARRIS, (Unadilla,) (Leopold Goldsmith and Jonas Harris,) dry and fancy goods, Main.
GOLDSMITH, LEOPOLD, (Unadilla,) (Goldsmith & Harris.)
Goldsmith, Oliver A., (Wells' Bridge,) farmer leases 70.
Greene, Geo., (Wells' Bridge,) (Leonard & Greene.)
Gregory, H. C., (Unadilla,) general merchant, Main corner Depot.
Griffis, Perry, (Wells' Bridge,) hop picker and farmer 50.
Griffis, Solomon L., (Wells' Bridge,) hop grower and farmer 50.
Haines, Chas., (Unadilla,) farmer 100.
Hallock, David, (Wells' Bridge,) farmer 16.
Hallock, Thos., (Unadilla Center,) farmer 100.
Halsey & Boorn, (Unadilla,) (G. L. Halsey, M. D., and C. A. Boorn,) drugs, medicines, stationery, wall paper &c., Main.
Halsey, G. L., (Unadilla,) (Halsey & Boorn,) physician.
HANFORD, CLARK, (Unadilla,) (D. Hanford & Co.)
HANFORD, DAVID, (Unadilla,) (D. Hanford & Co.)
HANFORD, D. & CO., (Unadilla,) (David, Clark and John Hanford,) carriage manufs., Bridge.
HANFORD, JOHN, (Unadilla,) (D. Hanford & Co.)
Harby, Thomas, (Unadilla,) (Townsend & Harby.)
Hard, Amos J., (Wells' Bridge,) farmer 235.
Harris, Asa, (Unadilla,) farmer 200.
HARRIS, JONAS, (Unadilla,) (Goldsmith & Harris.)
Hawks, Erastus B., (Wells' Bridge,) farmer 120.
Hawks, Henry L., (Wells' Bridge,) farmer 60.
HEADY, EBEN S., (Unadilla,) farmer 168.
Heath, ——, (Unadilla,) (Wilmot & Heath.)
Heliker, Henry, (Unadilla,) tailor, River.

HERALD, JOHN, (Unadilla,) foundry and machine shop, and manuf. of barn door hinges.

Hickok, Juliet, (Unadilla,) farmer 150.

Hire, Edgar A., (Rockdale, Chenango Co.,) farmer 72.

Holmes, Amos, (Unadilla Center,) farmer 121.

*HOME AND ABROAD, (Unadilla,) Main corner Bridge, G. A., Dodge, editor and prop.

Hughston, Robert L., (Wells' Bridge,) farmer leases 320.

Humphrey, Lorenzo, (Sidney Plains, Delaware Co.,) (*Palmer, Humphrey & Co.*)

Humphrey, Wm., (Sidney Plains, Delaware Co.,) (*Palmer Humphrey & Co.*)

Hutchinson, Milo, (Unadilla,) farmer 125.

Hyer, Geo., (Rockdale, Chenango Co.,) farmer 50.

Hyer, Schuyler, (Rockdale, Chenango Co.,) farmer 100.

Hyers, Henry, (Unadilla,) farmer 96.

IRELAND, LOUIS E., (Unadilla,) dentist, Masonic Block.

Jackson, Nathan, (Butternuts,) carpenter and farmer 85.

JENNINGS, EDSON S., (Unadilla,) (*Edson S. Jennings & Son,*) assessor.

JENNINGS, EDSON S. & SON, (Unadilla,) marble workers and farmers 94.

JONES, SAMUEL, (Unadilla,) barber and hair dresser, Main corner Brook.

Juckett, Elijah, (Unadilla Center,) farmer 200.

Judson, John, (Unadilla,) saloon, Main corner Bridge.

Lamb, John G., (Unadilla,) barber, Bridge.

Lamb, John S., (Wells' Bridge,) farmer 90.

Lampman, Giles, (Wells' Bridge,) mechanic and farmer 1½.

Lathrop, Lyman, (Wells' Bridge,) farmer 44.

Lathrop, Perlee, (Wells' Bridge,) mechanic and farmer 2½.

Launt, H. J., (Unadilla,) general merchant, Main.

LEHRBERG, MENDEL, (Unadilla,) (*Fuller & Lehrberg.*)

Leonard, Chas., (Wells' Bridge,) (*Leonard & Greene.*)

Leonard & Greene, (Wells' Bridge,) (*Chas. Leonard and Geo. Greene,*) blacksmiths.

Lesenn, Judson, (Wells' Bridge,) farmer 60.

Lesues, Alfred, (Wells' Bridge,) cooper.

Lewis, Mary, (Wells' Bridge,) farmer 110.

Lewis, Persifer M., (Wells' Bridge,) farmer 100.

Loomis, David P., (Unadilla,) lawyer, Main.

Luther, Martin B., (Unadilla,) farmer 152.

Mallery, Chas. W., (Wells' Bridge,) general merchant.

MATTICE, WM., (Unadilla,) prop. of Unadilla Hotel, corner Main and Bridge.

MAYER, JACOB, (Unadilla,) baker and confectioner, Main.

McOmber, Geo., (Unadilla,) farmer 100.

Mead, Wm. K., (Unadilla,) dairyman and farmer 180.

Meeker, Alanson H., (Unadilla,) harness maker, Main.

Merchant, Orlando, (Unadilla,) cooper, Bridge.

Merriman, Schuyler, (Wells' Bridge,) farmer 60.

MILLER, ALONZO M., (Unadilla Center,) dairyman and farmer 175.

Miller, Wm., (Sidney Plains, Delaware Co.,) farmer 150.

Mills, Erastus, (Unadilla,) farmer 97.

Monroe, Thos., (East Guilford, Chenango Co.,) farmer 150.

Moody, Josiah A., (Unadilla Center,)blacksmith and farmer 3.

Morse, Rosel A., (East Guilford, Chenango Co.,) farmer 150.

Mott, Leroy S., (Unadilla Center,) farmer 71.

Mulford & Stever, (Unadilla,) (*Wesley Mulford and Edson J. Stever,*) groceries, Main.

Mulford, Wesley, (Unadilla,) (*Mulford & Stever.*)

Myers, Ephraim, (Sidney Plains, Delaware Co.,) farmer 150.

Nichols, Edmond, (Unadilla,) farmer 35.

Nichols, Marble, (Unadilla,) farmer 75.

NORTH, SAMUEL, (Unadilla,) (*Thos. G. North & Co.*)

NORTH, THOS. G., (Unadilla,) (*Thos. G. North & Co.,*) hardware, stoves &c., Main.

NORTH, THOS. G. & CO., (Unadilla,) (*Samuel North,*) bankers, Main.

Odel, Anstin, (Rockdale, Chenango Co.,) farmer 25.

Odel, ——, (Unadilla,) physician, Main.

Osborn, Daniel, (Unadilla,) farmer 22.

Packard, Edward M., (Unadilla,) post master and coroner, Main.

PALMER, BENJ., (Unadilla,) farmer 96.

Palmer, Franklin, (Unadilla,) farmer 112.

Palmer, Geo. W., (Sidney Plains, Delaware Co.,) (*Palmer, Humphrey & Co.*)

Palmer, Henry, (Wells' Bridge,) tanner.

Palmer, Humphrey & Co., (Sidney Plains, Delaware Co.,) (*Geo. W. Palmer, Wm. and Lorenzo Humphrey,*) props. Unadilla Paper, Planing, Spoke and Saw Mills.

Palmer, Levi, (Unadilla,) farmer 100.

Palmer, Paul, (Unadilla Center,) farmer 81.

Palmer, Stephen, (Unadilla,) farmer 50.

Pearce, Henry T., (Wells' Bridge,) farmer leases of Joseph Wikes, 175.

Pearce, Oliver R., (Unadilla Center,) farmer 130.

Penny, Peter, (Unadilla,) farmer 130.

PERRIN, WM. J., (Wells' Bridge,) mechanic.

Pete, Frank, (Rockdale, Chenango Co.,) farmer.

Phelps, Horace G., (East Guilford, Chenango Co.,) stock dealer and farmer 230.

Phelps, James, (East Guilford, Chenango Co.,) farmer 80.

Phelps, Wm. H., (Unadilla,) farmer 50.

PLACE, RUFUS, (Unadilla,) farmer 100.

Pond, Ransom L., (Wells' Bridge,) farmer 117.

Post, Lemuel, (Wells' Bridge,) farmer 2.

Potter, Ransom, (Wells' Bridge,) farmer 145.

Quimbey, Eliza Mrs., (Unadilla,) dressmaker, Main.

Quimbey, Ransom, (Unadilla,) farmer.

Quimby, Stephen, (Unadilla,) farmer 40.

Quiney, Geo. M., (Wells' Bridge,) farmer 117.

Randal, Abel, (Rockdale, Chenango Co.,) farmer 107.

Redfield, Theophilus, (Unadilla,) farmer 140.

Reed, John, (Unadilla,) shingle maker.

Richards, Edward C., (Unadilla,) farmer 41½.

Robbins, Eli, (Wells' Bridge,) farmer 118.

ROBINSON, MARSHALL, (Unadilla,) (*Bailey & Robinson.*)

Rockwell, ———, (Unadilla,) (*Woodruff & Rockwell.*)

Rogers, Eber, (Rockdale, Chenango Co.,) farmer 100.

Rowle, Hartwell J., (Wells' Bridge,) restaurant.

Rowley, Abel C., (Wells' Bridge,) farmer 55.

Schofield, M. Rev., (Unadilla,) Episcopal clergyman.

Scofield, John S., (Unadilla,) farmer 140.

Scott, C. W., (Unadilla,) (*Warner & Scott.*)

Scott, E. W., (Unadilla,) brewer, Depot.

Seaman, James A., (Unadilla,) farmer 40.

Searles, Lester B., (Unadilla Center,) farmer 153.

Sherwood, David, (East Guilford, Chenango Co.,) farmer 50.

Sherwood, Nathaniel, (Wells' Bridge,) farmer 35.

Sisson, Alanson, (Wells' Bridge,) farmer 100.

Sisson, Christopher, (Wells' Bridge,) farmer 38.

Sisson, Francis M., (Wells' Bridge,) general merchant.

Sisson, Henry, (Wells' Bridge,) farmer 50.

Slade, Chas. L., (Unadilla,) farmer 76½.

Slade, Frederick, (Unadilla,) farmer 75.

Slade, Richard, (Unadilla,) farmer 100.

Smith & Dibble, (Unadilla,((*Perry Smith and Tustin Dibble,*) jewelers, Main.

Smith, Geo., (Unadilla,) farmer 50.

Smith, Gilbert, (Unadilla,) carpenter and farmer 5.

Smith, Jarvis C., (Unadilla,) farmer 193.

Smith, Kimbal, (Sidney Plains, Delaware Co.,) farmer 110.

Smith, Perry, (Unadilla,) (*Smith & Dibble.*)

Smith, Sylvester, (Wells' Bridge,) farmer 240.

Smith, Walter J., (Unadilla,) farmer 105.

Smith, Willet, (Unadilla,) farmer 110.

Spencer, Orange, (Unadilla,) farmer 57½.

Stebbins, Henry L., (Rockdale, Chenango Co.,) farmer 127½.

Stenson, R. A., (Unadilla,) (*Stenson & Weidman.*)

Stenson & Weidman, (Unadilla,) (*R. A. Stenson and Edward Weidman,*) blacksmiths, Bridge.

Stever, Edson J., (Unadilla,) (*Mulford & Stever.*)

Stimson, Wm., (Unadilla,) farmer.

Storms, Henry J., (Wells' Bridge,) farmer 60.

Strong, Charles L., (Unadilla,) fruit and fish, Main.

Sweet, Joseph, (Unadilla,) physician, Main.

Sweet, J. J., (Unadilla,) physician, Bridge.

Sweet, M. P., (Unadilla,) surveyor.

Taaffe, Mary Mrs., (Unadilla,) prop. of Central Hotel and dealer in millinery, fancy goods, stationery &c.

Taber, Lorin, (Unadilla,) cooper and farmer 60.

Talcott, Henry, (Rockdale, Chenango Co.,) farmer 180.

Teller, Rufus K., (Unadilla,) station agent.

THOMAS, GEO. W., (Wells' Bridge,) carpenter and prop. circular saw mill on Sand Hill Creek.

Townsend, Alexander, (Unadilla,) (*Townsend & Harby.*)

Townsend & Harby, (Unadilla,) (*Alexander Townsend and Thomas Harby,*) props. of Main Street Meat Market.

Trask, Parmenas, (Wells' Bridge,) farmer 40.

Truman, Jay E., (Butternuts,) carpenter and farmer 56.

UNADILLA HOTEL, (Unadilla,) Wm. Mattice, prop., corner Main and Bridge.

Vanschick, John H., (Unadilla Center,) farmer 86.

Vanschick, Peter G., (Unadilla Center,) farmer 62⅝.

Wait, Ahijah, (Wells' Bridge,) farmer 50.

Wait, Samuel, (Wells' Bridge,) farmer 96.

Wait, Thomas, (Unadilla Center,) farmer 117.

Walker, S. B. Mrs., (Unadilla,) tailoress and dress maker, Main.

Warner, J. M., (Unadilla,) (*Warner & Scott.*)

Warner & Scott, (Unadilla,) (*J. M. Warner and C. W. Scott,*) general merchants, Main.

Webb, James K., (Wells' Bridge,) farmer 120.

Webb, Richard, (Unadilla,) farmer 130.

Weidman, Edward, (Unadilla,) (*Stenson & Weidman.*)

Weidman, Peter, (Unadilla,) prop. Railroad Restaurant.

Wendall, Wm., (Unadilla,) (*Carver & Wendall.*)

Wheeler, Alonzo, (Unadilla,) photographer, Depot.

White, Wm. H., (Wells' Bridge,) station agent and post master.

Whitney, Henry, (Unadilla,) blacksmith, Depot.

Wickham, Wm. M., (Wells' Bridge,) farmer 112.

Widman, Maria, (Unadilla,) toll gate keeper.

Wilbur, Thos., (Wells' Bridge,) farmer 40 and leases 80.

Wild, Allen, (Rockdale, Chenango Co.,) farmer 25.

Wilds, L. A., (Rockdale, Chenango Co.,) farmer 125.

Williams, Abial J., (Unadilla,) harness maker, Main.

Williams, Wm. A., (Unadilla,) blacksmith, Water.

Wilmot & Heath, (Unadilla,) furniture dealers and undertakers, Main.

Wilson, John, (Unadilla,) farmer 50.

Winans, Walter, (Unadilla,) farmer 100.

Woodruff & Rockwell, (Unadilla,) groceries, Main.

Wysman, Jonas, (Wells' Bridge,) blacksmith and farmer 71.

York, Henry W., (Wells' Bridge,) painter and farmer 18.

York, James H., (Wells' Bridge,) painter and farmer 8.

Youmans, Jerome, (Wells' Bridge,) farmer 100.

Youngs, Clemens Rev., (Unadilla,) M. E. clergyman and farmer 100.

Youngs, Wheeler C., (Unadilla,) farmer 100.

WESTFORD.

(Post Office Addresses in Parentheses.)

Aker, Mary, (Westville,) farmer leases of Henry Baldwin, 130.

Aldrich, Daniel, (Westford,) farmer leases of John Shelland, 18.

Aldridge, Abel, (Westford,) refused information.

Andrews, Walter, (Westford,) justice of the peace and farmer 91.

Angel, Elbert, (Milford,) farmer 67.

Angel, Wm., (Milford,) farmer 95.

Ashley, Wm. O., (Westford,) mason and stone cutter.

Baden, Henry, (Westford,) farmer 20.

Baden, Margaret, (Westford,) farmer 70.

Baldwin, Aaron, (Westford,) farmer 144.

Baldwin, Almarin, (Westville,) farmer 108.

BALDWIN, D. I., (Westford,) farmer 160.

Baldwin, Eve, (Westville,) farmer 116.

BALDWIN, FREDERICK, (Westford,) farmer 85.

Baldwin, George W., (Westford,) farmer 126.

Baldwin, Hiram, (Westville,) farmer 500.

Baldwin, James, (Westford,) farmer 15.

BALDWIN, J. H., (Westford,) farmer 140.

Ball, Daniel B., (Westville,) shingle maker.

Ball, D. Mrs., (Westville,) milliner and dress maker.

Barnard, Daniel R., (Middlefield,) farmer leases of E. Briggs, 113.

Barnard, Nathaniel P., (Westford,) repairer of watches and jewelry, and farmer 40.

Becker, M. A., (Westford,) threshing and wood machine, and farmer 140.

Bell, John H., (Westford,) shoe maker.

Bentley, George T., (Worcester,) farmer 115.

Bentley, Moses D., (Worcester,) farmer 102.

Bentley, Perry C., (Westford,) preacher and farmer 100.

Bentley, Wm. R., (Westford,) farmer 55.

Bice, Andrew, (Westville,) dairyman and farmer 196.

Bidlake, Asa, (Westford,) farmer 65.

BIDLAKE, DAVID S., (Westford,) (*Dean & Bidlake.*)

Bissell, Charles H., (Westford,) supervisor.

Bolson, Abram, (Worcester,) hop raiser and farmer 120.

Boyce, Albert, (Westford,) farmer 30.

Bradley, Wm., (Westford,) farmer 50.

Brooker, Clay, (Schenevus,) (*with John Milks,*) farmer 185.

Brownell, Daniel, (Westford,) farmer 100.

BURLEY, GEORGE, (Westville,) farmer.

Burlingame, Billings, (Westford,) farmer 80.

Burton, Whitney, (Westville,) painter.

Campbell, Fenimore, (Westford,) farmer 82½.

Carey, Ira C., (Middlefield,) farmer 96.

Chase, Gilbert D., (Westford,) farmer 56.

Chase, H., (Westford,) farmer 120.

Cipperly, Wm., (Middlefield,) farmer 120.

Clark, Isaac, (Schenevus,) farmer 140.

Cleveland, Adlemorn, (Worcester,) carpenter and farmer 40.

Coats, Elbert, (Westville,) dairyman and farmer 400.

Cooper, Wm. J., (Westford,) hop raiser and dealer, and farmer 110½.

Cossaart, Harrison, (Westville,) farmer 120.

Cummings, Albert E., (Westford,) farmer 100.

Cummings, Orris, (Middlefield,) farmer 2.

Darling, J. M., (Westford,) prop. of Royal George and farmer 116.

Darling, Wm., (Westford,) farmer 80.

Davis, Charles, (Westford,) farmer 30.

DEAN & BIDLAKE, (Westford,) (*Edgar C. Dean and David S. Bidlake,*) merchants.

DEAN, EDGAR C., (Westford,) (*Dean & Bidlake.*)

Demelt, John D., (Worcester,) hop raiser and farmer 110.

Denton, Homer, (Westville,) carpenter.

Dickinson, George, (Worcester,) farmer leases of Edward Tipple, 159.

Diron, Anna, (Milford,) farmer 47.

Drake, John, (Westford,) physician.

Draper, F. P., (Westford,) dealer.

Draper, Hazer E., (Westford,) farmer 30.

Evans, Ransom, (Schenevus,) shoemaker and farmer.

Fasset, Hannah, (Middlefield,) farmer 75.

Flint, E. B., (Worcester,) hop raiser and farmer 100.

Flint, Norman, (Worcester,) hop raiser and farmer 70.

Francis, Sarah, (Westford,) farmer 58.

Galer, Jacob, (Westford,) carpenter, hop raiser and farmer 50.

Gano, David H., (Schenevus,) hop raiser, dairyman and farmer 130.

Gano, John, (Milford,) farmer leases 120.

Gardner, R. F., (Westford,) farmer 100.
Gaylord, G. C., (Westville,) groceries and liquors.
Goodenough, John, (Westford,) farmer 10.
Gove, George E., (Westford,) farmer 65.
GRANT, JAMES B. REV., (Westville,) pastor First Baptist Church.
Green, Rinaldo, (Schenevus,) hop raiser and farmer 85.
Griggs, Waldo, (Westford,) farmer 150.
Groff, Archibald, (Westford,) farmer 76.
Groff, John B., (Westford,) farmer 128.
Guage, Joseph, (Worcester,) farmer 50.
Guy, Henry, (Middlefield,) farmer 38.
Hall, Robert S., (Westford,) miller.
Hanor, George, (Westford,) farmer 100.
Haynes, Charles, (Milford,) farmer 130.
Herdman, David S., (Westford,) farmer.
Herdman, John, (Westford,) farmer 102.
Herrick, Alonzo, (Westford,) town assessor, hop raiser and farmer 155.
Holmes, Horace, (Westford,) farmer 100.
Holmes, Joseph M., (Westford,) farmer 260.
Holmes, Revilo, (Westford,) school teacher and (*with Joseph M.,*) farmer.
Howland, David, (Westford,) farmer 150.
Howland, Ira, (Westville,) farmer 7.
Howland, Wm., (Westford,) physician and surgeon, and farmer 80.
Hubbard, David, (Westford,) farmer leases of Philip Kiley, 53.
Hull, James, (Westford,) farmer 200.
Hunt, Benjamin D., (Westford,) mechanic and farmer 75.
Isman, Henry, (Middlefield,) farmer 54.
Ismay, Joseph, (Westford,) farmer 126.
Jewell, Charles H., (Westville,) justice of the peace and farmer 36.
Kaple, L. A., (Middlefield,) (*with Mrs. S.,*) farmer 120.
Kaple, S. Mrs., (Middlefield,) (*with L. A.,*) farmer 120.
Kinch, Thomas, (Westford,) farmer 205.
Kingsley, Wm., (Westford,) farmer 80.
Knapp, Edward, (Middlefield,) farmer 50.
Knapp, George, (Westford,) hop raiser and farmer 80.
Lansing, James E., (Westford,) farmer.
Lansing, Mary, (Westford,) farmer 80.
Manning, Wm., (Elk Creek,) dairyman and farmer 110.
Manzer, Sanford E., (Westford,) merchant.
Marks, Wm., (Westford,) cider mill and farmer 40.
McKellip, Wm., (Middlefield,) farmer 78.
McKlintock, David, (Westford,) farmer 200.
Menzer, Phila, (Westford,) farmer 90.
Metcalf, Hezekiah E., (Westville,) farmer 36.
Milks, E. B., (Schenevus,) stock dealer and farmer 160.
Milks, John, (Schenevus,) (*with Clay Brooker,*) farmer 185.
Misson, Wm., (Westford,) farmer 150.
Murphy, Michael, (Westford,) farmer.
Nellis, George, (Westville,) (*with Jacob,*) farmer 175.
Nellis, Jacob, (Westville,) poormaster and (*with George,*) farmer 175.
NELLIS, JOHN A., (Westville,) farmer 105.
Newton, E. & J., (Westville,) general merchants.

Northrup, Sophia, (Westford,) farmer 56.
Norton, Joel, (Schenevus,) cooper.
Norton, Margaret, (Schenevus,) farmer.
Norton, Stephen, (Schenevus,) farmer 100.
Palmer, Daniel M., (Westville,) dealer in hops, butter and wool, and farmer 56.
Palmer, Frederick, (Elk Creek,) farmer 100.
Palmer, Hiram, (Westville,) hop raiser and farmer 100.
Pank, Mathew, (Westford,) farmer 50.
Pank, Robert, (Westford,) farmer 117.
Pank, William, (Westford,) carpenter and farmer.
Patrick, Thomas, (Elk Creek,) dairyman and farmer 150.
Pearse, Eber, (Westville,) painter.
Pierce, Martin, (Westford,) farmer 59.
Platner, W. H., (Westford,) carriage manuf. and undertaker.
Pratt, George R., (Westville,) shoe maker.
Pratt, R., (Westville,) hotel keeper.
Prentice, E., (Westville,) farmer leases 160.
Preston, Adelbert H., (Westford,) school teacher.
Preston, Lewis E., (Westford,) hop raiser and farmer 125.
Preston, L. F., (Westford,) shoe maker.
Priddy, James, (Westford,) shoe maker and farmer 2½.
Prine, O. J., (Westford,) blacksmith.
Reynols, Almon, (Westford,) farmer 100.
Rider, John, (Westford,) farmer 110¾.
Roberts, G. N., (Westford,) farmer 212.
Roberts, Henry, (Westford,) farmer 40.
Roe, J., (Elk Creek,) shoe maker and farmer 2½.
Rose, Martha A., (Worcester,) farmer 40.
Roseboom, Garret, (Westford,) farmer 130.
Roseboon, Horace, (Westford,) farmer 100.
Roseboon, Robert, (Westford,) farmer 130.
Salisbury, Barnard, (Westford,) farmer 200.
Salisbury, Gardner, (Westford,) (*with Barnard,*) farmer.
Salisbury, John R., (Westford or Westville,) farmer 92.
Saulsbury, Philip, (Westford,) farmer 5.
Saxton, Raymond, (Milford,) farmer 170.
Saxton, S. N., (Westville,) retired farmer.
Shelland, David, (Worcester,) hop raiser and farmer 116.
SHERMAN, IRA, (Westville,) vice-president Schenevus Valley Agricultural Society, town assessor, hop raiser, dairyman and farmer 250.
SKINNER, GEORGE, (Westford,) librarian of Union Library.
Skinner, James B., (Westford,) hop raiser and farmer 93.
Skinner, Waldo, (Westford,) farmer 137½.
Skinner, Wm., (Westford,) farmer 120.
Snyder, Austin, (Middlefield,) apiarian, hop raiser and farmer 100.
Snyder, J. A., (Westford,) blacksmith.
Sornborger, Henry, (Worcester,) farmer 40.
Southard, Wesley, (Westford,) farmer 80.
Sperry, Jabez, (Schenevus,) farmer leases of E. B. Milks, 86.
Stilwell, S. B., (Schenevus,) farmer 102.
Sutherland, Nelson, (Westville,) shoemaker.
Thomas, James H., (Westville,) hop raiser and farmer 4.
Thompson, Beckwith, (Westford,) farmer 100.

Thompson, J. R., (Westford,) cooper.

Thurber, O., (Westford,) carpenter and farmer 97.

Tipple, John H., (Elk Creek,) dairyman and farmer 88.

Tipple, Peter J., (Schenevus,) blacksmith and farmer 20.

Tipple, Sylvester, (Worcester,) mason and farmer 70.

Townsend, Abner W. Rev., (Westville,) clergyman.

Treat, Elisha, (Westford,) butcher and farmer 8.

Treat, Stephen, (Westford,) farmer 130.

Tyler, C. B., (Westford,) farmer 80.

Tyler, W. H., (Westford,) merchant and postmaster.

Utter, Wm., (Westford,) commissioner of highways and farmer 163.

Vanderveer, Crosby, (Westville,) hop raiser and farmer 150.

Vanderveer, David, (Westville,) hop raiser and farmer 115.

Wales, Wm., (Westford,) farmer 150.

Waters, Simeon, (Milford,) saw and clover mills, and farmer 27½.

Watterman, Martin, (Worcester,) dairyman and farmer 100.

Webster, Noyes D., (Elk Creek,) farmer 62½.

Webster, Robert, (Westford,) mason and farmer 22.

Welden, Wm., (Westford,) hop raiser and farmer 80.

Wilber, German, (Middlefield,) farmer 100.

Wilber, Leroy, (Middlefield,) school teacher and farmer.

Wilber, Wm. O., (Westford,) farmer 140.

Willsey, Jonathan, (Westford,) farmer 235.

Wilson, Hiram, (Elk Creek,) hop raiser and farmer 146.

Wilson, Jacob, (Westville,) farmer 116.

Wing, George, (Westford,) town assessor and farmer 127.

Winne, Cornelius, (Westford,) overseer of the poor and farmer 120.

Wright, F., (Westford,) farmer 150.

Yeomans, Joseph, (Westford,) farmer leases of James McMullan, 52.

Youngs, Joshua, (Westville,) hop raiser and farmer 65.

WORCESTER.

(Post Office Addresses in Parentheses.)

Albert, Frederick, (Worcester,) resident.

Albert, John W., (Worcester,) farmer 136.

Alvord, Elisha, (East Worcester,) farmer 6.

ALVORD, JOHN, (East Worcester,) farmer 130.

Anthony, David, (East Worcester,) machinist and farmer 80.

Antis, Henry, (East Worcester,) farmer 32½.

Atkins, George, (Worcester,) farmer 25.

BABCOCK, W. W., (East Worcester,) prop. of East Worcester House and billiard saloon.

Bailey, Levi, (East Worcester,) farmer 116.

Baker, Sherman S., (East Worcester,) farmer leases 67.

Baldwin, Dewitt C., (South Worcester,) farmer 50.

Baldwin, Dorman, (South Worcester,) agent for Grover & Baker Sewing Machine.

Baldwin, Fredrus, (South Worcester,) lawyer.

BALDWIN, F. J., (East Worcester,) school teacher.

Baldwin, John S., (South Worcester,) farmer 116.

Barney, Ansel, (Worcester,) farmer 100.

Barney, William, (Worcester,) minister and farmer 70.

Barrett, James, (South Worcester,) farmer 1.

Baxter, Ormel, (East Worcester,) cooper.

Becht, Lewis, (East Worcester,) shoemaker.

BECKER, VOLNEY D., (South Worcester,) notary public, tanner and farmer 700.

Becker, Washington, (South Worcester,) lawyer and banker.

Belden, Amos D., (East Worcester,) farmer 80.

Bellew, George H., (South Worcester,) farmer 59.

Bellew, Joseph, (South Worcester,) farmer 110.

Bentley, Edwin, (Worcester,) farmer 127.

Bentley, Sylvester, (Worcester,) farmer.

Berner, Cyrus, (Worcester,) music teacher and farmer 60.

BERNER, HUMPHREY, (East Worcester,) boot and shoe manuf.

Bigelow, Cyrus, (Worcester,) painter and farmer 18.

Boiling, James, (South Worcester,) farmer 40.

Boiling, Lawrence, (South Worcester,) farmer 100.

Boiling, Michael, (Worcester,) blacksmith.

Boorn, G. O., (East Worcester,) farmer 100.

Q

Boorn, James E., (East Worcester,) (*J. E. & N. Boorn.*)

Boorn, J. E. & N., (East Worcester,) (*James E. and Nathan,*) blacksmiths.

Boorn, Nathan, (East Worcester,) (*J. E. & N. Worcester.*)

BOWEN, MILLARD F., (East Worcester,) (*Eckerson & Bowen.*)

Brady, Edward, (South Worcester,) farmer 160.

Brewster, Lois Mrs., (Worcester,) farmer 17.

Brotherton, H. Rev., (Worcester,) pastor of Baptist Church.

Brown, John C.,(Worcester,) saw and grist mills.

Brown, John H. Rev., (Worcester,) Presbyterian minister.

Bruce, Richard, (East Worcester,) farmer 102.

BRUCE, S. Rev., (South Worcester,) pastor of Lutheran Church and farmer 4.

Bucks, J. A. Mrs., (East Worcester,) milliner.

Bulson, George J., (South Worcester,) farmer 112.

Burnsides, Samuel, (Worcester,) farmer 100.

Butler, Rosander H., (Worcester,) farmer 200.

Butts, J. A., (Worcester,) cabinet maker, F. B. Rury, agent.

Cable, Walter, (East Worcester,) farmer 54.

Callahan, Michael, (Worcester,) farmer 60.

Campaign, Robert, (Worcester,) farmer 50.

Campaign, William, (East Worcester,) wagon maker and farmer 25.

Campbell, George, (East Worcester,) horse dealer.

Car, M. A. Mrs., (East Worcester,) (*Smith & Car.*)

Carroll, Charles, (Worcester,) farmer leases of Leonard Caryl, 54.

Carswell, Allen, (East Worcester,) farmer 50.

Casper, William, (East Worcester,) farmer leases of Isaac Harrington, 73.

Chamberlin, Charles R., (Worcester,) farmer 175.

Champion, John V., (Charlotteville, Schoharie Co.,) farmer 9.

Champion, Josephus, (East Worcester,) farmer 25.

Chase, William H., (Worcester,) farmer 100.

Childs, I. S., (Worcester,) shoe maker.

Cornish, S. H., (Worcester,) farmer 110.

Crippen, Eugene, (Worcester,) farmer 110.

Crippen, James M., (Worcester,) farmer 95.

Crippen, Schuyler G., (Worcester,) farmer 44.

Daily, Emerson, (East Worcester,) farmer 150.

Daley, Stephen, (Worcester,) farmer 85.

Dana, G. C., (East Worcester,) carriage manufacturer and undertaker.

Davis, Almon H., (Worcester,) mechanic, wagon maker and farmer 2.

Davis, Bradford, (Worcester,) farmer 2.

Davis, Cyrus, (Worcester,) farmer leases of William Sloan, 38.

Davis, —— Mrs., (East Worcester,) farmer 5.

DAY, LYSANDER, (Worcester,) farmer 104.

Dean, Robert, (East Worcester,) sawyer and wagon maker.

DECKE, M. S., (East Worcester,) (*Gott & Decke,*) inspector of elections.

De Long, Awry, (Worcester,) farmer 190.

Delong, De Witt, (Worcester,) telegraph operator A. & S. R. R., and express agent.

Dickinson, Silas, (Worcester,) carpenter and farmer 3.

Dickinson, William, (Worcester,) farmer 30.

Dorwin, Philip L., (South Worcester,) farmer 205.

Dox, David, (West Richmondville, Schoharie Co.,) farmer 65.

EAST WORCESTER HOUSE, (East Worcester,) W. W. Babcock, prop.

ECKERSON, ADAM, (East Worcester,) (*Eckerson & Bowen.*)

ECKERSON & BOWEN, (East Worcester,) (*Adam Eckerson and Millard F. Bowen,*) groceries, drug and variety store.

Fancher, Alva, (East Worcester,) farmer leases 166.

Fancher, Jedediah, (East Worcester,) carpenter and farmer 24.

Fancher, Stephen B., (East Worcester,) farmer leases of DeWitt C. Post, 114.

FENN, ALLEN B., (Worcester,) carpenter and farmer 10.

Ferguson, John, (Worcester,) farmer 111.

Fern, Edmund 2d., (East Worcester,) farmer 65.

Fern, George, (East Worcester,) farmer 105.

Ferris, William W., (East Worcester,) farmer leases 120.

Flint, Horatio, (Worcester,) farmer 60.

Flint, John R., (Worcester,) farmer 60.

FOLAND, ALFRED, (Worcester,) farmer 39.

Foland, Christopher, (Worcester,) farmer 122.

Fridendall, Barney, (East Worcester,) farmer 150.

Fuller, Elizabeth Mrs., (Worcester,) farmer 119.

Fuller, Joseph, (South Worcester,) farmer 100.

Fuller, Julia W. Mrs., (Worcester,) millinery, ladies' furnishing goods and dress making.

Gaige, Henry V., (Worcester,) farmer 104.

Gilbride, Daniel,(South Worcester,) farmer 117.

Gile, Stephen, (Worcester,) farmer leases of P. S. Tabor, 410.

Gilland, John, (South Worcester,) prop. of South Worcester Hotel and farmer 30.

Goodrich, Francis, (Worcester,) farmer 100.

GOTT & DECKE, (East Worcester,) (*G. S. Gott and M. S. Decke,*) general merchants.

GOTT, G. A., (East Worcester,) (*Gott & Decke,*) collector.

Grant, Orrin, (East Worcester,) farmer leases 23.

Grant, Samuel H., (Worcester,) lawyer and notary public.

Griffin, Harrison,(Worcester,) farmer leases 60.

Griggs, James, (Worcester,) carpenter and farmer 105.

Griswold, John J., (Worcester,) farmer leases 90.

Guernsey, Richard, (Worcester,) mechanic and farmer 3.

Gustin, E. L., (East Worcester,) lawyer and notary public.

Hadsell, Julius T., (Worcester,) mechanic.

Hall, James, (Worcester,) farmer 160.

HALL, ROBERT, (Worcester,) farmer 216.

Hall, William, (Worcester,) farmer 198.

Hanson, Catharine Mrs., (East Worcester,) farmer 50.

Hardy, John, (East Worcester,) blacksmith and farmer.

Harrington, Isaac, (East Worcester,) farmer 168.

Harrington, Jeremiah, (East Worcester,) farmer leases of Ezra Thurber, 160.

HARRISON, JOHN L., (South Worcester,) prop. of saw and grist mill, and farmer 10.

Hartwell, John F., (Charlotteville, Schoharie Co.,) farmer 100.

Hayner, Henry, (Worcester,) farmer 82.

Hayner, Martin, (South Worcester,) resident.

Hayner, Philip, (South Worcester,) farmer 102.

HAYNER, WILLIAM, (Worcester,) farmer 157.

Henry, George, (Worcester,) blacksmith.

Herrington, Catherine Mrs., (East Worcester,) farmer 160.

Herrington, David, (East Worcester,) farmer 120.

Herrington, Hiram, (East Worcester,) farmer leases 140.

Herrington, Jacob P., (East Worcester,) farmer 183.

Hill, John, (East Worcester,) farmer 46.

Holmes, John, (East Worcester,) farmer 4.

Holmes, Maria A. Mrs., (East Worcester,) milliner.

Holmes, Sylvester P., (East Worcester,) chair seater and farmer 140.

Hollenbeck, David, (East Worcester,) sewing machine agent and farmer 50.

Hollenbeck, Edwin F., (Worcester,) farmer 90.

Hollenbeck, John D., (Worcester,) stone quarry and farmer 325.

Hollenbeck, Peter, (Worcester,) farmer 220.

Hollenbeck, Peter, (East Worcester,) farmer 3.

Hoos, Levi, (Worcester,) farmer 100.

Houck, David, (South Worcester,) farmer 167.

HOWARD, FENTON, (East Worcester,) farmer leases 250.

Howe, Elmon, (Worcester,) drover and farmer 105.

Hoyt, Harrison, (Worcester,) confectionery and shell fish.

Hoyt, Lawrence, (Worcester,) poultry dealer.

Hudson, Edward M., (East Worcester,) veterinary surgeon and farmer 200.

Hungerford, Thomas, (East Worcester,) farmer 75.

Ives, Joshua, (Worcester,) farmer 84.

Ives, Josiah, (South Worcester,) farmer 45.

Ives, Orlando, (South Worcester,) farmer 78.

IVES, PHILEMON, (Worcester,) farmer 65.

IVES, TRUMAN S., (Worcester,) carpenter and farmer 84.

Ives, William B., (Worcester,) farmer 50.

Jaycox, Alexander, (East Worcester,) farmer leases 100.

Jaycox, Lorenzo, (Worcester,) farmer 4.

Jaycox, Myron, (East Worcester,) carpenter and farmer 20.

Jaycox, Samuel, (East Worcester,) (*with Isaac Wickham,*) farmer 133.

Jennings, Almon D., (East Worcester,) farmer 54.

Jennings, J. C., (East Worcester,) carpenter and farmer 100.

Johnson, James, (Worcester,) farmer 90.

Jones, Francis Rev., (East Worcester,) saw mill and farmer 39.

Jones, Jenkin Rev., (East Worcester,) pastor Baptist Church.

KNAPP, E. F., (Worcester,) prop. of Worcester House and livery stable, and farmer 12.

LA MOURE, I. W., (East Worcester,) groceries, provisions and confectionery.

La Moure, S. T., (East Worcester,) butcher, deputy sheriff and constable.

Lane, James, (South Worcester,) farmer 1.

Lape, Andrew W., (Worcester,) miller.

Lape, Daniel, (East Worcester,) farmer 8.

Lape, John S., (East Worcester,) farmer leases 230.

LAWYER, THOMAS M., (South Worcester,) deputy sheriff, overseer of the poor, constable, collector, bridge builder and farmer 114.

Leonard, William H., (Worcester,) physician and surgeon.

Lewis, R. B. Miss, (Worcester,) millinery.

Lobdell, Lucius, (Worcester,) farmer leases 140.

Lockwood, Jacob, (East Worcester,) farmer 50.

Lockwood, Philander, (East Worcester,) veterinary surgeon and farmer 15.

Lockwood, William, (East Worcester,) blacksmith, millwright and farmer 100.

Lovejoy, John, (Worcester,) farmer leases 180.

Maginnis, James, (Worcester,) farmer 150.

Maginnis, Patrick, (Worcester,) farmer.

Maginnis, Richard, (Worcester,) farmer 137.

Mann, Herman, (South Worcester,) farmer leases of Patrick Boiling, 129.

Marshall, Emory, (East Worcester,) farmer 158.

Martin, Charles, (South Worcester,) farmer 210.

Mattice, Henry, (East Worcester,) cooper and farmer 26½.

McClintock, Alexander, (Worcester,) farmer 97.

McClintock, James, (South Worcester,) farmer 115.

McClintock, John, (South Worcester,) farmer 240.

McClintock, William, (South Worcester,) farmer 114.

McConnell, Thomas, (South Worcester,) harness maker.

McCormick, Francis, (Worcester,) carpenter.

McDonald, Charles H., (East Worcester,) physician and dentist, and farmer 5.

McGregory, George, (East Worcester,) station agent A. & S. R. R.

Mereness, Charles H., (Worcester,) (*Isaac Mereness & Son.*)

Mereness, Isaac & Son, (Worcester,) (*Charles H.,*) general merchants.

Mereness, John D., (Worcester,) farmer leases 100.

Milks, Horace, (Worcester,) farmer 120.

Miller, Henry L., (Worcester,) carpenter and farmer 18.

Millias, Benjamin, (East Worcester,) farmer leases of Jane E. Smith, 160.

Millias, Sebastian, (Worcester,) farmer 90.

MITCHEL, RANSOM, (South Worcester,) (*with Raymond,*) farmer 200.

MITCHEL, RAYMOND, (South Worcester,) (*with Ransom,*) farmer 200.

Mitchell, John, (Worcester,) farmer 67.

Mitchell, Peter Jr., (South Worcester,) farmer 102.

Mitchell, Philip, (South Worcester,) farmer 250.

Mitchell, S., (South Worcester,) farmer 120.

Monfort, Isaac, (South Worcester,) farmer 10.

Monroe, Barnet, (South Worcester,) farmer 100.

Mooney, Michael C., (Worcester,) farmer 160.

Mooney, Patrick, (Worcester,) farmer 120.

Moore, Irvin D., (South Worcester,) farmer 290.

Mowers, William, (Worcester,) farmer 104.

Mudge, Ezra D., (Worcester,) carpenter and farmer 6.

Multer, Henry, (South Worcester,) farmer 300.

Multer, Jacob P.,(South Worcester,) assessor and farmer 240.

Multer, John D.,(South Worcester,) farmer 190.

MULTER, LEWIS, (Charlotteville, Scholarie Co.,) farmer 300.

Murray, Margaret Mrs.,(Worcester,) farmer 104.

Neer, Cyrus, (East Worcester,) assessor and farmer 163.

Nicholls, Henry, (East Worcester,) merchant tailor.

Niland, John, (East Worcester,) farmer 25.

Nisbeth, William, (Worcester,) carpenter.

Northrup, Alonzo H., (Worcester,) (*Russ & Northrup,*) farmer 6.

NORTHRUP, MARTIN, (East Worcester,) justice of the peace and pension notary.

Olmstead, Eben, (South Worcester,) general merchant and justice of the peace.

Olmstead, Ira B., (South Worcester,) (*I. B. Olmstead & Brother,*) postmaster and farmer 107.

Olmstead, I. B. & Brother, (South Worcester,) (*Ira B. and John,*) general merchants.

Olmstead, John, (South Worcester,) (*I. B. Olmstead & Brother.*)

Partridge, ——, (Worcester,) (*Wilcox & Partridge.*)

Payn, Austin, (Charlotteville, Schoharie Co.,) farmer 88.

Payn, Chester, (East Worcester,) saw and grist mills, and farmer 300.

Payn, George M., (Charlotteville, Schoharie Co.,) farmer 160.

Payn, Peter H., (Charlotteville, Schoharie Co.,) farmer 76.

Payne, Jacob, (East Worcester,) farmer 120.

Payne, Joseph, (Charlotteville, Schoharie Co.,) blacksmith and farmer 100.

Pepper, H. H., (East Worcester,) hop buyer.

Piatt, H. E., (Worcester,) farmer 50.

Pierce, Norman, (South Worcester,) farmer 148.

Pitcher, George O., (Worcester,) billiard and liquor saloon.

Platts, John, (Worcester,) farmer 25.

Platts, Peter, (East Worcester,) farmer 100.

Post, De Witt, (East Worcester,) groceries and clothing, prop. billiard saloon and farmer 149.

Power, William R., (East Worcester,) farmer 79.

Powers, David W., (East Worcester,) farmer 30.

Powers, Fordus, (East Worcester,) farmer 88½.

Preston, Joseph, (Worcester,) blacksmith.

Queil, John, (East Worcester,) farmer 250.

Race, Benjamin, (East Worcester.)

Race, Robert, (East Worcester,) farmer 105.

Race, William, (East Worcester,) farmer 120.

REIGHTMYER, DAVID F., (East Worcester,) farmer 112.

Ridge, Edward, (Worcester,) farmer 110.

Ridge, Francis, (Worcester,) farmer 90.

Rifenburgh, Andrew, (Charlotteville, Schoharie Co.,) farmer.

Rifenburgh, Harry C., (Charlotteville, Schoharie Co.,) farmer 115.

Ritton, Milo B., (Worcester,) farmer 135.

Roads, Emanuel, (Worcester,) saw mill and farmer 180.

Roads, William, (Worcester,) farmer 8.

ROADS, WILLIAM, JR., (Worcester,) farmer 50 and leases 130.

Robbins, C. B., (Worcester,) carriage maker and inspector of elections.

Robbins, Levi H., (Worcester,) farmer 140.

Robbins, Samuel, (Worcester,) cider mill and farmer 320.

Roberts, Alfred K., (Worcester,) painter and farmer 8.

Robertson, Alex., (South Worcester,) (*with Charles S.,*) lumberman and farmer 100.

Robertson, Charles S., (South Worcester,) (*with Alex.,*) lumberman and farmer 100.

Robinson, H. W., (Worcester,) judge of Court of Appeals, New York, and farmer 50.

Robinson, Milton M., (Worcester,) farmer 60.

Robinson, Samuel C., (Worcester,) farmer 120.

Rockefeller, John E., (East Worcester,) farmer 80.

Rockefeller, Orlando, (East Worcester,) farmer 83.

Rury, Alfred, (East Worcester,) farmer 33.

Russ, Abraham, (Worcester,) (*with Samuel,*) farmer 106.

Russ, Alonzo, (Worcester,) farmer 85.

Russ, Hamilton, (Worcester,) farmer 50.

Russ & Northrup, (Worcester,) (*William H. Russ and Alonzo H. Northrup,*) general merchants.

Russ, Samuel, (Worcester,) (*with Abraham,*) farmer 106.

Russ, William H., (Worcester,) (*Russ & Northrup.*)

Ryan, Thomas, (East Worcester,) farmer 8.

Salisbury, John H., (Worcester,) miller and farmer 62.

Schermerhorn, Simon P., (East Worcester,) farmer 71.

Scripture, Danvers A., (East Worcester,) farmer 61.

SHAFER, HENRY L., (East Worcester,) prop. of saw mill and farmer 110.

Shelland, Benjamin, (Worcester,) wagon maker.

Shelland, Isaac, (Worcester,) farmer 90.

Silvernail, Aaron, (Charlotteville, Schoharie Co.,) farmer 27.

Silvernail, John H., (Charlotteville, Schoharie Co.,) farmer 96.

Simmon, Andrew, (East Worcester,) farmer 100.

Simmons, David, (Worcester,) farmer 96.

Sisson, Jabez, (East Worcester,) blacksmith and farmer 14.

Skinner, John R., (Worcester,) farmer.

Sloan, Andrew L., (Worcester,) farmer 19.

Sloan, W. J., (Worcester,) merchant.

SLOAT, JOHN, (Charlotteville, Schoharie Co.,) farmer 232.

Smith, Abraham, (East Worcester,) farmer 106.

Smith & Car, (East Worcester,) (*Mrs. M. W. Smith and Mrs. M. A. Car,*) milliners.

Smith, Charles, (East Worcester,) U. S. treasury clerk.

Smith, Charles Mrs. (East Worcester,) milliner.

Smith, David B., (Worcester,) farmer leases of Harrison, 140.

Smith, Deveraux, (Worcester,) farmer 80.

Smith, F. M., (East Worcester,) physician.

Smith, George W., (Charlotteville, Schoharie Co.,) farmer 77.

Smith, Harvey C., (East Worcester,) farmer 96.

Smith, H. H., (Worcester,) (*Smith & Swartout,*) postmaster.

Smith, Jacob P., (Charlotteville, Schoharie Co.,) farmer 598.

Smith, Jane E. Mrs., (East Worcester,) farmer 306.

Smith, Jerry, (Worcester,) farmer 126.

Smith, John, (East Worcester,) farmer 180.

Smith, Marvin H., (Charlotteville, Schoharie Co.,) farmer leases 112.

Smith, Melvin A., (Worcester,) farmer leases of J. P., 150.

Smith, Michael, (Worcester,) lawyer and farmer leases of Leonard Caryl, 140.

Smith, M. W. Mrs., (East Worcester,) (*Smith & Car.*)

Smith, Nelson H., (Worcester,) farmer 100.

Smith, Rhoda Mrs., (East Worcester,) farmer 170.

Smith & Swartout, (Worcester,) (*H. H. Smith and A. Swartout,*) groceries, hardware, stoves, tinware, drugs and stationery.

Smith, Theobald, (Worcester,) farmer 7.

Smith, W. H., (Worcester,) farmer 120.

Snow, Alanson, (East Worcester,) prop. of East Worcester Woolen Mills and farmer 20.

Snyder, Egbert, (East Worcester,) (*Snyder & Son.*)

Snyder, Martin, (East Worcester,) (*Snyder & Son.*)

Snyder & Son, (East Worcester,) (*Martin and Egbert,*) stoves, tinware, hardware and cutlery.

SOMERVILLE, ROBERT, (Worcester,) farmer leases of Squire Hartwell, 125.

Spafford, Elisha, (East Worcester,) farmer leases 200.

Spencer, John, (South Worcester,) farmer 26.

Sperry, William, (South Worcester,) farmer 150.

Stam, George, (East Worcester,) carpenter.

Starkweather, David, (Worcester,) farmer 88.

STEVER, JOHN M., (East Worcester,) blacksmith, dealer in coal and overseer of the poor.

STEWART, JAMES, (South Worcester,) notary public, lawyer and farmer 100.

Stewart, William, (South Worcester,) physician and farmer 115.

Storrs, Nathaniel E., (Worcester,) farmer 137.

Strain, David, (South Worcester,) farmer 65.

Strain, Jacob, (S. Worcester,) farmer 114.

Sullivan, David H., (Charlotteville, Schoharie Co.,) lumberman and farmer 104.

Swartout, A., (Worcester,)(*Smith & Swartout,*) tinsmith and gunsmith.

Talbot, Hiram V. Rev., (East Worcester,) pastor M. E. Church.

Ten Broeck, Jeremiah, (Worcester,) blacksmith.

Terpenning, George, (East Worcester,) farmer 100.

Terrell, Isaac, (South Worcester,) wagon maker.

Thomas, Calvin, (Worcester,) farmer 46.

Thurber, D. W., (East Worcester,) (*D. W. & N. Thurber,*) farmer 500.

Thurber, D. W. & N., (East Worcester,) general merchants.

Thurber, Ezra R., (East Worcester,) farmer 250.

Thurber, George, (East Worcester,) produce dealer and farmer 11.

THURBER, GEORGE A.,(East Worcester,) telegraph operator, D. & H. Canal Co.

Thurber, N., (East Worcester,) (*D. W. & N. Thurber,*) post master and supervisor.

Tiffany, Lyman, (East Worcester,) physician.

Timbrook, William, (South Worcester,) blacksmith.

Tripp, Perry, (East Worcester,) farmer leases 20.

Utter, Albert D., (Worcester,) farmer leases 60.

Utter, Henry, (South Worcester,) clover mill and farmer 35.
Utter, James, (South Worcester,) farmer 61.
Utter, Lewis, (Worcester,) farmer 111.
Van Benthuysen, William, (Worcester,) saw and planing mills, cider press and farmer 10.
Van Patten, Frederick, (Worcester,) farmer leases of John, 164.
Van Patten, John, (Worcester,) farmer 202.
Van Valkinburgh, Cyrus, (Worcester,) (with Henry,) farmer leases 280.
Van Valkinburgh, Henry, (Worcester,) (with Cyrus,) farmer leases 280.
Van Wie, John, (Worcester,) farmer leases of D. W. Thurber, 86.
Vaughn, Eli, (Worcester,) farmer 96.
Vaughn, Niram, (Worcester,) farmer 60.
Walker, O. D., (Worcester,) furniture dealer and undertaker.
WARD, JAMES C., (Worcester,) farmer 55.
Warner, Benjamin, (East Worcester,) farmer 50.
Warner, D. W., (East Worcester,) grist, saw, planing and plaster mills, and farmer 10.
Waterman, Briggs W., (Worcester,) farmer 137.
Waterman, Charles O., (Worcester,) watches, jewelry &c., also town clerk.
Waterman, Elisha, (Worcester,) farmer 5.
Waterman, Hamilton, (Worcester,) station agent A. & S. R. R.
Waterman, J. W. Mrs., (Worcester,) farmer 185.
Waters, Daniel, (Worcester,) farmer 60.
WATERS, J. F., (Worcester,) mechanic and farmer 107.

Watterman, Paul, (Worcester,) farmer 90.
Webster, Owen, (Worcester,) farmer 100.
Wharton, Thomas, (Worcester,) farmer 121.
Whitbeck, John, (South Worcester,) farmer leases 100.
White, George I., (Worcester,) farmer 110.
White, Ichabod, (Worcester,) farmer 79.
White, Lewis, (Worcester,) farmer 179.
Whiting, Wm., (Worcester,) farmer 45.
Wickham, Isaac, (East Worcester,) (with Samuel Jaycox,) farmer 133.
Wickham, Mary Mrs., (East Worcester,) farmer 25.
Wilber, Briggs, (Worcester,) farmer 125.
Wilber, Enoch I., (Worcester,) farmer 125.
Wilber, Hamilton R., (Worcester,) farmer 126.
Wilber, John L., (South Worcester,) farmer leases 107.
Wilbur, Robert J., (South Worcester,) farmer 107.
Wilcox, Jacob P., (Charlotteville, Schoharie Co.,) farmer 60.
Wilcox, John D., (Worcester,) shoe maker.
Wilcox & Partridge, (Worcester,) gents' furnishing goods, boots, shoes and harness.
Wilson, Henry E., (South Worcester,) saw mill, lumberman and farmer.
Wilson, Julia Mrs., (South Worcester,) farmer 108.
Winegard, James N., (Worcester,) farmer 14.
Wood, Richard S., (East Worcester,) harness maker.
WORCESTER HOUSE, (Worcester,) E. F. Knapp, prop.
Wright, Lucy Mrs., (Worcester,) farmer 15.

Agricultural Statistics from Census of 1865.

TOWNS.	Winter Wheat bushels harvested 1864.	Oats, bushels harvested 1864.	Indian Corn, bushels harvested 1864.	Potatoes, bushels harvested 1864.	Tobacco, pounds harvested 1864.	Hops, pounds harvested 1864.	Apples, bushels harvested 1864.	Milch Cows, number of, 1865.	Butter, pounds made 1864	Horses, two years old and over, 1865	Sheep, number shorn, 1865.
Burlington.....	133	23436	7144	20640	256	89424	20939	2020	108304	533	3499
Butternuts.....	734	17993	13826	18227		31984	33217	2278	221815	638	4738
Cherry Valley.	548	28773	3030	21733		234765	14256	1334	87300	631	2266
Decatur.......		11779	2127	11634	50	60797	8613	634	63595	264	1475
Edmeston	327	21840	13825	19739		116250	21544	2078	84275	557	3677
Exeter..	130	15596	6264	12936	200	103628	19396	1564	53781	399	3408
Hartwick......	909	28621	11597	26162	500	166643	32484	1655	140271	605	3758
Laurens.......	187	19558	11838	15736	50	64083	25789	1382	150688	481	3542
Maryland.....	180	17164	3775	18402		163264	18703	881	103635	430	2575
Middlefield....	856	47440	19460	35726	1100	391861	35834	1797	170795	823	4017
Milford	174	19115	11857	19317	550	302594	21693	1110	120855	550	2775
Morris.........	262	14367	8467	13937	1170	63572	24891	1544	150609	464	3092
New Lisbon....	410	23438	8046	16101	60	67230	18365	1404	136872	514	3531
Oneonta.......	290	20053	13423	21033	70	110979	22077	1147	138236	501	2874
Otego.........	405	15870	13777	17147	1800	23924	23164	1449	133687	447	4399
Otsego	662	31585	11906	27032	1350	327923	31889	2223	145077	732	5212
Pittsfield.....	6	15189	9317	15903	135	50515	12082	1125	113770	381	4495
Plainfield.....	213	17717	7079	16128	8850	53911	16956	1792	18680	367	722
Richfield..	333	19267	5849	16081		192841	20931	1813	52332	484	2064
Roseboom.....	76	20496	2746	16603		166096	10003	953	83745	543	1893
Springfield :...	504	46043	9028	22879	1500	386088	21088	2011	93060	720	2015
Unadilla.......	1983	16891	16422	25855	3363	2200	25370	1523	202945	563	4606
Westford......	101	23945	5317	18841	800	170582	18254	923	102250	444	4278
Worcester.....	30	15597	4234	28168		110607	16721	1410	134622	647	1823
Totals.......	9453	530813	220354	475965	22104	3451761	519259	36040	2811199	12718	76674

ADDITIONAL STATISTICS FROM CENSUS OF 1865.

In addition to the above extracts we give the following *totals* for the County, as per returns for the several heads mentioned :

Cash Value of Farms, 1865, $23,253,671 ; *of Stock*, 1865, $3,509,123 ; *of Tools and Implements*, 1865, $819,092½ ; *Acres Plowed*, 1865, 74,033½ ; *Tons of Hay*, 1864, 114,494½ ; *Winter Rye*, bush. harvested in 1864, 18,724; *Barley*, bushels harvested in 1864, 22,731 ; *Flax*, acres sown in 1865, 175⅝ ; *Pounds of Lint*, 1864, 29,181½ ; *Honey*, pounds collected in 1864, 34,251 ; *Working Oxen*, number in 1865, 605 ; *Neat Cattle*, number killed for beef in 1864, 5,603; *Swine*, number of pigs in 1865, 10,137; one year old and over, 1865, 10,276; slaughtered in 1864, 11,476; pounds of pork made in 1864, 2,806,409 ; *Wool*, pounds shorn in 1865, 274,769; *Sheep*, number of lambs raised, 1865, 47,656; number killed by dogs, 1864, 614; *Poultry*, value owned, 1865, $36,851.77 ; value of eggs sold, 1864, $28,752.85 ; *Fertilizers*, value bought, 1864, $13,150.20 ; *Domestic Manufactures*, 1864, yards of fulled cloth, 5,839¼ ; yards of linen, 11,927¾ ; yards of flannel, 12,419¼ ; yards of cotton and mixed goods, 990 ; *Apples*, number of trees in fruit, 1864, 292,236; barrels of cider, 1864, 12,701½.

POPULATION OF OTSEGO COUNTY.

Census Returns for 1870, 1865 and 1860, showing
the Increase and Decrease in the last decade.

TOWNS.	1870.	1865.	1860.	Increase.	Decrease	Rate per cent. increase or decrease.
Burlington............	1476	1690	1818		342	19—*
Butternuts..........	2176	2245	2365		189	8—
Cherry Valley......	2338	2384	2552		214	8+
Decatur............	802	853	902		100	11+
Edmeston	1745	1793	1804		59	3+
Exeter.............	1256	1445	1570		314	20
Hartwick............	2343	2248	2496		153	6+
Laurens.............	1919	1885	1936		17	1—
Maryland..........	2402	2197	2228	174		8—
Middlefield.........	2876	2690	2825	51		2—
Milford............	2301	2208	2210	91		4+
Morris.............	2253	2191	2320		67	3—
New Lisbon........	1545	1649	1733		188	11—
Oneonta...........	2568	2363	2158	410		19—
Otego.............	2052	1883	1957	95		5—
Otsego............	4605	4292	4303	302		7+
Pittsfield..........	1468	1444	1480		12	1—
Plainfield	1248	1283	1354		106	9—
Richfield..........	1831	1665	1648	183		11+
Roseboom.........	1590	1719	1870		280	15—
Springfield.........	2022	2291	2390		368	11+
Unadilla...........	2555	2685	2702		147	5+
Westford..........	1300	1282	1382		82	6—
Worcester..........	2327	2231	2154	173		8+
Totals............	48998	48616	50157		1159	2+

*As it is not convenient to give the decimal expressing the
exact rate per cent., when the remaining fraction is less than
one-half, we have made use of the + sign to indicate that the
true rate per cent. is greater than that expressed, and when
the remaining fraction is greater than one-half, one has been
added to the integer, and the — sign used to indicate that the
true rate per cent. is less than the number by which it is
expressed.

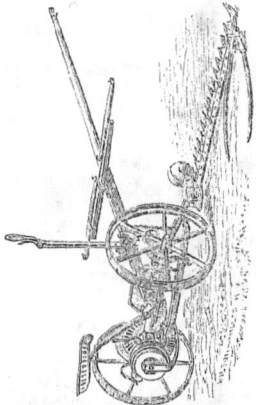
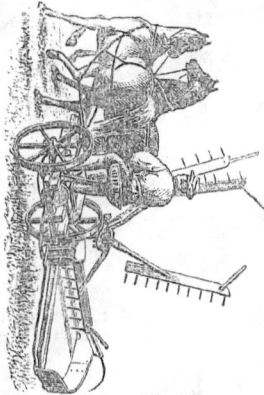

www.ingramcontent.com/pod-product-compliance
Lightning Source LLC
Chambersburg PA
CBHW070354270326
41926CB00014B/2538